Building Character in the American Boy

Building Character
in the American Boy

*The Boy Scouts, YMCA,
and Their Forerunners, 1870–1920*

David I. Macleod

The University of Wisconsin Press

Published 1983

The University of Wisconsin Press
114 North Murray Street
Madison, Wisconsin 53715

The University of Wisconsin Press, Ltd.
1 Gower Street
London WCIE 6HA, England

First printing

Printed in the United States of America

For LC CIP information see the colophon

ISBN 0-299-09400-6

To Margaret and Irving Macleod and Eleanor Sanderson

Contents

Tables   ix

Preface   xi

Acknowledgments   xix

Part I: Anxious Adults Confront a Changing World of Boyhood

1. Growing Up: Boyhood, Social Class, and Social Change   3
2. Character Building: Adult Ambitions and Concerns   29

Part II: Nineteenth-Century Beginnings: Early Forms of Boys' Work

3. Keeping Lower-Class Boys Off the Streets:
   The Mass Boys' Clubs   63
4. Shielding and Strengthening the Middle Class:
   The Start of YMCA Junior Departments   72
5. Forerunners of Scouting: Temperance Orders and
   the Boys' Brigades   83

Part III: Reorientation and New Forms of Organization, 1900–1920

6. Adolescence and Gang-Age Boyhood: An Ideology for
   Character Building   97
7. The Attempted Professionalization of YMCA Boys' Work   117
8. The Invention of Boy Scouting   130
9. The Organization and Expansion of the Boy Scouts
   of America   146

Part IV: Winning Public Favor and Building a Constituency

10. Boyhood, God, and Country: Creation and Defense
    of a Public Image   171
11. Winning Institutional Support and Volunteer Leaders   188
12. Recruiting a "Fine Lot of Lads"   212

Part V: Character Building in Practice

13. Camping: An Organized Setting for the New Boyhood   233
14. Adult Instruction and Boys' Responses   248
15. Group Experience, Membership Turnover, and
    Age Stratification   268

Conclusion and Epilogue   291

Notes   309
Index   390

Tables

1. Age and Sex of Pupils in Selected Indiana Sunday Schools, c. 1920   43

2. Associations Doing Boys' Work and Reported Membership, 1876–1900   78

3. Membership of the Boy Scouts of America, 1914–1922   154

4. Institutions with Which Boy Scout Troops Were Connected   191

5. Church Connection of Boy Scout Troops and Church Preference of Scoutmasters   194–95

6. Occupations of Scoutmasters in Selected Years, 1912–1921   207

7. Prior Experience of Scoutmasters in Selected Years, 1912–1919 210

8. YMCA Juniors at School and Work in Selected Years, 1904–1921   221

9. Ages at Which Boy Scouts Quit in 109 Local Councils, 1921 281

10. Ages of Boys Currently Enrolled in Boy Scout Troops, 1919–1934   282

11. Boys' Ages in Selected YMCAs, 1901, 1905   288

12. Ages of Boy Scouts and YMCA Juniors in 22 Rural Counties, 1923–1924   289

13. Ages of Boys Currently Enrolled in the Boy Scouts of America, 1967   292

Preface

In modern American culture the Boy Scouts are a familiar part of the furniture, somewhat like a comfortable old chair in the corner—not a rare antique that draws the attention of visitors but rather a well-worn fixture of the household that seemingly has always been there. The experience of Boy Scouting may be taken for granted because it has been so common; by the end of 1981, the Boy Scouts of America could report that since the BSA's founding in 1910 a cumulative total of 66,418,720 boys and men had been members at some point in their lives.* Many Americans would of course admit that Boy Scouting must once have been new and unfamiliar; some even know the movement's founding date. And yet most would find it hard to grasp that Boy Scouting in the 1910s impressed contemporaries as fresh and noteworthy—that it virtually exploded onto the American scene, growing from nothing in 1910 to 361,000 boys and 32,000 Scoutmasters by 1919, and from a few workers in a cramped YMCA office in New York City to an expanding bureaucracy with hundreds of employees. This book invites the reader to look anew at agencies such as the Boy Scouts—and through them at middle-class male adolescence—by returning to the years when those things were still just taking shape.

How can we explain such sudden and overwhelming success as the Boy Scouts of America enjoyed? How could a new organization transform itself within a decade into an established American institution? Part of the answer lies in the BSA's peculiar strengths—its appealing and standardized program, its strategy of replicating small units supervised by a promotionally aggressive bureaucracy, its ideological appeal to the Progressive Era middle class, and its usefulness to sponsoring agencies. But the Boy Scout movement did not burst upon an unprepared public without precedent or foreshadowing; far from being the first or only institution of its kind, Boy Scouting was the latest in a series of experiments—reaching back into the 1870s—at organizing activities intended to improve and strengthen boys or, in other words, to build their character. The BSA could never have established itself so rapidly except among a public already somewhat fa-

*Boy Scouts of America, *Annual Report* 72 (1982):89.

miliar with character-building programs and willing to try a new one. The most successful of these prior endeavors, the boys' work of the YMCA, was not a mere forerunner of Boy Scouting; it remained an important rival and a significant social program in its own right. One issue for this study, then, is how Boy Scouting was able to outgrow YMCA boys' work. More important, however, is the broader question of how and why the entire movement to build character in boys — the Boy Scouts of America, YMCA boys' branches, and a variety of lesser agencies — got started, took hold, and grew. Since these enterprises were rooted in middle-class Protestant anxieties about the rising generation, such questions in turn lead back to still broader issues — for example, how the lives of middle-class boys were changing and why middle-class adults worried about those changes. The search for explanation thus leads back in time and outward in scope far beyond the confines of the Boy Scout and YMCA programs.

In explaining the rise of these agencies, therefore, I have tried to locate the evolution of boys' work in its social and cultural ecology, tracing the interplay between external circumstance and internal decision-making as character-building agencies found, occupied, and exploited social and cultural niches. At the same time, I have tried not to let the reader forget the individual people involved and have sought to tell their story with the vigor and attention to human detail that we treasure in traditional narrative history. My method resembles the "political economy" approach to organizational analysis advocated by Mayer Zald, although possibly with greater emphasis upon the general social and cultural background of the era I describe.*

To be manageable within a reasonable space, such a comprehensive explanatory strategy demands strict limits upon the range of organizations studied. Accordingly, this study centers upon a cluster of closely related nonfarm, middle-class, predominantly Protestant, character-building agencies for boys. Two major organizations and one lesser one receive most of the attention. The YMCA began boys' work in the 1870s, amid evangelical alarm at urban immorality, then plunged in more seriously around 1900 as new ideas of child development took hold. The Boys' Brigade, a British import, fed on the militarism and social unease of the 1890s but failed to sustain its growth. Instead, Boy Scouting, another British import, welded the moral earnestness of Progressive Era Americans to the zeal for efficiency and increasingly militant patriotism of the 1910s, and won the public with a standardized program that retailed old verities to a consumer age. Sustaining a steady focus on these *middle-class* organiza-

*Mayer N. Zald, *Organizational Change: The Political Economy of the YMCA* (Chicago, 1970), esp. pp. 17–24.

tions dedicated specifically to *character building* for *boys* has necessitated sketchy handling of other phases of youth work that present inviting thematic parallels and contrasts: street boys' clubs and especially farm boys' and girls' clubs, which did not primarily serve the urban middle class; isolated team sports, which could not satisfy those who desired comprehensive character building; the Camp Fire Girls, Girl Scouts, and YWCA, whose development, thanks largely to stubborn misogyny among the male leadership of organizations for boys, had little influence upon the development of boys' organizations. A survey giving equal weight to all these different programs for the young would risk superficiality; simply juggling ten or a dozen varied organizations would become the main task of the book, and there could be no sustained consideration of their multifarious relations with other aspects of American society and culture. At the other extreme, limiting this study to Boy Scouting alone would have impoverished the analysis and obscured the movement's origins. By the compromise of limiting the core of this study to a few agencies, I have been able to explain and compare their organizational strategies and corporate ideologies quite carefully. This concentration has permitted me to explore a variety of broader themes that are common to these agencies but often not to other forms of youth work — such as the characteristics of middle-class boyhood and male adolescence, the masculinity problems of middle-class Protestant churchmen, and the changing values of the Protestant middle class itself — themes with interesting implications for the society and culture of the early twentieth-century United States.

While my thinking on many of these themes proceeded initially from boys' work outward, in this book my explanation of the origins and establishment of character-building agencies proceeds from the outside in — from the social and cultural setting inward to the genesis of the organizations, their exploitation of a social niche, and their success within it. The book begins with a broad overview of the sweeping changes in middle-class life and values that reshaped teenage boyhood and of the adult anxieties that underlay character building. There follow first an outline of the nineteenth-century origins of boys' work and then a fuller account of the great flowering of middle-class boys' work after 1900, with its new theories of boyhood and adolescence, thriving organizations, public acclaim, and successful recruitment of men and boys. The final major section of the book seeks to evaluate how well character-building agencies fulfilled their founders' expectations and what results the agencies achieved. In other words, it explores how character building worked out in practice — in the experiences of campers, in boys' ambitions, in their relations with adult leaders, and in their willingness to persist or eagerness to leave.

Basically, American character-building agencies developed in response to social and cultural changes that marked off first preadolescence and then adolescence as somewhat sheltered stages of life. These changes led various institutions and individuals, especially Protestant churches and laymen, to seek to strengthen and control middle-class schoolboys. Combining romantic nostalgia with new ideas from developmental psychology and modern organizational methods, YMCA boys' workers (following a professional model) and Boy Scout executives (taking a more bureaucratic approach) constructed thriving organizations and recruited adult volunteers and crowds of boys. Some of these boys were the dedicated enthusiasts adults hoped for; more passed rapidly out of the membership or took advantage of one or two aspects of the program while ignoring the rest. The Boy Scouts, highly successful at winning boys of twelve or thirteen, held few beyond the age of fourteen or fifteen. Yet recruitment of new boys was sufficient to maintain impressive and growing aggregate memberships; thus organizational momentum and the commitment of salaried staff who made boys' work a career insured that character building would receive vigorous promotion; and an enduring network of outside supporters, their faith bolstered by the close congruence between character builders' goals and the mainstream values of the American middle class, guaranteed continued financial support and public approval.

By now the focus of this study should be clear and so should its central thesis: that character-building agencies arose in response to middle-class men's concerns about teenage boys of their own social class and that those agencies prospered which organized most efficiently and most faithfully expressed middle-class values and concerns. If that is so, then the history of such agencies may offer a fresh if sometimes quirky perspective upon sociocultural matters reaching well beyond boys' work itself—notably the institutionalization of boyhood and adolescence and the changing values and ambitions of middle-class men in the Progressive Era.

Until recently, social historians have paid little attention to preadolescence and adolescence. Over the years, a modest literature on child-rearing has accumulated, but it has focused primarily upon infancy and early childhood. Although historians of social reform have written insightfully on subjects such as urban schooling, child welfare, the treatment of juvenile delinquents, and the crusade against child labor, these works have dealt most extensively with public policy issues, centered upon things done for —or to—the lower class, and given little heed to age differences as an issue in policy-making or a determinant of juvenile behavior. Without saying so directly, such works may have reinforced the common presumption that concern about adolescence must have centered first upon the lower class. While there has been some fine historical writing on college-age youth, not until Joseph Kett's recent work has a historian traced in detail the evolution of American adolescence.* Kett's study marks a major advance in understanding. Sensitive to cultural change and shifting nuances in middle-class views of the young, he makes it clear that modern adolescence — at least for boys — was an innovation of, by, and for the middle class. My work reinforces Kett's position on the origins of adolescence. The assumption that the most troublesome adolescents are lower-class males might lead one to expect that street boys' clubs should have been the first centers of alarm over adolescence. Yet initial concern about male adolescence *per se* centered on the middle class and took institutional form in agencies such as Boy Scouting and the YMCA junior departments. This book shows how one set of institutions for the young arose in response to very specific concerns and needs within the Protestant middle class.

In addition, the present study stresses the importance of small age differences and the evolution of narrowly stratified age grading in shaping adult strategies for controlling boys and in determining the boys' responses. Much confusion concerning adolescence and its history can be created by labeling as "adolescent" phenomena such as Boy Scouting that were in large measure preadolescent from the start or, worse yet, by casting the almost meaninglessly broad label "youth" over everything from the Boy Scouts to Students for a Democratic Society.** This book seeks instead to present the process by which adults sought to hold boys within a sheltered adolescence as a tug of war along an increasingly finely calibrated course.

While control was paramount in adult concern about adolescence, middle-class men also worried that boys from their own social class were growing up weak — and that fear in turn seems often to have been a projection of the men's anxieties that they were themselves unmanly. Although the study of women's social roles has produced a large and sophisticated body of historical literature, inquiry into American men's gender roles is still highly exploratory. The present study suggests that anxiety over effeminacy in boyhood should not be exaggerated, since adults cared more about controlling boys' values and behavior. Given the resistance women have encountered in seeking their rights, there is an understandable temptation to interpret males' anxiety over their own manliness as a reaction to women's activities, but the history of character-building agencies suggests that it was more directly a reaction to urban life. Once again, age

---

*Joseph F. Kett, *Rites of Passage: Adolescence in America, 1790 to the Present* (New York, 1977) is Kett's major work on the subject.

**Some of the differences between the German *Wandervögel* and the English and American Boy Scouts, for instance, reflect not only national differences in the management of adolescents but also the fact the German boys were older. Cf. John R. Gillis, "Conformity and Rebellion: Contrasting Styles of English and German Youth, 1900–33," *History of Education Quarterly* 13 (1973):249–60.

differences turn out to be very important. As this book will show, boys
striving for manliness cared particularly about the personal autonomy that
came with age; reaching for it brought them into potential conflict with
men who wanted to prove their own manliness by dominating a group
of boys.

The claim to build "character" — meaning strength and virtue of a conventional sort rather than personal distinctiveness — reflected the class ethos
of the early character builders, since they assumed the middle class held
a near monopoly on character. At the same time, they were especially eager
to *control* middle-class boys — which was what character building often
came down to in practice — and they regarded strength and virtue as vital
if the rising generation of the middle class was to maintain its social position. The issue of social control versus personal autonomy has figured
largely in the history of education, as revisionist historians of the past
two decades have stressed the development of bureaucratic school administration and the use of schooling to impose alien cultural hegemony and
social control upon immigrant and nonwhite children. There has been much
less attention to the question of how the schools affected native-stock,
middle-class children, and only recently have historians begun to investi-
gate teacher-pupil interactions and education outside the schools.* The
examination of character-building agencies for boys can make some
modest contributions along these lines. It shows how would-be educators
outside the schools reacted against standard educational practices as unbending and bureaucratic and yet were overawed and influenced by the
example of the schools — both in instructional approach and especially
in administration. Although the behavior of boys and their leaders in voluntary associations inevitably differed from what occurred in public schools,
the patterns are nonetheless revealing because the boys and men were acting more freely than school pupils and teachers. What these patterns suggest is that adult-imposed social control, when formalized and made explicit, had trouble winning voluntary assent even with middle-class boys
and familiar cultural values.

The Progressive Era has often been depicted as a time of particular
prominence for the American middle class, a period when political reformism grew out of middle-class culture and major organizational changes
reflected the emergence of a new middle class whose authority and social position rested upon specialized expertise. The history of character
building provides a revealing, if somewhat idiosyncratic, perspective upon
middle-class innovations and organizational activity in the Progressive Era.
It suggests the difficulty of grouping all such innovations — even those for
altruistic purposes — under the rubric of "reform." Programs such as the

---

*One can follow these issues in the *History of Education Quarterly*.

character builders', instituted by private bodies for conservative ends, are hard to link with political Progressivism. The rise of Boy Scouting and the YMCA fits the belief that America was developing an "organizational society"; but the history of these agencies shows that novel institutions could succeed without the high level of technocratic expertise sometimes attributed to new organizations of the Progressive Era.* The YMCA example shows how shallow professionalization could be in a marginal profession, while the fortunes of the Boy Scouts of America suggest that bureaucratic centralization worked better for organizational promotion despite erratic results at the grassroots.

The character builders' struggles as fledgling professionals and bureaucrats furnish a case study of the emergence of one small segment of the new middle class of white-collar employees and illustrate the difficulties — easily masked in retrospect — that individuals could face in trying to establish themselves within that class. Historical investigations of social mobility have tended to assume the exalted status of white-collar occupations, especially the professional, giving little heed to the problems of marginal vocations. Although this is a specialized study, it shows how leaders of one such occupation — boys' work — labored to make it securely middle-class. The character builders' recruitment patterns also cast some light on the processes by which social classes separated and suggest the value of using different dividing lines for different purposes. If volunteer service had become the mark of the middle class by the 1910s, Boy Scout experience would suggest drawing the line between white- and blue-collar workers. But if the criterion was willingness to pay for something like Scouting for one's children, then the line ran between skilled and semiskilled blue-collar workers and was fairly easily crossed from below.

While this book focuses most directly upon the institutionalization of boyhood and adolescence and the career paths and organizational activities of middle-class men, it also illustrates a variety of changes in middle-class American values extending substantially beyond boys and boys' work. Character building was, for instance, a translation into practice of the retreat from spirituality in mainstream Protestantism, a trend which troubled many boys' workers and yet which most abetted. This example shows that more was involved in secularization than just a shift in values; institutional imperatives — including the needs of churches and their boys' work auxiliaries to recruit large memberships — encouraged a tendency to stress affiliation as much as commitment. The character builders' programs also suggest a broader shift in middle-class ideology after 1900, from control by internalized values towards group participation as the favored mode

*Cf. Jerry Israel, ed., *Building the Organizational Society: Essays on Associational Activities in Modern America,* introduction by Samuel P. Hays (New York, 1972).

of American conformity. Yet their example furnishes a useful warning against overgeneralization, for character-building practice fostered weak group loyalties and continued to rely upon moralistic instruction and competitive pressures for individual achievement. In tracing changes in attitudes regarding foreign policy, one can turn to Boy Scout leaders of the 1910s for an example of how men trained to international good will in the prewar era retreated before the pressures of American nationalism during World War I. And it is evident that Boy Scout and YMCA camps both exemplified and helped to inculcate new attitudes towards the outdoors. From their days at camp, hundreds of thousands of boys learned an ambivalent attitude towards nature as a field for recreation, their values poised uneasily between preservation and use. While no single thread unites these diverse issues, in each instance character builders had to strike a balance between the enthusiastic idealism favored by middle-class moralists of the Progressive Era and the practical imperatives of competitive success.

The resulting posture was often awkward. Claims to build character could only exacerbate the Progressive Era penchant for professions of extreme idealism. And because they were dealing with young boys, character builders stated the ideals of their day effusively, without much adult reserve. Yet they could hardly do less, for the boys in question were present and prospective members of the middle class, presumed to be the future mainstays of the moral order. On the other hand, character builders had to establish a market for new and highly specialized services; they had to make careers for themselves, administer complex programs, and insure that their particular agency grew and prospered. Whatever their ideals, they could no more escape these practical necessities than could other members of the new middle class—rather less if anything, since their organizations and vocations were still so novel. Whether they were running summer camps, setting religious policies, or voicing patriotic sentiments, they had to avoid risk or offense, always considering what made for administrative efficiency and organizational growth. To a later observer, the early character builders may seem at times to have teetered indecorously, threatening to overbalance into simple gush on one side and cold-blooded organizational self-advancement on the other. Yet it was their novel and peculiar situation as purveyors of character and organizers of the young that left them looking so exposed and unsteady, for in other respects they were responding—even if a bit awkwardly—to common pressures of contemporary middle-class culture and careerism. Once the novelty of character building faded, its practitioners would settle down to steady practice of their vocation—their work generally respected, their fund raising routinely supported, and their agencies increasingly taken for granted as part of the ordinary fabric of American life.

Acknowledgments

The writing of this book has gone on so long that it seems I am indebted for its completion to half the people I have ever known; but certain individuals and institutions deserve special thanks. First in time was Don Holloway, my boyhood Scoutmaster, whose leadership of the 4th Oshawa left me with a high standard against which to judge Boy Scouting elsewhere. Years later, a series of mentors and friends directed my attention back towards the historical context in which programs such as Boy Scouting first arose. Jill K. Conway, then teaching at the University of Toronto, stirred my interest in late nineteenth- and early twentieth-century American society and culture. Study with Merle Curti, then engaged in investigating ideas of human nature in American history, set me thinking about character and the agencies which tried to build it. Above all, I want to thank Paul K. Conkin, whose critical guidance got me to write cogently and at more or less reasonable length on this subject, whose encouragement then helped me finish what became a first draft of the book, and whose support was vital in weathering the delays of rewriting and in bringing the book forward to publication. I am also grateful to Stanley K. Schultz, who read the manuscript at an early stage, and to Joseph F. Kett, who read it at a much later stage; each made extremely valuable suggestions. A host of friends and colleagues have given me generous encouragement and advice, some of it indispensable; I should especially thank Roger Simon, Jack Blocker, Jr., John Engram, Larry Reynolds, Charles Ebel, Eric Johnson, and John Haeger. The book's shortcomings are my own, since I have stubbornly sought my own solutions to most writing problems, but without the help and guidance of these friends and mentors many of those problems would have gone unrecognized.

None of this assistance would have mattered, of course, without sources for my research. I am grateful to the YMCA and especially to Virginia Downes, then librarian of the YMCA Historical Library, for giving me the run of the library's remarkable collection and for kindly providing a weekend pass which greatly speeded my work. Joseph W. Wyckoff, then Assistant to the Chief Scout Executive, Boy Scouts of America, gave me access to a treasure trove of unsorted BSA records from the 1910s and even lent me a desk behind his secretary's. Neither the YMCA nor the BSA is, of course, responsible in any way for my conclusions, but I appreciate their assistance in exploring their early history. I would also like to thank the staffs of the many libraries I have used, especially the helpful people in the Library of Congress Manuscript Room, Archie Motley of the Chicago Historical Society, Eleanor Pratt at the Seton Memorial Library and Museum, and J. A. Craig, who helped me find a useful collection at the Boy Scouts of Canada. Doris Miller, Joy Pastucha, and their efficient assistants in the interlibrary loan department of the Central Michigan University Library secured many of the obscure published materials which proved as vital as archival sources in rounding out a picture of early boys' work. Although the notes to this book acknowledge my huge debt to recent research by social historians, I should single out the work of Joseph F. Kett, whose pathbreaking articles on male adolescence helped orient me early in this project and whose subsequent writings have been an inspiration and at times a challenge. Jeffrey P. Hantover's dissertation, which I encountered late in my work, also spurred me to sharpen my arguments — both in agreement and in opposition.

The fourth year of a prize fellowship from the University of Wisconsin financed the start of research on this project. Nancy Hunt, Julie Downer, and a succession of student typists before them conscientiously typed the many drafts of the manuscript. Material now scattered through various chapters has appeared in articles in *Histoire sociale–Social History* and in the *Journal of Social History.*

The dedication reflects my loving gratitude to three people who shaped my character. But one huge debt remains. Beth Macleod has had to take my character pretty much as she found it. Without her love, advice, and patience I don't know how I would ever have completed this book.

I

Anxious Adults Confront a Changing World of Boyhood

1

Growing Up: Boyhood, Social Class, and Social Change

The character-building agencies for boys which rose to prominence in the decades around 1900 were curious organizations. Their declared ideals were singularly broad and seemingly timeless, and yet these organizations were in fact quite specialized, rooted in the experience of the late Victorian and early twentieth-century middle class. The YMCA proposed a fourfold plan of mental, physical, social, and religious development, while Boy Scouting imposed its famous oath and twelve Scout laws. Character building for boys embodied the diffuse idealism of the Progressive Era so effectively that a later, more cynical generation sometimes uses "Boy Scout" as a term of mild derision for a naive do-gooder. As such a falling out of fashion might suggest, character-building agencies were distinctly products of their formative era, marked by the conditions of those early years. Furthermore, they occupied a relatively narrow social niche, dispensing distinctive services to a selected clientele.

From the start, character builders specialized. Functionally, they relied upon recreational programs to nurture and discipline capacities which they summed up as character. Institutionally, they sought out a social niche left vacant by home and workplace, church and school, claiming to control and strengthen boys in ways that those institutions did not. And they defined their clientele quite narrowly, favoring white, middle-class Protestants like themselves and leaving the urban lower class to boys' clubs whose function was more to preoccupy street boys and prevent crime than to build character. YMCA and Boy Scout leaders paid even less heed to farm boys, leaving them to vocationally oriented corn and cotton clubs. The early character builders' militant Protestantism also kept Catholics away, even though Catholic youth work was fragmented and insubstantial until well after 1920. And leaders in boys' work insisted that girls be organized separately, lest they imperil the boys' manly character. Thus the YMCA and Boy Scouts left large areas of youth work to other agencies; however, by claiming to build character and concentrating their recruitment upon boys whom middle-class adults considered the most normal, morally wholesome, and socially respectable, the character builders staked out the

3

central, "normative" position in boys' work. By comparison, other agencies appeared narrow and limited.

The character builders were selective by age as well as class and sex; they wanted boys who were sliding out of adult control and yet remained within reach, whose characters were pliable enough to shape and yet firm enough to retain the impress of good influence. In the late 1800s, they concentrated on those from ages ten to sixteen; but around 1900, deciding that adolescents stood most in need of supervision, they fixed upon twelve through eighteen, making something of a fetish of the lower limit.

How, then, did such specialized organizations get started and take root? The answer is closely connected with their choice of clientele, for behind that lay a complex of social changes which had vastly expanded the non-farm middle class, altering family life, career patterns, and anxieties and expectations about the young. By the turn of the century, the lives of middle-class teenagers had changed, creating a large yet clearly delimited constituency for Boy Scouting and YMCA boys' work.

Both in reality and in the later memories of grown men, boyhoods a century ago varied widely — from farm to small town to city, from immigrant to native, and from lower to middle or upper class. With mingled bitterness and pride, what former farm boys remembered most was work. Hamlin Garland (1860–1940), a future chronicler of farm life and an early supporter of Boy Scouting, grew up on a succession of farms from Wisconsin to the Dakotas. His father, a transplanted Yankee, set a stern regimen; by age ten, young Hamlin plowed ten hours a day "like a hired hand." Winter gave some respite and a chance at schooling, but Hamlin spent most of his teens doing "a man's work on a boy's pay."[1] John Muir (1838–1914) could have envied Garland. From the day his family immigrated to a Wisconsin farm from Scotland when Muir was eleven, the future naturalist toiled for his father without time off for schooling, except one winter, until age twenty-two; his playtime was limited to a few hours each Sunday. Put to the plow — like Garland, "when [his] head reached but little above the handles" — young Muir nonetheless took pride that "none could draw a straighter furrow," and he toiled seventeen-hour days at haying time, driven "by foolish ambition in keeping ahead of the hired men." The closeness of farm families was a mixed blessing, for it was the closeness of labor under stern patriarchal dominance; Muir and Garland's fathers beat them severely. Overall, such boyhoods were at best, in John Muir's words, "hard, half-happy days."[2]

Yet there were second chances, since the sequence of education followed by work was not yet fixed. After limited country schooling, Garland attended a small-town seminary from ages sixteen to nineteen, though he still labored on the farm for half each year. At twenty-two, Muir left home and with surprising rapidity made up his missing education at the University of Wisconsin.[3]

Given a choice, most farm boys would rather have been village boys. Those boys had chores too, of course, but village life offered more variety — amusements, education, and strivings for culture. Villagers were on the average more prosperous than farmers and kept work and leisure in better balance. During one blessed year that Garland spent in town, he tended several cows, horses, and a huge garden; but he also enjoyed swimming, berrying, baseball, lectures, and music. He even gained a townsman's taste for natural beauty, previously stifled by the drab round of outdoor toil.[4] Understandably, then, when later novelists such as William Dean Howells celebrated rural boyhood, they harked back to small-town life more often than the isolated farmstead.

Although work was part of growing up for working-class city boys, much as it was for farm boys, the rhythms of life were different in the city. Education was less intermittent and stages of life came in sequence, with less doubling back.

The upwardly mobile, in these circumstances, had to be little engines of ambition. Soon after arriving from Galicia, Harry Golden (1902–1981) became a straight-A school pupil, sold papers every evening, began delivering telegrams at age eleven, and sold sheet music on the streets Saturday evenings. Like his friends, he left day school at fifteen, but he continued his education through college at night, later going on to stock promotion, journalism, and matzoh barrel punditry.[5]

Leonard Covello (b. 1887) had to swim against a tide of indifference towards education among his parents and compatriots from Italy. When he took a job at age twelve, delivering bread at five each morning before school, his father commented approvingly: "Good. You are becoming a man now." Already friends were leaving school to help their families. Covello lasted into high school, but eventually the combination of jobs with schoolwork wore him down, and he too quit. Until that point, his career was sadly typical. What was unusual was that he returned a year later, graduated, won a scholarship to Columbia, and eventually became a New York high school principal.[6]

The pattern which Covello broke was more strictly sequential than traditional farm boyhood: city boys first went to school full time; then they took part-time jobs but still came to school each day; and finally they took full-time jobs which displaced schooling altogether or crowded it into evenings. Gone was the seasonal alternation of work and schooling, except for summers, and gone for most boys the doubling back to get more education.

The day-to-day lives of working-class city boys — at least ambitious ones — were much more fragmented than those of farm boys. Their fathers did not wield the same overriding authority as the farmer-taskmasters. Their mothers had a stronger hold emotionally, yet this spurred boys forth into the world dreaming of returning rich to repay her sacrifices. And outside influences abounded. Golden ran errands for prostitutes, and Covello and his friends engaged in constant foraging that verged on theft; at the same time both boys nurtured imagination in the world of books and welcomed efforts to raise their ambitions. Golden developed an appetite for middle-class amenities from a small-scale boys' club run by his employer. Covello learned Bible verses at a one-woman mission called the Home Garden. He later reflected that every day he lived in "different worlds. There was my life with my Aviglianese neighbors. My life on the streets of East Harlem. My life at the Home Garden with Miss Ruddy. Life at the local public school. Life at whatever job I happened to have. Life in the wonderworld of books. There seemed to be no connection. . . . Yet I was happy."[7] Middle-class moralists never quite knew what to make of this; the raffish promiscuity and fragmentation of urban life troubled character builders, with the result that they tended to screen out the urban lower class from their organizations.

Unlike lower-class or farm boys, those from the nonfarm middle class were relatively free of pressures to help support the family. Though tensions sometimes marred their lives, these most often reflected high expectations for career achievement and emotional closeness between parents and children.

Autobiographers among them remembered glorious expanses of free time. Growing up in Sacramento as the son of a paint merchant, Lincoln Steffens (1866–1936) enjoyed remarkable liberty. After school and all day Saturday, from ages eight to fifteen, he regularly rode off on horseback to seek adventure in the countryside. Two flamboyant pioneers of American Boy Scouting were likewise middle-class city boys who spent long hours outdoors. Daniel Carter Beard (1850–1941), the future National Scout Commissioner, was raised in Kentucky, just across the Ohio River from Cincinnati, by indulgent parents who left him free to roam the woods and river with his friends. Ernest Thompson Seton (1860–1946) grew up in Toronto, the son of an emotionally distant accountant recently arrived from Britain. From ages ten to fifteen, Seton's imaginative life centered in wooded ravines at the edge of town, where he built a little cabin and spent long hours in nature study and Indian fantasy. These tastes later brought him fame as a writer of animal stories and Chief Scout of the Boy Scouts of America.[8]

All was not well with these three boyhoods, however. Seton grew up full of rancor at his father, a tyrant so exploitive — in the son's retelling — that he billed young Seton for his upbringing, charging 6 percent interest at maturity. In reality, the father's sins were more commonplace; cold and overbearing, he tried to force the boy's career plans into a conventional mold, forbidding him to think of nature study. Seton, who went through puberty late and suffered the social handicaps that slow development entails, fled outdoors for solace, only to find one day that tramps had obscenely defiled his cabin. In his maudlin recollection, this defilement ended his prepubertal idyll, presaging the onset of sexual desires which terrified him.[9] On the other hand, Beard idolized his father, a distinguished artist, and was shattered at age fifteen when his father moved to New York in search of commissions, leaving young Dan to complete his teens in Cincinnati with his mother. While Steffens's relations with his father remained warm, his poor schoolwork and a bout of drinking led the father to pack him off to military school at age fifteen.[10] For all three men, their outdoor boyhood remained in memory as a bright idyll set against darker hues; it was a vision that Seton and Beard never quite transcended.

Other boys from white-collar families grew up without such a wrenching sense of loss at boyhood's end. Especially for those born after 1900, prolonged schooling gave life a stable uniformity; as if on a long, broad pier, they walked far out into their late teens before plunging off. School left ample time for play and chores and even part-time jobs, and nothing outside of education imposed the urgent demands that work did on poorer boys. It was in this spare-time world of limited commitments that the character builders would find their market.

Jesse Davis (1871–1955) kept busy, yet only his schooling was considered essential. As a small boy in New York, he filled the woodbox and drove the cow to pasture, but only because his stepfather, a Baptist minister, thought work was good for him. The family had private means and left young Jesse plenty of time to climb hills and gaze at clouds. A move to Detroit when Davis was twelve soon launched him into high school; in his spare time, he went roller skating, built a gymnasium with friends in imitation of the YMCA, and met girls through the church young people's society. Though few boys graduated from high school in the 1880s, Davis went on to college and a career in high school teaching.[11]

A generation later, Bruce Catton (1899–1978) remembered boyhood as a pleasant limbo, "waiting for the morning train" that took him off to college and fame as an historian. The village of Benzonia, Michigan, where his father headed an academy, provided winter hills for sledding and summer woods to roam. In his teens, Catton played in the band, joined a young people's society, and belatedly took a summer job his last year home; on the whole, the years passed serenely, marked by little more than rising anticipation.[12]

B. F. Skinner (b. 1904), the future behaviorist, passed a more restless boyhood in Susquehanna, Pennsylvania. He and friends tried the usual projects — building huts, stringing telephones that failed; in the same spirit, he became a Boy Scout underage at nine and remained until fourteen. Once in high school, Skinner took more or less distasteful part-time jobs because his father thought they would be good for him. He grew bored with small-town life but took for granted that he would finish high school and go on to college.[13]

Despite the varied activities of middle-class boys, Skinner's reaction suggests a mixed verdict on their contentment. Although parents no longer pressured boys to help support the family, relations between fathers and sons did not automatically achieve intimacy. Jesse Davis's stepfather took him hiking and fishing and won the boy's friendship, but neither Skinner nor Catton's fathers mastered modern, affectionate parenthood so easily. They gave their sons opportunities, demanding only personal achievement in return, and yet a residue of stiffness remained. Catton recalled regretfully: "He was a warm-hearted man, but somehow he was out of my reach; our relationship was slightly Biblical. . . ." Skinner was readier to blame: "[He] read about, and yearned for, a good father-son relationship, but did not know how to enter into one."[14] In such an atmosphere—where easy friendship seemed called for and yet was wanting, and where boys were sometimes bored—substitute relationships with Scoutmasters and YMCA workers could flourish.

Of course, there were many other kinds of boyhood between 1850 and 1920. Black boys, for instance, faced biases unknown to white youths. Ironically, the most famous boyhood of the period—Theodore Roosevelt's—was untypical. He passed a solitary boyhood struggling to beat down asthma and build up his spindly frame, eventually overcompensating to a degree contemporaries found admirable.[15] This solitary striver from the gentry became a hero to middle-class character builders and the model of manly earnestness to his generation. However, it was a boyhood such as Catton's which the middle class came to regard as the norm. Such boys would stay in school, pressured towards achievement and decency, ripe for organized activity.

Beneath the diversity of experience remembered by autobiographers were broad economic and social trends. Farmers, the urban lower class, and the nonfarm middle class each developed distinctive characteristics in work, income, and child rearing, which eventually gave rise to separate worlds of boys' work: 4-H for farm boys, boys' clubs for the lower class, and self-professed "character-building" agencies for the middle class. At the same time, social changes swelled the urban working class and vastly expanded the middle class.

As textbook writers tell us, economic growth transformed nineteenth-century America into an industrial giant. In the process, agriculture's share of the labor force plummeted from 72 percent in 1820 to 27 percent by

1920, while that engaged in manufacturing, mining, and construction reached almost 25 percent by 1870 and rose to 34 percent by 1920. Areas of white-collar employment started small but grew even faster. Trade, finance, education, professions, and government employment accounted for just under 10 percent of the labor force in 1870 but reached 19 percent in 1920.[16] Associated changes increased per capita income much faster than in the early 1800s.[17] Victorian Americans were building a margin of prosperity that let them do more for their children and demand less immediate economic returns.

These benefits were unevenly distributed, however. The northeast and Great Lakes states had 70 percent of all manufacturing jobs in 1899 and a per capita income well above the national average. Income distribution among individuals was strikingly unequal; the top 30 percent earned 56 percent of all personal income in 1910, whereas the bottom 30 percent received 14 percent.[18] Farmers and farm workers averaged only 37 percent of the national mean income per worker in the 1890s and 47 percent in the 1920s and 1930s, while incomes in manufacturing and mining were much higher and white-collar workers did better still.[19] Although there was some overlap, the average white-collar worker earned more than twice as much as his blue-collar counterpart from the late nineteenth century through the early 1910s. Although this differential dropped during World War I, it remained substantial (about 5:3 in industry in 1920) and rebounded to 2:1 by the late 1920s.[20]

As incomes rose, increasing numbers of parents could forego the labor or earnings of their teenagers and invest instead in preparing them for success. Accordingly, when character builders proposed safeguarding parents' investment by strengthening their sons' morality and ambition, the idea found its largest appeal where income and movement off the farm were most advanced — the northeast and Great Lakes states — and among parents who could best afford prolonged training for their sons — the non-farm middle class.

Economic growth brought mass immigration, sharpening the old-stock middle class's sense of its own distinctiveness. Clustering in cities of the Northeast and Middle West, immigrants made their maximum impact upon old-stock perceptions in areas where the unsettling effects of economic and urban growth were most advanced. Immigrant strangeness and poverty inspired prejudice; yet nativism was only an extreme manifestation of something more basic: the recognition by members of the old-stock, Protestant middle and upper classes that they had a distinctive social and cultural identity which they now insisted was coextensive with Americanism.[21]

Coinciding with mass immigration came rapid urbanization, which rolled like a shock wave across American culture long before most Americans were city dwellers. In 1820, only 693,000 Americans (7.2 percent) were urban even by the Census Bureau's generous definition; that is, they lived in towns of 2,500 or more. But that number swelled fourteenfold to 9,902,000 by 1870 (25.7 percent) and reached 54,158,000 by 1920 (51.2 percent). Many of these people still lived in smallish towns, but what fascinated and appalled contemporaries was the mushrooming of great urban centers, aglitter with opportunity and danger; New York (3,437,000 by 1900) and Chicago (1,699,000) were perceived as the glory and terror of their day.[22]

Not just immigrants felt the cities' strangeness; native-born Americans did as well. Like the masses of foreign-born, most of them had come from somewhere else, from farms and villages and other cities. For these people, as much as for immigrants, city life was disorienting. Much of the population was alien; and beyond the jarring clatter of wagon wheels on cobblestones, the dirty air and sooty walls, the sheer "impersonality and bustle" of city life wore people down.[23] The impression of contemporaries was that the native-stock middle class sought refuge by retreating to "little islands of propriety."[24] The early YMCAs were just such islands, offering Protestant religiosity and sheltered sociability to young white-collar workers. In Richard Sennett's view, eventually most middle-class men took refuge in family life, increasing their sense of distinctiveness as they retreated to middle-class neighborhoods and then to their own suburbs once streetcars opened up mass commuting.[25]

Starting before the Civil War, middle- and upper-class Americans reached out with voluntaristic schemes — ranging from Sunday schools and tract societies to YMCAs and children's aid societies — intended to counter urban disorder and restore the moral order of the small community. These endeavors underlined class distinctions, however, for moral reformers soon divided their clientele along class lines: YMCAs and Sunday schools for the middle class and boys' clubs and mission schools for the lower class. Within large cities, middle-class Protestants were setting themselves apart.[26]

Yet it is well to remember that much of the middle class still lived in smaller towns. While the proportion of Americans in cities over 250,000 grew from 7.9 percent in 1870 to 19.6 percent by 1920, the number in towns and cities from 2,500 to 50,000 also rose, although more slowly, from 12.5 percent in 1870 to 20.2 percent by 1920.[27] Compared to larger centers, small towns and cities seemed islands of tranquil stability, dominated by a cohesive middle class. Yet for young people they were often way stations, as countless youths moved on in search of wider opportunities.[28] In smaller places where the middle class dominated and residents felt overshadowed and threatened by big-city culture, middle-class consciousness took the form of community defensiveness, and adults struggled to keep their young people loyal to the values of the town.

The emergence of a distinct, relatively self-conscious middle class was a protracted process, however. By the 1850s, Republican orators saw northern society as ideally a world of independent farmers, artisans, and merchants — a "middle class, neither rich nor poor. . . ."[29] Faith in work as discipline and self-expression fortified the "middling, largely Protestant, property-owning classes" against the idle dissipation they feared among laborers and men of wealth alike. And the voluntary associations of the socially dominant Protestant churches provided a distinctive "form of ethno-class identification. . . ."[30] This sense of separateness was still rudimentary, for observers regarded the middle classness of northern society as a mass phenomenon; but post-Civil War social changes broke the illusion of consensus and set the urban middle class apart.[31] Immigrants organized their own unions, political machines, churches, and charities. Protestant churches in the cities became increasingly, in Gregory Singleton's phrase, "mere middle-class institutions."[32] Meanwhile farmers organized separately to protect their interests, until by 1900 it was clear that they and the urban middle class did not share a common destiny.

Within the cities, economic developments marked off the growing middle class more sharply from those above and below them. At the upper edge, the postwar growth of vast fortunes created a class of plutocrats who estranged themselves more sharply from the middle class than had the antebellum mercantile elite, spurning even the old gentry families of lesser fortunes — some of whose scions adapted by becoming leaders in the professions, exemplars to the upper middle class. Genteel manners became a badge of middle-class respectability, and genteel culture heroes such as Theodore Roosevelt lent middle-class aspirations a certain dignity.[33] Sadly, at the lower edge of the middle class, the enormous expansion of factory production imperiled the status of artisans who had been accepted as part of the independent middle class at midcentury. Some found their skills displaced or degraded, while wage work and factory discipline eroded their independence.[34] Manual occupations no longer seemed to shade gradually up into the middle class.

In broad outline, these developments were obvious and class divisions clear; ordinary factory hands were far removed from white-collar workers. But where to draw the main demarcation line in the broad zone between them was less certain. Were there natural boundaries in this social landscape or merely open plains sloping gradually upward? A convenient and reasonably definite dividing line, much used in American studies of social mobility, has been that between white-collar and blue-collar workers. Yet a recent student of the turn-of-the-century American class system, impressed by differences between American and European patterns, has proposed a three-tier classification for the United States, one which downplays the collar line. According to Jürgen Kocka, the most striking divisions were those between executive, managerial, and highly placed professional workers on the one hand and lower level white-collar workers on the other and between skilled blue-collar workers on the one hand and the mass of semiskilled and unskilled blue-collar workers on the other.[35] In this schema, the skilled blue-collar and lower-white-collar categories do not quite coalesce, but they overlap.

Was the collar line as indistinct as Kocka suggests? Certainly it was weak by European standards, since America lacked either the sharp European distinction between white-collar and blue-collar schooling or the great European government bureaucracies which reflected prestige upon all white-collar work. In America, where preindustrial traditions of mercantile or bureaucratic status were weak, income mattered more; and this made for considerable overlapping in class position, since American clerks — including men — generally earned less than skilled blue-collar workers. Outside the factory, German and English visitors found to their surprise that they could not be sure which were blue-collar workers, since many changed their clothes at the end of the day and wore a suit and tie to go home. Nor could observers have judged by the workers' destinations, for skilled workers often lived in the same neighborhoods as office and sales workers.[36] Yet real status differences remained. Much to the disgust of blue-collar workers, a $15-a-week clerk often thought himself much above a $25-a-week mechanic. On the job, clean hands and a white shirt conferred superior status. Although the actual term "white-collar" was little used before 1900, late nineteenth-century usage distinguished clearly between wage and salaried workers — basically the same as blue-collar and white-collar. High school students questioned in 1913–1914 regarded white-collar work as distinctly superior thanks to shorter hours, paid vacations, and the hope of moving into management or independent business.[37] Doubtless these students hungered for the rewarding business and professional careers in the upper strata of the middle class; but even low level white-collar jobs tended to be subsumed under the rubric "middle-class" and drew prestige from being thus lumped together with high-status occupations.

Was the distinction between blue- and white-collar work of great importance? The question may seem a muddle, arguable either way. But it is significant that the best arguments for each side focus on different aspects of life. Those against the primacy of the collar line — and by implication, in favor of Kocka's rival classification system — center on consumption patterns as determined by income. Both skilled blue-collar and low level white-collar workers earned considerably more than unskilled workers and considerably less than executives or established professionals. Hence skilled blue-collar workers could afford to buy the same clothes and live in the same neighborhoods as low level white-collar workers. On the other hand, the argument in favor of the collar line's importance rests on matters of status, self-conception, and aspiration. Blue-collar workers, after all, could buy suits, white shirts, and ties; but they had to hang them in the locker while they worked. Similarly, only white-collar workers kept up the middle-class claim — with its overtones of genteel beneficence and professional ambition — that their work was a form of "service." And white-collar workers were much more likely, as we shall see, to carry this self-conception into volunteer service after work.

As later chapters will show, involvement in character building conformed neatly to this distinction between consumer behavior and work-related social roles. When it came to deciding whether to let one's son join the Boy Scouts — essentially a consumer decision — there was no significant difference between skilled blue-collar and low level white-collar workers; in each case, their boys were substantially less likely to be Scouts than were the sons of business and professional men but substantially more likely than the sons of semiskilled or unskilled workers. On the other hand, when it came to giving volunteer service or seeking a paid job with some character-building agency, there was a definite collar line, for Scoutmasters and YMCA boys' workers were almost all men from white-collar backgrounds — ranging from lowly clerks up through fairly substantial businessmen and professionals. By contrast, men from blue-collar backgrounds of any sort were rare in the early years.[38]

Under the circumstances, to attempt a proscriptive definition of the Progressive Era middle class would be to enter a minefield of contention. But because this book focuses on the concerns and activities of the sort of men who became Scoutmasters, Boy Scout executives, and YMCA boys' workers, the term "middle class" will be used to encompass all white-collar workers except the wealthiest businessmen. Among the boys, ambitious sons of skilled blue-collar workers also deserve inclusion; but otherwise even highly skilled blue-collar workers will be excluded from statements about the "middle class" unless specifically mentioned.

Certainly the number of people who were unambiguously middle-class multiplied in the decades around 1900, and they began to organize themselves along vocational lines. White-collar workers made up 17.6 percent of the male labor force in 1900 and 21.4 percent by 1920. Specialized training schools for certain professions appeared in the middle or late 1800s; occupations ranging from accounting to law organized national professional associations; and a host of specialties — among them boys' work — sought status as separate professions by the early 1900s.[39] More than just an effort to gain advantages for specific occupations, the drive towards professionalism became the most common way of affirming middle-class identity and elevating the status of white-collar workers.

At the same time, organizations that employed much of the middle class grew enormously and turned to bureaucratic management. And in the long run, reasonably well-placed employees could also derive status from identification with a large organization. The late 1800s saw the formation of giant corporations, culminating in a wave of mergers between 1898 and 1902. Government at all levels grew in size and complexity, as did universities and social welfare agencies. In each case, the problems of large-scale organization spawned administrative hierarchies and bureaucratic rules. Management soon passed from owners and founders—whether entrepreneurs or, in the case of nonprofit agencies, charismatic innovators—into the hands of paid administrators. Outside of business, superintendents ran city schools; paid staff took over boys' work; and even Protestant churches adopted business methods.[40]

Historians and sociologists have seen in these developments the rise of a new middle class whose members earned a living by exercising a certain skill, backed by a position in an organization or membership in a profession, whereas the old middle class owned and managed property as independent entrepreneurs. But observers have disagreed as to the nature and significance of this new class. Some describe it as a powerful, dynamic grouping. Robert H. Wiebe portrays the new middle class as consisting of "those with strong professional aspirations" plus "specialists in business, in labor, and in agriculture"—all fired by optimism based on new knowledge and eager to solve the problems created by disorderly economic and urban growth.[41] Gregory Singleton has shown substantial continuity between leaders of this new class and the voluntaristic Protestant activism of an earlier generation. Tracing a sample of prominent managers and professionals from the 1880s, he found the majority belonged to "British-origin Protestant denominations" and had fathers who were active in Protestant voluntary organizations.[42] Echoing the old code of the public-spirited gentleman, the new middle class claimed public influence through service as well as expertise. C. Wright Mills offers a different perception. For Mills, the modal member of the new middle class is the clerk, a petty functionary imprisoned in the iron cage of bureaucracy, his work routinized and his salary held to a level little better than blue-collar wages. Even managerial positions and the professions, in Mills's view, became increasingly bureaucratized.[43]

There are problems with either view of the new middle class. Mills ignores the power of those near the top and undervalues the advantages enjoyed by male white-collar workers through the 1920s. On the other hand, Wiebe and Hays ignore the common soldiers of the white-collar army and underestimate the constraints on the higher ranks. Much as Mills describes their situation, salaried professionals often lacked autonomy.[44] Nor were new middle-class careerists immune to market forces, since they had constantly to search out markets for their services.

The rise of character-building agencies was closely related to these developments. Most obviously, an expanding urban middle class, rooted in the British-origin Protestant denominations, provided the main source of boys, adult volunteers, and paid workers. Since voluntary association-alism played a major role in middle-class culture, boys and men of this class were eager joiners, numerous enough by 1900 to form a mass mar-ket yet jealous enough of their class identity to want selective recruitment. Perhaps remembering the ideal gentleman as a man of character and cer-tainly hoping to prepare their own boys for business and professional suc-cess, middle-class adults believed that they could make boys strong and virtuous.

Boys' work itself was another new middle-class career. The YMCA, for instance, followed organizationally the pattern which Singleton traced in individual terms; beginning as a Protestant voluntary association run by amateurs, it grew into a huge organization run by paid experts. Leading boys' workers displayed the dynamism of Wiebe's new middle-class career-ists, claiming unique expertise regarding adolescent boys; but lower-level boys' workers struggled simply to establish careers. The successes and fail-ures of these men tell us much about the fate of ordinary members of the new middle class, its followers as well as leaders.

Still, why did middle-class adults decide to help middle-class boys in particular? The answers lie in changing patterns of child rearing, in the boys' changing social environment outside the home, and in adult anxie-ties outlined in the next chapter.

With growing prosperity and urbanization, nineteenth-century families shrank dramatically, as birthrates approximately halved between 1800 and 1900. Although family size declined among all classes, the urban Protes-tant middle class led this change. Already by 1855, according to a study of Buffalo, New York, and its environs, the families of professionals and other highly skilled white-collar workers were nearly 25 percent smaller than those of other social groups. Between 1890 and 1910, the proportion of couples in a large sample of northern whites, both urban and rural, who had four or more children declined from 37 to 18 percent in the pro-fessional class, 39 to 21 percent in the business class, and 46 to 31 among skilled blue-collar workers; the decline was from 54 to 38 percent among the unskilled and 56 to 46 among farm owners.[45]

The significance of this trend was both negative and positive. Nega-tively, it reflected parents' decreasing reliance on children for farm labor or an extra paycheck. As the urban household became a refuge for relaxa-tion and emotional support, a few children made it homelike, yet a horde of noisy offspring did not. More positively, having fewer children enabled middle-class parents to engage in affectionate, personally intensive child rearing and keep each child in school longer. Presumably, reducing family size in order to invest more in education appealed particularly to the upper strata of the new middle class whose careers depended upon education and skills. But such a strategy heightened parental anxieties; for as families shrank, the investment in any one child rose. Once the household was no longer a workplace, moreover, its child-rearing functions stood out, vulnerable to criticism.[46] Meanwhile, children were more and more exposed to outside influences, especially from peers. Hence anxious parents strove to protect their investment and looked to outside agencies, eventually including character-building organizations, to help train their offspring and channel the children's social contacts.[47]

Even before family size shrank, Protestant child-rearing advice called for close attention to each child and steadiness of purpose. Nineteenth-century advice lost much of its sternness as writers recognized that it was mothers who did the day-to-day child rearing.[48] Gone for many children were the frequent beatings and erratic rages of farm fathers. Conflict and inconsistency did not disappear altogether; foreign travelers remarked on both the brash independence of American children and parents' spasmodic efforts at suppression. Yet Jacob Abbott, the pre-Civil War era's most popular writer on child rearing, urged strong, steady, early guidance, leading to disciplined self-direction.[49] This ideal of character eventually carried over, though much diluted, into boys' work in the form of pledges to marshal inner resolution.

The post-Civil War decades saw a declining emphasis upon rules, discipline, and arbitrary authority, as parents retreated into emotionally intense families. Fearing that society was overpressured, writers urged mothers to make childhood a sheltered idyll, accommodated to the child's needs and desires. So as not to stifle her child's impulses, a mother was to use substitution rather than confrontation; a boy who drove nails into furniture, for instance, should have blocks instead. Even more clearly, the psychologist G. Stanley Hall's child study movement of the 1890s, which attempted to record children's actual behavior and ideas, brought home the message that children differed from adults and that parents must adopt a child-centered form of management.[50]

Impulse and inspiration won freer rein. As Daniel T. Rodgers has noted, children's literature fled the mundane world of steady, self-denying habits and petty virtues for a realm of sentiment and impulsive heroism. Edward H. Griggs, whose *Moral Education* (1905) was widely read by character builders, warned against teaching ethics like arithmetic; rather, moral educators should foster "generous instincts . . . [and] an heroic attitude toward difficulties."[51]

Still, old themes of steadiness, order, and juvenile submission continued. Adults simply kept a looser rein, relying less upon overt command than upon manipulation or direction of the child's nature and environment. Horace Bushnell, a leading Congregational theologian of the mid-1800s, argued that a child raised within an ordered, loving Christian household could easily avoid depravity; like Abbott, Bushnell believed that "family government" grounded in steadiness and order would foster self-control. One could cite Griggs for quite similar advice.[52] And as we shall see in chapter 6, character builders held similar views regarding teenagers, whose adolescent instincts they hoped to channel. Character-building theory was an extension, inspired by Hall's psychology, of the trend in child rearing towards manipulation of young people's impulses and surroundings.

Although manipulative, middle-class child rearing grew less authoritarian than that of other classes. Investigators in 1930 found urban middle-class families more egalitarian than farm families, united more by positive emotions and less by shared labor; city children spent more time away from home and yet confided more easily in parents.[53] Parents in such families welcomed their sons' membership in outside agencies such as Boy Scouting. Recent research has also found a consistent, though modest, difference between middle-class child rearing, which stresses self-direction, and a working-class style, which favors conformity to authority.[54] Many boys' workers certainly *thought* there was such a difference, since they judged lower-class boys capable of obeying rules but not of forming inner strength of character. By contrast, although character builders insisted that middle-class boys meet adult expectations, they also presumed that such boys would be guided by internalized values or, increasingly, by the influence of a controlled environment and managed peer groups. This approach suited a new upper middle class whose work demanded self-direction yet had to mesh with that of others in large organizations.[55]

Somewhat anomalously, schooling lagged behind these changes in child rearing, remaining rooted in patterns established before the Civil War. At that time, urban schoolmen had led in the movement to impose order and regularity on children, reacting sharply against the jumble of ages in one-room rural schools. City superintendents separated pupils into graded classrooms where the teacher demanded uniform attention to a single lesson, backed by rules prescribing silence and rigid posture.[56] As women moved into teaching, advice on classroom discipline softened, yet in practice the emphasis on order and system persisted. Joseph Rice, an 1890s critic of classroom rigidity, met a teacher who insisted, "How can you learn anything with your knees and toes out of order?"[57] Even after 1900, the schools' main concession to adolescent restlessness was to add extra-curricular activities *after* school hours. Observers in the schools of Muncie, Indiana, in the 1920s found classroom instruction "thoroughly regimented," with "practically all movement . . . forbidden. . . ."[58]

Inconsistencies in the socialization of middle-class children—notably this disparity between trends towards flexibility in child rearing and con-

tinued rigidity in schooling—left a wide opening for character builders
to seek a middle path, purporting to give boys' needs and impulses free
play yet also promising order and discipline. Boy Scouting, for example,
struck some shrewd balances. The Scout oath embodied the new inspirational approach to moral education, while badges recognized the traditional claims of steady effort. The motto, "Be Prepared," called for careful preparation for the sort of sudden heroics which now filled boys' stories.
In general, early character builders stressed steady habits; their successors
shifted towards heroic ideals and somewhat greater spontaneity.

The turn to recreation in order to build character reflected not only
shifts in child rearing but also changing attitudes towards work and play.
In preindustrial America, workdays were long but the pace was irregular,
and one seldom spent whole weeks stretched drum-tight by work. New
economic opportunities and pressures changed that, however, so that work
took on new value and intensity. Antebellum American men looked to
work as an outlet for their finest strivings and as a goad to discipline
and self-denial; it was a school of character where boys and men learned
to obey the marching orders of the will.[59]
With rising prosperity, though, the hours of work per week gradually
declined; and for the middle class a week of summer vacation was commonplace by 1920.[60] Since the leisure of the young now seemed less anoma-
lous, prosperous parents who vacationed at a lakeside hotel would pay
to send a son to camp. Instead of spending more time with their children,
some parents took up recreations of their own and compensated by paying
so their children could do the same. This was no reversion to preindustrial
casualness, for work and leisure both grew more intense; as working hours
shortened, the pace of work accelerated. Nor was this pattern confined
to adults, for critics complained of overpressure in the schools. In reaction, a few middle-class ideologues such as Henry Ward Beecher began,
soon after the Civil War, to celebrate repose and idleness; but the main
currents in recreation raced past such pools of quiet and on towards busy
activity. As work grew more intense and driven, men looked hungrily to
leisure time as a compensation for work. As such, leisure had to be *spent;*
mere absence of work was insufficient.[61]
Recreation took on new earnestness. It is notorious, for instance, how
seriously turn-of-the-century Americans took team sports. As moral conservatives, character builders regretted that boys had lost the old-fashioned
discipline of work. When they began organizing activities for boys, their
initial preference for improving talks, gymnastic exercises, and military
drills made it clear they wanted recreation to substitute for work in demanding disciplinary effort.
For children, play came to seem both natural and necessary. Romantics

already celebrated the sunny playfulness of children; also, as will be discussed in chapter 6, evolutionary theories becoming popular around 1900 further legitimized play, explaining it as a recapitulation of the work of primitive mankind. In this transmutation, play became the proper work of children, promising moral benefits under proper supervision. Both work and schooling, in this view, were imposed from outside, whereas children at play lived out their instincts. So if morality was a matter of free intention, then play would be the best setting for moral education.[62]

Protestant moralists gradually changed their attitude towards literary fiction as well. Formerly, they had denied legitimacy to any but unbuffered confrontations with the sober realities of life. For instance, officials of the Bloomington, Illinois, YMCA boasted in 1884 that for their boys' story hour they rejected all tales which had "an air of romance" and confined themselves "to such as we know to have been strictly true."[63] By the late 1800s, however, play became a rehearsal for adulthood and imaginative literature a source of moral inspiration. Character builders extended this logic into the teens, supervising adolescents' recreation and trying to mold their fantasies as well.

Middle-class boys needed supervised recreation, character builders believed, because their lives had changed. As they spent more and more years under conditions of full dependence and tutelage, they were becoming what boys' workers by 1900 would label "adolescents." To understand the rise of character-building agencies which sought out such youths, we must return to the patterns of boys' lives and follow the emergence of schoolboy adolescence.

Anthropologists and sociologists have explained adolescence or youth (a broader term) as a necessary concomitant of modern industrialized society, basing this claim upon comparisons between modern Western and premodern or non-Western societies. Ruth Benedict blamed adolescent storm and stress upon "discontinuous cultural conditioning." In our society, she argued, because the demands of childhood differ greatly from those of adulthood, adolescence is a troubled time of transition, whereas in societies with continuous conditioning, children gain early experience with adult roles and pass fairly smoothly into adulthood.[64] S. N. Eisenstadt and his sociological allies assert that in modern Western societies, the youthful peer group has gained salience as a bridge from more or less uncritical acceptance within one's family to the impersonal achievement demands of adult society. In Eisenstadt's scheme of things, agencies such as the Boy Scouts stand between the peer group and the adult world; they offset the narrow training of the schools, offering "expressive activities" and a "common youth-adolescent identity," while at the same time fostering respect for adult authority.[65]

Though plausible in broad outline, such highly generalized explanations cannot account for the step-by-step emergence of specific cultural patterns in specific historical settings. Extended schooling was a precondition of modern adolescence, for instance, yet rural schools differed markedly from urban; and character builders mediated more often between church and peer group than between school and peer group. The broad term "youth" likewise obscures vast differences between preadolescents, adolescents, and college-age youths which are vital to understanding how agencies for boys' work began.

A framework more sensitive to incremental change comes from demographers who view relations between young people and adults as a function of the two groups' relative size. In this vein, it is significant that the ratio of boys to men declined markedly between 1870 and 1920. In 1870, there were 724 white boys below age *12* for every 1,000 white men ages 21 through 64. By 1920, one had to include teenagers to reach a similar ratio: there were 716 white boys under age *19* for every 1,000 white men 21 through 64. Relative to adults, small boys and teenagers *combined* now bulked no larger than preteenage boys *alone* in 1870. If we consider the economic and supervisory burdens borne by adults, by 1920 it should have been as easy—purely in terms of numbers—to keep both teenagers and smaller children dependent as it once had been to manage only the younger ones. A lesser shift may also have drawn attention to teenagers; while the overall share of the population under nineteen was declining, the ratio of white boys 12 through 18 to those 0 through 11 rose slightly from 460 to 1,000 in 1870 to 520 in 1920.[66] Not only was it becoming more feasible for adults to supervise everyone under 19; teenagers now bulked slightly larger within that group.

Conveniently—since boys' work began in the late 1800s—the decades after 1870 saw a particularly rapid decline in the ratio of boys to men. From 1850 to 1870, the ratio of white boys ages 0–18 to white men 21–64 fell only .25 percent a year. But between 1870 and 1900, it dropped .88 percent annually, slowing a bit to .61 percent from 1900 to 1920.[67] And the trend was most advanced by 1870 in the Northeast, where boys' work first became established. There were 785 white boys 0–18 for every 1,000 white men 21–64 in New England and 927 in the Middle Atlantic region, compared to 1,083 in the Great Lakes states, 1,248 in the South Atlantic states, and 1,304 in the East South Central region. The Great Lakes states, where boys' work soon caught on, saw a sharp decline to 643 boys per 1,000 men in 1920, on a level with 628 in New England and 653 in the Middle Atlantic states. In the two southern regions, the ratios remained higher (893 and 981 for whites) and boys' work lagged.[68] It was where and when boys were fewest relative to adults—in the North, the cities, the middle class, and the twentieth century—that a protected adolescence took root and character-building agencies flourished.

Demography provides a summary explanation of the rise of modern adolescence. However, attitudes as well as age ratios had to change for the concept to emerge.

Certainly modern adolescence is not totally without precedent. Indeed, adolescence threatens to become a historical perennial; historians have diagnosed forms of it among eighteenth-century New Englanders, seventeenth-century London apprentices, sixteenth-century Bristol apprentices, and fifteenth-century Florentines. Alarmist descriptions of *adolescentia* by Protestant reformers of the 1500s drew upon writers as early as Augustine and Aristotle.[69] Yet John Gillis, writing on Europe, and John and Virginia Demos, describing America, assert that adults did not recognize adolescence as we know it, centering on ages fourteen to eighteen, until the late 1800s. Instead, these writers distinguish a longer, less sharply defined precursor stage which they call "youth."[70]

The issue is partly one of definition. If one sees adolescence merely as a time between childhood and adulthood when the young are somewhat unsettled, then it has existed for centuries. Puberty as a developmental transition is universal. Western culture after the Reformation stressed sexual repression and religious conversion; and children of the past were not simply little adults, so their socialization was necessarily somewhat discontinuous. But there was little of Erik Erikson's "psychosocial moratorium" based upon extended formal education.[71] Apprentices, for instance, worked alongside adults and were expected to model themselves upon their masters. Nor was youth so compressed in time as modern adolescence; most accounts show it underway around fourteen and lasting into the mid-twenties or beyond.[72] In general, to trace the emergence of modern adolescence is to follow the separation of a narrower, more sharply defined period of life from a broader transitional stage less thoroughly segregated from adult life.

Such a broad youthful stage was evident in eighteenth-century New England, where Jonathan Edwards condemned the "company keeping" of "young people" from fifteen or so through their twenties.[73] The use of "youth" for ages fifteen to about twenty-five lasted well past 1800, its breadth reflecting the fact that young people's lives had not yet settled into an orderly sequence which could be subdivided.[74] Instead of gradually shedding restraints one by one, male youths of the early 1800s switched statuses abruptly but erratically. Yankee farm boys often left to work for wages in winter but returned to labor under their father's authority during planting and harvest. Midwestern farm boys stayed home more; yet in both regions, schooling was seasonal, with rural youths sometimes returning during slack winters until late in their teens. On the other hand, the many teenagers who fought in the Revolution and the Civil War paid an abrupt and brutal farewell to boyhood. Scions of the best families entered business young, to the point that Tocqueville claimed that in America "there is, strictly speaking, no adolescence; at the close of boyhood the man appears. . . ."[75] Evangelists likewise demanded early commitments. Overall, youths of the 1800–1840 period had no guarantee of a sheltered adolescence.

Growing boys mingled with a great variety of ages. Large families meant that most boys had siblings a good deal older or younger than themselves. At district schools, pupils ranged in age from six to twenty. Militia companies and self-improvement societies admitted teenagers into the company of young men; informally as well, teenagers hung around young people in their twenties with an easy familiarity impossible today. And of course work brought close contact with adults.[76]

In the end, though, industrialization and urbanization narrowed age contacts, reducing the likelihood that boys would work alongside their fathers and undercutting other forms of tacit adult control as well. Arrangements whereby established merchants took promising young clerks as boarders or informally apprenticed them were breaking down by midcentury under the press of numbers and the growing separation of the middle and upper classes. Businessmen looked instead to impersonal institutions, such as the YMCAs and ultimately the high schools, to control and screen their clerks.[77]

Early independence began to seem dangerous by midcentury; moralists charged that early responsibilities opened young men to urban corruption. A New York clergyman, George Bethune, complained in 1854 that young clerks were "forced to become men before they cease to be boys. . . ."[78] Bethune's answer was self-education and self-discipline through the YMCA, but the trend in succeeding decades ran towards a different solution; conceding the independence of young men, middle-class adults concentrated on lengthening control and indoctrination of teenagers *before* they went to work.

Before midcentury, the regimen of dependency and careful preparation had applied mainly to children under twelve. As it extended into the teens, adult attention began to focus upon the frontier where control was growing but still in doubt. From the 1870s onward, common usage defined youth narrowly as fourteen to nineteen, and adult concern centered increasingly upon the time around puberty. By the late 1800s, teenagers were seldom fully independent, since most lived at home whether they worked or merely attended school.[79] In child rearing, the mixture of steadiness and order with qualified indulgence of children's impulses carried over into the teens. Insofar as this approach presumed childish innocence and malleability, however, it courted disillusionment at puberty, spawning schemes like boys' work to distract boys from their new impulses which alarmed adults.

In religious training, the extension of dependency came as a reaction against early nineteenth-century practices which cut short the process of conversion—demanding decisions within a few fevered days and reaping a great harvest of teenage converts but exacerbating fears that youths were impulsive and overly emotional. Revivalism lost some of its appeal towards 1840, for by then perhaps 75 percent of the population was church-affiliated.[80] Since they had little hope of winning Catholic immigrants, Protestant churches were increasingly limited in recruitment to the children of their present members. Accordingly, by midcentury the emphasis swung away from sudden conversion towards the mild and steady socialization of children and teenagers. The logical culmination was Horace Bushnell's proposal for Christian nurture: "That the child is to grow up a Christian, and never know himself as being otherwise."[81] A conversion would therefore be unnecessary. This view was highly controversial when first enunciated in 1846, but over the next half century a compromise evolved within mainstream denominations which made conversion a relatively early, *pro forma* culmination of Christian nurture, preferably "in early to middle adolescence." As such, it should not be too jarring; there must be nothing, warned a committee of boys' workers in 1912, "that awakens any sort of hysterical response." And by then it was quite acceptable to elide conversion altogether. In a 1913 survey, 99 of 127 YMCA boys' workers claimed to have grown "gradually into the Christian conception of life"; only 47 even experienced a recognizable turning point.[82]

While Bushnell wrote about the Christian family as if it could exist in utopian self-sufficiency, the new emphasis on nurture took forms outside the family. First was the Sunday school; it originated as a way to help the poor, but as Protestant churches shifted towards internal recruitment, it became "the nursery of the church."[83] At first, older youths served as teachers; however, very soon Sunday school officials set up classes to hold teenagers in pupilage, and the effort to prolong Sunday school attendance continued through the nineteenth century until by 1900 it was a rare dissenter who objected that adolescents should not be kept "in the children's place."[84]

To provide for teenagers who felt too old for Sunday school, congregations sometimes formed young people's societies. In the 1880s, these coalesced into national organizations and members poured in. The largest was the nondenominational Christian Endeavor Society, founded in 1881; the Baptist Young People's Union and the Methodists' Epworth League each claimed half a million members by the early 1900s.[85] As the membership aged, a gap opened between these societies and the Sunday schools that churchmen had to bridge if Christian nurture was to be sustained. One answer was church-sponsored boys' work.

Sunday schools, character-building agencies, and young people's societies were all extensions of Christian nurture, since each reduced experience to a form of adult-supervised training, a process of "perpetual becoming."[86] Age grading helped by fostering a sense of progress while in fact prolonging dependency. So did the reduction of religion to morality, which discouraged spiritual adventuring. Thus Norman E. Richardson, a professor of religious pedagogy, told Scout leaders that religious educators should tell a boy only what was directly useful for morality at his present age.[87] Not surprisingly, boys lost interest in theology. A Unitarian minister observed ruefully: "The days are gone by when the eager boy had half a dozen theological problems hung up, like herbs, in his mental attic to dry, and occasionally took one down and chewed a leaf of it with a friend coming home from school."[88] Even the much older members of young people's societies were mired in functionless "endeavor"—pledge-taking, literary meetings, worship services, and bits of busywork around the church.[89] Similarly, character builders urged endless preparation and stressed morality rather than spirituality.

Changes in secular schooling likewise led towards prolonged pupilage, but by a roundabout route: first schooling grew more intensive, and then it grew longer. Towards the mid-1800s, in search of factorylike efficiency, city school officials instituted graded classes and sought to advance pupils from grade to grade at uniform ages, although age mixing remained substantial until about the 1890s.[90] Increasingly, city schools eliminated laggards in their teens who towered over younger classmates. City pupils could no longer attend seasonally; instead, they were to attend full time every year, finish, and leave soon after age fourteen, with the result by 1860 that many more farm than nonfarm children in the North remained in school at ages fifteen to nineteen.[91]

Education soon lengthened, however, as the growth of white-collar occupations produced a demand for employees with the deportment and skills that high schools tried to inculcate. The growth of bureaucratized corporations, civil service systems, and rudimentary professional licensing all put a premium on certified credentials. Education became a screening system. Nationwide, public high school enrollment shot up from 110,000 in 1880 to 519,000 in 1900 and 2,200,000 by 1920. By 1900, although some worthwhile blue-collar opportunities remained, most boys of fourteen or fifteen who quit school ended up in "dead-end" jobs.[92]

Accordingly, the years fourteen through seventeen became critical as never before. For parents, the first question was whether a son would remain in school. In 1919, 86 percent of all fourteen-year-old boys attended school, but only 32 percent of the seventeen-year-olds. Secondly, would he keep up to his grade level? "Retardation," as contemporaries called it, averaged 30 to 40 percent in big-city schools of the early 1900s.[93] Under the old, irregular rural system, ambitious boys could make up lost ground later, but the graded city schools were like crowded stairways on which few who fell behind caught up again. As late as 1920, only 16 percent of American seventeen-year-olds graduated from high school.[94] During their middle teens, therefore, boys faced increasingly irrevocable choices. Ambitious parents who could afford it favored a protected adolescence, curbing any turbulence or independence that might distract their sons from steady preparation for success.

A boy's chances of spending adolescence in high school depended heavily upon his family background. Around 1920, a study of four cities found that children of professionals were more than twice as likely to be in high school as those of building tradesmen and twenty times as likely as laborers' children.[95] Ethnicity also played a role, in part through differences in social class; in 1920, only 37 percent of sons of foreign-born parents were still in school at age sixteen, compared to 54 percent of sons of native parents.[96]

In balancing costs and benefits, strategies varied. The native-stock middle class tended to keep children attending school and living at home longer than other groups; even prosperous German immigrants, who had more children, did not keep them at home as long. In lower-class white families, certainly among Polish, Italian, and Irish families, children's wages often provided the margin of comfort, and boys commonly expected to quit school as soon as possible. Family pressures were particularly acute for boys, since girls could not earn as high wages and so stayed in school somewhat longer.[97] Ambitious boys could compromise by taking part-time jobs to stay in school, but as Leonard Covello found, the combination was wearing. In general, urban lower-class and farm parents tended to maximize immediate economic returns and scant their sons' schooling, whereas a schoolboy adolescence came to be characteristic of middle-class urban teenagers, particularly British-stock Protestants.

There was one conspicuous exception to this dichotomy, however — the small number of black boys living in northern cities by the late 1800s and early 1900s. Superficially, their lives resembled those of middle-class white teenagers who were developing a schoolboy adolescence. The families of longtime black city dwellers were small. Black migrants had high hopes for themselves and their sons; the boys stayed in school much longer than white immigrants and were less likely to have paid jobs.[98] A good many, moreover, tried to join character-building agencies. But the promise of education seldom paid off for blacks, as many northern cities would not even hire black teachers, and low teenage employment among blacks resulted from discrimination as well as choice. In boys' work too, as we shall see, blacks faced intermittent discrimination. A major reason why black parents did not — indeed, could not — pack their children off to work to help the family was that unlike immigrant parents whose ethnic groups had established firm footholds in certain blue-collar occupations, black families could not readily guide their sons into secure jobs; racism and small numbers blocked the growth of black vocational enclaves. Consequently, when black boys found work, they did so on their own and kept most of their wages; and they left home early.[99] While blacks appeared willing to invest in prolonged adolescent dependency and educational preparation, the supports and rewards were missing, as were the familial vocational networks of established immigrant groups. Black boys were on their own.

Progressive reformers worked to give all children—especially those of the immigrant lower class—a more sheltered childhood; yet this often meant altering rather than eliminating class inequality. Central to their efforts was the dual crusade for compulsory education and against child labor. School attendance laws began to take hold after 1900, although their effect was limited primarily to northern children under fourteen. However, as lower-class children attended in larger numbers, inequality moved inside the school, where educators channeled pupils they thought unpromising into separate programs.[100] Child labor laws were the other side of the coin. By the late 1800s, children ran machines in textile mills, sorted coal in mines, dashed about with change and packages in stores, delivered telegrams, peddled newspapers, slaved over piecework at home, and—as always—labored on farms. Gradually the belief spread that urban jobs were debilitating and dangerous. Still, in 1912 only nine states' laws met the National Child Labor Committee's minimum standards, including reliable proof of age and a ban on factory work before fourteen. As measured by the census, the first substantial decline in child labor came in the 1910s, though exactly how substantial remains uncertain.[101] Rising prosperity and technological changes may have made it easier to do without full-time child labor. Starting soon after 1900, for instance, telephones, cash registers, and conveyor belts eliminated Western Union boys and messengers in stores.[102] But part-time jobs continued, such as delivering groceries or setting pins in bowling alleys, and combining school and work can hardly have made working-class teenagers' lives less harried. Prohibitory legislation and the labor market could, after all, force a sort of sheltered childhood but not equalize incomes. Some middle-class boys took part-time jobs, to be sure, but they did so as a form of cultural nostalgia, as in the case of B. F. Skinner, or else to earn spending money or pay their way to college, as did Bruce Catton. The money was for their own use; they were not expected to help support the family.

Other Progressive Era reforms likewise worked to increase lower-class dependency without eliminating social inequality. Curfew ordinances and laws against smoking stigmatized the bravado of street boys, and juvenile court judges penalized obstreperous behavior, again primarily among the lower class.[103]

Dependency was already much more prolonged and unequivocal among the middle class. Indeed, the middle-class high school students became the model of adolescence as it was supposed to operate; they had literally to school themselves to patience, practising the virtues of "achievement, purity, and self-restraint" long thought vital to self-advancement but now doing so within institutions devised for their extended nurture. Parents demanded repayment "not in wages but in obedience to the demands of school and society." [104] They, along with educators, churchmen, and character builders, all wanted steady, unhurried development.

By the early 1900s, believers in protected and extended nurture had achieved a measure of success. Urban middle-class teenagers lived much more narrowly dependent lives than working-class or farm boys or youths of their own class a century before. Dependency, in turn, supported age grading by making differences in age stand out as mileposts in an otherwise featureless landscape and by preventing the intrusion of responsibilities demanding sudden maturity.

Development of a relatively protected adolescence both fed upon and strengthened the growing sense of middle-class identity. Sacrifice for one's children became another mark of middle-class status or aspirations; relying upon children's pay was considered as disgraceful as sending a wife to work. Smaller families enabled middle-class parents to give each child closer attention, and experts urged them to make allowances for the child's stage of development; a protected schoolboy adolescence extended this concern into the teens. With Sunday schools and mild conversions, the Protestant churches of the urban middle class took the lead among religious bodies in moving towards a protected upbringing, although their age grading still lagged sufficiently that church youth workers had to scramble to catch up with expectations boys had formed in other areas of life.

Age grading and dependency interlocked more fully in the public school system, where would-be white-collar workers had to advance on schedule with their age peers. Much as Eisenstadt described it, the schools' emphasis on secondary relationships drove pupils into peer groups in search of personal anchorage; and now that graded classrooms brought together so many pupils all about the same age, peer groups could be sharply stratified. While graded schooling gave a sense of progress to mitigate dependency, its extension made for a finicky peer culture, sensitive to age differences. To fill their new leisure, moreover, schoolboys increasingly took refuge in sports; this offered them tokens of achievement but further sharpened age grading, since physical capacities increase conspicuously with age and competitive sports magnify such differences.

The trend towards uniformity in timing of major life transitions enabled the young to be more precise in their age expectations. Boys grew touchy about marks of age status such as long pants at puberty.[105] And peer groups narrowed. As we shall see, the pattern of easy association between boys of fourteen or fifteen and young men of twenty or twenty-one carried over into early YMCAs, but YMCA leaders soon found that young men who worked full time had little left in common with full-time schoolboys. By the early 1900s, two or three years' difference in age effectively divided boys.[106]

In all these changes, the nonfarm middle class stood out. While much of the urban pattern of age grading applied to all classes, lower-class boys were more apt to fall behind their age group at school and yet move ahead of it in going out to work. Perhaps as a result, they accepted fairly casual age grading in boys' clubs. For country boys, age mixing persisted in ungraded schooling, farm labor, and sometimes social life as well.[107]

The separation of middle-class boys into age-graded peer groups was at once a blessing and a burden to character builders. Their programs would have been unthinkable without a constituency of dependent adolescents in need of recreation; yet the boys' sensitivity to age differences made them hard to hold. Pervasive age grading had reoriented the issue between adults and boys; instead of a few convulsive struggles for autonomy, there were endless little tests along a finely calibrated course. The boys wanted more tokens of maturity, yet had no intention of demanding total independence. Adults wanted to hold the boys back but not to cripple their initiative.

Basically, character builders were ambivalent towards adolescents. On one hand, they wanted to foster initiative and achievement; on the other, they wanted obedience and sustained dependence. They desired broad preparation for white-collar success yet retained a lingering regard for the tough virtues of the old-style, work-bound boyhood. They admired the vigor of sturdy street boys yet sought to guard middle-class boys from contamination by the lower class. To these conflicting ambitions and anxieties we must now turn.

2

Character Building: Adult Ambitions and Concerns

Character builders set broad goals. For a sense of their scope, consider what an American Boy Scout promised: "On my honor I will do my best: 1. To do my duty to God and my country, and to obey the scout law; 2. To help other people at all times; 3. To keep myself physically strong, mentally awake, and morally straight." And the Scout law obligated him to be trustworthy, loyal, helpful, friendly, courteous, kind, obedient, cheerful, thrifty, brave, clean, and reverent. The YMCA was equally ambitious, seeking to improve "the spiritual, mental, social and physical condition" of men and boys.[1] This was no narrow mandate.

The YMCA's fourfold plan of spiritual, mental, social, and physical improvement stands as the best brief summary of character builders' goals. Its elements are evident in the Boy Scout oath, especially the third clause, which was added under YMCA influence. S. W. Hopson, a Denver Scout executive, argued that no boy could "score in life" unless he rounded all four bases, ending with the spiritual.[2] Since character builders believed that morality demanded both social and religious training, the fourfold formula can be simplified still further to a balance of strength (mental and physical) and virtue (social and religious).

Broad preparation was tailored to the needs of middle-class schoolboys whose careers, ideally, would be open-ended and whose development, therefore, must not be limited or narrowly vocational like that of blue-collar workers. As managers and professionals in adulthood, they would be rated more on character and personality than on strictly technical capacities. Thus character builders, regarding the academic program of the schools as too narrowly intellectual, set themselves to provide a supplement.[3] Definitions of balanced development were somewhat arbitrary, however, since no one could specify, for instance, precisely what level of religious development equalled what level of physical culture. So character builders took refuge in comprehensiveness, piling up plans and statements in muddled profusion. Indeed, they never managed a clear definition of the word "character," assuming instead that everyone knew what they meant.[4]

The term in fact had a long history of shifting uses. Originally meaning reputation, character came to signify intrinsic qualities, commonly with connotations of solidity and value. By the early 1800s, "character" in this sense seemed a "configuration of moral qualities gradually molded in each person."[5] At first the assumption was that everyone must shape his or her own character; but just as the introspective struggle for conversion gave way to Christian nurture, so character became something which adults could foster in the young.[6]

Virtue and strength converged in nineteenth-century ideas of character. With the spread of belief in steady nurture, "character formation" began displacing religion as the primary basis for "learned moral behavior" at home and school.[7] By the 1830s, child-rearing advisers urged mothers to supervise small children constantly, embedding moral precepts in the child's conscience, while temperance and other reform societies soon began to inculcate more public virtues among the older population. Steady moral habits from both sources grew increasingly vital for obtaining credit and prevailing in small business. At the same time, middle-class careerists looked to character as the inner power which drove them upward. Strength merged with virtue in the Victorian association of physical health with moral character which underlay expressions such as "healthy minded" and turned boys' workers to exercise for building character.[8] Theodore Roosevelt, the BSA's Chief Scout Citizen, epitomized the ideal of moralistic energy and forceful conventionality.

By the late 1800s, it seemed, "character" was becoming commonplace as the meaning of the term shifted. Formerly the distinctive attribute of gentility, it now appeared attainable by any boy of decent family. But in evolving a class identity, the middle class attenuated and homogenized gentry styles, weakening "independence of character and . . . individuality."[9] The older notion lingered on in celebrations of forceful individuality such as William James's description of character as "the mental or moral attitude in which . . . a voice inside says: 'This is the real me!'" In Erik Erikson's terminology, James valued "a sense of identity."[10] However, the notion of character which was common by the late 1800s reduced it to a compendium of conventional virtues and strengths such as those enumerated in the Boy Scout oath and law; and it was this form that character builders sought to foster.

The logic of early character building rested upon a popular psychology which conceived the mind as being composed of several major faculties: intellect, emotion, will, and sometimes conscience. The faculties in turn comprised a host of separate powers; for example, memory, attention, observation, deduction, and many others made up the intellect. Like educators, character builders believed such powers could be "improved individually — as muscles are improved — through exercise."[11] Character, then, was balanced development of these powers. The main change over time was an almost endless extension of the capacities — moral, muscular, and social as well as intellectual — which character builders hoped to strengthen. Indeed, Sir Robert Baden-Powell, Boy Scouting's founder, prescribed exercises in everything from thrift to good eyesight and thoughtfulness.

Since they believed it was the will which actually moved a person to action and suppressed base urges, Victorian writers exalted it above other faculties. But because the will could not remain switched on at every moment, steady self-control depended on transforming efforts at self-improvement into reliable habits. Baden-Powell's motto, "Be Prepared," encapsulated this view of character as stored capacity to act. Since exertion strengthened and disciplined the will while building up subordinate powers and rendering their use habitual, effort was the core of old-fashioned character building.[12]

Techniques to strengthen powers and get a purchase on the will shifted over time. Midnineteenth-century writers, reflecting contemporary individualism, poured forth advice to young men demanding extreme self-control: the least deviation from evangelical morality — a glass of beer, an impure thought — betrayed a debased will and formed a fatal precedent.[13] But as adult attention and concern shifted towards younger boys and such boys remained fully dependent longer, earnest adults moved to a training mode designed to exercise boys' powers and build good habits directly. The old-style teacher's fondness for drills in spelling and arithmetic left as its residue a faith in repetitive effort to discipline the faculties. Even a few hours a week promised great benefits. As the Rev. Charles Morrell of the Boys' Brigade put it: "The habits of obedience taught in the drill-room are not forgotten in the Sunday school or the home. . . ."[14] Although Morrell spoke of habits, his argument relied on a loose faculty psychology in which words describing the form or results of mental activity acquired the status of entities able to produce the effects they described. Thus military drill exercised the power of attention, which then would function in any situation demanding attention.[15] Though generally subtler, similar assumptions underlay most character building. In line with shifts in child rearing, twentieth-century boys' work grew more manipulative and group-oriented. By following the natural course of boys' development and channeling their instincts, character builders sought to foster both energy and control without the strain of fiercely willed achievement against resistance. Yet steady training continued as an antidote to adolescent turbulence, though the atmosphere grew more relaxed. Indeed, all three modes — earnest advice, steady training, and management of instincts in a group setting — intermingled in twentieth-century character building. The Boy Scout law, for instance, set forth ideals; badge work purportedly strengthened boys' powers; and Boy Scout leaders claimed to harness the gang instinct. Each technique would contribute to all-round development.

All was not so positive, however, for beneath these gleaming ambitions bulked an iceberg of anxieties and ambivalence. At one moment, character builders lamented that middle-class schoolboys were flabby and effeminate, at another, that they were pushy and undisciplined. The trouble was that character builders demanded both strength and control: boys must be manly yet dependent, virtuous without femininity in a culture which regarded women as more moral than men. These contradictions were embedded in the role which adults now demanded of middle-class boys. Such boys were to seek achievement but only as a form of preparation, for they must stay in school. They should know their place and yet be bright and take initiative. When, however, might initiative turn into excessive self-assertion? When might virtue and obedience become effeminacy and weakness? With its goal of balanced growth, character building was an anxiety-driven struggle to have it both ways.

The character builders sometimes decried the whole drift of modern life. Ernest Thompson Seton, Chief Scout of the Boy Scouts of America, charged that "many Americans" had grown "degenerate. We know money grubbing, machine politics, degrading sports, cigarettes . . . false ideals, moral laxity and lessening church power, in a word '*City rot*' has worked evil in the nation." Baden-Powell likewise excoriated British society, comparing it to late imperial Rome.[16] In effect, boys' workers transposed all sorts of anxieties about modern life onto urban youth. The image of the wicked city was fixed in popular culture, and moral conservatives used the concept of urbanization as shorthand for unsettling social change.[17]

As a result, character builders ignored evidence that rural poverty and intermingling of ages and classes precluded the sort of sheltered adolescence they wanted for urban teenagers. A. N. Raven, a pastor from rural Pennsylvania, protested in 1898 that country boys went unsupervised. A friend claimed "there was not a low thought, desire, or motive, that he was not familiar with at the age of fifteen years." On slow days, "the 'hired man' and the boys would gather in the barn and talk such language as he now knew to be . . . the lowest of mankind." Raven urged rural clergymen to provide something like the Boys' Brigade.[18] But early character builders assumed that farm boys were morally solid, and public opinion agreed. In the 1910s, as Congress moved to support clubs for farm children, character builders began to admit that dirty stories passed as freely in the sunshine of the swimming hole as in the shadow of the elevated; but Boy Scout and YMCA workers still concentrated upon small-town boys and only belatedly decided it was wrong for farm boys to be "worked much like the hired help."[19]

Youth workers agreed that city boys of all classes were underworked compared to farm boys. Burning off energy got boys in trouble, however, as the growth of crowded, impersonal cities generated demands for social control. The new juvenile court statutes which most states passed between 1900 and 1917 defined a great range of offenses, such as truancy and incorrigibility, which multiplied the circumstances in which city youngsters could seem defiant of control. J. Adams Puffer, a widely read writer on gangs, pointed out that if rural youngsters plundered an orchard, the owner chased them himself, whereas boys who stole from a city fruit stand risked arrest. His point was a boys' work commonplace.[20]

Adults did not trust city boys to play unsupervised. As late as the 1920s, cities from Homestead, Pennsylvania, to San Antonio, Texas, barred pupils from school playgrounds after hours. The movement to supply playgrounds for small children which began in the 1880s belatedly provided for older youngsters; but there were not enough staff to watch boys closely, and playgrounds remained primarily for younger children.[21] Recreation surveys of the 1910s and 1920s found swarms of seemingly idle children on city streets. Accordingly, boys' workers promised to turn "aimless play" into "play with a purpose."[22]

Left to their own devices, older youths turned to commercial entertainment. Scandalized youth workers deplored saloons, dance halls, theaters, pool rooms, cigar stores, and amusement parks, and at best distrusted movies and professional sports.[23] Rooted in Protestant moralism, these antipathies were by no means exclusively class-related. Anthony Comstock, the notorious moral crusader, wrote exhaustively on dangers to respectable young people. Even innocuous commercial amusements inspired distaste, as nostalgia for the simplicities of an imagined village life led youth workers to favor the homemade and anachronistic—folk dances at Jane Addams's settlement house or woodcraft for Boy Scouts. Franklin K. Mathiews, the BSA's Chief Scout Librarian, waged intemperate war on sensational fiction, charging that it was "blowing out the boy's brains" with dreams of effortless triumphs and near-criminal escapades.[24] Commercialized amusements menaced middle-class investment in the young, luring them off the path of delayed gratification; thus the answer was to build a rival world of recreation.

The logic was environmentalist, leading to the sentimental conclusion that there were no bad boys, only bad surroundings. This became another commonplace of the Progressive Era, as a 1916 survey found that most newspaper editors blamed the "boy problem" on urban immorality and lack of recreation.[25]

But boys' workers had no doubt that certain boys were uniquely tainted —primarily, street boys and, secondarily, working-class or working boys, although these adults did not always distinguish the two groups carefully. Street boys included newsboys, bootblacks, and scavenging urchins, commonly presumed to be homeless or else from brutalized or broken homes;

in reality, they often came from ordinary working-class families and secured steadier jobs as they grew older. Still, they gained a taste for cigarettes and crap shooting which alarmed club workers, and such boys accounted for far more delinquency than boys tied to jobs in stores and factories.[26] Working-class or working boys seemed less rootless; those under fourteen were still in school, and older ones had regular jobs. Yet they were free to roam after work, and observers often confused them with street boys or simply lumped the two together as "lower-class." An easy assumption of middle-class moral and religious superiority reinforced the distinction between middle-class boys and all others considered beneath them. "We should strive to get the *Christian boys,* as we need their help," advised Francis Board of the Buffalo YMCA, "and then go after those who are not so fortunate as to have Christian homes, and are obliged to work in our stores and factories."[27]

Club workers believed that lower-class parents simply could not control their children. According to one estimate, 80 percent of street boys' parents were "addicted to vicious if not criminal habits."[28] Other observers were more sympathetic, but they assumed that even the best parents lost control of boys who got regular jobs. The truth was that family stability remained high among immigrants, but it was also true that few boys stayed inside their crowded tenements come evening.[29]

From midafternoon to late evening, the streets of tenement districts swarmed with children; and it was here, moralists believed, that urban recreation was most deficient. Jacob Riis, a longtime proponent of boys' clubs, reported fourteen purchasers under age fourteen in three and one-half hours at one saloon. Gang members were "perfectly happy" to be "chased round the block by the cop. The quintessence of joy is theirs to go swiping things from the corner grocery. . . ."[30]

Even to sympathetic observers, street boys' lives were a distillation of the bad effects of city life — a wretched example for middle-class schoolboys. To middle-class parents and youth workers, unguarded contacts threatened the results of careful nurture; S. A. Taggert, YMCA State Secretary for Pennsylvania, warned in 1879 that Sunday school boys were "on the streets getting an education in the other direction."[31] Thus the character builders' goal was to get boys from "good" families away from bad influences and under supervision. Because of Scouting, a BSA news release later boasted, boys were "no longer loafing in billiard parlors or among boys that tend to exercise a harmful influence over them."[32]

A rare dissenter, active in a YMCA women's auxiliary, argued that insulation was poor training for social leadership; a Christian boy should "'test his mettle' by contact with other boys from less favored homes that he may . . . prove an inspiration to those with whom he mingles."[33] This was the traditional code of the American gentry class; but few boys' workers believed that "less favored" boys would tamely defer to lads in well-pressed knickers.

Basically, character builders reacted to social disorder by retiring to fixed positions and doubling efforts to keep the garrison loyal. In recent years, revisionist historians have pointed to social control as a central — sometimes *the* central — goal of American reformers.[34] However, they have assumed that it was imposed by the upper and middle classes upon those beneath them. Yet in the case of character building, as in many religious and moral reform movements, social control was imposed by the middle class upon itself, or rather upon its own young people. Rather than remake the lower class, character builders kept respectable boys apart and strengthened them for leadership in later life. This strategy matched the experience of many Progressive Era reformers who had sheltered upbringings and then sallied forth, armed with moral certitude, into an imperfect world.[35] But protectiveness was part of a broader process: the growth of middle-class class consciousness, defined in part by agencies for moral and religious surveillance. Character building directed towards the children of one's own class came out of a long Protestant tradition. As the revivalism of the 1830s focused inward towards self-control and the conversion of the believers' own families, revivalists ended up appealing primarily to the middle class; temperance groups affirmed their members' middle-class superiority; and Sunday schools served mainly church members' children.[36]

Social tensions fanned middle-class zeal to strengthen the ramparts. To nervous newspaper readers of that class, the 1870s, 1880s, and 1890s were decades of unprecedented strife, as the new scale of American life transformed the working class into a faceless, shadowy menace; sitting in one's parlor, one read of violent deeds a thousand miles away.[37] Reflecting the fusion of middle-class and Protestant identity, churchmen were prominent alarmists. Josiah Strong's bestselling *Our Country* (1886), written for the American Home Missionary Society, portrayed America as riven by class divisions and unrest.[38] While missionary outreach was one response, Protestants also assuaged their fears by fortifying the institutional structure of middle-class life. This, rather than the better-known Social Gospel, was the churches' primary reaction to social change. And character-building schemes were part of that reaction.

Reinforcing class-based anxieties was the nativism of the 1890s and 1910s, which culminated in 1920s legislation to stem the flow of immigrants. Character builders seldom voiced bald antagonism, although a Boys' Brigade editor charged ethnic politicians with "superstitious and often priest-led egotism. . . ." But character builders were mistrustful; far from being fit companions, immigrant boys in their eyes were among the "perplexing problems" that middle-class boys must prepare to face as adults.[39] Like strands in a single rope, Protestantism, an ethnocentric

Americanism, and middle-class consciousness bound character builders to their constituency.

The fact that character builders sought to protect middle-class boys from lower-class contamination does not mean they thought such boys were perfect or even close. Complaints of minor vices such as Sabbath-breaking suggested little more than fear that church boys might get out of line. But YMCA men also reported substantial drinking and sexual activity in high schools of the 1910s; in one city, a boy chosen for the Y's organizing committee got too drunk to attend his interview.[40]

Nor did writers on youth regard the moral situation as ideal outside big cities. As we shall see, character builders looked back longingly to an idealized boyhood in preindustrial small towns, yet adults worried that contemporary small-town boys were growing up in idleness, rank as weeds in vacant lots. Henry S. Curtis, a leader in the recreation movement, praised Boy Scouting as "the salvation of the village boy," warning that idle village boys were learning "to smoke cigarettes, to shoot craps, [and] to tell smutty stories. . . ." In the little town of Cheney, Kansas, moral conditions before the YMCA arrived were "anything but wholesome," claimed a Y leader. The young people showed "a marked absence of ambition and a prevalence of low ideals. Frivolous amusements were the regular thing. . . . Just as in your town and mine a lot of good character-building material was going to waste."[41]

Men who grew up in small towns mostly agreed. B. F. Skinner stated flatly that his time "was not spent in interesting ways."[42] Clyde Brion Davis, a writer who grew up in Chillicothe, Missouri, around 1900, reported that boys plagued adults with pranks that ranged from slingshot ambushes to painting swastikas on the town water tower. For want of recreational amenities, boys drowned while swimming in the muddy river or were mangled hopping freight cars. Even a local minister's feeble attempt to enlist them as New Century Knights attracted a drove of recruits. Small towns, in short, were tailor-made for Boy Scouting; boys were hungry for diversion, and adults had reason to divert them.[43]

Similar considerations applied in suburbs, where boys loafed around stores, ice-cream parlors, and street corners. Writing in 1909, a housewife even argued that suburban children were under less control than city or country youngsters, since fathers went off to work downtown and policing was light.[44]

With all the faults of small towns, Boy Scout and YMCA leaders were more willing to mix social classes there than in big cities.[45] Whereas estrangement ran along class lines within the cities, character builders in small towns saw the greatest menace as external, coming from the cities. Thus middle-class defensiveness was transmuted into community defensiveness. This is a partial explanation of the seeming paradox that character builders launched their movements upon a flood of rhetoric about big-city corruption and yet recruited best in smaller places. Admittedly, many smaller cities had saloons and theaters, but it was easier to blame trouble on outside contagion. Large cities were growing faster than smaller communities, and newspaper accounts of urban vice inflamed imaginations. Living among populations that were on the average more native-born and Protestant, suburbanites and villagers were both awed and repelled by the polyglot metropolis. According to the common interpretation, vice crusades, prohibition, and immigration restriction constituted a backlash by native-stock, small-town Protestants — in alliance with much of the urban middle class — against urban elites and immigrants.[46] But small-town defensiveness ran deeper than cultural alienation. Local boosters feared stagnation; and parents, teachers, and churchmen knew that able young people would move on to college and the cities. There seemed very little time to teach teenagers the "right" morality, strengthen them to seek success, and insure that they would carry with them the values of their native setting. Therefore the ramparts character builders manned in largest numbers were those around the smaller cities, towns, and villages.[47]

Much of what troubled them, of course, was common to teenagers wherever they lived. In particular, teenage sexuality frightened adults. YMCA secretaries polled in 1898 agreed that masturbation was the most frequent sin of boys. Yet youth workers told themselves the practice was abnormal and dreamt up alibis for "good" boys — tight pants, local irritation, or sliding down bannisters. Only in 1919 did a YMCA manual concede the practice was virtually universal among teenage boys.[48] To make matters worse, high schools spawned a new pattern of informal contacts between boys and girls which unnerved many adults. In a 1912 survey, only 19 percent of a large sample of churchmen and youth workers blamed sexual sins on the theater — that bugaboo of days gone by — whereas 42 percent claimed actual knowledge of "wrong relations" among high school students, 52 percent had heard rumors, and only 6 percent suggested unconcern by failing to answer.[49] Just as religious guidance of the young progressed from individual conversion towards environmental control, so the idea took hold that adults could control youthful sexuality by supervising young people's recreation. Character builders in particular relied upon large doses of vigorous activity.

Underlying fears of teenage sexuality was a pervasive fear of precocity, by which adults meant any adultlike behavior or proclivity, especially passion or self-assertiveness. Worried that young people were growing up too fast, Progressive Era adults used "precocious" as a term of opprobrium.[50]

Their concern had a real, though limited, physiological basis. Since at least 1870, the average age of menarche in Europe and North America has gradually declined. If these changes can be extrapolated back into the earlier 1800s, and if the trend among boys paralleled that for girls, by the late 1800s boys entered puberty younger than they had a half century before.[51] By the 1910s, the median age of pubescence for American boys was about fourteen, though of course individuals varied widely.[52] Instead of accepting the inevitable, however, alarmists railed against precocity; for as puberty arrived ever earlier, it menaced the hope of shielding children from contamination. And to compound adult uneasiness, North American boys of 1920 averaged more than two inches taller at age fifteen and at least fifteen pounds heavier than their counterparts of 1880. Their eventual stature only slightly exceeded their fathers', but they approached adult height and weight much younger, with the increment concentrated right around age fifteen. Increasingly, therefore, boys of fourteen or fifteen were likely to strike adults as outsized and oversexed. While a full explanation of this trend towards earlier maturation is elusive, the trend was most advanced among the urban upper and middle classes, the very classes most alarmed about precocity.[53]

Precocity drew criticism as early as the 1830s, but only in the later 1800s did hostility towards it acquire a social base as children of the nonfarm middle class stayed longer in school, foregoing the partial independence a paycheck brought them. Teachers, reformers opposed to child labor, and churchmen eager to keep boys in Sunday school all worked to prolong dependency.[54] And character builders continued the flight from precocity. While street boys' clubs gathered in urchins at age seven or eight, nineteenth-century Boys' Brigade and YMCA leaders focused on ages ten through fifteen; and as efforts to lengthen juvenile dependence continued, Boy Scout and YMCA workers of the 1910s raised their intended age range to twelve through seventeen or eighteen.[55]

The incongruity is obvious: just when the trend towards earlier physical maturation was proceeding apace, within the age range most affected and among the social classes where the trend was most advanced, adults were trying hardest to prolong dependency. Fear of precocity and the concept of modern adolescence developed together.[56] Indeed, tension over precocity was inherent in the situation of middle-class schoolboys—advancing academically, increasingly mature physically, restless for diversion, yet held in tutelage. Control was less automatic than on the farm, less clearly rooted in family discipline and necessary tasks. Yet urban adults who were accustomed to manipulating the child's nature could not fall back on blatant coercion. Thus when adults spoke of building character, they were also busy elaborating unobtrusive, relatively noncoercive controls.

Character builders believed the difficulty was that existing agencies of control—home, school, and church in particular—were only partially effective. The answer was to supplement the available forms of guardianship.

In simple terms, boys' work came third in a three-stage sequence. In the early colonies, family and community socialized the young directly; transmission of property and vocational skills through inheritance or apprenticeship kept them under the control of a father or master. In the eighteenth century, however, these arrangements, never strong in some colonies, began to break down, and by the early 1800s social critics charged that parents, churches, and apprenticeship were failing in moral nurture.[57]

In the second stage, adults turned to intensive early nurture to prepare children for a degree of youthful independence. Formal organizations also took up some of the task of socializing older children. School reformers pushed for a single public system, charging that parents and uncoordinated schools failed to control youngsters and teach them proper skills and values. Similarly, churchmen cited weak home instruction as a reason to form Sunday schools. By midcentury both kinds of school were well rooted in northern middle-class life. As a back-up system to control lower-class children, there were houses of refuge, juvenile reformatories with more than twenty thousand inmates nationwide by 1857.[58] Initially, then, the response to weaknesses in home and community management of the young was to develop formal organizations for training and control.

In the third stage, nearing 1900, concern increased that teenagers were adrift and uncontrolled. The economic basis for even partial independence was eroding, and adults seemed to feel that the only substitute for social function was deliberate social control. But existing laws failed to curb youthful misbehavior, and reformatories were cruelly repressive. So reformers looked for ways to control youths without removing them from home. Although the juvenile courts which started soon after 1900 provided only a parody of family-style discipline, they put a majority of those charged on probation, letting them live at home.[59] Boys' workers likewise helped boys for a few hours after school rather than attempting to displace the family. Boys' work was part of a trend away from massive institutions for social control and towards more flexible agencies to supplement existing arrangements. Preoccupation with public policy has led historians to neglect this noncoercive, voluntaristic wing of the movement to control the young; yet it touched more lives than did juvenile courts. Delinquency prevention was the boys' clubs' raison d'etre; Boy Scouting and the YMCA also traded on fears of delinquency, promising to keep good boys from going bad. More important for character building, critics saw shortcomings in the institutions trusted by the middle class—not just the family but public and Sunday schools as well. As Progressive social thought turned towards enviromental solutions to social problems, character builders proposed to supplement the schools and churches, patching the cocoon these agencies had tried to weave around boys.

In fact, a boys' work consensus along these lines spread throughout the

English-speaking North Atlantic. The Boys' Brigades and Boy Scout movement both originated in Britain. Canadians were prominent in American
boys' work; and YMCA boys' branches in the U.S. and Canada were under
common supervision until 1912. Conversely, American psychological theories and club work were influential in Britain and Canada. In all three
countries, character builders played upon social anxieties to establish their
new specialty. Educators and churchmen had criticized the home and community for years; character builders simply repeated the litany and went
on to point out shortcomings in schools and churches as well.

Complaints about the weakness of the family are hardy perennials. Still,
Victorian Americans saw cause for alarm. As communities lost cohesion,
people looked to parental nurture as the basis of social order. Yet most
nonfarm families ceased to be units of economic production, leaving observers unconvinced that child rearing and emotion would suffice to bind
a family together without other functions.[60] Boys' workers were critical
not merely of lower-class parents but also of middle-class fathers for being
too busy to spend time with their sons.[61] Without claiming to be surrogate
parents, they made clear there was a huge gap in supervision.

Family weakness was a long established concern, however. More central to the case for boys' work was the idea that public and Sunday schools,
developed to supplement family nurture in the management of children, were inadequate to control teenage boys and needed supplementing
themselves.

The basic problem with the schools was simple. While work had brought
a measure of independence to nonfarm boys, full-time jobs (except street
trades) generally meant adult surveillance and long hours. Ironically, prolonged schooling gave many schoolboys far more free time. A favorite
computation was to take the hours in a week, deduct those spent in school,
asleep, and eating meals, and then announce some staggering remainder
as free for play. Baden-Powell came up with fifty hours a week, while
the BSA's James West claimed that "school provides leadership for only
about one thousand of the five thousand hours a year a boy has for activity."[62] Such claims were effective; even the A.F.L. praised Boy Scouting
for supervising boys after school and in summer when there was "absolutely no control."[63]

The schools' extracurricular activities might have taken up some of the
slack, but they could never fill all a boy's free time and they were still
very rudimentary when boys' work agencies first started up. As the early
high schools labored to establish academic reputations, teachers frowned
on distractions from study. Besides, many were women with little interest
in boys' sports, and would-be coaches among the men often knew little
about the new team sports.[64] Athletics were fairly common before 1900,
but mainly under the boys' own management. Although some teachers

sponsored orchestras and literary societies, such groups often were tolerated rather than supported by nineteenth-century school authorities. A majority of high schools did not officially sponsor football and basketball until at least the 1910s, and many other activities waited until the 1920s. Even then, a survey of 140 village high schools found that 16 percent had no basketball team, 32 percent no literary society, and 40 percent no other clubs.[65] In any case, boys twelve to fourteen were still in elementary school, where sponsored activities were few indeed. Despite the organization of public school athletic leagues in a few cities, many boys of the 1910s had no sports whatever through the schools.[66] Boys' work was part of the same broad trend as school activities and the playground movement; in each case adults turned young people's spontaneous activities to adult purposes of control. Yet because the trend was not far advanced, ample room remained for boys' work.

The character builders' opportunity reflected also the difficulty with which regular classroom instruction adapted to demands for control and nurture of the young. Antebellum public schools imposed a good deal of essentially Protestant moral training; however, with classes ranging up past sixty pupils, teachers in late nineteenth-century cities had to set modest goals. Superintendents such as William Torrey Harris of St. Louis made the demands of the school system — punctuality, attention, obedience, and silence — moral objectives in their own right. Other simply confessed inability to impose moral control. An 1890 survey found that the average big-city pupil spent only 2 percent of his elementary schooling learning "morals and manners."[67] Turn-of-the-century educational changes brought renewed interest in moral education, but the proliferation of gimmicks such as stereopticon lectures suggested loss of faith in ordinary classroom methods.[68]

Character builders reproached the schools for narrow formalism. Schools taught the three Rs, said Baden-Powell, but not character, helpfulness, and civic duty. YMCA men sometimes blamed the lack of religious instruction, but the goal of all-round development suggested a more basic deficiency: schooling was only intellectual. James E. Russell, dean of Teachers College at Columbia University and a prominent supporter of Boy Scouting, remonstrated: "The state seems to have overlooked the fact that intellectual power is as great an asset to the crook as to the honest man."[69] Thus the rationale for boys' work was to a degree anti-academic, even anti-intellectual.

If schools failed to control boys fully, the teachers' problems were mitigated by the power of the diploma. Churches and Sunday schools, however, had no such built-in leverage. Churchmen became the leading supporters of character-building agencies because they needed help in holding teenage boys.

As liberal Protestants elevated moral stability above purely spiritual considerations, they came to regard mere church affiliation and attendance as evidence of commitment. Therefore the "'progressive' church of the late Gilded Age" busily marshaled its members into "associations for self-improvement or recreation."[70] This impulse reshaped church life as much as anything the Social Gospel recommended. These were not necessarily institutional churches catering to slum dwellers; the goal more often was to make the churches into hives of activity for the regular members and their children, with a program for every age and sex.

But teenage boys were more than just another age group, for their restiveness threatened the strategy of passing children smoothly through Sunday school on to full church membership. Overall, Sunday schools grew faster than the school-age population from 1878 to 1916, although they fell behind from 1896 to 1905.[71] Yet this success would not benefit the churches, boys' workers believed, if the boys quit once they reached their teens. The Rev. John Quincy Adams, a founder of the Boys' Brigade in America, stated the case in 1891: "In recent years there has been much discussion over the relation of the church to young men. Much less has been said regarding the boys, but any careful observer must have noticed that the trouble begins with them. Soon after the age of twelve, a large number of them drift out of the Sunday school and away from the church. Here is 'the missing link' in our church work."[72]

Such concern was widespread by the early 1900s. Sunday school writers and boys' workers proclaimed variously that Sunday schools lost 60 to 80 percent of their boys between ages twelve and eighteen. For most observers, the initial loss from ages eleven or twelve to fifteen or sixteen was most serious.[73] And most teenagers did not quit because they had joined the church, for estimates in 1905 and 1913 held that two-thirds or even three-quarters left without passing into full communion.[74]

High dropout rates persisted through the 1910s, for a survey of 256 Protestant Sunday schools in Indiana around 1920 found huge losses among teenage boys (see Table 1). Whereas twelve-year-olds made up 10.1 percent of all male Sunday school pupils aged six through twenty, fifteen-year-olds accounted for only 5.6 percent and eighteen-year-olds for just 2.5 percent. In other words, there were only 55 percent as many fifteen-year-old boys in Sunday school as there were twelve-year-olds and 24 percent as many eighteen-year-olds. The girls' membership also declined but much less rapidly, as can be seen by the higher percentage of girls still in Sunday school in their late teens. At age fifteen there were still 74 percent as many as at age twelve, and 41 percent as many remained at age eighteen. As a result, the ratio of boys to girls in Sunday school declined sharply with advancing age, from 80 boys for every 100 girls at age twelve to 59 at age fifteen and just 48 by age eighteen. These effects, moreover, were more

Table 1
Age and Sex of Pupils in Selected Indiana Sunday Schools, c. 1920

Age	Male		Female		Ratio of Male Pupils to Female (Female = 100)
	N	(%)	N	(%)	
6	547	7.4	650	6.5	84
7	601	8.1	741	7.4	81
8	712	9.6	776	7.8	92
9	697	9.4	815	8.2	86
10	719	9.7	870	8.7	83
11	778	10.5	890	8.9	87
12	754	10.1	946	9.5	80
13	639	8.6	803	8.0	80
14	557	7.5	835	8.4	67
15	415	5.6	704	7.0	59
16	334	4.5	576	5.8	58
17	253	3.4	503	5.0	50
18	183	2.5	384	3.8	48
19	121	1.6	272	2.7	44
20	127	1.7	223	2.2	57
Total	7,437		9,988		

Source: Walter S. Athearn et al., *The Religious Education of Protestants in an American Commonwealth* (New York, 1923), p. 289.

marked among urban than rural boys. Reflecting the weak youth programs of country churches, the rural Sunday schools surveyed enlisted a somewhat smaller proportion of all the children in their communities than did urban churches, but they held onto those boys they enrolled. Whereas urban Sunday schools had only 51 percent as many fifteen-year-old boys as twelve-year-olds and 19 percent as many eighteen-year-olds, the rural Sunday schools still had 75 percent at age fifteen and 51 percent at age eighteen. Although the Sunday schools lost pupils of all sorts with advancing age, it was clear that the gravest failure to retain members occurred with urban boys.[75]

Pessimism regarding the Sunday schools' loss of pupils created a market for boys' work as churchmen sought church-related programs to keep boys interested and loyal. Consequently, character builders concentrated on the early teens, where the loss began; they focused on nonfarm boys, whose sensitivity to age gradations led them to drop out sooner than farmers' sons; and they treated boys' work as more urgent than girls' work, since girls stayed on longer in Sunday school.

What was wrong with Sunday schools? Churchmen and character builders blamed boredom and failure to allow for age and sex differences. The widely used International Uniform Lessons imposed the same weekly Scripture passage for all ages, making for dull instruction. Also age grouping was lax; Eugene C. Foster of the *Sunday School Times* estimated that half the boys who quit did so "because they had to sit in a class with the 'kids.'"[76] Another concern was that Sunday schools were too effeminate for boys. Most teachers were women—73 percent in the 1920 Indiana survey—and by a form of guilt by association, even male teachers were suspect; a Boy Scout executive complained that they were not forceful.[77] Above all, boys' workers complained that Sunday schools were too sedentary. George J. Fisher of the YMCA told the Religious Education Association: "The weakness of the Sunday school is that it is a society for sitting still, while boys were not made to sit still."[78]

The churches' other major agency for youth, the young people's society, had lost momentum by the 1900s and promised little help with boys. For all the talk of Christian "endeavor," involvement offered a mere simulacrum of purposeful activity, and eventually the pretense wore thin. Character builders had long attacked the societies as sedentary and sissified; and the idea of "girls giggling over the boys and the boys passing notes to the girls" offended men who believed that boys could be manly only when no girls were around.[79] Unquestionably, teenage boys stayed away; various studies from 1900 to 1920 found a 61 to 75 percent female membership in young people's societies. A majority of members in the senior societies were eighteen or older, and yet intermediate societies were rare.[80] This failure to attract teenage boys left a huge gap in church programs for the young—one which boys' workers rushed to fill.

Certainly the churches' difficulties with boys gave character builders their great opening. But their remedy was the same whether the problem was commercialized amusement, precocious sexuality, idleness after school, or boredom with Sunday school: boys needed vigorous, sex-segregated recreation under a man's supervision. It would distract them from base urges, reinforce parental nurture, and bind them in gratitude to the church or other agency responsible.

This concern for masculinity points to another preoccupation of character builders; counterbalancing worry that boys were out of hand was fear that middle-class boys were growing weak and effeminate—a disastrous possibility in a country whose models of manliness were heroes like Andrew Jackson and Daniel Boone. By the mid-1800s, moreover, economic opportunity and the ideology of free competition led the middle class to regard growth in character as being, in large part, a matter of marshaling one's inner resources to get ahead.[81] Hence character builders wanted more than just control; they also wanted boys to develop strong powers and a firm will.

Conscientious Victorian males were troubled over how to assert themselves as men. Since impulsive physical action led easily to drunkenness and fornication, moralists espoused a counter-ideal of the "Christian gentleman . . . continuously testing his manliness in the fire of self-denial." Self-restraint was essentially negative, however, and exposed reformers to jibes that they constituted "the third sex."[82] Then, in the wake of the Civil War, styles of masculinity grew more abrupt and self-assertive—it was an era of beards and boots—but also more narrowly practical, as former reformers opted for unreflective action in place of broad idealism. In line with this cult of action and in an effort to play down the negative implications of Protestant asceticism, men turned to muscular Christianity. At its finest, as enunciated by the English novelist Charles Kingsley, it defended "the divineness of the whole man" and inspired American YMCA leaders to seek all-round development of young men.[83] But it easily degenerated into mindless strenuosity, justifying the cult of games which submerged English schools in athleticism and spread to America by 1900. This functionless strenuosity soon permeated church work, the object not to accomplish anything in particular except to show that boys could be both manly and Christian. Manliness, in Joseph Kett's words, came "to signify less the opposite of childishness than the opposite of femininity."[84]

By the 1890s, however, such assertive masculinity seemed problematic. Thus Theodore Roosevelt denounced "the over-civilized man, who has lost the great fighting, masterful virtues," then warned the wealthy to seek the "strenuous life" and not permit their sons to grow up in "slothful ease. . . ."[85] Others shared Roosevelt's concern for boys, as the 1890s spawned a new interest in cadet training. Even William James, a leading anti-imperialist, proposed "a moral equivalent for war." Reciting the "horrors" of a world without strenuousness as depicted by militarists—"a world of clerks and teachers, of co-education and zo-ophily"—James endorsed "the central essence of this feeling" that "human life with no use for hardihood would be contemptible." He proposed drafting "gilded youth" off to "coal and iron mines, to freight trains, to fishing fleets in December," there to "get the childishness knocked out of them. . . ."[86] Vastly milder but similar ideals underlay Boy Scouting.

In both Britain and America, gentlemen like Roosevelt and James infected the middle class with their dread of national enfeeblement. In Britain, upper-class fear of rival empires gave Boy Scouting its initial impetus. In America, however, the main dangers seemed to lie *within* the country.

One symbolic shock was clear: the purported closing of the frontier by 1890 punctured the dream of endless space for manly self-assertion. Yet to an era rife with notions of survival through superior fitness, wilderness appeared a vital source of virility and toughness. Roosevelt and other gentlemen like Owen Wister who headed west in the 1880s found an outlet for frustrated energies and a refuge from commercial specialization that was undercutting the gentlemanly ideal of well-rounded character. Millions who did not go west escaped vicariously in western novels such as Wister's *The Virginian* (1902). Team sports flourished as a form of outdoor life adapted to the new age of shrunken space and rule-bound organization, but the hordes of spectators dismayed activists like Roosevelt and Baden-Powell. Boy Scouting appeared to be a better substitute for the vanished frontier.[87]

In marked contrast to the frontier stood the world of urban white-collar work, where alarmists worried that soft living and salaried dependence sapped manly character. Unnerved by sedentary jobs, men thronged YMCA gymnasiums. Even more unnerving might have been the prospect of being a lifelong employee—an affront to traditional notions of manly independence—since opportunities for self-employment appeared to be declining towards 1900.[88] But the new deference to experts after 1900, the growing power and prestige of large organizations, the security and authority attached to jobs within such organizations, and the new cult of team players and efficient managers soon made promotion up the organizational ladder a respectable career.[89]

Fears concerning women added to the masculine sense of confinement and weakness, although these anxieties also should not be exaggerated. Women's rights did begin to undercut the simplistic equation of masculinity and power. Women invaded the white-collar world, trebling in numbers there from 1900 to 1920. Male anxieties were exacerbated by the "race suicide" panic of the early 1900s, as alarmists led by Roosevelt blamed women for reducing birthrates to levels which would leave the old stock too weak to hold its own against immigrants.[90] Men felt they must respond assertively, for the ideology of social equality left masculinity as one of their few unambiguous distinctions. Lee F. Hanmer of the BSA executive board was adamant that Scouting must be different for boys than for girls: "The men are the fighters," he insisted, whereas "the women are the home-makers." Yet his colleague Mortimer Schiff conceded that "women are in many cases more virile than men."[91] Like Theodore Roosevelt, male character builders displayed extreme concern for sex differences, aggressiveness, and energy—only a lavish outpouring proved that one had enough.[92]

Still, we must beware of seeing the history of boys and men as a simple reflex of alarm at changing women's roles. Boys chafed at dependency based on age as much as loss of masculinity. Nor should too much be made of occupational encroachment, since most of the new women white-collar workers got low-level clerical jobs or entered "women's professions" such as teaching, while men rose into supervisory posts.[93] Male clerks and teachers perhaps suffered embarrassment, but vocational discrimination shielded other white-collar men.

Echoing C. Wright Mills's pessimistic view of the new middle class, Jeffrey P. Hantover explains Boy Scouting's popularity as a reaction — especially by lower-middle-class men — to loss of independence, insecure status, and the apparent feminization of white-collar work. Although leading small boys may seem an unlikely way to reassert the sort of strenuous, aggressive masculinity traditionally valued by American men, Hantover argues that men became Scoutmasters in search of status and masculine self-affirmation.[94] Many mercantile employees did become Scoutmasters; but this explanation does not account for Boy Scouting's strong support among upper-middle-class men and boys. Nor does it explain why adults worried at least as much about controlling boys as about fostering masculinity.

Still, character builders clearly worried that urban middle-class boys were turning soft. According to a book on Boy Scouting for church use, "absence of the woodpile, the vegetable-garden, [and] the carpet-beater" made Scouting essential. Schooling seemed too sedentary and narrowly intellectual to engage boys' energies: "The public school fails in will-training," claimed William Byron Forbush, a leader in church boys' work, "because it gives the will no exercise."[95]

Boys' workers also asserted that boys needed manual training and vocational guidance because they no longer worked alongside their fathers. While some schools had manual training as early as the 1880s, the BSA's Dan Beard complained that instruction was "perfunctory." As high schools enrolled a wider range of students, educators in search of "social efficiency" added manual training and vocational courses; but as Beard implied, these often fell into arid formalism. James West told teachers in 1916 that schooling failed to help boys find careers — and Boy Scouting might assist.[96]

Male critics blamed a large measure of the schools' faults on feminization. The percentage of women teachers rose from perhaps 59 in 1870 to 86 by 1920, and even in the high schools 65 percent were female by 1919–20. The remaining men suffered guilt by association; David R. Porter, the YMCA's leader in work with high schools, jibed that women teachers were "more manly than the men."[97] Moderate critics conceded that women teachers were fine for smaller children but agreed that boys over twelve needed men as models — a distinction which dovetailed neatly with the twentieth-century character builders' practice of enrolling boys at that age. Coeducation further galled the schools' more extreme critics because girls inconveniently outperformed boys scholastically.[98] Boys' work was accordingly to be a sex-segregated refuge, with men as leaders.

The schools' shortcomings might have mattered less, had character builders not worried that middle-class home life was also overfeminized because fathers were preoccupied with business. New conceptions of the model family, intensely devoted to child rearing, spawned expectations of close involvement which fathers like B. F. Skinner's recognized but could not meet. Even the touchy task of purity instruction fell by default to mothers.[99]

Complaints that mothers were too lenient dated from well before the Civil War, but late nineteenth-century styles in maternal nurture struck critics as turning blatantly sentimental. The enormous popularity of Frances Hodgson Burnett's *Little Lord Fauntleroy* (1886), the hero pictured in long curls, lace collar, and velvet suit with knee pants, furthered what many decried as the fashion of treating young boys as pretty little children.[100] Character builders took alarm. Edgar M. Robinson, who supervised YMCA boys' work in the U.S. and Canada, verged on panic in his denunciation of the boy who has been "kept so carefully wrapped up in the 'pink cotton wool' of an over-indulgent home, [that] he is more effeminate than his sister, and his flabby muscles are less flabby than his character."[101] Character builders accepted "that a boy normally belongs to his mother until he is ten or twelve" but insisted upon masculine leadership thereafter. "The REAL Boy Scout is not a 'sissy'," boasted James West. He "adores his mother" but "is not hitched to [her] apron strings."[102]

Even more subject to criticism than the home or school was the Sunday school. Complaints of women teachers and the Sunday schools' physically passive program masked the broader fear mentioned earlier that religion itself was unmanly. During the nineteenth century, the imagery and doctrines of the major Protestant denominations turned—as Barbara Welter describes them—"more domesticated, more emotional, more soft and accommodating—in a word, more 'feminine.'"[103] Calvinists in a sense lost their nerve; Protestant morality stressed self-denial, traditionally a female virtue; and increasing numbers of women took up church service work. By 1916 only 40.5 percent of Protestant church members were male.[104]

Boys got the message that religiosity threatened masculinity. Tales of boyhood written in the late 1800s made it clear that "real" boys squirmed their way through weekly applications of soap, Sunday school, and sermons. Henry Cabot Lodge observed that boys "had a wholesome dislike of the youthful prig—especially if he was a religious prig, for they felt that such boys must be insincere and they drove him out from among them." A boys' worker at the Toronto YMCA in 1884 felt obliged to reassure his lads that "a real boy . . . need not cease to be a boy because he is a Christian."[105]

Churchmen responded with calls for a "manly" religion. For adult males, most major denominations formed brotherhoods between 1880 and 1910.[106] For boys, there were large doses of muscular Christianity; hence the enthusiasm for church clubs, Sunday school athletic leagues, the YMCA, and imported British militancy — from "Onward Christian Soldiers" to the Boys' Brigade and Boy Scouts.[107]

But the threat of weakness was seen as going beyond any one institution to embrace the whole of modern urban life. Luther Gulick of the YMCA warned that urban parents "are frequently pained to find that their children have less power and less vitality to endure the rough side of life than they have themselves. . . . Families who live in the city without marrying country stock for two or three generations . . . later are unable to rear strong families. . . ." Ernest Thompson Seton blamed urban growth, industrial specialization, and the rise of spectator sports for turning "such a large proportion of our robust, manly, self-reliant boyhood into a lot of flat-chested cigarette-smokers, with shaky nerves and doubtful vitality." As these complaints indicated, weakness and perversion virtually replaced sin in this era of nervous masculinity.[108]

Fears of enfeeblement drew upon nineteenth-century theories of depletion. In the Gilded Age, nervousness or neurasthenia (weakness of the nerves) became for alarmists virtually a "national disease." George M. Beard described it as an affliction of "the in-door-living and brain-working classes" and warned against overpressure in the schools — a concern echoed by Boy Scout writers in their prediction of "neurasthenia or even insanity" unless boys had varied physical exercise. Victorians believed that "overstimulation of one faculty drained the others of vitality."[109] Since sexual and intellectual overactivity were the two great bugbears, teenage schoolboys seemed acutely in danger.

To Victorian moralists, the most depleting sin was masturbation, a menace to health, vigor, even sanity. And as we have seen, character builders worried a lot about this form of teenage sexuality. There is a huge historical literature on fear of masturbation and an appalling record of painful treatments to restore "nerve force." A milder and doubtless more common cure was to divert energy to other organs and build up a reserve of vigor.[110] Although by 1900 informed writers had abandoned the most lurid tales, they still purveyed fears of depletion based upon confusion between semen and sex hormones. The 1911 Boy Scout handbook described it as "the sex fluid . . . that makes a boy manly, strong, and noble."[111] So character builders fostered exercise, urging heroic efforts at clean living. Purity was power — all the more essential if big corporations and mass immigration were constricting business opportunities. A Boy Scout must grow up "free from every blemish and stain," *Scouting* magazine insisted, for "only then will he be fully equipped to . . . fight the battles of business life."[112]

Mental overstrain purportedly ranked second only to masturbation as a drain on vitality. By a quirk of phobic illogic, adults assumed that any boy they thought unmanly — the studious or unathletic — must masturbate.

Not only did the "bookworm" face jeers from schoolmates, character builders joined the chorus, West boasting that the Boy Scout was not "a puny, dull, or bookish lad. . . ."[113] H. W. Gibson, YMCA boys' secretary for Massachusetts, blamed "unnatural, hot-house forcing" in the schools "for the highly nervous and sexually passionate adolescents. . . ."[114]

These anxieties converged in character builders' loathing of precocity as a little bestiary of inbred horrors: debility, nervous prostration, and degeneracy. Concern centered on middle-class boys, for boys' workers seldom worried that precocity weakened tough little street boys. Fear of precocity drew upon anxiety to keep middle-class teenagers dependent, unintellectual, and asexual. By stressing physical strength and playing down other adult capacities, character builders hoped, paradoxically, to conserve boys for long-term development.

A comparison with agencies for girls may help elucidate the boys' workers' goals. Girls' work did not directly influence early boys' work, but the founders borrowed heavily from boys' work, and the resulting similarities and differences reveal much about expectations for each sex. Until about 1909, YWCA secretaries did little work with girls under sixteen, but then developed programs of athletics, outdoor life, literary studies, and domestic skills. Juliette Gordon Low founded the Girl Scouts in 1912, modeled upon Baden-Powell's English Boy Scouts. Luther Gulick and his wife began the Camp Fire Girls the same year. As a veteran boys' worker anxious to maintain sex differences, Gulick declared it would be "fundamentally evil" to copy Boy Scouting; since girls must learn "to be womanly," the "domestic fire" became the group's symbol.[115]

Many concerns applied to both sexes, for sex roles tended to converge as middle-class adolescents spent their days in high school. Girls' workers were eager to end physical passivity; also like the Boy Scouts, the girls' groups gave achievement awards, although they put a bit more emphasis on group endeavor.[116]

There were also explicit differences, however, summed up in 1918 by a writer on Girl Scouts who asserted that in adapting Scouting "to the psychology of the young girl it has been recognized that boys like to be boys, while girls do not like to be girls. They are fundamentally little women, and the surest way to win their interest is to open to them the pursuits of women so modified as to insure to them the rewards of achievement."[117] Some of this was window dressing, yet Girl Scouts had to win badges such as homemaker or laundress in order to reach first class rank. The Gulicks sought even more definitely to suffuse household tasks with an air of romance and lead girls towards community involvement in ways consistent with homemaking, such as employment before marriage and club work after.[118] Ironically, whereas boys' workers favored strict sex segregation, girls' workers endorsed supervised coeducational recreation, since girls had to orient themselves towards marriage. Camp Fire Girls earned honors for dancing and coed hikes, and Girl Scouts had a badge for social and folk dancing.[119] In line with traditional expectations, girls were to be more self-abnegating than boys. Whereas Boy Scouts won advancement only for earning and saving money, Camp Fire Girls could also earn $3 to give away. Boy Scouts raised produce and sold it during World War I; Girl Scouts gave theirs to the school lunchroom.[120] At the same time, concern to keep girls placidly content ran as a refrain through girls' work. The head of Girl Scouting in Pittsburgh urged that "the home-maker of tomorrow . . . must be made efficient in her task and happy in it." A YWCA club leader warned that girls were "liable to moods of irritability, depression, and excitement," and the Camp Fire Girls' final law was: "Be happy."[121] In steering girls towards service and domesticity, girls' workers feared melancholy and dissatisfaction. Boys' workers, on the other hand, said little about happiness; they expected boys to put on a cheery face, subdue emotion, and work off restlessness through exercise and achievement.

On the whole, girls aroused less adult alarm than boys—a fact which explains why girls' work started later than boys' and was initially much less extensive. Girls, it seemed, had more continuous socialization and adapted more smoothly to adult expectations. They stayed a little longer in high school and a good deal longer in Sunday school (see above, Table 1). After classes each day, they mostly went straight home, whereas boys hung about on the streets. Consequently, by one contemporary tabulation there were twenty times as many groups doing boys' work as girls' work in 1910.[122]

In training girls directly for adult roles, girls' work programs resembled the forerunners of 4-H, founded in the 1900s and 1910s to inspire farm children to raise superior pigs, corn, and cotton and to cook, sew, and can better.[123] Programs for girls and farm children reinforced traditional patterns of continuous socialization, whereas the training of middle-class boys was unavoidably discontinuous. Extended education laid the groundwork for success, yet it was only indirectly related to boys' future occupations and there was no gradual edging into adult roles. Parents, teachers, and character builders all wanted such boys to be obedient, submissive school pupils. But since men were supposed to be self-assertive, adults also expected boys to burst with energy. The only way for character builders to have it both ways was to displace the boys' energy and achievement drives into boyish sports or anachronistic woodcraft, neither of much utility in modern adult life. This is not to say that continuous training was in fact better, for the future farmer or housewife's preparation all too often led down a narrow path in life. But discontinuous training for the sake of broad development exacted a price in restless strivings that adults stigmatized as precocious.

Character builders wanted to forestall precocity without coercion, to control and shield boys while building up their masculinity. How, then, could these divergent goals be reconciled? For inspiration, character builders looked to semimythical models of an ideal boyhood, yearning for a rural world where strength and virtue flourished in easy harmony. According to Ernest Thompson Seton, every American boy of the early 1800s "could ride, shoot, skate, run, swim; he was handy with tools; . . . he was physically strong, self-reliant, resourceful. . . ." In addition, he respected his superiors, obeyed his parents, and was "altogether the best material of which a nation could be made."[124] This was a world that never quite existed—Seton had never known the numbing monotony of field labor or the turbulent indiscipline of country schools; but it was gone in any case, and character builders had to reckon with the town boy's leisure.

Popular novels of small-town boyhood were more to the point. These were exercises in nostalgia. Although farm fathers of the early 1800s demanded that their sons work hard from an early age, by the 1850s the spread of public schooling and the growth of small towns had opened up a more leisured boyhood. Between home and school there was time for energetic play, sometimes highly structured, imitating the adult militia, for instance, but also very independent of adult control and free of adult responsibilities. In Utica, New York, as Mary P. Ryan describes it, boys of twelve or fourteen published their own newspapers, mimicking the adult press right down to "misogynist humor and ethnic slurs" yet also full of puerile interjections such as, "Horse chestnuts are fine things to pelt girls with." The boys indulged in high-spirited mischief, digging holes in the streets and overloading the butcher's sausage machine with garlic, to the point that "the term *boy* was often synonymous with prankster in the pages of the Utica press." Organized sports such as "base-ball" were just catching on in Utica by 1860.[125]

This was the kind of boyhood which popular novelists of the Gilded Age, remembering their own youth before the war, idealized and made the model of normality. The heroes of antebellum children's books had been moral paragons; but in the postwar context of assertive masculinity, authors depicted boys as vigorous, impulsive—though relatively harmless —savages. Thomas Bailey Aldrich popularized the new view in 1870 with his *Story of a Bad Boy* who got into scrapes over fibbing, fighting, and petty thievery; Aldrich thought him better than boys without spunk. Adults in such stories half admired the pranks, applying the by then familiar excuse: "Boys will be boys." Aldrich and other writers such as Charles Dudley Warner and Mark Twain established the boy-book as a familiar

genre, while popular painters exploited similar themes.[126] Boy-books re-
minded adults of their vanished playtimes and the seemingly protected
world of midnineteenth-century rural America, for the boy's small town
was free of sexuality, commercial vice, or class conflict. Even Huck Finn,
the rural equivalent of a street Arab, never seriously corrupted anyone,
though he did teach Tom Sawyer to smoke. Drawing upon romantic distaste for modern industrial civilization, sentimental authors portrayed small-
town boyhood as a golden age.

Unlike Louisa May Alcott's *Little Women* (1868–69), whose ideal girl-
hood revolved around the home, boys in these books formed a separate
world of boyhood. Although they played forerunners of baseball and football, more of their energy went into sledding, skating, swimming, fishing,
and foraging expeditions to the woods. Much modified, these activities
were to form the outdoor phase of Boy Scouting. The boys reportedly
formed their own pecking order, and a newcomer would have to fight all
challengers.[127] Boys' values differed from adults', for "real" boys disliked
schooling and sermons. With a little half-humorous hyperbole, these elements added up to a rudimentary culture of boyhood that was reassuringly unprecocious.

Boy-book youths appeared amoral at times, but there were compensating virtues. According to William Dean Howells, small-town boys had a
crude sense of honor, lied only when absolutely necessary, and always
respected women. Howells explained the paradox that virtues coexisted
with moral insensitivity by suggesting that the laws of boyhood came down
from "far-off savages." Though leavened with whimsy, his explanation was
serious. Charles Dudley Warner asserted flatly: "Every boy who is good
for anything is a natural savage." Thus boys in these books were presented
as having the "primal, vigorous instincts" of the savage without the vices
or virtues of civilization.[128] Free from women and their sentimental morality, such boys seemed to inhabit an ideal male world, a refuge from over-
civilization and effeminacy.

Rivaling the boy-books as accounts of ideal boyhood were stories of
English schoolboy life, notably Thomas Hughes's *Tom Brown's School
Days* (1857). Englishmen believed they had invented the sheltered, games-
playing boyhood; and Americans were much impressed. An American
clergyman who visited Britain in 1858 claimed: "They had no such boys
in America. [American boys] are all premature men; they never pass through
the intermediate stage of football and cricket and schoolboydom."[129] On
the average, English public schoolboys were older than those in American
boy-books, but they were cloistered in an all-male world governed by the
senior boys and seemed more securely boyish than American teenagers.
Sports in England had become an obsession by midcentury, as masters
tried to keep boys energetic and stamp out masturbation. From these

schools, muscular Christianity spread throughout the English-speaking world, promising strength harnessed to morality.[130]

An idealized schoolboy life influenced boys' work through many channels. Most significantly, Baden-Powell drew upon his experiences as a Charterhouse boy in designing Boy Scouting. *Tom Brown* was hugely popular in America. (Theodore Roosevelt thought every boy should read it, along with Aldrich's *Story of a Bad Boy*.)[131] American writing on boys teemed with British references, and British and Canadian-born men figured prominently in American character building, notably three who supervised Boy Scouting's transit to America in 1910: Edgar M. Robinson, then head of YMCA boys' work, had grown up in New Brunswick; Ernest Thompson Seton, the BSA's Chief Scout, was an English-born Canadian; and John L. Alexander, the main author of the early Boy Scout manuals, came from Scotland.

Belatedly towards 1900, Americans developed their own schoolboy life, as prep schools such as Choate and Lawrenceville won considerable eclat. Novels of American prep school life won great popularity in the early 1900s, but the British model remained more influential in boys' work.[132]

Either model of boyhood — small-town playtime or schoolboy athleticism — suggested ways to keep boys unprecocious while bolstering their masculinity. If character builders were to impose authority without breaking wills, they had to find means that seemed natural to boys. What better in an age of popular Darwinism than woodsy savagery? Or what more appealing than team sports? Summer camp even combined the boarding school and backwoods. Gradually, character builders took over things that boys already did, meanwhile adapting a longstanding form of social control: the stereotyping of women and minorities as irrational and dependent. Ideally, boys would learn to see themselves as vigorous yet immature — hearty, heedless lads too busy to essay impurity or claim adult prerogatives.

By the 1890s adults were complacently embracing an artificial cult of the "bad boy." Thus a writer for *Leslie's Weekly* transmuted the traditional rogue's progress, from stealing candies to robbing stagecoaches, into praise of Admiral Dewey, who went from hooking apples to seizing the Philippines: "By the older people of his native town, George Dewey is remembered as a harum-scarum lad. . . . He could swim better than most boys of his age, and found pleasure in climbing such trees as contained the earliest apples. . . . It is observed that young Dewey was not over-particular whose orchard he visited, either." The "good" boy fell under suspicion of "moral precocity." John Johnson told readers of *Popular Science Monthly* that any boy of fourteen who had "no instinctive impulse to maim a ground squirrel" with his slingshot was abnormal.[133] With serious troublemakers, though, admiration evaporated. Bruno Bettelheim has sketched the ambivalence of uneasy adults: "It may take the form of contempt if youth does not fight back (they are weak) or of hostile anxiety if it does (they are delinquent)." When fearful that middle-class boys were weak, Boy Scout leaders welcomed those with "energy enough to get into trouble," but they loathed real hooligans.[134]

Boys did have to fight, for Americans associated manly effort with combat. Theodore Roosevelt urged Boy Scouts to keep the playgrounds free of toughs, and a YMCA physical director even suggested that boxing would make boys "Christlike and manly." Though reluctant to endorse recurrent fisticuffs, the *Handbook for Scout Masters* praised a fight as "one of the greatest institutions that savage man has invented" for subduing a bully.[135]

All in all, character builders propounded a small boy's view of masculinity, suited to a period in life when boys were turned loose to reinforce each other's fears of seeming weak. Roosevelt's friend Cecil Spring-Rice once observed: "You must always remember that the President is about six."[136] (Age eight or ten might have been closer.) Yet Roosevelt epitomized manliness to his generation. Nostalgia for small-town boyhood likewise centered on the time between early childhood and puberty, from six or eight to twelve or fourteen.[137] Taken together, the popularity of boy-books, Roosevelt, and Boy Scouting all suggested a hunger for perpetual early boyhood.

If purity was power, preadolescent boyhood seemed the ideal time to build masculinity, while virility was still untainted with genital sexuality. To depict boys as savages reinforced the point, since Americans stereotyped Indians as violent but not lascivious.[138] Echoing a long tradition that civilization enfeebles and corrupts, this view of boyhood fitted in with popular Teutonism; boys were the heirs of the Tacitus's German tribesmen — strong, pure, youthful forest dwellers whose virtues stood in sharp contrast to the effete decadence of city people.

Character builders troubled by teenage sensuality, weakness, and indiscipline concluded that they should prolong boyhood into the teens. After 1900, as concern about teenagers crystallized around the new concept of adolescence, this desire to prolong boyhood became a central theme in character building. In effect, character builders proposed a trade. By remaining in school, middle-class boys had accepted prolonged dependency; now they would accept closer control of their spare time as well. In return, adults would assure them of their masculinity and busy them with sports and outdoor ramblings, compensating the youths for loss of independence with a simulacrum of manliness. The boys could, however, reject this bargain at any time simply by dropping out of adult-sponsored boys' work agencies, since membership was wholly voluntary. And as later chapters will show, character builders often did better at winning adult support than at holding boys.

Few organizations have only a single purpose, yet few have espoused more open-ended goals than those implied by the fourfold plan of character building for boys. The resulting programs soaked up middle-class anxieties and norms like blotting paper and were colored by commonplace values of the Progressive Era.

This middle-class relationship was complex. On one level, for instance, the character builders' preoccupation with strength and control reflected the immediate needs of churchmen who hoped to hold boys by convincing them that religion was manly. At a deeper level, character building institutionalized the ambivalence of middle-class Americans who celebrated energy, drive, and ambition, yet treasured discipline and social control.[139] A common complaint of the Progressive Era was that the middle class was under siege from above and below, its income and opportunities eroded by the extortionate gains of both organized labor and massed capital. Such middle-class defensiveness underlay the character builders' determination that boys from good families grow up strong and disciplined. Yet middle-class spokesmen commonly refused to admit class interest, blandly defining their own values as normative and classless.[140] So, too, character builders claimed that their organizations epitomized American democracy; yet the ideal boyhood they promoted was in fact anchored to middle-class yearnings.

Whether to classify character building for boys as itself a Progressive reform is less certain. In working through voluntary associations, character builders used a technique common among Progressive reformers, especially those from the middle class for whom action through private organizations was the preferred way of exerting social control. But voluntary associationalism was long established among the middle class and not unique to Progressive reform.[141] As for political Progressivism, its link with character building was distinctly tenuous. Both movements, it could be argued, had a primarily middle-class base; but in the case of Progressivism that claim is open to challenge. Although the gentry and middle class provided most of the leaders and reformism functioned substantially within their world view, the same social classes also furnished most of the leading opponents of Progressive reform. Furthermore, recent studies show that leading Progressive politicians did not draw reliable support from middle-class voters except insofar as many of those politicians were Republicans who profited from the loyalty to Republicanism of the northern Protestant middle class. A more direct, personal tie between character building for boys and Progressive reform politics is hard to trace, because leading character builders voiced many of the same concerns as cautious reformers but were not closely connected with politicians except for Roosevelt.[142]

What character builders shared with many Progressive leaders was an ethos, a yearning, a moral tone and organizational style rooted in middle-class Protestant culture. They shared with many of these reformers a "frame of mind," a set of attitudes and assumptions common to much of the Protestant middle class in the Progressive Era, which historians have incautiously identified with political Progressivism but which was in fact rather broader.[143] Like contemporary businessmen, professionals, and Progressive politicians, character builders believed both in individualism and in loyalty to the group or organization. Although religious faith was losing its urgent immediacy for much of the Progressive Era middle and upper classes, a strenuous moralism, descended from Protestant religiosity, powered the rhetoric and judgments of middle-class public figures in that era.[144] While character builders, like most of their contemporaries, were too conservative to jettison religious faith altogether, in shifting priority towards earnest moralism, strength, and citizenship they epitomized the basic assumptions — if not always the professed values — of mainstream middle-class Protestants in the Progressive Era.

Insofar as character building for boys had affinities to political Progressivism, it was closest to those forms with substantial middle- and upper-class support, notably Theodore Roosevelt's 1912 Progressive Party and local campaigns for city manager and commission government. Like character builders, politicians from those campaigns conflated morality and efficiency. Much as boys' work had roots in Protestant moral earnestness, so Progressive leaders brought it into politics, never more blatantly than in 1912 when Roosevelt's supporters sang "Onward Christian Soldiers."[145] While Progressive leaders made a fetish of technical expertise, it was only in the 1910s that this began to displace moralism as the rationale for exercising power, and even then efficiency and morality seemed in harmony.[146] As later chapters will show, character builders likewise shifted towards technocracy, confident that social science remained the handmaiden of traditional morality.

Like boys' workers, Progressives commonly believed that reform should begin with the young. Moralists of all political stripes could support child welfare measures modeled on the middle-class norm of a sheltered childhood.[147] Child labor opponents sought to remove lower-class children from the world of work, playground enthusiasts tried to get them off the streets, and juvenile court supporters worked to shield delinquents from adult criminal procedure. In each case, reformers favored a protected environment separated from adult life, just as character builders did for middle-class teenagers.

Ideally, Progressive Era youth workers wanted to copy the virtues not only of middle-class child nurture but of bygone small-town life as well. At its most literalistic, such nostalgia inspired the formation of William R. George's highly publicized George Junior Republic (1895) and similar model communities with their own political and economic systems where neglected or delinquent boys were to practice obedience to law, hard work, and small-town democracy.[148] Progressive educators shared the longing for a setting which would teach useful skills and social discipline. Through classroom activities which echoed the preindustrial "household and neighborhood system" of production, John Dewey hoped to inculcate "a spirit of social cooperation and community life. . . ."[149] As character builders practiced it, summer camping was yet another experiment with forming temporary communities away from modern life.

Nostalgia for an imagined Arcadia of close-knit little towns pervaded Progressive Era culture. Almost obsessively, intellectuals expostulated on the need to recover a sense of community, moral order, and social control. In a lighter vein, songs such as "Down by the Old Mill Stream" and "In the Good Old Summertime" celebrated the small town as a place of "innocent romance and decent fun. . . ."[150] Progressives recoiled from the class strife of the 1890s. Thus George Creel, the Progressive generation's foremost propagandist for Americanism, closed his reminiscences of boyhood with a paean to small-town democracy: "No dividing line between the rich and poor, and no class distinctions to breed mean envies. The wealthiest merchant stood behind his counter, and the banker walked home of an evening with the round steak for supper tucked under his arm." Creel remembered the consensus as essentially moral: "Character was the bed rock on which the community rested."[151]

Nostalgia for small-town boyhood was a cultural synecdoche, epitomizing the dream of a simpler, self-contained existence with clear rules. Boys —like women—were cultural surrogates, expected to remain loyal to traditional values while men's lives changed. Character builders could not understand boys like Leonard Covello whose lives careened between immigrant parents and native-stock teachers, street life and the boys' club. They wanted boyhood all of a piece.

Ironically, like most Progressive reformers, character builders sought the values of preindustrial life by the methods of the new organizational society. While they strove to prevent the fragmentation of middle-class boys' lives by supporting the values of home, school, and church, they added one more affiliation to lives which already cut across many institutions.

Nor could boys' workers actually recapture a lost Arcadia. Leo Marx points out that America's pastoral ideal bore the seeds of its own destruction, sanctioning conquest of the wilderness and "economic and technological development—up to a point. The objective, in theory at least, was a society of the middle landscape, a rural nation exhibiting a happy balance of art and nature." But economic development did not stop; it continued until the pastoral ideal was only a sentimental memory. The *Handbook for Scout Masters* might propose restoring the virtues of farm boyhood, but Boy Scout leaders wanted tightly controlled energy, not bucolic placidity.[152] So they went back beyond farming, invoking boyish savagery, and sought to balance two extremes—the forest against the city.

Basically, character building was a complex, sometimes inconsistent mixture of modern theories and techniques, rural nostalgia, and contrived primitivism. While longing for a simpler time, many reformers of the Progressive Era also recognized the promise of modern life; and so, though very tentatively, did some character builders. The YMCA's primary answer to boyish problems—"a new conception of manly, muscular Christianity"—though born on the elm-shaded playing fields of English public schools, was reshaped to fit an urban setting of gymnasiums and swimming pools.[153] Around 1900, as we shall see, character builders borrowed new ideas from developmental psychology to form a full-blown ideology of character-building methods; but they still yearned for the moral uniformity of preindustrial small towns and the all-around development those towns purportedly had fostered.

II

Nineteenth-Century Beginnings:
Early Forms of Boys' Work

3

Keeping Lower-Class Boys
Off the Streets: The Mass Boys' Clubs

Nineteenth-century boys' clubs were among the first and most rudimentary forms of boys' work — a hasty, often improvised translation into action of the dismay with which Protestant moralists and men of wealth regarded lower-class city boyhood. Since club workers set essentially negative goals — to get boys off the street and out of trouble — club programs were severely practical, designed first and foremost to interest masses of boys and keep them harmlessly occupied rather than to inculcate advanced moral and religious ideals or to develop any great strengths. Character was not the main objective.

Consequently, the resulting boys' clubs are not central to this book, which concentrates on agencies that served middle-class boys and made bolder claims — to build character. Indeed, the two streams of boys' work defined themselves against each other. Club workers took poor boys whom the YMCA and Boy Scouts largely passed by, espoused simple, direct programs, and contrasted their mission to the easier task of aiding "pampered" youths. Character builders, on the other hand, dismissed street boys as precociously immoral and described the goal of middle-class boys' work as character formation, not *re*formation.[1] The training they offered was less immediately practical; the virtues they propounded were more ambitious; and on the average, the boys joining their organizations were a bit older. But a brief account of the boys' clubs is a good starting point for an understanding of boys' work, since the clubs represent its most basic form as a preventive response to city ills; one can then see what the character builders added.

The term "boys' club" applied to many different institutions. The most important were the mass clubs which enrolled boys by the hundreds, but there were many smaller ones, usually sponsored by a church or some other charitable or religious agency. Common to all was a sense of mission to the poor in which Christian and philanthropic motives intertwined with fear of class strife and social upheaval.

Many boys' clubs stemmed from efforts to adapt Protestant church work to urban problems. The English example was important, inasmuch as British experiments with religiously oriented clubs dated from the 1860s and 1870s. In America, city missions proliferated in the 1870s and 1880s, backed by wealthy businessmen, as Protestants sought to convert slum dwellers. But these undertakings won over few lower-class men; so the missions added social services, including boys' clubs, and sought a more malleable clientele among the young.[2] The first boys' club to be called such originated in 1876 at the Wilson Mission in New York City. With help from the railroad magnate E. H. Harriman, it grew into the Boys' Club of the City of New York, the largest in the country. The club movement in New England owed its early impetus to the Committee for Christian Workers, an association of city missionaries formed in 1886 by the Reverend John C. Collins which established twenty clubs. As Protestant church work for the poor served increasing numbers of Catholics and Jews, those in charge played down proselytizing. Accordingly, despite their sponsorship, most mass clubs avoided overt religious instruction. And not until the late 1890s did any number of Catholic boys' clubs appear in response.[3]

By the mid-1880s a few Protestant congregations, calling themselves institutional churches, began to supply an ambitious program of classes and clubs for all ages, open to members and nonmembers alike. Innovations took place in working-class churches or in fashionable parishes such as J. P. Morgan's St. George's Episcopal, which had been surrounded by tenements as immigrants moved in but had kept its wealthy vestrymen. St. George's Boys' Club began in 1884, and other churches followed—until in 1892 Jacob Riis could list 31 boys' clubs in New York City, 27 sponsored by some church, mission, or church-related agency.[4] Church clubs were often small, serving boys from the congregation one or two nights a week; but a number of churches sponsored clubs for their poorer neighbors, and a few of these became true mass clubs. Boys' clubs were less controversial than full-scale institutional churches, and boys proved easier to recruit than adults.[5]

Secular reformers soon took up the club idea. As social settlements multiplied in the 1890s, they quickly formed both boys' and girls' clubs. An interest in juvenile reform led women's clubs to back ventures such as Milwaukee's Boys' Busy Life Club and prod school officials to take up the cause. By 1914, New York City had more than five hundred small clubs under Board of Education auspices.[6]

Without institutional backing, many mass clubs relied heavily on individual supporters. A few clubs, such as William McCormick's Olivet Boys' Club in Reading, Pennsylvania, were financed and run by the same man. Others depended on men of wealth; public appeals for funds were surprisingly rare before the 1910s. Instead, club superintendents sought to emulate Massachusetts' Fall River Boys' Club, which secured a building worth $85,000 from Matthew C. D. Borden, a local cotton manufacturer, or the club in Pittsfield, which received two buildings from Zenas Crane.[7]

It would overstate the case to represent the boys' club movement as an alliance of the upper and lower classes against the middle, but that was more true than in other forms of boys' work. Mass clubs and institutional churches relied heavily upon wealthy donors. A few of the men who ran the clubs were well-to-do volunteers, while others came from the lower middle class. But many city missionaries were simply uneducated converts who found wealthy sponsors, so men who entered club work through the missions were often lower-class.[8] Charles Stelzle and Thomas Chew, two leading spokesmen for boys' clubs in the early 1900s, both had quit school young—Chew at twelve to toil in a textile mill, Stelzle at eleven to make artificial flowers. Stelzle became a machinist, then entered church work at a mission in Minneapolis in 1895 and wrote a widely read book, *Boys of the Street: How to Win Them.* Chew became a YMCA janitor, and in 1890 took over a small boys' club organized by a city missionary in Fall River. With Borden's help, he made it a huge enterprise and later served as president of the Federated Boys' Clubs. Despite this success, he never quite shed a suspicion of middle-class institutions like the YMCA.[9]

Benevolence and social control were mingled in the motives of boys' club enthusiasts. We saw in the last chapter how middle-class adults reacted to street boys with shock and even revulsion. Simply being found upon the street was enough to convict boys of delinquency in many a juvenile court. Proponents of a curfew wanted to force them back indoors, around whatever radiator or cookstove served as the family hearth, but club workers knew that boys needed a more positive alternative; they understood the hunger of deprived boys for innocent fun.[10] Yet men like Chew and Stelzle, who had sought and found personal respectability, also had a sturdy working-class appreciation of the need for order and discipline in boys' lives.[11]

Street boys made it plain that they could be controlled only by meeting their hunger for diversion; they would not sit still for preaching. Reportedly, boys pitched mud at New York's Wilson Mission until the people inside tried starting a boys' club.[12] Admittedly, such tales were staples of boys' club propaganda, but they reflected the boys' itch for active fun.

Club workers maintained that existing agencies had little influence. The Sunday schools had lost the lower class, and public schools imposed only limited, mechanical controls. Charles Keith, assistant secretary of the Boys' Club Federation, held that no teacher burdened with fifty pupils of alien class and culture could shape boys' lives outside the classroom. And William McCormick, who prided himself on taking the boys' point of view, asserted bluntly that they found five hours in school "an extremity of torture."[13]

Above all, there existed the fear that restless youths would turn to crime. Boys' club enthusiasts proposed to enroll boys well before their teens, keep them busy, build decent habits, and forestall the drift towards trouble. According to club workers, admiring reporters, and police, boys' clubs markedly reduced juvenile delinquency; a favorite argument compared the $2 cost per boy to the $120 needed to keep a prisoner in jail.[14] Although untested by direct evidence, such claims won wide acclaim for the clubs.

Related motives included the hope that benevolence would reduce social tensions and prevent mass upheavals. This was a prominent theme in the social Christianity of the 1880s. Jacob Riis remembered when Tompkins Square, the site of the Boys' Club of the City of New York, "was taken from a mob by the police, a mob carrying red banners. . . ." This occurred July 25, 1877, at the height of that year's railroad strike, during which juvenile delinquency seemed about to ripen into mass revolt as boys in their late teens demonstrated or rioted in cities across the country. "To-day," Riis boasted in 1902, "Tompkins Square is the quietest street in the city. The boys' club simply made good citizens."[15] This was transparent puffery, but the same consideration doubtless helped the club remain E. H. Harriman's favorite charity. In addition, wealthy supporters hoped the clubs would foster working-class efficiency. Settlement workers likewise sought social peace by preparing children of immigrants to be citizens of a democracy. And as concern about immigration rose in the 1910s, club workers played up the clubs' value for Americanization.[16]

Since the basic rationale for mass clubs was preventive, club workers used simple methods to get boys off the streets and generally set their sights lower than middle-class oriented character builders. The first clubs gave street boys a substitute home for the evening, noisy and crowded yet equipped with amusements that prosperous boys took for granted. In fact, John F. Atkinson proposed calling his the "Boys' Club and Pleasant Evenings."[17] To start, organizers rented rooms, bought games and books or volumes of illustrated papers, turned on the lights, and waited for boys to swarm in. Any youngster who refrained from tearing up the place was welcome.[18]

Visitors marvelled at the resulting crowds. The clubs in Meriden, Connecticut, and Worcester, Massachusetts, each enrolled nearly 800 boys in 1889, of whom 75 to 120 showed up on an average night. In 1904, the Boys' Club of the City of New York claimed registration of more than twelve thousand and daily attendance of nearly two thousand.[19] Since the mass club went for crowds and did not demand deep commitment, it became for most boys a place to drop in on now and then.

Controlling such crowds was like riding a tiger. Indeed a set piece in writing on club or mission work was the opening night battle to see "who was master."[20] Accounts reaching print usually ended with the boys' worker triumphant, ejecting the troublemakers by main force, although *Work With Boys* published a lugubrious fiction about a young volunteer who lost control and was killed when someone threw a brick. The moral was to take command at once, but even then peace was not guaranteed. One evening two years after the Chicago Boys' Club started, a speaker was part way through an illustrated lecture when a restless wit raised the cry, "Somebody's sitting on me silk hat!" The crowd chimed in until the speaker turned off the lantern. He tried repeatedly to resume, but the boys defied control until the police arrived. They cleared the hall and forced one urchin to surrender a folding chair he was smuggling out under his coat. A club spokesman called the meeting a success, but he did not say for whom.[21]

An occasional fracas gave boys' workers a chance to show how tough they were, but none wanted a steady diet of confrontation. So club leaders turned to a simple system of rewards for good behavior and deprivation for rowdiness. Instead of attempting to inculcate ideals, they used simple conditioning to impose good behavior by carrot-and-stick methods: a boy had to wash his hands before he could get a book; he paid in clean speech and self-discipline for gymnasium privileges. To enforce habits of concentration, club directors ruled that no boy could remain in the room without something to occupy him. At least in theory, lectures and magic lantern shows forced the boys to sit still and pay attention, while refreshments raised the stakes by forcing rowdies to weigh the pleasures of disruption against the loss of sandwiches. Thus early club workers spent their best efforts enforcing habits of cleanliness and patience which middle-class character builders took more or less for granted. The boys might develop more advanced capacities—but almost in spite of themselves, if one were to believe the club workers. Frank Mason of Boston's Bunker Hill Boys' Club explained that games would habituate a boy to persistence and "unconsciously arouse . . . thought and perception. . . ."[22] Club discipline took the same behaviorist approach, seeking simply to condition boys to obedience. William Taylor of Rochester's Brick Church Institute explained, "Some of the roughest and toughest [boys] have become some of the best, because having come into a square stand-up and knock-down fight with the powers that be, and having been worsted, they have submitted."[23]

Reluctance to try ambitious character building reflected an unflattering assessment of street boys. Chew found contact with so many apparently hopeless cases discouraging; the boys gave him little sympathy, and discipline had to be autocratic (he used a whistle to direct movements). Because the clubs offered deprived boys temporary use of books, games, and tools, preventing theft became a preoccupation it never was for Boy Scout or YMCA leaders. A manual training teacher at the Chicago Commons settlement house found the only way to stop boys from stealing tools was to threaten cancellation of the class; but with the season's end the *quid pro quo* vanished, and so did the tools.[24] Even without thefts, some volunteers were shocked that the boys did not share their principles. Walter T. Stern, who coached sports at the Boys' Club of the City of New York, reported that the boys "naturally did not vouchsafe to me any ideas which would emanate from well trained minds" and had no interest in maintaining "the strict amateur standing of the amateur sportsman. They desired always to play for some stake . . . [but] were easily dissuaded from playing for money and perfectly satisfied to play for a prize instead."[25]

A further indication of the early club workers' low expectations was their avoidance of religious instruction. John F. Atkinson complained that New York's clubs were mere playrooms; however, proselytizing scared off Catholics and Jews. His Chicago Boys' Club, one of the few which evangelized openly, began operations in 1901 among Italian newsboys of the Loop but had to relocate, and by 1911 was 66 percent Protestant. To YMCA critics who carped that club work was "not Christian," the editor of *Work With Boys* replied: "If we were able to rescue Johnny and Willie from drunken parents; to take Tommy and Jimmy from the streets, . . . we have but imitated One whose religious teachings are largely summed up in the words, 'He went about doing good.'"[26]

Club leaders defined their work against that of the YMCA socially as well as religiously. Some expected the Y to recruit all the "best" boys and then skim the cream of their members as well. A lady club worker regretted that "as soon as a boy gets so he will take off his hat and stop spitting on the floor the YMCA gets him."[27] At first Chew saw this in a positive light, believing that boys' clubs should "drill the awkward squad and fit them to join the army of young men who were already organized in church, temperance and Christian organizations." He expected to pass boys on at age fourteen, but soon found that few joined "the Y.M.C.A. or other societies [because] they were not wanted and could not have made themselves at home in any of them."[28] Therefore the Fall River Boys' Club developed its own clubs for older youths, a parallel social world to carry lower-class boys to adulthood. This walling-off reflected resentment of middle-class bias, a feeling which sharpened over time. The Fall River Club had "little room to spare for the boy of cultivated parents or of comfortable home," and by the 1910s some clubs adopted rules to bar such boys.[29] More positively, a director of the Boys' Club of Indianapolis asserted proudly in 1914 that the club did not duplicate YMCA, Boy Scout, or church work: "We are mining for the raw material, while they are working on a more finished product."[30]

As Chew's remarks suggested, the clubs' preventive approach led them to take boys much younger than the YMCA or Boy Scouts. Once the clubs began to hold onto older boys as well, a very broad age range resulted. In 1904 Chew's club had 280 boys (19 percent) ages eight and nine, 402 (27 percent) ages ten and eleven, 485 (32 percent) twelve and thirteen, and 333 (22 percent) fourteen and over. The Chicago Boys' Club in 1910 had 30 boys under age six, 825 from six to twelve, and 965 over twelve.[31] Unlike character builders, club leaders gave little heed to age as a factor in personal development, because the slum boys' immediate needs crowded out other considerations. The early mass clubs concentrated on those under fourteen, who seemed more controllable. Although this preference for pre-adolescents weakened somewhat after 1900, the continued presence of younger boys perpetuated elementary methods.

Changes in the 1900s and 1910s brought boys' club practice a little closer to that of the character builders. Yet boys' clubs remained distinctive and separate from middle-class boys' work. Organizationally, in fact, the two streams diverged still further as mass club directors developed a sense of separate identity. A number joined other boys' workers from the Northeast in 1898 to form the General Alliance of Workers with Boys. They had to contend with the "cheerful omniscience" of college-educated settlement workers, but they persevered, held separate sessions, and were "so eager and so humble . . . that they soon won a better appreciation both for themselves and their work."[32] In 1905, a committee of the Alliance sponsored formation of the Federated Boys' Clubs (later the Boys' Club Federation and then the Boys' Clubs of America). Membership was limited to nonsectarian mass clubs with at least 100 boys, though some settlements joined as affiliates. The General Alliance's magazine listed 74 mass clubs in 1905 — 63 in New England or the Middle Atlantic states, 7 in the Midwest, and 4 scattered. By 1911, the FBC had 110 clubs with 108,063 boys, including some settlement clubs; in 1915 there were 85 "distinct" boys' clubs. The federation had no administrative control over clubs but encouraged basic standards.[33]

Gradually, club leaders tried to shed the rescue mission image. In 1907, Frank Mason attacked the stereotype of the boys' club member as a "ragged urchin with dirty face, bad manners, [and] oafish disposition. . . ." Mason insisted that his boys, while sometimes destructive, were not of "distinctly evil tendencies." Otherwise, he commented with a trace of special pleading, clubs would have been unfit for ordinary boys.[34] As facilities improved, club leaders began to stress attracting working-class and working boys instead of street boys, although the main shift was one of age, as clubs signed up older boys with steady jobs who resented the label "street boy."[35]

These changes encouraged club leaders to talk of building character, but their expectations remained modest. William Taylor offered a surpris-

ingly guarded assessment of "Character-Making" at his church club: although the boys learned not to wreck furniture and long-term members
showed other improvements, it was "the exceptional boy in which these
results [were] sufficiently pronounced to cause anything like a glow of
real satisfaction. . . ."[36]

In career terms, expectations were likewise modest. Early club leaders
hoped to make boys "into good, honest, working men," and this emphasis continued.[37] Few clubs could afford serious vocational programs, but
most had manual training to build habits of obedience, industry, and accuracy. The Chicago Boys' Club had classes in carpentry, printing, cob-
bling, and basket weaving but not advanced mechanics or white-collar
skills — even though the club's star members were ambitious youths who
attended night school or high school or hoped to do so.[38] Although a
committee of the Boys' Club Federation urged in 1920 that boys be introduced to "the business and service possibilities of life," subsequent discussion favored inducing most to learn a trade.[39]

Manual training was one of many activities that proliferated after 1900
under pressure from the boys, who tired, Stelzle warned, of nothing but
games and socials. As in other forms of boys' work, variety became the
nostrum for high dropout rates. While many small clubs limped along
with sadly restricted programs, boys at the largest clubs could play nearly
every game imaginable (except cards), study drawing, play in the band,
act in plays, debate the tariff, go on outings, or merely attend story hour.[40]
Clubs lagged far behind the YMCA in physical training, but 92 out of
152 had gymnasiums by 1920.[41]

The mass clubs also drew a bit closer in spirit and program to the public
school and settlement clubs, whose spokesmen recognized the influence
of immigrant cultures as well as poverty upon boys and consequently cherished somewhat higher expectations for them. At New York's College Settlement, for instance, boys could join the Hero Club to receive pointers
on success or the Knights of the Round Table to learn chivalry.[42] Using
volunteer leaders, school and settlement workers divided the boys into
separate clubs of fifteen to thirty members, all about the same age. Since
this was not rescue work, the leaders could concentrate on teenagers and
favor the ambitious, unlike mass club superintendents who kept open house
every night. Intensive guidance got results, for the memoirs of successful
immigrant boys are studded with tributes to the way such club work gave
them wider culture and enhanced ambitions.[43]

After 1900, some mass clubs introduced rudimentary age grading and
divided boys into small groups led by former members or student volunteers. But superintendents had trouble finding help; and rescue-minded
directors continued mass methods, arguing that more intensive approaches
such as Boy Scouting required too much manpower and could reach only

a fraction of the needy boys. Even the Chicago Commons settlement still used game rooms as a "dumping ground" for crowds as late as 1922.[44] Ultimately, intensive work with teenagers remained more characteristic of middle-class character builders.

Mass club programs grew like houses built without blueprints, one room at a time. Superintendents tried whatever would keep boys off the streets, and the pressures of riding herd on crowds obliterated the distance needed for theoretical detachment. At a time when middle-class character builders were aspiring to professional status, many boys' clubs superintendents still saw themselves as the practical mechanics of boys' work, practitioners of a craft with few universal standards. Discussions at Boys' Club Federation meetings focused narrowly on specific program ideas; and descriptions of the ideal boys' worker stressed qualities such as cleanliness, patience, good humor, and love of boys—all personal attributes entailing no claim to professionalism.[45]

Preoccupation with providing recreation to fill boys' leisure hours was not unique to the clubs, since all boys' work sought to keep boys busy and out of trouble. But the mass clubs' rescue mission imposed special limitations upon their directors' ambitions to go further. The fragmented, narrowly practical focus of leaders' concerns reflected the clubs' origins as an ad hoc response to the grimmest sort of urban boyhood. To impose upon the polygot throngs who crammed their rooms the sort of small-town moral consensus of which character builders dreamed would have been a herculean labor; by not pushing boys too far, club leaders could accommodate diversity. The strengths and virtues they promoted were simple, partly because they lacked resources but also because derogatory assumptions about street boys lowered their expectations. Since club workers lacked equipment and feared boisterous disruptions, they encouraged sedentary pastimes and elementary crafts. Boys' clubs did less than Boy Scouting and the YMCA to build physical strength through gymnastics, sports, or woodcraft; club leaders saw less need for this, since street boys seemed less prone to weakness than were middle-class boys. Although club leaders eventually talked of building character, they relied upon carrot-and-stick methods to improve behavior, whereas middle-class character builders worked with older boys in smaller groups, imposed pledges, preached moral ideals, and sought all-round development of boys' faculties.

4

Shielding and Strengthening the Middle Class: The Start of YMCA Junior Departments

Unlike the boys' clubs, YMCAs did not start out to serve boys. Indeed, it was only after they established their special mission to young, mostly white-collar men — and young men only — that YMCAs turned to boys' work, partly in reaction to the exclusion of boys under sixteen from membership and partly as a feeder for the older group. The resultant junior departments then sought out a class of boys more suited to YMCA needs than those the boys' clubs welcomed.

The first YMCAs arose from the convergence of two responses to city life: mission work and young men's self-improvement societies. A clerk named George Williams founded the first Young Men's Christian Association in London, England, in 1844, banding his friends together to keep their faith unsullied by the city. The idea spread to the U.S. and Canada, where YMCAs sprang up in major cities during the 1850s, combining libraries and literary societies with prayer meetings and Bible classes. Older businessmen who valued discipline for their clerks backed the young men's initiative.[1] Although city Associations sent delegates to state and international conventions (U.S. and Canada), they remained independent; and each level — city, state, and international — raised its own budget.[2]

Many Associations of the 1850s and 1860s imposed only a maximum age, commonly forty, and accepted teenagers as full members. Sumner Dudley, a future boys' worker, was an active member of the Worcester YMCA at age fourteen. As Y leaders grew older, however, maximum age limits disappeared, while minimum age limits — usually sixteen — became common by the 1870s. By the 1880s, many YMCA officers claimed youth only because those "that wait on the Lord shall renew their strength. . . ."[3] Teenagers seemed out of place beside them.

Few Associations did separate boys' work in the 1860s and 1870s. Many YMCA secretaries (the Y's paid officers) hoped to lead a broad crusade in which they and men who joined the YMCA would win all ages to Christ. The few YMCAs which tried boys' work did so as a form of home mission;

members established Sunday schools or set up rooms with books and games to lure deprived lads away from warm-air gratings.[4] These experiments anticipated the work of boys' clubs; but they entailed no recognition of the needs of boyhood as such, for poverty, not age, made street urchins objects of solicitude. Boys' work remained peripheral, with only 48 of 666 Associations active in 1879 (see Table 2).

By then, YMCAs were developing a more focused sense of mission to middle-class young men. As the light-armed cavalry of the Lord, the first YMCAs skirmished ahead of the churches into the city wilderness. But after a time, they settled into camp, built imposing headquarters, and concentrated upon bringing young men within their walls. Starting in the late 1860s, YMCA leaders from New York City promoted "work for young men only" under the rubric of "the fourfold program"—spiritual, mental, social, and physical. In the process, they discouraged outside enterprises such as boys' meetings and mission schools.[5] The New Yorkers blamed the frequent collapse of local YMCAs on failure to provide activities to hold members once converted; lonely young men away from home needed wholesome recreation to fend off temptation. Under the guidance of the YMCA's International Committee, located in New York, the fourfold approach gradually displaced the more exclusively religious programs of men like Dwight Moody, who began his evangelistic career with the Chicago YMCA.[6] Y men struck a compromise between revivalist and antirevivalist Protestants, as secretaries continued to run evangelistic meetings for young men but increasingly stressed the kind of gradual growth in character preferred by antirevivalists. From the fourfold program it was a short step to the assumption that YMCAs should enlist "average" young men and not the poor, who had special problems and could not pay for expensive facilities. City YMCAs were established in the business district, enrolling many clerks, some mechanics, and almost no laborers.[7]

Gymnasiums, introduced originally to compete with those attached to saloons, became the great attraction by the 1890s. Vigorous exertion assuaged young clerks' fears of losing virility because they did sedentary work and answered to a boss's beck and call. More important, it was both an outlet for energy and a form of self-discipline; even alcohol could not surpass exhaustion as a cure for business tensions or restless cravings.[8]

Luther Gulick, the YMCA's first international secretary for physical work, went beyond these simple benefits to develop a rudimentary "philosophy" of physical education which became a rationale for the expanded YMCA program. Echoing the classical idea that man "is a unit," Gulick argued the Y must train "the whole man. . . ."[9] To symbolize this unity, Gulick proposed the red triangle, which the YMCA adopted as its emblem in 1895; the three sides stood for man's physical, mental, and spiritual nature.[10] Its adoption confirmed the YMCA commitment to character building through balanced development.

The new programs transformed the Y. By 1900, 77 percent of city YMCAs had gymnastic facilities, as even small Associations made that investment. Full-size buildings also contained a meeting hall, library, and rooms for games and classes. As paid secretaries took over most operations, reducing members to paying customers, there was less reason to exclude boys.[11] Still, boys' work did not thrive until it was reoriented to fit the new-style YMCA.

Initially, boys forced the Y to serve them. In Poughkeepsie and Buffalo, for instance, so many drifted into the YMCA building that Y officials eventually gave them a room to use. Many of these boys came from respectable families and might once have joined as regular members but now were barred by the minimum age limit.[12] Even so, secretaries feared rowdiness; Chicago's YMCA cut back in 1888 because its rooms were crowded with boys whose "ill behavior" interfered with "the enjoyment of young men."[13] Apparently young men no longer tolerated boys of fourteen or fifteen the way they once had.

Early boys' work received little systematic promotion. Powerful leaders such as Cephas Brainerd, chairman of the International Committee, feared that appointing an international secretary for boys' work would weaken the primacy of programs for young men. Therefore supervision fell to lay committees at the state level, and not until Sumner Dudley took a one-third-time position with the New York State YMCA in 1892 did any state hire anyone to help.[14] At the local level, general secretaries disliked taking time from their main work, and few volunteers rushed into anything so wearing as boys' work. Henry Webster, who started the first regular boys' program in the New York City YMCA, combined it with a full-time job and many other projects and worked himself to death by age thirty-eight.[15]

For boys' branches to take hold and grow under such unpromising circumstances, they had to fit in with the YMCA's other work; that is, they had to reject the boys' club model and become "a feeder" for the parent Association by recruiting middle-class teenagers.[16] YMCAs which had served the underprivileged reorganized during the 1880s to bar all but those they desired "to hold and train for future usefulness," relegating street boys to annual newsboys' dinners and other sporadic charity.[17] Street boys needed to be "civilized," not admitted to the YMCA, warned a secretaries' manual in 1892. Robert R. McBurney, secretary of the New York City YMCA, put it more positively: "It is our business to reach the average young man and the average boy. It most places the Children's Aid Societies and kindred organizations are making special efforts to reach the lower classes of boys."[18] Thus YMCA leaders defined their task against that of the rescue agencies, just as boys' club leaders saw their mission as reaching those whom the YMCA ignored.

Part of the shift was simply a change in rhetoric, since many Associations already served fairly respectable boys. For instance, in Poughkeepsie, New York, in 1882 all but 16 of 630 boys who came to YMCA entertainments reputedly also attended Sunday school.[19] Even the best-behaved boys, however, were apt to turn rambunctious when assembled in boys'-club-sized throngs, and some boys' meetings attracted a very mixed bunch. Of 700 juniors at the Harrisburg, Pennsylvania, YMCA in 1880, 12 percent were fatherless or runaways; 66 percent were sons of railroad employees, mechanics, laborers, saloon keepers, livery men, or the unemployed; and only 21 percent had fathers in professions or mercantile pursuits.[20] In 1885, junior departments were still in a transitional stage. Of 48 YMCAs, 13 gathered "the better class" of boys, 10 reached a "medium class," 12 claimed success with all classes, 2 reported partial success, and 14 said "the classes will not mix. . . ."[21] But by 1890, the chairman of the New York State YMCA's boys' work committee reported that boys' branches in his state served mainly "the middle and upper classes."[22]

Financial considerations encouraged reorientation; expensive facilities had to be used as many hours as possible, and working boys competed for the crowded evening hours — whereas schoolboys came in earlier when the gymnasium stood idle. These boys brought in extra cash without necessarily requiring extra staff, since as late as 1900 only 11 percent of the boys' branches had their own paid officer.[23] Although later boys' work ran deficits, many junior departments of the 1880s and 1890s reported modest profits. As late as 1904, E. M. Robinson complained that boys' branches neglected religious programs in favor of gymnasium classes because fees and parents' gifts made such classes profitable.[24] Certainly there was a connection between building gymnasiums and starting boys' work, since few YMCAs tried to attract boys without one: 8 percent in 1890 compared to 38 percent of those with gymnasiums. This was partly a matter of city size, since larger YMCAs could afford both gymnastics and boys' work, but even in cities of 10,000 or more, 40 percent of YMCAs with gymnasiums tried boys' work, compared to only 16 percent of those without.[25]

High gymnasium fees, compounded by the cost of tights for gym wear, discouraged the poor. In 1893, the thirteen junior departments in New York state which lacked gymnasiums charged a median fee of $1.00; in the other thirty-seven boys' branches, the median was $2.50, and ten asked $5.00 — more than three days' wages for a laborer. YMCA secretaries argued that boys must not get something for nothing, but they did not mind prosperous fathers "pauperizing" their sons by paying the fees.[26]

YMCAs were still getting boys off the streets, but not in the same sense as boys' clubs. Parents who paid substantial fees wanted their sons protected, so instead of uplifting the unwashed, YMCA boys' workers now protected prosperous boys from rubbing elbows with them. "If the Association seeks the lower classes of boys it must do so exclusively," warned McBurney, "as it could not reach safely the middle classes in the same place."[27] Character builders particularly feared class mixing in large cities, where lifestyles and values seemed to differ drastically by class. Defining junior department work as "preventive," H. E. Crowell of Rondout, New York, urged reaching all classes "so far as possible, especially in the smaller places, where there is little class distinction." But he cautioned against "introducing an element in our large cities which may contaminate the boys who have always been surrounded by good influences."[28]

These attitudes help to explain why big-city YMCAs were slow to start boys' work. Of YMCAs that had gymnasiums by 1890 and so could easily have tried boys' work, only 36 percent did so in cities over 100,000 compared to 53 percent in cities from 50,000 to 100,000.[29] It was hard for downtown YMCAs in metropolitan centers to bring in middle-class boys from distant homes, whereas smaller cities had middle-class neighborhoods within easy reach. This pattern would persist: while big cities fostered mass clubs, smaller places proved better recruiting grounds for middle-class character builders.

The YMCA decision to favor middle-class boys was not of course just financial. It reflected the increasing defensiveness of the late nineteenth-century middle class as well as an attitude of "assumed dominance," a faith that middle-class Protestant culture should and would dominate American life.[30] Through character building, YMCA men reaffirmed that middle-class, Protestant values were normative for America; however, they did so by bolstering the superiority of boys from good families and training them for moral and social leadership, rather than by imposing middle-class ways upon the lower class. If, as Protestant churchmen still hoped, they were to establish a Christian America, the rising generation of their own class had to be held at all costs.[31] Thus the policy of favoring middle-class boys found justification as a holding pattern for "those who will be our general secretaries, pastors, missionaries, and businessmen."[32]

YMCA men certainly found the results more satisfying when they enlisted white-collar boys. A boys' branch which recruited the "better" class got 80 to join a church and 120 to enter the adult YMCA, whereas another large branch which concentrated on street boys could report only that the boys became cleaner and smoked and swore less — a mere 6 or 7 converted and 10 joined the Association. A patient worker could wait "until the books be opened by Him, who saith: 'Inasmuch as ye have done it unto the least of these, ye have done it unto me.'"[33] But most leaders wanted something for the current year's report.

With middle-class recruits, character builders felt justified in serving fewer boys. Many were happy to cut back on turbulent mass meetings; YMCA leaders advised starting with selected Sunday school pupils. John D. Chambers of Toledo urged: "Do not so generally or publicly advertise . . . that the rougher element shall be attracted; rather make [your meeting] known by personal effort among the better class of boys."[34] Most junior departments, accordingly, were much smaller than boys' clubs, averaging 60 members in 1890 and 76 by 1900. Boys' work grew mainly through an increase in the number of departments from 48 in 1879 to 401 by 1900, with 30,675 boys enrolled (see Table 2). Boys' workers still had trouble winning support, however, and until about 1900 were innocent of any theory to explain why the early teens were crucial to building character. That year Y leaders estimated that they enrolled 3.5 percent of all American young men but only .5 percent of the boys.[35]

YMCA secretaries and laymen who experimented with boys' work before 1900 were surer of class than age. They recognized youth as a time of promise, but youths over sixteen were still regular YMCA members, while mass evangelism and mission schools had led many Y men to subsume boyhood under childhood. Thus the New Hampshire state YMCA boasted in 1880 of converting children, young men, and the middle-aged but did not mention boys. Awareness of boyhood as a separate and critical stage between the sheltered life of childhood and the relative independence of young manhood grew slowly out of concern that boys encountered moral dangers very young and out of a need to rationalize YMCA practice.[36] Lacking a clear rationale, boys' workers experimented widely but gradually settled on an age range which averaged some two years older than the boys' clubs' core constituency, primarily because they expected middle-class boys to remain under parental control longer than street boys. With older youths, Y men then proceeded to develop what became the standard character builders' strategy of playing up the boys' vigor while prolonging their dependency.

Early mass meetings drew throngs as mixed as the boys' clubs' gatherings. In 1882, Poughkeepsie's YMCA welcomed 162 boys ages 6 to 9, 303 ages 9 to 14, and 160 from 14 to 16.[37] Selective recruitment generally narrowed the age limits; but in 1885 these still varied hugely from one YMCA to another: 6 to 13; 6 to 15; 7 to 16; over 8; 8 to 15; 8 to 16; 9 to 16; 10 to 15; 10 to 16; 10 to 17; 10 to 18; 11 to 18; over 12; 12 to 16; 12 to 17; 12 to 18; 12 to 19; under 16; over 14; 14 to 17; 14 to 21. The list grows wearisome. After surveying the confusion, I. E. Brown, state YMCA secretary for Illinois, proposed settling upon ages 10 to 16. Younger boys might better stay home, he felt, while about age 10 boys began "to drift out upon the streets, to make up the knots of eager debaters on matters of

Table 2
Associations Doing Boys' Work and Reported Membership, 1876–1900

Year	City YMCAs Reporting[a]	YMCAs Doing Boys' Work	Boy Members
1876	—	21	—
1877	—	32	—
1878	—	39	—
1879	666	48	—
1880	554	77	—
1881	536	79	—
1882	484	114	—
1883	561	151	—
1884	599	144	—
1885	664	148	—
1886	708	158	—
1887	733	158	—
1888	777	162	—
1889	815	178	—
1890	807	190	11,455
1891	836	228	14,300
1892	777	266	17,941
1893	722	252	15,924
1894	730	307	17,610
1895	742	328	19,817
1896	707	338	21,232
1897	676	265	17,284
1898	601	296	19,434
1899	596	344	23,405
1900	589	401	30,675

[a] Totals of city YMCAs were inflated before 1879. A few railroad or other specialized YMCAs had junior departments, but city YMCAs did almost all the boys' work.

Sources: Young Men's Christian Associations of North America, *Year Books* (New York, 1877–1901).

games and sports, and to come within the outer circles of temptation to bad language and its cognate evils." He put the maximum at 16 as "the first limit of young manhood" and the age that most YMCAs received full members.[38] Brown's proposed limits, which approximated the median of those then in use, straddled the age of puberty but encompassed primarily preadolescents.

The spread of gymnastics helped hold older boys and drive out those too small to use the gym. Attitudes were changing; Y juniors no longer were passive children who sat through lantern shows but were instead sturdy fellows who liked exercise. In 1882, a YMCA writer could still address

his readers, "Ah, little children," and an Association advertised entertainments "for the little folks." In 1883, a speaker moved a YMCA conference
with a lachrymose account of a dying "child"—a boy of fifteen years.[39]
But as perceptions changed, stories of sinless little sufferers struck boys'
workers as morbidly sentimental. They distinguished sharply between childhood and boyhood, playing up the popular image of energetic, rambunctious boyhood to counter fears that middle-class boys had grown too soft
for social leadership.[40]

First, YMCA men were determined the involvement of women had to
end. Many YMCAs of the 1880s had women's auxiliaries, a number of
which ran the local boys' work and favored charitable projects for poor
boys.[41] Prevailing theories of child nurture proclaimed women's superiority with small children, but men thought women too soft for older boys.
As boys' branches abandoned rescue work and took up gymnastics, the
women quit or were forced out.

Increasingly, YMCA leaders favored older boys who might soon become full members. Since these boys resented having swarms of "kids"
around, some junior departments divided at age fourteen.[42] As late as
1901, only 43 percent set a minimum age as high as twelve; but small boys
stayed away. A survey of 57 east coast YMCAs found a pattern very different from the boys' clubs: there were only 99 boys ages eight or nine
and 1,096 ages ten or eleven, compared to 3,249 ages twelve or thirteen,
3,478 ages fourteen or fifteen, and an undetermined number older still.[43]

And yet more seemed necessary to hold the other boys. Should Y men
go through the motions of sharing power? Although many who did simply chose boy officers or composed a slate and put a boy up to nominating
them, Y men were uneasy, since they were still just learning how to control
boys unobtrusively.[44] The secretaries' manual warned that formal organization led to a boyish fascination with mechanics during which concentration on adult purposes dribbled away. Indeed, almost half the junior departments in 1885 were without any gestures towards self-government.[45]
But as boys' workers gained confidence, they learned to rely more upon
guidance and manipulation and less on overt dominance.

Maintaining control was doubly vital because teenagers might still take
independent action. In the 1870s, a highly evangelistic Young Converts'
Association led by teenagers sprang up around Indianapolis. By 1880, this
group began to challenge YMCA jurisdiction by advocating independent
Youths' Christian Associations. The youths involved were no younger than
many who had joined the first YMCAs, but they felt out of place now
or were barred from full membership by new age limits. The YMCA's
national magazine argued, however, that youths too young to join the adult
YMCA needed supervision; most YMCAs withheld support, and the
group died out by 1894.[46]

Even so, boys' workers remained fearful of losing independent-minded teenagers. Sumner Dudley at first tried to integrate potential breakaways into the adult YMCA by taking them to conferences, but they could no more gain full participation there than in local Associations. Therefore Dudley decided, starting in 1885, to stage separate conferences for older boys. These were exercises in functionless leadership at which delegates read papers on inspirational topics, preferably after advance censorship to curb feelings of self-sufficiency. When young Louis Kilmarz warned against *"know every-thing ism* [and] pride," the men in charge wanted his speech printed for wider distribution.[47] Adults easily headed off independency. At the first Connecticut conference, when the delegates proposed an independent organization of boys' branches, Dudley shunted the idea aside; and such incidents soon ceased.[48] The boys settled in as acquiescent consumers or else quit the YMCA.

The activities which boys purchased by joining the Y were much like those for men, since both groups used the same or similar facilities. YMCA secretaries fell back upon the fourfold formula used for men, asserting that boys needed balanced, all-round development.[49] In practice, this meant going beyond boys' club rescue work and trying to strike a balance between the inculcation of religious and moral ideals and the provision of activities to build up strength and keep boys entertained.

Reorganization promised to make YMCA religious work more intensive, for at mass meetings boys could profess conversion painlessly, even repeatedly, just by raising their hands. In small groups the stakes went up dramatically.[50] Starting with picked Sunday school boys, YMCA religious enthusiasts formed "praying bands" of ten or twelve boys and set up training classes where boys learned the techniques of personal evangelism.[51] YMCA workers held weekly religious meetings and Bible classes, often judging their effectiveness by the numbers of boys who accepted Christ.[52]

This did not mean that Y men staged psychodramas of repentance and salvation, for they tried to embed conversion in the broader process of character building. The proper tone for a boys' meeting was positive, "full of life and vigor"—even if it led incongruously to "that peace which passeth all understanding."[53] There was no agonized waiting for the Spirit; indeed, Y men expected boys from good families to grow "quietly up into the Christian life." Bible study followed the same matter-of-fact, moralistic pattern.[54] High-pressured evangelism was more common at camps and older boys' conferences, but even there much time went to sports and routine YMCA business. Although YMCA juniors still made decisions for Christian living, their leaders had accepted the nineteenth-century compromise between conversion and Christian nurture.

Striking a balance between religious training and what I. E. Brown called the "secularities" was not easy, since it was easiest to hold boys by giving them what they wanted, namely recreation.[55] In 1890, 92 percent of the boys' branches reported some religious feature; 77 percent held prayer meetings and 44 percent had Bible classes. Variety, however, was easier in recreation. Only 5 percent managed three different forms of religious activity, whereas 67 percent had three or more kinds of "secular work." YMCA men claimed that boys joined the Y because of "the good times they have. It then becomes an easy matter to get them to attend their Gospel meeting."[56] Although in 1884 the conservative head of boys' work at the Toronto YMCA described the new tactic sarcastically — "To tickle them first and save them afterward" — attendance at religious meetings was in fact substantial.[57]

In any case, to safeguard Christian nurture it was imperative to keep boys occupied and forestall sin; YMCA men always praised the busy businessman and saw sin as a spare-time activity. George H. Robinson of the New York YMCA boys' work committee maintained that boys' work was "largely a matter of prevention."[58] Thus boys' workers felt justified in offering a good deal of boys' club-style amusement, especially since the boys hungered for diversion. The YMCA in Joliet, Illinois, for example, claimed that occasional evenings of entertainment doubled membership. Association men tried harder than boys' club directors to make the evenings educational, however, and entertainment shaded off into admonition — especially against impurity and alcohol.[59]

This improving impulse was especially apparent in the educational features copied from the adult YMCA. Nearly half the junior departments had reading rooms in 1890, and 39 percent had separate libraries. Literary and debating clubs set boys to considering topics such as which offered the best hope for advancement — farm, store, ship, or office.[60] But schoolboys had less need than ambitious clerks for self-education, and towards 1900 hobby clubs replaced most of the literary societies. Although the International Committee promoted vocational training, middle-class boys seemed more in need of character and general development. By 1900, only 32 of 401 junior departments offered formal education, and few boys took part.[61]

During the 1890s, physical training overshadowed all else. YMCA Christianity became more and more muscular, until by 1900 88 percent of the boys' departments had gymnastics. Even before Detroit's YMCA had a boys' branch, high school students came down to the gymnasium to watch; once the Y was open to them, they and boys in other cities flocked to do as young men did. In 1900, at least 71 percent of all juniors nationwide signed up for gym classes despite paying higher fees than if they merely attended religious and social gatherings.[62]

Though team sports were popular, YMCA officers at first preferred to put the boys through long gymnastic drills and exercises, "the play instinct being crushed as largely as possible without driving them away."[63] As described in nineteenth-century advice books, character required control of all errant impulses; thus drill built character better than play. But Y men, led by Gulick, eventually recognized that sports could teach vital attributes for middle-class boys, such as willingness to follow rules and strive for symbolic rewards. Since football was too violent, a young instructor at the YMCA's Springfield College, James Naismith, invented basketball in 1891. Almost at once it swept the Associations.[64] The YMCA had taken a step away from coercive methods towards meeting what soon came to be called boys' natural needs.

Taking youths somewhat older and from a higher social class than the boys' clubs, YMCA workers protected their chosen few and tried to bolster the boys' superiority by building their physical strength and fostering such classic middle-class virtues as disciplined effort and a decent concern for religious and moral ideals. Even activities designed to attract boys took on an effortful tone, and YMCAs did far more religious proselytizing than the boys' clubs. Yet Y secretaries had no integrated strategy; and while they imitated the men's program, hoping to train the boys' various faculties, the boys themselves pressed for gymnastics and sports. Hobby clubs displaced more serious self-education. Gym classes lost some of their grim purposefulness as boys played more sports. Character builders concluded that if a middle-class boy's success depended on schooling, his leisure did not need to be directly instrumental; he might better broaden himself and develop his capacities without growing up too fast.

5

Forerunners of Scouting: Temperance Orders and the Boys' Brigades

Each YMCA or mass boys' club was an independent agency, offering a variety of programs which had developed locally and in consequence might vary a good deal from place to place. Other forms of boys' work began, however, with the formulation of a standard program for use by existing organizations, notably churches, which wanted to sponsor small groups of boys. Requiring few facilities beyond a meeting hall, these standard programs had great potential for growth, since untrained amateurs could simply follow the preplanned program — always provided that the agency in charge gave adequate supervision. The most successful application of this approach, Boy Scouting, did not originate until 1908; but nineteenth-century temperance orders and the Boys' Brigades offered standard programs which foreshadowed many aspects of Scouting. Although these programs were narrower than Scouting's and their leaders never built up an adequate supervisory apparatus, they broke a path for the more imaginative and better organized Boy Scout scheme to follow.

The originators of the first standard programs took a narrower view of boys than YMCA boys' workers did. Early temperance and cadet leaders used mental and physical exercises, grounded in a rather simplistic faculty psychology, to teach both strengths and virtues. Like YMCA men, they favored middle-class boys, but the range of capacities they trained was much more limited.

Many juvenile temperance societies had weak programs, some because they began as byproducts of adult reform with little thought to the special needs of young people. In line with the intense moralism of antebellum child rearing but primarily in order to marshal all ages beneath their banners, crusaders for causes such as antislavery as well as temperance set up juvenile auxiliaries. The first such group of consequence in the temperance field, the Cold Water Army, marched in the Washingtonian teetotal movement's parades of the early 1840s but dwindled once the excitement passed.[1] The Cadets of Temperance was an offshoot of the adult Sons of Temperance, founded in 1846 when Wyndham H. Stokes of Germantown, Pennsylvania, made over the men's program for use by boys. In much the same way, in the 1870s the International Order of Good Templars spawned the Juvenile Templars. In both cases the parent body ignored the young as long as adult membership was rising and only turned to children when the organization's prosperity began to ebb.[2] Formed more or less as afterthoughts, the Juvenile Templars could claim no more than 19,457 members in 1885, and the Cadets merely 5,500.[3]

Other temperance schemes existed merely to administer pledges to Sunday school pupils. The Loyal Temperance Legion, founded by the Women's Christian Temperance Union in the late 1870s, pledged 240,000 children against liquor, profanity, and tobacco by 1890, but provided no ongoing activities.[4]

Even the more ambitious schemes centered on taking the pledge, which usually proscribed smoking, swearing, and especially drinking. Juvenile Templars, for example, "most solemnly" promised never to "make, buy, sell, or use, as a beverage, any spiritous or malt liquors, wine or cider." The emphasis upon drink rather than tobacco was unrealistic—a clear indication that juvenile temperance groups responded to adult fears more than to boyish practices—since even before the advent of the cigarette, many more boys chewed or smoked than drank.[5]

Faith that the exercise of pledging benefited even small children rested upon the assumption that they had the same faculties as adults, though less developed, and that these faculties would grow stronger with use. Ideally, according to faculty psychologists, a moral decision involved the intellect, emotions, and will plus the composite power of conscience. First the intellect presented the facts of the case, and these aroused favorable or unfavorable emotions; then the conscience passed judgment, using both reasoning and emotion; and finally the will chose among possible motives and put one into effect.[6] Sinners, however, gave way to appetites and passions or else weakened their moral sense by lack of exercise. Thus the best precaution was to reach each boy as young as possible, store his memory with proper facts, train his emotions to hate evil, and strengthen his will by frequent firm resolutions. It scarcely mattered that a boy would not fulfill his pledge for years, since the business of deciding was good exercise for the will.

Since the rest of the program served mainly to reinforce the pledge, the program generally did little more than imitate rituals that the adult temperance orders had copied from the Masons and Odd Fellows. Forceful reiteration was supposed to impress lessons upon children's memory, while songs and regalia—usually just a badge—added emotional power. As a tonic for the will, Juvenile Templars chanted their firm resolution: "The conflict is raging, 'twill be fearful and long, / But we'll gird on the armor and be marching along."[7]

The underlying strategy was protective; temperance workers barred any child whose "immorality and insubordination might exert a bad influence. . . ."[8] In other respects, however, they were less selective than later character builders, for they often tried to enroll both sexes and all ages. Even though any drinking by middle-class children centered among teenage boys, temperance workers showed little awareness of peer pressures and relied upon individualistic indoctrination begun very young. The Cadets of Temperance recognized the distinctiveness of youth by limiting membership to boys from twelve to eighteen, though they later admitted girls, but the Juvenile Templars optimistically prescribed an age range from five to sixteen.[9]

A few temperance men realized by the 1880s that existing organizations were too narrow. The Rev. Wilbur F. Crafts, a Presbyterian social reformer, tried refurbishing a Sunday school auxiliary called the Look-Up Legion so as to build all-round character. "We want one-idea men," he explained, "but not one-idea boys."[10] Crafts added ten more virtues to the pledge, and gymnastics and military drill to the program. A few temperance men followed him into full-scale boys' work by forming cadet corps. Howard H. Russell, the future superintendent of the Anti-Saloon League, organized some of the first Boys' Brigade companies in America.[11] But most temperance men still tried to inculcate moral precepts without offering recreation.

Single-purpose pledging continued long after 1900, mostly in Sunday schools. The main change in the early 1900s — reflecting a stronger perception of boys as different from adults — was a shift in emphasis towards the more boyish vice of smoking as the primary target. Cigarettes, which came into wide use after 1880, introduced mild tobaccos which boys tolerated better than those in cigars. Alarmists transferred onto the young "cigarette fiend" all the traits of laziness and criminality hitherto reserved for drunkards: "Began smoking at 10. Mind shattered at 14."[12] But a single-minded crusade against smoking was no way to win boys; character builders found they had to take a broader approach.

Although mainstream boys' work offered a richer variety of activities, boys' workers continued to exact pledges. In boys' clubs, pledges were infrequent and rudimentary. For example, members of the Chicago Boys' Club promised "to behave in a quiet and orderly manner," and boys caught shooting craps signed promises to stop.[13] With middle-class boys, more was expected: Boys' Brigade cadets had to promise to shun tobacco, liquor, and profanity; and nineteenth-century YMCAs often imposed the same pledge.[14] Negative pledges came to seem narrow and constricting, however, and violations were embarrassingly obvious, as Brigade boys often smoked.[15] Character builders responded after 1900 by transmuting pledges into broader, more positive affirmations; boys now promised to strive after general ideals instead of forswearing a few specified sins. The new ap-

proach suited the middle-class taste for vague idealism; it fitted in with
the shift in juvenile fiction from plodding virtue to heroic endeavor; and
it reflected the shift in child-rearing from prohibitive commands to redirec-
tion of children's drives. The Boy Scout oath became the most renowned
of these new broad-form pledges. Although Scoutmasters and YMCA
workers still waged unobtrusive war against tobacco, the new pledges
sidestepped openly declared confrontation with the boys and virtually
eliminated direct perjury by sticking to safe generalities.[16]

Thus pledge-taking survived, adding a strain of moral idealism to the
general atmosphere of effort for effort's sake, shielded from immediate
practical consequences, which pervaded character building. But the inculcation of moral rules was no place to start attracting boys. Most character
builders began instead with recreation and added moral instruction as best
they could.

An early recourse along those lines was military drill. Leaders in the
1890s used it to keep boys busy the way a later generation fell back on
basketball; if such men ran out of ideas, they simply marched the boys
around the hall. But boys' cadet corps were more than an easy expedient;
they were both the stunted descendants of generations of volunteer drill
companies and the immediate offspring of rising religious and political
militancy among the middle class.

Before the Civil War, the American militia consisted mainly of voluntary units, privately financed, gaudily uniformed, and officered by members of the social elite or recruited from particular ethnic groups. Voluntary units nearly disappeared after the war, but the turbulent railroad strikes
of 1877 spurred a resurgence, as new regiments filled with young men eager
to defend the social order. In addition, election campaigns brought out
uniformed young men to parade for their party. Yet the National Guard,
as it was now called, was also becoming more professional by the 1890s,
with officers discarding their fancy uniforms and imitating the regular
army. In 1903, the Dick Act made the Guard part of the national military
establishment.[17] Whereas once there had been no clear line between mere
hobbyists and serious militiamen, now fancy-dress flourishes came to seem
amateurish and eventually childish. Therefore men who still liked fancy
drill and uniforms turned to boys' cadet corps to indulge their taste for
pageantry.

As Joseph Kett has noted, youths in their middle and late teens had
joined the volunteer companies of antebellum America, and their younger
brothers had formed juvenile auxiliaries. Boys had run these on their own,
often acquiring uniforms and wooden guns.[18] But all that changed by the
1890s when juvenile reformatories, churches, high schools, and YMCAs
organized cadet corps — now keeping the boys firmly under adult com-

mand.[19] The pattern was common in boys' work and sports: at first boys spontaneously imitated the activities of young men; then adults took over, offering better facilities and organization, but demanding persistence and obedience in return.

To use military drill for moral uplift might have seemed somewhat incongruous. But military rhetoric permeated late Victorian Protestantism. The image of Christian endeavor as a battle came naturally to temperance advocates—hence the Cold Water Army and Cadets of Temperance. Reformist crusades, followed by the Civil War, supplied a fund of intensely felt metaphor to evangelists like Dwight Moody and hymn writers like George Duffield ("Stand up, stand up for Jesus! ye soldiers of the Cross"). Crossing the Atlantic, these American influences reinforced the vogue of muscular Christianity in Britain and proved especially appealing to men engaged in missions to the young. "Onward Christian Soldiers" was written for a mission Sunday school, and the Boys' Brigade began in a Glasgow Sunday school.[20] Thus amplified and fused to youth work, the rhetoric of Christian militancy then re-echoed to America, where some churchmen took it literally and assuaged their fears of weakness by organizing drill corps. By 1894, for example, Detroit's churches had 27 companies with 694 members, mostly men.[21]

In an era when church magazines thundered anathema on strikers, the line was very thin between the rhetoric of "Onward Christian Soldiers" and the class defensiveness and nationalism of the middle and upper classes. Military training for the young promised social stability; and in the 1890s schoolboy cadet corps enjoyed a considerable vogue, especially after 1893, when the G.A.R. endorsed military instruction in the schools. Although some of the impetus came from fear of foreign powers, labor disputes did more to convince the well-to-do they needed a strong army and National Guard. By one count, Guardsmen intervened in 328 strikes or riots from 1886 to 1895. Cadet training promised not only to instill respect for authority but also to prepare future soldiers.[22] At its peak in 1896, there were some thirty thousand schoolboy cadets in New York City alone. Their numbers shrank as social tensions lessened, but private cadet companies continued, and military academies for boys thrived.[23]

Although the Boys' Brigade drew strength from British fears of weakness among the empire's future soldiery, its origins owed more to church concerns. William Smith—a Glasgow businessman, Dwight Moody convert, and officer in the Territorials (somewhat like America's National Guard)—had trouble keeping order in his Sunday school and turned to drill in 1883, hoping to interest the boys and convince them that Christianity was manly.[24] The resulting program was like oatmeal for breakfast—solid but unexciting. Under Smith's guidance, the Brigade forebade technical military training; his purposes were "Discipline and Religion!"[25] The movement found a livelier publicist, however, in Henry Drummond, an evangelical lecturer, geologist, and propagandist for athletic Christianity, who had ostensibly reconciled Christian faith with Darwinian science. Following a similar tactic, soon to be commonplace among boys' workers, Drummond maintained that the Brigade reconciled religious training with the boisterous nature of actual boys: "Call these Boys *Boys,* which they are, and ask them to sit up in a Sunday-school class, and no power on earth will make them do it, but put a fivepenny cap on them and call them soldiers, which they are not, and you can order them about till midnight." Reality never matched Drummond's hyperbole, but the Brigade reached a total of 53,486 boys in Britain by 1906.[26]

In various places, American clergymen heard of Smith's idea and founded companies. John Quincy Adams, a Presbyterian from San Francisco, formed the first supervisory corps in 1889; but the Californians were too isolated to run a national movement. Chicago-area clergymen seized control in 1894 and formed the United Boys' Brigades of America, which drew in many independent outfits, although the Methodists maintained their own Epworth Guards.[27]

Adams saw Brigade work as essentially a means to stem erosion of the Sunday school. A company Bible class was part of the program, and Brigade officers claimed to usher 12 or 13 percent of their boys into church membership each year. On this basis, the program won wide praise in the early 1890s.[28] But the 1894 reorganization sowed dragon's teeth, for the new leaders broke with British methods and militarized the Brigades, drawing upon the same nationalism and social insecurity which fueled the campaign for military training in the schools. The long-run effect was to weaken the organization, prevent broadening of its program, and offend potential sponsors. In the short run, though, the UBBA thrived, reaching twelve to fifteen thousand boys by 1896.[29]

Whereas the British Brigade recruited extensively from the upper stratum of the working class, the leading evangelical churches in America were more exclusively middle-class, and Brigade officers favored recruits from their own Sunday schools.[30] The UBBA served mainly high-status denominations; the frequency with which companies met in the First Congregational or First Presbyterian church attested to the members' respectability.[31] Fancy uniforms accentuated this selectivity. British cadets merely wore a cheap belt, cap, and haversack over their street clothes, whereas American outfits cost $5 to $8 and included striped pants unusable for street wear.[32]

Proponents of military drill expected great things. Former President Benjamin Harrison described schoolboy cadet corps as nurseries of strength and social discipline: "A military drill develops the whole man, head, chest, arms, and legs, proportionately; and so promotes symmetry. . . . It teaches quickness of the eye and ear, hand and foot; qualifies men to step and act in unison; [and] teaches subordination. . . . If rightly used, it will wake [boys] up, make them more healthy, develop their pride, and promote school order."[33] Drill, then, did more than furnish exercise; it exacted formal symmetry, close attention, and obedience—qualities akin to "character" which were much admired by adults, but which cost boys a fair measure of constraint.

In enforcing adult standards of posture and decorum, military enthusiasts showed little awareness that growing boys would pass through different stages, not all of which might strike their elders as comely. The UBBA set age limits at twelve to eighteen, but there was nothing sacred about those, for the Brigades had trouble holding older boys and lowered the minimum to ten by 1912.[34] To expect boys so young to perform the same drills as adult soldiers ignored developmental changes; indeed, General Oscar Perrigo of Connecticut seemed genuinely surprised and angered when boys grew tired on parade.[35]

Behind the Brigade officers' fondness for drill stood a narrow ideal of character as something unimaginative, fixed, and dependable—rooted in habits as reliable as the total abstainer's. The cadet promised not to smoke, drink, or swear; methodical drill would teach him diligence, order, and obedience; and rapid maneuvers on parade would strengthen specific powers such as alertness. Of all these virtues, obedience was paramount. General O. C. Grauer of Massachusetts explained that military work "subdues and controls the contentious spirit of the boy; teaches him to obey and enables us to hold him under influences that . . . lead him to become a loyal soldier of Jesus Christ."[36]

The military model made for a thin diet of activities. Weekly meetings centered on learning individual drill movements according to U.S. Army regulations, plus whatever formations twenty to one hundred boys could carry out. Parades, competitive inspections, and drill contests offered more of the same. Mock battles furnished an occasional outing, complete with powder burns and cuts. Beyond this, imagination flagged; the captains who tried signaling or first aid reduced these to showpiece drills, and non-military features were sporadic: an address, an entertainment, a field day.[37]

Brigade leaders were torn between belief in effort as a form of discipline and the new idea that they must arouse the boys' interest. They were trying to have it both ways, using drill to attract members and then to teach persistence at something a bit monotonous. In practice, boys got restless, so that discipline off parade was often erratic as they sought release after the constraint of drill. Thus a captain considered it cause for congratulation when his boys completed an entire evening's display program without any throwing of chairs or destruction of property.[38] Yet the only solution for boredom the editor of *Brigade Boy* could suggest was still more demanding maneuvers: "Mix up commands. Rip out four or five movements all to be done at one command and in succession, and your boys will begin to show signs of interest in you."[39] Although the UBBA represented an advance over temperance groups, boys still wanted more variety.

The military emphasis also led to neglect of religious training. It took more than a Brigade officer's claim that "promptness and obedience are the great elements in a Christian life" to make marching a religious exercise.[40] Though company Bible classes were fairly common, attendance was erratic, since the boys took a thin sugar-coating of drill one day and the Bible study pill another. A good many captains sloughed off religious responsibility onto the pastor, who seldom did much. Perhaps a third of Brigade officers were Guardsmen, whom church officials suspected of recruiting more for the Guard than for the church.[41] While it was common in boys' work for the recreational bait to become the main course, few entrées aroused such uneasiness as military training.

After the American Brigades' initial surge of growth in the 1890s, they entered a decade of accumulating difficulties, followed by decline. Membership shrank slightly to twelve thousand in 1909 and fell off drastically thereafter.[42] Not only did the narrow program fail to hold boys; administrative disarray confined the Brigades to isolated pockets of enthusiasm, and amateurish militarism alienated potential adult backers.

The Brigades and temperance orders were part of the upsurge in nationally organized associations which began before the Civil War. As new organizations proliferated, associationalism came to seem the "most powerful" of "moral agents."[43] Simply by forming a new organization, the Brigade was in the line of progress, or so men such as E. A. Girvin of the California group believed.[44]

Yet amateur management was inadequate. The old temperance orders were quite unstable. Local clubs united in state divisions, which in turn formed a national body, but there was no systematic central supervision; local groups began and died on their own. The UBBA was very similar in structure, except that the organizational pyramid was military, which may have weakened it still further. In place of the British Brigade's elected committees, the Americans in 1895 erected a full military hierarchy — with a colonel for each few companies, a major general for each state, and a commanding general elected annually.[45] This elaborate chain of command left an amateur organization vulnerable to weak links. To make matters worse, national headquarters shifted depending on the commander's hometown, from Chicago to Pittsburgh in 1901 and then to Baltimore in 1908. Each time, the UBBA boomed locally and withered elsewhere.[46]

Symptomatic of the Brigades' localism was their failure to require a common uniform; some companies wore Civil War blue, while others sported khaki garb with upswept Australian bush hats or the flat-brimmed U.S. Army version.[47] State officers could not afford to travel, and headquarters provided no instructional materials. Thus most captains saw no reason to forward dues to their superiors, and a vicious circle resulted: for lack of money, the UBBA never hired an organizer who might have raised an adequate budget. Instead, the officers gloried in unpaid good works and feared professionalism as an interference with their hobby.[48] That threat was real, since few laymen could challenge the power of an executive secretary; yet only those boys' work agencies which accepted the risk prospered.

Without a strong superstructure, the UBBA could not compensate for turnover at lower levels the way the Boy Scouts of America did by recruiting fresh volunteers and spreading the program nationwide; companies clustered in a few cities, suburbs, and large towns. Unlike the BSA, the UBBA never gained a monopoly; many boys belonged to unaffiliated church corps, and Catholic boys' workers—many of whom liked the disciplinary rigor of drill—formed cadet groups of their own, including in 1916 a Catholic Boys' Brigade in New York City.[49]

As hobbyists, Brigade officers could indulge their own inefficiency and ignore pedagogical innovations. They were in no way cosmopolitan; their military model was the localized National Guard. Yet with even the Guard changing and other forms of youth work seeking professional standards, the Brigades' leadership came to seem not merely amateur but amateurish. S. F. Shattuck, the only American officer in close touch with the British Brigade, complained that fancy titles and gaudy uniforms attracted "shallow natures."[50] Although many captains were earnest churchmen, some used military trappings to act out frustrated ambitions. Colonel W. C. Groom of Urbana, Illinois, compensated for failure to get into West Point by organizing cadet corps, and General Perrigo's uniform would have passed muster in a Viennese operetta.[51]

The Brigades' military emphasis strained relations with the churches upon which they depended for recruits and meeting places. Even with successful Bible classes, it was hard to see why midweek activities should be military; yet American Brigade officers flaunted their militarism. Henry P. Bope, a Pittsburgh businessman who headed the UBBA from 1901 to 1908, praised "Anglo-Saxon aggressiveness," and most companies used dummy or real rifles for drill, with blank shells and bayonets for mock battles.[52] Military training for schoolboys had its defenders among the clergy, such as the Right Reverend Samuel Fallows, presiding bishop of the Episcopal church; but critics found it incongruous that a church-sponsored club should equip boys with bayonets or use the church basement to stage a mock battle complete with cannon and corpses.[53] Despite a fondness for martial images and a shared hostility to alcohol, the WCTU opposed the Brigade idea. Consequently, churchmen who tried cadet training for want of anything better turned to Scouting or other forms of boys' work once these became available.[54]

With the passing of the troubled 1890s, public support for cadet training waned. By the early 1900s, the peace movement was socially respectable, boasting such names as Andrew Carnegie and Jane Addams. Peace advocates charged that cadet training imbued boys with militarism, and the National Education Association firmly opposed compulsory military training in the schools. Opponents of military drill complained that it shaped boys to adult tastes rather than their actual needs. D. A. Sargent, director of the Hemenway Gymnasium at Harvard, argued that boys should learn broad coordination through free movement; drill, he said, actually harmed their development.[55]

Nor could cadet enthusiasts count on support from regular Army officers, since Army men looked askance at cadets who thought they knew all about soldiering. The Brigades' mock battles taught the wrong lessons, for tactics were of the glorious sacrifice school: a rout of boys charged across open fields while the other side blazed away from the hilltops. They trained to lose the battle of Gettysburg; in one engagement the colonel was killed three times over.[56] Ambitious young Army officers who were trying to establish the regular Army's primacy over the militia on the basis of superior technical competence scorned such foolishness. They wanted to train young men, not schoolboys.[57]

National Guardsmen were potentially more supportive; indeed, they provided much of the Brigades' leadership. Yet the UBBA repeatedly strained relations by aping their uniforms. When Illinois passed a law against wearing uniforms resembling the state militia's, Brigade leaders let the law virtually eliminate the UBBA there.[58] Thus military enthusiasts managed to damage the Brigades' standing as church auxiliaries without finding an alternative base of support.

Other troubles arose simply because boys' work was so new in the 1890s. Churchmen feared for the furniture and were unforgiving of lapses of discipline. Boys grew impatient with the character builders' stodgy beginning efforts, yet parents worried about the things their sons liked best—long outings and sham battles. By the time all parties grew accustomed to boys' work, more appealing organizations were on hand.

Already in decline, the Brigades could not hold their own against the Boy Scouts of America, founded in 1910 and—as we shall see in chapters 9 and 10—aggressively promoted nationwide. Even in Britain, where the Brigade survived as a major boys' work agency, it fell behind Boy Scouting. The UBBA hung on around Baltimore, but only as a dwindling relic. James West, the Chief Scout Executive and one-time treasurer of the Brigade regiment in Washington, D.C., commented in 1921 that the UBBA had once had fairly strong leaders but that the program now was "woefully lacking."[59]

From a later perspective, the temperance groups and Brigades did seem sadly limited. Their programs were narrow and had a weak hold on boys. Yet they introduced a good many men to boys' work and foreshadowed major elements of Boy Scouting, which addressed some of the same social concerns, provided a standard pledge and program, and organized troops as church auxiliaries.

Character building suffered from a split agenda which was particularly acute in these early decades: religious and moral instruction on one side, disciplined activity and recreation on the other. The two modes of training were hard to integrate, and character builders often settled simply for striking a balance. Thus the nineteenth-century YMCA tried to keep gymnastics and sports from hopelessly outweighing worship and religious education. Hampered by narrow programs, the temperance orders and Boys' Brigades each lapsed into one-sided formalism. Temperance workers offered little beyond pledges and homilies, while Brigade officers often let military training become an end in itself, damning their character-building efforts in the eyes of many churchmen. Boy Scout leaders eventually struck a better compromise: they retained a broad-form pledge for moral uplift, made their activities innocuous by banning overtly military training, and explicitly left religious instruction to the churches, thereby avoiding undue expectations.

In general, nineteenth-century character building was small-scale, loosely organized, and unsure of its rationale beyond getting control of boys early to forestall sins and strengthen their faculties. Moral education was heavy-handed, and efforts to make recreation a surrogate for work resulted in stodgy fun. The twentieth century was to bring more appealing programs, new psychological ideas, tighter organization, professional standards, and far broader public support.

III

Reorientation and New Forms
of Organization, 1900–1920

6

Adolescence and Gang-Age Boyhood:
An Ideology for Character Building

"The period of Boyhood or the Gang period corresponds racially to the tribal period, and is characterized by the development and dominance of gang influence over the boy's whole allegiance. The early Adolescent or Chivalry period is racially parallel to the Feudal or Absolute Monarchial period with its chivalric virtues, vices and actions."[1] These words from the 1914 *Handbook for Scout Masters* were no mere metaphor to character builders. After floundering in confusion, unsure even what age group to serve, they found an ideology to explain their efforts—based upon the notion that boys recapitulated the development of the race as they grew older, progressing upward as instincts implanted during each past culture epoch emerged in sequence. Character builders now promised recreation and training adapted to the boys' cultural level. These ideas took hold among YMCA boys' workers around 1900, spread from there to Boy Scouting, and ushered in two decades of rapid expansion during which character-building agencies rose to prominence on the American scene.

Character builders stressed particularly the importance of adolescence as a troublesome yet promising stage of life, the last great formative period before adulthood. Accordingly, YMCA and Boy Scout officials resolved to work only with boys age twelve through eighteen. They were optimistic that they could suppress undesirable drives and channel the others to good ends. At the same time, the portrayal of adolescents as turbulent and erratic increased concern about middle-class boys; for if instincts were to blame for teenage problems, then all classes were at risk and not just the urban poor.

Rivaling adolescence for attention was a slightly younger yet overlapping stage of development: "gang-age boyhood." Whereas the word "adolescence" suggested difficult teenagers, "boyhood" evoked pleasant images of small-town life. Indeed, the theory that boys of ten or twelve to fourteen or sixteen had an instinct to form gangs and recapitulate the lives of barbarians was essentially an updating of established notions of small-town boyhood—now applied to slightly older boys than the central figures in most nineteenth-century novels celebrating village boyhood. Many character builders now believed that they could control boys well into their teens and solve problems of adolescence by manipulating the gang instinct.

It may seem curious that religiously oriented boys' workers greeted evolutionary theories of boyhood with such enthusiasm. Yet by 1900 most liberal Protestants, towards whose theology many boys' workers were drifting, and many moderates as well had accepted optimistic, non-Darwinian versions of evolution portraying progress as a law of nature. Indeed, Henry Drummond, the Boys' Brigades' best-known supporter, was a renowned proponent of the belief that the world's advance towards altruism resulted from the action of divine will through nature.[2] Though it was left to others to develop a fully evolutionary theory of boys' work, that theory posited that individual growth towards altruism recapitulated the progress of the human race, which many Protestants now saw as divinely directed.

The lore of boyhood and adolescence gave character builders confidence and helped them mark off a field for themselves. With their new-found developmental lore, YMCA boys' secretaries tried to become boys' work professionals, while Boy Scout executives spread a standard program nationwide with an assurance that it suited the nature and needs of adolescent boys.

The stereotype of adolescence as a time of storm and stress had roots in European romanticism, the youth-oriented evangelism of nineteenth-century America, and Victorian fears of youthful sexuality. As chapter 1 has indicated, however, adults did not explicitly recognize adolescence as we know it until the late 1800s. Except by a few educators and physicians, the word itself was rarely used until the 1890s, when G. Stanley Hall (1844–1924) and his many students and popularizers produced a detailed description which they trumpeted as a great discovery. Hall had passed a difficult youth, struggling against the desire to masturbate and yet exalted by vast ambitions; his writings on adolescence preserved all the anguish and yearnings, inflated to massive scale by his ambition to be an intellectual system-builder.[3]

After studies in Germany, Hall became a psychologist and president of Clark University, which he made into a small factory for child study. In an effort to ascertain what was natural at each stage of a child's development, child study enthusiasts went out, much like anthropological field workers, to administer questionnaires and gather reports on children's play, ideas, and physical development. Hall then mounted the results upon a loosely evolutionary framework. But these never showed the neat patterns which he expected; and towards 1900 he and colleagues turned their child study method to the scrutiny of teenagers.[4] In a flood of articles and 1,300 pages of florid prose entitled *Adolescence* (1904), Hall maintained — more by repeated assertion and sheer mass of erudition than by reasoned argument — that adolescence was an age of upheaval corresponding to mankind's leap from savagery to civilization.

The notion that youngsters resemble culturally the adults of earlier societies was not new with Hall; German educators had previously applied it to curriculum design. But Hall posited an actual, biologically inherited link between the child and past cultures, resting his argument upon reports that the human fetus develops in sequence the physical traits of long extinct ancestors. From Ernst Haeckel, Hall got the idea that the process continues after birth; he concluded that children recapitulate as instinctual drives those mental traits which proved useful for survival during each successive epoch of the past. Since anthropologists believed that cultures advance through a fixed series of stages, Hall expected that sequence to provide a normative guide to child development.[5]

Each stage of growing up, in Hall's view, began with a massive infusion of new instincts. Ages six and seven were years of crisis, leading to a period from eight to twelve during which a boy was a relatively unimaginative, unemotional, and individualistic replica of early pygmies. Then after a virtual new birth, the adolescent emerged, a recent evolutionary product similar to men of ancient and medieval times — imaginative, emotional, capable of idealism and sympathetic participation in community life, but still not fully modern.[6]

Hall's description was awash in romanticism, buoyed by a vision of the adolescent as the hope of the race. Adolescence was "the infancy of man's higher nature, when he receives from the great all-mother his last capital of energy and evolutionary momentum."[7] It was a time of upheaval and confusion, for the teenager had to master a flood of instinctual forces while beset by undertows from the past, and then try to ride the crashing waves farther up the beach than anyone before him. Hall subscribed to the Lamarckian view that acquired characters were biologically inheritable but must be added on at the *end* of individual maturation. Thus late adolescence — after eighteen, in Hall's view — was crucial to racial advancement, for only then could new characters be acquired.[8]

Before that time, Hall urged a conservative regimen under which recapitulation prescribed how boys *ought* to live. Adolescence was "the most critical stage of life," as failure to assimilate new instincts "almost always" led to "retrogression, degeneracy, or fall."[9] And that outcome would be doubly disastrous because greater virtues grew out of lesser ones. "[If] the higher Christian values are built on savage virtues," argued the YMCA's E. M. Robinson, savage instincts must be "given proper opportunity for expression." Furthermore, warned Hall, impulses denied catharsis "during their nascent periods" would break out later to disrupt adult life.[10] Character builders insisted, accordingly, that boys must live out their instincts through active, supervised recreation.

Hall's theories reinforced longstanding antipathies towards precocity by apparently demonstrating that young people must remain juvenile until late adolescence. Hall turned to race history for "norms against the tendencies to precocity in home, school, church, and civilization. . . ." In his ponderous way, he blamed "urban life with its temptations, prematurities, sedentary occupations, and passive stimuli just when an active, objective life is most needed. . . ." This thinking encouraged character builders to hold older boys back from maturity; boys' work was analogous to imperialism, which Hall described as the "ethnic pedagogy of adolescent races." [11] Hall considered adolescence virtually paradisaic in its power for personal development, and he wanted the angel with the fiery sword to bar the inhabitants from leaving Eden. The task, as YMCA boys' workers put it, was to insure "adequate growth in every line before the specializations of later life." [12] Thus the ideology of adolescence meshed with the YMCA's fourfold plan for personal development.

Hall's ideas also confirmed existing preferences in recruitment. The best youths, he said, were middle-class, since they could afford slow development, whereas according to G. Walter Fiske, a leading writer on boys' work, "the working boy . . . short-circuits from childhood to manhood. . . ." [13] Hall's ideal adolescence would have been impossible without a large class of economically dependent teenagers who could forego work for the sake of broader development.

For such boys, a sheltered adolescence promised enhanced strength and virtue, as new instincts purportedly opened adolescents to altruism and religious faith. Using the questionnaire method, Hall's student Edwin Starbuck seemingly confirmed that youth was the time for religious conversion. His study lent a sense of urgency to character building, concluding "that if conversion has not occurred before 20, the chances are small that it will be experienced." [14]

The promise of adolescence was marred by anxiety, for Hall posed the same alternative as the revivalists of his youth: adolescents must either rise or fall. "The dawn of puberty . . . is soon followed by a stormy period," he asserted, ". . . when there is peculiar proneness to be either very good or very bad." [15] Researchers claimed that crime and conversions peaked at the same age. [16] The idea of youth as a critical juncture was not new, but Hall's psychological rationale tied it firmly to puberty and made the crisis universal.

Strength was at issue; for a protected adolescence promised vigor in later life, whereas precocity aroused fears of debility. Hall and other writers encouraged protective delay by fostering the misleading stereotype of the clumsy, vulnerable adolescent who outgrew his strength yet must attempt nothing that smacked of finesse. Hall warned against early development of fine skills like piano playing, while a leading YMCA physical director cautioned that training small muscles before large ones could lead to nervous breakdown.[17] As these examples indicate, genetic psychologists and boys' workers agreed that adolescent psychological and somatic developments were bound together by a web of reciprocal influences and manifested themselves through mutually interacting changes in mental states, brain fibers, nerve connections, and physique. Hall was fascinated with studies of growth rates, and boys' workers dreamed of surgical shortcuts to moral improvement through tonsillectomy or other unspecified operations.[18] Much of this concern was euphemistic, for the coupling of soma and psyche that character builders feared most was "self-abuse," as they called it. Hall loathed masturbation, believing that reabsorbed semen gave one strength. Starbuck, Hall, and the YMCA's Luther Gulick all asserted that a boy's sexual nature opened the door to conversion. Thus a boy who abused his sexuality cut the taproot of faith.[19]

Adolescence, then, seemed a time of promise; yet in Hall's teaching, that promise was a mixed blessing, beset with longstanding fears of youthful immorality. Adults took comfort, accordingly, in an overlapping but more reassuringly vigorous and childlike image of the early teens as the "gang age."

While Hall assumed that childhood in the form of boyish savagery ended about age twelve and adolescent changes began, many writers modified his timetable and granted boys a few running steps before the adolescent leap by positing a lengthy boyhood or "gang" age, variously estimated at ten or twelve to fourteen, fifteen, or sixteen.[20] By implication, it was more securely juvenile than early adolescence.

Certain authors elaborated considerably on the parallels with race history. The 1914 *Handbook for Scout Masters* used Lewis Henry Morgan's sequence of savagery, barbarism, and civilization, and included a table comparing modes of subsistence with stages of "boy life" which produced the surprising intelligence that twelve-year-olds loved gardening. George W. Fiske described ten to fourteen as the gang or tribal period; thirteen to fifteen as the chivalric period; and fourteen to eighteen as the age of the constitutional monarchy.[21] Writers such as Fiske believed that recapitulation was social as well as individual and hence that wider cooperation should unfold as boys grew older.

Recapitulation reinforced a familiar image of the young—the notion that boys were savages. This became a common rationale for camping; Ernest Thompson Seton even founded little tribes, explaining that the boy from ten to sixteen "is ontogenetically and essentially a savage."[22] Just as Hall's version of adolescence echoed established ideas about youth, so the gang age incorporated the popular image of rambunctious boyhood; but it added a new emphasis upon group socialization and focused on older boys, a shift which matched the lengthening dependency of schoolboys.

Belief in the ubiquity of gangs drew upon quasi-anthropological studies of boys. Writing in 1898, Henry Sheldon showed that boys maintained semiformal organizations without adult guidance, particularly athletic clubs and gangs engaged in tribal activities such as hunting and stealing. John Scott, a YMCA secretary, reported that 70 percent of all boys ten to eighteen belonged at some time to a spontaneous group of five or more boys, which he called a "gang."[23] Such studies exaggerated participation by defining gangs loosely, but they convinced adults that moral education would have to take account of peer influences.

It comforted adults to think the gang stage overlapped adolescence. In his popular *Lawrenceville Stories* (1909–1911), Owen Johnson applied the old boy-book conventions to a prep school for boys twelve to eighteen, whom he called "adolescent" yet described as a "lot of semibare savages."[24] Among character builders, similar inconsistency was common. Luther Gulick, for instance, explained that adolescents liked camping because they were in the savage stage.[25] In effect, character builders were claiming that adolescents were still just little boys.

Traditionally, gangs — being viewed as packs of lower-class delinquents — had a poisonous reputation among the middle class, and yet most boys' workers were favorable to the gang instinct, some remarkably so. Henry F. Burt, who led boys' clubs at Chicago Commons, asserted expansively that he would as soon break up the family as the gang.[26] Other enthusiasts for the gang instinct distinguished more cautiously between actual predatory gangs, which could be dangerous, and the underlying *instinct,* which could be turned to good ends. Character builders already knew of gangs in the slums; what the anthropology of boyhood convinced them was that middle-class boys also had an instinct to form groups — an instinct which adults could use. This instinct added a stabilizing sense of structure to boy life as they saw it, for investigators assumed that gangs had leaders whom adults could influence. Furthermore, they traced gang-age activities to other instincts which in principle could be enumerated and safely channeled so that boys would, for instance, obey migratory instincts as hikers instead of truants; also predatory and combative instincts would find harmless outlets in woodcraft and sports.[27]

We have seen that the idea of boys as savages was not new; but recapitulation theory gave it a more scientific-sounding basis, reassuring middle-class adults that sheltered schoolboys were in fact bursting with energy. Men who worried that the nation would lose vigor after the closing of the frontier could have found a comforting parallel to Frederick Jackson Turner's celebrated theory of American history. On each successive frontier, Turner believed, civilization re-evolved through the major stages of human culture, emerging better than anything before.[28] If the closing of the frontier precluded repetition of this drama on a national scale, recapitulation theory promised that boys would still repeat it in small groups and thus gain strength to surpass their predecessors. Gang-age boyhood could be seen as a surrogate frontier, right down to its outdoor activities. On a more mundane level, belief in a gang instinct bolstered the conviction that boys needed an all-male refuge to live out their savage impulses. Boys' workers stopped apologizing for taking boys away from home. "Out among his peers God intends that he shall go," wrote William Byron Forbush, a student of Hall's and a leading theorist of boys' work, "to give and take, to mitigate his own selfishness and to gain the masculine standpoint which his mother, his nurse, and his school-teacher cannot give. . . ."[29]

As Forbush's words suggest, the group nature of gang life accounted for much of its appeal to adults. In this, the enthusiasm for gangs was typical of Progressive Era opinion, for in areas as far apart as social theory and children's stories, the years around 1900 saw a new recognition of human interdependence. Charles Cooley, for example, argued that urban society must find substitutes for the primary group ties of small-town America; meanwhile for boys, stories of teamwork in sports, school, and Scouting displaced tales of individual derring-do.[30] Reform ideology stressed social responsibility, and character builders echoed this. Gulick hoped playgrounds would build a "corporate conscience," while the head of Sea Scouting praised his program as a way to teach "modern conscience," that is, group cooperation.[31] To moralists in an age of business trusts and political bosses, the subordination of individual greed to social welfare seemed problematical. The man of character who set his course by an inner gyroscope of principle and ambition could no longer leave the consequences to an invisible hand; for the public rhetoric of the day made "selfish" and "self-serving" terms of opprobrium, whereas "unselfish" and "public-spirited" were common words of praise.[32] After 1900, therefore, "altruism" and "service" became character builders' catchwords, and boys' workers emphasized citizenship training. Their new concern faithfully reflected the Progressive fashion in politics or, as Forbush complacently described it, "the recent national revival of righteousness."[33]

A more fundamental force for change was the emergence of a corporate society increasingly dominated by large organizations in business, education, and government. Such organizations needed individuals who worked well with others and followed rules. Ambitious parents wanted their sons trained not as solitary strivers, hardened for the entrepreneurial scramble of the old middle class, but rather as managers and group workers, socialized to pass smoothly into the new bureaucratic and professional middle class. Educators moved to meet the new demands for group socialization, mainly by sponsoring extracurricular activities; however, character builders were ahead of them.[34]

And yet there was a revealing exception: the Boys' Brigades remained bastions of individualism. Blustered H. P. Bope, the UBBA's commander in the early 1900s: "Altruism may come some day. It is not here yet and it is not wanted yet. The world is yet too practical . . . , fierce in competition, with little mercy and less pity for those who are trampled underfoot in the struggle for livelihood, and therefore our teaching must be practicable. . . ."[35] For Bope, business was a struggle of each against all, not a team effort. Admittedly, cadets had to learn to march together, but they cooperated only at the level of mechanical uniformity.[36] Boy Scout and YMCA officials were more predisposed to favor group socialization since they worked as employees within large organizations on whose boards of directors sat leaders in corporate business and organized philanthropy. By contrast, Brigade officers were disorganized amateurs, jealous of their own prerogatives, suspicious of bureaucracy, and incapable of effective cooperation.

Sociological theorists of adolescence such as S. N. Eisenstadt depict peer groups not merely as a refuge from role confusion and an outlet for deviant values but also as a potential source of community orientation and a way station between the uncritical personal acceptance of family life and the impersonal, achievement-oriented norms of adult work life.[37] Character builders espoused a similar yet more uncritically functional view of gang life. What they sought was not, of course, altruism in the sense of selfless concern for others, but rather the ability to work cooperatively; they believed a boy took the vital first step when he joined a gang, just as the race first formed bands and then slowly built up more inclusive political units. Elbert K. Fretwell of Teachers College, Columbia University, told Boy Scout executives in 1922: "One who isn't loyal to his gang, of course, can't grow up into a man loyal to society. . . ." J. Adams Puffer, a reform school principal, even suggested that young thieves might be on the path away from crime if they stole as a gang instead of each for himself.[38] While adolescence was seen as opening possibilities of truer altruism, that seemed a more autonomous virtue than cooperation; and the image of the brooding adolescent suggested independence as opposed to group conformity.

Character builders believed they could use the gang instinct because boys would follow like savages wherever their chief led. Few men could become true gang leaders, but theorists of boyhood offered advice on imperialism: form artificial gangs, or take over existing ones and rule through the native leaders, subverting any who prove recalcitrant. Thus the *Handbook for Scout Masters* described the Boy Scout patrol as "an organized gang under boy leadership and adult supervision. . . ." Seton compared this approach to the British and Roman policy of governing tribes through their chiefs. Ideally, one had only to win the "key boy" and the rest would follow.[39]

This cult of the leading boy made it clear that character builders did not denigrate individual achievement — far from it. Traditionally, the man of character was a self-acting striver, although a conformist in personal morals and style. Despite their group methods, character builders remained in awe of the type, as is evident from the many awards they offered boys. The difference was that now they recognized the group context of achievement and made group leadership an end in itself. Character-building programs, accordingly, had to reconcile personal accomplishment and group loyalty. Team sports, widely used by the YMCA, promised to teach the virtues of modern business: cooperation within the firm and competition against outsiders.[40] Since advocating sports would have undercut their own program, Boy Scout leaders instead encouraged boys both to cooperate in patrol or troop activities and to earn badges for individual achievement, in the latter case competing to win the most awards.

While it would be rash to revive debate over Riesman's contention that American values have shifted over the long haul from inner- to other-direction, the changing views of character builders do suggest a shorter-term shift in middle-class opinion around 1900. Americans have long been ambivalent towards unrestrained individualism. After a period of burgeoning industrialization when aggressive entrepreneurship was glorified and social problems mounted, a partial return of the pendulum was natural. Biographical articles published in middle-class magazines from 1904 through 1913 played up social virtues such as unselfishness and patriotism, while celebrations of forceful, aggressive characteristics declined.[41] Yet achievement values remained prominent. So too in character building for boys, the early 1900s saw new enthusiasm for group life and social responsibility. Yet gang life was expected also to foster aggressiveness and achievement. In practice, as we shall see, individualism prevailed and group bonds were weak. If such inconsistency was widespread, Riesman may have mistaken a shift in ideology for one of personality.

Despite enthusiasm for gang life, the new lore of adolescence had a more immediate and striking effect on boys' work practices, since it spurred character builders to try to recruit older boys. The main constituency for nineteenth-century YMCA boys' work had centered on the gang age — about ten to fifteen or sixteen, though with wide variations.[42] But adolescence stirred greater alarm; hence twentieth-century character builders set the minimum age limit at twelve and made a point of barring anyone younger. Furthermore, they tried to hold boys far into adolescence — preferably until sixteen or eighteen. The YMCA pioneered; led by E. M. Robinson — the Y's first international secretary for boys' work (U.S. and

Canada) — YMCA junior departments specialized in boys from twelve to sixteen, later eighteen. "Adolescent" became a catchword, widely used to impress the public. And when-Boy Scouting reached the U.S., its American organizers followed the YMCA lead. Whereas British Scouting initially accepted younger boys, the Boy Scouts of America barred any under twelve, lest they limit the movement's "effectiveness in dealing with adolescent problems. . . ."[43]

North American character builders predicated exclusive enrollment of boys twelve and older upon Hall's dramatic account of adolescence as a virtual rebirth, the time when adult character first began to take shape. This premise undermined the nineteenth-century presumption that habits formed early and thus the younger that boys could be enlisted for moral indoctrination the better. Adolescence, according to twentieth-century Boy Scout leaders, was the "critical" period in a boy's life, the age when he was most "plastic," the time for making "life decisions."[44] According to James West, a "thorough analysis of the boy problem" would find "that the most difficult ages are thirteen, fourteen, and fifteen and sixteen; perhaps of those four the more difficult are fourteen and fifteen."[45] But such judgments rested on more than just Hall's theories. As we have seen, ages fourteen and fifteen were indeed "difficult," for those were the years when boys had to move on to high school and settle down to steady advancement. Yet boys that age had inklings of independence, and many did in fact quit Sunday school. Most also passed through puberty about then. To worried adults, therefore, the early and middle teens boded unsettledness and immorality; character builders took Hall's ideas as their warrant to reach out for teenagers and bar the younger boys.

Still, why did they choose to admit boys at twelve instead of fourteen or fifteen? Nineteenth-century usage had leaned towards fourteen as the start of youth; and while twelve had traditional religious significance, the average age of puberty for boys was fourteen or so. Apparently Hall's influence was decisive, overriding the views of writers who regarded the gang age as preadolescent and consequently set the beginning of adolescence at fourteen or older.[46] Yet once accepted, the division at age twelve inspired fierce commitment. When Ernest Thompson Seton proposed a woodcraft scheme for boys eight through fifteen which would have treated them all as preadolescent, E. M. Robinson responded that the proposed age range would be to Seton's fellow boys' workers "like a red rag to a bull. . . ."[47] Luther Gulick was especially dogmatic: "We believe that there is a marked line of division between manhood and childhood, and that this division in the majority of men occurs about twelve years of age."[48]

At bottom, character builders simply found an early start at age twelve the safest choice. A few boys might reach puberty by then, and character builders wanted the others securely moored, morally and socially, before the floodtide of adolescence could rip them loose. Thus the 1914 *Handbook for Scout Masters* announced that Scouting would help boys "from the pre-adolescent period of boyhood through the changes of adolescence to young manhood. . . ."[49] Besides, many character builders preferred gang-age boys, and their programs were juvenile enough that raising the age of entry to fourteen would have cost them half their members. In the war against precocity, age limits represented a compromise between the adult desire to hold boys back and the boys' desire to push ahead. Age twelve came close to adolescence without barring too many potential recruits.

As the choice of twelve for a starting age suggested, character builders were drawn to adolescence and yet wary of it. Fascinated but fearful, they circled around its possibilities, edging in and darting back, never at ease but convinced by Hall that adolescence glowed with promise as well as danger. Adolescent emotionalism in particular seemed all too likely to run off into sensuality; yet it held out a promise of moral and religious enthusiasm if carefully managed. Taylor Statten of the Canadian YMCA warned that turbulent feelings in adolescence could "dethrone reason and moral lapses ensue."[50] The trouble, said *Scouting* magazine, was that teenagers had adult powers and passions without strength to control them. Yet boys' workers distrusted young people who tried, in the parlance of a later day, to stay cool: "The masklike, impassive face at this age," Forbush warned, "is a sign of loss of youth or of purity."[51] Accordingly, character builders tried to preempt the teenager's imagination with approved fantasy and packaged idealism, a process which discouraged respect for adolescent rationality. A Sunday school text written on these principles announced frankly: "The method is to beautify and glorify rather than to clarify."[52] Men decided that teenagers were at the right culture epoch for flimflam romanticism, anachronistic and simple-minded. Elements of Tennyson and temperance rituals mingled in a host of church-related chivalric orders, while Boy Scout symbolism presented the strange spectacle of moralized knights who saved their pennies like good tradesmen and kept their armor on all day to answer service calls.[53]

American Boy Scout leaders sought to foster adolescent idealism by inculcating patriotism, making the Boy Scout oath and law the centerpiece of Scouting, and tentatively urging Scoutmasters to draw upon adolescent hero-worship.[54] In practice, however, the busyness which Boy Scouting fostered amounted to an effort to prolong boyhood and dilute or circumvent adolescence. Men who mistrusted emotionalism, sexuality, and independence wanted to lead teenagers like frightened horses past the fire: "You can sum up the whole philosophy of reaching and holding boys for all that is noble and right in one work — preoccupation," explained the *Handbook for Scout Masters*. Fear of adolescent brooding prompted a camp committee for Queens in New York City to warn that during "the moody hours of twilight" boys were prone to "great thoughts" and must be kept busy. In more general terms, James West stated that Scouting "takes the boy . . . when he is beset with the new and bewildering experiences of adolescence and diverts his thoughts therefrom to wholesome and worthwhile activities." Two other Boy Scout officials asserted that absorbing activities would "short circuit" the sex impulse.[55] Since the activities were those favored by smaller boys — woodsy ramblings rather than team sports — and since the gang age which Boy Scouting mimicked through its patrol system was basically preadolescent, plainly the BSA's strategy was to prolong energetic, asexual boyhood while delaying and distracting boys from adolescent problems.[56]

YMCA secretaries also worked to prolong boyish innocence, but their desire to convert boys led them to sponsor an attenuated adolescence as well. This meant nothing rash, since they worked within the context of Christian nurture and kept in close contact with religious educators who were trying to apply child-centered pedagogy to church work. To both groups, Hall's portrait of volatile adolescence was a promise and a warning, goading them to seek early religious commitments but intensifying fears of easy passion run amok. Forbush cautioned against "the hot night atmosphere" of a superficial revival; and most boys' workers agreed on the need to avoid what Forbush stigmatized as "forced precocity." Like Edwin Starbuck, they preferred that growth be smooth and "the end . . . reached without a hitch."[57] Tactics differed, however. Sunday school writers preferred to hasten decisions, reducing them to mere affirmations or mileposts on the broad and level road to faith. Henry Robins of Rochester Theological Seminary urged securing a decision before "the storm and stress of the pubescent crisis, when there are enough other matters to occupy attention."[58] YMCA workers were more prepared to wait and then provoke a mild crisis, though they insisted that adolescents must not brood. "Boys from thirteen to eighteen are passing through tremendous . . . changes," cautioned Fred S. Goodman, the International Secretary for Special Religious Work. "The less they think of their feelings and the more their thoughts go out in loving regard for their Master, their parents, brothers, sisters, and companions, the better."[59] Since the possibility of a teenage identity crisis troubled yet attracted YMCA character builders, their remedy was a compromise: an innoculation to produce a mild form of the disease and forestall emotional turmoil or deeper experiences.

Both major character-building agencies favored steady, unhurried growth for boys, and both promised to address adolescent problems; but they followed different strategies. The YMCA combined gymnastics and team sports with limited yet direct confrontation of adolescent crises, whereas the Boy Scouts relied more upon distraction and gang-age recreations.

Recapitulation-based theories of gangs and adolescence gave character builders their first semblance of scientific expertise and allowed them to define theirs as a unique service — recreation and moral guidance psychologically suited to the nature of boys at their most critical period. On this basis, YMCA boys' secretaries and Boy Scout executives sought to find a secure footing in the new middle class. Like many members of that class, especially professionals, they wanted autonomy and a chance to serve but lacked power and money; in such circumstances, technocratic indispensability was their best card. If leaders in a new vocation were to stake out a market and fence it off as their preserve, they had to claim special knowledge.[60] Boy Scout leaders had to guarantee their program's soundness if they were to sell it nationwide, while YMCA boys' workers had to establish their speciality within the YMCA and demonstrate competence that outsiders would respect and pay for. Much of this purported expertise amounted to little more than renaming familiar ideas about boys; still, that made the new ideology of boys' work all the more acceptable. For a nascent profession, nomenclature is a first step; doctors, for example, categorized and labeled long before they cured.

The new ideas strengthened longstanding hopes and fears and gave existing practices the blessing of science. If adolescents had to integrate a flood of new instincts, they must remain dependent on adults — just as did middle-class high school students. Hall's warnings of teenage unsettledness recalled the troubled passage of conversion, while his prescription of a steady, even regimen echoed the spirit of Bushnell's Christian nurture. Hall made it clear that teenage sexuality was unavoidable, but his romanticism suggested a program of sublimation through religious idealism and enthusiastic activity; the adolescent could be a young Galahad. Hall's ideas reinforced detestation of precocity and linked it to fears of weakness. The working child lost the benefits of adolescence, and the delinquent who tasted adult vices courted degeneracy; but in Hall's view, so also did the middle-class boy who was too obedient or bookish too soon. On the other hand, recapitulation theory promised that the boisterous, unprecocious lad could draw upon lavish stores of ancestral energy. The new theories further rationalized the postponement of work by bolstering the growing adult regard for play as a school of virtues formerly identified with work. Instinct theories culminated this trend by investing play with structure and purpose, explaining it as a recapitulation of activities that had been work for the boys' distant ancestors. Hall's theories held that because instinctually driven activities were natural, they would elicit the effort character builders still believed vital to train the will. Thus play became the proper work of boyhood, to the point that George Johnson, who surveyed the city of Cleveland's recreation in 1915, warned that "the boy without play is father to the man without a job."[61]

The gang age combined nostalgia for rural boyhood with the contemporary vogue for primitivism and outdoor vigor as an antidote to debility. The fantasy of escape from women now seemed psychologically justified as a need for masculine leadership and group experience. Thornton W. Burgess told readers of *Good Housekeeping* that "as a member of a Boy Scout patrol, under the right kind of a Scout Master," a boy would have the "two natural cravings of boy nature gratified" — the need to "belong to a 'gang'" and the impulse to "worship a 'hero'. . . ."[62] Supervised gang membership in turn promised to lead boys through broadening group loyalty on to the good citizenship which was the Progressive ideal.

This is not to say the new ideas merely restated the familiar and had no practical impact. Not only did character builders seek an older clientele; the belief that boys had to live out ancestral instincts infused a new naturalism and breadth of interest into character-building programs. The twentieth-century Y boys' branch was livelier than its Victorian forerunner; and in church meeting halls, the repetitive drill of Boys' Brigade cadets gave way to Scouting's varied activities.

Conveniently, though, recapitulation theory forced no wrenching break with past practice except banishment of boys under twelve. Hall believed that culture epochs offered an escape from the circularity which besets instinct psychology; for without some such independent evidence, the only clue to an instinct's nature is behavior — which is precisely what the instinct is then used to explain. However, he also suggested that race history and child development could explain each other, thereby opening the door to the comfortably circular belief that the structured activities of small-town American boys must reflect some ancestral practice and hence be natural. Thus Puffer suggested instinctual origins for baseball: "The boy . . . likes to run, to dodge, to throw accurately and hard, to hit any quick-moving object with a club, because for ages his ancestors have been getting their food by swift running and quick dodging, by accurate throwing and deft hitting of objects with clubs."[63] This naive *a priori*ism reveals a significant truth: despite its apparent novelty, recapitulation theory had extremely conservative implications. It justified holding boys back from independence and gave nostalgic traditions of boyhood presumptive authority — whatever *was* was right; only modern urban life was "unnatural."

Although William James exaggerated in claiming "there is no 'new psychology'," child study was a capacious mold into which flowed recycled elements from traditional psychology.[64] In their zeal to explain broad developmental patterns, genetic psychologists bypassed the problem of accounting for individual mental acts. Hence familiar concepts survived more or less intact. Character builders still imposed pledges to train the will, although these were now transmogrified into affirmations of adolescent idealism. Character building still meant strengthening the faculties—or "symmetrical boy development," as a YMCA book phrased it.[65] Boy Scout requirements tested generalized capacities such as ability to judge number, weight, and distance. Forbush even published a table of instincts developed by each form of boys' work; he credited his own Knights of King Arthur with fostering courage, emulation, imagination, imitation, love, loyalty, and physical abilities.[66] These were simply traditional mental powers with a built-in drive, rather like the carriages with motors produced by early automakers.

More important than any specific lesson was the confidence that leading character builders gained from psychologizing. Thanks to child study, the *Handbook for Scout Masters* claimed, "the mind of the boy becomes like an open book. What was once an enigma to our fathers is now most easily understood, and the work has therefore been placed on a firm foundation. . . ."[67] This faith was essential to changing boys' work from a hobby to a career upon which men would stake their futures.

Alternatives to recapitulation theory in education and psychology did little to shake this confidence, since character builders blurred theoretical distinctions, believing the practical implications all pointed the same way. Boy Scout and YMCA leaders ignored the progressive educators' emphasis upon teaching small children but applauded conservative innovations such as physical education, manual training, and vocational guidance. Among psychologists outside Hall's circle, only William James was reasonably familiar to boys' workers, who took his ideas simply as a call to the strenuous life. Describing character as consisting "in an organized set of habits of reaction," James urged: "Seize the very first possible opportunity to act . . . in the direction of the habits you aspire to gain."[68] This advice tied in neatly with Boy Scouting's daily good turn and busy program. James's views had unsettling implications for the theory that boys lived out ancestral instincts, for he explained mental activity as an interaction between an individual and his environment without positing an elaborate instinctual inheritance. Character builders initially ignored this possibility, however. Not until the late 1910s did alternatives to Hall's theories begin to influence them, and even then they clung to the faith that adolescence and the gang instinct were master keys to boyhood.

This faith helped character builders clear a space for their work. The notion of a gang age sharpened their critique of weakness and effeminacy in home, school, and Sunday school, enabling them to insist that boys needed an escape. F. A. Crosby of the Chicago YMCA judged parents weak in the very skills for guiding adolescents on which boys' secretaries prided themselves: Bible teaching, sex instruction, and boy psychology. As for Sunday schools, E. M. Robinson charged in 1911 that only three out of sixty teachers of older boy classes "knew the meaning of the word adolescence, to say nothing of its significance. . . ."[69] He complained that teachers mixed boys of all ages and supplied sedentary programs. Agreeing that church methods had failed to "keep their grasp upon boys at their age of greatest need," William Byron Forbush put forth boys' work expertise as the remedy.[70]

Character builders were well ahead of most school officials in making a major division at age twelve. The first educational innovation to deal specifically with the twelve to fifteen age group was the junior high school. Its proponents wanted to free young adolescents from the childish regimen of the primary grades and yet hoped, as did character builders, to keep them "boys and girls a little longer."[71] Educators at first had tended to believe that adolescence began around fourteen; but then they, again like character builders, stretched it down to twelve in order to bridge the gap from childhood to the high school age.[72] While curricular concerns predominated in the junior high school movement, innovators also sponsored sports, clubs, and student assemblies. In this respect, they staked out some of the same territory as boys' workers, but such schools were still uncommon during the formative years of boys' work—at most a few dozen before 1910 and perhaps eight hundred by 1917.[73] They did not undercut boys' work and sometimes provided a market for it by admitting the YMCA or Boy Scouts as auxiliaries.

Character builders had discovered an untenanted social niche. As schooling lengthened, leisure time for many boys expanded, and parents and churchmen wanted it supervised. Hall's ideas intensified fears of precocity and crystallized anxiety about youth around the concept of adolescence. Furthermore, boys from middle-class homes seemed to need toughening. By claiming programs tailored to adolescents, character builders staked out a constituency; and in promising to harness the gang instinct, they undertook to keep boys safely juvenile and vigorous.

Ideas articulated within the culture epochs framework brought the various forms of boys' work close to a unified ideology of method. A flood of books propounded similar ideas about boyhood, adolescence, character building, and religious education.[74] Even the occasional skeptic about recapitulation agreed upon the sudden change at adolescence and the social propensities of gang-age boys.[75] Among the character builders deeply influenced by Hall's ideas were William Byron Forbush, founder of the Knights of King Arthur for church boys and author of *The Boy Problem,* the best known early guide for church-based boys' work; Luther Gulick, another student of Hall's, who launched the rapid expansion of YMCA boys' work towards 1900, helped form the Boy Scouts of America, and with his wife founded the Camp Fire Girls; Edgar M. Robinson, who took over YMCA boys' work in 1900 and did much to organize the BSA in 1910; and John L. Alexander, a former YMCA boys' secretary who wrote large parts of the BSA's early manuals. Among theorists of Sunday school work, developmental ideas of adolescence passed as common coin. In the playground movement, recapitulation also figured prominently. Henry S. Curtis, secretary of the Playground Association of America, took a doctorate with Hall; and Joseph Lee, the PAA's longtime president, was a fanatical enthusiast for the "Big Injun age" and boyish gangs.[76] While organizational rivalries sometimes intruded, shared presuppositions disposed other youth workers to favor the Boy Scouts and YMCA.

Although boys' workers never achieved equivalent organizational unity, the General Alliance of Workers with Boys, founded in the late 1890s, brought together leading YMCA secretaries, some prominent club workers, and a scattering of men interested in settlements, juvenile courts, and church work. Under William Byron Forbush's guidance, the Alliance, which claimed 800 members in 1909, built a rough consensus around instinct psychology and the culture epochs theory. Its journal, *Work With Boys,* spread the new ideas to some three thousand readers.[77]

A small band of Catholic boys' workers stood apart. Since character building was a task for the offices of the Church, early Catholic boys' work was limited to combating the lure of outside agencies. The Rev. George E. Quin, who published a guide in 1908, urged thirteen as the minimum age in order to get boys old enough to leave parochial school, but he had little interest in gang life or adolescent crises. Only about 1920, in the postwar rush of enthusiasm for Catholic social service, did Catholics move closer to Protestant and secular boys' work.[78] Once culture epoch ideas diffused among them, though, the concepts persisted; for as late as 1941 the founder of the Catholic Boys' Brigade, Kilian J. Hennrich, periodized boy life from ten to thirteen as the "Big Injun Age," thirteen to fifteen as the "Gang & Loyalty Age," and fifteen onward as the "Adolescent Age."[79]

Outside of boys' work, agencies for girls varied in their response to the idea of adolescence. In the YWCA, it caught on suddenly around 1909, leading to a vast expansion of girls' work and age limits from twelve to eighteen.[80] The Camp Fire Girls, founded in 1912, leaned heavily on recapitulation in its Indian symbolism; Luther Gulick described the program as a subsitute for tribal societies' recognition of the "adolescent crisis"; and recruitment eventually centered on ages twelve to fifteen, with separate programs for younger and older girls.[81] The Girl Scouts, on the other hand, copied Baden-Powell's early age limits and let girls in at ten.

This made sense, since girls matured faster; still, it alarmed American Boy Scout officials.[82]

Of more immediate significance to boys' work was the division between mass club workers and middle-class character builders. Club workers were interested in the gang age, but Hall's version of adolescence failed to shake their preference for younger boys, since his prescription of prolonged, sheltered nurture did not correspond to the realities of lower-class life. According to Thomas Chew, the years from nine to thirteen were best for mass club work. After that, boys grew hard to manage, with the result that as late as the 1910s some superintendents expelled them at fourteen. For these men puberty marked a time when boys turned troublesome; it was not an age for influencing character. Other superintendents kept older boys on, but described the whole age span from five to eighteen as "critical."[83] Club workers in settlement houses were often highly educated and consequently more receptive to academic psychology, commonly grading boys by age; but even they felt no exclusive calling to serve adolescents.[84]

Instead of coalescing into a single profession, the different forms of boys' work grew apart after the early 1900s. Once the Boy Scouts of America started in 1910 and boys' clubs and YMCA junior departments multiplied, the number of paid boys' workers grew rapidly. They could now find colleagues within their own organization; rivalries developed, and loyalty to one's own agency assumed paramount importance. In 1911, the General Alliance gave up the struggle for unity and *Work With Boys* passed into the hands of the Federated Boys' Clubs.[85]

Separation reinforced the mass club workers' commitment to a severely practical approach. E. W. Krackowizer, who took over *Work With Boys* in 1911, derided social scientific claims to expertise, while his successor, William McCormick, argued that university psychology courses might be "an impediment" to club work.[86] Mass boys' clubs eventually had to enroll teenagers, as delinquency centered in the teens and older boys, some now jobless or in school, wanted to stay on. Yet club leaders continued to profess primary concern for younger boys, criticizing Boy Scouting because it left them out. Under 1944 rules, the Boys' Clubs of America required member clubs to admit at least boys aged eight to fifteen.[87]

By the 1910s, Hall's reputation had waned among educators. In embryology, recapitulation was collapsing, and the doubts reached social scientists; but character builders were slow to react.[88] E. L. Thorndike moved to direct criticism by 1913 of Hall's belief in "nascent periods" when instincts sprang to life.[89] But to have followed Thorndike's psychology would have forced character builders to reconsider their special mission to adolescents, and they clung to that mission. Indeed, much consensus prevailed through the 1910s. A 1913 YMCA report on boy life broke with Hall by describing children as born with unformed capacities which developed in response to stimuli, yet it echoed Hall's views on adolescence and contemporary lore on gangs. In Boy Scouting, though novice Scoutmasters showed little interest, the paid executives made much of instinct psychology.[90]

Although aspects of John Dewey's views found occasional echoes among character builders, these were mostly coincidental until the late 1910s. Dewey shared their desire to find children a substitute for the lost benefits of rural life, but he proposed a process of guided inquiry intended to develop thoughtful citizens of an industrial society. Not only was this concern to make activity a source of reforming insight alien to most boys' workers, but he started long before age twelve and believed that human planning could supersede any sequence of culture epochs.[91] On the whole, character builders preferred Hall's conservative Lamarckism to Dewey's social reconstruction.

Boy Scouting drew praise from progressive educators but little direct involvement until the late 1910s, when Dewey's colleagues at Teachers College, such as Elbert K. Fretwell, an expert on extracurricular activities, became boys' work oracles. William H. Kilpatrick's "project method," by which children planned group undertakings, enjoyed a vogue among Boy Scout executives, since it narrowed Dewey's ideas down to a manageable formula which they could use to supplement the BSA's official program.[92] Within the YMCA, Abel J. Gregg, who designed boys' work programs for the International Committee, became a disciple of Kilpatrick in the 1920s; yet the effect was to reconfirm the group methods called for by gang theory.[93]

Practicality reigned as H. W. Hurt of Teachers College revised the *Handbook for Scoutmasters* in 1919 to emphasize the basics of running a troop. What theory appeared centered on familiar, somewhat Jamesian concepts such as interest and habit; but the new handbook also preserved established views of gang life and adolescence. Speaking at a 1924 Boy Scout conference, Fretwell described character building as "writing habits [into] the nervous system," yet he and his colleagues also discoursed on adolescence and the gang age, stressing the need to use boys' instincts.[94] Boys under twelve were still barred, and headquarters put off providing separate programs for boys under twelve or over fourteen. Clearly, though, practicality and activism were in the ascendant. In that sense, the sunny tradition of boyish vigor had triumphed over the cloudy, romantic image of brooding adolescence.

Once established, basic attitudes persisted within boys' work and outside it. While social scientists increasingly stressed that adolescent changes came gradually, popular faith in sudden transformations at puberty remained strong.[95] Stereotypes of adolescence in our own time still owe much to Hall; and as late as 1947 the *Handbook for Scoutmasters* included a traditional description of adolescents' vulnerability. Long before then, however, the idea of a universal gang instinct had lost support. Thrasher's famous 1927 study of gangs in Chicago returned to the old view of them as pernicious growths from slum soil, and this remains the common opinion today. Yet the group emphasis remained prominent in middle-class boys' work; and the idea of boyish savagery still crops up, at least as metaphor, in writing on boyhood and Scouting.[96]

The historian Samuel P. Hays describes a major innovation of the early decades of our century as the growth of "technical systems," large organizations or clusters of professionals which undertake empirical inquiries and use knowledge to plan for social change.[97] Theories of adolescence and gang life did not make character-building agencies into anything so grand. The need for supervised recreation (the boys' hunger for activity and the adult desire to control and strengthen them) created a market for boys' work. What recapitulation-based psychology did was explain how character-building programs, by supplying recreation suited to crucial developmental stages, could serve that market. Although the promise of special knowledge encouraged boys' workers to try to professionalize their calling, organizational rivalries cost boys' work the necessary critical mass, and character builders remained primarily consumers of expertise whose guiding principles mixed academic theory and popular belief. Yet the combination of a market, claims to special skills, and competition for members set character-building agencies on the road to rapid growth.

7

The Attempted Professionalization of YMCA Boys' Work

Development of a boys' work ideology formed part of the struggle to create a new profession. Since each Association was formally independent and programs varied somewhat from town to town, bureaucratic centralization was unsuited to the YMCA. Ideally, leading boys' workers hoped that professionalization would establish basic standards and yet enable boys' secretaries to design their own programs; but in practice, most had to scramble like small businessmen simply to keep their programs afloat.

Even the general secretaryship (the job of running a local YMCA) was originally an unstable occupation. In 1883, for instance, there were 322 secretaries; in two years, 327 joined these ranks, but 250 quit. Many were young and virtually untrained. When A. G. Knebel, aged eighteen, arrived to run the YMCA at Corsicana, Texas, in the late 1890s, his only preparation was a six-week apprenticeship in Waco. He had to clean the rooms and raise his own budget, a task so hard that one man he solicited kicked him.[1] This sort of initiation stirred a poignant hunger for training to forestall errors and earn a stronger claim upon the public for support.

The first boys' secretaries' status was even more tenuous. As lay initiative died off towards 1900, large YMCAs began to hire assistants to run the junior department. But the big-city general secretary who met with leading businessmen on the board of directors was no model for a struggling subordinate who spent his time with boys. Tenure was brief; of 59 men who took the job in the 1890s, only 12 lasted three years. Their duties were mostly custodial, supervising the rooms and arranging meetings. And they could claim no special expertise, for descriptions of the ideal boys' worker stressed purely personal qualities: "He should be . . . a manly Christian . . . with a cheerful face, a hopeful heart, unlimited patience, and with all this a good disciplinarian."[2] Professionalization was vital if boys' workers were to become more than mere assistants. To gain some autonomy, they would need to fence off a social area — in this case adolescence — and claim special competence to define reality within that area.[3]

A combination of systematic promotion and unplanned expansion in the years around 1900 established YMCA boys' work as an embryonic profession with the beginnings of training, some common knowledge, and a growing work force. The promotion flowed initially from the YMCA's Springfield Training School in Massachusetts, later Springfield College, which had begun in 1885 as a normal school for church workers. The YMCA section grew into a separate college under the leadership of three unusual YMCA men who tried to reconcile evangelical Protestantism with the scholarship of German and American graduate schools. Laurence Doggett, who held a Leipzig Ph.D., served as president and built a curriculum around biology, sociology, psychology, and religious education. William G. Ballantine introduced students to the unsettling findings of recent Biblical scholarship and urged them towards social service. And Luther Gulick, a medical doctor who served as the YMCA's international secretary for physical education while teaching at Springfield, tried to transform physical directors into professionals skilled in anatomy, hygiene, and physical diagnosis. Despite such ambitions, Springfield trained only a fraction of all secretaries.[4] The college stirred controversy, for fundamentalist students had a troubling adjustment; one man threw his Bible on the floor during a class on evolution and shouted "he was through."[5] Still, ideas from Springfield spread rapidly among boys' workers, since they offered a rationale for boys' work as an independent specialty.

In the late 1890s, Gulick extended his campaign for professional standards to boys' work. After studying with Hall, he began to teach about the gang instinct and adolescent hero-worship. He spoke on adolescence at conventions and ran training sessions for physical directors, who then did much of the boys' work.[6] Gulick left in 1900 to become principal of the Pratt High School in Brooklyn, but other instructors at Springfield developed courses in adolescent psychology, physiology, and methods of work among boys.[7]

The college made a major contribution to boys' work by training Edgar M. Robinson (1867–1951), the Y's first international secretary for boys' work. Robinson had entered boys' work as a volunteer while running the family store in St. Stephen, New Brunswick, and made a name for himself with evangelistic camps and conferences. "I was full of zeal and intolerance," he recalled much later, "and burdened with the one idea of making Christians of all the boys with whom I came in contact."[8] After much indecision, he left the store, became half-time boys' secretary for Massachusetts, and enrolled at Springfield in 1898. What he learned there gave his beliefs such a wrench that he lapsed into despair and packed to leave; but Doggett dissuaded him, and Ballantine's views won out. Meanwhile Gulick gave him new ideas about boys which he seized upon with a convert's conviction. Before this, Robinson later confessed, he had relied on

Scripture and dogma, whereas Gulick led him to seek "scientifically sound" principles. He wrote an essay on "Boys as Savages" and built a career on Gulick's ideas.[9]

Boys' work needed Robinson. During the 1890s, it was left to state committees. At the international level (U.S. and Canada), departments for physical, educational, army, railroad, foreign, and student work vied for funds, while boys' work was ignored until Robinson and Gulick emerged as spokesmen. Robinson stressed the needs of boys from good homes, warning that public concern would focus on the gamins served by boys' clubs unless the Y pushed character building.[10] In 1900, he addressed the YMCA Employed Officers' Conference, where J. F. Oates documented the failure of YMCA evangelism among young men; Robinson responded that the Y must shift from adults to adolescents. A singer followed with "'Twas in the Days of Careless Youth," speakers urged hiring an international boys' work secretary, and delegates pledged $1775. The International Committee appointed Robinson as secretary.[11]

He propagandized so relentlessly on the importance of adolescence that the YMCA's national magazine protested: "There is danger that conversion will be regarded, as . . . 'an adolescent phenomenon,' and that conversion after the period of adolescence is not only improbable, but impossible."[12] Robinson's tall, angular form became a familiar sight at YMCA gatherings. Younger boys' secretaries gave him respect bordering on awe, though some outsiders considered him too radical. He complained of "stand pat" men, notably big-city general secretaries; but by 1913 he had five international secretaries for boys' work, while state YMCAs hired forty-nine boys' secretaries by 1919. Robinson stayed with the International Committee until 1920, when he left to run the YMCA world committee for boys' work.[13]

The one serious brake upon Robinson and his colleagues' ambitions was the cost of boys' work. Although it was economical in the 1880s when it fitted into unused nooks and crannies in the adult program, once it became a major undertaking run by salaried men it showed huge deficits, since boys' fees were lower than men's. The Salt Lake City YMCA, for instance, lost $6.13 per boy in 1907 but only $2.47 per young man, and made a profit of $3.33 from each businessman.[14] And yet boys were eager to join, or their parents wanted them to. Furthermore, boys' work figured prominently in Y fund-raising and brought in substantial donations. Accordingly, the junior departments began to make up for their late start, as the ratio of boys to men in city Associations rose from .129 in 1900 to .398 by early 1921. The number of boys' secretaries employed by local YMCAs soared from 43 in late 1900 to 107 by early 1904 and 637 by early 1921.[15] Although hardly a mass profession, boys' workers gained the numbers to form a distinct group within the wider YMCA secretaryship.

The increase in junior memberships was almost as marked: from 30,675 in 1900 to 103,570 in 1910 and 219,376 in early 1921. By then there were also 41,384 Hi-Y members in affiliated high school clubs.[16] Figure 7.1 shows the growth from year to year. Note that the vertical scale is logarithmic. As a result, the steepness of the slope between any two years represents the *rate* of growth in membership over that period—the steeper the slope, the greater the annual percentage of increase. The overall rate of growth between 1890 and 1920 was 10.6 percent per annum. But one can see that the line rises especially sharply around 1900. From 1890 through 1898, growth was only 5.5 percent a year, whereas from 1898 through 1903 it went up to 20.1 percent per annum. Expansion slowed thereafter, but some of the new momentum was sustained, with growth averaging 8.7 percent a year from 1903 through 1920–1921.[17] Part of the surge in

Membership in Thousands

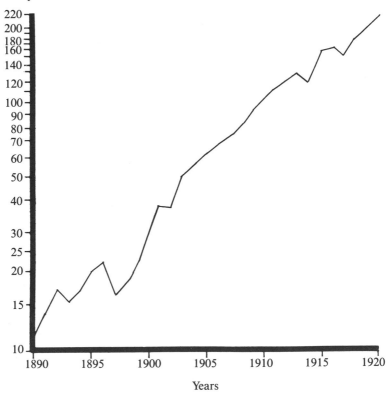

YMCA Junior Memberships, 1890–1920. (Semi-logarithmic scale.)
Sources: See Table 2 and notes 17 and 18 to this chapter for exact membership figures.

membership around 1900 probably represented growth held back during the 1890s depression, but this was also a time of major new beginnings for YMCA boys' work. The number of junior departments nearly doubled from 296 in 1898 to 578 in 1903. Those were the years when Gulick and Robinson spread their new ideology of boys' work based on recapitulation theory, and a cadre of professional boys' workers, however weak, came into being.

Although the number of boys' workers rose sharply, rapid turnover betrayed frustration. During the 1910s, more than a fifth quit each year. Still, a small core of permanent workers developed soon after 1900, for one-third of boys' secretaries in 1907 were still boys' secretaries in 1925.[18] These men wanted to upgrade their vocation, but they faced a vicious circle common to developing professions: to improve their colleagues, they needed to stem the flow of ill-qualified transients, which was impossible until the job offered more satisfactions; but the men could hardly demand better pay and status without improved qualifications.

To the new middle class, professionalism seemed to promise security and prestige. Most professions stressed esoteric competence based on broad technical or scientific knowledge, but some — notably the clergy — drew prestige from association with the sacred and from the serious affairs with which they dealt. By 1900, architecture, dentistry, engineering, accounting, law, and medicine had acquired the institutional appurtenances that sociologists associate with professions: training schools, university affiliation, and professional associations. The Progressive Era spawned new specialties such as city planning and social work; and marginal professions such as librarianship and teaching were in a state of perennial becoming.[19] In an era of specialization, boys' workers' aspirations were typical; but they entered the race for professional status with handicaps characteristic of marginal professions.

Self-improvement was hard, for boys' secretaries led harried lives, "drowning" in detail and worn down by pressure.[20] They had to run summer camps, organize Bible classes, invent projects to keep boys busy, and — above all — control the boys. Ironically, men who were supposed to build solidity of character fell prey to "nervous strain."[21] Boys' workers had little contact with educated men and little time for reading; a majority of Y boys' workers in Massachusetts spent sixty hours a week in the building. Nor did their specialty win much respect; in some Associations they doubled as janitors and general assistants.[22] Salaries averaged $803 around 1910 — below a physical director's pay and well below a general secretary's. Boys' secretaries claimed they could not afford a family, and few saw the job as a "life-work."[23] Since fitness depended upon rapport with boys, they were haunted by fear of being discarded in middle age. Instead of planning lifelong careers in boys' work, most men moved up within the YMCA or else left.[24]

Like schoolteachers, boys' secretaries lost status by association with youngsters. Billy Burger, New York state boys' secretary, described some of his early colleagues as "boisterous, . . . immature in judgment, hasty in decision, and idealizers of boyhood." They "got on famously with younger boys and the goody-goody type of older boy. But most men rather tolerated than respected them." Thus David R. Porter felt obliged to assure recruits, "The man who loves boys is not a freak incapable of other matters. . . ."[25] Insofar as boys were children, to work with them was apt to be considered an affront to masculinity, not an affirmation of it. Hence the insistence with which boys' workers trumpeted virility and Christian manliness. To concentrate on adolescents was to move up a notch in prestige — as from elementary to high school teaching — by serving an older clientele.

Professionalization promised a similar enhancement of prestige. John L. Alexander, the former head of boys' work at the Philadelphia YMCA, in 1912 expressed the hope that by combining academic theory with direct experience the boys' secretary could become the local expert on adolescents, to be consulted by pastors, judges, and teachers; E. M. Robinson proposed that such a man's status might equal a clergyman's.[26] Thus skill with adolescents promised authority — both as a technical expert and as a priestlike counselor during one of life's great crises.

To many young men, the promise apparently outweighed the difficulties. Some new boys' secretaries wanted to give social service; many avowed a desire to save souls and help adolescents avoid moral dangers. A large number were former juniors or volunteers who liked the work. Too often, however, the job looked promising because men could drift into it with little preparation. To those from modest backgrounds, it was a step up, somewhat like a high school teacher's position without a college degree. Only 18.5 percent of new recruits from 1909 to 1913 were graduates, although half claimed some college work. Many secretaries had nagging deficiencies in the common culture of educated men. Billy Burger admitted a fondness for big words to compensate for lack of formal education; others confessed to frequent mispronunciations.[27] Nearly a third of those who quit boys' work went back to school, indicating they were undereducated or had used the job as a stopgap just as nineteenth-century students had often taught school. Many new boys' workers were too young to command respect — 64 percent from 1909 to 1913 under twenty-five. They came mainly from the lower middle class; 48 percent had low-level business experience, a number as salesmen or stenographers. Thirty-five percent came straight from school or college, and 17 percent from religious or philanthropic work; yet the business ethos was strong — about half who left YMCA work took a job in business. This looked bad for a profession engaged in religious and social education. A YMCA report complained that some men "are a little undecided whether they shall go into Boys' Work or the Ministry, or moving picture business, or sell fish."[28]

In most nascent professions a few men took the lead to recruit better candidates and upgrade training. Robinson played this role in Y boys' work, along with David R. Porter, a Rhodes scholar who headed the International Committee's high school division. Porter tried, though with limited success, to recruit college graduates. By 1906, moreover, one-sixth of all boys' secretaries had studied YMCA work at Springfield. Still, this was a far cry from the established professions' insistence upon specialized course work and degrees.[29]

Symptomatic of weak professionalism was heavy reliance on self-education. Robinson's journal, *Association Boys,* nagged subscribers to read, and a few men founded the Order of the Hour Glass in 1911 to promote daily study. Men without college experience were urged to start with history and biography, so they could converse with high school students and businessmen. Technical reading included Hall's *Youth;* Le Bon's *The Crowd;* and Forbush's *The Boy Problem.* Only a third of the secretaries enrolled, however, and few read widely.[30]

Most boys' secretaries got their formal training belatedly in summer. Both the YMCA's Lake Geneva Summer School in Wisconsin and the conference center at Silver Bay, New York, had full-scale summer institutes by 1908. Sessions ran two weeks, and the full program took three summers, proceeding from basic methods to principles of "boy life" and community outreach. Silver Bay's second-year course for 1908 offered Bible Study, Religious Pedagogy, Social Aspects of the Religious Life as Related to Adolescents, and Municipal Sociology as It Relates to Boyhood and Genetic Psychology. Summer schools provided a forum for YMCA leaders and eminent outsiders such as Walter Rauschenbusch. Boy's workers flocked there for encouragement, with as many as 80 percent attending one time or another.[31]

To further the sense of professional identity among boys' workers, twenty-nine men met in 1905 at a call from Robinson to form the Association of Boys' Secretaries of North America—its stated purpose to make boys' work "more scientifically correct" and consider "the Boys' Work Secretaryship as a profession." A majority of secretaries joined by the mid-1910s.[32]

By the usual criteria—"a high degree of generalized and systematic knowledge"; a respectable level of general culture; formation of a full-time occupation, training school, and professional association—YMCA boys' work was moving towards professionalism by 1920.[33] The institutional arrangements were in place, if a bit rickety. Yet most boys' secretaries boasted only a thin veneer of knowledge and culture, although many professed the sort of aggressive commitment to their field expected by sociologists of the professions. Boys' workers were apt to make such declarations as: "If I ceased to be a Boys' Work Secretary I'd leave the Association. . . ."[34] They professed scorn for general secretaries as mercenaries preoccupied with fees and for physical directors as mere technicians. Boys' workers pursued their own projects so relentlessly that in 1919 Canadian YMCA authorities felt obliged to remind them of their duty to the larger Association.[35] They were indeed more open than other YMCA men to new ideas from psychology and sociology, but much of their assertive professionalism was defensive bravado, since other YMCA men had more pay and power.

In any case, the appurtenances of professionalism were one thing, the practice quite another. Boys' workers of the early 1900s were enthusiastic improvisors. Besides the inevitable basketball teams, they started clubs for polo, fencing, and canoe building; imposed anticigarette and personal purity pledges; and sponsored choirs, bands, a weather bureau, woodworking shops, cadet corps, mock elections, and a McKinley Memorial Club.[36] All this activity kept the boys busy, but it drained off energy in random directions, whereas professionalization implied a more consistent strategy. Most successful professions cohere around a "nuclear skill" or cluster of skills which define the core of professional practice.[37] Despite intense experimentation, YMCA boys' secretaries found no such core; the task of building character remained too diffuse.

The most basic dilemma was how to combine large-scale boys' work with a role as priestlike counselor. Nineteenth-century YMCA boys' workers had predicated character building upon admitting limited numbers of boys and getting to know them well. Later boys' secretaries still saw their job in highly personal terms; but unlike the amateurs who preceded them, they had to enroll enough boys to justify their salary. And that forced them to routinize their work.

A 1913 report urged boys' secretaries to accept the situation and emphasize their supervisory role. They were told to impress the directors by arranging groups "so as to use equipment continuously."[38] More importantly, they should use their knowledge of adolescence to claim authority over other secretaries in dealing with boys—a difficult task, although physical directors did concede limited supervisory rights. A more promising tack was to train adult volunteers to lead small groups of boys, but junior departments were short of volunteers.[39] Hence many secretaries followed Robinson's advice to let adolescents teach Bible classes and lead other boys to Christ. After the early 1900s, however, the proportion of boy leaders to total membership declined slightly.[40] Because their sense of professionalism rested in part upon skill in leading boys, secretaries hesitated to admit that amateurs could do the job.

Another apparent solution was standardization, as YMCA men in the 1910s were caught up in the nationwide infatuation with scientific management and decided they could improve efficiency by designing a set program with measurable outputs. A commission of the Association of Boys' Secretaries asserted boldly that it would be easier to standardize "principles of work based on adolescent psychology" than to set uniform fund-raising procedures. Enthusiasts wanted a "definite standard . . . with regard to physical development, moral training, recreation, intellectual stimulus, [and] at which period special effort shall be made to secure definite decisions for the Christian life. . . ."[41] In an era still buoyed by faith in progress, standardization carried more positive implications than today. What Y men wanted was not mediocre sameness or stop-watch Taylorism but rather the leveling upward of performance to a higher standard. To an era in search of social cohesion, standardization suggested the hope of common bonds. Also, standardized tests were sweeping the schools; and the rapid spread of Boy Scout troops, led by volunteer Scoutmasters, convinced YMCA leaders that they needed a program with which they could trust amateurs to lead groups of boys.[42]

The Canadian YMCA led off the experimentation in 1915 with Standard Efficiency Tests, followed the next year by an American Standard Program — revised in 1919 and renamed the Christian Citizenship Training Program. Unlike Boy Scouting, the YMCA programs tried to measure character-related outcomes directly. Following the Y's traditional fourfold plan, the authors devised detailed sets of questions to measure a boy's physical, intellectual, religious, and social "efficiency."[43] The CCTP group leader was to interview each boy, awarding points for achievements in each area, and then plot the scores on a chart with two crossed axes like a giant X. When the four points were joined, the lines formed a quadrilateral — more or less lopsided according to how badly, for instance, the boy's religious score fell short of his physical one. Thus the perfect boy was a big square. After bringing each boy to a "wholesome discontent" with his misshapen self, the character doctor prescribed remedial activities.[44] The year's program consisted of group training, usually under church sponsorship, followed by a second charting.

In the end, the attempt to systematize quasi-professional standards generated unmanageable complexity. The charting proved cumbersome, and requirements such as an all-night vigil to focus adolescent idealism were hopelessly artificial.[45] The Canadian version had some success in church use, but financial problems after World War I and pressure from YMCA authorities to re-emphasize boys' work within the Y building forced the organizers to turn it over to church boards. The American version did not catch on until simplified forms appeared.[46] In neither country could the YMCA match the appeal of Boy Scouting's standardized program.

If standardization was not the answer to the boys' secretaries' search for self-definition, neither was their more personal role as religious mentors. On the surface, a smooth evolution seemed under way. Boys' secretaries at their 1913 conference assured themselves that their goal was to bring boys to Christ, but their methods were shifting as they sought to use psychology to foster steady growth of Christian character. Secretaries held fewer evangelistic meetings—an average of fourteen per junior department in 1900 and 1910, but only seven in 1920. Meanwhile, the percentage of boys' branches which ran Bible classes rose from 49 in 1900 to 80 in 1910 and 1920; and boys' workers changed the courses to fit their conception of boys' natural interests, even developing one on Scripture in athletic phrases, and downplaying exegesis in favor of moral instruction.[47] Y men compromised between growth and conversion by holding meetings to urge boys to take a "Forward Step"; the biggest was accepting Christ, but boys who had already done so were urged to take a further step such as teaching a Bible class or renouncing a bad habit. In modish terminology, conversion became "not an end, but a process" through which boys sought "social realization" for their faith.[48]

E. M. Robinson warned against neglecting either "welfare service" or "spiritual results," and yet striking a balance proved difficult, as secular concerns increasingly predominated. Robinson himself complained that boys' secretaries were so intoxicated with the new wine of psychology that many decided theology "was a theory while psychology was a fact, and theology ought to be modified to fit psychology. . . ."[49] Perhaps a more serious problem was that boys' secretaries got caught up in administration and recreational activities designed to attract boys, and they neglected religious work. This was compounded by growing "timidity," partly a reluctance to force the pace of adolescent development but also an inability to muster the hard-shelled nerve required to demand conversions.[50] Gradualism thus became an easy out. Accordingly, while decrying the old practice of counting conversions like notches on one's Bible, David Porter urged secretaries at their 1920 convention to do something definite. Yet that assembly could not decide what to stress. The delegates adopted tests of religious efficiency that ranged from old-fashioned evangelism—getting boys to join the church and lead others to Christ—to new-fashioned social service: "Have we contributed definitely towards a growing community consciousness of responsibility for the influences affecting boy life?"[51] Hearing no specific trumpet call, boys' secretaries scattered in different directions. Some abandoned evangelism during the 1920s in favor of educational programs to build character, while others still sought conversions; in the South, for example, YMCA Bible classes were still common in the 1950s.[52]

Despite this trend towards secularization, boys' secretaries could not simply turn to social service as their core skill, for social outreach posed complications of its own. Nineteenth-century boys' workers had simplified their task by retreating inside a middle-class constituency; now their successors started admitting that the Kingdom was delayed by bad social conditions —not just dirty books and juvenile street roving but poverty and poor housing as well. If they were to be local experts on adolescents, boys' secretaries felt they had to look outside their own walls. As a first step, a few ran community surveys, a common Progressive device to raise public awareness. In 1909, secretaries from around the country descended upon Detroit for a week, and then each reported on a topic: playgrounds, schools, street trades, fornication and prostitution, and so forth.[53] The faith in public opinion was typical of contemporary reformism, as was the attention given vice and squalor. Other projects were likewise cautiously Progressive. Boys' workers sent lists of current laws dealing with the young to legislators, and they supported juvenile courts. Sometimes they set up demonstration playgrounds and got the city to take them over.[54] On the whole, though, these undertakings were a bit dilettantish, since conservatives controlled the YMCA and the boys' workers' social concern was too diffuse to spur a radical reconstruction of their jobs.

Other forms of outreach addressed the failure of regular boys' work to reach boys who lived some distance from the Y building or in towns too small to afford one. The first attempts, called "equipmentless work," began in rural counties and in Tulsa, Oklahoma, in 1909. The men involved did welfare work and promoted church clubs throughout their communities.[55] In their zeal to decentralize boys' work, Y men also helped launch Scouting in America. But only Minneapolis and Chicago among big-city YMCAs developed full-scale community programs. Boys' secretaries preferred short campaigns such as the career decision days they ran in high schools, since more sustained projects meant wrenching changes and perhaps problems with lower-class boys.[56]

Boys' secretaries mostly settled for modest programs within their own buildings, such as letting affiliated church clubs use the pool or making new efforts to recruit working boys. During 1919–1920, boys' workers found jobs for 17,133 boys, enrolled 12,446 in educational classes, taught first aid to 19,999 and sponsored 632 Boy Scout troops.[57] The basic goal, though, was still to bring in boys to use the meeting rooms and gym, "the objective being the rounded development of every member, and the maximum use of equipment." The opening report at the 1913 assembly claimed that "unless there is a carefully organized and administered work in our membership within the building, other boys' work within the community is weakened very largely."[58] The illogic of this proposition merely highlighted the strength of the conviction.

Local YMCAs enjoyed a construction boom from 1900 through 1929 which gave boys' workers space to expand operations without pressure to conceive of changes. A secretary admitted in 1920: "The use of $100,000,000 worth of property theoretically designed to serve the complex all-round needs of boys and men is yet an unsolved problem in human engineering."[59] And yet the boom rolled on.

Expansion did nothing to mitigate the boys' secretaries' sense of drowning in detail. Summer camp, Bible classes, entertainments, community outreach, and special projects all took time and led to superficiality; still, a man who worked intensively with a few boys and let membership shrink could lose his job. Market pressures hopelessly compromised professionalization, and the breakdown of any sort of unified boys' work profession deprived boys' secretaries of leverage from professional standards independent of the YMCA. Instead, they competed with other agencies for members. This brought pressure from the general secretary, who needed large enrollments to hold down deficits; one boys' worker bitterly reported that the man running his Association talked only of $5 and $8 boys.[60] The need to attract boys, combined with failure to impose order on proliferating activities, left boys to choose like diners at a smorgasbord; the secretaries complained their work was little more than the "selling of privileges."[61] This was the reverse of professionalization, since professionals normally expected to substitute their better judgment for the client's untutored wishes. Accordingly, Y men in the 1910s tried to compel boys to take a balanced program by imposing pledges of all-round participation and recruiting boys who would forego the gym and pool.[62] But those facilities were what boys and their parents would pay for. Like many marginal professions, YMCA boys' work needed more market power before its practitioners could impose their standards.

Those standards were none too firm in any case, since the level of expertise among ordinary boys' workers was modest, and they could not agree upon a core of professional practice. Boys' secretaries accepted the goal of fourfold development — mental, physical, spiritual, and social — yet gave the four vastly unequal emphasis. Thanks to market pressures, physical training outweighed everything else.

Boys' secretaries had a strong group sense by 1920, but so did other marginal professions which had reason to be defensive. Turnover remained high. Boys' secretaries chafed at close supervision by the general secretary; many left for Boy Scouting, where they could head their own local operation.[63] Indeed, the size of their exodus shows that professionalization was no panacea for their problems.

Y boys' workers were also hurt by slowness to adapt ideologically. As Progressive opinion swung away from moralism towards efficiency and bureaucracy in the early 1910s, Y men had trouble going along. Their standard programs failed to match the appeal of Boy Scouting. Then in the 1920s, the alliance between Protestantism and social reform weakened and fundamentalism emerged, exposing strains within the YMCA between reformers and traditional religionists.

The boys' secretaryship stabilized slowly. By 1931, median tenure had risen to 4.8 years, and half the men were college graduates. But their median age was only 29.6, and salaries remained low. Theirs was still a marginal profession, yet even partial professionalization was costly and curbed expansion, while Boy Scouting surged ahead with a standard program for amateurs.[64]

8

The Invention of Boy Scouting

As the previous chapter suggests, while YMCA boys' secretaries labored towards professionalism, their work began to be overshadowed by the successful transplantation of Boy Scouting from England. Although the new import filled much the same social niche as the Boys' Brigades, it had better organization and a livelier program. Compared to the YMCA, it was more centralized and standardized. And it had a great allure for boys around ages twelve or thirteen. These traits all went back in some measure to Boy Scouting's British origins.

Its rapid success on both sides of the Atlantic reflected contemporary enthusiasm for manly outdoor vigor. More importantly, however, Boy Scouting drew upon anxiety to mold the rising generation into a cohesive, hard-working citizenry — patriotic, disciplined, and conventional in values. Despite a dose of romantic individualism in the movements' origins, success brought centralization of authority. By tracing the fortunes of Boy Scouting's two most immediate American precursors and the movement's early days in Britain, we can gauge the relative strength of impulses towards individualism, spontaneity, and submergence within nature on one hand and towards social, moral, technological, and organizational control on the other — both within Boy Scouting and within wider spheres of British and American life.

The founders of the two American groups, the Woodcraft Indians and the Sons of Daniel Boone, confused the issue of Boy Scouting's origins by each claiming to be its true begetter. But their claims are plausible only if one assumes that romantic individualism triumphed in Scouting. Their schemes are of interest primarily as alternatives to Boy Scouting, examples of cultural and organizational approaches which did not take firm root in Progressive Era America.

The Woodcraft Indians, the more influential of Boy Scouting's American forerunners, was the creation of Ernest Thompson Seton (1860–1946), a naturalist and illustrator who had won fame as a writer of animal stories. His group originated in 1902, when Seton invited boys to camp at his estate in Connecticut and published a series of articles in the *Ladies' Home*

Journal on woodcraft and Indian-style camping. But the roots lay deeper, for Seton had grown up with few boyhood friends and a father whom he remembered as stingy with affection yet lavish in demands for filial submissiveness. Turning to art and nature study as an escape, Seton grew into an impassioned defender of wild nature and youthful playfulness against the utilitarian demands of modern society. Through boys' work, he tried to relive his boyhood and alter its outcome. Yearnings for recognition, independence, and immersion in nature made him a contentious figure—he identified with the lone wolf and signed letters with a paw print—and an affront to respectability—he seldom bathed or cut his hair.[1] But those yearnings also nerved him on occasion to swim across the currents of his age.

Seton came upon his Indian motif from two directions. First, he was concerned not merely to preserve resources for man's use, the reigning form of conservation, but also to defend the ecological balances of nature in the wild. The American Indian, he believed, had lived in harmony with those balances, whereas the white man destroyed them. Second, in reaction against his father, Seton exalted natural drives; this predisposition, combined with an interest in animal behavior, led him to embrace Hall's instinct psychology and the idea of boyish savagery.[2] Yet instead of seeing "savagery" as merely a rung on the ladder to civilization the way Hall did, Seton came to value Indian life as an end in itself, until by 1915 he proposed a Red Lodge for men to learn the "spirit of Indian religion. . . ."[3]

The initial goals of the Woodcraft Indians were more modest but still unconventional, since Seton avoided ordinary utility, moral indoctrination, and regimentation. Basically, his was a loosely organized plan for camping out, with Indian ceremonies, games, and awards. Instead of pursuing vocational training or the usual hobbies, boys could earn awards, called "coups," for single feats of campcraft, nature study, or track and field. Whoever won twenty-five became a "sachem," and fifty made one a "sagamore"; otherwise there was no formal hierarchy of promotion. In place of overorganized team sports, Seton designed his own, such as a simulated deer hunt with tracking irons to leave a visible trail. When E. M. Robinson saw the Indians in action, he marveled at Seton's ability to give fantasy substance, with boys chasing excitedly after burlap deer. In the evenings, Seton led in songs, Indian dances, and storytelling around the council fire and solemnly gave each boy an Indian name.[4] Although Seton dominated by sheer personal presence, his plan differed from most previous boys' work in making all offices elective. Costumes were individual, not uniforms. Seton also departed from character-building precedent by making little effort to inculcate conventional morality, piety, and patriotism. Since he believed that young savages were unready for abstractions, the laws he propounded for his Indians were merely rules for an orderly camp. He was skeptical of established verities, and the qualities he praised were simplicity of life, reverence for nature, and delight in the arts.[5] In trying to foster an appreciation of beauty, Seton blended stereotypically feminine virtues into his version of manliness. Indeed, the agency most influenced by Seton's ideas was the Camp Fire Girls, which used awards like his to glamorize domestic skills and Indian ceremonial to draw out girls' aesthetic inclinations.

Seton's proposals also intrigued boys and boys' workers. His novel of boyhood, *Two Little Savages* (1903), which he crammed with information on nature study and Indian-style camping, became one of the most widely read and remembered boys' books of its generation.[6] Many boys' workers suspected that Seton's plans would only work when he himself was present; but a number of YMCA boys' secretaries organized tribes, the Y's standard programs of the 1910s borrowed extensively from his ideas, and those for younger boys in the 1920s used an Indian motif.[7]

Still, the Woodcraft Indians never took root independently. Although Seton issued manuals and magazines lauded his plans, he never set up any supervisory mechanism, and few tribes operated outside the YMCA.[8] Had Boy Scouting not come along in 1910, Seton's plan might have gone further, but the organization was probably too flimsy.[9] Exaltation of the Indian also aroused resistance; and the organizers of the Boy Scouts of America thought Seton's plans deficient in moral indoctrination.[10] Not only did the Woodcraft Indians lack the organizational efficiency to prosper in Progressive Era America; the scheme also lacked commitment to the technological progress and economic growth so highly valued in white American culture, and it disappointed the moral earnestness of the time. Only as a supplement to more conventional YMCA boys' work did it win wide acceptance.

Daniel Carter Beard (1850–1941), the founder of the Sons of Daniel Boone, identified himself with a central symbol of American nationalism —the pioneer scout. Raised in Kentucky, he posed as the last link with the world of Daniel Boone. In fact, as we have seen, he grew up just across the river from Cincinnati. An illustrator and free-lance writer and an acquaintance of Seton, he took up backwoods camping in adulthood, moving socially on the fringes of the fashionable world of outdoorsmen and big game hunters. He began the SDB in 1905 as a circulation-building device for *Recreation* magazine.[11]

Beard's forte was gadgetry. Starting in the 1880s, he wrote how-to articles for boys: how to camp out, new ways to fish, and so forth. His *American Boy's Handy Book* (1882) sold well for years. Beard had a weakness for the sort of design that required two trees spaced just right and forty straight poles; but he gushed enthusiasm, and boys daydreamed over his plans. The SDB was in this fanciful vein, since Beard's guidance consisted almost entirely of plans for gadgets and games such as simulated gander pulling on bicycle.[12]

For his grander aims, Beard fell back on nativism and hypermasculinity. Against Seton's Indians he set up the ideal pioneer, boasting that the SDB's "soul" was "essentially American. We play American games and learn to emulate our great American forebears in lofty aims and iron characters. . . ." Beard maintained that outdoor life would build toughness: "We want no Molly Coddles," he proclaimed.[13]

Despite such bombast, the SDB was merely one of many clubs with which magazines filled their children's pages, and it led a precarious existence. Crowded out of *Recreation* in 1906, Beard shifted to the *Woman's Home Companion* but fell out with the editors in 1908. Renamed the Boy Pioneers, his plan was featured for a few years in the *Pictorial Review* and lasted into the 1920s on a small scale as an activity for boys too young for Scouting.[14] To make the SDB even less stable, Beard did not at first require adult control, since a magazine club could not be too demanding. But without adult leaders to supply new ideas and enforce persistence, most SDB groups collapsed once the boys tired of the novelty.[15]

Failure to develop a full program or any real organization doomed the Sons of Daniel Boone. Yet unlike Seton, Beard was to survive in Boy Scouting as a figurehead because his emphasis on technique in outdoor life and his fervid patriotism fitted in with Boy Scout ideology.

Boy Scouting in its finished form was created by a British general, Robert S. S. Baden-Powell (1857–1941), who set out to enrich Boys' Brigade training and ended by founding a movement which overshadowed the Brigade. Fascinating to boys, Scouting also soothed ruling-class fears of imperial weakness and social unrest.

This blending of strengths owed much to the personality and career of Baden-Powell, who had advanced himself by spicing basic conservatism with a dash of unconventional adventurousness. Born to a prosperous family, Baden-Powell was raised by a strong-willed mother after his father died in 1860. Sent to Charterhouse School, he was a compulsive joiner, relentlessly cheerful; yet he spent hours roaming the woods alone. Joining the army, he cultivated prominent men and advanced rapidly; but he tired of mechanical drill and tried his hand at reconnaissance, learning to love the flannel-shirt life of the South African veld. Over the years, he saw action against the Zulu and the Matabele, took part in an expedition against the Ashanti in West Africa, and observed fighting along the North West Frontier of India. From this experience, Baden-Powell came to regard war as something of a game in which most of the casualties were natives. When he secured his own regiment, he turned to military scouting to enliven training, transforming men without "strength of character [or] . . . resourcefulness" into self-reliant scouts. In 1899, he published a lively, anecdotal little book, *Aids to Scouting for N.C.O.'s and Men,* full of training games such as Spider and Fly which later appeared in Boy Scout manuals.[16] Boy Scouting was to echo these aspects of Baden-Powell's career, breathing the public school spirit without the elitism of school sports (which Baden-Powell had escaped in the woods), promising discipline without the stultification of endless drill, and turning military scouting into a game for boys.

Baden-Powell became a national hero when the South African town of Mafeking, under his command, withstood a cautious Boer army for 217 days. He had bungled in letting his force be entrapped; but the defense was a stirring episode in an otherwise inglorious little war. When news of the relief of Mafeking reached London on May 18, 1900, the city went wild in an outpouring of jingoistic hysteria that coined a word — "mafficking." Baden-Powell's jaunty nickname, "B-P," began to pass into public usage as his personal trademark. Meanwhile the story spread that one of his officers had formed a boys' messenger corps at Mafeking; and *Boys of the Empire* serialized parts of *Aids to Scouting* under the title of "Boy Scouts."[17] Baden-Powell had only to turn his fame to civilian account.

His direct involvement in boys' work began when the Boys' Brigade enlisted him to inspect parades. Finding Brigade drill mechanical and unappealing, he concluded that it scared off boys; accordingly, he set about designing a supplement for the Brigade along the lines of *Aids to Scouting*.[18] Although a preliminary outline published in 1906 met with a lukewarm response from the Brigade's leaders, this lack of enthusiasm may have led Baden-Powell to consider developing a wholly independent program. A meeting with Seton encouraged him to go it alone and suggested some ways to enliven the proposed activities. In May of 1907, Baden-Powell issued a leaflet which outlined a comprehensive program of discipline, observation, woodcraft (a term from Seton), health, patriotism, chivalry, and lifesaving. The leaflet also suggested that sponsors form boys into units for Scouting: six or more to a patrol under a boy patrol leader, and four or more patrols to a troop under an adult Scoutmaster.[19] Meanwhile Baden-Powell sought support in high places, winning expressions of approval from such famous advocates of military and patriotic training as Lord Roberts and Admiral Charles Beresford. YMCA men arranged a lecture tour, and the press lord C. Arthur Pearson agreed to publish a handbook.[20]

A trial camp in 1907 demonstrated that despite its sober purposes, Scouting would also furnish exuberant fun for boys. B-P taught by practice and games, following Seton's example; and at night he was the life of the campfire, telling stories and dancing around the flames leading African chants.[21] The new handbook, *Scouting for Boys,* was equally zestful. Baden-Powell called the chapters "Camp Fire Yarns," illustrated them with his own sketches, and threw in unedifying tidbits calculated to appeal to boys, such as a little melodrama about a diamond thief, with directions on how to simulate his hanging. The book captured Baden-Powell's public persona and welded it to his program: unsystematic, determinedly cheery, decent yet with a touch of the professional soldier's callousness. Issued in 1908 and pushed by Pearson, who was a master of popular journalism, the handbook sold famously.[22]

The basic program was simple: a boy made promises and worked to pass tests. On becoming a Scout, he promised on his honor: "1. To do [my] duty to God and the King. 2. To help other people at all times. 3. To obey the scout law." In brief form, the Boy Scout law prescribed: "1. A scout's honour is to be trusted. 2. A scout is loyal to the King, and to his officers. 3. A scout's duty is to be useful and to help others. 4. A scout is a friend to all, and a brother to every other scout. 5. A scout is courteous. 6. A scout is a friend to animals. 7. A scout obeys orders of his parents, patrol leader, or scoutmaster without question. 8. A scout smiles and whistles under all circumstances. 9. A scout is thrifty." The Boy Scout motto, "Be Prepared," was based somewhat immodestly upon Baden-Powell's much publicized initials. American Boy Scout officials later endowed the oath and laws with Mosaic import; but the laws came late in Baden-Powell's planning, and he regarded activities as more important for character.[23] The tests required boys to qualify as "tenderfoot," "second class," and "first class" Scouts. To become a tenderfoot, a boy had to take the oath and know: the laws, signs, and salute; four of seven knots; the composition of the Union Jack and how to fly it. To reach second class, he must know simple first aid and signaling; he had to track half a mile in twenty-five minutes or describe the contents of a shop window observed for one minute; he had to cover a mile in twelve minutes, alternately running and walking. Further tests required him to lay and light a fire (with two matches) and cook meat and potatoes; also he must have sixpence in the bank and know the sixteen points of the compass. A first class Scout had to swim fifty yards, bank one shilling, signal sixteen letters per minute, take a fourteen-mile hike, perform more advanced first aid, do more elaborate outdoor cooking, read a map correctly and draw a sketch map, tell directions without a compass, demonstrate skill with an axe or make something with wood or metal, judge distance, size, numbers, and height within 25 percent, and train a tenderfoot. Once past these required tests, a Boy Scout could earn badges for ambulance work or proficiency as a cyclist, signaler, seaman, marksman, master-of-arms, pioneer, or stalker.[24] There was more to Boy Scouting than this cluster of outdoor and military skills; Scoutmasters were free to add sports and other activities. They were also expected to teach moral and patriotic virtues and motivate Scouts to practice self-improvement and the daily "good turn." But the tests were central; through them, Baden-Powell hoped to strengthen and discipline boys' faculties.

Ironically, the full program never caught on in the Boys' Brigade.[25] Part of the problem was that the officers preferred drill to Scouting's encouragement of boyish initiative. But a more basic principle was involved: to superimpose a whole program, brought in from outside, upon the work of an existing boys' work agency was to undermine that agency's raison d'etre. Although Boy Scout troops were to operate under the sponsorship of other institutions, these were mostly churches, schools, and service clubs — seldom rival boys' work agencies.

Baden-Powell had strong incentives to push ahead with his program. His army career lost momentum within a few years of Mafeking, as superiors doubtful of his competence named him to high-ranking but less and less significant posts, first as Inspector-General of Cavalry and then as commander of the Territorials (a form of militia) in the northern three counties of England. Doubtless Baden-Powell sought a new public role. There were less personal reasons as well, for Baden-Powell shared with much of the British ruling class a growing alarm at loss of social control, widening class divisions, and waning imperial power. As soon as he revealed his plans to solve social and political problems by raising hardy, disciplined boys, he won enthusiastic establishment support.

Fear that Britain would go the way of Rome was strong among Tories and prominent in Baden-Powell's 1907 leaflet. Popular Social Darwinism, reduced to the catchphrase "survival of the fittest," fortified fear that Germany's growing power boded Britain's ruin and that China and Japan would one day trample Europe under. The Boer War dealt British self-confidence a wound that bled long and never quite healed. It stirred especial concern about the condition of working-class youth, since many army recruits had to be rejected as unfit and many even of those accepted performed badly. At the same time, surveys by Charles Booth and Seebohm Rowntree exposed the squalor of lower-class life and triggered a spate of books warning of national deterioration beginning in boyhood.[26] Baden-Powell echoed these concerns; disturbed by his troops' inability to cope with army rations, he even saw signs of imperial decay in their wretched teeth. Rather than social forces, he blamed "PREVENTABLE deterioration . . . owing to ignorance on the part of parents and children. . . ." The problem as he saw it went beyond the physical, for he was appalled by the hysteria of football crowds and warned that the raucous entertainments of the urban masses were destroying the stolid British character. To restore manliness, Baden-Powell proposed to make boys "PERSON-

ALLY RESPONSIBLE" for their own health and strength.[27] Scout games and badge work would make boys bright and energetic yet steady and unexcitable, ready to serve the empire.

Boy Scouting's stress on duty reflected burgeoning upper- and middle-class fears of lower-class restiveness. Not only had the 1906 elections brought in a Liberal government which Baden-Powell feared would cut the military, but the Labour Representation Committee elected twenty-nine M.P.'s. Like most urbane conservatives, Baden-Powell claimed that everyone wanted a humane society, but he told boys that socialists "made life a kind of slavery for everybody, and left the country an easy prey to a stronger one." Redefining snobbery, he wrote acceptance of the status quo into the fourth Boy Scout law: "A scout is a friend to all, and a brother to every scout, no matter to what social class the other belongs. . . . A scout must never be a SNOB. A snob is one who looks down upon another because he is poorer, or who is poor and resents another because he is rich. . . ."[28] In a society where class distinctions were sharper and more blatant than in America, less blurred by ethnic and racial variety, Baden-Powell clearly intended Boy Scouting as an agency of class control. Through Scout badge work, he encouraged ambitions suited to working-class status: farming in the colonies, a steady trade, a place in the armed services—in these niches Boy Scouts would find security and serve the empire.[29]

Lest anyone think established institutions adequate to manage boys, Baden-Powell and his supporters voiced complaints much like those of American boys' workers. The Earl of Meath, a member of Baden-Powell's advisory board, decried "neglect of control" by parents of all classes. And the Sunday School Union admitted losing 80 percent of boys by age fourteen or fifteen. Accordingly, Baden-Powell offered Scouting to keep "the wilder spirits" in line and decreed that all Boy Scouts must attend some form of church service.[30] As for the schools, Baden-Powell complained that they gave "book instruction" but not "character education." Although clubs, charities, and Brigade companies catered to boys outside school, Baden-Powell estimated with fair accuracy that they reached only one boy in eight. The rest, he warned, were "becoming 'hooligans' and ultimately 'wasters'. . . ."[31]

Baden-Powell's remedies grew out of English traditions and his own experiences. Boy Scouting's use of play for serious ends was a logical extension of the Victorian elevation of sport to a realm of worklike earnestness and moral gravity. More influential still was the assumption, widespread by the late 1800s, that schoolboy values could govern adult life. Schoolboy stories exalted health, strength, and ready action over reflection as the keys to character, foreshadowing the Boy Scout motto, "Be Prepared." That motto and the promise of a daily good turn echoed the Victorian vogue of chivalry, which the English gentry misconceived as a sort of medieval service ethic.[32] Even more than gallantry, though, the public schools stressed peer conformity and discipline mediated through older boys. As a former Charterhouse boy, Baden-Powell tried to replicate this system by grouping Boy Scouts into patrols; he wanted to spread the public school spirit to the lower social orders. Although he downplayed team sports because they reduced many boys to spectators, even that was a return to an older form of schoolboy life when boys had roamed the woods before sports eclipsed all else. Spreading from the public schools down through church and chapel, a new protected, supervised boyhood — symbolized by uniforms and outdoor recreation — was reaching into the lower middle class and even the upper reaches of the working class.[33] Like the Boys' Brigade, Boy Scouting was yet another agency of control, through which Baden-Powell hoped to extend supervision even further down the social scale.

As a conservative bred to the English class system, Baden-Powell thought of a "character" as a social type and urged Boy Scouts to classify people "by their faces, their walk, their boots, hats, clothing, etc."[34] This outlook, familiar to readers of English detective fiction, reflected a lively sensitivity to signs of social class, region, and occupation. Accordingly, in building character he tried to mold a composite social type, with the public school-boy's sportsmanship and sense of duty, the middle-class boy's thrift and diligence, and a working-class boy's sense of his place.

The last thing Baden-Powell wanted was inwardness or complexity that might tempt boys out of their proper roles; he was a missionary for the schoolboy cult of action.[35] Like Boys' Brigade and temperance workers, he saw character as a bundle of faculties and powers to be strengthened. In particular, he believed that mental powers and even eyesight improved greatly with practice. Thus Boy Scout requirements such as the shilling bank deposit were to foster good habits, while a host of others — from memorizing the contents of shop windows to estimating distance and learning to cover a mile in exactly twelve minutes — were designed to strengthen observation and memory. Once these powers became habitual, Baden-Powell asserted, "a great step in the development of 'character' has been gained."[36]

Boys who were alert yet disciplined would, he and others believed, make efficient citizens. Thus Boy Scouting drew support from the contemporary vogue for national efficiency — an irritation with complacency, party politics, and imperial decline which united a broad spectrum of men in the Unionist and Liberal parties. Boy Scouting's promise to promote class harmony, strengthen the Empire, and improve the masses pleased social imperialists such as R. B. Haldane, the Liberal who was Secretary for War, and Joseph Chamberlain, the Unionist who favored modest domestic reforms and imperial consolidation. Haldane encouraged Baden-Powell to leave the army and give full time to Scouting; and C. Arthur Pearson, whose news-papers beat the drum for Chamberlain, promoted the infant movement.[37]

Articulate working men were apt to be skeptical, however, for they saw imperialism as a costly impediment to social reforms at home—especially to the sort of social welfare programs that Baden-Powell himself opposed. As a national hero, B-P's popularity to some extent transcended class lines. Although few working-class groups shared the middle and upper classes' often jingoistic enthusiasm for the Boer War, the great majority of work-ing men were more likely to be indifferent than vociferously opposed to the war; many joined in the rejoicing when Mafeking was relieved and hailed Baden-Powell as the hero of the day. Yet B-P's personal charisma, though lovingly burnished in succeeding years, was bound to fade a bit with time; it could never wholly dispel the cynical mistrust with which the working masses regarded the military and political schemes of the rul-ing elite.[38]

Not surprisingly, critics of Boy Scouting concluded that training effi-cient citizens meant preparing boys for war. In the militarized atmosphere of Edwardian England, it was easy to believe such charges, especially when a few Boy Scouts attended reserve army maneuvers in 1909 and others won a small field gun at a Boy Scout rally. This militarism aroused resis-tance among the working class whom Baden-Powell hoped to win; ambu-lance work was far more popular than marksmanship in working men's clubs. Since he also believed that mechanical drill was poor training for initiative, Baden-Powell tried to keep it to a minimum, mixed in a good deal of first aid and other reasonably pacific pursuits, and insisted that his boys were "peace scouts" like the Royal Canadian Mounted Police.[39]

It was true that Boy Scouts received no technical military training—though Baden-Powell encouraged rifle practice and urged Scouts to prac-tice leading a running target by sighting along the staves they carried. But he clearly saw Scouting as *pre*liminary. With unusual frankness, he told an aide to the Governor General of Canada that he wanted "all boys to become Boy Scouts from 11 to 14 and then to become proper Cadets from 14 to 18. If this is done . . . in all colonies, we shall establish a standard and bond throughout the cadets of the coming Imperial Army."[40] In Brit-ain and Canada, retired military men and militia officers held half the top Boy Scout posts; and conscriptionists, including Sir Edmund Elles, the first Chief Scout Commissioner, hoped to win recruits for the army reserves through Scouting. According to Samuel Moffat, an American Boy Scout official who observed British Scouting in 1914, the movement was "semi-military," and Scoutmasters drilled the boys like army men.[41] It would take the carnage of World War I, which decimated Britain's Scoutmasters and former Boy Scouts, to make British Scouting unambiguously non-military.

Clearly the basic Boy Scout program grew out of Baden-Powell's experience in military reconnaissance; one cannot explain otherwise the mélange of activities from signaling to outdoor cookery. Some had little value to civilians, yet Baden-Powell thought they would be useful on the empire's frontiers. Besides, the idea of faculty discipline — that powers exercised in one context are fully transferable to another — justified nearly any form of training that appealed to boys. Thus the Boy Scout program grew by accretion around a core of military scouting.[42] And because Baden-Powell set such store by his sociopolitical goals, borrowings from other boys' workers consisted of techniques more than purposes.

This pattern was evident in Baden-Powell's dealing with Seton. Seton's influence led Baden-Powell to broaden slightly his plan to transport *homo faber* to the wilds, adding a bit of romantic appreciation of nature to the features based on military scouting; but nature study remained peripheral. Baden-Powell also copied some of Seton's games, campfire rituals, and use of totemic imagery (Boy Scout patrols had animal names and cries), although he substituted Africans for American Indians. But Seton looked to the outdoors to uplift man's spirit, whereas Baden-Powell treated it as a training ground on which to practice specific skills and play games reminiscent of military scouting. Baden-Powell used primitivism for a dash of color, but he saw no spiritual value in it. He distressed Seton by emphasizing conventional morality and adding vocationally oriented proficiency badges to the outdoor program. Seton wanted to break with the values of industrial America, whereas Baden-Powell's ideal Boy Scout went out to serve the British Empire and never cut his ties to the society he left behind.[43]

Baden-Powell learned far less from Beard, since he heard only belatedly of the latter's work. Still, both men were militant patriots (if for different flags), and their plans dovetailed sufficiently for the *Woman's Home Companion* to run extracts from *Scouting for Boys* on Beard's page after he left the magazine.[44]

Though British YMCA men helped Baden-Powell launch Boy Scouting, their boys' work was undeveloped and did not influence Scouting in Britain the way the American YMCA's junior programs would affect Boy Scouting in the United States. Boy Scouting's major debts to British boys' work were to boys' clubs and the Boys' Brigade. The idea that working-class boys needed supervised activities owed much to the example of English boys' clubs, which had flourished since the 1880s. Leaders such as Charles Russell of Manchester shared the Americans' hope of turning gang life to advantage, though whether Baden-Powell got the idea from English or American sources is uncertain.[45] In structure, Boy Scout troops were modified Brigade companies, broken into patrols and given a more varied program. Also like Brigade companies, many troops were church-affiliated, although Bible classes disappeared as citizenship training displaced religion.

Baden-Powell's knowledge of American developments was spotty, but all the more inspiring because he tended to exaggerate American successes — notably Seton's. He had heard of self-governing clubs and read Forbush on *The Boy Problem* and Stelzle on *Boys of the Street.* Though he had not read Hall by 1907, he could learn the main drift of Hall's theories through Seton and Forbush; more important, he had encountered the concept of boyish savagery and gangs. The lore of adolescence was slower taking hold in Britain, although it was in familiar use among Boy Scout leaders there by 1915 or so.[46] Initially, American boys' work was most influential for its group orientation, woodcraft techniques, and purported success with working-class boys.

Samuel Moffat was sharply critical of British Scouting because the boys were "mostly preadolescent" — a major shortcoming in the eyes of an American character builder.[47] Yet this pattern was not simply the result of negligence or failure to appreciate the gospel according to Hall; it followed logically from Baden-Powell's purposes and the nature of the Boy Scout program. It also proved, as we shall see, very hard for American Boy Scout leaders to reverse.

In the beginning, unconsidered expedience played a part; boys of nine or ten were easy to recruit. Only after much debate among British Scout leaders and growing recognition that the presence of younger boys repelled older ones did Baden-Powell raise the age of admission to eleven — and by then the practice of enlisting boys even younger was well entrenched. The boys' clubs offered a precedent, but more important was the belief that the very young were still malleable, whereas older youths were "lost capital" for national advancement.[48] Besides, if Boy Scouts were to become cadets at fourteen, as Baden-Powell initially contemplated, they had to start Scouting young.

Baden-Powell's program was in actuality most attractive to preadolescents; by the late 1910s scarcely one British Boy Scout in ten was past age fourteen.[49] As later chapters will show, uniforms and outdoor rambles appealed most to boys of eleven or twelve; boys that age were eager to try cautious adventures away from home. Moreover, Erik Erikson's outline of developmental stages suggests that such boys would be preoccupied with developing a sense of industry; they would work at learning a packet of disparate, circumscribed, even questionably useful skills such as those in Boy Scouting, provided that adults assured them these were valuable.[50]

For their part, boys' work innovators had a striking preoccupation with preadolescent boyhood; in a limited sense, some were themselves Peter Pans who never grew up. Baden-Powell, Seton, and even Beard had talent, but none was deep; boyish enthusiasm and an instinct for boys' tastes won them an audience. Seton and Beard in particular kept going back obsessively to boyhood. We have seen that Seton, lonely as a boy, looked to the Woodcraft Indians for vicarious compensation; Beard based his writing career on his Ohio Valley boyhood, retaining through life a schoolboy's pack rat mind and naive jingoism.[51] Baden-Powell, on the other hand, was adept at using his boyishness while transcending it. He carried off the performance at Mafeking with the insouciance of a schoolboy playing tricks on a rival house and exuded through life a relentless cheeriness. But that was a well-honed public persona. Unlike Seton and Beard, he did not neglect administration and rush off to be with the boys; he understood adult forms of power.

A related pattern merits attention, however. Though Baden-Powell went off to a life of adventure, he remained — like many Victorian men — a boy before his mother, presenting accomplishments for her approval. He and four brothers remained remarkably under her domination; the first to break ranks and marry — beginning "the selfish ordinary life of earning and spending for himself alone," as his mother put it — did so at age forty-five.[52] Baden-Powell married at fifty-five. It is notorious that British boarding schools did not prepare boys for easy relations with women; and the purity advice which inundated conscientious American boys was equally inhibiting — notably the injunction to counter sensual desires by thinking of mother. Many pioneer boys' workers, including Sumner Dudley, E. M. Robinson, and Dan Beard, married late or not at all, while the YMCA's Billy Burger confessed to a "mother fixation" which made it hard to transfer his affections to his wife.[53] Nor were these isolated problems, for sex role anxieties had infected broad reaches of the middle and upper classes. Accordingly, some boys' workers favored boyhood's cameraderie, secure masculinity, and freedom from new emotional entanglements; fascinated and a bit conflicted themselves regarding the years before puberty, they encouraged boys to make a partial break from home into the gang stage but then to stay there rather than go on and become involved with girls. Boy Scouting's popularity with men as well as boys suggests that this reaction was common.

The preference for preadolescents marked woodcraft groups more than the YMCA. Seton showed most interest in boys eight to fifteen, while Beard complained that older boys were self-assertive. Baden-Powell let Scouts remain to age eighteen, but made his basic appeal to preadolescents; he wanted boys who were still frank and open.[54] Since introspection was superfluous if boys were to learn their duty and do it, the last thing he wanted was a soul-searching adolescent identity crisis. Only later did Baden-Powell become concerned about "keeping touch with [youths] at the critical age between boyhood and manhood. . . ."[55] In the late 1910s, he began a program of Rover Scouting for boys in their late teens, but few joined up.[56]

From the start, Boy Scouting walked a fine line between spontaneity and control. English Scout leaders boasted that the movement began with boys, not men. Though overstated, the claim had merit, for boys read *Scouting for Boys* and rushed to find their own Scoutmasters. By late 1910, headquarters claimed 100,298 Boy Scouts in Britain. Scouting offered boys a respite from formalized schooling and the stifling domesticity of the Edwardian middle class. In the words of Leslie Paul, an early Boy Scout, "the movement took the side of the natural, inquisitive, adventuring boy against the repressive schoolmaster, the moralizing parson and the coddling parent. . . ."[57] Soon, however, boyish initiative was submerged as adults took over. Churchmen, hopeful of controlling urban youth, grasped the opportunity and made churches the leading sponsors of troops.[58]

Administratively, Boy Scouting started out relying on local enthusiasts, but Baden-Powell soon moved to impose centralized control. A major break came in 1909 when, charging insubordination, Baden-Powell sacked Sir Francis Vane, a radical Liberal who had been Scout Commissioner for London. Accusing Baden-Powell's group of militarism and dictatorial methods, Vane led ten or twenty thousand boys into a rival British Boy Scouts, but the group withered, and Baden-Powell sustained his authority.[59] He set up an Advisory Council and Executive Committee with himself as chairman and left the army in 1910 to lead Scouting full time. Boy Scout headquarters also set up a hierarchy of nonelective County Councils and Local Associations, but effective power lay with County or District Commissioners appointed by headquarters.[60]

In its administrative structure, Boy Scouting followed a conservative's model of the British social order: an elite held national power, lesser gentlemen ran matters locally, and parents and Scoutmasters participated but had limited power. Unlike Americans, the British felt that to use paid organizers betrayed flagging zeal. Hence, except for clerical drudgery, volunteers did most of the work; two-thirds of the Scout Commissioners were military men, mostly retired.[61] Parents were represented on troop committees and Scoutmasters on district associations, but neither had a say in appointing commissioners, and headquarters further insulated itself from below by subsisting on badge and equipment sales rather than dues.[62]

Splinter groups broke off in later years — Ernest Westlake's Order of Woodcraft Chivalry in 1916 and John Hargrave's Kibbo Kift Kindred in 1920 — but these remained small. Their leaders cared more for social causes or woodcraft than for organization; inspired by Hall and Seton, they combined literalistic faith in recapitulation with zeal for picturesque outdoor life to brew heady draughts of romantic primitivism.[63] Scouting was ginger beer by comparison.

Despite the Boy Scouts' popularity, Baden-Powell's ultimate targets — working-class boys — remained elusive. Since working-class opinion was not all of a piece and was seldom highly ideological, working-class boys were not all immune to the excitement of Scouting. But there were practical obstacles to their recruitment. The cost of uniforms deterred many. Scoutmasters were scarce in poor areas, and some did not trust lower-class boys with the responsibility Baden-Powell envisioned.[64] In addition, Boy Scouting's religious affiliations bypassed the unchurched masses, and the taint of militarism alienated left-wing parents. More generally, Scouting's patriotism and middle-class morality ran up against the deep-seated cynicism with which most working-class people regarded official pieties. Nor did boys themselves necessarily care to trade a measure of freedom for the promise of respectability. Baden-Powell held up middle- and upper-class styles of boyhood as models, while decrying lower-class pleasure-seeking. Not surprisingly, he attracted the middle class plus individuals within the upper stratum of the working class who wanted to claim respectability.[65] Still, the balance of initiative and deference which Baden-Powell desired in working-class boys seemed equally valuable for middle-class boys just entering their teens.

Enthusiasm for British novelties had already set American boys marching with the Boys' Brigades, so Boy Scouting was sure to cross the Atlantic, though in what condition remained uncertain. Baden-Powell hoped to make Scouting a force for imperial consolidation and to that end toured Canada for two months in 1910; but he took a relatively hands-off attitude towards American Boy Scouting and managed only a single day in New York.[66]

As we shall see, though, similarities in British and American culture and careful organization by Boy Scouting's American leaders insured that many of British Scouting's leading characteristics carried over to the United States. The tone of militant patriotism, the concern for individual efficiency within a nationalistic context, insistence on uniformity and centralization of authority, and the attraction of Scouting for preadolescent boys — all these traits of British Scouting took root in America, with due allowance for American nationalism and the preoccupation of American character builders with adolescence. U.S. Boy Scout leaders did not, however, attempt the offhand style of the English gentleman amateur; the American Boy Scout movement was run by salaried staff who treated Scouting and its ideals with a seriousness reminiscent of the work ethic.

It may seem odd that a British import flourished where American woodcraft organizations had not. But many leading Americans were Anglophiles; reformers copied English social innovations such as the settlement house; and Baden-Powell's efforts to socialize boys for a stable social role went over better in Progressive Era America than anachronistic yearnings for frontier liberty. Given the urgent striving for mastery that marked American notions of masculinity, Seton's rejection of dominance over nature, of white superiority over Indians, and to some degree of rigidly conventional morality was too extreme for a mass movement. On the other hand, Beard's berserker spirit (he preferred Davy Crockett's cocksure motto, "Be always sure you are right, then go ahead," to Baden-Powell's sober, "Be Prepared"), though attuned to American dreams of individualistic frontier manhood, was too anarchic and willful for an age groping towards social control.[67] Boy Scouting promised a manageable, centrally administered program.

9

The Organization and Expansion of the Boy Scouts of America

Boy Scouting began in America as a hasty improvisation by YMCA men to head off misuse of Baden-Powell's ideas; yet it soon became the most centralized of boys' work agencies, dedicated to spreading a single program across the land. Since they could not rely on Baden-Powell's prestige, the American organizers strove to make the program itself a well-known product of uniform quality. Whereas the English relied on gentlemanly amateurs whose social standing could bolster their authority, American Boy Scout leaders turned instead to formal organization with paid staffers whose power stemmed from their positions in an administrative hierarchy. Efficiency was becoming a catchword in American industry, education, and philanthropy, but it was not to result from self-direction by workers or teachers; instead, administrators imposed standards.[1]

None of this was evident in 1910, however. A few YMCA secretaries used *Scouting for Boys* to spice outings, but Boy Scouting could easily have fallen prey to military enthusiasts and become just another cadet corps.[2] Instead, E. M. Robinson took responsibility for its promotion in the U.S. He was looking into Scouting as a portable program for community work when he learned in May of 1910 that the Hearst newspapers hoped to exploit Boy Scouting as a circulation gimmick and that William D. Boyce, a Chicago publisher, had already incorporated the Boy Scouts of America and was seeking a Congressional charter. Boyce, who was out of his depth, agreed to let the Y take over; the charter attempt failed but left the BSA a legacy of ambition.[3] YMCA help enabled Boy Scouting to catch on fast, as boys' secretaries promoted the scheme and tapped YMCA supporters for help. John L. Alexander, a Y boys' worker, became managing secretary, and BSA headquarters occupied YMCA offices in New York City.[4]

At first, Robinson thought of making the Boy Scouts of America a YMCA satellite; but the BSA needed broader support to establish itself as the only legitimate Boy Scout movement. Accordingly, Robinson invited men interested in child welfare to meet in June. Although none came as official representatives, those present included men affiliated with the

Red Cross, Big Brothers, *Outlook* magazine, public school athletic leagues, and a number of other organizations. The meeting elected a committee on organization with Seton as chairman; Lee F. Hanmer, Associate Director of Recreation for the Russell Sage Foundation, as secretary; and George D. Pratt, a wealthy YMCA layman, as treasurer. In addition, Seton chose Robinson, Luther Gulick, Jacob Riis, Dan Beard, and Colin Livingstone, a friend of Boyce who was a Washington banker with good Republican connections. As this list shows, men of varied interests who worried that city life was ruining boys were eager to support the BSA.[5]

Upon this broad base, Robinson laid foundations for a monopoly of Boy Scouting. The main threat to the BSA's dominance came from militaristic imitators. Some misunderstanding was inevitable, as *Harper's Weekly* had recently introduced Americans to "England's Boy Army." But William Verbeck, the head of a boys' military school, had formed the National Scouts of America on lines avowedly more military than Baden-Powell's, and Peter Bomus, a retired colonel, headed a similar scheme. Robinson preempted their support so effectively that both gave up and accepted honorary posts in the BSA.[6] One obstacle remained — the American Boy Scouts, launched by the Hearst papers in May 1910. Hearst disowned the scheme, charging fraud, yet it hung on under little-known leaders. BSA officials complained that their rivals drilled boys with rifles and sent them out to solicit funds, trading on confusion with the BSA. Much of the impetus behind the drive to make the Boy Scouts of America the only legal form of Boy Scouting stemmed from a wish to eliminate these competitors.[7]

Meanwhile Robinson and Seton were busy securing publicity. Articles appeared in magazines; Minute Tapioca sponsored half a million booklets; and Seton patched together his own writing and some of Baden-Powell's to form a Boy Scout handbook. Baden-Powell himself came in September for a brief laying-on of hands which showed that the BSA stood in the true line of succession.[8]

With so many distractions, however, the organization and program remained in disarray. Power rested legally with a self-perpetuating Board of Managers. In addition, there was a ceremonial National Council and Seton as Chief Scout. Baden-Powell, who was impressed with the American initiative, described the BSA as a great "combine"; yet like many holding companies, it was a hasty conglomerate, lacking internal cohesion.[9] Seton clung to his Indian program instead of Baden-Powell's format; the managing secretary lost track of troops; and Scoutmasters gave up in confusion. Clearly it was time to standardize the program and organize the "combine" more efficiently.[10]

The managers turned to the Sage Foundation, which was trying to make philanthropy businesslike. They secured money to hire a new executive secretary and chose James E. West (1876–1948), who came highly recommended for efficiency. West combined driving energy with nagging insecurity, for he had grown up in an unloving orphanage. Although partially crippled, he worked his way through law school, was active in the Washington, D.C., YMCA, and worked for the government before entering private practice in 1906. Eager to right wrongs he had known as a boy, West campaigned for playgrounds and a juvenile court in Washington. Through *Delineator* magazine, he hunted homes for orphans, and a campaign he organized spurred Theodore Roosevelt to call the 1909 White House conference on dependent children.[11] As an executive, West proved aggressive, conscientious, and inflexible. He took over in January of 1911 determined to reorganize the BSA to correspond with the best administered social agencies.

West's appointment insured that Baden-Powell's charismatic leadership would have no American equivalent. The BSA enlisted Roosevelt as Chief Scout Citizen, but he merely issued occasional statements of support.[12] That left only Seton, and West's editorial board shunted him aside, asserting that in "this country the individuality and personality of one man cannot sum up in itself the genius of this organization in its entirety. . . ."[13] The ambition to see Scouting dominate American boys' work was incompatible with dependence on one man's enthusiasms; instead, the BSA adopted West's bureaucratic style.

"My first problem," West recalled, ". . . was to make sure as a lawyer that I knew which way we were going."[14] To spell out the rules, he had three committees set up: one to standardize the oath, laws, and promotion requirements; a second on badges; and a third on organization. West recruited members from other social agencies but made most decisions himself.[15]

Characteristically, he called not merely for changes but for "the absolute adaptation of this idea to American conditions."[16] Somewhat to Baden-Powell's displeasure, the BSA altered the Boy Scout badge by superimposing an eagle on the fleur-de-lys. West secured Jeremiah Jenks, a leading proponent of immigration restriction, to chair the committee which overhauled the oath and laws.[17]

More was involved than just substituting Uncle Sam for John Bull. The BSA played up civic and moral values and de-emphasized imperial rivalries, for few Progressive Era Americans shared Baden-Powell's apocalyptic fears. Rather, they saw separate, manageable, primarily domestic problems, of which the boy problem was one. Since Americans believed that social order depended upon the moral behavior of self-directing individuals, Boy Scouting's moral code mattered more than it did in Britain. Accordingly, West's committee made the oath more comprehensive: "On my honor I will do my best: 1. To do my duty to God and my country, and to obey the scout law; 2. To help other people at all times; 3. To keep myself physically strong, mentally awake, and morally straight." The third part, which was new, incorporated the YMCA stress on all-around development. The Boy Scout laws also became more inclusive. The first nine followed the British pattern, though the BSA adopted a simplified formula which made them easier to memorize: "1. A scout is trustworthy. . . . 2. A scout is loyal. . . ." and so on through "12. A scout is reverent. . . ." The last three — brave, clean, and reverent — were wholly new. The committee excised references to hostility between social classes, a subject Americans disliked mentioning in front of children. To dispel fears of militarism, the BSA also softened the strictures on discipline. The committee even muted B-P's frenetic cheeriness: no American Boy Scout "smiles and whistles under all circumstances," as Baden-Powell's eighth law had required; for literalistic critics said such a boy would be insufferable.[18] In general, the changes produced a bland, inoffensive text.

There was one major change in the other requirements; on the advice of YMCA men, the minimum age was raised to twelve to insure recruitment of adolescents. Otherwise, the tests for tenderfoot, second, and first class rank remained much the same, though the committee spelled them out more precisely and added a woodcraft requirement at Seton's instance. One addition attested to the formalism of American Boy Scouting: a first class Scout had to furnish "evidence that he has put into practice in his daily life the principles of the scout oath and law."[19]

Merit badges proliferated. By mid-1911 there were literally fifty-seven varieties, open only to first class Scouts, from Agriculture and Angling to Swimming and Taxidermy. A hierarchy of ranks rose above first class: a Life Scout had to win five specified badges; a Star Scout earned five more; and at the top perched the Eagle Scout, the "all-round perfect scout" who had amassed twenty-one badges.[20]

Once the program was settled, the BSA issued a new *Handbook for Boys* to make Boy Scout practice "throughout America . . . uniform and intelligent."[21] It included articles by sixteen individuals and six agencies or committees. The result was safely impersonal, since almost all Baden-Powell's lively writing disappeared, although several spirited articles by Seton survived. Further publications followed as West brought Boy Scouting "to a definite, a very definite organization. . . ."[22] In 1912, the national office bought a magazine, *Boys' Life,* to reach individual Boy Scouts. Starting in 1913, *Scouting* magazine offered adult leaders news and advice, a *Handbook for Scout Masters* appeared, and in 1916 the BSA began issuing pamphlets on merit badge subjects. Samuel Bogan, a veteran Scouter, observed that the publications seldom sparkled but were technically excellent.[23]

It was symptomatic of the BSA's organizational approach, even of its character-building methods, that its basic texts avoided any one personal style. In Max Weber's terminology, Baden-Powell's charisma had been routinized very fast.[24] Standardization also shunted aside Seton, a would-be charismatic leader, and left West supreme as the man who ran the administrative apparatus.

After the 1911 revisions, the main Boy Scout requirements remained nearly unaltered for decades. This simplified distribution; once the program was set, West could concentrate on building a system to control its use and sell it nationwide. Throughout this task, the steady trend of decisions conformed to two principles: power should be centralized, and it should be exercised by paid staffers.

West's appointment forestalled decentralization. The YMCA men in charge during 1910 had expected to set up state and regional offices, but West formed a Committee on Permanent Organization to reconsider.[25] Its members had the professional organizer's viewpoint, since many were executive heads of social agencies. West received a crucial warning against copying the YMCA's multilevel structure from Richard C. Morse, secretary of the Y's International Committee, who had had to battle for power with state and big-city YMCA leaders.[26] Over substantial local opposition, West's committee advised against regional, state, or district organizations; no center of authority must intervene between national headquarters and municipal Boy Scout councils.[27] Centralization reflected the best business practice of the time, but such utter refusal to countenance intermediate offices was unusual. It suited the BSA's identification with American nationalism; but at bottom it was an extreme reaction to the centrifugal tendencies of voluntary associations, in which state or local units which acquired their own lay supporters and independent funding often demanded corresponding autonomy.

To keep local councils in check, the executive board decided that no council's jurisdiction should cross municipal boundaries.[28] Although exceptions multiplied by the late 1910s, this policy initially favored suburbanites and hampered Boy Scouting in the central cities by impeding allocation of resources on a metropolitan basis. New York posed the problem in reverse; its huge size demanded decentralization, yet locally powerful Boy Scout leaders resisted so strongly that in 1915 the national executive board determined to intervene and divided the city among independent borough councils.[29] Overall, BSA policy was to prevent the growth of huge local councils that could become independent power centers.

The BSA was a closed corporation, since headquarters chartered the local councils. These in turn sent representatives to the National Council, which seldom challenged the paid staff. Guided democracy spared the BSA the turbulence that roiled YMCA conventions. On many issues

West's executive board simply made its own decisions after a brief survey of the field.[30]

The board members were men of wealth and substance, several of whom spent more than twenty years on the board. They met monthly; between times West consulted a subcommittee of Lee Hanmer and George Pratt. Pratt, who came from a Standard Oil family, was a conservationist, spokesman for Americanism, and West's closest ally. When Hanmer, a specialist in child welfare, resigned in 1915, John Sherman Hoyt of American Car and Foundry took his place. Other long-term members included Mortimer Schiff of Kuhn Loeb and Company, who helped with finance; Frank Presbrey, who owned an advertising agency and advised on publicity; and Colin Livingstone, who became president of the BSA. In addition, the board in 1911 included boys' workers and military men: Seton; Beard; Robinson; William Verbeck; Peter Bomus; plus George W. Hinckley, who ran the Good Will Farm for boys in Maine; and Seth Sprague Terry, who chaired the YMCA International Committee on Boys' Work. The other members were William D. Murray, a YMCA layman and New York lawyer, and two more businessmen, Benjamin L. Dulaney and Milton A. McRae.[31] Businessmen soon predominated, while representation of specialists in boys' work and related fields shrank. The seven members who left by 1917 — Seton, Robinson, Terry, Hanmer, Hinckley, Bomus, and Verbeck — had all been involved in boys' work, child welfare, or rival Boy Scout groups. Of eighteen new men who joined by 1921, all but a few were businessmen. Jeremiah Jenks was a professor and consultant on public issues; John H. Finley was Commissioner of Education for New York State; George W. Goethals had been in charge of building the Panama Canal; and Charles P. Neill was a former U.S. Commissioner of Labor. Theodore Roosevelt, Jr., and George W. Perkins, Jr., were sons of famous fathers soon to gain prominence themselves in business and government. The other twelve new board members were leading businessmen, five of them bankers. Like Theodore Roosevelt, they saw benefits in the increasing scale of American organizational life. Just as businessmen pressed churchmen to become efficient, so these men favored businesslike methods in the BSA; but because they were not boys' workers, they generally accepted guidance by West.[32] Over the years, their support strengthened Boy Scouting's tacitly conservative cast.

Financially, headquarters relied on wealthy donors, six of whom provided 71 percent of the $69,984 budget in 1913. Three were board members: Pratt, Hoyt, and Schiff. The rest were practitioners of the gospel of wealth — Andrew Carnegie, John D. Rockefeller, Jr., and Mrs. Russell Sage — who wanted to put philanthropy under trained administrators.[33] Their support freed the national office to consolidate its power independently of local Boy Scout leaders.

While the superstructure grew, however, troops were collapsing. Scoutmasters tried to learn Scouting from the manuals and got discouraged; by 1913 two-thirds had quit. Nor did the rest necessarily follow the official program, for observers noted unearned promotions, underage Boy Scouts, and military-minded Scoutmasters with sabres.[34] Clearly the men needed local supervision. Though federations of Scoutmasters might have sufficed, the executive board wanted leading citizens who would lend more prestige and keep an independent check on the Scoutmasters.[35]

The common procedure in forming a council was for someone, often the YMCA secretary, to call a meeting of "men who represent the important interests, be they commercial, financial, religious, educational, or whatever."[36] In Chicago, speakers ranged from Jane Addams to the head of the Illinois National Guard. In smaller towns, business and professional men came, plus church and school officials.[37] The BSA tried, in short, to replicate the local power structure, particularly as it affected boys. Boy Scout councils resembled the centralized school boards which contemporary reformers favored; in both cases the organizers assumed that successful men were disinterested and "representative." It was typical that when the BSA's Ludwig Dale organized a council in Dayton, Ohio, he "spoke to" teachers and foremen but "interviewed" businessmen, while the head of National Cash Register supervised the organizational plan.[38]

With the advent of local councils, Scoutmasters came under local supervision — by a volunteer Scout Commissioner in small towns or a paid executive in large cities. Each council also had a Court of Honor to examine boys for first class and merit badges. Yet two-thirds of all troops had no local council in 1912.[39]

Since West wanted tighter national control of the membership, the executive board decreed, as of October 1913, that every Scoutmaster must register all his boys annually. Each Boy Scout paid twenty-five cents. The board acted unilaterally, expecting protest, but resistance was scattered and easily dismissed.[40] Though the dues covered almost half the headquarters budget by 1916, central registration was even more important as a system of control. The plan made it clear that local leaders held no vested interest, since local councils and Scoutmasters both had to reregister each year. "Oh how fortunate it is that we put that last provision in it," West later exulted, explaining that the "burden of proof was always on the other fellow, to show why the commission should be renewed."[41] Central registration was not foolproof, but the BSA gained closer control over its membership than the Brigades or YMCA ever had. American Boy Scout leaders drew a sharp line between members and nonmembers; unlike the YMCA, for instance, they reserved their big attraction, camping, for bona fide members.[42]

Few voluntary agencies had as accurate a view of their own operations. Even YMCA reports did not reveal turnover in membership, while other associations inhabited a dream world, recording new members but seldom striking those who quit. As a result, statistical honesty was no better in church work than in stock promotion; a student of young people's societies estimated in 1917 that 45 percent of their reported membership was "water." At first the BSA did no better, reporting an inflated total of 300,000 Boy Scouts, but West wanted a truer count.[43]

The results were a shock (see Table 3). There were only 103,395 Boy Scouts in 1914, most of them new, and only 35 percent reregistered for 1915. Although the BSA claimed 376,537 boys by 1920, turnover reduced the significance of this figure, for the persistence rate was still under 50 percent. Turnover was equally great among Scoutmasters. Throughout the 1910s, Boy Scouting remained in a promotional phase, stronger at the top than the bottom, with the national office floating high upon a wave of publicity.

It was clear that the BSA could recruit boys but had trouble holding them. Blaming the frequency with which troops collapsed when the Scoutmaster quit, headquarters decreed in 1914 that each Scoutmaster must recruit a troop committee of men to share responsibility and find a replacement if he left. The BSA stopped issuing troop charters to Scoutmasters, granting them first to troop committees and then to the institutions which sponsored the troops. An interlocking system resulted. Troop committees were represented on the local council, which in turn oversaw the committees; both checked on Scoutmasters; and councils, committees, and Scoutmasters all had to be reauthorized by the national office every year.[44]

Volunteer supervision failed to make troops permanent, however. The average committee met at most twice a year, and only half the troops founded in 1919 lasted two years. Especially for troops outside council areas — 51 percent in 1919 — national headquarters continued to serve as a surrogate local council.[45]

Whereas British and Canadian Boy Scout officials were apologetic about interfering with local initiative, their American counterparts gloried in centralized administration as evidence of efficiency.[46] The years 1914 to 1919 saw consolidation of power by the paid staff and rapid growth of the BSA's central administration, even though that administration often had a weak hold on local Boy Scouting.

National headquarters in New York City was a cross between a head office and and a mail order house. The BSA's organizational structure approximated the line-and-staff pattern common in business, but the line — that is, the hierarchy of officials who administered the basic Boy Scout program — was discontinuous. A large Administration Department — sixty-seven people in 1916 — processed registrations and answered policy questions by mail. A National Court of Honor, composed of volunteers headed by Dan Beard and assisted by clerks, verified that badge recipients had

Table 3
Membership of the Boy Scouts of America, 1914–1922

Year	Boys				Scoutmasters and Assistant Scoutmasters[a]			
	New	Reregis- tered or Carried Over[b]	Total	Persis- tence Rate (%)[c]	New	Reregis- tered	Total	Persis- tence Rate (%)
1914	89,270	14,125	103,395	–	5,338	3,133	8,471	–
1915	99,394	35,937	135,331	35	9,729	3,604	13,333	43
1916	130,053	55,198	185,251	41	13,346	5,290	18,636	40
1917	204,359[d]	76,685[d]	281,044	41[e]	–	–	25,919	–
1918	238,149	139,428	377,577	50	–	–	28,391	–
1919	194,515	166,275	360,790	44	–	–	31,827	–
1920	229,321	147,216	376,537[f]	41	–	–	–	–
1921	121,769	269,613	391,382	72	–	–	33,472	–
1922	240,859	192,136	432,995	49	24,620	17,114	41,734	51

[a] Some years' reports listed Scoutmasters and Assistants separately, others listed them together, and a few omitted them altogether.

[b] The BSA generally carried over some members who had failed to reregister.

[c] This represents the percentage of boys on the membership rolls at the end of the previous year remaining there at the end of the current year.

[d] Since contemporary figures are not available, these come from the 1964 annual report and are only approximately consistent with the rest.

[e] BSA, *Annual Report* 8 (Mar. 1918):22 claims 50 percent reregistrations but also reports 38 percent for 1916. My computations differ.

[f] The BSA made a particular effort in 1920 to weed out lapsed members.

Sources: Boy Scouts of America, *Annual Report* 6–13 (Feb. 1916–Dec. 1923); 55 (Mar. 1965).

been tested by the proper local authorities. Otherwise supervision of local operations fell to a tiny Field Department which had only two full-time and eight part-time field workers in 1916, plus a director, Samuel Moffat. Since expansion took precedence, Moffat's men concentrated on organizing new councils rather than helping existing ones.[47] Despite formal centralization of authority, a wide gap remained between the national office and local officials, some of whom thought national headquarters "arbitrary in its rulings."[48]

Staff functions expanded erratically. There was an editorial force of seven by 1916, but departments to deal with specialized facets of the program developed more slowly. Only in 1916, thanks to gifts from wealthy supporters, did the BSA acquire an Education Department to promote training for Scoutmasters and executives. A small Department of Camping followed the next year.[49]

Staff departments which ran as businesses grew faster as Boy Scout officials sought to advertise their product and protect its reputation. Hence the alacrity with which they purchased *Boys' Life,* a small magazine with the temerity to claim it was the semiofficial organ of the BSA. Hence also the creation of a Library Department under Franklin K. Mathiews, a Baptist minister who waged intemperate war against the flood of cheap "Boy Scout" books published in the early 1910s. In 1913, the BSA started its own series, "Every Boy's Library."[50] These publishing ventures helped the organization reach nonmembers, but also gave the executive board recurrent headaches because they failed to generate self-sustaining profits.[51] Like many businesses, the BSA expanded for reasons that were in part defensive and then had trouble with the resulting acquisitions.

The most troublesome division was the Supply Department. Again, its expansion was partly defensive; endorsement of products to be sold through ordinary retailers failed badly, as knives broke and knapsacks lost their straps. Besides, West wanted to control the badges and uniforms, and the executive board hoped for a source of income.[52] The first catalogue came out in 1914; by 1918 gross receipts totalled $555,346. Uniforms were sold through retailers where there was a local council to monitor sales, but the boys had to order badges from New York. Since the Supply Department pushed sales of accessory gadgets until the fully equipped Boy Scout rattled when he walked, headquarters seemed mercenary, and reports spoke defensively of service to the movement. Actually, profits never rose above 5 to 12 percent, while failure to run the department on genuinely commercial lines deprived it of working capital, since the BSA siphoned off profits to help the movement.[53] In both Publications and Supply, it proved very hard to run a profit-making operation as part of a philanthropy. Ironically, because losses seemed unconscionable in quasi-commercial departments, such departments kept expanding in search of greater efficiency. Because of this process and the massive correspondence generated in supervising Scoutmasters by mail, the BSA had a far larger headquarters staff — 282 in 1919 — than most voluntary associations.[54]

As the administrative apparatus grew, so did West's power; his title soon changed from Executive Secretary to Chief Scout Executive. Contemporary bureaucracies tended to overcentralize, and advisors on management presumed that only the "personal contact and individual ability [of] a man of enormous energy" could hold together a large enterprise.[55] But West added a driving ambition all his own, fusing concern for boys with a sense of personal mission until he scarcely distinguished between Boy Scouting and himself. His compulsive work habits pushed efficiency to the brink of inefficiency. He so routinized operations that men from the Bureau of Municipal Research gave his office their highest praise: it was, they said, the closest they had ever seen to Sears Roebuck. Yet they suggested that he take a vacation.[56] As late as 1917, he claimed to read every Scout-master's registration; and he kept subordinates on a short rein, running headquarters departments "on a sort of time clock basis" in the words of a man who declined a chance to head the Education Department.[57] Major decisions attested to West's influence over policy as well. Like a company president dealing with his directors, he used the power of infor-mation to squelch proposals by individual members of the executive board.[58] West's power marked the BSA's divergence from British Boy Scouting. The British could not understand giving a paid employee such authority, while Americans thought that less reliance on social status and more on managerial expertise would have strengthened English Scouting.[59]

In America, bureaucracy met little effective resistance. In 1914, Arthur Carey, a wealthy amateur, presented a memorial signed by Scoutmasters, teachers, and public men which decried neglect by the BSA of Scouting's moral aspect, alleging that external organization had outstripped the spirit of Boy Scouting.[60] But Carey's romanticism clung tenuously to the fringe of the BSA, and such protests were rare. The main dissenters among the national leadership were Seton and Beard, who clumsily tried to defend outdoor adventure against what they saw as encroachment by a soulless organization. Seton lost heavily in West's rise to power, as the National Council made it explicit in 1913 that the Chief Scout was only honorary head of the BSA. He never understood the staff's preference for a largely impersonal handbook and chafed at continued use of his chapters. Mount-ing tensions culminated in the executive board's decision to forestall Seton's resignation by leaving his post vacant in 1915.[61] A tangle of principle, per-sonality, and organizational strategy lay behind the ouster. Seton's British citizenship, Indian rituals, and distaste for American nationalism seemed to opponents to threaten the BSA's public image. He irritated associates with charges such as the claim (not wholly unreasonable) that Boy Scout staves were really dummy muskets.[62] Above all, Seton felt the BSA had been commercialized and overregulated; he longed to keep his panache paramount. Indeed, Seton later described West cruelly as a "man of great executive ability but without knowledge of boys . . . who, I might almost say, has never seen the blue sky in his life."[63] Yet Seton and Carey's in-tensely personal methods did not suit men bent on expansion.

The Seton controversy strengthened calls for discipline. West told Boy Scout executives, "We are part of an organization, or a large machine. . . ." And the BSA's president, Colin Livingstone, warned in 1920 that public argument weakened the movement.[64]

These admonitions had some force by then, for in 1916 the BSA finally won a Congressional charter. Although its sponsors assured a Texas con-gressman that the corporation would not be national, the charter was quite broad, giving the BSA exclusive rights not only to its emblems and badges but to all "words or phrases now or heretofore used by the Boy Scouts of America. . . ."[65] Congress also banned civilians from wearing uniforms which resembled those of the armed forces, while exempting the BSA.[66] Federal legislation thus made the BSA a national institution of a sort and provided the legal basis for its monopoly of Boy Scouting.

West promptly took legal action against the United States Boy Scouts (the old Hearst group with a new name). Under pressure, the USBS reorganized in 1918 as the American Cadets. Its control fell to men more interested in 100-percent Americanism than in boys' work, and the Cadets followed the crest of postwar nativism into oblivion.[67]

With groups seeking to run Boy Scouting semi-independently, West was equally unbending. Though he styled the BSA a "movement" rather than an organization, he forbade any independent superstructure above the troop level. To ethnic groups wanting their own organizations, the most he would concede was appointment of volunteer commissioners to work up interest; the troops still had to come under local council control.[68] Even E. M. Robinson met refusal. As relations with the BSA worsened and YMCA troops lapsed, Robinson proposed in 1918 a YMCA branch to be called Red Triangle Scouts. West replied flatly that special insignia were illegal. As a result, Y men grumbled that the BSA used its charter to club rivals.[69]

West's intransigence reflected a desire to protect not only the BSA's power but also its standards. He differed sharply from Baden-Powell, who hoped to keep slower boys interested by rewarding effort as well as proficiency. Such an idea, though reasonable to an old Charterhouse boy who had himself been a poor student, made little sense to an American whose schools used tests to grade masses of children. West believed Boy Scouting would forfeit respect unless its awards represented a single standard; his comparison was a Harvard diploma.[70] Though he criticized hidebound schooling, he coveted the recognized status of school credentials.

Actually, pressure to uphold standards came from many sources. The boys' propensity to cut corners stiffened resistance by the committee on badges and awards. After 1914, for instance, Eagle Scout candidates could choose only ten of twenty-one badges; the rest were prescribed. Scoutmasters kept asking that one of their boys be exempt from some test, most commonly swimming. After the first years, the committee always refused, even if this meant disqualifying handicapped boys.[71] The committee's outdoorsmen, notably Beard and his friend Frederick K. Vreeland, disliked West's administrative "mechanism" and hoped by high standards to strike at "swivel-chair woodcraft."[72] Yet unchecked demands for virtuosity would have hobbled the BSA, limiting badges to a tiny elite.

West's own commitment was not so much to high standards as to uniform ones; personally insecure and obsessed with detail, he needed fixed standards. He tried to do all the long-range planning in one burst early in his tenure and then, like many executives, immersed himself in administration, resisting major product innovation as zealously as Henry Ford. When Baden-Powell instituted separate programs for younger boys and those past fifteen or sixteen, West resisted, citing the BSA's mission to "the adolescent boy between the ages of 12 and 18."[73] West regarded the handbooks as a contract with the public that the BSA would do nothing unexpected; the definiteness and fixity of the program contributed largely to its popularity.[74]

Ironically, administrative rigidity eventually went beyond West's wishes. In 1922, when he urged exemptions for handicapped boys, local executives gave a mixed reaction; they also resisted proposals that second class Scouts be permitted to earn a few merit badges, arguing that the present first-class-only rule was hard enough to administer without making exceptions.[75] The BSA's administrative system built in conservatism, for men who had to enforce standard requirements wanted them kept simple and stable.

With the Congressional charter, the BSA entered a new phase. Its 1917 report said that emphasis thus far had been on the program's soundness; now it was time to expand numerically.[76] This distinction between standardization and expansion proved false, since growth soon slowed; but it conveyed the organization's basic strategy: fix the product's quality, secure a monopoly, and sell the idea nationwide. After time out in 1917–1918 for war work, Boy Scout officials turned to the task of improving distribution and firming up controls at the local level.

Boy Scouting had grown unevenly, lagging in the South, where poverty, fundamentalism, and racial discrimination made stony soil, and in the far West, which lay beyond easy eastern influence. Though headquarters wanted better field service, commercially oriented departments and war work had taken precedence.

The executive board finally took action in 1919, naming Dr. George J. Fisher Deputy Chief Scout Executive and Director of Field Work.[77] Fisher, then head of the YMCA's physical department, was familiar with the Y's county extension program and wanted to bridge the gap between BSA headquarters and the troops; unlike other head office employees, he had influence with the board.

Fisher divided the U.S. into twelve districts. Each had a committee of local Boy Scout officials, but the committees' duties were advisory and promotional, "not administrative or legislative. . . ."[78] Their main task was to collect payments from local councils to finance the field service. Field executives appointed by the national office did the real work; acting under Fisher's instructions, they had only to "consult" with the regional committees and "as far as possible be guided by their advice."[79] Thus the BSA avoided the YMCA's independent state committees and extended the central bureaucracy down to the regional level. West was reluctant to see changes, but except for the interposition of Fisher, administration still ran along the "single track" that led to his desk.[80]

The field executives' first duty was to set up local councils with paid executives — the panacea for substandard Scouting. Fisher flirted with the impractical idea of having a council in every city or county with 20,000 or more people, but a new plan in 1921 permitted councils to cross county lines, blanketing the country with 1,157 councils, of which 742 were yet to be organized. The percentage of troops under council rose from 49 in 1919 to 83 in 1925. In addition, BSA headquarters had been pressuring existing councils since 1917 to hire a paid executive. By 1921, such councils already constituted 70 percent of the total.[81]

The new organizing drive culminated the BSA's emancipation from its YMCA matrix and exacerbated strains which had accumulated over the years since West took over. As soon as the first councils moved out of YMCA buildings, some secretaries bitterly resolved to "make themselves inconspicuous" in the Boy Scout movement.[82] Yet as late as 1915, ten of the BSA's thirty-five volunteer Special Field Commissioners were Y men. Relations grew tense between West and Robinson — who disliked the BSA's militant patriotism, organizational exclusiveness, and rapid growth. Then Fisher's appointment capped a series of transfers that sapped YMCA boys' work. Five of the six district heads of BSA field work in 1918 had YMCA backgrounds, and Fisher estimated in 1920 that a quarter of all Boy Scout executives were former YMCA workers.[83] Association men complained of colleagues who built up Boy Scouting in their town and then shifted allegiance, often at high pay; others who had promoted the movement resented being pushed aside by a Boy Scout executive. Though relations generally remained courteous, the two agencies vied for boys and financial backers, especially in small towns and in the West and South where the BSA was expanding. Boy Scout executives competed aggressively, and an occasional Y man blocked formation of a Boy Scout council by organizing his own standard program or using local influence.[84]

The Boy Scout executive's job was much more promotional and administrative than that of a YMCA boys' secretary. The local executive was the key to the whole BSA system of standardization, for he supervised the local council and especially the Scoutmasters. He also ran the council camp and did promotional work, raising funds, securing press coverage, and cultivating community and church leaders. Although some men yearned for more than administration and led a troop on the side, their basic job was not to lead boys; *Scouting* magazine warned against turning the council headquarters into a "hang-out" for Scouts. Certainly the public saw Boy Scout executives as organizers.[85] Like school administrators or YMCA general secretaries, these executives worked mainly with men and hence enjoyed somewhat higher prestige than most teachers or boys' workers — one reason why so many Y men switched.

Increasingly, though, new executives entered Boy Scout work from jobs in business rather than education or boys' work. Recruits described in *Scouting* from mid-1915 through 1917 were 25 percent Y workers, 22 percent schoolmen, 13 percent from social services or playground work, 10 percent businessmen, 5 percent clergy or church workers, 9 percent other professionals, 3 percent just out of college, and 13 percent from unspecified backgrounds. A 1924 study of 193 current Boy Scout executives found a marked shift, as 60 percent now came from business, 18 percent from the YMCA, 11 percent from other forms of boys' work, 9 percent from teaching, and 3 percent from the clergy.[86]

This shift reflected the BSA's growing ability to go it alone through internal recruitment. Typically, businessmen entered the movement as volunteers, became enthusiasts, and went on to paid Boy Scout work; in later years, volunteer experience became mandatory.[87] This pattern weakened any lingering commitment to a common boys' work profession, since internal recruitment selected for an interest specifically in Boy Scouting rather than broader social or professional concerns. YMCA converts and former church workers lauded the religious opportunities in the Boy Scout movement; but executives generally prided themselves on a hard-headed, businesslike approach and sometimes contrasted the BSA's efficiency to the haphazard methods of clergymen and others they considered sentimentalists.[88] To be businesslike, they believed, was to be manly. But this bravado was laced with anxiety, for young recruits worried about their ability to impress older, wealthier businessmen: would they dare approach "hard boiled eggs"?[89] Accordingly, training conferences devoted long sessions to salesmanship and record-keeping intended to impress businessmen with one's efficiency.[90]

Boy Scout officials eventually decided they must standardize the executives' training. In 1916, the BSA began to hold training conferences, often with West present to lay down the law; if there was no set policy, he told the men to "work along until we do standardize and make available to you, a program that is to be followed."[91] As his words indicated, the trainees learned rules and procedures. They also picked up psychological terms intended, one executive explained, to impress educated businessmen. Starting in 1925, headquarters put all new executives through a set program which took four weeks to cover basic educational ideas, administrative routine, and the training of Scoutmasters.[92]

Like other boys' workers, Scout executives were promoters; but unlike others, they were links in a bureaucracy. As Lynn Marshall has observed, "American 'bureaucracy' differed from [Max] Weber's ideal . . . for Weber emphasized professionalization and life tenure in officeholders," whereas in the American version, which Marshall traces back to the Jacksonian era, "men were fitted to [the] system," and large organizations were staffed with "mobile interchangeable operatives." Other writers have elaborated the distinction between "bureaucratic discipline" and "professional expertness."[93] Thus Boy Scout officials took their cues from BSA regulations rather than the norms of a broader boys' work profession. Hence some of the lone wolf impression they made upon outside boys' workers. Hence also their limited training, centered on BSA procedures; YMCA men were much more likely to have specialized academic training.[94] The BSA valued knowledge of boyhood, but program design centered at headquarters.

In developing district and local offices, Boy Scout officials tended, like nineteenth-century educators, "to favor simple military or industrial models in which uniformity of output took precedence over functional differentiation."[95] Outside the national office, Boy Scout executives all did much the same tasks; few could specialize. Since the BSA was so much smaller than the public school system, Boy Scout officials inevitably lagged behind educators in introducing more modern forms of bureaucracy with "greater specialization of function within the hierarchy. . . ."[96] In the BSA, uniformity and centralization went together.

With its staff of interchangeable executives, the BSA extended central authority to the local level more effectively than most national associations, relatively few of which had employees in local units. Though paid by the local council, Boy Scout executives were agents of the national BSA whose careers, promotions, and eventually pensions came from the larger organization.[97]

No amateur could speak with such authority as an agent of the national body. West told a training session: "We are paid executives not legislators, but it is our power and responsibility . . . to keep those who are working with us as legislators, guided properly. . . ."[98] Indeed, the executive determined in large measure who served on the local council. By the 1920s, this practice was common among philanthropies. Often board members had value only "as names with financial or social weight. Frequently executives seemed to feel that the non-interference of a board was an asset. . . ."[99] W. J. B. Housman, who took over Boy Scouting in Newark in 1916, simply dismissed a council he disliked. In another extreme instance, the council president in Toledo, Ohio, resigned when a "bigger" man came along; the new man owned a car and drove the executive to meetings.[100]

Executives displaced the volunteer Scout Commissioners. As transient employees, executives enforced directives better than amateurs with local roots, who sometimes misunderstood, ran short of time, or turned contrary-

minded. Commissioner Thompson of St. Louis proved especially troublesome. Though enthusiastic, he seldom answered letters and sometimes mis-
represented Boy Scout policies; he embroiled the BSA with the musicians'
union and offended West by smoking in public.[101] In rejecting the British
model of administration by local gentlemen, the BSA took a large step
towards centralization. Once paid executives became common, the average commissioner either turned professional or found himself, like Seton,
with drastically curtailed duties. His personal standing could be helpful,
and he might head the local Court of Honor to pass boys on their badges,
but his powers were limited; in many cities the post turned purely
honorary.[102]

Scoutmasters were less easily controlled. Early on, some even challenged
local councils on the grounds that they, not the council, did the actual
work.[103] Fisher warned executives that Scoutmasters might criticize them
and try to take away their leadership. Although a good many executives
held Scoutmasters' round tables, they often mistrusted such gatherings,
fearing the men would usurp the local council's power.[104] Presumably the
council accepted guidance better.

Outside the cities, Scoutmasters accustomed to freedom did not necessarily want a local council. The impetus to form one frequently came from
the BSA's field service rather than community sources, and organization
sometimes proceeded without much local consultation. Most community
leaders liked Boy Scouting, but a small 1923 survey found less criticism
where there was no local council; respondents complained of BSA financial campaigns and pressure to follow inflexible rules.[105]

An executive could arrogate too much power, but the presumption at
headquarters was in his favor. Since the BSA needed churches and other
institutions to furnish meeting places and sometimes recruit Scoutmasters,
it had to accord these troop sponsors, in West's careful words, "a certain
degree of independence." Hence he rebuked an executive who forced a
church troop to take in outside boys.[106] When an executive asked bluntly
which was supreme, however, the troop committee or the local council,
West refused to state categorically that a council was bound by any decision of a troop committee. Executives who felt a troop was run wrongly
did not hesitate to remove it from its sponsoring institution. There was
no dissent when Hutchinson of Denver urged his colleagues to be independent and not to beg.[107]

Supervision did strengthen adherence to standards, but executives fought
a hard battle and were unsure how far to press their demands. Some emu-
lated school superintendents, while others favored a looser rein with volunteers. Some executives imposed examinations with printed questions for
boys seeking promotion; others settled for informal quizzing. Some demanded strict accounting of all troop activities, others only general re-

ports. Efficiency contests among the troops were common. Yet 75 percent compliance with his directives made an executive an instant authority in the eyes of his peers on the subject of managing Scoutmasters. In desperation, some executives tried to circumvent the Scoutmasters by requiring reports directly from the patrol leaders and troop scribes.[108] Amid the constant pressure to form new troops, raise funds, and replace the many Scoutmasters who quit each year, executives had trouble keeping the remaining men in line. So strong were the pressures to be a promoter that one canny executive decided he could get better statistical results by ignoring existing troops altogether and putting all his effort into forming new ones. West could only urge him to divide his time.[109]

Zealous Scoutmasters sometimes adopted the bureaucratic style themselves, but they were exceptional; standardization often broke down at the Scoutmasters' level, particularly among novices who signed up expecting an instantly successful program. Boy Scout publications, averring that anyone could learn as he went along or find experts to help, lured men beyond their depth, especially before there was a handbook for Scoutmasters. Having confused imposition of standards with the provision of guidance, BSA officials were surprised and irritated when Scoutmasters pestered them for advice. "We need practical men," grumbled Moffat. "If we had these instead of such a great proportion of the goody-goody kind, there would not be such a great demand for a Scout Master's Manual."[110] Once the manual was published, it seemed even truer that anyone could lead a troop. After all, Sunday school teachers and ill-trained instructors in the public schools managed with little more. Just as school examinations tested knowledge of the textbook and instruction focused on preparing for the exams, so in Boy Scouting the handbooks prescribed the program, and advancement through that program became the measure of success. Scoutmasters were vulnerable to distraction, however, as fear that boys might quit led them to expedients that departed from the standard program.[111]

Like Moffat, many local executives had trouble grasping just how basic Scoutmasters' problems were. Certain requirements such as first aid were especially daunting. "Many good scoutmasters have avoided the subject," observed the editor of *Scouting,* "until their troops were at the point where second class first aid looked like an impassable wall."[112] Basic training had to be paramount as long as the BSA was committed to rapid growth. Lorne Barclay advised executives to leave theory to headquarters; the Scoutmasters' school he ran while executive for New York City "was nothing more or less than a troop of scouts" where the men learned signaling, knot tying, and camp cooking. "They made hunter's stew so that they could do the thing with their own hands. . . ."[113] Even so, it was hard to get men to evening meetings; attendance ran 65 percent. Many executives were better promoters than educators, for in 1919 only 56 percent of all local councils reported courses for Scoutmasters. Of forty-two courses reported in detail, about half went into boys' work theory. Almost all discussed the ideals of Scouting and the tenderfoot requirements; most then dealt selectively with subjects such as first aid and signaling that gave Scoutmasters trouble. By the 1920s, headquarters insisted even more upon standardized, practical courses; still, many remained quite theoretical, and it was hard to get men to attend.[114]

Widespread employment of local executives somewhat improved the BSA's stability. In 1925, 57 percent of Boy Scouts outside council areas quit or saw their troop collapse, compared to 42 percent under council supervision.[115] If this success seems modest, we should imagine the schools' attrition rates if schooling had been wholly voluntary and had counted little towards getting a job.

The BSA did not simply standardize and then expand; it did both together. Thus Mark M. Jones, a hired consultant, could criticize it simultaneously for an essentially promotional approach and for inflexibility. His report, submitted in 1927, praised the BSA's guidance of adolescents but urged more scientific self-examination, since Boy Scouting was so popular that it spread on sentiment alone. Jones also criticized top Boy Scout leaders for putting too many matters beyond compromise and basing policy on personal preference; he felt that West still did too much. Scoutmasters required help adjusting to local conditions, Jones believed, and boys needed a more varied and individualized program.[116]

Baden-Powell had designed a standard program, but the BSA took uniformity and centralization still further. The English Boy Scout organization incorporated aspects of the squirearchy, whereas the BSA imitated business and mass education. Baden-Powell relied on Britain's established social order; and as a national hero, he had reserves of authority that freed him to innovate. By contrast, West owed his power to the administrative apparatus; he was personally stubborn, and as an American he had more faith in formal organization than social order. Because other institutions sponsored troops, Boy Scouting called itself a movement. For that reason, however, West felt impelled to guard its authority all the more fiercely, until the BSA became more jealous of its prerogatives than the more self-sufficient YMCA. Whatever the cost in richness of texture, though, West's approach aided expansion, for by 1920 the BSA had already outgrown YMCA boys' work.

The history of boys' work casts light from an unusual angle upon the processes of institutional change in the Progressive Era, for character-building agencies were popular innovations whose success confirms criticisms of the best-known synthesis of Progressive Era institutional developments. This historiographical approach, espoused by Robert Wiebe and Samuel P. Hays among others, stresses the emergence of a "new organizational society."[117] Hays summarizes the process as involving the growth of "technical systems" and the spread of "functional relationships." Technical systems, he claims, "mobilize vast resources . . . to conduct focused empirical inquiry; and plan long-range strategies" for social change. Functional relations develop with the formation of economic and professional associations and the sharing of knowledge among specialists, who strive "to influence the surrounding environment through technical expertise."[118] With less theoretical pretension, various historians have also noted the rapid consolidation of large corporations around 1900. Hays and other historians have traced the application of the corporate model in the ambitions of Progesssive Era municipal and school reformers: elite groups tried to impose centralized control, vest it in a small board of directors, and delegate administration to hired experts, usually headed by a powerful manager or superintendent.[119]

In many respects, the rise of character-building agencies offers yet another example of these processes at work. YMCA boys' secretaries developed professional ambitions that set them apart from boys' club workers. Nationally, the BSA adopted the corporate model in reaction against YMCA decentralization. Locally as well as nationally, the BSA assembled boards of prosperous, well-placed directors and turned management over to a paid executive. Salaried character builders might thus appear to have been representative members of what Wiebe calls "the new middle class," heady with "consciousness of unique skills and functions," and eager to "fulfill [their] destiny through bureaucratic means."[120] But problems arise if we try to apply Hays and Wiebe's ideas too precisely, for theirs is a highly idealized model of change based upon the most advanced bureaucratic and professional ideologies of the Progressive Era.

Certainly the level of expertise among character builders was modest, and they were too preoccupied with immediate problems to "mobilize vast resources" for "focused empirical inquiry." Borrowed psychology helped character builders gain self-confidence and impress outsiders, yet it often masked old-fashioned moralism, which was still an effective basis for institutional authority. To be sure, the early development of the BSA matched the turn from moralism towards efficiency which observers have noted in Progressive Era ideology around 1910 to 1912.[121] But it did not bring full-blown technocracy, for standardization narrowed curiosity, and the rush of expansion kept Boy Scout leaders too busy to study their social environment. In 1924, H. W. Hurt chided Boy Scout officials and the service clubs which backed them for plunging ahead and organizing local councils in most cases without even a community survey.[122] Boy Scout leaders simply took the program, staked their claim to a bonanza, and mined it. Real technocratic expertise—as opposed to the appearance—may, in short, have been less central to Progressive Era institutional innovations than Hays believes.

Furthermore, as a recent critic of Wiebe's ideas has noted, professionalization and bureaucracy commonly conflicted, since professionals chafed at controls.[123] In boys' work, the two forms of organization functioned as alternatives, with YMCA boys' secretaries trying to professionalize and Boy Scout executives becoming administrators and promoters. At best, one could argue that both groups were professionals but that Boy Scout executives resembled engineers in their weak professional ethos and overriding loyalty to the organization, whereas Y boys' workers resembled teachers and social workers, for whom service to clients took precedence over technical efficiency and organizational fealty.[124] Far from leading to the cooperation based on functional similarity which Wiebe sees as typical of the new middle class, bureaucratization reduced cooperation across agency lines. Wiebe overlooks these difficulties because he regards Progressive Era bureaucratization as having a professional ethos. But the BSA's standardization bore little resemblance to the constant, expert readjustment which Progressive ideologues thought would characterize bureaucracy at its best.[125] Yet the BSA, though relatively nonprofessional, competed so well with YMCA boys' work that a good many boys' secretaries became Boy Scout executives. Contrary to common belief, these facts suggest that professionalization was and is no certain path to vocational advancement and indeed may have surpassed other modes only in a few spectacularly successful cases such as medicine. The social landscape of the twentieth century is littered with stillborn professions, while others have gained only a dwarfish maturity, stunted by meagre pay and status. The example of boys' work suggests that market-oriented bureaucracies like the BSA have done better at claiming social space and rewarding their functionaries.

Boy Scouting's success in outstripping Y boys' work was more than just a triumph of bureaucracy over professionalism, however; it also depended upon extensive use of volunteers. Rank amateurism was doomed to fail, as the Boys' Brigades demonstrated; but a carefully controlled form of voluntarism was essential for mass character building. To win support from community leaders, boys' workers gave formal authority to boards of laymen; and to lead the boys, they recruited volunteers. More than simple necessity was involved, for Americans believed in the moral superiority of unpaid service and the practical superiority of businessmen. How then to avoid rivalries? The Boy Scout answer was simple: draw a line across the bureaucratic hierarchy. Above it, Boy Scout executives were not to lead boys in person; below it, Scoutmasters were not to share administrative authority. As Roy Lubove has noted, voluntarism, "traditionally viewed as a duty of the citizen in a democratic society, . . . was becoming instead a privilege granted by philanthropic agencies to those who accepted their discipline."[126] Some Scoutmasters resented their powerlessness, and reliance on volunteers weakened enforcement of standards; still, the division worked fairly smoothly. No such simple solution was open to the YMCA, since boys' secretaries, like many marginal professionals, stressed the service component of their work and often regarded volunteers as competitors, thereby restricting YMCA expansion. Similar problems must have been common in the Progressive Era. By switching to paid probation officers, for example, juvenile court authorities virtually guaranteed that these officials would be spread too thin to be effective.[127] The conclusion is obvious: in an era when social expenditures, public and private, were limited, professionalization was no panacea. Voluntarism, though slighted by historians, represented a vital alternative without which no agency could give large numbers of people close personal attention.

Further complicating any simple view of bureaucracy and professionalization as the master keys to Progressive Era social changes — including success in boys' work — was the overriding need for social innovations to find a market. Indeed, boys' clubs thrived without much professional ethos or centralized bureaucracy because fear of lower-class rowdies guaranteed them financial backing. Once committed to serving adolescents, the YMCA and Boy Scouts had to attract and hold teenagers — who became increasingly demanding customers, unwilling to settle for an hour's drill or scraps of ritual. The resulting pressures condemned YMCA boys' secretaries to harried lives, whereas Boy Scout executives could concentrate upon promoting a single saleable program. Since boys did not pay the full cost of it, however, there was a second market for boys' work: character builders also had to win adults to pay the bills and help lead the boys. When we examine the character builders' publicity efforts, their religious and political ideologies, and their choice of constituencies, we will see much that had little to do with attracting boys but had everything to do with winning adult backers.

IV

Winning Public Favor
and Building a Constituency

10

Boyhood, God, and Country: Creation and Defense of a Public Image

A nascent profession or a new bureaucracy has to find markets for its services; and as other chapters describe, American character builders assiduously courted particular constituencies. Yet to tap a mass market, the Boy Scouts in particular needed a corporate image which looked more or less the same to all audiences—not too confining but specific enough to set the BSA apart. A reasonably sophisticated rationale for boys' work methodology, such as Hall's ideas provided, was vital to win supporters who were already interested in youth. Mass recruitment, however, demanded a public image which tied boys' work to basic middle-class American concerns and values. Outdoor activities figured prominently in publicity, since they attracted men and boys alike. Still, an appealing program was not enough; character builders believed their goals must sound more serious than fun and friendship. Their work must claim to serve values closer to the central trends of American ideology. Indeed, lofty aspirations would make up for shortcomings in actual performance.

Judging by their high turnover rates, boys were more likely than adults to detect such shortcomings. But they were not the primary targets of boys' work publicity. While Boy Scouting's uniform, its publications, and its reputation for outdoor adventure all attracted them, boys had little interest in the movement's abstract pieties; most joined because their friends did. Accordingly, it seemed to American character builders that the key to expansion was simply to have enough established groups for boys to join; in keeping with their preference for adult initiative, character builders assumed that boys would flock to accept adult direction once they had the opportunity. Hence boys' work publicity concentrated upon impressing adults, to whom character builders looked for volunteer leaders, institutional sponsors, and above all money.

YMCA and Boy Scout publicity techniques differed markedly, however. Because YMCAs sponsored many activities besides boys' work and because local programs varied, YMCA boys' work never received centralized, systematic promotion. The YMCA promoted a few highly publicized programs nationwide, notably its popular Father and Son Day, but basically each local Association was its own advertisement. Localized publicity worked fairly well; a 1923 survey found that respondents praised the YMCA's camps and conferences, instruction in Bible knowledge and social service, and promotion of clean sports and recreation. In addition, they praised Association direction of the gang spirit and lauded the father and son dinners.[1] Boys' secretaries in large cities complained, however, that the boys' branch carried the other departments, winning approval and donations without a commensurate share of the budget.[2] Boys' workers could not capitalize fully on the popularity of their specialty, since the general secretary handled community relations for the Association as a whole.

Boy Scout leaders had an easier task, since they could project a single, sharply focused image of Boy Scouting nationwide. In fact, at the national level the story of boys' work publicity is mainly the story of the Boy Scouts; for the BSA used extensive self-advertisement to transform itself almost instantly from an innovation into an established institution. In 1911, headquarters hired a newsman, John Price Jones, who sent ready-made articles to religious periodicals and newspapers across the country, although the Boy Scout movement already received reams of favorable news coverage. West also won endorsements of Boy Scouting from national figures, church bodies, and the National Education Association. In lieu of actual investigation, these commendations could be brandished as proof of Scouting's value to boys.[3]

The best local publicity involved keeping the boys visibly active, thereby demonstrating that boys' work built masculinity and kept adolescents safely occupied; as presented for public admiration, the boys were to appear bustling and energetic, not passive or effeminate. Since YMCA activities centered around the gymnasium and pool, the Y easily identified its programs with the strenuous life of the Christian athlete; the lad in gym shorts was safely occupied. Boy Scout executives set about creating a similar impression a good deal more deliberately. They saw to it that local papers carried regular reports of Boy Scout activities, particularly hikes and camps.[4] They staged rallies where Scouts displayed skills to please the proud parents; the boys lit fires, waved signal flags, and swathed victims like mummies in the elaborate bandages then in vogue. A field meet in Hartford, Connecticut, drew two thousand Boy Scouts and three thousand spectators. According to *Scouting*, "the schedule was followed with precision, which convinced everybody of the efficiency of the organization." Certainly the purpose of all this was not to interest boys but rather to impress adults — so much so that the editor of *Scouting* suggested sympathetically that someone should have warned the Scouts, "Boys, this is an ordeal, like getting married. . . ."[5]

In any case, the boys may have dreamed of adventures no boys' worker could deliver, for a flood of cheap "Boy Scout" books exploited the movement's aura of romance. Did boys find the real thing tame after vicarious struggles with villainous prospectors or raging forest fires in these novels? Even Tom Slade, the in-house hero of the BSA's own books, went "on the rampage" in stories of World War I.[6] More typical of what the BSA approved, however, was a much more restrained series, "Under Boy Scout Colors," which ran in *St. Nicholas* during 1917. In the course of a camping trip, the Scouts were shown performing feats such as giving first aid to motorists whose car had overturned.[7]

At first, headquarters made much of Boy Scout heroism in real life. The National Court of Honor decorated Scouts who plunged into water, fire, or the path of runaway horses. Increasingly, though, accounts of Boy Scouting for adult consumption played down the incidence of unplanned adventure, lest parents take fright. S. A. Moffat warned that one drowning could spoil a year's work in the public mind.[8] Accordingly, the emphasis shifted from spontaneity towards careful control.

As the BSA turned to bureaucratic standardization, its adult-oriented publicity stressed steady advancement rather than sudden heroics, making the Boy Scout program itself the object of admiration and promising the kind of solid, progressive achievement that educators and parents wanted from schoolboys. Writing in the *Review of Reviews,* a supporter suggested that Boy Scouting stirred the same competitive zeal as sports but was "constructive" instead of just "piling up a score. . . ."[9] It was, in short, a worthy surrogate for work.

More than other activities, service projects laid claim to public support while affirming the boys' middle-class status. Herbert Hoover, his generation's leading technocrat, looked to organized, voluntary service as the American way of progress—a safe alternative to fundamental social change.[10] Echoing the public spirit of the old gentry class, voluntary service was becoming central to middle-class self-affirmation, whether codified in professional ethics, advertised by business firms, or ritualized in Rotary and Kiwanis. To bestow service, rather than receive it, was to assert one's personal respectability. Hence BSA officials strenuously resisted any implication that participation in community chest drives marked their movement as a charity, for Boy Scouts *gave* service.[11]

One of the YMCA's weaknesses was its failure to enlist boys for such displays. Y juniors led gymnasium or Bible classes, but because the Associations did not use boys for conspicuous public campaigns, people did not call upon them for ushering or handbill distribution the way they did the Boy Scouts.

Y boys' workers did more themselves. In campaigning for such things as juvenile courts and playgrounds, they espoused a cautious brand of Progressive reformism — one that remained deeply rooted in Protestant moralism. In little Cheney, Kansas, for instance, the coming of a YMCA purportedly transformed the town. "Now, in 1912 sentiment against tobacco, profanity and loafing is so strong in Cheney that these vices are greatly diminished even among the older people," reported a YMCA official, "and it is said there has not been a dance in the town for three years."[12] In keeping with chamber of commerce Progressivism, the final proofs of Cheney's reformation were a new town hall and cement sidewalks. This was the Progressivism of the reforming mayor and the prohibitionist, lacking the nationalism which contributed so much to Scouting's popularity.

Boy Scout executives shared the YMCA's service-oriented concept of good citizenship but shied away from personal involvement in social action; instead, they stressed that Scouting trained boys for public service. This claim was somewhat forced, since Baden-Powell's program was most directly suited to training military scouts. Even during World War I, skills such as first aid and signaling were of limited utility on the home front.[13] But Boy Scout leaders could claim that Scouting developed boys' faculties and readied them to act; and nobody noticed that Boy Scout service projects made little use of Scout training.

Group service magnified the Boy Scouts' daily good turn and impressed it firmly upon the public's attention. Most troop projects were fairly prosaic; Boy Scouts took gift baskets to the poor or ushered at church and school gatherings. But other group undertakings enabled Boy Scouts to show especial ingenuity and alertness. For example, a troop in Middletown, Ohio, mined a winter's coal for a widow. In another town, when a thunderstorm came up while an audience was at the Chautauqua, Boy Scouts turned up all the seats in the open cars parked outside; the owners rode home dry, and the local paper took note.[14] In addition, a few good turns won nationwide attention, notably the Boy Scouts' labors during Ohio Valley floods in 1913 and their efforts to protect suffragettes from the mob who attacked them as they marched down Pennsylvania Avenue before Wilson's inauguration.[15]

When numbers were vital, a Boy Scout council could summon throngs of boys to hunt for missing children or march in parades. Headquarters officials preferred that the Scouts direct traffic or hold back crowds along the way, but the boys commonly marched themselves. In either case, these spectacles had little to do with regular Boy Scouting, since executives commonly bypassed the troops and mobilized only "the neatest appearing Scouts" under their own leadership.[16]

Perhaps as a result, public service became an intermittent ritual; by one calculation, service projects averaged six hours a year per troop in 1928. Yet Boy Scout leaders had reason to fear resistance from parents or boys if they demanded more.[17] During World War I, BSA bond drives which called upon the Scouts to push hard for a week or so were fairly successful, whereas a scheme to have Boy Scouts raise gardens — which required them to grub along for an entire season — failed because the boys got bored.[18] Besides, Boy Scout leaders shared the Progressive Era weakness for brief crusades in which everyone pledged good intentions; as distant descendants of evangelical revivals, such campaigns sought moral satisfaction for the participants more than practical results. Boy Scouts in Pittsburgh, for example, signaled the date of fire prevention day from the city's tallest building by wigwag, semaphore, and heliography, then distributed 100,000 safety first cards. In Minneapolis in 1920, Boy Scouts directed city traffic for fifteen minutes as part of a campaign for auto safety.[19]

Results did not matter greatly, since Boy Scout officials valued service projects primarily for their effect on the boys and on public opinion. Through Boy Scouting, future business and professional men had their first introduction to the formalized service activities of Rotary and Kiwanis. They joined a long line of clubs in displaying middle-class paternalism by giving Christmas baskets to the poor. And the class symbolism was clear when Boy Scouts took their cleanup campaigns to immigrant neighborhoods. A photographer captured a couple of dozen adults and children who had gathered to watch while two Boy Scouts, stiffly uniformed, swept up a tiny pile of trash. A third Scout held back the crowd with outstretched arms, but the little throng showed no disposition to surge forward; they stared blankly — not at the Scouts but at the camera.[20]

As the service projects indicated, Boy Scout officials were desperate to insure that their program be taken seriously. In particular, the national leadership wanted to impress upon the public that Boy Scouting's outdoor activities served serious purposes. "This program," West claimed, "holds the interest of the boy and makes possible the accomplishment of the real objective of scouting, which is character development and training for citizenship."[21]

Following the same strategy as in their organizational decisions, West and his colleagues tried to standardize the public's understanding of their goals. The revision committee made the American oath and law much more comprehensive than the British; then West sent copies to presidents of major universities, ostensibly for comment but actually too late for anything except praise. Over the years, BSA publicity reiterated that Boy Scouts pledged themselves to be trustworthy, loyal, helpful, and so forth, until Franklin Roosevelt could quote the Boy Scout law in a radio talk without even bothering to explain his reference.[22]

On sensitive issues such as religion, social equality, and militarism, the BSA followed a similar practice, reducing policies to formulas which reappeared year after year in reports and speeches. Wanting everyone to like the BSA, West sent copies of these policies to opponents of the movement such as Eugene V. Debs, who was sufficiently impressed to suggest that socialists reconsider their condemnation of Boy Scouting.[23]

The twelfth Boy Scout law illustrated the care that went into these statements. Lest the BSA give offense, West put it on record as resolutely favorable towards God but noncommittal on specifics: "A scout is reverent. He is reverent toward God. He is faithful in his religious duties and respects the convictions of others in matters of custom and religion." A rare critic, William Byron Forbush, complained that this could mean "everything or nothing."[24] Even so, it said more than West had planned; revisions were nearly complete before William D. Murray persuaded him to add the words, "is faithful in his religious duties." Headquarters coupled the law with a disavowal of responsibility: it was up to the "institution with which the boy scout is connected [to] give definite attention to his religious life." The BSA also promised that no troop would require boys of another denomination to attend services "distinctively peculiar" to the host church. A superbly balanced statement of the American way towards God, the twelfth law was, West believed, responsible for much of the BSA's success.[25]

An occasional believer suspected indifferentism, including Colin Livingstone, who complained of "the desire to soft-pedal the religious question in Scouting. . . ."[26] When faced with such criticism, West pointed to the BSA's constitution, which prescribed that only men who subscribed to the BSA's religious policy could be Scoutmasters. Few Americans resisted a mere acknowledgement of God's existence, but headquarters did bar a few hundred conscientious disbelievers over the years.[27]

If Boy Scout leaders as a group had a level of ultimate concern, it was Americanism rather than religious faith, for Protestants had long identified their values with Americanism, and the priorities were easily reversed. The BSA's official position was explicit about those priorities: "The recognition of God as the ruling and leading power in the universe . . . is necessary to the best type of citizenship, and is a wholesome thing in the education of the growing boy. No matter what the boy may be—Catholic or Protestant or Jew—this fundamental need of good citizenship should be kept before him."[28] The BSA, in other words, upheld what recent scholars have labeled a "civil religion"—not as a prophetic faith standing in judgment upon actual American practices but as a celebration of the American way of life, in which a decent measure of religiosity plays an important but subordinate role. The power of Americanism to submerge rival faiths can be seen by comparison with France, where Catholicism, Protestantism, and secular patriotism were so thoroughly at odds that French Boy Scouting split into three bodies.[29]

The YMCA's religious credentials were much more apparent yet for that reason potentially more troublesome, with Catholics shying away, some Protestant clergymen fearing the Y would trespass on church prerogatives, and others cherishing high expectations of YMCA evangelism which were later disappointed. The YMCA shift from high-pressure evangelism towards moral education and social service caused little trouble in the 1910s, as most ministers still praised the YMCA. Although a few complained the Y lacked spirituality, it took an old-fashioned Calvinist to condemn the Associations' cult of the "strong and efficient moral man."[30] By the 1920s, however, the retreat from evangelism grew too obvious to miss and cost the YMCA support from conservative Protestants.[31] By promising less, the BSA ran fewer risks.

Just as Boy Scouting was open to every creed, so BSA publicity portrayed it as democratically concerned for every kind of boy. Despite the organization's primarily middle-class base, Boy Scout leaders insistently presented Scouting as an answer to juvenile delinquency. The hero of *The Making of a Scout,* a BSA-sponsored movie produced in 1913, was "raised in vicious surroundings. . . ."[32] The Chicago Board of Education endorsed Boy Scouting as a remedy for youthful crime, and that claim was a major argument in the BSA's drive for a Congressional charter.[33] Yet the promise to fight delinquency was a boys' work commonplace with a significant qualification—that Scouting would prevent boys from going bad rather than salvage those who already had. West would not publicize troops in reformatories for fear of offending "the average boy."[34] A cartoon in the annual report for 1916 showed potential recruits smoking and shooting craps; but they were curiously respectable misdemeanants, for each wore a collar and tie. As the respectability of the membership became clear, the interest of child welfare workers waned, and BSA publicity stressed the typical Boy Scout's fine character as evinced by the good turn. Yet forms of publicity which demanded dramatic contrasts, such as movies or cartoons, continued to tell of gang boys transformed.[35]

Boy Scouting gained wide acceptance as the epitome of democracy. Whites who noticed the exclusion of Southern blacks were mostly Southerners who applauded it. All other boys were free to join. They had to join on the BSA's terms; immigrant boys, for instance, took their tests in English, but that was part of the movement's Americanizing function. Like public schoolmen, Boy Scout leaders equated democracy with uniformity —quite literally, since the uniform ostensibly made all Boy Scouts equal. The Committee on Americanization edited all mention of class conflict out of the Boy Scout law in 1911, even deleting Baden-Powell's demand that boys be loyal to their employers, lest that preclude union membership.[36] The BSA's determined nonrecognition of class barriers touched a responsive chord, for many Americans saw in the threat of widening class divisions a portent of social unrest and rents in the seamless web of American nationhood. Like many Progressives, Boy Scout leaders believed that middle-class standards were classless.

Perhaps the BSA's greatest image-building triumph was its appropriation of the symbols of American nationhood. The process began early; Livingstone and West enlisted William Howard Taft as honorary president in 1911, and thenceforth the country's chief executive always held the post.[37]

Above all, the uniform — which closely resembled the army's — identified the Boy Scouts with national service. A full outfit included a flat-brimmed hat with a high crown, khaki shirt and coat, olive drab belt, and shorts or breeches with leggings, puttees, or stockings. Colors varied slightly, and not every boy bought the same items, so early troops paraded in motley drab; however, acquisition of full uniforms soon became a test of commitment.[38] Councils could require them by 1918, and a revised version became mandatory in 1922. The uniform was conspicuous because it was worn for every Boy Scout activity. Even boys out hiking scrambled through the woods in full uniform, for leaders wanted all who met them to know that they were sepoys, not savages; the uniform made it clear that control outweighed free-ranging woodsmanship.[39] Yet there were critics who wondered why Boy Scouts dressed like soldiers. Did citizenship training necessarily imply preparation for military service, they asked. Despite the choice of uniform, that was a conclusion BSA officials did not want to concede. So closely, however, did patriotism, discipline, and military service seem to be related that Boy Scout leaders had trouble keeping them apart.

The BSA was harried on both flanks. The leaders dared not espouse vehement antimilitarism, for they had worked hard to preempt their military rivals' support. Army men regarded Boy Scouting with favor; National Guardsmen often became Scoutmasters; and Theodore Roosevelt had announced that Scouting would "make boys good citizens in time of peace, and incidentally . . . fit them to become good soldiers in time of war. . . ."[40] Yet the BSA could not ignore its other flank, for peace sentiment was eminently respectable before the war, and some churchmen worried that Boy Scouting would be just another cadet corps. Newspapers often portrayed Boy Scouts as juvenile militia, and early Scoutmasters dabbled with drill and rifle practice.[41] The BSA's leaders responded by deleting military references from the handbooks; they courted peace societies successfully enough to mollify the more conservative and secure regular donations from Andrew Carnegie, the most prominent and richest financial supporter of the movement against war.[42]

How, given these conflicting pressures, was the BSA to describe its goals? One formulation simply equated citizenship training with service, presumably civilian, and bypassed the military issue: "The call of the Community is service. This constitutes Patriotism to State and Country. The cry of the adolescent boy is Service. This means that citizenship, in its formation, begins with the twelve-year-old boy."[43] But Boy Scout officials could not duck the issue entirely. Instead, a compromise statement, first formulated in 1913 and widely echoed in local publicity, held that Boy Scouting was not military but taught "the military virtues such as honor, loyalty, obedience, and patriotism." G. Barrett Rich, Boy Scout Commissioner for Buffalo, New York, echoed William James in suggesting that Boy Scouting was "a moral equivalent for war."[44]

The shock of 1914 upset this balance, launching the BSA's leaders on a course towards greater militancy. Their first impulse, however, was one of horror, for they expected cultural and political progress to bring increasing altruism just as individual Boy Scouts grew up to service. *Boys' Life* published a strongly antiwar "War Issue." Cyrus Townsend Brady told boys that a soldier's job was "to kill and destroy . . . just that and nothing else."[45] British and German troops butchered each other in one illustration, while in another a Boy Scout led a female figure labeled "Civilization" toward "peace." Colin Livingstone urged parents to read the issue, and most Boy Scout leaders reacted favorably.[46]

Yet an antiwar position based upon spontaneous outrage could not be sustained, for the BSA was so committed to the stream of Americanism that it had to float with the current. The "War Issue" itself praised cheery German and British Boy Scouts who harvested crops or reported spies, and the back pages carried a Daniel Boone story in which two white men and thirty-seven Indians were slain.

The BSA's organizers had given hostages to fortune when they secured endorsements from Theodore Roosevelt and Leonard Wood, both bellicose advocates of military training for boys. The "War Issue" so enraged Wood that he quit the BSA's National Council. Relations with Roosevelt deteriorated until in late 1915 he charged that the BSA was "part of the wicked and degrading pacifist agitation of the past few years. . . ."[47] His anger was symptomatic of pressures along a broad front, for the war revived interest in cadet training, and by 1918, 15 percent of all high school boys nationwide had military drill.[48] Since full military training for young teenagers did not command wide public support, however, the BSA tried to placate men like Roosevelt and hold the center.

Accordingly, the executive board disavowed antimilitary sentiments in October of 1915: "It should be clearly understood . . . that the Boy Scout movement is not anti-military. The Boy Scout movement neither promotes nor discourages military training, its one concern being the development of character and personal efficiency of adolescent boys."[49] West accepted the major premise of preparedness advocates, arguing only that cadet training did not suit young boys who needed strength and discipline first. Spokesmen played up the physical benefits of boys' work and warned that army men scorned "toy soldiers," preferring recruits who had the outdoor skills that Boy Scout training gave.[50] This argument was tactically effective; the National Education Association praised the Boy Scouts in 1915 for remaining nonmilitary, yet New York State accepted Boy Scouting for partial credit towards cadet training.[51] In defending their program, however, Boy Scout leaders abandoned the principle that training citizens did not mean training future soldiers. Quite the contrary, official reports boasted of Boy Scouting as a force "for preparedness," since it built character and helped boys learn "a citizen's responsibility." In case of war, former Scouts would volunteer "in larger proportion than other boys . . . [and] prove themselves more virile and efficient."[52] By mid-1916, West let troops march in preparedness parades; and long after the war he repeated the same formula: Boy Scouting was "neither military nor anti-military."[53] The corollary was that it could be *pre*military.

It is hardly surprising that Boy Scout leaders compromised their antiwar stand, since most of their contemporaries did so too. Faith in individual good will could not confront the demands made upon citizens by a modern state. Thus two Boy Scout officials described militarism as a belief in "cold, deadly competition between men, in which the clever adversary outwits or outmaneuvers his less unscrupulous or less aggressive opponent. . . ."[54] Obviously, few people could love such a jackbooted ogre. But the massive armies of modern warfare consist less of war lovers than of ordinary citizens, often conscripts, doing what they have been told is their duty. And the BSA's handbooks celebrated American citizen-soldiers who had gone to war reluctantly but surprisingly often.[55]

The national office resisted feebly as more and more Scoutmasters drilled their troops. In 1917, the board forbade "technical military training and drill," but an executive got a laugh when he asked West what "technical military training" meant.[56] West exempted anything common to army and civilian life, including some kinds of drill. The BSA's new manual of drill in fact sold out, and troops celebrated the war with parades on a scale unknown before and unequalled since.[57]

Yet it must be emphasized that basically the BSA's equivocation succeeded. West and his colleagues bent enough to forestall serious rivalry from cadet training, which they believed would stultify the young; yet they prevented Boy Scouting from degenerating into a cadet corps. As public opinion shifted, Boy Scout leaders counterbalanced their opposition to cadet training with increased stress on patriotism and "the proper attitude of mind towards duly constituted authority. . . ." After 1917, Scoutmasters had to be citizens or have declared their intention to become citizens, and non-American boys had to swear allegiance before joining.[58]

With help from Seton, West even mollified Roosevelt without agreeing that boys should start military training at age fifteen. Seton delighted in puncturing Americans' "noxious self-satisfaction" about their past, but he kept quiet in public and angered only a few zealous patriots on the BSA's executive board.[59] His undoing began in 1914 when the board learned that the Chief Scout was still a British subject. The news did little harm, as it appeared in a small newspaper item about his wife, a suffragette who won her cause in Connecticut, only to be denied the vote because of Seton's citizenship. But when Seton delayed becoming an American citizen, the board forced him from office.[60] There the matter might have rested, except that Seton chose the week of a BSA fund drive late in 1915 to issue a statement protesting continued use of his name and accusing West of having destroyed Scouting's imaginative elements. West replied with gusto that Seton "was in harmony with the views of anarchists and radical socialists on the question as to whether the Boy Scouts of America should stand for patriotism and good citizenship. . . ."[61] The board followed with a press release charging that Seton had opposed putting a chapter on patriotism in the handbook. At this point, Roosevelt intervened to call off the dogs, since he disliked West's personal attacks on Seton; but he was pleased by the evidence of the BSA's Americanism and issued a long statement of support.[62] Among the board members, only Robinson—himself Canadian—chided West and suggested that Boy Scouts needed to learn the difference between patriotism and jingoism.[63] But Robinson soon had to resign when the BSA's federal charter required American citizenship. After that, nobody remained to oppose militant Americanism.

When the U.S. went to war, this Americanism grew even more insistent. Boy Scout officials distrusted German-born Scoutmasters and in a few cases expelled men who refused to help the war effort. Some executives encouraged their Scouts to spy on malcontents. Except for Beard, however, the BSA's national leaders avoided hysteria.[64]

The bulk of the war effort was more positive, as Boy Scout officials seized upon the idea of using boys as bond salesmen. The boys had a hard task, since the authorities, fearing the Scouts might undercut the regular canvass, held them back until the last week. As "gleaners after the reapers," Boy Scouts had to tap their parents and others who had subscribed already but might still respond to a boy's importunities.[65] Organizational problems and individual indifference kept many troops from participating; not quite half took part in the third Liberty Loan campaign, and only 7.1 percent of all Boy Scouts sold ten or more bonds.[66] But the national office kept the pressure on, until some Scoutmasters worried that the regular program was being crowded out. And the Boy Scouts' aggregate achievement was substantial; they distributed 20 million government flyers, scoured the woods for black walnut needed for war production, and sold $354,859,262 worth of bonds.[67] The result was a public relations triumph. In 1919, when the BSA mounted a nationwide campaign for funds and members, the wartime Secretary of the Treasury, William Gibbs Mc-Adoo, served as campaign chairman.[68]

All this success left YMCA boys' work in the shade. West, who often clashed with Robinson, told Seton — of all people — that Robinson was an internationalist and the Y was not "committed to a program for good citizenship. . . ."[69] West exaggerated, but it was true that YMCA boys' work never matched the BSA's strident nationalism. In setting priorities, Y boys' secretaries followed the pattern of Association life, which was civic and evangelical before it was national; at the same time they saw themselves as part of a world church movement. They did not ignore the war, for they got boys to promise $2,700,000 for YMCA service to the troops. Nor could they ignore the BSA's success; these were the years when Y men were launching their Christian Citizenship Training Program as a response.[70] But the YMCA's undemonstrative version of good citizenship in daily life could not match the focused intensity of Boy Scout patriotism.

Boy Scouting thus entered the 1920s as an agency of aggressive Americanism. Labor unrest, the Red Scare, and rising nativism all fueled concern among the BSA's prosperous supporters. *Scouting*'s editor urged that in a time of strikes boys must learn "self-reliance"; and when Cincinnati police struck in 1918, Boy Scouts helped direct traffic. Although unwilling flatly to condemn strikes, West suggested that "aggressive introduction of scouting into all our industrial sections . . . will help to solve all our industrial problems." He warned Chicago businessmen that "Neglected Boyhood Breeds Bolshevism."[71] Similarly, the Hartford *Times* said that Boy Scouting would salvage future Wobblies. Closely linked to fear of labor radicals was suspicion of immigrants. Reflecting fear of German-Americans, Italian-Americans, and others with seemingly divided loyalties, McAdoo praised the BSA as "one of the most potential agencies we could employ to Americanize America. . . . The war put dynamite and explosive under the hyphens. . . ."[72] During 1920, Boy Scouts distributed cards inviting immigrants to apply for citizenship. With help from local Boy Scout officials, Beard stirred up a storm by attacking foreigners and revealing that Lorne Barclay, the BSA's Director of Education, was still a Canadian citizen. Though the executive board backed Barclay, it threatened to remove the Richmond, Virginia, council's charter for having an English executive.[73] In addition, Theodore Roosevelt, Jr., helped the BSA win support from the new American Legion, then aggressively antiradical and jingoistic; and the grave of his father — who proved more manageable dead than alive — was the goal of an annual pilgrimage led by Beard. As "character and citizenship" became the standard formula for Boy Scouting's goals, public figures virtually ignored the outdoor program to praise the BSA as a force for patriotism.[74]

As war fever dissipated, headquarters tried to reduce confusion between

Boy Scouts and soldiers and yet retain premilitary discipline and an intensely patriotic image. By 1923, headquarters was urging replacement of the army-style outfit with a more boyish neckerchief, shirt, and shorts. On the other hand, the BSA continued to prescribe "a moderate amount of drill" based on army regulations, and the BSA's intense Americanism persisted despite the waning of postwar political anxieties.[75] Through the 1930s, the *Handbook for Scoutmasters* warned: "A suspicion of disloyalty must not remain unchallenged. . . . It is intolerable that a man commissioned by the National Office, should make an utterance or give instruction which the Scouts interpret as unpatriotic." Unless "perfect loyalty of the Scout leader is established," he should be dismissed.[76]

Although initially more military than the BSA, British Boy Scouting moved in a different direction as Baden-Powell recoiled in dismay from Britain's terrible losses in World War I. Hoping to foster peace and fend off Bolshevism, he reoriented Boy Scouting towards cautious internationalism and poured his energy into jamborees that brought together Boy Scouts of all countries. The BSA responded somewhat reluctantly to these initiatives, since West hated compromising with foreign Boy Scout movements on religious policy and the BSA was riding a wave of nationalism.[77] But Mortimer Schiff, whose banking connections gave him an international perspective, pressed for cooperation; American Boy Scout leaders took pride in their boys' performance at the 1920 jamboree; and West agreed that international Scouting was a dike "against the rising tide of Bolshevism. . . ."[78]

The growth of Scouting was part of a worldwide tendency for adults to form what S. N. Eisenstadt calls "totalistic organizations" to cope with rapid cultural change by inducting the young into a supervised world of recreation with prefabricated values.[79] While many countries developed state youth groups, the Boy Scouts flourished in open corporate societies such as Britain, France, and the U.S., where private agencies inculcated patriotism on a semiofficial basis.

The BSA's wartime exploits served not merely to demonstrate the boys' Americanism but also to show off their masculinity; for patriotic service with military overtones had long signified manliness. Ironically, the war also benefited the Girl Scouts and revived a nagging fear among the BSA's national leaders that Girl Scouting would undermine the Boy Scouts' image of masculinity.

From the start, West had opposed Girl Scouting. In 1911, he and several colleagues, including Seton and John L. Alexander, helped Luther Gulick and his wife design a program for the Camp Fire Girls which emphasized domestic skills and an Indian-maiden image for the girls. The Gulicks' scheme was designed to fill a social niche similar to Scouting's while averting any suspicion that the girls were imitation Boy Scouts. Initially the

Camp Fire Girls' membership vastly outgrew Juliette Low's fledgling Girl Scout movement, founded in 1912. But the war gave Girl Scouting a huge boost. Its leaders, who derided the Camp Fire Girls' ceremonial robe as a "fantastic nightgown," adopted a khaki uniform much like the boys'.[80] During the war, Girl Scouts sold war bonds and marched in parades, just as the boys did. When several thousand marched through Boston in 1919, a reporter wrote approvingly: "Marching with military precision that won the plaudits of thousands of spectators, . . . the young girl soldiers manifested every evidence that they are just as militaristic as their brother scouts."[81] Girl Scout membership swelled from just 5,000 in 1915 to 50,000 by 1920. In numbers, the Girl Scouts did not overtake the Camp Fire Girls until 1930, yet by the late 1910s they were getting most of the publicity, and the BSA's leaders worried.[82]

Boy Scout opposition to Girl Scouting increased after 1917, but it had only limited practical results. Disliking the term "Girl Scouts," Baden-Powell had christened the British equivalent "Girl Guides" and insisted upon separation to the point that the Guides were not to talk to Boy Scouts in uniform; but his friendship with Mrs. Low forced him into uneasy neutrality in the American dispute.[83] Within the BSA, alarm centered at the top, where the problems of maintaining a stable, unimpeachably masculine image nationwide were most apparent; the national leadership, which barred women from any authority within the movement, feared the taint of effeminacy.[84] At the local level, boys were skittish—the more so as the Girl Scouts' admission of girls at age ten threatened to make Scouting seem childish as well as unmasculine—but on the whole their fears were manageable. As for the local Boy Scout executives, many regarded smooth local relationships as more important than the BSA's overall image and cooperated freely with the Girl Scouts. Others put pressure on Girl Scout leaders to convert to the Camp Fire Girls, and in Butte, Montana, one man even censored local newspaper coverage of Girl Scouting. Still, such interference was only intermittent. West kept pressing the Girl Scouts' leaders to change the group's program or at least its name, but without result.[85] Apparently patriotism and control of the young mattered more than affirmation of masculinity, since many local leaders of the BSA, unlike West, accepted that either sex could be Scouts.

The BSA's wartime shift towards 100-percent Americanism raises again the question of the character builders' political affiliations. Initially, the BSA's values were a moderately conservative amalgam of classic American virtues, tinged with the all-encompassing Progressive rhetoric of the early 1910s. These values then turned more distinctly conservative in the late 1910s as the Progressive consensus disintegrated. Like most character builders, Boy Scout leaders believed that personal failings cried out

for cure more urgently than did social problems. Thus West blamed social ills on individual selfishness, and Scout service consisted of short-
term projects which would not lead, even by implication, to changes in
the social order.[86] Boy Scouts in uniform symbolized the purported class-
lessness of American democracy, while by good turns and patriotic demonstrations they acted out the good-neighbor, good-citizen virtues of
small-town America. Believing in an ideal, harmonious America, Boy Scout
officials were less apt than Y men to criticize American society, not that
either went very far. The BSA supported conservation, and troops sometimes aided prohibition drives, but otherwise headquarters forbade partisan involvement.[87]

Nonpartisanship suited Boy Scouting's vaguely Progressive image. Many
self-styled reformers also wanted to bypass partisan politics and favored
efficient administration such as West gave the BSA. We may thus locate
the BSA on the conservative edge of the Progressive movement. Concern
for the young, a middle-class aura, support for conservation, and zeal
for personal and bureaucratic efficiency all fit with such a view of Boy
Scouting. Like West, many Boy Scout leaders saw character building as
an alternative to partisan discord. Lorillard Spencer, Jr., Scout Commissioner for New York, told the press that the U.S. would gain more from
training boys for citizenship than from "sensational muckraking, which
is often only party politics."[88]

By 1920, though, the BSA's exXcutive board had a decidedly conservative
and partisan complexion; except for a couple of southern Democrats, the
members were virtually all Republicans, though most were not active politicians. Beard criticized the board's failure to name McAdoo, a leading
Democrat, to membership, suggesting the failure smacked of politics and
adding that he did not care how many Roosevelts were appointed. He had
a point, for by 1920 a good many members of the board had some connection with the late president, and one was Roosevelt's son.[89] This affinity
came easily, since West and his colleagues had courted the president assiduously and shared his liking for the strenuous life, nationalism, and
large-scale organization. In some ways the BSA paralleled—at a distance
—the political evolution of its Chief Scout Citizen. By the mid-1910s, big
businessmen took over the executive board, and social reformers faded
out. Beard's single tax days were long gone, and Seton—whose views struck
his colleagues as betraying a tinge of woolly radicalism—was forced out.
Late in his life, Theodore Roosevelt turned more conservative and bellicose than he had been for years. Similarly, the BSA took up the crusade
in wartime, though without Roosevelt's bloodlust. And in later years West,
like many old Progressives, was to dislike the New Deal for relying upon
government instead of private initiative, although he kept quiet about it
in public.[90]

It would be rash, however, to conclude that Boy Scouting simply followed the course of the Progressive movement, since that would mean identifying a broad political tendency (Progressivism) with a mere portion of its conservative wing — that exemplified by Theodore Roosevelt. Any such linkage assumes that there was a single Progressive movement and that boys' work had a degree of political coherence which in fact it lacked.[91] Woodcraft offered a respite from political problems, after all; and many top Boy Scout officials were not remotely Progressive. To include such staunch conservatives as Lorillard Spencer or Colin Livingstone in the movement would make almost everyone a Progressive. The most that should be said is that the BSA's Americanism bent more easily towards the right than towards the left.

The YMCA could at least as definitely be identified with Progressivism — a localized, civic version which blended mild reformism with Protestant morality and a faint echo of millenial hopes for American society. Ironically, the YMCA's one venture in a more nationalistic vein — its wartime management of canteens for soldiers — brought few benefits; Americans attacked the canteen service as mercenary, while in Canada a boom-bust pattern of fund raising led to huge successes during the war followed by postwar penury which forced abandonment of programs with which Y boys' secretaries hoped to match Scouting.[92] Then by the 1920s, as fundamentalism divided the churches and Protestant reformism no longer seemed so surely and simply part of the American way, the YMCA found its ideological support running off into separate shallow channels, whereas the BSA's drift towards the right kept it in the mainstream of middle-class political belief.

For competitive purposes, the Boy Scouts' sharply defined and demonstratively patriotic image served better than the less precise impression people had of YMCA boys' work. Furthermore, the uniformed Boy Scout, busy with helpful projects, personified boyish energy under close adult control, whereas YMCA boys were adolescent consumers of services — and adults liked boyish vigor better than adolescence with its reputation for moodiness. Boy Scouting had its weaknesses, to be sure. Among working-class populations the BSA's attenuated military style was a liability. Moreover, around 1920 YMCA men began to criticize the BSA for neglect of religious training; and a 1925 study in Los Angeles found that "many parents" echoed the YMCA's charges that the BSA was "not religious."[93] A distinct public image, in short, entailed costs as well as benefits. Yet a 1923 survey of prominent people in suburbs and small towns found the BSA a bit ahead of the YMCA in the race for approval. Respondents praised Boy Scouting's "hikes and camps and participation in patriotic and civic celebrations." They singled out visible good deeds such as police duty at parades. Despite YMCA criticism, Boy Scouting won praise both for its "non-sectarian character and appeal to all classes" and for its value in church work. Those questioned said the BSA helped steer boys through adolescence. Eighty-eight percent of 197 respondents spoke favorably of Boy Scouting, compared to 77 percent of 217 who discussed the YMCA.[94]

Still, these differences were slight. Ultimately, the BSA owed its success at least as much to strong organization and program as it did to public image. In local competition, Boy Scout executives relied primarily on claims that their program was technically superior and that Y boys' work duplicated theirs.[95]

There is evidence, moreover, that the BSA's high seriousness did not reach everybody. A Scoutmaster complained in 1922 that parents viewed Boy Scouting as "only sport and fun." Interviews in 1940 with 250 men who did not contribute to the BSA found that a quarter missed the organization's character-building goals "and saw 'companionship, pleasure, and sports' as scouting's only benefits to boys."[96] Headquarters took these results as evidence of failure, even though the fun of Boy Scouting was an indispensable ingredient in its success.

Yet a survey of noncommunicants is a poor measure of a church's appeal; to see why character-building agencies prospered, one must examine their constituency. The early years were crucial; for from then on, boys' workers could rely upon established custom and Americans' enthusiasm for noncontroversial good works.

11

Winning Institutional Support and Volunteer Leaders

A good public image was vital, but character builders had to translate it into active support. The BSA needed meeting places for its troops and volunteers to run them. Headquarters wanted an institutional sponsor for each troop to provide continuity, recruit leaders, and perhaps help with money. In addition, the local executive had to recruit a council of prominent men to establish Boy Scouting's position in the community. YMCA boys' work made fewer demands upon lay support, since salaried staff did much of the work and boys paid to join. Still, junior departments needed volunteers to run clubs and classes; and as Y men moved into community work, they had to find high schools to accept Hi-Y clubs and churches to sponsor Christian Citizenship Training groups. In the long run, YMCA boys' secretaries weakened their cause by concentrating upon building-centered projects and failing to build a base of lay involvement to rival Boy Scouting's.

As we shall see, support came most easily from middle-class institutions with responsibilities towards the young (churches and to a lesser extent the schools), from ministers and teachers, and from the business and professional community. Most men who took an active role did so not merely because they had been won over by the YMCA's or the Boy Scouts' public ideology but also because they wanted to control boys, build up a church or school, act out the middle-class code of service, bolster their own status, or foster community stability. Mere ideological congruity was insufficient; churchmen in fact distrusted the YMCA as a potential rival. Outside supporters wanted a boys' work program that would complement and not supplant their own work or that of their church or school.

Churches and churchmen formed by far the largest single market for character-building programs because, as chapter 2 explained, mainline Protestant churches in towns and cities were losing boys in droves and had nothing comparable to the schools' promise of vocational advancement to hold them. Churchmen needed help to keep the boys in Sunday school and convince them that Christianity was manly.

A variety of undertakings testified to the churchmen's concern. All kinds of "boys' clubs" (not the same as street boys' clubs) sprang up within churches, mostly after 1900; a number began as Sunday school classes which added recreation. City-wide Sunday school athletic leagues also proliferated after 1904.[1] Many of these schemes were ill-coordinated, however, and churchmen were unused to sustained organization across denominational lines such as athletic leagues required. Thus there was a great opening for both the Boy Scouts and the YMCA, which had organizational superstructures ready to use.

Young clergymen were especially anxious to demonstrate the manliness of Christianity, because as spokesmen for the softer virtues, ministering to disproportionately female congregations, they found that men often condescended to them as fit only for a ladies' tea. Unlike big-city clergymen who ran large churches, moreover, young ministers starting out in small towns lacked prestige and needed projects to justify their time. Lacking the authority that once had armored the clergy, they would settle for mere "contact" with potential male parishioners and some affirmation of their own masculinity.[2] Obsessively, boys' work enthusiasts reiterated that ministers must show themselves *real* men with "virile manhood." The Rev. H. A. Jump offered the intimidating advice that every clergyman should master one sport "so as to beat all the boys in the parish at it."[3]

Cautious souls wanted something more original, however. After all, why was baseball with the minister better than baseball without him — unless he owned the bat? With a patent program of boys' work in his pocket, he owned the rules. Cadet companies were one answer, as we have seen; but they often bored the boys and provoked opposition, driving clergymen to other expedients. Some of the resulting programs were modest, such as the Captains of Ten, a system of handicrafts. Others promised miracles: Perry Edwards Powell offered a *Solution of the Boy Problem* through his Knights of the Holy Grail, while David Jemison boldly subtitled his Kappa Sigma Pi manual *The Boy Problem Solved.*[4] Unimaginative authors copied from the temperance orders and composed systems of bookish chivalry; they founded the Knights of Methodism, the Epworth Court of Arthur, the Knights Crusaders, the Knights of Valor, and more prosaically, the Junior Order of Messenger Boys. These schemes were monotonously similar, offering a cheap manual, a few suggested activities, and extensive ritual. Occasional church workers tried one patent method after another, throwing away the discards like half-used bottles, until the boys must have concluded they were subjects of an experiment.[5]

William Byron Forbush, a Congregational minister, founded the best-known chivalric order, the Knights of King Arthur, in 1893. Forbush went on to study with G. Stanley Hall, confirming a belief that chivalry uniquely suited adolescence, and soon made himself an authority on church-based boys' work. Under the supervision of the minister, who played the role of Merlin in Forbush's program, KOKA boys passed through three degrees: pages promised obedience, watchfulness, and service; esquires pledged purity, temperance, and reverence; and knights joined the church. The boys initiated degree recipients with pageants based on Tennyson's *Idylls of the King* and hymned heroic purity of heart and body; one castle (the equivalent of a troop in Scouting) even built a round table in pie-shaped wedges, one per boy. For recreation Forbush proposed camping and manual training; but his main goal was to bring boys under the personal guidance of the minister as Merlin.[6] Chivalry also afforded clergymen a genteel version of masculinity, for Forbush hoped to avoid the coarseness of boyish savagery. The Rev. William Brosard, for instance, could not control the boys in a Missouri lumber town. Hikes failed when the boys slipped off to smoke or hunt rabbits, which they ate "without salt!" Yet Brosard claimed that through the KOKA he got these Huck Finns to address each other as "your gentleness" and "Fair and courteous Knight Sir Gawain."[7]

Without field workers, the KOKA enrolled only a total of only 125,000 boys from 1893 through 1923.[8] But the multiplication of such schemes showed that churchmen wanted a Sunday school supplement that worked better than the Boys' Brigade.

Boy Scouting met this need without requiring a gymnasium, while the badges and uniforms impressed boys that they were joining something bigger than a church club. As a result, the Boy Scouts outgrew all competition, until a survey of city churches around 1924 found that 46 percent had Boy Scout troops, whereas only 33 percent had other clubs for boys. In villages, Scouting was often the only form of church boys' work.[9]

In turn, the BSA depended heavily upon the churches. From 1912 through 1921, they sponsored about 52 percent of all Boy Scout troops (see Table 4); in 1921, 50 percent of all troops met in churches. And these figures may have understated the BSA's dependence, for James West estimated in 1916 that "over 80%" of troops had some connection with a church or Sunday school.[10]

Initially, a striking number of ministers — primarily in small towns — led troops themselves; 29 percent of all Scoutmasters in 1912 were clergymen.[11] Ironically, Boy Scout officials were displeased at this, fearing that clergymen-Scoutmasters would hurt the BSA's image of manly, businesslike efficiency. BSA men complained that ministers moved about a lot, leaving troops to collapse behind them. Sad to say in view of the clergymen's desire to prove their masculinity, Boy Scout executives looked down upon preachers as inefficient sentimentalists. S. A. Moffat was especially caustic: "One of these fellows wrote in the other day, believing that he had accomplished the aim and object of the scout movement, and was entitled to an honor medal because . . . his patrol leader was baptized with

Table 4
Institutions with Which Boy Scout Troops Were Connected

Institutions	1912 (%) (N = 5,140)[a]	1917 (%) (N = 13,248)	1921 (%) (N = 17,619)
Churches	52.1[b]	51.6	51.6
Schools, public	7.5	16.9	7.4
Schools, private or parochial	.3[c]		1.2[d]
YMCAs	6.1	3.5	1.3
Boys' clubs	1.0	.6	.3
Miscellaneous	5.5[e]	9.1[f]	8.4[g]
Community troops	—	6.4	19.3
None	27.6	—	—
Not definitely reported	—	12.0	10.4

[a] There were 1,777 other troops from which information had not been requested.
[b] Listed as Sunday schools.
[c] Parochial schools.
[d] Private schools, .9%; parochial schools, .3%.
[e] Settlement houses, 1.3%; playgrounds, .3; others, 3.9%.
[f] Public institutions, 3.6%; associations, 1.1%; libraries, .5%; asylums, .3%; playgrounds, .3%; YMHAs, .2%; office buildings, .1%; others, 3.0%.
[g] Associations, 1.9%; industrial plants, .6%; Rotary Clubs, .5%; American Legion, .3%; asylums, .3%; YMHAs, .2%; Knights of Columbus, .2%; playgrounds, libraries, secret societies, Kiwanis, and Elks, .1% each; others, 3.9%.
Sources: Boy Scouts of America, *Annual Report* 3 (Feb. 1913):20; 8 (Mar. 1918): 46–47; 12 (May 1922):139.

his scout shirt on in the tank at the Baptist Church. . . . Of course, I am not interested in the kind of shirt he wore, the only practical thing I would like to find out is whether or not he learned to swim fifty yards before he got out."[12] For their part, ministers lost enthusiasm as the BSA extended local council control into smaller cities and towns. Distant supervision by denominational Sunday school boards had not prepared them for a local executive who claimed authority over one of their programs; in one instance a church simply stopped Boy Scouting "till the County Council dies." Although clergymen continued to serve as Scoutmasters — the absolute number rose until 1918 — their relative proportion among all Scoutmasters fell to 16 percent by 1921 and 10 percent in 1925 as the BSA quietly discouraged their recruitment.[13]

Some tension was inevitable between Sunday school and Boy Scout officials, since each group feared being used by the other. Boy Scout officers worried lest Scouting become mere bait for Sunday school attendance. When congregations limited troop membership to their own boys, Boy Scout officials protested; yet if church troops admitted outside boys, as most did, the leaders were forbidden to proselytize.[14] West and the BSA's badge committee discountenanced a proposed Bible study badge for fear of seeming, like the YMCA, to rival Sunday schools.[15] These policies tried to please everyone; but committed believers suspected indifference — the more so as Scoutmasters often held Sunday hikes without providing for worship. Some troops were in fact quite independent, since church sponsorship was often pro forma and Boy Scout executives sometimes moved troops around.[16] Towards 1920, as a result of rising tensions, religious educators toyed with organizing their own midweek activities and barring outside agencies like Boy Scouting from the Sunday schools. Still, most troops kept some affinity with their church, as five out of six Scoutmasters in 1921 avowed the same denomination as the host church, and nine out of ten Boy Scouts attended Sunday school.[17] Boy Scout officials responded to criticism with a mixture of endorsements and concessions. Aided by wartime service, Boy Scouting secured endorsements from bodies favorable to the BSA's interdenominational tolerance and Americanism — including agencies of the Northern Baptist, Episcopalian, Presbyterian, Congregationalist, and Methodist churches plus the Federal Council of Churches. West hated to ban Sunday Scouting, since some Scoutmasters worked Saturdays; but the BSA's national council compromised by decreeing that Boy Scouts who stayed home for church must not lose credits. Decades later, church youth workers still complained that most churches merely gave troops a place to meet.[18] And yet that was what Boy Scouting needed.

The YMCA might have been expected to fare better; but by promising intensive religious work, Y boys' secretaries raised expectations higher than they could always meet and aroused a fear of rivalry as well. Although the YMCA enjoyed wide support from Protestant laymen, the clergy feared that lay evangelism would become a substitute instead of a feeder for the church. Secretaries referred boys to interested pastors, but ministers complained the new recruits did not appear. Nor did boys' workers help relations by implying that they knew more about adolescents than did the clergy.[19] For their part, churchmen complained that Y secretaries neglected spirituality amid the detail of their work. A few also disliked the content of YMCA Bible lessons, but criticism of the Y for modernism was still a thunderhead low on the horizon in the 1910s.[20]

What clergymen wanted of course was support for church programs. A good many Associations shared their gymnasium and pool with Sunday school clubs. YMCA men also organized Sunday school athletic leagues and training classes for church club leaders. They found to their regret, however, that these services did not build up YMCA membership the way church-sponsored troops built up the BSA.[21]

As we have seen, YMCA efforts to go a step further by promoting a complete program for church use failed. The Christian Citizenship Training Program was hopelessly complicated. Judged by stricter religious standards than was Boy Scouting, it also stirred initial criticism for failing to require boys to accept Christ as their personal Savior. Simplified versions came into use in city churches in the 1920s, but the Associations never really challenged Boy Scouting's primacy.[22]

In the 1910s and 1920s, YMCA men made a further effort to go where the Boy Scout movement flourished in the suburbs and small towns. Although the resulting clubs drew their leaders mainly from the schools, friction arose with local clergymen. With no cushioning period of local experimentation, a YMCA secretary would come in from outside the community to launch the program, sometimes alarming ministers who charged that the Y duplicated their work and yet was less religious. The BSA, on the other hand, operated more smoothly. Local men usually founded the first troops and ran them for some time; only when the bait had grown familiar did the hook appear—in the person of a county Boy Scout executive. Though some clergymen then took alarm, the BSA kept a huge lead over the YMCA in small-town churches.[23]

The core of the character builders' church support came from the established denominations of the native-stock middle and upper classes who regarded their moralistic Protestantism and Americanism as virtually synonymous. Presbyterian, Congregational, and Episcopal churches sponsored 15, 10, and 8 percent respectively of the church troops in 1917, whereas their shares of the country's church membership in 1921 were only about 5, 2, and 2 percent (see Table 5). Significantly, these were the three most socially prestigious denominations.[24] White Methodist churches, a fairly prosperous connection, were the next most overrepresented, accounting for 29 percent of church troops compared to 14 percent of church memberships. White Baptist and Christian churches supported just about their share of troops, although Northern Baptists were much more active than Southern. Lutheran and Catholic churches supported far fewer troops in 1917: 2 and 3 percent respectively. Catholic troops reached 10 percent by 1921, but this was still far below the Catholic share of church members, about 25 to 28 percent in 1921.[25] The denominational preferences of Scoutmasters, including those who led nonchurch troops, were very similar (see Table 5). In 1921, Episcopalians, Congregationalists, Presbyterians, and Methodists were greatly overrepresented; Baptists served roughly in proportion to their share of church members; Lutherans were mildly underrepresented; Roman Catholics were greatly underrepresented; and there were almost no black Protestant Scoutmasters. In short, Boy Scouting drew upon the same denominations whose laymen had long backed the YMCA.

Table 5

Church Connection of Boy Scout Troops and Church Preference of Scoutmasters[a]

Church Connection	Church-Connected Troops			Scoutmasters' Preferences		U.S. Church Members[b]	Index of Participation: Scoutmasters[c]
	1915 (%) (N = 3,716)	1917 (%) (N = 6,833)	1921 (%) (N = 9,090)	1917 (%) (N = 12,392)	1921 (%) (N = 16,839)	1921 (%) (N = 46,242,130)	1921
Methodist	31.5	28.7	27.4[d]	27.7	26.7	14.2[d]	202
Presbyterian	18.1	15.5	15.3	15.1	14.1	5.2	294
Baptist	12.8[e]	10.5[e]	10.2[e]	11.5[e]	10.4[e]	10.2[f]	109
Congregational	12.5	10.4	7.4	8.3	6.2	1.8	372
Episcopalian	10.7	8.1	7.6	9.5	9.0	2.4	404
Christian	4.4	4.9	4.7[g]	4.0	4.9[g]	3.5[g]	149
Mormon	2.9	2.3	4.2	1.4	2.6	1.3	219
Lutheran	2.4	2.4	3.3	3.0	3.6	5.3	72
Reformed	2.4	2.2	1.7	1.6	1.3	1.1	129
Roman Catholic	1.3	3.3	10.3	3.6	7.6	38.7[h]	21
Jewish	1.1	.8	1.4	1.3	1.8	.9[i]	221
Other churches	—	10.8	6.5[j]	6.9	5.1[k]	15.5[l]	30
Not listed or none	—	—	—	6.1	6.6	—	—

[a] Includes all Scoutmasters but only church-connected troops.

[b] Membership figures offer only a rough comparison with denominational preference.

[c] Divide the proportion of Scoutmasters favoring each denomination by the proportion of all church members in the respective denomination and multiply by 100. Scoutmasters reporting no denominational preference are excluded.

[d] Includes Methodist Episcopal and Methodist Protestant but not A.M.E.

[e] Includes almost no Negro Baptists; see f and l.

[f] Includes only white Baptists, since there were almost no black troops.

[g] Listed as Disciples or as Christian.

[h] Overstated relative to Protestants; see note 25.

[i] Very approximate—probably too low.

[j] Absolute numbers: African Methodist Episcopal, 24; Evangelical Association, 79; Evangelical Synod, 22; Salvation Army, 4; Unitarian, 32; United Evangelical, 34; Universalist, 39; other, 359.

[k] Absolute numbers: African Methodist Episcopal, 27; Evangelical, 126; Salvation Army, 7; Unitarian, 91; United Evangelical, 43; Universalist, 75; other, 493.

[l] Includes "colored" Baptists, 6.7%; "colored" Methodists, 3.0%; other, 5.8%.

Sources: BSA, Annual Report 6 (Feb. 1916):39; 8 (Apr. 1918):44–47; 12 (May 1922):139; Statistical Abstract of the United States, 1922 (Washington, 1923), pp. 70–71.

Although data for YMCA volunteers are unavailable, the denominations of boys who made commitments at YMCA conferences and of Canadian churches which used YMCA standard programs were very similar to those of Boy Scouting's backers. Of 706 boys who pledged themselves to Christian callings at YMCA conferences in 1920, for example, 30 percent were Methodist, 25 percent Presbyterian, 13 percent Baptist, 12 percent Congregationalist, 5 percent Lutheran, only 4 percent Episcopalian (the one major difference), and 11 percent other denominations.[26]

Since character builders followed the modern method of seeking social discipline through specialized associations, it is tempting to apply Richard Jensen's and Paul Kleppner's distinction between modernizing pietistic denominations (such as the Congregationalists, Presbyterians, and Methodists) and traditionalist liturgical groups (such as most Lutherans and Catholics).[27] Within this framework, most character builders would be classified as modernizing pietists. But the pietistic denominations were also quintessentially middle-class churches; and the prominence of Episcopalians (purportedly liturgical) among Boy Scouting's backers suggests a simpler explanation: upper- and middle-class groups most favorable to Americanism also backed the BSA. YMCA support was more narrowly pietistic, but that is merely to say that the Associations' lingering evangelical earnestness apparently scared off Episcopalians.

Practical concerns reinforced the effects of social class, for the denominations which led in support for Boy Scouting already relied heavily upon auxiliary agencies to train and hold their young. Of all major denominations in 1906, the Congregational, Presbyterian, and Methodist had the highest ratio of Sunday school pupils to adult members.[28] They sponsored young people's societies, and the Episcopalians had boys' brotherhoods. Starting in the 1890s, however, Sunday school growth slowed in the northeastern U.S.; it virtually ceased in Congregational and Episcopal churches by 1916 and soon leveled off among Methodists, Presbyterians, and Northern Baptists as well, though it continued among Southern Baptists.[29] Similarly, Christian Endeavor within Congregational churches fell from 204,000 members in 1895 to 134,000 by 1916, and the Methodists' Epworth League began shrinking in the mid-1910s.[30] Thus men from these churches were very receptive to any new agency which might help in holding boys.

Support for Boy Scouting did not demand Social Gospel sympathies. In fact, churches committed to social service more often sponsored other clubs better suited to needy boys. Yet cautious clergymen joined service clubs and favored modest social programs such as Scouting.[31] Many churchmen who backed the BSA took a very positive view of American boys and society; in their Sunday schools "ideals of heroic living" and "habits of Christian service" displaced repentance. Franklin D. Elmer, a Northern Baptist minister, wrote that Scouting gave boys an appreciation of Washington and Lincoln, "of Paul, mission's frontiersman," and of Jesus, "the Master Scout, whose life may be best interpreted for a boy in terms of observation, service, and the twelve great laws. . . ."[32] Boy Scouting, in short, fitted in with a moralized, Americanized creed.

The BSA policy of treating all faiths as equal echoed the mainline Protestant assumption of denominational consensus. But men who believed their church unique in dogma or mission wanted no blurring of distinctions. In addition, the BSA's Americanism eroded ethnic loyalties. Therefore Lutherans whose churches were theologically or ethnically conservative distrusted the BSA; the United Lutherans' boys' work committee commended Boy Scouting in 1918, but the conservative Missouri Synod withheld even grudging sanction until the 1940s. To groups which shunned unredeemed society, the Boy Scouts threatened submergence; nor did sectarians mad for salvation see much need for recreation. Seventh Day Adventists, for example, shunned the movement. Although the Southern Baptist convention endorsed Boy Scouting in 1923, BSA men found the "very conservative" pastors a problem.[33]

Among Catholics, boys' work of any sort was weak. The Church concentrated upon building parochial schools, with boys' programs strictly an afterthought to forestall non-Catholic friendships among boys who attended public schools or left school to work. Much of what passed for boys' work was so heavily instructional and liturgical that it resembled Sunday school more than midweek recreation. Priests, moreover, were less likely than Protestant pastors to become Scoutmasters. In his *Boy-Savers' Guide,* the Rev. George E. Quin insisted that no priest should join in the boys' sports; he must always remain "their condescending superior."[34] Catholic boys' work was thus a concession rather than a cause.

Throughout the world, Catholics worried that the Boy Scout movement was Protestant. In France, Catholic Boy Scouting did not begin in earnest until after 1920; and French Canadians—who feared submergence by English Canadians—did little Boy Scouting before the 1930s.[35] The Boy Scouts' middle-class ethos might explain some Catholic indifference in the U.S. but not the fact that in 1915 Catholic parishes sponsored only forty-eight troops. Many priests saw Boy Scouting as "Episcopalianism or Presbyterianism transfigured" and controlled by the YMCA. The BSA would foster contact with non-Catholics and give boys "the impression . . . that one religion is as good as another."[36] After all, BSA publications said as much. Hence the few bishops who endorsed Boy Scouting insisted that each troop have an official chaplain.[37]

The strength of Americanism began to erode Catholic resistance in the United States as the BSA lived down its YMCA connections and won praise for wartime service. The National Catholic War Council, a sometimes controversial agency that Americanized immigrants and provided social services, actively promoted Boy Scouting; and Catholic troops multiplied.[38] Yet traditionalists opposed the NCWC, and Catholic boys' workers divided. Some believed that without Catholic troops, boys would "follow the crowd to non-Catholic institutions. . . ." On the other side, Kilian J. Hennrich, a diehard who revived the Catholic Boys' Brigade in 1920 to rival Scouting, argued that separation was essential to combat "naturalism."[39] In a few smaller cities, anti-Catholic and anti-Jewish bigotry fenced off Boy Scouting as a Protestant preserve, but Catholic attitudes themselves primarily determined Boy Scouting's degree of success within the Church.[40] As postwar enthusiasm subsided, Catholic Boy Scouting lagged, until by 1930 only 7 percent of church troops were Catholic. By then, however, it was clear that the BSA stood firmly against Communism beneath the banners of God and Country; and when Boy Scout officials promised to stop interdenominational services, the bishops backed the BSA strongly.[41]

Mormons and Jews reacted more positively than most minorities, since they saw in the BSA's Americanism a help with their identity problems. The Mormons, who wanted to prove their Americanism and yet bolster group loyalty, made Boy Scouting part of their church program for youth. Jews took a different tack; although most rabbis except the orthodox liked the Boy Scouts, many resisted separate troops and urged their boys to seek wider social acceptance by joining community troops.[42]

The YMCA had less chance to grow beyond its Protestant base. Most priests were hostile. A good many Catholics and Jews used the Y anyway, but their presence troubled conscientious secretaries. One man agreed to teach a Bible class of Jewish boys if he could try to prove that Jesus was the Messiah, but such zest for combat was rare; most secretaries felt the same inhibitions against proselytizing that Boy Scout leaders did.[43] The BSA's Americanism made a broader platform.

No other institutional sponsors matched the churches' importance, not even the schools. Educators generally had a good opinion of character-building agencies, but they were less troubled than churchmen by fear of losing contact with boys and were better able to organize their own recreational programs.

Ideologically, schoolmen certainly were receptive, as the 1910s were years of triumph for advocates of education for "social efficiency." A celebrated report on *Cardinal Principles of Secondary Education,* issued by a committee of the NEA in 1918, argued in terms familiar to boys' workers that the socializing role of other institutions had declined and the schools must take up new tasks, including training for citizenship, use of leisure, and ethical character.[44]

High school principals, moreover, were eager to curb teenage independence. In particular, they waged war upon high school fraternities, which the NEA excoriated for giving teenagers a feeling of self-sufficiency and undercutting the schools' system of rewards. Despite repression, fraternities had spread to more than a third of all high schools by 1905.[45]

Conveniently, YMCA clubs offered a "substitute" that would be easy to control; and educators praised the YMCA's influence for discipline, sportsmanship, and scholarship.[46] On the other hand, the Y's obvious Protestantism caused trouble in religiously mixed communities by threatening to taint the schools' professed neutrality in religion. YMCA organizers had to win entry by stressing morality, organizing big campaigns with schoolwide assemblies for "clean living, clean speech and clean sports."[47] At times YMCA secretaries used pressure tactics; David R. Porter, the YMCA's international secretary for high schools, even grumbled that recalcitrant principals were "probably out of sympathy with the purpose of the school" and should be fired.[48] With time, however, Y men learned moderation and accepted that Bible classes would have to be held away from school. Although most chapters remained small, Hi-Y grew to 2,303 clubs with 65,546 members by 1924.[49]

Elementary and high schools also sponsored Boy Scout troops, as teachers cherished the usual hopes of better discipline. Taking advantage of the vogue for citizenship training, BSA officials stepped up their courtship of school authorities around 1916—so successfully that a 1920 survey of North Central Association high schools found that 55 percent had a Boy Scout troop.[50]

Nonetheless, relations between school and Boy Scout officials remained a bit standoffish. Three-quarters of city school systems let Scouts use school property for free, but school officials were reluctant to take responsibility for troops. Although 17 percent of Boy Scout troops met in school buildings in 1921, only 7 percent were under school sponsorship (see above, Table 4). This pattern was to endure, as school troops never approached in number those sponsored by churches.[51]

Since character builders had long sniped at the schools for arid formalism, Boy Scout officials could never quite shake off their fear that Scouting in a classroom setting would remind the boys of work.[52] West also feared the power of the local school authorities; after one experiment, he refused to charter school boards as Boy Scout councils, complaining that the state already wielded power enough over children. Although some executives favored schools in order to balance their lopsided dependence upon churches, West concluded that religious bodies were more manageable and supported troops more reliably.[53]

From the teachers' viewpoint, Boy Scouting came in from the outside, professing a rival expertise in managing the young and sometimes engaging nonteachers to lead the school troops. Lacking a sense of proprietorship, educators seldom mentioned Scouting when they discussed extracurricular activities.[54] Like clergymen, male teachers suffered from imputations of effeminacy, yet in seeking to efface that impression they had options besides leading Boy Scout troops, such as coaching school teams. Besides, teachers saw teenagers all day; unlike ministers, they had no need to invent contacts and might instead have craved a respite after hours.[55] In any case, for the majority who were women the aggressively masculine Boy Scout movement was no help, since it threatened to fence them off from boys. Hence the Chicago Teachers' Federation, one of the few teachers' groups run by women, condemned the BSA in 1912 for usurping a function of the schools. Still, male teachers did account for 11 percent of all Scoutmasters in 1919—enough for the editor of *Scouting* to urge a moratorium on criticism of the schools.[56]

Other institutional sponsors for troops can be dismissed briefly. Baden-Powell overestimated the willingness of other boys' workers to follow his lead, for duplication led to rivalry. Only the YMCA sponsored any large number of troops—6 percent in 1912—and this dwindled to 1 percent by 1921 as relations with the BSA soured (see above, Table 4). Boys' club directors greeted Scouting as useful yet insufficient by itself to civilize poor boys. However, the BSA's control over its program prevented them from borrowing freely without organizing regular troops—which then threatened the sponsoring agency's identity, since boys' club members who joined a troop became first and foremost Boy Scouts. Besides, Scouting was expensive for lower-class boys. As a result, boys' clubs sponsored only sixty-one troops by 1921. The Hartford, Connecticut, boys' club went so far as to expel boys who became Scouts, for resentment of the BSA's intransigence mounted during the 1910s.[57] William McCormick, the editor of *Work With Boys*, complained in 1917: "Some Boy Scout leaders whom we have tried to amiably discuss the movement with have bristled up and walked out. They will brook no questioning. They will admit no criticism."[58] In general, only those organizations, such as churches, which had an independent function that would be supported and not threatened accepted Boy Scouting gracefully.

In theory, Boy Scout leaders demanded an organized constituency. Dr. Fisher argued that "the only way to get leadership" was to rely on institutions that were "permanent in the community, such as church and school."[59] Nonetheless, the 1921 annual report listed 19 percent community troops. In small towns these were often extensions of Protestant church work formed by pooling boys from several congregations, but a number of troops may actually have been without institutional sponsors.[60]

Boy Scout executives were occasionally tempted to go it alone. Noting how small-town institutions, locked in bitter rivalries, sometimes prostituted Scouting to gain a mean advantage, some of the new county executives of the 1920s frankly favored independent troops.[61] In larger centers, zeal for homogeneous Americanism encouraged the formation of "cosmopolitan" troops to break down "the old bigotry" and teach boys "the patriotic spirit. . . ." Even some Catholic boys disliked church troops: "They want to be in the school and to meet with one another, and they do not seem to mind having an Italian boy over an American boy or otherwise."[62] Despite such reservations, sponsored troops far outnumbered independent ones.

Instead of running individual troops, men who sought community integration often worked at a higher level, forming a second boys' work constituency above the schools and churches. Such men sought behavioral conformity throughout the community rather than structural assimilation; by underwriting supervisory bodies and drawing together adult leaders rather than boys themselves, they avoided thrusting youngsters into groups with those from different backgrounds.[63]

Businessmen who backed character building acted in accordance with a principled class ideology and not just narrow self-interest; they sought social decency as they saw it and an orderly environment for business rather than specific advantages for their own firms. The YMCA had a long tradition of support by businessmen who valued its services to white-collar men and its socialization of middle-class boys and young men. Boy Scouting inherited much of this support; although the BSA did not serve businessmen as directly as the YMCA, it pleased them by giving boys conservative citizenship training and fostering individual achievement through badge-winning.[64]

Individual firms seldom sponsored troops or clubs. Although the BSA encouraged industrialists to start troops for young employees, only 102 were in operation by 1921.[65] Railroad YMCAs had a long history, and secretaries tried in the 1910s to set up industrial equivalents. But what support YMCA and Boy Scout leaders received for directly company-related programs — several million dollars for buildings in the YMCA's case — came mainly in quasi-paternalistic one-company towns. After the Ludlow massacre, for instance, small YMCAs graced the Colorado Fuel and Iron Company's installations. Industrial and railroad Associations enrolled few boys, however.[66] Occasional firms welcomed separate YMCA clubs for boys, and a few businessmen dispensed Y memberships to render worthy lads "more efficient," but in the long run rising school attendance doomed boys' work for employed boys.[67]

Until the 1920s, businessmen helped most readily as private individuals, for the Gospel of Wealth applied only to private fortunes; corporate managers had learned to seek profits ahead of good public relations, and their reluctance to give to philanthropic agencies continued down to World War

I. The YMCA, however, was the one significant exception to this parsimony; railroad YMCAs had breached it before 1900, YMCA building campaigns of the 1904–1916 era drew heavily upon corporate gifts, and several big-city YMCAs of that era even secured about one-fifth of their donations for current expenses from businesses.[68] Although war work and the community chest movement of the 1920s began to make corporate philanthropy more common, throughout that decade the YMCA still greatly outdid most charitable agencies in securing corporate gifts; in some large cities, these made up a third or more of all donations to the Y's current expense fund. The Boy Scouts were also quite successful; in 1928, their Boston council obtained 6 percent of its donations from business corporations and the Chicago council 25 percent.[69]

Among men without personal fortunes, the ideology of service took hold in the 1910s and 1920s as an affordable equivalent to the Gospel of Wealth; rooted in the old gentry code rather than the crass power of heaped-up dollars, and trumpeted as every layman's duty by the prewar Men and Religion Movement, service justified the social standing of the new middle class.[70] Business and professional men served others in their vocations, they believed; by volunteer service they extended this good work into their leisure hours and displayed a degree of local influence. In so doing, they preferred supervisory positions, where the authority was.

From the BSA's standpoint, recruitment of business-class volunteers was a genuflection before the principle of voluntarism and a promise to local elites that centralized power would not ride roughshod over their concerns. Much as the federal government in its economic mobilization for World War I employed dollar-a-year men from business and turned to pricing and propaganda rather than fully coercive controls, so Boy Scout officials clung to the principle of local authority and the notion that private businessmen could do anything better than anyone else.[71] Americans mistrusted the centralized power represented by a paid executive. Accordingly, BSA officials went on naming prominent men as Scout Commissioners long after the duties of the office had dwindled to mere ceremony. Boy Scout executives filled local councils with leading businessmen and managers rather than preachers or teachers who actually worked with boys. The councils met at most a few times a year, yet these gatherings certified that the BSA had local roots.[72]

The greatest need for businessmen as volunteers was financial. In its pre-World War I drives to raise building funds, the YMCA pioneered the technique—later imitated by the Boy Scouts and community chests—of intensive ten-day campaigns during which large numbers of volunteers, mostly businessmen, solicited contributions from thousands of potential donors. At the top of a military-style hierarchy, directing the campaign, were "leading industrialists, merchants, and financiers"—the same sort of men whose presence on YMCA boards of control guaranteed the Associations such strong corporate backing.[73] The BSA sought similar men for its local councils. Since half the money in successful Boy Scout fund drives came in large sums at the start, council members had to be well enough connected to fish the local pools of wealth. By the 1920s, indeed, social agencies of all sorts chose their directors for fund-raising potential.[74]

Unlike boys' clubs, which sometimes served as one man's hobby or some rich man's monument, middle-class agencies usually had collective leadership. Many of the same men served on a host of local boards, including both the Boy Scouts' and the YMCA's.[75] In theory this could have curbed duplication, as it did in Spokane, Washington, when the Boy Scout executive rashly tried to bypass the churches and the YMCA boys' secretary promptly announced a CCTP program for church use. Local men of means intervened and arranged a dinner at which the BSA man proclaimed that churchmen could make any religious use of Boy Scouting they wished, while the Y secretary agreed to drop his plans. In most towns, though, businessmen enabled competition to persist by patiently supporting every agency that sounded worthy.[76]

Middle-class support took more organized form after the war as newly founded service clubs — Rotary (1905), Kiwanis (1914), and the Lions (1917) — spread rapidly. Together with the older fraternal orders and the new American Legion, they sought to perform visible community service without disturbing established institutions. There were 741 Legion troops by 1925, and the Elks, Knights of Columbus, Kiwanis, Rotary, and Lions all sponsored troops; by 1930 civic and service clubs outdid the schools in their support of troops.[77]

More ambitiously, the leading clubs sought to command the heights of local boys' work. Communitywide father and son dinners or an annual "boys' week" displayed a comprehensive, mildly paternalistic solicitude.[78] Rotary, the most prestigious club, staked its claim to overall authority by sponsoring surveys of patterns of boy life in the community, often with YMCA help. This ambition to get involved at the supervisory level profited Boy Scouting hugely in building up its superstructure, for Rotary organized more than half the local councils in the United States.[79]

The community chest movement, backed by businessmen who tired of fund drives every other week, further regularized business-class support of boys' work. Although Boy Scout and YMCA leaders held back at first, asserting that character building was a higher calling than the charity dispensed by the relief agencies initiating the drives, such scruples evaporated once boys' work supporters won power on the fund committees; 42 percent of all Boy Scout councils took part by 1926. Boy Scout and YMCA involvement helped direct the chests' philanthropy towards the comfortable classes.[80]

Patterns of troop sponsorship showed how concern about uncontrolled boys created a market for boys' work. Protestant churches, with a tenuous hold on boys, experimented widely; public schools, which had other means of control, gave some support; and employers, who had the paycheck for discipline, felt little need of boys' work. Within the upper tier of boys' work's backers—those who supported its superstructure—the character builders' public ideology mattered more; businessmen and their clubs supported the Boy Scouts and YMCA as a contribution to social welfare and general social stability. Then as character-building agencies became well established, habit, fashion, the community chest, and organizational momentum carried them along.

Because the business ethos pervaded character building, labor leaders were suspicious. For their part, YMCA boys' secretaries anticipated difficulty finding "Christian" representatives of labor. S. C. Britton of St. Louis "stumbled upon . . . a member of the Machinists' Union" who helped him, but most secretaries launched their programs for working boys without such consultation.[81]

The BSA's relations with labor started badly. *Century* magazine greeted Boy Scouting as a cure for strikes, and prominent supporters of the movement said as much in public.[82] Labor leaders, who assumed the worst of a uniformed movement founded by a general, saw their suspicions confirmed when they read Baden-Powell's antiunion fulminations in the first BSA manual. The IWW hooted Baden-Powell and West off a platform in Portland, Oregon.[83] More seriously, the AFL took note of incidents such as the rash action of a Scoutmaster from Des Moines, who became incensed at bootblacks raising their price to ten cents for state fair week and brought in Boy Scouts who knocked the rate back to a nickel. By late 1911, several mine unions and five state federations of labor had formally condemned Boy Scouting.[84]

BSA headquarters expunged Baden-Powell's diatribes from the manuals and began something between a holding action and a courtship. West met with AFL officials, who then reported to their 1912 convention. They liked the Setonian aspect of Boy Scouting—outdoor life as an antidote to "the strain of modern industry"—and praised the movement for distracting "adolescent" boys from impurity. Yet the report voiced lingering fears of militarism and recommended only that the federation "not denounce" the BSA.[85] World War I ended overt opposition even by militant unions, but mutual suspicion hung on. During the strikes of 1919, *Scouting*'s editor felt obliged to warn that scabbing was not a good turn.[86] Unionists still thought that Boy Scouts marching in formation were being conditioned to the drums of war. One executive told of a speech to labor leaders in which he assured them that Scouting was unmilitary; but then a magic lantern picture appeared on the screen with Boy Scouts drawn up in "fine array in columns of fours . . . and I slipped out in the dark." [87] By the 1920s, Dr. Fisher, who headed the BSA Field Department, was urging local councils to find moderate labor representatives; but local executives were indifferent or feared antagonizing their business allies. Labor leaders were not named to the national executive board, and union locals seldom sponsored troops. [88]

Not surprisingly, the volunteers who helped lead the boys came from the same milieux which gave the Boy Scouts and YMCA so much organized support. Teachers helped with Hi-Y; ministers or laymen led church troops; and even when sponsorship was weak, volunteers came mainly from the lower strata of the same business and professional classes which supported the superstructure of boys' work.

YMCA secretaries sought "virile men" of "contagious Christianity" to lead clubs and classes; but boys' branches were "greatly lacking in this leadership — both as to quality and quantity," according to a 1913 study. [89] As marginal professionals, Y secretaries resented being undersold by volunteers who followed "foolproof instructions"; one disgruntled Y man attributed Boy Scouting's rapid spread to its "spectacular" program and use of "very low grade" leaders. [90] Some secretaries would have liked to put volunteers through intensive summer training; even the authors of the Christian Citizenship Program, intended to rival Scouting, warned never to start without "a reasonably trained leader." [91] Such attitudes must have intimidated potential volunteers.

Those who did step forward were predominantly middle- but not upper-middle-class. Bible class leaders of the 1920s were mainly teachers, young businessmen, and older boys. A study of town and village YMCAs found that most volunteers were young (66 percent under thirty-five), well educated (73 percent with some college or normal school), and middle-class (52 percent in the professions, 12 percent each in trade and mechanical pursuits, and 8 percent farmers). Of the professionals, 70 percent were teachers and 18 percent clergymen — a reversal of the pattern among Scoutmasters and further evidence that men wanted a program which supplemented without threatening their particular specialty. Teachers found that the Y's religious flavor added something missing in their classrooms, whereas Boy Scouting — which was educationally oriented — did better among ministers. There was also a pecking order, for the ministers and teachers were younger and lower in social prestige than the businessmen who controlled the YMCA county councils. [92]

Although many Boy Scout executives shared the YMCA secretaries' critical attitude towards volunteers, the BSA could not do without them and thus tried to curb rivalry by sharply defining authority and functions: the executives led men, whereas Scoutmasters led boys.

What sort of men, then, consented to lead the boys, and why did they volunteer? Personal motives are of course hard to decipher in the mass; however, most Scoutmasters, like YMCA volunteers, were recognizably middle-class. They were young, with a median age of thirty-one in 1921, and had substantially above-average education; in 1912, 64 percent claimed some college experience. As the BSA grew, the proportion declined but in 1921 still stood at 48 percent. Meanwhile the percentage who had attended high school or business college rose from 20 in 1912 to 32 by 1921. By contrast, as late as 1940 only 10 percent of all American men claimed college education.[93] Blue-collar workers were greatly underrepresented, for in 1912 only 3 percent of Scoutmasters worked at a mechanical trade (see Table 6). As the BSA grew, the proportion rose, but merely to 13 percent by 1921. Common laborers remained rare: 238 in 1921 (1.5 percent), compared to 382 physicians. Even including those reported as having some unspecified occupation or none, blue-collar workers made up just 18 percent of Scoutmasters in 1921. By contrast, nonfarm manual workers comprised 44 percent of America's male labor force in 1920. Farmers were even rarer as Scoutmasters — 4 percent in 1921, although farming employed 30 percent of the male work force. On the other hand, white-collar workers — clerks, businessmen, professionals, semiprofessionals, and students — accounted for 75 percent of all Scoutmasters in 1921. The group was hugely overrepresented, for white-collar workers amounted to only 21 percent of the male labor force in 1920.[94]

In general, then, Scoutmasters were young men of modest but respectable social status, middle- to lower-middle-class. The one major shift during the 1910s was away from clergymen towards more commercial men as the BSA evolved from an offshoot of religiously oriented boys' work towards a movement for good citizenship (see Table 6). The annual report for 1921 classified 38 percent of Scoutmasters as mercantile, a catchall category that included both substantial businessmen and lowly clerks but probably a preponderance of young men in junior positions.[95] Professional men were plentiful. Doctors, lawyers, and engineers made a fair showing, 7 percent of the total; but ministers and teachers were more numerous, at 16 and 9 percent respectively. These were two of the lowest paid professions, although their standing with boys was respectable judging by a poll of 1920s high school pupils. These teenagers rated clergymen high in prestige, even though small-town pastors — who were those most likely to be Scoutmasters — were notoriously insecure in status. The students ranked teaching at the bottom of the professions but still above blue-collar jobs.[96]

The Scoutmasters' class background was no accident; it is a sociological commonplace that white-collar workers are more likely than blue-collar ones to be joiners, and they were better able to volunteer for Boy Scout

Table 6
Occupations of Scoutmasters in Selected Years, 1912–1921

Occupation	1912 (%) (N = 6,868)[a]	1915 (%) (N = 6,731)[a]	1919 (%) (N = 14,728)[a]	1921 (%) (N = 16,002)[a]
Clergyman	28.7	24.4	19.5	15.5
Mercantile	18.7[b]	25.8	42.1	38.0
Teacher	9.9	11.7	11.0	9.4
YMCA	5.7	2.6	.5	.4
Student	3.9	3.5	1.7	2.2
Mechanical	3.1	10.3	11.0	12.6
Lawyer	2.7	2.2	1.7	1.5
Doctor	2.1	3.0	2.3	2.4
Government worker	—	2.2	2.5	2.3
Professional engineer	—	1.0	1.7	3.0
Journalist	—	.8	.5	.8
Farmer	—	—	—	3.6
Laborer	—	—	—	1.5
Miscellaneous	25.1	12.4	5.6	6.9[c]

[a] N includes only Scoutmasters who were classified by occupation.
[b] Clerks and salesmen, 9.5%; own business, 9.2%.
[c] Various occupations, 3.3%; social worker, 1.6%; physical director, .8%;
army or navy, .7%; no occupation, .4%; YMCA, .1%.
Sources: Boy Scouts of America, *Annual Report* 3 (Feb. 1913):19; 6 (Feb.
1916):39; 10 (Apr. 1920):53; 12 (May 1922):142.

service. Since they generally worked somewhat shorter hours, were less
physically exhausted, and were less pressed financially, white-collar workers could better afford the time, effort, and sometimes expense required
to lead a troop. BSA officials sought out middle-class recruits, and men
of that class found volunteer service appealing or at least expected of
them. Boy Scout executives spoke mostly to service clubs, church bodies,
and college groups; for slum troops they often brought in outsiders rather
than hunt up local men.[97] Thus a BSA report explained the "evident high
character" of Scoutmasters by saying they were "clean men . . . largely
college men." And Ormond Loomis, Boston's Boy Scout executive, singled out the dedicated bourgeois as the ideal Scoutmaster: "The man with
a calling, whether that be professional, business or otherwise, has something
to contribute, because life to him is 'real and earnest.'" With no apparent
irony, Loomis added that such a man probably needed "constructive leisure to avoid nervous breakdown."[98]

What would-be Scoutmasters were seeking from the movement—and
often not finding, for annual turnover was 51 percent as late as 1924—
varied widely. After tabulating the conventional, rather stereotyped mo-

tives stated on their application forms by 432 Chicago Scoutmasters of the 1910s, Jeffrey Hantover concluded with pardonable understatement that the results did "not lend themselves to explanatory parsimony."[99] The purposes most often mentioned — to help boys (79 responses), follow an interest in boys or boys' work (67), teach citizenship (53), and foster manhood (44) — were unrevealing or merely echoed the BSA's own statements of purpose.[100]

Some Scoutmasters had narrower interests of a kind that one did not enter on an application. There were lecturers who hungered for an audience, parliamentarians who loved formal meetings, and coaches who wanted a team.[101] No single thread ran through these enthusiasms, but the first two were mostly middle-class and all were harmless, although they detracted from outdoor Scouting. One urge, however, was widespread and troublesome. Judging by complaints about men who wore National Guard uniforms and brandished revolvers, a good many Scoutmasters were throwbacks to the Boys' Brigades — frustrated civilians who wanted to play soldier or weekend militiamen who sought more authority.[102] Still, their excesses were extensions of the militant Americanism that the BSA itself encouraged. A few men wanted to prove they could beat the toughest boys. Others caused a very different kind of alarm; Judge A. B. Cohn, Scout Commissioner for Toledo, warned that the man "is too often admitted [who] calls his scouts 'dear' and 'paws' them." To minimize scandal, BSA headquarters maintained a "red tab" file of men not to be accepted as Scoutmasters.[103] But no such quirky urge — despite the homophobic suspicion that has hovered around the image of the Scoutmaster — could explain why thousands of men volunteered each year.

Many young men wanted a form of social anchorage and an outlet for their energy. Thirty-five percent of Scoutmasters were single, many doubtless still trying to establish themselves, and only 36 percent had sons — of whom only a fraction could have been Scout age.[104] Most men therefore did not take up Boy Scout service to help their own sons; more likely, they sought some of the satisfactions of fatherhood without irrevocable commitments. Lonely men found friendship, but more than that, young men not yet well established in their communities or in their own estimation found an acceptable role as Scoutmasters. Ministers, teachers, and clerks who wanted proof of masculinity may have been disappointed when Scouting proved to mean riding herd on small boys at weekly meetings; still, it held out at least the promise of outdoor life. The men may have hoped to relive their own boyhoods, repeating outdoor joys or making up for what they missed. It is noteworthy how often the promise that "the boys will make you young" figured in remarks on Scoutmastership; men reported they wanted "to be a boy with the boys."[105] The wish to be a child again was a staple of Victorian sentimentality, here transmuted into the nervously masculine idiom of the early 1900s. Nostalgia for boyhood was an obvious reaction against the pressures of white-collar careerism.

Merely spending time outdoors was unlikely to be considered enough to make one a man, however; as an adult, one demonstrated masculinity and social respectability in responsible undertakings. Boys' work was one such project open to young men, a modest opportunity for altruism and leadership. Many Scoutmasters had in fact already tried some form of work with boys and turned to Scouting as a better method. In 1912, only 16 percent reported no relevant experience whatever (see Table 7). At least 25 percent had taught Sunday school. Many had done other boys' work: 12 percent in the YMCA, 11 percent in clubs for church or street boys, 5 percent in the Brigades, and 2 percent in the KOKA. Still others were ministers or teachers. And these were minimum figures, since the BSA reported only one form of experience per man. A number may have been seeking a more vigorous, masculine, and socially prestigious alternative to teaching Sunday school—a common form of service but one that was dominated by women (73 percent in an Indiana survey of the 1920s) and less selective socially than Boy Scouting (only 43 percent of male Sunday school teachers in that survey held white-collar jobs).[106]

Certainly recruiters found it best to present Scoutmastership as a chance to help boys. The men responded with statements about "social service" and descriptions of Scouting as a way "to develop the boy and help him to help others" or to foster 100-percent Americanism.[107] For young business and professional men to offer service of some sort was unremarkable, since they claimed a commitment to do more than just make money. The concept of service also had religious roots, but secular concerns led a good many men to choose Boy Scouting. For those from the native-stock middle class, the BSA's support for social discipline and patriotism had an obvious attraction, since theirs was the social class and ethnic group which most zealously supported militant Americanism. Furthermore, Boy Scouts were familiar youths, much less threatening than boys' club urchins.

Involvement in Boy Scouting was not, therefore, a variant of noblesse oblige in the sense of succoring the downtrodden. For Scoutmasters, service was a way of planting themselves more firmly in their own class. As members of the new middle class—which most were—they had to locate themselves socially and advance by displaying the proper qualities rather than by control of property. Ministers, teachers, and ambitious clerks had to convince themselves and others that they were worthy men. Civic service demonstrated respectability; experience with people might aid one's career; and community activities were a professional man's substitute for advertising. For a century, marginal members of the middle class had anchored their own status by participating in associations headed by prominent men.[108] Ambitious Scoutmasters could also hope to meet important

Table 7
Prior Experience of Scoutmasters in Selected Years,[a] 1912–1919

Area of Experience	1912 (%) (N = 6,917)	1915 (%) (N = 7,067)	1917 (%) (N = 12,392)	1919 (%) (N = 15,176)
Boy Scouts	6.9	12.8	34.4	39.8
Sunday school	24.6	14.3	11.2	12.0
Boys' club (church or street)	11.4	18.5	10.7	6.7
YMCA	11.8	10.7	7.8	6.7
Teaching	7.7	4.9	4.9	5.0
Military	—	2.6	3.4	6.2
Boys' Brigades	5.2	1.8	.9	.7
Ministry	—	2.9	.8	2.1
Knights of King Arthur	2.1	—	—	—
Playground	1.3	.1	.2	1.0
Miscellaneous	12.4	5.3	3.7	1.8
None	15.9	1.9	1.5	9.9
No record	.7	24.2	20.4	8.0

[a]Only one form per man. Non-Scout forms increasingly went unrecorded.
Sources: Boy Scouts of America, *Annual Report* 3 (Feb. 1913):19; 6 (Feb. 1916):39; 8 (Apr. 1918):40–41; 10 (Apr. 1920):52.

men who served on the local council. Potential recruits were "more impressed" when a council member approached them than when the executive did, for service, status, and sometimes self-advancement then beckoned all at once.[109] Similarly, Scoutmasters and YMCA men preferred respectable youngsters in part, one suspects, because the parents might be worth knowing. A Canadian Boy Scout official summed up the advantages: "The recognized public service of the Scoutmaster gives a standing in the community. The circle of acquaintances and friends made through the boys is always worthwhile."[110]

The difference between Scoutmasters and members of the local council shows that while character building centered on the middle class, that term obscures a world of complexity. Some of the confusion about support for Progressive Era movements can be alleviated by recognizing that leaders and followers formed a pyramid, in this case one of age and status. At the top in character-building agencies were wealthy members of the governing boards who financed national headquarters; below them were the men who sat on Boy Scout local councils and YMCA boards of directors, not necessarily rich but generally middle-aged and well connected. Next came the Scoutmasters and Bible class leaders, still above average in education and social status and including a number of upper-middle-class businessmen and professionals but in the main young, from the lesser professions and the lower ranges of the white-collar world. Leading YMCA secretaries and Boy Scout executives resembled local council members in power and status, but the run-of-the-mill were more like the Scoutmasters or YMCA volunteers they once had been. The carping of paid boys' workers at volunteers suggested an uneasy recognition of similarity in age and social background; only the tenuous authority of their organizational position and some shreds of professional expertise distinguished the salaried staff. Below the professionals and volunteers, at the base of the pyramid, came the mass of boys who were — as we shall see — disproportionately but not exclusively middle-class. Participants at lower levels of the pyramid gained satisfaction from membership in a respected organization and recognition by those next above them. They could hope to rise in social status and organizational position as they grew older. The effect of such a pyramid was to reserve final authority for prominent, prosperous individuals but at the same time to assimilate others as willing, subordinate participants. If similar patterns obtained within most community-based organizations, it is no mystery how lower-white-collar and even some blue-collar voters came to support elite-dominated urban reform — especially in small cities where they were more likely, through associational memberships, to feel an integral part of the community; certainly character builders recruited best in such places. More to our point, it becomes evident how character-building agencies, ruled by men of money and position, nonetheless enjoyed an expanding mass membership.

12

Recruiting a "Fine Lot of Lads"

It is of course intellectually risky to infer the characteristics of an organization's members from those of its leaders; still, like their leaders, Boy Scouts and YMCA juniors were disproportionately middle-class, although less exclusively so. Some of the same social processes were at work. Since the 1920s, studies have found the lower class less likely than the middle class to join voluntary associations. In addition, blue-collar joiners have tended to favor recreational or expressive associations rather than those seeking specific goals through social or political action.[1] From the boys' viewpoint, however, Boy Scout or YMCA membership was recreational, whereas for adult volunteers it was more socially purposive. Thus one could have predicted that more working-class boys than men would join, but not as many as middle-class boys. In the case of character-building agencies, however, enrollment patterns also had historical roots in decisions — made before 1900 and sustained thereafter — to favor middle-class boys and guard them from lower-class contamination. An upsurge of confidence led character builders of the 1910s to reach out for lower-class boys; yet these sporadic efforts were only partly effective, marred at times by condescension and defeatism and hampered by the fact that many lower-class boys found the programs costly and culturally alien.

Black youths were hard for character builders to reach, since they were disproportionately poor and at the time still heavily rural; however, their neglect also reflected the casual racism which permeated contemporary British and American culture. YMCA men gave minstrel shows at camp and even parodied a "colored" YMCA, laughing at the education committee's purported obsession with chicken-raising. The first American Boy Scout handbook included Baden-Powell's mnemonic device for "N" in Morse code, a cartoon of a "Nimble Nig" (the dot) chased by a crocodile (the dash).[2] Although seldom as blatantly nasty as Baden-Powell's joke — indeed generally fairly mild by the standards of the early twentieth century, when vicious racism pervaded much of white American culture — heedless bigotry was commonplace among character builders.

The most direct damage came from southern intransigence and fear of losing white enrollments. By deciding to sanction no black troop without local council approval, the BSA's executive board gave southern whites a veto which they were happy to use. Not even a black group's offer to rename themselves "Young American Patriots" could budge the board.[3] Bolton Smith, a Memphis banker who served as the board's expert on race relations, answered a critic by stating that "as long as the grown people are willing to stand for lynchings of colored people," it was hopeless to expect public support for giving them Boy Scouting. To admit black boys "would lose us many white Scouts. . . ."[4] Outside council areas, the BSA simply refused to register black troops, as West foresaw "great mischief . . . if we permit the organization of colored troops in some very small community, even with the consent of the superintendent of schools and other representative people. Suppose this small community eventually becomes part of a county council or district council—it would work havoc and be an unnecessary embarrassment to overcome."[5] Even when opposition to black Boy Scouts began to wane, access to uniforms which resembled the army's remained a sticking point; Boy Scout officials in Richmond, Virginia, threatened a public burning of Scout uniforms if black boys were allowed to wear them.[6]

The northern situation was more complex. Since the 1880s, some boys' clubs had enrolled black and white boys together; and integrated Boy Scout troops mixed immigrant and black youngsters in cities such as Buffalo and Philadelphia.[7] Most troops, however, were smaller, more socially cohesive and middle-class than boys' clubs; hence black Boy Scouts belonged mainly to separate troops with black Scoutmasters. Although much segregation within the Boy Scout movement followed more or less automatically from the prior segregation of the institutions which sponsored troops, some was deliberately imposed in addition. BSA officials in Camden, New Jersey, were concerned when a black clergyman promoted Boy Scouting so successfully that more than a fifth of the local Boy Scouts were black. The council responded by cutting the county into ten districts, nine of them geographical and the tenth "a division of all the colored troops" with a representative on the council. "They have taken it as a compliment," claimed a local officer, "and although some . . . did not like segregation . . . they have swallowed it. . . ."[8] Camden was unusual, for by 1926 there were only 4,923 Boy Scouts under black leadership in 108 councils. Even allowing for integrated troops, blacks were underrepresented. A survey in the late 1920s found that in ten northern communities 5.7 percent of the boys were black but only 1.9 percent of the Boy Scouts.[9] This poor representation possibly owed as much to poverty, however, as to direct racial exclusion.

Louisville, Kentucky, had some five hundred Boy Scouts in black troops by 1924, with an advisory council of prominent black men answerable to the white council. Further south, however, Boy Scouting for blacks was virtually unknown before 1926, when the BSA persuaded the Laura Spellman Rockefeller Foundation to finance a promotion campaign.[10] One by one, southern councils accepted blacks, though some imposed a delay before black Boy Scouts could wear the uniform. Stanley Harris, field executive for the South, estimated that by 1939 50,000 of the nation's 1,449,103 Boy Scouts were black.[11]

The YMCA pursued a similar separate-and-not-quite-equal policy but succeeded with it sooner in the South. City Associations north and south formed "Colored" branches; as in the BSA, final authority rested with white boards of directors. When Jesse Moorland, secretary of the International Committee's Colored Men's Department, took up organizing in 1898, he found white community leaders indifferent; but large gifts from Julius Rosenwald of Sears, Roebuck broke the impasse in the 1910s and spurred construction of "Colored" YMCA buildings nationwide. Advocates of equality objected that these structures fixed segregation in stone; contemporary philanthropists, however, typically supported schemes for black uplift which reinforced racial separation.[12] Although in 1916 the International Committee finally hired a secretary for black boys, George W. Moore, Moorland complained that state and local boys' workers gave only limited help. Boys' work for blacks grew slowly, mostly in "Colored" YMCAs, until by 1920 they enrolled 3 percent of YMCA juniors.[13]

E. M. Robinson was dismayed that the BSA barred black boys in the South; yet when Moore designed a substitute for Boy Scouting to be called the Lincoln Guild, Robinson delayed implementation, demanding centralized authority on the grounds that "colored people are less responsible than white. . . ."[14] Moorland opposed the plan as a "'Jim Crow' organization," and Moore's successor, Henry K. Craft, rejected it outright. Craft further irked Robinson by opposing construction of a "Colored" YMCA in Boston which would have expanded boys' work but might have eliminated blacks from the parent Association. "I asked him plainly if he was ready to victimize 99% of the colored boys in order that 1% might mix with the whites," reported Robinson, "and he said he was."[15]

Character builders' relations with immigrant and lower-class boys (the two categories overlapped in their minds) were more complicated. Character builders were hopeful of recruiting such boys and making them over. But the boys' slowness or reluctance to remold themselves on native-stock Protestant lines reinforced a lingering suspicion that these boys were inferior and must be kept separate from those of "better" families.

The Honolulu YMCA furnished an extreme example of character builders' problems in trying to remake boys. Waldo Shaver, the boys' secretary there, said it was sad to get a boy almost to accept Christianity and then receive a letter "saying that he cannot stay longer in the program because his parents are Buddhist, and cannot stand the break between the parents and the son." In dilute form, similar tensions troubled relations with Catholics; according to a New York state survey published in 1910, they were five times less likely than other boys to be Y members.[16]

The BSA's Americanism was almost as troubling as the YMCA's Protestantism. In negotiations with ethnic groups, Boy Scout officials showed little sympathy for immigrants' desires to preserve their culture. The Polish National Council backed out of a 1914 agreement to merge its Boy Scouts with the BSA, demanding instead special rules and a handbook in Polish.[17] Immigrants' memories of European conscription led them to fear their sons had been inveigled into military training. Because faith was intimately bound up with the mother tongue, many foreign-speaking Catholics also assumed that Boy Scouting, conducted all in English, went against the Church. Many tried to keep their boys from joining, and executive Doan of Cleveland saw mothers in tears because they had failed. Yet when he asked about issuing literature in immigrant tongues, there was none available. Ray Wyland of the BSA's Department of Education was sympathetic, but prevailing theories of Americanization called for English-only instruction.[18]

Character building came most directly between parents and children if it cut into the time boys worked to supplement the family income. Thus a Scoutmaster in Manhattan found that Italian boys saw no point in earning their uniforms; they thought they should spend their time helping their fathers truck, since Italian parents commonly believed that duty to one's family took precedence over recreation or even individual self-advancement.[19]

Some immigrants' sons became Boy Scouts anyway, often in separate troops. Worcester, Massachusetts, for example, boasted Arabic, Armenian, French, Italian, and five French Canadian troops. Such boys could face discouragement, however, since many Scoutmasters considered them less able or dependable than other boys. Klaas Oosterhuis, Scoutmaster at Chicago Commons, judged the full Scout program "too hard and comprehensive for our Italian boys. . . ."[20] Many immigrant families clung to preindustrial habits that character builders, eager for order, punctuality, and standardized achievement, found troubling. I. S. Southworth, an executive from Long Island, let patrols from one of his troops — made up of a "high type of boys" — hike by themselves; but his other troop consisted of Polish and Italian boys. "I cannot run that troop on the patrol system," he claimed. "I have to conduct it more on the old idea of the boys' clubs." L. L. Mc-Donald of Chicago was equally blunt: if three nineteen-year-olds had not reached first class, that was normal in his view, since they were "just ordinary Hungarian boys." A 1928 study by the BSA found no difference between troops in poor neighborhoods and those in "so-called 'better' districts" but admitted that Boy Scout leaders had "not expected good Scouting from some of our foreign districts."[21]

This strain of nativism was apparent when the BSA recruited outside experts. To head the committee revising the program in 1911, the executive board chose Jeremiah Jenks, intellectual leader of the 1907 Immigration Commission which stigmatized recent immigrants as inferior; and to assess Boy Scouting's success in the 1920s, the BSA picked Henry Pratt Fairchild, a leading foe of immigration who wrote *The Melting Pot Mistake*.[22]

YMCA men preferred economic and moral rather than nationalistic criteria, but they too passed a missionary judgment upon lower-class boys. Thus Fred Rindge of the International Committee felt obliged to say that "deep sea dredging" would not bring up "all slime and filth, for many a boy 'Groping for the right, with horny calloused hands, and staring round for God with blood-shot eyes,' will prove a perfect jewel when refined."[23] Rindge's jumbled rhetoric betrayed the character builders' uncertainty whether to try to salvage lower-class boys or avoid them.

Caution limited social outreach, since middle-class parents wanted their sons protected. "Boys of good morals should not be exposed to contamination with boys who have grown up without good home training," insisted *Association Men* in 1900. Although twentieth-century YMCA workers reached out to working boys, they did so on a segregated basis — to the point that some men believed if a schoolboy wanted to join a club with employed boys, "the request should be endorsed by his home; and his school principal should be advised of the circumstances."[24] Boys' secretaries were even warier of street boys; a few tried Bible classes or admitted gamins for a cleansing dip in the pool before the week's water was emptied, but most left them to other agencies.[25] In general, secretaries continued the pre-1900 three-tier system: favor schoolboys, admit working boys, and shun street boys.

Boy Scout enthusiasts gloried in rough brands plucked from the burning, such as Antonio Draginetti of Chicago's stockyards district, who had once attacked a teacher with an axe but then found a place in Scouting and rose to be a patrol leader.[26] Despite the BSA's promises to combat delinquency, however, sponsorship patterns and residential clustering kept roughnecks out of most troops. In addition, Scoutmasters were deterred from social experiments by parents who said a "rotten apple contaminated the lot" and threatened to remove their sons. Indeed, Boy Scout officials were careful to describe their program as "formative rather than reformatory."[27] In a few towns they took boys on probation from the juvenile court, but this practice could still be selective; in Toledo, for instance, they took only the "most promising." Even when they did recruit in the slums, YMCA and Boy Scout leaders were mostly "skimming the cream."[28]

To square their practice with professed concern for the underprivileged, character builders espoused a comforting belief that they could teach the better boys to help the others. Thus *Scouting* magazine suggested: "Whether or not there is a Juvenile Court in your town, your Scouts should be urged to take a friendly, helpful attitude towards boys who are less fortunate." Speakers at YMCA older boys' conferences expressed similar ambitions to redeem their working brethren.[29]

One wonders how many boys risked a beating to assert class superiority. Perhaps they were safer under the racial code of the South, for some white boys there coached black youngsters on Boy Scout requirements and gave them used uniforms once the BSA permitted black troops.[30] In general, boys themselves were less tolerant of social mixing than their Scoutmasters; they preferred to stay in homogeneous groups and were prepared to blackball boys they thought inferior. Winifred Buck, for instance, found in club work that department store cash boys voted to bar all newsboys. Similarly, a Scoutmaster who admitted a foreign-born street boy met fierce opposition from native-born Scouts.[31] It was therefore easier for leaders simply to avoid social diversity.

Cost, of course, barred many boys. Even employed boys who joined the YMCA came from families in the upper tier of the working class, where financial pressures were less intense; they commonly kept a couple of dollars a week for themselves, whereas other working boys gave over all but their small change at home. A YMCA commission reporting in 1913 asked despairingly: "[How] can a lad earning from $3 to $4 a week pay for privileges that would mean privation in the home?"[32]

Although Boy Scout officials tried to control costs, these proved hard to keep low. In 1914, troops could use a stripped-down uniform for $2; but the regular outfits ran up to $6, and boys outgrew them or reduced them to "hikers" by long wear. After wartime inflation, a 1920 estimate put a new Boy Scout's expenses at $20 to $30 for the uniform and two weeks at camp.[33] The total was too high, since one week was more common than two; still, the expense could deter parents of limited means.

BSA officials liked having boys earn their own uniforms, and some Scoutmasters tactfully arranged for all boys in the troop to do so through cleanup work or door-to-door sales, thereby avoiding the stigma of charity for the poorer boys. But money-raising schemes caused endless headaches, since BSA officials did not want the boys to peddle anything while in uniform.[34] By the 1910s, paying jobs were hard to find for middle-class boys of twelve or thirteen; Boy Scout officials struggled just to enforce the requirement that second class Scouts earn and deposit a dollar in the bank —"the first work of their lives" for many boys.[35] To Boy Scouts who received allowances, earning money had become an artificial task, a ritual of faith that diligence in petty enterprise still led upward to success.

The assumption—typical of Progressive Era abhorrence of special privi-

lege for rich or poor — that standardization and a common uniform made
Boy Scouting democratic obscured the facts of selective recruitment. To
the charge of ignoring poor boys West answered that Boy Scout officials
treated everyone alike. A few executives realized that this approach worked
against disadvantaged boys. L. L. McDonald of Chicago, for instance,
took special pains to recruit Scoutmasters from lower-class areas.[36] For
the most part, however, the BSA in its early years of rapid growth followed
the course of least resistance regarding enrollment.

Although the degree of selectivity in Boy Scout recruitment was not
immediately apparent, Beard for one had the impression that Scouts belonged "to the 'better class' of boys." They were a "fine lot of lads," he
said, "but apparently they were a fine lot of lads before they joined."[37]
David Snedden, an educational sociologist, judged in 1917 that Boy Scouting was "largely restricted to urban (including village and suburban) boys
of middle class parentage and good or fair home environment."[38] Snedden exaggerated if he excluded all working boys, for a Scoutmaster estimated that one-fifth of the Boy Scouts in Paterson, New Jersey, held factory jobs. Yet that was still a low figure. William McCormick, a club leader
hostile to the Boy Scouts, believed the movement attracted "the white-
collared, blue-necktied boy who loafs in your office" but not "the boy
who comes from the factory at night with smudged face and empty dinner
kettle."[39] In short, informed if not unbiased observers agreed that the BSA
recruited few lower-class boys.

More solid information comes from surveys, although few cover the
years before 1920. The best study for the 1910s is that of Jeffrey Hantover,
who tried to trace the occupations of fathers of some 1,200 Chicago Boy
Scouts and succeeded with half. Professional men, managers, and officials were substantially overrepresented (about 2:1 compared to these occupations' shares of Chicago's male labor force), skilled workers and clerical
and sales workers less so (4:3 and 6:5 respectively). The semiskilled were
underrepresented (1:2), and the unskilled more so (1:3). A 1918 survey of
1,505 Minneapolis-area Boy Scouts yielded similar conclusions, though
the class differences were a bit less striking. In both cities, the higher his
father's vocational status, the more likely a boy was to be a Scout. Just
as in Britain, the Boy Scout movement in the U.S. had trouble attracting
boys below the topmost tier of the working class. Indeed, these statistics
may slightly overstate the BSA's early success with lower-class boys, since
the figures were gathered during the wartime upsurge in blue-collar incomes which may temporarily have made it easier for lower-class boys
to afford Scout membership.[40]

It is noteworthy that there was little membership difference between lower
white-collar and skilled blue-collar workers' sons. In regard to Boy Scouting

—and a good deal else, one suspects—the two groups behaved much the same. Compared to the sons of semiskilled workers, both groups were much more likely to join the BSA and imbibe its conformist, achievement-oriented ethos. Thus Boy Scouting may have represented a channel of upward mobility. These statistics do not, however, support the theory that lower-middle-class marginality was the primary incentive for parents to enroll their sons, since fathers higher in the middle class were in fact more likely to have boys in Scouting. But no doubt they too had worries about their sons' futures. What these statistics suggest about the older generation is that lower white-collar and skilled blue-collar workers behaved similarly as consumers, both paying the cost for their sons to become Boy Scouts. But the men's attitudes towards their own social roles remained different, as even skilled blue-collar workers were much less likely to become Scoutmasters. Class distinctions seemed less striking among the boys.

Most Boy Scouts were still in school; an Indiana survey found only 4 percent who had quit. Admittedly, the boys were young, but it still is striking that only 15 percent had paid jobs, mostly as part-time delivery boys or salesmen; a mere 3 percent held blue-collar jobs. Many Boy Scouts would later attend college, for Ray Wyland found in 1926 that 40 to 50 percent of male students at some twenty-eight colleges had been Boy Scouts.[41]

Further studies confirmed the Boy Scouts' above-average socioeconomic backgrounds. A 1928–1930 survey of 917 boys in ten communities, mostly large cities, found that the average Boy Scout's family had 5.1 members living on $241 a month, whereas non-Scouts' families averaged 5.7 members with $208 income—29 percent less per person.[42] Studies of Connecticut Boy Scouts in 1928–1929 by Jerome Davis and of high school students in 1933 by Ray Wyland likewise demonstrated that Boy Scouts tended to come from above-average socioeconomic backgrounds. Catholic boys' involvement remained low; Davis found Protestant and Jewish boys nearly four times more likely to be Scouts. Significantly, class differences extended beyond mere enrollments, for Davis and Wyland both found that Boy Scouts from higher socioeconomic backgrounds stayed longer than others in Scouting and were a good deal more likely to advance in rank. They also had a much better chance of getting to summer camp.[43] Prosperous boys, we may conclude, received more from Scouting and were more committed to it.

Although one cannot read these results directly back into the 1910s, it is unlikely that Boy Scout recruitment was broader then. And yet the BSA's membership probably had always included a number of boys from outside the middle class. The movement broadened from the base upward as such boys grew up to become Scoutmasters. There were changes from the top down, too, as headquarters officials felt secure enough by the 1930s to encourage troops in "less chance" neighborhoods. A survey of 195 councils in 1933 found only 193 special troops in delinquency areas and 130 in settlements; however, there were also 148 in state industrial schools, plus 406 in orphanages and institutions for the handicapped, who now could win special badges.[44]

Unlike the BSA, the YMCA began in 1904 to record and publish how many of its boys were at work or in school—an easy task, since junior departments separated the two groups (see Table 8). Although YMCA boys averaged somewhat older than Boy Scouts, the proportion who worked for a living never rose much above 25 percent except during World War I, which temporarily swelled the number of boys at work. About half the juniors were grammar school pupils, and a quarter were high school students. These figures leave out Hi-Y members, however. If we include them, only 16 percent of the members for 1920–1921 were at work, while 40 percent attended high school and 44 percent were in grammar school. By comparison, of all American boys aged twelve through seventeen—the YMCA's range for juniors by 1920—only 8 percent in 1910 and 16 percent in 1920 were enrolled in high school. YMCA juniors tended therefore to be disproportionately middle-class, for the children of professionals, proprietors, and managers were more likely to remain in high school than those of blue-collar workers.[45] Admittedly, the fact that so many YMCA boys were in grammar school reflected their age more than their social class, yet the growth of Hi-Y showed where the room for expansion was.

Local reports confirmed that YMCA juniors were predominantly Protestant, native-stock schoolboys from the more respectable neighborhoods.[46] Yet a good many boys' secretaries of the 1910s made serious efforts to enlist working boys, forming an Employed Boys' Brotherhood which paralleled Hi-Y and running large campaigns of vocational guidance open to working boys outside the regular membership.[47] These efforts met with some success. In the mill town of Holyoke, Massachusetts, 38 percent of the juniors were Catholic and 55 percent foreign, mainly French Canadian.[48] According to the federal census, the nationwide percentage of boys aged fourteen and fifteen who were gainfully employed fell from 41 in 1910 to 23 in 1920, although both figures—especially that for 1920—probably understate the number of boys who worked.[49] Despite this apparent decline in youth employment, the proportion of working boys among YMCA juniors held steady at levels between 20 and 25 percent (see Table 8). Part of the reason, to be sure, was that junior departments were taking in more older boys, but Y workers were also reducing their favoritism towards the middle class.[50] For their part, working boys wanted recreation. YMCA programs must have seemed less constraining to them than Boy Scouting, since the YMCA practice of selling services for a fee allowed them some of the freedom as consumers which they expected their new spending money to bring. The Associations did not entirely break out of their white-collar

Table 8
YMCA Juniors at School and Work in Selected Years, 1904–1921

Report Year	At School		At Work	
	N	(%)	N	(%)
1904–5	33,247	80	8,474	20
1906–7	40,370	76	12,874	24
1908–9	50,122	77	15,387	23
1910–11	68,078	77	20,152	23
1912–13	76,631	75	25,641	25
1914–15	90,798	77	27,127	23
	Grammar School		High School		
	N	(%)	N	(%)	
1916–17	60,348	49	32,599	26	30,216	25
1917–18	58,104	41	31,187	22	53,690	38
1918–19	74,823	50	37,660	25	36,574	25
1919–20	88,015	47	46,510	25	53,259	28
including 38,034 Hi-Y	88,015	39	84,544	37	53,259	24
1920–21	102,934	53	54,036	28	38,261	20
including 41,384 Hi-Y	102,934	44	95,420	40	38,261	16

Sources: YMCAs of North America, *Year Books* (1904–21).

constituency, however, since they recruited mostly office boys and clerks but few industrial workers.[51] William McCormick complained enviously that the "millions spent upon vast Y.M.C.A. plants" reached only a select group of working boys—those "fired by ambition" and "well brought up."[52] He had a point, for white-collar lads who joined the Y averaged longer schooling than other working boys and more often claimed definite career plans. Apparently the dream of rising at least to head cashier flickered on among young clerks and made the YMCA ethos more congenial than it was to other working boys.[53]

At the other end of the socioeconomic scale, character builders did well with upper-class boys. The Y's college-based student department had a thriving prep school division. And private schools sponsored 152 Boy Scout troops in 1921, many more in proportion than the public schools. Although an occasional Scoutmaster found rich boys restive, Scouting—with its vaguely military air and nonutilitarian outdoor activities—reached upward from the middle class more easily than downward.[54]

By way of contrast consider the Chicago Boys' Club's membership in 1911. Thirty-four percent of the boys' fathers were "mechanics," 45 percent laborers, and 21 percent "not regularly employed."[55] While character-building agencies gradually broadened their appeal, they clearly started from a very different base than boys' clubs.

Nor did character builders abandon their mission of protecting "good" boys from the rabble, for expansion was carefully segregated. Boy Scout troops met separately, and institutional sponsorship produced a relatively homogeneous membership within each troop. The YMCA achieved much the same result, though rather less gracefully, by keeping programs for working boys and schoolboys entirely separate.

Lower-class boys were unlikely in any case to drift easily into Scouting or the YMCA. Neither storefront nor immigrant churches commonly sponsored troops. Furthermore, blue-collar families were somewhat less settled than others, and lower-class boys, like their parents, were seldom joiners by habit. Primary ties did not therefore draw them into formal memberships. Since such ties are preeminent in leading people to join voluntary associations, low membership perpetuated itself.[56]

The logic of character building was nearly circular: unto him that hath shall be given. Still, the circle was a wide one. Character-building agencies were integrating sons of the most prosperous blue-collar workers into the middle class. This was a small but significant part of a broader process by which better paid blue-collar workers have partly retained and partly regained some of the status enjoyed by independent artisans a century and a half ago. The main social barrier, although a permeable one, lay between skilled and semiskilled workers. Discrimination against blacks, slowness to win immigrants, and condescension towards lower-class boys all narrowed the character builders' constituency. Even so, the boys were less uniformly middle-class than their leaders. Not all were in training for leadership; some were "just ordinary Hungarian boys."

We must remember that ultimately membership depended upon the boys' own choices—in particular upon whether they found a given group congenial. While character builders generally assumed that boys would join if they could, in actuality that was far from certain.

In Britain the class flavor of the Boys' Brigade and Boy Scouts put off lower-class boys, who were cynical about the official pieties those agencies represented. Sex segregation showed the public school influence, and the uniforms served—as did school uniforms—to distinguish sons of middle-class parents and self-consciously respectable artisans from the "rabble." Cadets marching in the slums faced the singsong, "Here comes the Boys' Brigade / All smovered in marmalade, / A tup'ny'apenny pill-box / And 'arf a yard of braid." And Boy Scouts met the jeer, "Here come the Brussel Sprouts / —The stinking, blinking louts."[57]

In the U.S., where class divisions were blurred by an overlay of racial and ethnic distinctions, uniforms did not carry such unmistakable class connotations, but they did brand boys as goody-goodies. To walk down any street in a Boy Scout uniform was to risk mocking whistles; to do so in a tough neighborhood was to court real humiliation. Even in little Lockport, Illinois, Boy Scouts had to "beat up several gangs of the town toughs before it was safe . . . to appear alone in uniform on the street."[58] It was bad enough when the uniforms featured knickers, which were less grown-up than long pants but which boys at least wore into their teens; it was worse towards 1920 when headquarters began pushing shorts, which were cheaper yet so mortified the poorer boys that Scoutmaster A. H. Durieux of Paterson, New Jersey, reported they flatly refused to go bare-kneed.[59]

BSA publicity played upon the class distinction implied by the uniform, contrasting smartly clad Boy Scouts to shabby loafers. In one instance, some Memphis newsboys reportedly were so incensed to find their photo used as Brand X in a Boy Scout circular that they threatened court action. According to a local paper, BSA officials smudged out the boys' faces, and the "newsies" organized a troop; still, other lower-class boys who detected condescension no doubt remained hostile.[60]

As YMCA men learned, the problem was not just one of outreach; even had they spent more time recruiting in the slums, they would have met many indifferent or unfriendly boys. Like the Boy Scout uniform, YMCA religiosity challenged the tradition of unbuttoned, Babe-Ruth-style masculinity. After surveying boys in Los Angeles, Emory Bogardus concluded that a religious program "is bound to meet with scorn from many boys. . . . Any rough-neck will always call a less rough-neck a 'sissy'. . . . The 'Y' boy needs special guidance in coping with this problem without compromising his own developing manhood. . . ." Character building ran counter to a lower-class tradition which "valued physical prowess, spontaneity, and defiance of authority rather than self-restraint and an orientation toward abstract goals."[61]

Factory boys puzzled Y men by their apparent hedonism and lack of ambition, which led to the conclusion that they had no ideals and worked only for money.[62] This curious complaint revealed the gulf of incomprehension between middle-class careerists and blue-collar boys. These youths, having less reason than schoolboys to bear a yoke in the hope of future prospects, were in fact less docile and harder to enlist for Bible study; the few who joined the Y sought tangible benefits, mostly gymnasium privileges.[63] Clarence Robinson, the International Committee's secretary for working boys, found that after a hard day, factory boys wanted sleep or easy entertainment rather than self-improvement; their gym classes had to be lighter, with more games than for schoolboys. To boys short of money, moreover, Association fees seemed mercenary compared to the boys' clubs' nominal charges; YMCA stood for "Your Money is Cheerfully Accepted," they joked.[64]

Working boys alienated from middle-class norms did not find Boy Scout ideals and activities any more appealing. A New York Scoutmaster reported that most boys at his church settlement disliked the laws and stayed away; only the timid who felt unsafe other nights showed up.[65] Many lower-class boys doubtless found the boys' clubs' less intrusive style more congenial. Nor could they see value in skills so far removed from earning a living; activities such as the woodcraft program made it clear that Boy Scouting put off independence. Scout leaders agreed boys were likely to quit when they left school; as West noted, such boys believed they had had all the discipline they needed. A Scoutmaster reported poignantly that a number of his troop members had left school and met other working boys: "I have lost them as far as I can see; they abandoned me; they abandoned everything."[66]

In addition, Scouting's outdoor program was an acquired taste for center-city boys. Club workers sometimes had to labor to generate interest in camping, as city boys, their minds "warped by constant excitement," perversely found nature unnatural and longed for Coney Island.[67] Other outdoor amusements seemed more manly, especially the sports favored by young working-class men; factory towns swarmed with baseball teams, for example, and Boy Scouting could not compete.[68]

Middle-class boys moved more easily into character-building groups, since both the leaders and their values were familiar. Recent studies suggest that patriotism is strongest among middle-class families; this was probably true in the 1910s as well, for political cynicism and radicalism were most apparent among children of immigrants.[69] Studies since the 1920s have also reported that middle-class parents tend to encourage self-direction in their children more strongly than do working-class parents.[70] If this is so, then middle-class boys would have been familiar with the kinds of personal resolves that YMCA secretaries tried to get them to make. Boy Scout requirements for promotion similarly demanded a desire for personal achievement of a conventional sort, although Wyland found that Boy Scouts who won badges were not significantly more successful at schoolwork than their peers.[71] Perhaps other boys simply stuck to what paid — school and part-time jobs — whereas Boy Scouts could afford to be hobbyists and joiners.

Concern for outreach was primarily a big-city phenomenon; character builders recruited more easily in smaller places where the middle class was more solidly in control and class divisions looked less menacing. By 1920, there were 302 Boy Scouts per 100,000 people in council areas with more than 500,000 inhabitants, compared to 847 in councils with populations from 25,000 to 50,000. Even in places too small to have a local council, Boy Scouting did better than in big cities. In 1921, 6.4 percent of all troops were in cities over 1,000,000, compared to 9.6 percent of the country's total population; 18.3 percent were in cities from 100,000 to 1,000,000, which had 16.4 percent of the nation's people; 14.9 percent were in cities from 25,000 to 100,000, compared to just 9.8 percent of the entire population; 19.8 percent were in towns from 5,000 to 25,000, which had only 11.4 percent of the country's people; and 19.2 percent were in small towns from 1,000 to 5,000, compared to just 8.6 percent of the population. Only in tiny hamlets and the open countryside did the troops thin out, with 21.4 percent of them serving 44.3 percent of the total U.S. population.[72] Admittedly, these figures slightly overstate the Boy Scouts' success in small towns, since city troops were sometimes larger and village troops might include farm boys; however, even city troops seldom went over 32 boys, and the fact is few farm boys became Scouts.

It should be no surprise that the BSA did better in small towns than in big cities. Just as municipal reformers failed to centralize administration of the largest cities, scoring their triumphs in smaller ones where there was a more cohesive elite to back their programs, so Boy Scout organizers could not contact all the men who mattered in a large metropolis simply by addressing a few clubs; nor, despite the formation of district committees, could they reach into all the subcommunities of a big city.[73] In smaller places the clergy, school officials, and civic boosters cooperated more easily in support of both the Boy Scouts and the YMCA. Another problem in big cities was the large number of Catholics and immigrants — though the ethnic and religious makeup of cities was less important than simple size in predicting Boy Scout or YMCA enrollment, perhaps because native-stock Protestants redoubled their efforts where they were outnumbered.[74]

At this point we should remember the fears that underlay character building. In big cities, middle-class adults worried that their boys would be corrupted by the pernicious example of lower-class teenagers. In small towns, the potential contagion seemed more likely to be external, seeping in from the cities. This does not mean that class favoritism disappeared among small-town character builders; however, because the poor seemed less alien there than in the cities, Boy Scout and YMCA officials felt they could mix boys of all classes more freely.[75] Many more small-town than big-city ministers became Scoutmasters, presumably because they had the time and thought they could reach the local boys. Although boys' work owed much of its early impetus to the shocks of city life, character building looked most promising where the boys were still within fairly easy reach and seemed less in need of reformation than of mere protection against contagion from outside.

After a fast start in the cities, by the late 1910s Boy Scout troops were spreading faster in small towns than anywhere else.[76] More small-town and suburban boys stayed in school than city youths or farmers' sons, and they were often bored and restless. Unlike big-city churches, those in small towns and the larger villages would not launch major boys' work schemes on their own; but unlike the impoverished little rural churches found in hamlets and out along country roads, they could afford modest ventures.[77] Hence small-town boys and churchmen both welcomed Boy Scouting. The suburbs had other advantages for the movement; indeed, much of what passed for small-town boys' work was actually suburban. Social organization there tended to center around churches and schools, and the relatively high social status of the population eased recruitment. In fact, suburbs siphoned off some of the potential leaders of city boys' work, since high-status commuters did much of their service at home in the suburbs.[78]

Even more than Boy Scout leaders, YMCA boys' workers recruited best outside the largest cities. In 1919–1920, only 166 YMCA juniors enrolled per 100,000 inhabitants in cities of more than 500,000 people and 316 in those from 100,000 to 500,000. Wherever smaller cities had YMCAs, however, Association boys' work nearly matched Boy Scouting's popularity. Cities from 50,000 to 100,000 had 589 Y juniors per 100,000 of population; those from 25,000 to 50,000 had 816; and those from 10,000 to 25,000 had 1,385. Many small cities had no YMCA of course, but even if we include *all* cities — with or without a local Association — the Y still recruited best in medium-small cities: 528 boys per 100,000 population in cities from 50,000 to 100,000 and 548 in those from 25,000 to 50,000.[79]

It may seem strange that YMCA boys' work fell so far behind the Boy Scouts in big cities. But one should remember that in the nineteenth century, Associations in smaller cities began boys' work first. Early boys' workers did not want the promiscuous throngs of big-city boys' clubs. Nor did the Y's Protestantism and building-centered program make it easy to penetrate the subcultures of a metropolis. Whereas small-town YMCAs specialized in boys' work, the huge central YMCAs catered to transients and men who worked downtown; few boys made the trip from respectable neighborhoods.[80] Although most large Associations had outlying branches, they could not cover the city the way Boy Scout troops could. Since more than half the membership of most YMCAs came from less than a mile away, those in smaller cities drew a larger fraction of their city's population.[81]

On the other hand, very small towns could not afford YMCA buildings, and Y men had difficulty adapting their large-scale, building-centered programs. Thus the BSA had the suburbs and villages virtually to itself, enrolling about seven times as many small-town boys as the YMCA by the early 1920s.[82] Only in medium-sized communities could Y boys' work match Scouting.

When considering farm boys, Boy Scout and YMCA leaders turned hesitant. Initially, they saw little need for character building among lads whose pastoral virtues served as a foil for city vices. The country boy was less precocious than his city cousin, claimed W. H. Babcock, a YMCA county secretary, because hard work and social isolation kept him from becoming a "little man like the shop boy."[83]

Although concern about farm boys increased towards 1920, leaders in agricultural education found urban character-building programs unappealing. The promotion of leisure-time activities such as woodcraft which were not directly productive made sense to an urban middle class whose adult and boyhood tasks differed sharply. But farm life enthusiasts wanted boys to toil like their fathers; they saw vocational education as the answer to their boy problem and worried that glimpses of the more exciting, prosperous, leisured world of the cities would lure boys off the land. They were right to worry, for few rural high school boys really wanted to farm. In response, leaders in demonstration education such as Seaman Knapp proposed a carrot and blinders. Club life would fix the blinders, beguiling members into spending their free time working plots of land, while in place of the carrot educators dangled high profits realized by scientific farming. Starting soon after 1900, boys' and girls' corn and canning clubs spread under the aegis of the Department of Agriculture, won further federal aid through the 1914 Smith-Lever Act, and eventually took the name "4-H."[84]

The YMCA did not meet this challenge head on. "County" YMCAs tried a few 4-H-type programs but put their main effort into remedying the social isolation of rural life — an approach which threatened farmers' control of their sons. County work grew slowly, with 17,867 boys enrolled for 1920–1921.[85]

BSA officials were reluctant to meet 4-H-style competition on its own ground for fear of turning recreation into drudgery. In revising the program in 1911, they added several merit badges for farming but resisted pleas from Willett M. Hays, Assistant Secretary of Agriculture, to add large doses of vocational training for farm boys.[86] They did not want to beat paddles into plowshares.

Besides, the BSA was slow to modify its group emphasis, as West and his colleagues insisted that all boys needed "gang" experience.[87] William D. Boyce stepped into the gap in 1915 with *Lone Scout* magazine, which purveyed a blend of Setonian woodcraft with regular Boy Scouting. Though Boyce developed no real organization, individual boys were enthusiastic

Lone Scouts, often publishing their own magazines. But interest waned when the BSA bought Boyce out in 1924 and brought Lone Scouting under close adult control.[88] Two years later, the BSA hired O. H. Benson, a leading organizer of farm clubs, to develop rural Boy Scouting. Benson retained the rural educator's suspicion of troop Scouting's gregarious good times, warning that if farm boys became "too social and urban-minded they [would] desert their parents and the farm life. . . ." The Lone Scouts, he promised, would keep them individualistic, isolated, and agrarian.[89]

According to a 1925 estimate, 34 percent of American boys lived in the open countryside but only 6 percent of the Boy Scouts—and the latter estimate may have been high.[90] As we have seen, farmers were poorer on average than townsfolk and had larger families; thus the pressure to get their sons to work and keep them at it was very real. Charles Galpin, a rural sociologist, warned Boy Scout executives that "the old farmer" wanted to keep his son away from others and hard at work. The farmer did not mind his boy being a Lone Scout, since it "didn't cost very much . . . and it didn't bring him into the company of strangers very much." But leaders in agriculture were "far from enthusiastic" about regular troop Scouting.[91] Farmers were not joiners, and their churches were organizationally impoverished, with some lacking even Sunday schools. What club life the countryside afforded came mostly through farmers' organizations, which did not separate age groups and were "more of a family affair" than those in the village.[92] Bogged down by incessant labor, many farmers resisted anything that did not promise an immediate economic return—even schemes for scientific farming, let alone social uplift or church-sponsored recreation. Therefore they did not follow when Main Street merchants started a citified church auxiliary such as Boy Scouting; its control centered among business and professional men whose relations with country folk were often distant and occasionally hostile.[93]

Farm boys proved hard to interest and assemble in any case. They evinced less interest in hiking and nature study than village youngsters, since they saw enough of fields and woods already; what they really wanted were team sports. Also the boys were busy, and without all-weather roads they had trouble reaching meetings.[94] The YMCA adapted a bit more easily, as sports fitted naturally into its program; even so, a survey of rural and suburban counties in 1924 found that just 17 percent of the Boy Scouts and 29 percent of the YMCA juniors came from farm families. And the Y was not organized in most counties.[95]

Overall, character builders found their prime constituency among white, native-stock Protestants in the smaller cities and in towns and villages. They had trouble reaching out to boys who were literally or figuratively alien. Farmboys and Catholics, for instance, were under disciplines of work and worship such that farmers and priests initially greeted Boy Scouting and the YMCA as threats to their control of boys. It was fitting that character-building agencies — which balanced between nostalgic and modernizing urges — found their firmest footing not in big cities where social change seemed to rush forward almost unmanageably, nor among the farmers who embodied tradition for the urbanite, but in towns and villages in between. It was there, as Joseph Kett has noted, that the institutions of adult-sponsored adolescence first flourished.[96]

V

Character Building in Practice

13

Camping: An Organized Setting for the New Boyhood

Having won public acclaim for their organizations, found adult supporters, and selected boys to their liking, what would Boy Scout and YMCA
men actually do with the boys and how well would they hold them? The
top leaders never lacked ambition, hoping as they did to strengthen the
boys' physical, mental, social, and religious faculties while also remedying
the ills of adolescence and reconstructing an ideal boyhood. But success
in organization, publicity, and recruitment furnished no guarantee that
they could realize their goals for boys; how character building would work
in practice and how the boys would respond remained to be seen. This
chapter focuses on the one setting in which YMCA and Boy Scout leaders
had more or less complete — though very temporary — control of boys. Returning to the mundane world of weekly meetings, the next chapter will
then assess the character builders' efforts to teach skills and moral values.
And the chapter beyond that will hazard a summation of boys' group experiences and their reactions to Scouting and YMCA boys' work as they
grew older.

It may seem strange to have described so much of boys' work with little
mention of camping. Yet camping must be treated separately, since character builders used it to form a world apart where they could recreate an
ideal boyhood. On one level, the summer camp was the culmination of
their ambitions, one of those ideal institutions in which Progressive Era
Americans sought to reshape personal values and social relationships. Yet
on another level, camping was a separate activity with a history of its own,
oddly peripheral to the week-to-week operations of most character-building
agencies.

Certainly camping was no simple return to nature; character builders
favored a settled existence with few hardships, and they insisted that outdoorsmanship was not an end in itself. Sometimes the promise of summer
camp was a bribe to hold boys through a year's dull meetings. Generally,
though, boys' workers viewed hikes and camps as part of their strategy
of building character by meeting boys' "natural" needs under supervision

until adult values became second nature. Outdoor life would toughen boys; yet by cloistering the youngsters in pastoral surroundings, camps would also keep them dependent and safe from city vices. Carefully buffered contacts with tame wilderness would enable campers to vent their boyish savagery under close control. Camp programs would encourage boyish activism; yet campfire rituals and natural beauty would induce mild cases of adolescent romanticism. The hope was to strengthen boys and yet protect them, to keep them boyish and yet reap certain benefits of adolescence. Because such balances were hard to maintain, however, camp leaders increasingly adopted a cautious, highly organized approach. Summer camps began as a series of improvisations but soon settled into standard routines.

Early enthusiasts touted camping as a cure for the enervation, nervousness, and fears of effeminacy which distressed the late nineteenth-century urban middle class. Along these lines, William H. H. "Adirondack" Murray, a Boston clergyman, popularized camp life as a cure for exhaustion. The minister would return, he wrote in 1869, "swarth and tough as an Indian, . . . depth and clearness in his reinvigorated voice. . . ."[1] Similarly, John Muir prescribed life in the wilds as the perfect balm for nervous strain brought on by city life. Promotional literature for camps applied this argument to city boys whose robust growth seemed problematic—the prosperous because of schoolroom pressures and parental pampering, the poor because of deprivation. Well-to-do parents were pleased to see their sons return from private camps "brown as berries," while for slum children Jacob Riis claimed that a week in the country produced "most remarkable cures. . . ." And camp directors of all sorts boasted of their boys' hearty appetites.[2]

Organized camping was more than just an escape from the city, however. Its format drew elements from holiday outings, camp meetings, farm summers, military encampments, hunting trips, and boarding school and resort life.

The first YMCA camps of the 1880s were simple outings to hold boys' interest in summer—rather like three-day picnics, with swimming, games, and big meals.[3] The boys camped out as a practical matter, just as pioneers, soldiers, and worshippers at camp meetings had done for years. Only gradually did boys' workers come to think of camping as an activity in its own right; then terms like "boys' camp" and "camper," still considered neologisms in the 1880s, shed their quotation marks.[4] Full-fledged Y camps remained uncommon until the 1890s, when Sumner Dudley and E. M. Robinson promoted them as places to convert boys. Thus the YMCA camp, which the secretaries' manual of 1892 still defined as simply "a more extended outing," began as an excursion that took roots.[5]

Boys' club and charity camps evolved more slowly, combining aspects of one-day outings with placement schemes which sent tenement children off to farms. By 1882, one such placement venture had grown into the *New York Tribune* Fresh Air Fund. Related projects, such as Cleveland, Ohio's, Children's Fresh Air Camp and Hospital, provided group outings; and in 1893 the Milwaukee Boys' Club held the first boys' club camp, although the idea spread only slowly thereafter.[6] Many club directors preferred to send lower-class boys to farm settings where they could work as well as play.[7] Besides, many people suspected that tenement children did not appreciate the woods. In his hyperbolic way, Seton told how a "benevolent rich man" treated a crowd of slum boys to a day in the Catskills. The boys soon huddled "in groups under the bushes, smoking cigarettes, shooting 'craps,' and playing cards, — the only things they knew."[8] Woodsy camping at first was class-based, dependent upon suitable tastes, income, and leaders.

The rapid growth of private camps reflected this class base, for they were logical extensions of expensive boarding schools which sequestered boys in pastoral seclusion; camps extended this tutelage year-round. A couple were under way by 1880, and twenty or so followed by 1900 — all but one in the Northeast. As camp leaders sold parents the idea that organized camp life was better than having sons hang around a resort hotel all summer, private camps became more and more like schools, with gymnastics, handicrafts, dramatics, nature study, academic tutoring, and achievement awards. Just as popular authors made the doings at elite boarding schools the epitome of schoolboy life, so magazine writers glamorized the private camps.[9] Increasingly after 1900, the YMCA imitated them.

Organizers of short-term camps for church groups turned not to schools but to temporary assemblies as their models: revival meetings, chautauquas, and military encampments. Making no pretense that the camp fitted into its natural surroundings, most chose a flat field and drew the tents up in a square. Boys found little seclusion, for visitors wandered freely around the campsite; the Knights of the Holy Grail even invited parents to rent nearby cabins.[10] Camp leaders often turned to army men for technical advice; however, Brigade camps went to extremes, slavishly following military routine from reveille through the posting of sentries at night. Beguiled by this apparent rigor, the officers let the boys have most of their time free; not surprisingly, most boys reveled in swimming, baseball, and pranks, but shy or awkward youngsters suffered without supervised activities. Although many non-Brigade camps adopted semimilitary discipline to keep track of the boys, most camp directors recognized it as only a framework within which to set a program.[11]

Under the circumstances, early camps developed no fervid mystique of wilderness or woodcraft. The private camps were too settled, while the leaders of short-term camps were still preoccupied with technical problems such as how to arrange latrines. Providing a cheap and varied diet proved especially hard; understandably, boys grumbled when a Brigade camp served the same menu every day.[12] When campers roughed it, they did so mostly from necessity. At pre-1900 YMCA camps they slept in earth-floored tents and cooked over open fires, but these were simply facts of camp life and occasioned neither praise nor blame.[13] The vogue of wood-craft came later, in reaction against sedentary tendencies.

Men who ran lakeside excursions were content with Arcadian settings. When a Brigade officer described the route to camp in 1892, his fancy was pastoral: "meadows and running brooks, and rural homes, embowered in trellised vines. . . ." Around 1900, however, as E. M. Robinson became taken with the possibilities of adolescence, he seized upon the idea of inspiring awe: "One cannot see the boy upon the seashore in the storm, when the waves are pounding in," he wrote, without seeing the boy's "flashing eye, the deep-drawn breath, the tense muscles. . . ."[14] In accord with increasing romanticism in character building, camp leaders' preferences in landscape shifted towards the sublime. As for nature study, though, most camps that pursued it at all did so in an academic manner.[15]

Camp organizers were at pains to show that boys would not imbibe rudeness from the wilds. "Sunday was a sweet experience," reported Dudley. "Although in the woods, the bars were not let down, but we were all in the Spirit." Peter Blos has noted in preadolescent boys a resurgence of "pregenital" behavior — scatological joking, slovenly grooming, and so forth.[16] In modern slang, "grossing-out," especially regarding bodily functions, becomes important to boys — perhaps as a way of handling anxiety about their own physical changes. Modern Boy Scout camps are likely to indulge this impulse. Turn-of-the-century camps offered youngsters of that era a very limited outlet; but Robinson, though enamored of boyish savagery, opposed any surrender to coarseness. He warned against "that tendency to rudeness and smartness which characterizes some camps, where the butter is called grease, the milk cow juice, or meat the corpse."[17]

Supervision was the key to group camping. As we have seen, much of boys' work involved taking things that boys already did and translating them onto a slightly larger scale. In summer, most boys who could went out at least occasionally to nearby woods. Even in a big city such as Cleveland, a 1915 survey of grammar school boys found that 25 percent camped and 45 percent hiked, even though only 3 percent were Boy Scouts.[18] Organized camping added a new sense of adventure; instead of sticking close to home, boys might go to a lake forty miles away.

Accordingly, close supervision was vital to calm parents' fears — fears which early camp leaders exacerbated by their evident jitters. Thus the organizers of a YMCA excursion in 1882 gave disquieting assurance: "We shall use every possible care to prevent accident. . . . Should anything, however, unforeseen occur, we shall immediately apprise the parents by dispatch."[19] Even in the 1910s, continuing parental anxiety necessitated visits by the Scoutmaster before some families let their boys attend. As a final reassurance, camp directors had to concede a visitors' day when parents could overrun the site, plying their sons with sweets and disrupting the schedule but verifying that the boys were all right.[20]

As parents relaxed a bit, group camping caught on after 1900. By 1924, there were 713 private camps, mostly in New England, and 535 organizational camps, spread across the country and varying somewhat in character as their sponsors' goals varied.[21]

YMCA camping epitomized in extreme form the odd combination of fee-based membership and earnest evangelizing which narrowed the parent Associations' recruitment. Y camps started fairly cheap — $3.50 to $5.25 a week in the early 1900s — but even this would have strained a workingman's budget, and elaborate facilities brought higher fees. By 1911, the New York State YMCA's Camp Dudley charged $7.50 a week for a minimum of two weeks, plus $8.50 rail fare from New York City. Boys would want the camp uniform at $4.00; a trip to Montreal added $10.00; and optional tutoring cost $1.00 a week. Although private camps charged more, even YMCA fees sufficed to deter many middle-class families. Camp attendance rose from 3,459 in 1900 to 16,690 in 1915 — less than 15 percent of all Y juniors. A rare critic complained, "While the boys' secretary goes off to the country with a few of his boy members, the rest of them go to the devil at home."[22]

High fees imposed arbitrary selection, but a tradition of smallish camps facilitated the YMCA quest for religious commitments. The early camps were small enough — from six or seven boys to seventy or so — to become pressure cookers. On Sumner Dudley's first outing, the six other campers bent all their efforts towards winning one unconverted lad who was "providentially" present.[23] Hoping that boys would idolize their counselors, camp directors changed around 1900 from middle-aged volunteers to college students — "athletic Christian young men who were full to the brim of fun and sport. . . ." Secretaries boasted of campers who came determined only to have fun and left as professing Christians.[24]

Campfires were the established time for conversion. They began with rousing choruses, then passed by way of college songs to hymns and religious talk. Efforts built up all week towards the climactic Sunday evening. Two Y workers described the scene at Brooklyn's Camp Tuxis: "The boys have been away from home for some time. They are unusually thoughtful and tender. The stars twinkling overhead, the sighing of the breeze in the tree tops, the breaking of the waves on the rocks all tend towards turning the mind of the boy towards the God of nature. . . . A few of the older and more manly boys give their personal testimony and now and then a tear falls unheeded down some cheek. It is the critical hour that settles a boy's destiny and many a spot on old Tuxis has witnessed the surrender of a boy's life."[25]

This atmosphere lingered for decades, but gradually stories and stunts took over the campfires as secretaries turned for religious effect to brief vespers in the tents. Conversion rates of 90 percent had led to massive backsliding, for the leaders had exploited confusion between the wind in the trees and the Holy Spirit. Although conversions remained more prominent than in regular Y work, camp directors followed the trend away from encouraging emotional adolescent upheavals.[26]

Camp Sundays changed slowly. Originally they included a soap bath, worship, Sunday school, letter writing, perhaps a walk. The first break at Camp Dudley came when the boys got permission to swim quietly as they rinsed the soap off; then they were allowed calisthenics before the evening meeting. As late as 1915, however, the flagpole at Massachusetts' Camp Becket bore each Sunday a pennant inscribed in red: "Remember."[27]

Camp directors maintained surveillance by grouping the boys five or ten to a tent with an adult leader. The purpose was more than just religious, for Y men after 1900 thought of camp life as a force for social adjustment and turned the many against the few with point systems under which misbehavior lost the group points. Gang life also sanctioned hazing, especially in the name of masculinity and sexual purity. Since Robinson considered nightshirts effeminate, at Camp Dudley anyone wearing one was fair game. One weekend a distinguished clergyman came up to preach. At bedtime he strolled out in his nightshirt to enjoy the breeze, whereupon a camper raised the hue and cry, and an eager horde poured forth to assault the D.D.'s dignity.[28]

As camps expanded, organized programs reinforced social pressures. Large camps acquired tennis courts, rifle ranges, workshops, libraries, and darkrooms. Athletics grew more organized; cabins underwent daily inspection; and Camp Dudley offered a camp letter for ten achievements modeled on Seton's coups. Spurred on by Boy Scouting and the private camps, Y men made their work more educational. Camp Dudley divided the morning into periods of instruction in woodcraft, campcraft, swimming, sports, and school subjects. The result at many camps was a regimented schedule from compulsory morning dip through vespers.[29]

Campers lived comfortably in cabins or tents with board floors. Cooks and caretakers relieved them of most chores, until there were camps, complained Robinson, "where almost everything is done for the boy except the eating of his meals." Ironically, side trips became necessary for "camping experience."[30]

Boy Scouting was different because outdoor activities were an integral part of the program rather than a separate treat for a few boys. Yet BSA officials believed in standardization, and they too moved towards a highly organized style of camping, divorced from ordinary troop activity. Significantly, Seton and Beard—the BSA's main proponents of unadulterated woodcraft—had little say in these arrangements. As Chief Scout, Seton wanted to make woodcraft an end in itself, whereas his associates saw it as merely a means. Seton campaigned unavailingly for higher tenderfoot standards and more outdoors knowledge on the part of Scoutmasters. He chafed at the standard program, demanding more ceremony and symbolism. But his colleagues thought him narrow, dismissed his yearning for undiluted woodcraft as "fanatic idealism," and edged him out.[31]

Seton's enthusiasm grew once he left the Boy Scouts. He revived his Indian program, added elements for girls and adults, and founded the Woodcraft League, securing a distinguished council, which included John Burroughs, Hamlin Garland, and John Alexander. Philip Fagans, a YMCA boys' worker, became executive secretary. The League reached some five thousand members and sputtered along for years in YMCAs and boys' clubs, but organizational laxness and perhaps the eccentricity of Seton's ideas barred sustained growth. In later years, with the Buffalo Wind blowing ever stronger through his imagination, Seton moved to Santa Fe, founded an institute for the study of Indian wisdom, and died there in 1946.[32]

Beard was never as important to the BSA as Seton, but he never fell as far from grace either. Robinson recruited him in 1910 while rounding up potential rivals to the new Boy Scout movement. He became National Scout Commissioner, wrote regularly for *Boys' Life,* and feuded with Seton over who had originated the Boy Scout idea. Beard believed that frontier scouts were the most American of men and hence that Boy Scouting must actually have begun with his Sons of Daniel Boone. It was white man versus Indian as he and Seton squabbled, each convinced that the other's ideal was a bloodthirsty wretch. Beard also outdid the rest of the executive board in charges that Seton was an un-American monarchist. Personal rivalry and nativism thus destroyed the alliance of the board's two leading outdoorsmen.[33] Beard sniped at headquarters for three decades, grumbling about red tape and commercial interests.[34] But his colleagues made clear that he was a mere figurehead. A small man with a white Vandyke beard and a face wrinkled by ninety summers before he died, "Uncle Dan" came to ceremonial occasions arrayed in buckskin, awed the boys with frontier yarns, and dubbed Eagle Scouts with a real bald eagle's claw. He was popular with youngsters (when asked to name the greatest men alive, 1,200 St. Louis schoolchildren placed him twelfth, just behind Mussolini, "Hoot" Gibson, and Marconi), but as far as influence upon BSA policy went, he was a walking totem pole.[35]

Seton affected Boy Scout imagery more deeply, for BSA men laid on more and more Indian ceremonial in the years after his dismissal, as if to make up for lost romance.[36] Otherwise, neither man proved very influential within the BSA. Yet their personal fortunes alone do not explain why romantic woodcraft failed to prevail. More telling were the rival influences of Baden-Powell's plans and YMCA-style camping. To Baden-Powell Scouting was basic training; his lessons in observation, memory, and signaling stemmed from army experience, not nature study. American Boy Scout leaders, though more appreciative of nature, agreed that outdoor activities were primarily means to build character.

Outdoorsmanship bulked large in the BSA's official program but not Seton's intense variety. Of twenty-four requirements to reach first class rank, a majority had some connection with outdoor life; but more than half, such as first aid, had everyday value as well. Nature study was limited, as only one test called for identifying trees or animals. Of fifty-seven merit badges, only nine definitely included woodcraft. Ironically, merit badges at times appeared to rival woodcraft; according to John A. Styles, the chief Boy Scout executive for Canada, Scoutmasters complained that badge seeking interfered with outdoor Scouting.[37]

The chance to get outdoors probably lured more boys and men into Scouting than anything else; yet many Scoutmasters could not get out on weekends and would not let the boys go alone. While strong troops hiked frequently, the complaints of boys who quit the movement indicate that weak troops had nothing but indoor meetings. Still, by 1928 a majority of troops hiked at least once a month.[38]

These hikes were mostly one-day outings, although some extended into weekend camps, and a few were quite adventurous. Even if the Scoutmaster had camp experience, the first overnight hike offered great opportunities for mischance. A troop led by Stuart Walsh, an early Chicago Scoutmaster, returned from its first foray cheerful yet exhausted from fighting mosquitoes, with two lads clad in blankets because their wet clothes had fallen into the fire. The level of adventure depended of course upon the Boy Scouts' ages and the regional topography. Walsh took his boys in summer to woods where houses were so close that they showed through the trees in winter; however, he also hiked the Indiana dunes with robust Scouts and camped in the snow. The dunes in turn paled when he went as Boy Scout executive to Seattle and soon was leading chosen boys deep into the Olympic rain forest.[39] Far more common, though, were Saturday hikes which had few pretensions to romance but did offer the satisfaction of minor exploits and misadventures recollected in tranquility. The tenderfoot in Walsh's troop whom an older Boy Scout lured into heating his unopened can of beans in the fire furnished a memorable tale with an explosive climax. Ideally, one-day hikes were camps in miniature, as Guy

Shorts, an Oklahoma Boy Scout, described: "We started about a quarter of nine. We had some time on the way. My rubbers came of [*sic*] three or four times. We stopped and rested at the bridge a mile and a half out. We got there about half past eleven. First we pitched tents. And then we cooked dinner. I had four weiners, [*sic*] one pie. After dinner we played 'Capture the Flag'. Our side won. We stayed till sixe [*sic*] o'clock. We took the tents down and packed up and went home."[40]

Hiking and camping exposed the character builders' ambivalence towards young teenagers. Good boys, it seemed, led too soft a life, and character builders wanted to toughen them; yet doctors warned that overstrain in adolescence would drain vitality. Dr. John Lovett Morse of Harvard told Scoutmasters that young boys "because of the energy required for growth and the relatively small size of their heart, are very liable to be seriously injured by over-exertion. . . ."[41] Inconsistency resulted; Boy Scout officials at first advised issuing boys their own rations on the theory they needed a little hardship but then worried about indigestion and constipation. In the end, most camps hired a cook. Caution sometimes verged on alarmism; for example, Dr. Fisher warned not to let boys swim twice a day, because loss of heat was loss of life.[42] In that context Boy Scouts were viewed as vulnerable adolescents rather than hardy savages. On the other hand, some Scoutmasters did demand too much. "A foot-weary, muscle-tired, and temper-tried, hungry group of boys is surely not desirable," warned the YMCA's H. W. Gibson in the 1911 Boy Scout handbook. "There are a lot of false notions about courage and bravery and grit . . . and long hikes for boys is one of the most glaring of these notions." Similarly, the 1920 *Handbook for Scoutmasters* complained that "many Scoutmasters pick out a nice camping place about seven miles away and spend a large part of the time hiking along a road, with more or less luggage, going to the place and getting back. The boys become tired, the younger ones lag behind, they are interested in nothing but the next well or a place to rest. . . ." The *Handbook* advised going by trolley.[43] At the cost of making Scouting less challenging to older boys, the Boy Scouts themselves forced Scoutmasters to strike a balance that favored the younger ones.

Full-scale camps were more exciting to the boys, some of whom cried when they had to go home.[44] At first, however, many could not camp; in 1915, for instance, less than a quarter of Philadelphia's Boy Scouts attended summer camp. Some could not afford it, although this was less a problem than in the YMCA, since pre-World War I camps kept fees down to $2.50 to $5.00 for a week.[45] More serious was the shortage of local council camps and the failure of many Scoutmasters to run their own. Campsites were hard to find, since public parks were crowded and noisy. Once the Boy Scout movement became known, leaders could rent or borrow land, but decades elapsed before a good many councils secured their own permanent site. And yet by 1920, as council camps multiplied, almost 45 percent of all Boy Scouts, 167,677 boys, spent a week in camp.[46] Allowing for turnover, a majority of those who had been members for a year got to go. This was perhaps the greatest achievement of the BSA's early years: the movement made a brief camp experience available and affordable to far more boys than YMCA or private camps.

In general, the trend in Boy Scout camping ran to cautious, large-scale enterprises. We have seen that some of this caution stemmed from exaggerated fears of adolescent vulnerability, but inexperienced Scoutmasters did make some troop camps genuinely dangerous. At one such camp there were no ditches around the tents, surface water drained into the muddy spring, and five boys had powder burns from blank cartridges.[47] Although things were seldom quite that grim, poor food, inadequate equipment, and a disorderly program were common. B. F. Skinner, who was a Boy Scout in the mid-1910s and generally liked camps, wrote home from one that went wrong: "We aren't having a very good time after all. All day today the wind has blown very hard and one of the tents fell in. . . . My stomach is all out of order and yesterday I vomited twice and last night we had a circus. I woke up in the night and heard Raphael Miller vomiting outside the tent. That started Bob Perrine's. . . . Then I started in again. . . . They haven't given us a full meal since we've been here. Today they had half boiled potatoes, weak coffee and bread. . . . If I had a good excuse I'd come home but I don't want them to think I'm homesick. . . ."[48] No wonder BSA manuals harped on sanitation.

More than sickness, drownings forced better supervision. Lives were lost because Scoutmasters stood lifeguard fully dressed or went in with the boys. When the number reached twelve in 1916, headquarters named L. L. McDonald, a former Y worker who was Chicago's Boy Scout executive, to be national camp director. He set some standards, and safety improved; by 1918 a troop could lose its charter for holding an unsanctioned camp.[49]

These pressures discouraged backwoods camping, as even Beard warned that every boy seemed intent upon suicide. Nobody took the *Boy Scouts' Diary* seriously when it promised: "When matches are forgotten [the Boy Scout] laughs and proceeds to kindle a fire by rubbing two sticks together. . . ."[50] Instead, one group joked about kindling a Dan Beard fire whenever they used kerosene. At large camps the boys often slept on cots and occasionally in cabins. Many camp directors lined up the tents or cabins with parade square precision; others scattered them around a central site; still others formed them in a circle, so they could see in on rainy days. But seldom were the tents placed in woodsy seclusion; the whole crowd stayed together at the main campsite.[51] Dining halls were common at the larger camps; and a good many camps followed YMCA practice by providing baseball diamonds and tennis courts. Towards 1920, Boy Scout officials felt obliged to warn against running summer "boarding houses"; to add a touch of adventure, camp leaders tried overnight trips like those at YMCA and private camps.[52]

More than simple caution shaped Boy Scout camp life, for the BSA inherited a hodgepodge of camping styles from fresh air farm to military encampment; these outweighed romantic woodcraft and led for the most part toward large, highly organized camps. Some Boy Scout camps followed the military routine of reveille, taps, and daily inspection in uniform; a few even posted sentries at night.[53] Boy Scouts set up encampments on state fair grounds, and visitors streamed through these showcase campsites. Even regular camps incorporated family vacations at first, for executives reluctantly let Scoutmasters bring their wives provided they kept them in seclusion and visited only after ten P.M.[54] The war revived the fresh air farm idea, as Boy Scouts took up food production by working for nearby farmers. This anachronism enjoyed surprising popularity, at least among some leaders, for 22 of 249 council camps reported in 1920 that farm work formed a major part of their program.[55] Mostly the trend was towards YMCA-style camps with a fully planned program and paid leaders. Association men were the main source of expertise; concern for health and safety favored camps run by professional staff; and permanent camps could accommodate boys whose Scoutmaster worked all summer.

Like Y camp leaders, the men who ran large Boy Scout camps planned the boys' whole day and used point systems to spur activity.[56] A typical day began with reveille at 6:30, following which the boys had flag salute and setting-up exercises or else a dip. Then they ate breakfast, tidied up, and underwent inspection. A couple of hours of instruction and Scouting practice followed, then a swim or boating and dinner. After a rest or lecture, there were Scout games, hiking, and more instruction, followed by more swimming. The games were particular favorites with the boys—a sort of glorified hide-and-seek drawn from Baden-Powell's military training and Seton's hunting play, with boys crawling through the underbrush, taking each other prisoner, and trying to break through the enemy's lines. Flag-lowering ceremonies, supper, and camp games filled the early evening, and the day closed with a council fire.[57] The idea was to keep boys busy—and they loved the bustle. Skinner reported home in high spirits in 1915: "Everything runs like clockwork. This afternoon we had water races and tomorrow a quoit tournament. Thursday we have a game of 'lost battalion' and Friday we are going to give a show and invite the people around the lake. Not an idle moment. We have sentry duty and Ebbe [his brother] is on to-night. . . . It's great and nobody kicks."[58]

The evening campfire, when boys slowed down somewhat, carried much of the day's moral and emotional weight, just as at YMCA camps. The *Handbook for Boys* pictured the scene in familiar terms: "The huge fire shooting up its tongue of flame . . . , the company of happy boys, and the great, dark background of piny woods, the weird light all over, the singing, the yells, the stories, the fun, and then the serious word at the close, is a happy experience long to be remembered."[59]

The mood was less serious than at YMCA camps, though, for Boy Scout leaders aimed more to circumscribe and vent boyish savagery than to grapple with—let alone encourage—adolescent crises. Moral instruction based on the Boy Scout law was less intense than the YMCA quest for conversions, and although ceremonies might be impressive—an Indian initiation ritual at the camp for suburban Philadelphia prescribed a day-long fast—they tended to be somewhat superficial without religious goals. By design, they served to "avoid the torsions of certain high-tensioned initiations which are dangerous to boys in the adolescent stage." A parent who observed the wrong kind found it "a mixture of lodge ritual and cannibal torture, planned by the older boys whose ideas were not inspired by Boys' Life, St. Nicholas, nor the American Boy."[60] Indian ceremonies offered a way to ritualize hazing and avoid such excesses. Still, within limits camp leaders let gang pressures run their course. Thus boys who did not fit in could expect harrassment; nicknames such as "Professor" or "Yellow" stuck.[61] A writer for St. Nicholas assumed complacently that a fat Boy Scout was fair game, to be paddled out of bed in the morning with a sneaker. In addition, practical jokes enlivened camp life, and not just against misfits; Boy Scouts at one camp tried to haul the Scoutmaster out of his tent by pulling his cot with a rope but were foiled when he tied it to a tree. Accordingly, some Boy Scout leaders promoted decidedly boisterous fun at campfires. An executive from Birmingham, Alabama, described with mock dismay how the chief entertainments were "boxing and wrestling and other rough forms of sport, with the contestants in a semi-nude condition, and their faces streaked with dirt and perspiration." Such measures allowed boys to reassure themselves collectively regarding their masculinity, while deflecting boisterous or rebellious urges into sanctioned disrespect—the practical joke on the Scoutmaster—or more commonly into competition among the boys.[62]

Counterbalancing these forms of release, however rowdy, was the even stronger urge to circumscribe and channel boys' activities. Boy Scout executives believed they could do this most safely and efficiently at council camps they ran themselves. Although British and French Boy Scout leaders advocated informal camping by separate troops, American Boy Scout executives resisted—in part because few Scoutmasters would sacrifice their vacation (often only a week or two) to take their troop to camp but also because American executives simply did not trust Scoutmasters. Baden-Powell decried the lack of adventure at BSA camps; yet after hearing a French Boy Scout leader advocate small-scale camping, American executives responded that nothing Scoutmasters did so often caused them public embarrassment as troop camps.[63] An improving impulse, narrowly conceived, enhanced the executives' distaste for troop camps. Since advancement in rank had become the standard of good Scouting, executives saw camp as a precious time for instruction and promotion. They thought the boys were "not getting anywhere" at troop camps because they "do just as they please," whereas council camps could have high school teachers direct classes and doctors and foresters talk to the boys.[64] Kansas City even got an old Barnum and Bailey man to run the campfires. The result was that council camps far outstripped troop camps; 124,477 Boy Scouts attended council camps in 1920, for example, compared to 43,200 at troop camps.[65]

Council camps submerged the individual troops. Though the median camp size in 1918 was just over sixty boys, many were larger; and with most boys staying only a week, the bigger camps ran a thousand or more through in a summer.[66] Many big camps used paid counselors plus a floating force of volunteers. Few Scoutmasters accompanied their boys, especially since camp officials tented boys from different troops together, undercutting the men's authority.[67] A few executives compromised by giving troops limited autonomy, while the central camp provided certain meals, swimming instruction, and a mammoth campfire every other night.[68] But most council camps of the 1910s and 1920s operated on a mass basis.

In the long run, the BSA's zeal for centralized efficiency proved harmful, since it sapped troop initiative in getting boys to camp and undercut the ties of friendship among troop members which were vital to make short-term camps cohere as temporary communities. By the late 1920s, Boy Scout camping was in decline. Executive O. C. Alverson of Sacramento complained that only a fraction of all Boy Scouts attended council camps, a few from each troop; in only 19 percent of troops did more than half the Scouts go to camp. In 1940, less than a third of all Boy Scouts camped for a week or more, though two-fifths camped for one to six days — low figures for a movement ostensibly dedicated to outdoor life.[69]

An ambivalence implied by pastoral views of nature was characteristic of character building: much as boys' ungoverned instincts were to be moderated and kept within bounds, so too the wilds were to be tamed or else fenced off and entered only on brief forays. Thus YMCA and Boy Scout campers went to the woods but drew their tents and cabins up in squares or circles like settled communities. Thus also each day was scheduled, and camp leaders rationed access to the wilds; fearful of overstrain, they permitted only occasional excursions to test the boys' endurance of backwoods tramping, amateur cookery, and lumpy ground beneath their blankets.

Under these circumstances, boyish activism found vent in a decidedly instrumental view of nature, symbolized by the restless hatchet. The BSA's supply department promoted these weapons for sale, and every gadget-happy Boy Scout longed to have one at his belt. The tradition of blazing trails, the use of wood for rustic bridges and fences, and the constant search for firewood all encouraged a slash-and-burn style of camping. Much to Seton's annoyance, Beard liked to show off his skill at throwing hatchets at trees; yet Seton himself casually suggested the way to climb a tree was to fell another tree against it.[70] Such prodigality did little harm in the Yukon—but not in Palisades Park near New York City, where Boy Scouts stripped birch trees as high as they could reach; they even did it in all innocence for publicity photos. To cure the little hackers of their addiction, Boy Scout officials often had to impose strict rationing—one hatchet per patrol.[71]

Boy Scout attitudes were understandable, since conservationists had barely dented the assumption that nature was a boundless storehouse. Americans were firmly in the grip of production-oriented values, and many conservationists set little value on wilderness; they merely wanted efficient use of resources.[72]

Although Boy Scout leaders shared the Western belief in man's dominance over nature, they did more to teach conservation than other boys' workers. In 1907, a Brigade magazine published with approval a photo of a boy who shot forty birds, while the Agassiz Association, which had promoted nature study since 1875, made it synonymous with specimen collecting. Nor did young boys incline towards conservation. "I do not believe," William Dean Howells commented, "that boys are ever naturally fond of nature. They want to make use of the woods and fields. . . . A dead horse will draw a crowd of small boys . . . when they would pass by a rose-tree in bloom with indifference."[73] The BSA sought to change all this and stop Boy Scouts from stealing birds' eggs or picking wildflowers; instead, they were to observe birds and plants in the wild. Boy Scout leaders disagreed, to be sure, over how far to go. William T. Hornaday, a prominent naturalist, sought Boy Scout support for closed seasons and posting farms off limits to hunters, whereas George Pratt preferred to preserve game for gentlemen sportsmen. On the whole Pratt prevailed, although a few Boy Scouts won the medal which Hornaday offered for lobbying for his measures. Several states arranged for Boy Scouts to plant trees or fight fires, although nothing sustained resulted.[74] Conservation was at best a piecemeal crusade with little sense of ecological interdependence, yet Boy Scouts did begin to realize the woods did not exist to be ransacked.

Like nature, camping was for use; character builders wanted an ideal community in which to foster boyish activism and perhaps reap a small harvest of adolescent idealism. In practice, camp directors relied primarily upon careful scheduling and incessant busyness. They fitted camping to middle-class tastes in recreation by making it a boyish surrogate for work — steady, structured, and mildly demanding.

Despite these broad similarities, summer camps took on distinctive features of their organizational parents. YMCA camps built up additive programs for fee payers and exploited adolescent idealism. The BSA brought centralization and efficiency to mass camping. Camping did not, however, represent a full culmination of either agency's goals; it was only a temporary interlude, and, as we have seen, even Boy Scout camps did not involve all BSA members.

This fact exemplifies one form of a basic boys' work dilemma: character-building agencies could arouse great enthusiasm, yet they had a slippery hold on their massive memberships. As we shall see, it proved difficult to combine mass recruitment with deep and lasting commitments; no voluntary association could truly satisfy romantic yearnings for a substitute community.

14

Adult Instruction and Boys' Responses

Despite the attractions of summer camp, success or failure for character-building programs rested ultimately with the year-round routine of meetings. In those, much as they did at camp, Boy Scout officials tried to channel boyish activism into recognized achievement, YMCA men grappled cautiously with problems of adolescence, and both groups sought to educate boys morally. The results were mixed, however, as enthusiasm was hard to sustain week after week, and formalism often took over.

Boy Scout officials channeled boys' activities most directly through the promotion requirements; boys in first-rate troops came under great pressure to advance.[1] Buffalo, New York's, Court of Honor (the group who examined badge seekers) went so far as to propose a Double Eagle rank requiring forty-two badges, to prevent even Eagle Scouts from relaxing. Anyone who reached the new rank would be "so near the perfect, all-round Scout that he [would] go for the full fifty-seven, even if it [were] necessary to take special training." Although headquarters rejected the proposal, it reflected the tendency of Boy Scout leaders to equate personal growth with advancement in rank and character with "personal efficiency."[2]

For certain boys Scout awards posed an exhilarating challenge and perhaps an escape from peer pressures towards sameness. One fourteen-year-old made the cover of the BSA's fourth annual report by advancing from tenderfoot to Eagle Scout in twelve months, winning twenty-eight merit badges en route. Alatau T. Wilder of Honolulu accumulated fifty-five merit badges. Starting, he said, with those which any boy could win "right off the bat," he hunted up tradesmen to help him with skills such as printing and practised relentlessly for difficult badges such as archery. He walked, he said, "hundreds of miles chasing arrows. . . ."[3] While few Boy Scouts rivaled Wilder's dedication, a good many obviously liked the sense of order provided by a graded series of awards like those in school. In 1920, 629 boys earned Eagle badges, one for every 600 Boy Scouts nationally, and the proportion of Eagles was rising rapidly. A few Scouts, of course, cut corners—to the point that Boy Scout officials began to worry that badge-hounds were doing superficial work; but prodigies of speedy badge accumulation continued to be celebrated in Boy Scout publicity as evidence that Scouting taught ambition.[4]

On balance, Boy Scout officials worried less about boys cutting corners than about their failure to advance. "Some of us have quite a bit of trouble," complained one Scoutmaster, "pushing the ordinary tenderfoot into second and first class and getting him to pass the tests with any degree of thoroughness." Another man found that if "work is the order of the day, then there is some grumbling, 'We want some fun,' but if some fun is provided, more is wanted, and Scouting . . . seems to be pushed to the wall by all but a few. . . ."[5] Team sports posed an enticing alternative — and not merely from outside the movement, for a good many Scoutmasters turned to sports to hold their boys.[6] Rapid advancement was uncommon; in 1919, only 5 percent of Boy Scouts in first class councils had won merit badges, 7 percent more had reached first class, 20 percent were second class, and 68 percent were still tenderfeet. By 1925, 20 percent had reached first class or higher, but 54 percent still were tenderfeet.[7] Any growing organization has disproportionate numbers of junior members, and weak instruction held back some Boy Scouts; but many evidently did not strain to win promotion. Only among a minority did BSA requirements harness and strengthen the "sense of industry" which Erik Erikson singles out as the great developmental achievement of the preadolescent years. Insofar as twentieth-century American "masculinity has been associated with an instrumental orientation, a . . . focus on 'getting the job done,'" Boy Scouting may also have secured more mixed results in inculcating masculinity than its founders wished.[8]

The achievements demanded to reach first class rank were in some measure forced, for character builders had by no means abandoned the ideal of formal discipline — the notion that boys could strengthen their will, and specific mental powers as well, by doing difficult and sometimes unappealing tasks. Baden-Powell had included requirements expressly to strengthen powers such as observation and memory. How else could one justify learning such arcane skills as tracking and semaphore signaling? Regarding the first class requirements, a Scoutmaster commented: "The great thing seems to be that in getting mastery over material things . . . you are also helping to get a mastery over self. That is character. . . ."[9] By the 1910s, however, many of the boys who joined character-building groups were uninterested in teeth-gritting self-improvement; for middle-class boys the route to success ran upward through the grades in school, and they were used to spending spare time at play, not work.[10]

Boy Scouts had to learn a hodgepodge of skills, some of which must have seemed arbitrary and difficult now that they had lost their unifying rationale as training for military reconnaissance. First aid particularly intimidated boys. BSA officials worried that doctors expected too much;

yet Dr. W. N. Lipscomb of the Red Cross complained that most Boy Scouts were "remarkably weak in three important essentials, namely wounds and their care, the proper use of the tourniquet, and artificial respiration." [11] Boy Scouts found cooking a challenge as well. Other difficult tests derived from military scouting, such as Scout's pace, which required boys to cover a mile in exactly twelve minutes by alternately running and walking. The tracking test was likewise artificial, as Boy Scout officials had to use all sorts of aids, including paper, corn, chalk marks, and blazes. After first aid, the other great stumbling block was signaling, a military carryover which required much memorization. [12]

Since the BSA had grown so fast, many Scoutmasters had not mastered Scouting's skills and in their insecurity tried to teach boys the way they remembered having once been taught, with lectures and rote memorization. Thus many Boy Scouts could recite the points of the compass sing-song fashion with no real grasp of what, say, "east northeast" meant, even though headquarters campaigned against "the usual routine methods of school instruction." [13]

Training for merit badges was even harder to come by, so that Boy Scouts virtually had to cut corners in the early years because they could seldom find instruction. Although pamphlets were available for each badge by 1920, these focused closely on how to pass the tests. Boy Scouts were tempted to memorize just enough to satisfy their examiners, who were commonly indulgent. Scoutmaster Charles F. Smith of Staten Island, for example, explained that boys in his area took the Firemanship badge because the fire chief merely asked a few simple questions. [14]

In reaching first class rank, the major hurdle was to impress one's Scoutmaster. Thereafter, a Boy Scout needed little more than verbal recall when he appeared before the local Court of Honor. If his first class hike map was just a "smear," he might be sent back to do it right, but boys seldom failed these showpiece examinations. [15] Where testing was rigorous, Boy Scout officials copied the school practice of examinations with answers straight from the text, in this case the handbook. Rote responses sufficed because many of the requirements merely asked boys to describe or explain, and others were impossible to test indoors. [16] Even though headquarters increasingly pressed for practical demonstrations, the battle for standards remained a tug of war on slippery footing in which the examiners sometimes pulled for the boys.

Without experimental evidence, it is impossible to be certain what boys learned beyond the obvious bits of skill and information on which they were tested. Did Boy Scouting nurture broader capacities? Although the faculty psychology upon which Baden-Powell based his program is now discredited, exercises such as reporting what was in a shop window (an alternative to tracking) could have strengthened the boys' ability to memorize

—but only if Scoutmasters taught mnemonic strategies. It is clear that the requirements did not encourage broad intellectual growth; Boy Scouts developed limited skills based on rule-of-thumb methods and did a surprising amount of memorization. Although Boy Scout leaders criticized the schools for formalism, in practice they fell into a formalism of their own—changing the subject matter without eliminating the teachers' fact fetishism. Thus the badge for Personal Health, which more boys earned than any other in 1920, merely required a Boy Scout to memorize disconnected rules and bits of information on matters such as the effects of alcohol and tobacco, the value of walking as exercise, and the effects of hot and cold baths. Like much school instruction, badge work relied heavily upon the child's "magpie" ability to accumulate facts without understanding the principles underlying them.[17] The logic involved seldom reached beyond what Jean Piaget has called "concrete operations"; it almost never reached Piaget's level of "formal operations," which includes the systematic enumeration of logical possibilities in solving a problem, the use of abstract categories and symbols, and the generation and testing of hypotheses. Perhaps this was just as well, since the ability to perform formal operations does not develop in most children until ages eleven to fifteen and then unevenly; indeed, perhaps half the American adult population cannot reliably perform them.[18] By sticking to the level of concrete operations, Boy Scout requirements remained logically accessible to all twelve-year-olds. On the other hand, the requirements did not stretch boys' minds logically—although they did introduce new subject matter—and older Boy Scouts may well have regarded the arbitrary rules they had to memorize as being beneath their new-found powers of logic.[19]

Still, hope of promotion led some boys onward. Ideally, once a Boy Scout reached first class standing, merit badges would encourage him to broaden his interests; but certain specified badges were required for further promotion. To become an Eagle Scout, a boy had to earn badges for First Aid, Personal Health, Public Health, Life Saving, Pioneering, Cooking, Camping, Civics, Bird Study, Pathfinding, and Physical Development or Athletics, plus ten he chose himself. In practice, therefore, ambitious Boy Scouts kept to the path which led to advancement, with the result that the twelve required or alternate badges for Eagle Scout made up 46 percent of all badges earned in 1920. Ten others, headed by Swimming and Firemanship, accounted for another 39 percent. Only 15 percent of the awards went for the remaining thirty-seven badges. The popular optional badges were ones which could be won rapidly. The badge for Swimming recognized a skill that many boys already had, while Firemanship was easy because fire officials did not want boys to meddle in firefighting. A minority of Boy Scouts did explore new interests or further their hobbies, but most cannot have spread themselves widely. In 1920,

Boy Scouts earned a total of 7,099 badges for Handicraft, Carpentry, and Craftsmanship but only 3,896 for the other sixteen hobbies and vocational skills for which there were badges. Scientific, cultural, agricultural, and vocational badges were not popular. And in any case, most Boy Scouts could not spread themselves widely because so few won badges of any sort; 376,537 Boy Scouts shared just 65,728 merit badges in 1920.[20] Rather than encouraging experimentation, the badge system bypassed most Boy Scouts and herded the rest along a single track in search of extrinsic rewards.

Few YMCA juniors came up against requirements as elaborate as those in Boy Scouting, since most boys' branches offered a string of activities with no extrinsic goals. Yet YMCA boys proved no more interested than Boy Scouts were in balanced, all-round development. It appeared that many boys had to be pressured before they would do anything outside the physical department. Thus boys who joined the Bronx YMCA in 1916 expecting only to play basketball had to promise to develop themselves mentally, socially, and spiritually as well as physically, and to help make "the Bronx an ideal place in which to live, work, and play." If they skipped Bible class, the secretary threatened expulsion. A. R. Freeman reported that this method eliminated most "pool-sharks, gym-hounds, water-rats, and stunt artists" — or at least forced them to sham.[21] For the few boys who enrolled, the CCTP tests exerted similar pressures, as most boys scored high on the physical section and were told they needed religious improvement.[22] Repeatedly, though usually gently, boys' secretaries urged their charges to put more effort into educational, social, and religious activities. Since YMCAs in effect sold privileges for a fee, however, the customers exerted considerable counter-pressure. Boys enrolled in respectable numbers for Bible classes: 37 percent of total junior membership in 1909–1910 and 35 percent in 1919–1920. But more than twice as many flocked to gymnastics and sports: 78 percent in 1909–1910 and 79 percent in 1919–1920. Equally revealing were changes in the physical program. Exercises in the 1890s had been almost as disciplinary as drill; now fun seemed vital. For boys twelve to fourteen, the 1920 physical directors' manual suggested only twenty-five minutes of calisthenics and formal instruction, then twenty-five minutes recreation and a twenty-minute swim. Socials and entertainments also increased from fourteen per junior department in 1909–1910 to twenty-four in 1919–1920, whereas only 9 percent of the boys joined educational clubs in 1919.[23] Clearly, boys in search of diversion unbalanced the Y's fourfold character building.

Confronted with adult prescriptions for self-improvement, in short, neither Boy Scouts nor YMCA juniors rushed to comply, although they did respond — somewhat erratically — to extrinsic rewards and pressures. Boys' workers needing members had to offer an entertaining program.

In a sense, the battle pitted purpose against technique, for character builders were trying to teach ideals — which they identified with formal precepts — through programs which stressed athletics and outdoor recreation. James West conceived the Boy Scout program as a sort of giant vise designed to hold boys while adults "poured in" values. More plausibly, character builders saw activity programs as ways to bring boys under their influence.[24] Yet personal contacts were not very sustained. So moral education fell back upon a kind of formalism more suited to boyhood as then conceived than to adolescence. Instruction in approved values and respect for authority reinforced the experience of following rules and accepting adult leadership.

Certainly formalism pervaded Boy Scout training in patriotism and civics. When a troop ceremoniously burned a desecrated flag, for instance, they earned high praise. To win his Civics badge, a Boy Scout memorized disconnected information about the formal structure of government: the provisions of the Constitution, the Declaration of Independence, the voting and naturalization laws, plus the methods of election or appointment and terms of office for all executive, legislative, and judicial officers within whose jurisdiction he lived. Such training repeated the "catalogues of civic information" which children learned at school.[25] Then as now, children learned to abhor political divisiveness; they learned nothing of how to effect political change or apply such principles as freedom of speech in practical situations. In that respect, Boy Scouting's formalism went beyond even contemporary Progressives' abhorrence of traditional partisanship; since the Civics badge gave no hint that citizens might seek personal goals or social changes through politics, its net effect was conservative but not thoughtfully so. Scout instruction encouraged boys to retain a child's view of government as a benevolent officialdom which could set everything right; it did not spur the critical thinking or grand idealism often associated with adolescence.[26]

It is unlikely that many Boy Scouts reacted cynically to this, since most were too young to sense the implications and came from comfortable families likely to be sincerely patriotic. Boys of the early 1900s responded enthusiastically to traditional patriotic symbolism; when asked to name their personal exemplars, many more schoolchildren in 1902 and 1910 picked national heroes than in the 1940s and 1950s.[27] Boy Scouts were receptive therefore to the demonstrative patriotism of World War I; in the words of a troop paper describing a parade: "It was a grand and glorious feeling to march behind the martial music and made us feel like really and truly soldiers."[28] On the other hand, Boy Scouts were also a bit young to take permanent shape politically. Recent studies have found that American teenagers tend to pass from naively authoritarian towards more differentiated political views with increasing age.[29] Although later critics alleged that Boy Scouts too easily accepted authoritarian leadership, many young Scouts were unready to demand autonomy and would grow more thoughtful with advancing age.[30]

At most, Boy Scout training merely reinforced existing attitudes, for patriotic rituals took only a fraction of most troops' time; only one Boy Scout in two hundred won the Civics badge in 1920, and many Boy Scouts ignored the wartime bond drives.[31] A sizable number of Scouts went on to the service academies, but the proportion at civilian colleges was almost as high.[32] Although the BSA may have inspired some boys to serve their country, it recruited the type who would have done so anyway.

Patriotic indoctrination did not figure as largely in YMCA work. As befitted the YMCA's cautious interest in civic reform, however, some local Associations had mildly venturesome programs to foster social awareness among older boys, to the point of running the junior department as a model city. In 1915, two thousand YMCA juniors studied C. C. Robinson's course, "Christian Teaching on Social and Economic Questions," learning that political life required difficult decisions. But most citizenship training oversimplified political reality. E. M. Robinson expected boys to learn "honest, upright, intelligent, nonpartisan and altruistic citizenship."[33] Yet the idea that good men could all agree to solve problems through morality and efficiency, although a staple of contemporary rhetoric, did not equip teenagers to understand partisanship or class interests. On the rare occasions when they encountered a mild radical, secretaries were nonplussed. What was one to do when a high school senior who was "a very fair athlete" left the church and espoused a kind of Christian socialism because he opposed warfare and private enterprise? In this instance, the secretary dodged the issues by getting the boy to make "a clear cut decision to make Christ master of his life, expressing his willingness to let theories and doctrines work themselves out later."[34] Even older boys were not supposed to think *too* deeply.

As social training, service projects offered an alternative to dogmatic instruction, yet they involved most boys only sporadically. Older boys who led YMCA gym squads or Bible classes made up only a fraction of the membership. Otherwise, older boys shared in highly formalized conferences and campaigns for clean living. And if younger boys undertook service projects, they set themselves modest tasks, as when a group of Torontonians aged eleven to fifteen resolved to stamp on discarded cigarette butts to stop young smokers from retrieving them.[35]

Service by Boy Scouts was more publicly visible but not necessarily more sustained. Although many Boy Scouts did individual good turns, group service averaged less than one whole day a year. Boys who took part in cosmetic ventures must have imbibed the notion that good citizenship consisted of ritual gestures. Yet it might have been futile to have expected more, since early adolescents have a tendency to assume that merely expressing an ideal is sufficient to attain it.[36]

Boy Scout moral training emphasized conformity to others' expectations and obedience to authority. The Boy Scout laws portrayed the ideal Scout as trustworthy, loyal, helpful, friendly, courteous, kind, obedient, cheerful, thrifty, brave, clean, and reverent. Explanations appended to each law drove the points home. Thus the eighth law elaborated on cheerfulness: "[A Scout's] obedience to orders is prompt and cheery. He never shirks nor grumbles at hardships." Similarly, a Boy Scout was loyal "to all to whom loyalty is due: his scout leader, his home, and parents and country." Although the tenth law called upon the Boy Scout to "stand up for the right against the coaxings of friends," there was no suggestion of resisting adults in authority. The oath and law comprised a litany of conventional virtues, each worthwhile yet bound together by no single principle such as the Golden Rule. They offered little help in dealing with complex questions or resolving contradictions, such as instances when, for example, obedience might require performing an unkind act.[37] Like badge work, moral instruction was additive, to some degree rote, and potentially productive of simplistic thinking. The BSA's annual report for 1916 claimed one could tell a boy all he needed to know about life in one three-hour sermon; the reason *Boys' Life* published stories was simply to add flavor and bulk. Although some Scoutmasters discussed the implications of the oath and law with their boys, Scouts were to accept the text without question; in many troops they simply memorized it and recited it at meetings. Since the central injunction was to do one's duty, Boy Scout morality stood firmly in the conservative tradition of Baden-Powell and Roosevelt against the antiformalistic, increasingly subjective morality sometimes associated with Progressive Era movements more liberal than Boy Scouting.[38]

As in assessing Scout badge work, however, we must consider the cognitive abilities of Scout-age boys. In the six-tier hierarchy of moral development propounded by Lawrence Kohlberg, Boy Scout morality contained elements of state three, in which "good behavior is that which pleases or helps others and is approved by them." The predominant logic was that of stage four, characterized by "orientation towards authority, fixed rules, and the maintenance of the social order. . . ."[39] Stage five reasoning, which was not encouraged by the Boy Scout oath and law, goes beyond conventional morality to take a social-contract, utilitarian approach looking towards the universal moral principles of stage six. A study in the late 1960s found that the modal form of moral statement among middle-class urban American boys aged thirteen was stage three, followed by stage four. Thus Scouting once again was well adapted to boys of twelve or thirteen and did not risk incomprehension by those unready for more abstract and all-inclusive moral principles. By age sixteen, however, this study found stage five moral reasoning most common, suggesting that by the middle teens Boy Scouting's moral code was in a measure retrograde.[40]

Still, reasoning is one thing and behavior quite another. Thus the question remains whether Boy Scouting's conventional morality had a cutting edge in practice. Certainly it impinged on things that boys actually did. The Boy Scout oath and law had substituted safe generalities for the dangerously specific temperance-style pledges against smoking which the Boys' Brigades had trouble enforcing; but Scoutmasters chastised smokers informally, and a good many troops expelled them. Nor would BSA officialdom sanction "bad-boy" high jinks. A New Jersey Scoutmaster who condoned theft of watermelons by boys in his troop was expelled.[41]

On the other hand, few Boy Scouts found themselves backed into a corner except for some offense as detectable as smoking. To be sure, teachers and parents sometimes shamed a boy with reminders of his oath, occasionally overusing this "whip" until he turned against Scouting.[42] Yet Scoutmasters generally exercised forbearance. Although they fairly often made anonymous good turn reports part of troop meetings, Boy Scouts did not come under severe pressure to perform. Of twenty-eight New York City men who reported to the BSA in 1911, only five asked parents or patrol leaders whether the boys lived up to the Boy Scout law. Only ten described good turns; most mentioned help with home or church chores or school discipline, while four told of boys who gave first aid, shared lunches, or helped people across streets.[43] Such chores involved an element of sacrifice; as a reluctant Boy Scout explained, if boys did "girls' work about the house . . . the other fellows [would] find it out and call [them] sissies. . . ."[44] But these chores were the sort of things that many boys were doing already before they joined the Scouts.

There is reason to doubt that the oath and law much affected Boy Scouts' behavior. Arthur Carey, a leading Sea Scouter who took Scout ideals very seriously, found that "practically none" of a group of Boy Scouts "could do more than repeat the headings of the twelve laws; many of them could not repeat the oath accurately, and one of them could not repeat it at all." Daily instruction during a long cruise secured an obligingly "spontaneous response," but few boys underwent such intensive evangelizing.[45] Ambitious boys saw that approval came by winning badges. When Boy Scout executive Portz of Wheeling, West Virginia, complained in 1920 that he had a thirteen-year-old Eagle Scout who never took part in community service unless pushed, Portz's colleagues echoed his comments, complaining that ambitious Boy Scouts were preoccupied with self-advancement. In theory every first class Scout had to "furnish satisfactory evidence that he has put into practice in his daily life the principles of the scout oath and law," but in practice the Court of Honor settled for routine endorsements from parents and teachers.[46] The BSA's Committee on Merit Badges, Awards, and Scout Requirements virtually gave up the pretense of an inquiry in 1916 and charged local Courts of Honor instead with "impressing upon" candidates the principles of Scouting.[47] Boy Scout leaders clearly had not solved the problem of inculcating precepts through an activity program.

As evidence of success, character builders turned to testimonials. The *Church Gleaner,* for instance, published a boy's statement that Brigade membership gave him "better muscles, straighter shoulders and better carriage," and helped him "as Jesus to overcome temptations. . . ." Scoutmasters told of boys transformed, such as "Billy," a paroled thief who became "a splendid fellow . . . with a clean, well-formed body and an eye that can look straight into yours."[48]

Systematic evidence, nonexistent before the 1920s, was inevitably less positive than isolated examples. In 1928, on the basis of contrived tests which gave schoolchildren detectable opportunities to cheat, Hugh Hartshorne and Mark May concluded that Boy Scouts did not differ significantly from other boys in their propensity to cheat; the desire to succeed overbore moral compunctions. The Boy Scouts were not alone in this disappointing performance, for Sunday school pupils did no better. The results suggested strongly that teaching boys a list of virtues did not change their behavior.[49]

In response to these and other criticisms, the BSA hired a sociologist, Henry Pratt Fairchild, to compare Boy Scouts' and non-Scouts' delinquency rates and character development. Even allowing for favoritism in the courts and shortcomings in Fairchild's statistical procedures, fewer Boy Scouts were delinquent — although this probably came about more because potential delinquents did not join the movement than because Boy Scout membership reformed them. When it came to measuring character, Fairchild did not test actual behavior; he sent out ten investigators, each of whom was to get to know 90 or 100 boys in one community and rate them on the "conduct habits" enumerated in the Boy Scout law. Fairchild supplied no criteria for scoring, leaving raters to use their own judgment and to solicit opinions the way a Court of Honor did from parents, teachers, Boy Scout officials, pastors, and occasionally other boys. Judged this way, Boy Scouts substantially surpassed non-Scouts. But Fairchild was talking past the movement's critics, for what his approach measured most directly was merely the ability of boys to secure adult approval — and Boy Scouts came from respectable families. Fairchild himself found the results ambiguous; because Boy Scouts clearly outranked non-Scouts in socioeconomic background, he could not say whether they owed their higher character ratings to Scout training or to initial advantages.[50] There was no easy way to prove that "good" boys had been made better.

YMCA secretaries persisted in seeking deeper commitments than Boy Scout leaders, yet they too had problems with pro forma responses; increasingly they turned to discussion methods as a remedy. The "life questions" courses of the 1910s led from problems of schoolboy life to discussion of fraternities, liquor and tobacco, profanity and slang, lying, cheating, gambling, work attitudes, social service, politics, sex, and religion. "On few of the questions . . . is there an absolute right or an absolute wrong," cautioned Jeremiah Jenks, who wrote a widely used manual. "The man who can secure the hearty goodwill and liking of the boys . . . has secured a hold that . . . will be worth far more than the inculcation of any opinion." Attitudes had changed since the 1870s, when a YMCA writer said the "fatal malady of discussion" ruined Bible teaching.[51] Yet even now, when boys started behaving as critical-minded adolescents, their leaders reimposed the old formalism. At the Newark, New Jersey, YMCA, according to a conservative observer, Jenks's course "did more harm than good as the groups became mere ethical societies with no Christian purpose whatever. In one case a group of this kind had to be stopped, and that with great difficulty. . . ."[52]

YMCA men took some chances, since romantic notions of adolescence seemed to dictate a new reliance upon teenage enthusiasm. Overall, though, moral instruction meant inculcating standard formulas. "The revolt against formalism" that Morton White has traced among Progressive Era intellectuals did not transform boys' work any more than it did education. The weight of habits ingrained by generations of schooling was too great. Techniques became ends in themselves, and although the subject matter changed, rote learning continued.[53]

Character builders aspired to do more, for solving the problems of adolescence constituted much of their raison d'etre. The BSA's preferred solution, however, was distraction—which led back towards standardized programs and constant busyness. YMCA men were more eager to confront adolescent problems directly; but getting boys to do this took great effort, since few turned spontaneously to character-building programs in a quest for identity.

One issue which character builders were convinced adolescents must face was the choice of vocation. Yet most boys dodged the subject, and their professed choices were superficial. A 1924 study found only a .1 correlation between vocational goals stated by grade-school pupils and those same individuals' goals in college; nor could many high school students account for their supposed preferences.[54] Middle-class boys simply let the school system carry them along.

Character builders were in no position to provide serious vocational training. Boy Scout badges were too superficial; and YMCA educational programs, which were a carryover from the self-improvement efforts of young men's associations, had little appeal to boys who more and more expected the schools to give them all their training. In 1920, just 3 percent of Y juniors took YMCA classes; they were easily bored, and few Associations could offer highly technical instruction. Although Boy Scout officials hoped that their badges might lead boys to explore possible vocations, middle-class urban occupations went almost unrepresented, as most vocational badges were for farming or trades. Some of these were quite modern, such as Automobiling, but others were obsolescent or esoteric, such as Blacksmithing and Bee Keeping.[55] Such trades were unlikely to excite boys from prosperous homes, and members below first class rank were ineligible to win merit badges, with the result that Boy Scouts in 1920 earned only one vocational badge for every twenty-nine Scouts. Nor did winning badges signify systematic exploration of possible interests. When Scoutmasters meeting in 1917 quizzed a Boy Scout on why he earned merit badges, the lad was baffled; the best he could offer was that at first they seemed interesting, and he knew other boys who had won them.[56]

What character builders offered instead of specific guidance was middle-class aspiration. By the early 1900s, they realized the folly of advising a boy to take any job, work hard, and impress his employer; boys who did so drifted into "blind alley" jobs.[57] Agencies for lower-class boys, such as the crassly commercial American Cadets, still favored business practice of the sort that verged on street trades. But YMCA and Boy Scout leaders were far more concerned with keeping their boys in school.[58] As a result, even ostensibly specific vocational guidance concentrated upon implanting middle-class values. YMCA men had long steered their charges towards the ministry and Y work or else business and the professions. By 1910, as vocational guidance came into vogue among educators, Y secretaries began to experiment with administering questionnaires. Some of the questions probed the boys' interests, but mainly they forced boys to rate themselves on "enthusiasm, decision, loyalty, obedience, determination," and so forth — thereby routinizing adolescent introspection and imposing in disguised form the old middle-class credo that character was the key to success.[59] Such guidance was limited, in any case. At older boys' conferences, Y men pressed hard for delegates to commit themselves to Christian callings, yet these pledges numbered only in the hundreds annually; nor did they reflect deep thought, since most boys plumped obligingly for YMCA work. The main thrust was still to urge them on to college.[60]

In dealing with sexual urges—a subject more pressing than vocation for most boys—the obstacle was not indifference but rather shyness on both sides of the generation gap. Parents said little to their sons, to the point that even a reputed expert on sex hygiene admitted he had no idea how much his own son knew. "He is so normal, with such a beautiful, even disposition that . . . I hesitate to speak to him. . . ."[61] A few zealots were fearless—but with other people's sons. The Rev. Joseph Flint, a supposed purity expert, accosted boys on the playground if their "form and features indicated" that they were "going wrong."[62] The Rev. Guy V. Hoard, a KOKA Merlin from Crystal Falls, Michigan, actually devised hand signals for boys to assure him confidentially of their continued blamelessness. YMCA secretaries were more restrained yet often questioned boys during physical examinations or interviews. However, it took all their professional resolve for some men to muster the necessary nerve. Matthew Crackel of the Cleveland YMCA worked ten years before he would "touch the subject." He blamed his ignorance of conditions and fear of criticism or failure.[63] As amateurs, Scoutmasters felt less obliged to act. The Boy Scout law stressed purity, and individual leaders counseled boys in their troop; but most dodged the issue, so that few Boy Scouts came under serious pressure. In the early 1920s, only ten of forty-one rural YMCAs gave sex education; not even six of thirty-nine local units of the BSA could claim as much.[64]

When adults did summon up the nerve to act on these concerns, they covered their uneasiness with blustering or more often obfuscation. Baden-Powell echoed tales of madness and enfeeblement, blaming nocturnal emissions on incontinence and calling down the penalties of nature and the scorn of right-thinking men upon boys who masturbated. American character builders were more cautious and generally adopted one of three strategies: a sentimental idealization of purity, a circuitous approach by way of botany, or an ostensibly frank account, strong on internal plumbing and external cleanliness.[65] Appeals to keep pure for one's future wife were common, and boys were urged to think of girls as sisters or mothers—not an approach well suited to long-term sexual adjustment.[66] Pleasure never of course skulked across the stage. Since character builders preferred to dodge the whole business, boys often got only a lecture or two during which some physician told them all they needed to know for the next five years. This reticence reflected more than shyness, for purity enthusiasts wanted to ration out a minimum of information, much of it irrelevant, and shut off discussion before the boys got interested. Thus a YMCA pamphlet assured fathers that "all instruction shall be based upon . . . plant, bird, fish, and animal life. Wherever the boy, through right thought, is led to make analogies in human life, his questions will be truthfully answered." "With the average boy the subject is mentioned but once," reported Crackel. "The boy is given a chance to ask questions and his mind is set at ease." H. W. Gibson likewise discouraged repetition, saying it made boys "hardened and sophisticated."[67] Boys needed little wit, therefore, to realize that insistent questions or "wrong" reasoning would turn adults hostile; and so they looked to friends for answers.[68]

The repression of sexual desire epitomized the drive for self-mastery which pervaded character building, but boys had to be pressured to respond. Understandably, they volunteered little to adults, almost never mentioning masturbation when called upon to list their temptations. Yet those old enough were troubled by their new desires; Baden-Powell said he received floods of mail from boys grateful that someone had broken the barrier of silence. At a meeting in New York City, a YMCA boy asked anonymously, "Is a fellow healthy after he has conquered the temptation of impurity?"[69] Under pressure, some boys would break their silence, caught between their self-image as good boys and their secret behavior. Crackel got startling results once he subjected every boy in his department to an interview. For instance, a thirteen-year-old whose father was adamant that the boy was pure admitted, "I've got a habit I can't quit." Under Crackel's guidance, he became a Sunday school teacher and later reported he had the habit "licked to a standstill."[70] Boys could not easily fend off probing questions, since they accepted the rightness of demands for self-control; but only a minority faced such assaults upon their privacy. For most Boy Scout leaders and many YMCA men, the answer to adolescent sexuality remained distraction, supplemented only rarely with confrontation.

Ironically, activities that character builders looked to as distraction sometimes furthered sexual gossip by bringing together older and younger boys. Summer camp offered special opportunities, although the YMCA practice of putting a young man in every tent damped down ribald hearsay. E. M. Robinson warned that curiosity might lead boys in their early teens "to do what may range from simply unwise to the absolutely detestable."[71] Rules against nightshirts and suggestions that boys sleep fully clothed were designed to reduce temptations towards masturbation or exhibitionism. Robinson's fears suggest that there was some casual experimentation, normal for that age, but not that boarding school–type homosexuality was in evidence.[72]

On a major issue which recapitulation theorists predicted would be of concern to adolescents, YMCA men had a long tradition of involvement — seeking religious conversions quite boldly at camp and more cautiously back in the city. And yet traditional methods often failed to elicit deep commitment or even interest among teenagers. Since Sunday schools already held annual decision days at which young teenagers were pressured to accept Christ on cue, YMCA juniors were quite familiar with the step. Some, indeed, were so eager to please that at one mass meeting a speaker tricked them. Launching into what appeared would be an invitation to accept Jesus, he asked, "How many of you boys . . ." — while he paused, hands went up — "would like to have your heads cut off this afternoon?" [73] As we have seen, campfire conversions induced by social pressure could be equally superficial. A more basic problem with mass meetings in the city was simply that boys stayed away. The Montreal YMCA, for example, had 452 juniors in 1906 yet averaged only 31 at its religious meetings and eventually gave up. Bible classes were the substitute, suited to smaller groups and more conducive to thoughtfulness. Yet only 43 percent of juniors throughout North America joined Bible classes in 1920, and they attended on average only 12.6 sessions. [74]

As boys' secretaries wallowed in confusion over their religious role, many soft-pedalled evangelism, concurring with William Byron Forbush's warning that boys just entering adolescence would be "in agony" if dealt with "by 'personal workers'." Others tried to adapt by preparing better, making personal work less of a "flying tackle" at some unwary boy's soul. [75] And some followed the lead of E. M. Robinson and David Porter, who warned against mass appeals to preadolescents; belatedly realizing that few boys were fully adolescent at twelve or thirteen, some Y men began to concentrate more upon winning older boys. At the same time, they broadened the scope of their evangelism — concatenating issues of religion, vocation, and purity so that they would reinforce each other, drive home to adolescents the gravity of the choices they faced, and spur them towards a closely supervised and carefully modulated identity crisis. Indeed, as Y men lost the nerve to force dramatic conversions, they bore down all the harder on church affiliation and personal morality.

When wielded in haste, the new techniques of adolescent guidance produced their share of superficial resolutions reminiscent of old-style evangelism at its silliest. During the religious, vocational, and purity campaigns of the 1910s, secretaries and laymen would descend upon a high school and give every boy who agreed an interview during which — depending on the theme of the campaign — he was pressed to join the church, decide his life's work, or abjure bad habits — and sometimes all three if there was time. Arthur Cotton, the International Committee's secretary for high schools, suggested that interviewers take three minutes to establish friendly relations, twelve to consider problems, and ten to record a decision. C. C. Robinson, the committee's specialist on working boys, reported a session with a youth who wanted to be an auto mechanic. After suggesting where to get information, Robinson turned to religion. The boy admitted he never went to church, but when Robinson explained "the place that the church holds in civilization," the boy agreed "that he needed such influence in his own life. Here was a boy who in a twenty-five minute interview was brought without any difficulty at all to an absolutely new viewpoint with regard to the church and a statement of his willingness to identify with it."[76] Even campfire conversions never went that fast.

The standard programs of the 1910s refined the interview technique by tempting boys to see how they would score on a point system. Since they were rated on externals—activities, achievements, and so forth—the boys faced less intrusive inquiries than when confronted by old-fashioned personal workers. Even so, charting interviews produced many pseudo-decisions. During one purportedly typical session, for example, the boy admitted he "had never heard of the 'Three C's Campaign' with its 'Clean Speech, Clean Living and Clean Athletics,' but . . . said he would do what he could to promote such a campaign."[77] In this case, the interviewer shrewdly refused him points until he actually took part.

Yet the Y's insistent moralism, especially regarding masturbation, seized upon an issue which—unlike religion or vocation—was of fearful daily concern to conscientious boys. Anxious teenagers fluttered in like moths, fascinated by the confessional candor of talks with men who did not "know 'their case.'" Cotton reported that in Dallas high school boys stayed for interviews till after midnight, doing homework as they waited: "The memory of those needy boys and their intense desire to conquer sin will long remain with me."[78]

Y men formalized the link between moralism and conversion in the Forward Step technique, which became popular around 1910. At meetings each boy received a card asking him to check off some Forward Step: "1. Accept Jesus Christ as my Savior and Leader. 2. Unite with the Church. 3. Teach a Bible class. 4. Give systematically. 5. Do committee work. 6. Read the Bible and pray daily. 7. Give up the habit of _____."[79] In theory, this technique adapted conversion to religious nurture and made it milder by having it the first of a series of steps. But it was also a shrewd device to puncture complacency, playing upon the contrast between a boy's professed respectability and his failure to give service or end a nasty habit. E. M. Robinson explained: "[It] was found that Christian boys who were members of the church, and regular in attendance, were still victims of some pernicious habit, and to them, the determination, with God's help to overcome this habit, was the forward step they needed most of all."[80]

In a way, the Forward Step refurbished the old temperance pledge. And just as adults had used abstinence to affirm their own respectability, so self-consciously "good" boys—with a nervous sense of isolation—decried their classmates' failings. These included drinking; but smoking, being more widespread, became the easiest symbol. A Canadian boy described it as a sign of "accompanying habits," adding that "SMOKING IS THE KEY TO IT ALL. . . ."[81] Indeed, pious boys condemned smoking at least as much as illicit sex, since it was easier to confront and openly divided bad boys from good. Good boys also complained of "'mushing' or 'FUSS-

ING' . . . in the dark classrooms" at school dances. Two Colorado boys
told Arthur Cotton that few "fellows" danced "with clean thoughts" and
that "fussing in its first stages is very prevalent . . . and is rapidly advancing into worse."[82]

Scenting self-righteousness, a critic warned that YMCA boys could turn
smug: "Lord, I thank Thee I am not as other boys, inefficient, impure,
slack and casual. . . ."[83] This was possible; yet some Forward Steps were anything but exercises in complacency, for YMCA moralism recoiled upon
good boys troubled by their own insistent sexuality. E. M. Robinson watched
at one meeting as David Porter spoke "calmly, slowly and quietly"; then
Porter asked the boys to write out decisions as if Christ were looking over
their shoulder. Some responses were bland and stilted, but others were
very frank. One boy confessed his inability to follow Christ "so as to be
worthy of His love. I have really tried but failed time after time, but now
vow that I will not give up until I am entirely clean, pure, and worthy
of Jesus' love. I have another ideal which I will follow, that of being worthy of one dear girl. . . ." Another wrote: "As I listened to the awful meaning of your words, Mr. Porter, I seemed to have a trembling all over me.
I pray God that it was the exit of a personal sin and habit I have and
that I may let you know soon that I have conquered this and that Jesus
is my standard."[84] Such boys were vulnerable, for attacks on impurity fueled
their consciences with a potent mixture of religious and sexual guilt.

As YMCA men described it, the ideal outcome was a bracing sense of
moral resolution, based on purity. "We talked about strong manhood,"
a boys' worker recalled of one interview, "and how the boy could buy it
at the price of clean living. And we talked about God, and his place in
a boy's life." Years later, the boy returned from the war "able to look me
right in the eye" and announced that "through all his experiences he had
kept straight. . . ."[85] One model convert, a young "Hebrew," stated: "Before I came into contact with Y.M.C.A. fellows, I was a fellow without
a belief, a creed, an object, a purpose, a God. I was all at sea." Writing
from college, he closed a letter to the boys' secretary with a tag from Mc-
Guffey's *Reader:* "'Life is real, life is earnest.' Tell all the fellows I am
. . . praying for them."[86] This was earnestness for its own sake, not particularly thoughtful, directed resolutely outward towards action and away
from the introspection which adults mistrusted in adolescents.

On the other hand, many boys were proof against the Y's best measures.
In one Texas town, reported Cotton, YMCA work was impossible because
the "'Filthy Fifteen' . . . [were] the real leaders of the school . . . the faculty acknowledging their inability to check their vile practices." At a private school in New York, Francis Miller found no boy "even willing to
allow us to talk to him. So, throwing ceremony aside, Mr. Welty, of the
Cornell Association, went with me to a room where we cornered a fellow

and had a long talk." Yet the boy still balked, and Miller had to leave Welty still searching for "an opening."[87] More pervasive than direct resistance was timidity or indifference. As one lad complained, "Decent fellows at school stand as individuals; the fellows who are going bad go in the crowd. . . ."[88] An average of less than half the YMCA's juniors attended any given religious function; nor did high school campaigns fare better, especially if they faced a rival attraction such as a basketball game. Even at conferences of picked boys, only about half took a Forward Step, and the proportion was much lower during high school campaigns.[89] There was no trend away from "decisions for Christian life," but the recorded percentage of YMCA juniors who took the step remained small: 4.7 in 1909–1910, 4.0 in 1919–1920, and 6.8 in 1920–1921. According to YMCA reports, moreover, only about one-third as many boys went on to join a church.[90] Even if underreported, these figures indicated modest levels of religious participation, with zeal limited to a small minority.

In terms of more or less formal instruction, character builders had mixed success at reaching their professed objectives. This is true whether we consider the ideal of balanced development—physical, mental, social or moral, and religious—or the goal of solving adolescent problems.

In view of the flawed theory of faculty discipline underlying it, the goal of balanced development was probably unattainable. Physical development certainly won the most enthusiasm from boys. YMCA juniors exercised frequently. Although Boy Scouts received little systematic training and no more than one in one hundred and forty won Athletics or Physical Development badges in a given year, their meetings included games or drill.[91] Outdoor life promised exercise, and boys' prize essays told how Scouting taught "endurance," correcting a "stooped chest and rounded shoulders."[92] Yet the intermittent nature of hiking and camping precluded steady building of strength; Boy Scout leaders rightly feared overstrain if they suddenly demanded too great exertion.[93] While the best troops hiked and camped frequently, many others held little besides indoor meetings. Boys gained less intellectually than they did physically, since Boy Scout requirements were fragmented, and instruction and testing relied heavily upon memorization. At their best, YMCA discussion groups encouraged more thoughtful habits of mind, yet limited numbers of boys participated, and Bible study often meant learning isolated facts. Relatively few boys joined educational clubs. The results of moral and social education were likewise mixed, as boys gave sporadic service but did not respond in any easily verifiable way to instruction by precept. Boy Scouts were enthusiastic patriots, but Scouting probably did little more than channel existing values. Again, YMCA study groups fostered a wider-ranging consideration of social problems, but not many boys took part. Religiously, the outcome was also mixed. Few Boy Scouts encountered sustained proselytizing. The impact of YMCA evangelism was dramatic in individual cases yet limited in the mass. In each area of development, however, assessment is complicated by the boys' immaturity; physically, intellectually, and psychologically, many still had to pass through further stages of growth before adult criteria implicit in the fourfold plan would become applicable. In this regard the assumption of simple, linear, incremental growth which underlay the theory of faculty discipline was misleading.

Character builders recognized this possibility, regarding adolescence as a new beginning, but they were often too ambivalent about adolescent crises to apply the insight. It is worth recalling that to many character builders, the potential of adolescence for developing a sense of identity was less a promise than a threat—to be met by keeping boys busy and teaching them prefabricated values. Boy Scouting in particular offered no direct resolution to quandaries predicted by Hall's account of adolescence, such as what vocation to choose, what religious commitments to make, and how to manage sexual urges. Instead, Boy Scout leaders looked to preoccupation as their answer to adolescence, although the slowness with which boys advanced through the ranks suggests that the BSA's formal program accomplished little along these lines. YMCA secretaries addressed adolescent problems more directly, but they too put their best energies into simply keeping boys busy. When they interviewed boys, the purpose, explained a Canadian manual, was to "centre the boy's attention as much as possible upon objective interests and activities . . . in order to prevent . . . morbid and extreme introspection."[94] Given the distrust of self-analysis evident in prevailing stereotypes of vigorous, go-ahead masculinity, it is understandable that Boy Scout leaders did as little as they did to foster self-examination and is perhaps surprising that YMCA men did as much.[95]

Avoidance of adolescent issues was all the easier because the boys themselves dodged problems such as vocational choice and worried about impurity yet talked only under duress. Great swells of storm and stress did not roll visibly across the surface of their lives, both because they kept things to themselves and because Hall's account of adolescent crisis was overblown. Recent studies indicate that disruptive turmoil does not characterize most suburban teenagers; and Hall's romantic predilections probably led him to exaggerate both the crisis and the idealistic promise of adolescence in his own day.[96]

As we are about to see, moreover, many of the boys, especially the Boy Scouts, were simply too young to be fully adolescent. This made it doubly tempting for Boy Scout leaders to stress activities suited to gang-age boys. Once set, enrollment patterns perpetuated themselves as older lads grew restless and dropped out. To the boys, after all, social experiences mattered more than formal lessons. Thus the fate of character building depended upon how boys responded to the groups they joined and upon the ages at which they felt most content there.

15

Group Experience, Membership Turnover, and Age Stratification

Membership in YMCA boys' branches and especially in Scouting attracted boys who had begun to work free of parental controls but would still tolerate close supervision. For character builders tried, more or less openly, to wean boys away from their mothers; ritual gestures towards closer parent-child relations, such as father and son suppers, involved men only. Like schoolteachers, character builders wanted general support and no interference; they would not guarantee parents increased influence over their sons, although the BSA did pledge not to cultivate "an independence detrimental to the home."[1] Many parents were of course so happy to have someone take charge of their sons that BSA officials complained of their indifference. Yet almost never did Boy Scout leaders discuss sharing control; instead, they treated parents as consumers, inviting them on special nights to watch displays of Scoutcraft.[2] YMCA men likewise recognized, as E. M. Robinson put it, that boys wanted now and then to slough off "home restraints."[3] Camp leaders chose sites well beyond walking distance in order to discourage visitors, give the boys a sense of adventure, and prevent them going home. Boy Scout executives also supported evening meetings, despite objections that these weakened home life, because boys liked going out after supper.[4]

To earn their ticket out, however, boys had to accept fairly close supervision, since concern for control permeated boys' work. Character builders wanted group loyalty from boys, and they wanted it to last through adolescence. Thus the strength of group ties and the ages at which boys quit provide crude but telling indications of the character builders' success. Basically, as we shall see, they recruited boys more effectively than they held them.

A Boy Scout troop of twenty-four to thirty-two members was a reasonable size for maintaining boys' loyalty under adult control. In the early years, a few ambitious men formed troops several times as large, but the boys were partial strangers to each other, and the Scoutmasters had to run the troops like boys' clubs. On the other hand, troops could not be too small, for units of five or ten would have required an enormous force of Scoutmasters.[5] Indeed, a weakness of YMCA boys' work was its failure to form stable, troop-sized units.

Despite Boy Scouting's outdoor program, troop activities centered on the weekly meetings, to the point that some troops had little else. Since young boys joined a troop eager for new adventures, nothing disenchanted them more effectively than dull meetings in a church basement. That was what boys whose troops collapsed complained of; and Boy Scout officials agreed that troops fell apart primarily from failure to run meetings in a "decent peppy manner."[6] Accordingly, neophyte Scoutmasters spent the hour and a half each week in flight from one expedient to another, desperate to outrun the boys' boredom. At the end, all one such Scoutmaster could sigh was, "Well, I'm glad that's over."[7]

Since the BSA ethos favored standardization, experienced Scoutmasters turned to careful scheduling. A few outlined the entire year in advance. Thus Boy Scouts in Alpena, Michigan, knew that the five meetings in October of 1916 would feature successively business, a talk by a meteorologist, drill, an illustrated travel lecture, and a talk on thrift by a banker. A simpler approach was simply to have parliamentary-style business one week and Scouting practice the next.[8] The most common strategy was to use the same general outline each week and try to hold the boys by varying details and setting a fast pace. George G. Walker of Grand Rapids, Michigan, cut his meetings into twenty-minute blocks. The first included inspection, a flag ceremony, minutes, a talk on Boy Scout principles, and orders of the day. The next consisted of marching drill, the third of instruction for promotion, and the fourth of games and a story by the Scoutmaster. Closing exercises included good turn reports and another brief talk.[9] In all this, the boys depended upon the Scoutmaster to keep things moving.

A certain formality was not inimical to close ties among the boys. A Minneapolis troop, for instance, not only elected officers but also admitted new members by vote—with current Boy Scouts as their sponsors.[10] But many boys were bored by business meetings, and other kinds of formality kept the boys apart. Some Boy Scout troops were run like classes with the boys in rows or in an open square before the Scoutmaster.[11] Drill served as much to quiet them as to ready them for parades. Such a setting was no place to form close friendships; instead, boys made friends at play before the meeting or on weekend hikes. Yet the average troop met in borrowed rooms with no permanent clubroom and came together only once a week, perhaps thirty times a year. Worse yet, troops commonly shut down altogether in summer and had trouble reorganizing come fall.[12]

Troop cohesion thus depended heavily upon hikes and other outside activities, which brought active troops together at least monthly. Despite this, the centralizing zeal of ambitious Boy Scout executives led them to run rallies and service projects without regard for troop divisions and to discourage troop camping. Although not all his colleagues agreed, executive Steele of Baton Rouge, Louisiana, saw council camps as a direct antidote to "over-emphasis on troop loyalty."[13]

Despite these obstacles, veteran Boy Scouts formed loyalties strong enough to impede organization across troop lines. Even when they grew old enough to leave, some felt ambivalent and guilty.[14] Groups the size of school classes were familiar settings for boys; their Scout troops commanded modest but genuine loyalty.

YMCA governance was rather formal, as befitted large groups of partial strangers. Clubs elected officers, and many Associations set up committees for each phase of the program, with a boys' cabinet for oversight. At the state level, conferences brought together the secretaries' favorite future leaders. Altogether, a good many boys had leadership experience, although the proportion on committees declined from 9.7 percent in 1906 to 6.6 percent by 1921.[15]

In some cases boys made and carried out plans, but formal organization often proved artificial. Boys' conferences had little function beyond reassuring religious lads, as one delegate put it, that they were "not alone."[16] Within junior departments, secretaries practiced closely guided democracy. Harvey Smith of Brooklyn designed an elaborate system of self-government which he called "Tuxis City," but to prevent miscreants from escaping what he considered justice, he acted as defense attorney in all court cases. Most secretaries likewise insisted upon having their own way, until one disgruntled colleague complained: "All of the self-governing schemes that we have seen tried have either failed or are being perpetuated by the men who promoted them through their determined effort to keep up the appearance of a self-governing organization. In several places these men . . . simply handle the boys like a Punch and Judy show. This disgusts the serious-minded older boys. . . ."[17] Boys tasked with imposing discipline were caught between the boys' worker and their peers. The young judge of Tuxis City tried to avoid levying any penalties, but finally gave in to pressure from Smith. Other boys, according to a critical observer, became "priggish, selfish and unsympathetic toward the younger fellows."[18] The remedy, suggested a YMCA commission in 1913, was to simplify organization and stop giving boys disciplinary authority. Gradually YMCA men moved toward less formal arrangements centered on modest-sized, self-directing groups.[19]

It is significant that Boy Scouts' primary allegiance went to the troop, led by an adult, rather than to the patrol, led by a boy; for loyalty was arguably more diffuse and less intense that way than if bestowed upon a small group of friends. Despite the character builders' declared enthusiasm for gangs, the adult impulse to dominate proved too strong; even while adults recognized the importance of peer groups, they denied them the autonomy that made them important to teenagers.

The troops' weekly meetings gave patrols little chance to cohere. The multiplication of troop scribes, troop leaders, and other functionaries plus the addition of parliamentary touches to meetings reduced the salience of the patrol and its leader.[20] During the instruction period in many troops, each patrol did retire to a corner to work under its patrol leader. Yet all the boys often gathered in a single class led by the Scoutmaster. Even more disruptive of patrol unity, though rarer in practice, was the system of promoting boys school-fashion from one patrol to the next as they passed their tests.[21] Contests among patrols were common but involved mostly the accumulation of points by individual patrol members rather than group endeavor.[22] Scoutmasters were so anxious to edify, instruct, and control the boys that they made everything revolve around themselves, while patrol leaders were little more than monitors. One solution might have been patrol meetings separate from those of the troop, but Boy Scout officials insisted upon the inhibiting presence of an adult leader.[23]

The same pattern continued outdoors, as council camps submerged patrols as well as troops. Boys often had no advance idea with whom they would be tenting; only about a third had boys as tent leaders, and these were often older lads brought in for the purpose.[24] Hikes offered patrols a better chance to go off by themselves; some hiked frequently, and a few held weekend camps. But reports of behavior damaging to the movement's public image and complaints by protective parents stirred misgivings at headquarters, to the point that West opposed letting boys go into the woods alone "even for tree study."[25] A good many Scoutmasters ran hikes themselves and merely used patrol leaders to chivvy stragglers. As of 1922, the official BSA position was that boys should not go anywhere as a group without adult leaders present.[26]

Ignorance accounted for some failures to apply patrol methods, as only half the executives in 1918 claimed even to understand the patrol system. Unlike the British, Americans assumed that education occurred almost exclusively in classrooms; like schoolteachers, therefore, American Scoutmasters tried to run everything themselves. But more than thoughtlessness was involved, for boys' workers had never quite decided whether to use the gang instinct or subvert it. Many Boy Scout leaders argued that the patrol idea frightened parents and reduced efficiency. For his part, West insisted upon constant surveillance to maintain standards and refused to let patrol leaders administer tests on Scout requirements.[27]

Boys in their early teens needed supervision, to be sure. The cruelty of bullies was familiar to readers of *Tom Brown's School Days,* while even generous boys turned rule-bound and fractious when exercising power in a formal setting; for their political views were likely still to be naively authoritarian. A conspicuous weakness of the Sons of Daniel Boone was that the boys, encouraged by Beard to draw up their own laws, either ignored these rules or enforced them harshly. Thus Fort Deerfoot reported proudly: "Jay Geiss used to always want to have his own way but we ducked him so often that he is pretty well broke of it by now. . . ."[28] Disputes broke up forts, and Beard had to warn boys not to be too strict. Even under supervision, boys reveled in rules. Boy Scout troops which ran on parliamentary lines spent evenings entangled in procedural matters and were quite ready to blackball new members.[29]

Ideally, the patrol system operated less formally, striking a balance between juvenile tyranny and powerlessness; but few Scoutmasters needed their 1914 handbook's warning to take care "that the patrol leaders do not have too great authority. . . ."[30] The patrol leaders' tenuous position was apparent in the circumstances of their appointment. Although some Scoutmasters permitted free elections, many believed this made the patrol leader a poor conveyor of orders and either manipulated the vote in the best boys' work tradition or made the choice themselves. In itself, appointment probably enhanced a patrol leader's authority; a conference of patrol leaders voted unanimously in favor of appointment by the Scoutmaster. But a good many Scoutmasters shuffled their patrol leaders annually or even every six months, preventing any one from consolidating his authority.[31] They did not always name older boys either, since some thought it more democratic to have all patrol members the same age or found younger boys more malleable. Because his appointment violated the tendency of boys to choose older leaders, a young leader had to be exceptionally aggressive. "One of the smallest, one of the youngest boys of my first patrol is my troop leader," reported a satisfied Scoutmaster, "and he is able to thrash any other boy in his patrol. . . ."[32] Yet an older boy might not have had to fight. The obvious way to hold older and younger boys together was to give the older ones authority; appointment of younger boys meant that older ones could not be sure of rising in rank.[33]

Around 1920, disturbed at the frequency with which older boys dropped out, headquarters officials began to urge greater use of patrol methods.[34] But Lorne Barclay, director of the BSA's Educational Department, still described the patrol leader as primarily an assistant to the Scoutmaster, and local training courses prepared patrol leaders to work as instructors and monitors.[35] Some Boy Scout officials even encouraged patrol leaders to see themselves as a separate officers' caste, meeting apart and demanding salutes from ordinary Scouts. The notion of the patrol as a gang whose leader was part of the group remained in large measure theoretical; as late as 1924 only a fraction of American troops really used the patrol system.[36]

The American reluctance to grant older boys independent power contrasted markedly with Baden-Powell's belief in giving responsibility. This disagreement was deeply rooted in American and British culture. American Boys' Brigade captains delegated far less authority than their British counterparts. Similarly, few American boarding schools used the English prefect system, and those few avoided granting the sweeping powers (including the right to cane younger boys) customary in Britain. President Eliot of Harvard condemned the British system as "absolutely inapplicable in our country," unless the masters had "quite extraordinary control."[37] For their part, British boys' workers criticized American practices. William Smith, the Brigades' founder, urged American officers not to compromise their noncoms' authority. The British way did not aim at unbridled liberty — quite the opposite — for delegating authority made supervision more sustained, if occasionally tyrannical, whereas discipline in the U.S. Brigades was erratic. Baden-Powell likewise complained that American Boy Scouts were too "leisurely" and insisted that "the great step towards discipline" was "giving real responsibility to the patrol leaders and looking upon the patrol, not the troop, as the unit for discipline and efficiency."[38] Admittedly, he had to nag British Scoutmasters as well, but American observers agreed that British patrol leaders had far more power than their counterparts in the U.S.[39]

Baden-Powell and Smith had faith in a reasonably stable social order rooted in a hierarchical tradition. In delegating authority to older boys, they assumed a hierarchy based on age, confident that these subalterns would know their place.[40] Americans, on the other hand, saw their social order as artificial, dependent upon the cooperation of free individuals. Hence American Boy Scout leaders felt that boys needed careful watching and indoctrination before being turned loose as independent citizens. Hence also they relied more than the British upon formal regulations — from the oath and law to BSA policies — and less upon unwritten understandings such as those implicit in the patrol system.

This shift in emphasis also reflected a belief that American boys differed from British. Fearing that the English working class had gone slack, Baden-Powell put his primary emphasis upon fostering self-discipline, initiative, and individual intelligence, whereas American character builders stressed control. They agreed with Baden-Powell — and generations of European travelers — that the typical North American boy had ample intelligence and initiative but lacked "discipline" as well as "unselfishness, courtesy, etc., which Scouting may teach him." Accordingly, they emphasized Boy Scouting's moral ideals and strove to "restrain the excess of self-assertion" which they thought marked American boys.[41]

Boy Scouts appeared to live up to these differing expectations. S. A. Moffat marveled at how "amenable to authority" British Boy Scouts were: "In the English camps, I have never seen a boy come to his scoutmaster and clap him on the back, and treat him familiarly, and roll him in the dust, and so on, in the presence of visitors. . . ." A BSA executive who opposed the patrol system argued similarly that "English and French boys will obey orders quicker than the American boy. The American boy . . . wants to go his own way. . . ."[42]

American men and boys alike were troubled about authority. Boys wanted both freedom and security; they liked a Scoutmaster who did "anything that we wanted him to do . . . and yet he was pretty strict and when he gave an order he meant to have it obeyed."[43] But when Scoutmasters hesitated, there was trouble, as neither side knew how far to push. A disconsolate Boy Scout reported one such instance: "I have given the scoutmaster so many suggestions that he accused me of trying to run the troop. The next thing he tells me is that he is glad of the suggestions—but he never uses them and he never has a program. . . . I was kicked out tonight, just sent out for the evening, but I don't think that I will go back."[44]

Some men concluded that it was rule or ruin. And there were boys ready to test them, for writers told of cliques who wore out one Scoutmaster after another. In one Chicago troop "there was nothing but trouble during the two years [it] existed. The gang fairly ran things. . . . The other boys were afraid of them and were always trying to please the gang rather than the Scout officials. . . . Eventually when some of the members of the gang disobeyed orders at the summer camp, the whole gang bolted, and the rest of the troop seemed very half-hearted."[45] This was an extreme case, but it illustrates why Scoutmasters shied away from admitting tough boys and were leery even of letting patrols function as artificial gangs.

Jay Mechling, who has studied a highly successful 1970s Boy Scout troop at summer camp, has described its life there as a balance between substantial adult control on the one hand, with a high ratio of leaders to boys, and a fair measure of independence and responsibility on the other, especially for the older boys. Campfires provided little interludes of sanctioned rebelliousness through songs and jokes about spiting adult authority.[46] While one cannot pretend that teenage boys of the 1910s and 1920s were identical to those of the 1970s, insofar as most early Scoutmasters failed to strike that balance between maintaining supervision and granting independence, it is not surprising that they had trouble holding the boys' loyalty or sometimes even disciplining them.

YMCA secretaries faced some of the same problems as Scoutmasters in keeping control. One man complained: "[The boys] don't behave well. They are unnecessarily noisy and they have to be constantly scolded to keep them in order. It wears me out, and it is unpleasant for them. They soon lose interest and drop out."[47] Yet the problem was less troublesome than in Boy Scouting, as most activities stayed safely inside the building. YMCA men used boys with little hesitation as monitors and squad leaders to keep order in the locker room and "check hazing of small boys. . . ." A few juniors also taught Bible classes, although a boy reported that "being instructed by one whom they regard as one of themselves [was] at first hard to accept. . . ."[48] By the 1910s, boys' workers preferred distinctly older boys — sixteen and up — to lead those twelve to fourteen, because their authority won easier acceptance. Such boys were hard to recruit, however, since they were busy finishing high school, and the proportion of juniors serving as squad leaders fell from one in twenty-three in 1906 to one in thirty-three by 1921.[49]

Because so much YMCA activity took the form of classes for fee payers, juniors seldom knitted into anything like gangs, although special interest clubs made more intimate small groups. Y juniors were also less likely to know each other in advance than Boy Scouts. One purpose of the standard programs of the 1910s was to form cohesive small groups, but these programs caught on slowly. Only in the 1920s, through community programs, did the YMCA manage to take over many preexisting groups of boys instead of assembling new ones.[50]

Failure to generate enough close-knit peer groups was a weakness of Boy Scouting and an even graver obstacle to the success of YMCA boys' work. For recent studies suggest that schools are most important to adolescents as places to interact with peers; developing academic or even athletic competence matters less.[51] Since establishing oneself securely in a peer group is so vital for boys approaching adolescence — as character builders recognized in their theoretical enthusiasm for the gang instinct — boys probably cared less about the achievements recognized by Boy Scout badges or even the skills built up in YMCA gymnasiums than they did about the group ties they formed or failed to form. If those ties were weak, it would take a most enticing program or gifted leader to hold the boys.

On balance, character builders of the 1910s were as likely to subvert the gang instinct as to use it; they accustomed boys to large, adult-dominated gatherings. Like the student governments becoming popular in high schools, boys' work programs often reduced boys to puppets, while smaller, less formal groups such as Boy Scout patrols had little autonomy. The boys' responses to character building depended heavily, therefore, upon whether they liked the adult leader. Those whose fathers were distant may have looked to Scoutmasters and Y workers as guides and friends. How well, then, did the men measure up?

Although no exact answer is possible, we can ponder the constraints under which the men labored. Their hunger for control suggests a nagging lack of trust in boys. The insistence of Brigade captains upon military protocol was an extreme manifestation of the formalism some men used to keep boys at a distance. For their part, boys were often standoffish or troublesome, and few men can have succeeded without good-humored resignation. Thus a Scoutmaster wryly advised his colleagues never to be too tired to take the boys out hiking, since boys were the best friends a man could have—but not until he had done everything in their favor for about three years. Murray Brooks of the YMCA likewise suggested that young men would find volunteer work "good training in patience."[52]

A major problem was lack of time, for the Scoutmaster's job demanded far more than other forms of volunteer work such as teaching Sunday school, which took an average of just an hour and a half a week. Including preparation, one conscientious Scoutmaster estimated he needed thirty-five hours a month to run a weekly meeting and a monthly hike. The BSA's annual report for 1915 estimated that a Scoutmaster needed five to thirty hours a week. Yet on the average, Scoutmasters spent only five and one-half hours a week in 1912, and small-town Scoutmasters in the early 1920s averaged only three and one-half hours.[53] Boy Scout executive Hierault of Paterson, New Jersey, lamented: "I cannot find men who are willing to devote half an hour at night studying their scout work...." Ideally, boys got to know their Scoutmaster on hikes and at camp, yet mass camping undercut troop bonds and many men could not get out to hike.[54]

Lack of time fostered high turnover. Most Scoutmasters floundered the first year or so, and half left within a year.[55] The frequency with which men and boys quit made sustained contact the exception rather than the rule (see Table 2, above, on turnover). As late as 1921, only 42 percent of all Scoutmasters could claim more than a year's experience, and just 7 percent had more than five. Although time spent is a crude test of relationships, only a fraction of all Boy Scouts could have got to know their Scoutmaster very well. A survey of Los Angeles boys in the 1920s blamed many of the BSA's difficulties on untrained and impermanent Scoutmasters.[56]

Yet statistical summaries miss the kindness that boys received from individuals. Two letters on the same page of *Scouting* in 1915 displayed a range from dogged patience to merry ingenuity. One Scoutmaster reported that his troop had shrunk from eleven to six, "a very unambitious lot. They are rapidly developing the manners and morals of scouts, but when it comes to study or anything outside of a brainless game it is like teaching sparrows to do tricks in the woods." Still, he added, "there *is* a change in the ones who stick, and the compliments I receive from their former 'annoyees' give strength...." In a different vein, another man told of gathering his troop at his house for an evening hike; when it poured rain, he responded by running a burlesque track meet using Tiddleywinks, balloons, and feathers. Amid loud cheers, the troop's largest boys discovered that strength did not avail when hurling balloons. "After the last event was 'run off' . . . it was voted that the 'Parlor Athletics' had been a tremendous success."[57]

Certainly volunteers could be as close to boys as professionals; for many YMCA boys had far less personal contact with their leaders than did Boy Scouts. Except at camp, where college students served as counselors, and in rural work, which was decentralized, volunteers were lacking to run small groups. Among boys' secretaries, turnover approached the rates for Scoutmasters; and the paid staff supervised more boys than they could possibly know well—an average of 225 per man in 1919.[58] They could manage because the physical director and other specialists took over some activities; however, from the boys' viewpoint superficial contacts resulted, since they saw several men for an hour or two each week under basically instructional circumstances. Eventually personal guidance became another program item, routinized like the rest, until a commission found it necessary in 1913 to "urge upon all Boys' Work Directors the essential value . . . of the personal interview with each boy as he comes into the membership."[59]

Despite nostalgia for an imagined rural world so close and intimate that the community itself was a primary group, character builders inhabited a world of bureaucratic organization and segmental relationships—a world whose standards they actively fostered. Rather than countering the fragmentation of boys' lives as they cut across different institutions, boys' work added yet another affiliation. Even church-sponsored groups were seldom well integrated into the church program. What boys received was further exposure, above and beyond their schooling, to the circumscribed relationships and organizational settings of middle-class life.

Only rare boys centered a pattern of life on either the YMCA or Scouting. One such paragon assisted afternoons at the Louisville, Kentucky, YMCA: "He is hard as nails and wiry as a cat . . . and can put boys larger than himself flat on the mats," boasted the boys' secretary. "Saturday morning he teaches a Bible class and Sunday finds him in his Sunday school. . . . His evenings are spent in study—no time for cheap theaters and the like—and when his bed time comes it finds him tired and ready for sure enough sleep. In the morning he starts for school with a clear eye, ruddy cheek and quick step. . . . The Devil has no show with a boy like this."[60] Such incessant activism was what character builders dreamed of—adolescence tamed and channeled—but we may wonder whether it added up to a way of life or merely served as a distraction from commercial entertainment and sexual urges.

Perhaps more typical was young Nathaniel Alexander Owings, later a distinguished architect, whose family steered him into the Boy Scouts on his twelfth birthday, soon after his father died. The Scoutmaster, a cousin of his, "saw to it that scouting was not a passing phase, as it seemed to be in many families. For me it held the authority of a monastic rule: voluntary, self-imposed and fun." For five years, as he worked his way to Eagle Scout, "there were meetings in the church basement each week and camping on the White River on weekends." Owings was no paragon—the combination of Scouting, part-time jobs, and dates eroded his school grades—but he bounced happily from activity to activity.[61]

Despite their dream of solving adolescent problems by preoccupation, character builders had little hope of preempting all of most boys' leisure time. Most Boy Scout troops met only once a week. Although YMCA junior departments reported an average daily attendance in 1910 exceeding 28 percent of the total membership, that still left nearly three-quarters of the juniors uninvolved on any afternoon and evening.[62] Nonetheless, Boy Scout or YMCA activities unquestionably made a happy addition to a bustling life like Owings's.

For many boys, though, membership was merely a passing fancy. As we have seen, character builders recruited with great success. The BSA claimed 376,537 Scouts by the end of 1920, equal to 6.3 percent of all boys aged twelve through seventeen recorded by the 1920 census. The YMCA reported 219,376 juniors for 1920–1921, plus 41,384 Hi-Y members. These figures understate the range of boys' work, however, and overstate its depth, since between 1915 and 1920 only 35 to 50 percent of each year's Boy Scouts reregistered for the next year.[63] Turnover rates were just as high in the Boys' Brigades, while YMCA membership renewals above 50 percent were cause for congratulations.[64] As a result, many more boys had some brief YMCA or Boy Scout experience than appear on the rolls in any one year. About 9.6 percent of all eligible American boys were Scouts at some time between 1910 and 1920; another 7.8 percent were YMCA juniors—and these totals rose sharply in the 1920s.[65] Yet we should beware of overestimating the character builders' influence on the basis of cumulative memberships, keeping in mind that many boys lasted only a few months.

Some turnover was of course inevitable. Nearly 15 percent of the boys should have reached age eighteen each year, and others had to quit because their parents moved. Furthermore, organizational shortcomings forced out some boys; almost one-third of those whose membership lapsed in 1926 belonged to troops that collapsed. However, it was the boys' discontent which had precipitated the disintegration of many of those troops. So it remains fair to say that the majority of boys who quit did so deliberately, long before they had to. As late as 1927, more than 44 percent of Boy Scouts dropped out in their first year and just 5 percent in their fifth year or beyond.[66]

Although neither Scoutmasters nor boys were very articulate about why Boy Scouts quit, their comments indicated diffuse restlessness and boredom among the boys. In 1922, 707 former Boy Scouts from Toledo each gave one reason for leaving: 14 percent each blamed the lure of athletics and social life, poor leadership, or the collapse of their troop; 12 percent blamed boredom and lack of outdoor activities; 11 percent cited the press of other duties; 9 percent had moved; 7 percent mentioned conflict between older and younger boys; 6 percent cited lack of discipline; the remaining 13 percent blamed parental objections, the wrong class of boys in the troop, cost, sickness, expulsion, or other reasons. The dropouts claimed to like hiking and camping, and many complained their troop seldom ventured outdoors.[67] Scoutmasters surveyed nationally in 1924 and 1925 favored vague explanations such as "lost interest" (32 percent in the first survey and 22 percent in the second). They also blamed "other activities, work, school" (17 percent in each poll); moving from the neighborhood (17 and 19 percent respectively); age (10 and 6 percent); and other reasons (24 and 36 percent).[68] Perhaps stories of Scouting which filled the boys' heads with dreams of wilderness adventure and heroic escapades did not prepare them for the discipline of learning signaling and first aid or the routine of weekly meetings. The declared enthusiasm of dropouts for outdoor activities suggests that Boy Scouting's great practical weakness was a tendency to wither indoors amid the dull round of meetings in a church basement. A good many boys formed only weak troop loyalties and then left as outside activities beckoned.

Perhaps part of the problem was also that American boys were chronically restless. Certainly British Boy Scouting had much lower turnover (around 25 percent a year), although there is no way to tell whether British Boy Scouts stayed on because they were more disciplined and docile than American boys or because the patrol system held their loyalties.[69] In America working boys typically changed jobs every few months. Even a group of 1,115 ambitious boys who signed up for YMCA vocational guidance interviews in 1919 reported an average job tenure of only nine months. The same was true of part-time jobs; William Boyce estimated that his newsboys lasted an average of only five months.[70] Considering that the boys were free to come and go, perhaps Boy Scout leaders did well to hold as many as they did.

The YMCA had a somewhat different problem. The fact that "membership in most Associations meant a purchase of privileges" cut two ways.[71] It gave older boys a degree of freedom as consumers that Boy Scouts lacked, but insofar as they simply paid fees for swimming and basketball, their involvement was "calculative" rather than "moral" and hence less likely to be intense or lasting.[72] If they judged the benefits insufficient, they simply quit. This problem was not unique to the YMCA, for it affected Boy Scouting and was acute in boys' clubs. The trick, which not all boys' workers mastered, was to demand deeper involvement without frightening the boys off. YMCA secretaries were apt to ask too little or too much.

The Boy Scouts' restlessness was not merely random, for they and their leaders were engaged in a tug of war — in which the men tried to protract Boy Scout membership through adolescence while the boys balked with increasing vigor as they grew older. Since the boys' interest in Scouting centered on a narrow band of years, small shifts in age mattered enormously.

Boy Scout leaders knew they had an "older boy problem."[73] In 1922, almost 60 percent of the boys who quit Scouting were fourteen or younger, and 89 percent were sixteen or younger. Their median age was 14.5 (see Table 9). In other words, nearly three-fifths of all the boys who quit the movement had not yet reached their fifteenth birthday. And of course the median age of current members was lower still. In 309 troops studied in 1919 it was 13.8, and no more than 10 percent of the Boy Scouts were sixteen or older. There was little change over time; for in 1924–1925 and again in 1934 the median age was still only 13.9, although the proportion aged sixteen and above rose to 16.5 percent by 1934 (see Table 10). Basically, most Boy Scouts were just entering their teens. In 1919, 77 percent of those studied were ages twelve, thirteen, or fourteen; in 1924–1925, 72 percent were, and in 1934, 70 percent.

What happened was that Scouting attracted hordes of small boys but lost many fairly quickly and found few older recruits to replace the dropouts. Most Boy Scouts joined young — 67 percent at twelve or thirteen in 1925 — and lasted two years or less. Among a nationwide sample of 6,843 Boy Scouts who joined in 1915, the median period of membership was 19.6 months; only 6.7 percent stayed four years or more.[74] Some turnover stemmed from causes unrelated to age, such as a family move; but few boys joined or rejoined past age fifteen, and the older a new Boy Scout, the briefer his membership.[75] Scoutmasters agreed they could not attract older boys. The Boy Scout movement thus repeated the pattern of the American Boys' Brigades, most of whose cadets were twelve to fourteen and left when tin soldiering began to seem juvenile.[76]

Although the Brigades and the BSA established themselves as church auxiliaries with a promise to help hold boys in Sunday school, their efforts cannot have helped much, since boys quit Scouting and the Brigades about the same average age they left Sunday school. In fact, an Indiana survey around 1920 found that among Sunday school boys of Scout age (twelve through eighteen) the median age was 14.3, a bit higher than the Boy Scouts'.[77]

Despite the declared interest of BSA leaders in shepherding boys through adolescence, many of their Scouts must have been prepubescent. Several studies in the 1900s and 1910s found median or average ages of pubescence

Table 9

Ages at Which Boy Scouts Quit in 109 Local Councils, 1921

(*N* = 20,575)

Age	(%)
12	16.1
13	22.2
14	21.3
15	19.0
16	10.5
17	6.3
18	3.4
19 +	1.2
Median Age	14.5

Source: Boy Scouts of America, *Second Biennial Conference of Scout Executives, 1922: Report of the Commission on Scout Mortality and Turnover* (New York, 1922), p. 8.

ranging from 13.9 to 14.4, although normal boys varied two years or more in either direction.[78] On the basis of a few cases, Paul H. Furfey, a sociologist interested in boys' work, argued that boys quit Scouting when they entered adolescence. No such neat correspondence can have obtained uniformly, but the figures just cited suggest that most Boy Scouts departed before, during, or soon after puberty. By definitions which assume a rough correspondence between the onset of puberty and that of adolescence, most Boy Scouts were preadolescent or in early adolescence.[79]

Ironically, some of the BSA's problems stemmed from Scouting's enormous popularity with young boys, for it proved equally difficult — indeed almost impossible — to keep underage boys out and older ones in. In 1911, the BSA raised the minimum age from ten — Baden-Powell's initial choice — to twelve. Yet Scoutmasters who needed recruits, especially in small towns where enough were hard to find, routinely accepted boys under age twelve.[80] Southerners claimed their boys matured early; other men simply found ten-year-olds less trouble than older boys and easy to sign up. For their part, underage boys often lied in order to get in.[81] This constant downward pressure on age indicated that boys really wanted to join younger. B. F. Skinner joined when he was nine and stayed for five years, enjoying it hugely. A hint that paramilitary trappings attracted mainly youngish boys was the American Boys' Brigades' decision after 1910 to lower their minimum age to ten.[82] Although Boy Scouting appealed more broadly than the Brigades, its natural constituency consisted of gang-age boys on either side of twelve and not those aged fifteen or sixteen. One could indeed argue that Baden-Powell designed Scouting for that younger age group.

Table 10
Ages of Boys Currently Enrolled in Boy Scout Troops, 1919–1934

Age	309 Troops Nationwide, 1919 (%)[a] (N = 6,658)	Nationwide Registrations, Oct. 1924 to Apr. 1925 (%)[b] (N = 228,087)	Nationwide Registrations, Jan. 1934 (%)[c]
12	29.4	25.3	27.1
13	25.2	25.5	24.8
14	22.0	21.0	18.2
15	13.5	14.4	13.5
16	6.5	8.0	8.0
17	2.4	3.7	4.6
18	.6	1.3	3.9[d]
19+	.4	.8	—
Median Age	13.8	13.9	13.9

[a] Walter S. Athearn et al., *The Religious Education of Protestants in an American Commonwealth* (New York, 1923), p. 224.

[b] Boy Scouts of America, *15th Annual Report,* H. Doc. 109, 69th Cong., 1st sess., 1926, p. 148. These figures, based on about half the Boy Scouts, include both new Scouts and those reregistering.

[c] Ray O. Wyland, *Scouting in the Schools: A Study of the Relationships Between the Schools and the Boy Scouts of America* (New York, 1934), p. 71. Again, the figures include both new Boy Scouts and those reregistering. (*N* not available.)

[d] For age 18 + .

He eventually settled on eleven as the minimum age, and even then, underage boys clamored to get in. Although membership turnover was much lower in Britain than in America, even in the British Boy Scout movement most boys except for patrol leaders were gone by age fifteen or sixteen.[83]

In both Britain and America, Boy Scouting suffered from the Gresham's Law of boys' work: younger boys drive out older ones. Wherever population was large enough, boys preferred to stratify themselves by age; E. M. Robinson considered three years the maximum age span feasible in any one group. Thus a former Boy Scout explained that he quit because "we got a bunch of little kids in the troop and they wanted to be with us all of the time and we wanted to be by ourselves. And I guess we wanted to do different things."[84] Baden-Powell caught on quickly and began experiments with a distinctive form known as Rover Scouting for older boys. But few American Boy Scout troops were divided by age or reserved for older Scouts. Although Scoutmasters used older boys as instructors, they had to be eighteen to be Assistant Scoutmasters, and patrol leaders were on a short leash.[85]

In effect, as we have seen, Boy Scout leaders offered boys a trade: to accept sustained dependency in return for robust outdoor activities and assurance that they were manly fellows. The terms seemed reasonable to men who wanted to control boys and for whom masculinity was personally a more pressing concern than age; they could convince themselves that boyish restiveness derived primarily from threats to masculinity. But they had trouble delivering the outdoor adventure, and effeminacy turned out not to be the boys' paramount concern. When boys were asked why more did not attend Sunday school past age fifteen, a number did indeed complain that Sunday school was "only for girls" and that the teachers were women; yet more common were statements that boys felt "too old to go" and that Sunday school was "too 'kiddish'." Large numbers also complained that Sunday school was boring and gave boys "nothing to do."[86] Growing boys took gender at least partly for granted, whereas the prerogatives of age and freedom to seek their own recreation were still at issue and much to be desired. Effeminacy marked one as a sissy, to be sure, but so did submissiveness and failure to play the right sports or gain the measure of independence expected at one's age.

Older Boy Scouts could sense they were being held back; and as prolonged school attendance made boys fully dependent economically, they clung to tokens of maturity. The term "Boy Scout" was itself offensive; E. P. Hulse of the BSA's national office warned: "Kids of 15 down South when called 'boy' used to retort, 'If I'm a boy where did Jackson and Lee get their men?'" Teenagers from other regions lacked only this *Herrenvolk* cockiness. William McCormick of the Olivet Boys' Club in Reading, Pennsylvania, wrote that boys from age fourteen or so detested "make-believe" and ridiculed the Boys' Brigades. Scouting initially aroused a similar reaction from the boys' cabinet of the Toronto YMCA, who judged "that it savored too much of the 'tin soldier' idea. . . ."[87] The uniform, which appealed to younger boys as a step away from childish dress, became an embarrassment to older Boy Scouts; high school as well as working boys disliked its resemblance to army garb and cringed even more at wearing shorts. But Frank F. Gray, a Boy Scout executive from New Jersey, implied that this chastening function was deliberate; he excoriated "the boy who wants to dress up like a man. . . . Watch your boy's activities carefully and see that the boy is living a boy's life—not the life of a manikin. . . . Unless he is going to be a real boy, he can never be a real man."[88] Like Gray, many character builders tried to curb what they saw as precocity and conceit. Thus Franklin K. Mathiews, the BSA Librarian, recommended a novel about a lad with a "big head," whose deflating was "admirable." The boy failed to make first baseman and pestered his coach until he got to play as a substitute, only to make a crucial fielding error and strike out. After baiting by the coach, he admitted he was "rotten."[89] Yet what was insupportable pride to an adult may have been precarious self-esteem to a teenager.

Impatience with restraint increased in the midteens, when boys were still young enough to be under close control but old enough to try resistance. If extreme cases are revealing, it is significant that of forty-seven runaway Boy Scouts advertised in *Scouting* from 1915 through 1919, fully nineteen were age fifteen, eight were age fourteen, and seven each sixteen and seventeen, whereas only three were thirteen and just one was twelve; two more were age eighteen. This concentration around age fifteen is noteworthy; 72 percent of this little group of boys were precisely that age or within a year in either direction. This concentration in age apparently occurred because few older boys were still in Scouting, while younger ones were not yet bold enough to break for freedom; boys of fifteen or so were in between, old enough to be impatient for independence and yet young enough still to be under fairly close adult surveillance. Most boys around that age did not of course run away, but many did assert their independence with less risk by quitting Sunday school or Scouting.[90]

The reader may recall West's view that fourteen and fifteen were the most difficult ages. Besides being the years when a majority of boys passed through puberty, they were the time when boys could quit school and go to work or else go on to high school. Either way, Boy Scout officials agreed that boys were likely to mark the transition by quitting their troop.[91] The pressures and attractions of schoolwork and part-time jobs increased. By the late 1920s, high school sports and other extracurricular activities drew boys' interest away from Scouting, which no doubt seemed to them a carry-over from grade-school days. Worse yet, the uniform drew scorn in high school corridors. E. B. deGroot, Boy Scout executive for Los Angeles, reported that girls dismissed Boy Scouts as "little kids" and that in high schools with military training, "the R.O.T.C. will sometimes ostracize, or the girls will be encouraged to ostracize, every boy in high school that is not an R.O.T.C., who wears any other uniform or kind of badges."[92]

The girls' opinion was a sore point. For boys twelve and thirteen, sex segregation was fine; but by fourteen or fifteen a handful had girlfriends, and others were beginning to care what girls thought of them. Yet the founding fathers of the Boy Scout movement wanted boys to make the initial break from mother to gang life and then to go no further. Regarding an interest in girls as one more manifestation of precocity, many Boy Scout leaders discussed "the girl-struck boy" in pathological terms, worrying about the "girl problem" and how to treat older boys who were "infected" with "girlitis."[93] Only rarely did Boy Scout gatherings include girls, although a few troops reported that parties helped hold older boys. Joint hikes were out of the question — and besides, who could talk to a girl with dignity in a Boy Scout hat?[94] YMCAs occasionally compromised by holding ladies' nights, but not all girls liked such tame gatherings.[95] Admittedly, not all boys were interested in girls, yet BSA reports on the older boy problem stressed "the girl matter . . . almost in red ink." Oscar A. Kirkham, the executive for Salt Lake City, put the issue baldly: "My observation is that when the girl comes, the Scout goes."[96]

To compound the boys' restlessness, the BSA's outdoor program lost some of its appeal as boys aged. Although they continued to like full-scale summer camps, boys apparently lost interest in lesser outings and may never have cared much for technical woodcraft. Beard's Sons of Daniel Boone could earn notches in their fort's tally gun for outdoor feats; yet half the notches won were for baseball, and boys wrote Beard requesting something besides woodcraft. Boy Scouts likewise tended not to seek woodcraft badges.[97] We should remember, moreover, that Scouting transmuted the common activities of small boys, and older ones could doubtless recognize the basic style. Left to themselves, boys from twelve upward were much more likely to play baseball than go off to the woods. Boy Scouting had its own woodsy games, invented by Seton and Baden-Powell; but these resembled the simplified games, such as tag or hide-and-seek, that small boys played. Enthusiasm for Boy Scout games almost certainly declined with age; an 1896 study of Worcester, Massachusetts, schoolboys found that interest in hide-and-seek held steady through age thirteen but then fell off sharply, whereas interest in ball games rose steadily through the teens.[98] In making baseball their favorite recreation, boys broke with the old culture of boyhood described in boy-books; thus in avoiding sports, the Boy Scout movement was — despite its seeming novelty — somewhat old-fashioned as well as juvenile, although perhaps a welcome refuge for the unathletic. Besides baseball, many older boys hungered for football and basketball, which highly publicized high school and college athletics had made fashionable. This preference was evident in a 1920s survey asking 1,500 high school boys from farms and small towns to list their favorite recreations. Team sports received 1,755 choices, swimming 592, and hiking and camping combined only about 350.[99] Officially, the BSA discouraged team sports; unofficially, Scoutmasters often gave in and permitted them. Boy Scouts took baseball gloves to camp, and crack teams sometimes challenged other troops in football or basketball. But because league play was rare, sports remained a concession rather than one of Boy Scouting's central attractions.[100]

Boy Scouting probably suffered from comparison with athletics for another, less obvious reason as well: it provided little opportunity to achieve for the sake of the high school peer group. Whereas a star athlete's efforts brought renown to his team and to the whole school, the outstanding Boy Scout bore a suspicious resemblance to the studious pupil, who brought distinction to himself alone. Like the A-average student, the Eagle Scout labored assiduously at tasks imposed by adults; and like the outstanding school pupil's achievements, his successes might be used by adults to justify demands upon his peers for greater effort. At best irrelevant to the high school's prestige system and at worst reminiscent of zealous conformity to teachers' academic impositions, distinction in Boy Scouting had no assured place of honor in high school life.[101]

For Boy Scouts to quit in their midteens was no reflection upon the movement's extraordinary success with younger boys. Their departure simply showed that Boy Scouting fitted the world of British schoolboys or gang-age Americans more closely than that of American adolescents. Still, men who had given their best to a group of boys for several years found detachment painful. A New York Scoutmaster lamented that his boys, who had not cared for basketball when he first organized them, joined teams as they grew older. "Some of them are influenced by outside boys," he reported, "and they are going into poolrooms and starting to smoke cigarettes, etc. What am I to do in order to hold the boys together . . . ?"[102]

The proposition that Boy Scouting had limited appeal beyond the early teens found little support at BSA headquarters in the 1910s. Annual reports defined the Boy Scout age as twelve through eighteen, and *Scouting* asserted that the program was "big enough" to keep boys "indefinitely at work."[103] Scoutmasters and local executives, who were unconvinced, tried a variety of schemes to interest older boys, such as special training in first aid and civic service, or fraternal orders with quasi-Masonic ceremonies — another example of the faith that ritual would fascinate adolescents. But no innovation found the magic formula, and West discouraged major departures from the established program.[104] Although West's stand-pat approach won no big successes, supervision by paid executives did bring a modest reduction in turnover rates; and although the median age of Boy Scouts scarcely changed between 1919 and 1934, the percentage sixteen and older rose from 9.8 to 16.5.[105]

To interpret Boy Scouting as simply a form of masculine affirmation and ignore the vital factor of age fails to explain the countertradition among older boys that Scouting was juvenile. Historians should not try to explain male behavior as a mere reflex of alarm at whatever women were doing in a given period. The fact is that to Boy Scout leaders, control mattered more than masculinity, as shown by their reluctance to let boys hike alone and their unwillingness in the end to force a crisis over Girl Scouting. Likewise, to growing boys the increments of independence and self-assertion that came with age mattered more than a demonstrative yet cloistered masculinity. As age grading became more differentiated, boys stuck with friends their own age, ranked amusements by age, and grew impatient with what seemed juvenile. With other areas of freedom closing off, the boys looked to recreation as a field for self-assertion;

thus what seemed adventurous at age twelve could seem sissified three years later.

For a number of reasons, YMCA boys' work attracted a higher proportion of older boys than did the Boy Scouts. Instead of Scouting's standard program which appealed intensely but narrowly to gang-age boys, YMCAs offered varied activities suited to differing ages. Association programs infringed less upon the dignity of older youths; for there was no uniform, boys had some freedom to choose among activities, and the Y catered to their athletic interests. Basketball, the YMCA's enormously popular game, was preeminently a high school boy's sport. Equally important was the growing recognition of age differences within the teens; by 1920 Y men commonly divided boys around age fifteen.[106] After a slow start, separate Hi-Y and employed boys' groups multiplied towards 1920. Other special features for older juniors probably mattered less than these, since they often degenerated into puppetry. But boys' cabinets at least purported to exercise authority, and evangelistic conferences which centered upon older boys conveyed the message that such boys were important.

Whereas Scouting appealed intensely to youngish boys yet held few older ones, the Y enlisted fewer boys overall but a wider spectrum of ages. In a sample of YMCAs in 1901, membership held fairly steady from twelve through fifteen, then nearly doubled at age sixteen (see Table 11). Most new members that age were seniors; but boys of sixteen and seventeen soon began to feel uneasy among the men and stayed on as juniors, until by the 1910s reports defined the boys' work field as twelve to eighteen. Already by 1905, the median age of juniors at the Buffalo YMCA was 15.2, and 29.6 percent were sixteen or older (see Table 11). In Holyoke, Massachusetts, in 1917 the juniors' mean age was 14.9.[107] More significantly, from 1916 to 1921, 50 to 61 percent of all YMCA juniors were either in high school or out at work (see Table 8, above). This did not mean that all YMCA boys were postpubescent; when the secretary at New Britain, Connecticut, tried requiring that each new member be fully adolescent, he ended up with almost no one age twelve and a median age of 16.0 — a year above the usual figure.[108] Boys' branches had their share of preadolescents, but they also had more older boys than most Boy Scout troops. In twenty-two rural and suburban counties in the early 1920s, the Boy Scouts' median age was 14.3, whereas the YMCA juniors' was 15.5 (see Table 12). Forty-four percent of the Boy Scouts were under age fourteen, but only 25 percent of the YMCA juniors. On the other hand, almost 43 percent of the YMCA juniors were age sixteen or older, compared to just 18 percent of the Boy Scouts. Similarly, in Trenton, New Jersey, the Boy Scouts had twice as many junior high school boys as the YMCA, but the Y had six times as many senior high school boys.[109]

Table 11
Boys' Ages in Selected YMCAs, 1901, 1905

Age	Junior and Senior Members in 57 YMCAs, 1901 (%)[a] (N = 16,460)	Juniors in Buffalo, N.Y., YMCA, 1905 (%)[b] (N = 672)
8	.1	—
9	.5	—
10	2.5	—
11	4.2	—
12	9.6	9.4
13	10.2	16.2
14	10.9	20.2
15	10.2	24.6
16	18.6	19.0
17	17.0	9.7
18	16.3	.9
Median Age		15.2

[a]Edgar M. Robinson, "Age Grouping of Younger Association Members," *Association Boys* 1 (1902):4. The fact that most YMCAs still let boys join the senior Association at age 16 probably accounts for most of the increase at that age.
  [b]G. Barrett Rich, Jr., "The Boys' Work in Buffalo," ibid. 4 (1905):190.

Even so, Y men found older boys hard to hold. In their study *Middletown,* the Lynds reported that Hi-Y was the most successful religious club among high school boys but lacked prestige compared to fraternities and school clubs.[110] In many Associations, membership fell off between sixteen and twenty-one, since youths that age were caught in the middle, leery of being classed even remotely with small boys and yet not fully accepted by the men. As a result, towards 1920 YMCAs began forming separate groups for members from sixteen or eighteen to twenty-one.[111]

In practice, the link between character building and adolescence proved unexpectedly tenuous, especially as judged by midtwentieth-century standards. A recent summary singles out four major developmental tasks for teenagers: to mature physically, reach formal operational thinking, fit into the peer group, and develop relationships with the opposite sex.[112] While the YMCA and Boy Scouts provided physical exercise, neither group did much to advance the boys' thinking or guide their interest in girls, although YMCA men made some tentative gestures. Scouting drew boys into peer groups of a sort, but only a minority of boys formed intense or lasting loyalties. One could speculate, then, that failure to develop the possibilities of adolescence accounted for much of the turnover among older boys.

Modern expectations differ somewhat from the character builders' origi-

Table 12
Ages of Boy Scouts and YMCA Juniors in 22 Rural Counties, 1923–1924

Age Ranges	Boy Scouts (%) (N = 3,402)	YMCA Juniors (%) (N = 1,930)
10–13	44.0	25.4
14–15	38.1	32.0
16–17	15.8	33.6
18–20	2.1	9.0
Median Age	14.3	15.5

Source: H. Paul Douglass, *How Shall Country Youth Be Served? A Study of the "Rural" Work of Certain National Character-Building Agencies* (New York, 1926), p. 69. Douglass presented the data grouped into age ranges and not by single year of age.

nal hopes for adolescents; yet character builders fell short by their own standards as well as later ones. The BSA strategy of prolonging preadolescent boyhood worked splendidly to recruit boys of twelve or thirteen but failed to hold most any distance into adolescence. YMCA men aimed to foster an attenuated adolescence, heavy on adult-sponsored idealism and very light on sexuality. In this they enjoyed a measure of success; certainly they enlisted more truly adolescent boys than Scouting. Still, only a minority of YMCA juniors became converts or chose careers of religious service. Many juniors simply bought access to the gym and pool; they practised free throws or learned the side stroke, and if they tired of those, they simply left.

Despite their talk of fostering manliness, character builders of the 1910s also had difficulty bolstering such conventional masculine attributes as leadership, competitiveness, and successful achievement. Neither major character-building agency offered many of its boy leaders major responsibilities or much chance to act in any capacity without direct adult surveillance. Adult concern for control remained paramount. Although the YMCA had a substantial sports program, Boy Scouting avoided this, the commonest medium through which twentieth-century boys sought competitive achievement; neither the outdoor program nor badge-winning aroused the same dangerous but heady sense of contest. Although a few Boy Scouts did earn large collections of badges and a few YMCA juniors used Association training to hone their skills, neither agency inspired many boys to undertake sustained programs and carry them through to completion.

The dream of building character by fostering strength under close adult and peer control depended on striking that precarious balance—so vital to American dreams of achieving both personal success and social order—between individualism and personal achievement on one hand and conformity and group participation on the other. Yet character builders had trouble either harnessing boys' achievement drives or keeping them as members; the boys' individualism rendered voluntaristic social control relatively ineffective. Character builders did not inspire commitments strong enough to make recreation truly a surrogate for work.

Yet how, given their mediocre success at holding boys, could the BSA and YMCA have prospered the way they clearly did? The question is not entirely fair, since inactive members are numerous in most adult associations, and there was no reason for boys to be more committed than any other group. Besides, both the Boy Scouts and YMCA had cadres of enthusiastic members, and these were the boys the public saw. Nor were character builders immune to boys' desires; as we shall see, they eventually responded to the eagerness of younger boys by forming separate groups for those aged nine or ten. But the fact is that as creations of adult hopes and fears regarding adolescence—with a growing force of professionals or bureaucrats, an appealing public image, and prosperous supporters— character-building agencies soon gained organizational momentum almost independent of the boys they served. Such agencies needed to attract large memberships to prove their worth, but impressive aggregates sufficed; an agency would prosper as long as these kept rising, whether the boys who clicked the turnstyle stayed inside or soon went out again.

Conclusion and Epilogue

American Boy Scout enrollment patterns can help correct some plausible yet misleading assumptions about the course of adolescence in this century. Scouting today holds relatively few boys through their middle teens. A 1968 survey found that generally boys thought highly of Scouting, but those fifteen to eighteen were much more likely to pronounce it boring, childish, and restrictive. Likewise, a mother tells us sadly that her fifteen-year-old will not take public transit in uniform "because a scout, in uniform, traveling alone, is invariably the butt of ridicule."[1] A common presumption is that the Boy Scout movement must once have been much more successful with teenagers. The underlying belief is that middle-class teenagers once were markedly more docile, more like "ideal" adolescents, and that adult controls worked better sixty or seventy years ago than they do now that teenagers have grown sophisticated and restive.[2] There is, moreover, a general assumption among historians hostile to institutions for social control that such institutions work. Otherwise, why do they wax indignant about them?

Upon closer examination, however, the contrast between past and present proves largely illusory. Cub Scouting has grown, to be sure, and Boy Scouts now swarm in at age eleven. But younger boys had always clamored to join; only the policy barring those under twelve kept them out. Among Boy Scouts and Explorers aged twelve and up, the proportion fourteen and older changed surprisingly little over the years: 45.4 percent in 1919, 49.2 in 1924, 48.2 in 1934, and 43.4 in 1967 (compare Table 13 and Table 10, above). In fact, because the BSA continued to grow, it enrolled an increasing share of all American boys aged fourteen through seventeen — about 4.2 percent in 1919, 6.6 percent in 1934, and 9.0 percent in 1967 — although the proportion fell off sharply in the middle and late 1970s.[3] Since this upward trend stemmed from increased urbanization and suburbanization, better organization by the BSA, initiation of an Explorer program for older boys, and better recruitment of minorities, it does not prove that traditional Scouting grew more attractive to older boys. But neither does it suggest that the BSA was once very successful at retaining such boys and later failed. Rather, the evidence shows that Scouting *never* held

291

Table 13
Ages of Boys Currently Enrolled in the Boy Scouts of America, 1967

Age	Cub Scouts, Boy Scouts, and Explorers (%)	Boy Scouts and Explorers Age Twelve and Older (%)
8	20.0	—
9	18.4	—
10	11.9	—
11	14.4	—
12	11.5	32.7
13	8.4	23.9
14	6.1	17.4
15	4.1	11.6
16	3.0	8.4
17	1.8	4.9
18+	.4	1.1
Median Age	11.0	13.7

Source: Boy Scouts of America, *58th Annual Report, 1967,* H. Doc. 287, 90th Cong., 2nd sess., 1968, p. 121. Since 1949, the minimum age for Boy Scouts had been eleven. To make a fair comparison with the pre-1949 enrollment patterns reported above in Table 10, however, it is essential to consider only those boys aged twelve and older. The total number of boys counted in 1967 is not available, but the sample appears to have been very large, perhaps all the boys registered.

many boys much beyond fourteen or fifteen. In 1967, the proportion of Boy Scouts and Explorers (among those twelve and over) who were sixteen or older was only 14.4 percent, but in 1924 it had been 13.8 percent. Although the median age of Boy Scouts and Explorers twelve and older was only 13.7 in 1967, even in 1924 and 1934 it had been only marginally higher at 13.9 (again, see Table 13 and Table 10, above).

Where does this flurry of statistics leave us? One conclusion is that for middle-class boys of the early twentieth century, age grading was already more finely calibrated than catchall terms such as "adolescence" imply. One can certainly distinguish between adolescence on the one hand and boyhood—or the gang stage or preadolescence—on the other, even though in period usage the gang stage and early adolescence overlapped confusingly. E. M. Robinson's judgment that three years formed the maximum age span for a boy's group suggests the value of thinking in units about that size. Just as they do today, middle-class, nonfarm boys moved through the teens in cohorts no more than three years wide, feeling quite superior to the next younger cohort.[4] As Boy Scout leaders discovered, what was exciting for boys of twelve or thirteen seemed trivial or childish by fifteen or sixteen. YMCAs held a wider age range, but they subdivided the boys by age. Boys' clubs likewise divided up internally, although lower-class boys may have been less stratified by age in everyday life than were middle-class boys.

In the decades around 1900, as schooling engulfed teenagers, they looked to recreation for self-assertion. Teenage boys developed definite tastes and a jealous regard for the status marks of increasing maturity, however factitious these became.[5] And their standards grew more demanding over time. Although one can explain the shift away from drill in boys' work as the result of new theories of child development, as alternative recreation became available boys grew much less tolerant of drill by 1920 than they had been in 1890.

This does not mean there was a full-fledged youth culture among middle-class teenage boys of the 1910s.[6] Their removal from the mainstream of economic life met one precondition for the rise of modern youth cultures; and by holding to certain roles for each age, they were forerunners of a sort. Yet they were not very self-conscious about these roles, and they were not forerunners of a single youth culture; they were instead internally divided — as young people remain to this day. Recent historical interest in male and female sex roles and in the changing context of youth must not obscure the fact that the young have not seen masculinity or youth whole; especially since the late 1800s, they have subdivided each condition by age and social class.

A related conclusion is that we cannot accurately sum up the history of twentieth-century adolescents simply by saying they have grown more restless, precocious, or sophisticated. They have, to be sure, and adult authority has weakened somewhat. But many of our would-be agencies of control are not new; they date from the years around 1900 when adult concern about adolescence sharpened and focused on the early teens. And these institutions were — as agencies of control — partial failures from the start. I have singled out middle-class boys' work, but a similar argument is conceivable regarding boys' clubs, juvenile courts, even high schools.[7]

Is this judgment a bit severe? Character builders had obvious successes: boys in large numbers gained a taste for camping and learned to swim and play basketball; to hundreds of thousands trapped in drab little towns or sterile suburbs, the Boy Scout movement and the YMCA offered stimulation and excitement. But character builders had grander ambitions: they wanted boys to strive earnestly for adult-sanctioned achievement and act according to predetermined moral codes. Some YMCA juniors did indeed make dramatic resolutions, and some Boy Scouts reached Eagle rank. But high turnover, slow advancement in Scouting, and frequent avoidance of the YMCA's educational and religious programs all suggest a guarded response by many boys. One need not accept the extreme premise —

fashionable today in studying oppressed groups—that "youth makes its own history" to realize that by quitting when dissatisfied, boys put pressure upon the institutions with which adults hoped to control them.[8]

How reflective was this response of boys' attitudes in other areas of life? The career value of education and the schools' coercive powers reduce the value to the historian of such simple measures as dropping out, at least in studying middle-class boys. Still, one may wonder what such boys would have done if free to act. Boys' work is valuable for that reason as a window onto their world. Restless or apathetic, many faced a life that constrained without quite holding them. Nor were the boys alone, for Americans of the Progressive Era recurrently dreamed of a stable world of rooted relationships—all the while employing the new techniques of commerce and bureaucracy. Character builders, with their nostalgia for a bygone village world, were no exception. If boys took an instrumental attitude towards group membership, they were typical of many Americans who were learning to manage segmental relationships, often to gain from them, and to shrug off those that seemed unprofitable.

One could conceivably argue that the relative absence of revolutionary upheaval in the United States during the 1910s and 1920s demonstrates that the Boy Scouts and YMCA did succeed—in the broadest sense—as agencies of social control. But such an assertion confuses intentions with results and is inherently incongruous in view of the vast array of weightier influences against revolution in America. The revolutionary potential of the character builders' disproportionately middle-class constituency was distinctly limited in the first place; nor can one make much of the counter-revolutionary power even of the BSA—the more overtly political of the two agencies—considering that it enrolled primarily boys of twelve or thirteen, occupied only a fraction of their spare time, and held them on the average less than two years. Rather, the relative lack of revolutionary potential in the United States helps explain some of the features that distinguished character-building agencies there from the highly politicized youth groups in many other twentieth-century nations: a fairly flaccid ideology based upon presumed consensus, tacit rather than explicit discrimination by social class and ethnicity (though not by race), a gradual decline in such exclusivity, comparatively low levels of regimentation, and perhaps the decline in personal commitment that sapped membership as American boys grew older.

After 1920, character builders began a tentative and frequently reluctant readjustment of their programs to accommodate boys' actual desires and new ideas on child development. Moving downward in age proved the easiest adaptation.

Intellectually, the fashion of the 1920s stressed early influences upon personality. Freud, J. B. Watson, and John Dewey in very different ways all emphasized the power of events occurring long before adolescence. As Hall's reputation waned, other psychologists rejected his contention that a whole new instinctual heritage welled up in the teens. The idea that building character meant forming habits, implicit in boys' work since the first temperance groups, now paraded in scientific garb, with Elbert K. Fretwell of Teachers College telling Boy Scout executives that building character was simply writing habits onto the nervous system.[9] Logically, then, one must start the process early. H. W. Hurt, a colleague of Fretwell's who designed the Cub Scout program, drew upon the work of George Mead to describe the growth of character as an interplay, begun in infancy, between the child and its environment—such that boys began to think independently by nine, and habits could harden by twelve. E. S. Martin of the BSA's Editorial Department was ready by 1924 to claim, "The years between 8 and 12 are formative years in a boy's life."[10]

Organizational considerations also prompted change. Alfred Chandler has argued that large firms, after initial rapid growth and subsequent consolidation, expand "into new products to insure maximum use of corporate resources. . . ."[11] This was more or less the pattern as the YMCA moved into boys' work in the 1880s; and it clearly was the sequence as the Boy Scouts and YMCA moved towards work with younger boys in the 1920s. But the main impetus to change was more immediate: boys under twelve encroached upon the program for older boys.

Under Baden-Powell's venturesome leadership, the British and Canadians began forming Wolf Cub packs for young boys by the mid-1910s. But American Boy Scout leaders hesitated. In reworking Scouting for America, the organizers of the BSA had rendered its rules rigid and portentous: the oath became a statement of ideals; standards for promotion (at least in theory) were not to be relaxed to reward effort as Baden-Powell had intended; and the age twelve minimum, far from being an ad hoc compromise like Baden-Powell's eventual choice of age eleven, purportedly embodied the developmental verities of adolescence. Much of this difference stemmed from the BSA's bureaucratic rigidity, intensified by West's *apparatchik* insecurity. But also, because American society was ostensibly more leveled and competitive than Britain's, Americans anchored themselves by formal definitions. West and his colleagues, accordingly, greeted the Wolf Cub idea with skepticism; persisting in the conviction that the early teens were crucial, West worried that English Cubbing would undercut the BSA's work with adolescents.[12] Baden-Powell, who regarded Scouting as straightforward training of powers needed in manhood, intended through Cubbing to train boys equally directly to be good Scouts. But West feared that Scouting would bore boys who had toyed with it as Cubs; American Scout leaders disliked the Cub imagery, based on Kipling's *Jun-*

gle Books; and they believed that boys should stay under direct parental supervision until age twelve.[13]

After much delay, investigation of ways to meet these objections got underway in 1925. As in other matters, the BSA executive board rejected Baden-Powell's charismatic approach and turned to certified experts, employing an educator and psychologist, Harold W. Hurt, and adding an Advisory Committee which included such distinguished names as John Dewey and E. L. Thorndike. Hurt's program, which began experimental operation in 1929, was for boys nine through eleven; as it evolved over the next several years, the Cubbing program was intended not to duplicate Boy Scouting, and it safeguarded the childlike qualities of the Cubs (the early term for Cub Scouts) by keeping them in their own neighborhood under the supervision of parents and Den Mothers, who assisted the Cubmaster. Cubs could not camp overnight, nor were their dens permitted even the limited autonomy of Boy Scout patrols.[14]

In the long run, the market proved immense, although like regular Boy Scouting, the initial Cubbing program held boys back a bit more than some wanted. Enrollment did not grow rapidly until the 1940s, after program revisions, the change in name to Cub Scouting, and the return of economic prosperity. Then in 1949 the BSA lowered the age limits for Cub Scouts to eight through ten, recognizing the program's juvenility. Swollen by the postwar baby boom, Cub Scout membership surpassed Boy Scouts and Explorers combined in 1956 and ran neck and neck with them through the early 1970s. The point is not that teenagers had changed but that the BSA had tapped a huge new market. Massed in age-graded classes at school, yearning to emulate older boys, and yet neglected by planners of extracurricular activities, preteenagers swarmed into Cub Scouting and Little Leagues — both of which mushroomed after 1945.[15] Whether or not they consciously shunned adolescents, volunteer leaders and coaches had little stomach for generational skirmishing after a day's work; they liked boys who were young enough to be malleable and eager to enter the circumscribed yet satisfying world of achievement promised by Cub Scouting and the Little Leagues.[16]

With boys fifteen through seventeen the situation was different, since regular Boy Scouting was supposed to suit them; and the BSA's national leaders were slow to admit it might not. Having learned by 1924 that boys who joined at twelve remained Scouts longest, BSA officials concentrated recruitment there; however, few openly challenged West's conviction that Boy Scouting was elastic enough to fit all ages twelve to eighteen.[17] Decades had to pass and West retire in 1943 before the BSA did much of anything special for older boys. Sea Scouting, for many years the only senior program, received so little promotion that only 8,043 boys belonged in 1930.[18] The first Explorer plan, promulgated in 1935, did not remove boys from their troop; instead, those aged fifteen and older formed separate patrols to carry on a more adventurous version of regular Scouting. Older boys showed little interest. But the Explorer idea took on new life in the late 1940s when headquarters authorized separate units and a program that addressed the accepted needs of adolescence, stressing vocational guidance and including ambitious service projects and a social life with girls. In 1949, the BSA lowered the entering age for Boy Scouts to eleven and Explorers to fourteen. Exploring became the BSA's main answer to adolescence, with regular Scouting for preadolescents or very young adolescents. In 1968, girls could become Explorers.[19]

Ultimately, BSA officials recognized that boys changed too rapidly to group them more than three years deep. The 1949 shift in age limits also amounted to an admission that Boy Scouting and Cub Scouting both appealed most to boys a bit younger than the BSA first tried to enlist. The effort to stave off adolescence had failed; at best the long tug of war had ended in a draw.

Although the BSA's new efforts at a sponsored adolescence were not entirely successful, Exploring was small only by comparison with the BSA's other branches. The number of Explorers or other Senior Scouts grew from 55,951 in 1944 to 488,324 by the end of 1973—slightly more than one-fifth girls. Meanwhile, Cub Scouting mushroomed from 412,871 in 1944 to a peak of 2,486,706 at the end of 1972; and regular Boy Scouting grew more slowly from 1,002,255 to a peak of 1,949,229 by the end of that same year.[20] Compared to younger boys, those in their midteens remained reluctant to don a BSA uniform; yet in absolute numbers the organization enrolled more adolescents than ever.

Each branch of the movement held boys fairly well. Among Cub Scouts, the annual persistence rate (which could not exceed 67 percent if the age range was three years) rose to a median of 52 percent for the decade 1965–1974, while the rate for Boy Scouts and Explorers combined was 64 percent.[21] But passing boys along proved tricky; each form of Scouting became a separate compartment. Only 41 percent of a 1959 sample had been Cub Scouts at the time they joined the Boy Scouts, although a good deal of the problem lay with the repetitiveness of the Cub Scout program, which bored many boys by their third year of membership; the institution in 1967 of a separate Webelos Scouting program for ten-year-olds markedly raised the rate of graduation into Boy Scouting.[22] Still, sustained commitment to the Boy Scout movement counted for less than the boys' immediate interest (or lack of it) in the separate programs.

Other indices of commitment also show mixed results. From 1969 through 1973, just one Boy Scout in twelve reached first class rank each year, about the same as in 1921; yet nearly one in fifty-seven became an Eagle Scout, many more than earlier. Surprisingly, only 45 percent attended summer camp in 1973.[23] Traditional Scouting, it seems, inspired more enthusiasts than ever but also left many Boy Scouts relatively untouched.

Worried that the Boy Scout movement was out of tune with the times and that boys wanted more obviously practical activities, the BSA rewrote its 1972 handbook to emphasize urban skills and opened up a potpourri of achievements by requiring merit badges before a boy reached first class — thereby diluting Boy Scouting's traditional outdoor emphasis.[24] The assumption that because Americans were predominantly urban, Scouting could grow best by appealing to big-city boys was misconceived, however, since many of the Census Bureau's urbanites were actually from smaller cities and towns where traditional Boy Scouting had thrived. Sapped by economic recession and shrinkage of the Scout-age population, BSA membership dropped alarmingly; by the end of 1978, it stood at 1,787,791 Cub Scouts, 1,123,300 Boy Scouts, and 392,178 Explorers. Both absolutely and relatively, Boy Scouting declined most sharply of the three branches. Believing that this drastic shrinkage of membership was traceable in part to the BSA's tinkering with its program, traditionalists led by William Hillcourt introduced a new handbook in 1979 which turned Boy Scouting firmly back towards the woods.[25]

Although no miracles ensued, Boy Scout membership apparently stabilized, standing at 1,101,262 at the end of 1981. Meanwhile, Cub Scout enrollments declined a bit further to 1,643,179, but Exploring grew to 499,595. Among those Boy Scouts who remained, indicators of commitment to traditional Scouting rose slightly, with one Boy Scout in eleven reaching first class rank in 1981, one in forty-four becoming an Eagle Scout, and 48 percent camping for six or more consecutive days.[26] Still, the level of commitment remained modest, and BSA membership had stabilized at a level far below that of the early 1970s.

Along with the schools, the BSA suffered from the aging of the baby boom and its replacement by a much smaller cohort of children born in the late 1960s and early 1970s. Between 1970 and 1981, the number of American boys aged eight through ten fell 18.5 percent, while the number of those aged eleven through thirteen declined 15.8 percent. But Cub Scout enrollments fell more sharply — by 32.6 percent — from 2,438,009 to 1,643,179, and Boy Scout membership dropped off even more precipitously — by 42.5 percent — from 1,915,457 to 1,101,262. After holding approximately steady through the 1960s, the BSA's ability to recruit and hold boys had weakened grievously in the mid-1970s. Whereas the Cub Scouts in 1970 enrolled 38.4 percent of all American boys aged eight through ten and the Boy Scouts 30.3 percent of those eleven through thirteen, by 1981 these shares had fallen to 31.7 and 20.6 percent respectively. Starting from a much smaller base, the Explorer program expanded from 329,192 or 2.7 percent of all American boys and girls aged fourteen through sixteen in 1970 to 499,595 or 4.5 percent by 1981. Almost all of that increase, however, resulted from the admission of girls beginning in 1968. Whereas few had joined by 1970, more than 200,000 were Explorers by 1981.[27] Recruitment of older boys thus showed little increase. Overall, the Boy Scout movement remained most popular among quite young boys; but especially for those of Boy Scout age, its attractiveness had apparently declined substantially.

Like the BSA, the YMCA eventually found its largest enrollments among preteenagers. By the late 1920s, groups of Friendly Indians (boys under twelve) operated alongside Pioneers and Comrades (twelve to fourteen and fifteen to seventeen). In 1930, the Y's membership included 83,000 boys under age twelve and 232,000 aged twelve through seventeen; by 1960, there were 621,000 and 472,000 respectively.[28] Although teenage membership had risen, younger boys by then formed the largest market.

Mass recruitment of preteenagers should not, however, obscure the continuities between early boys' work and that of recent decades. Character builders have continued to cherish their predecessors' dream of setting goals for youth, including those long past twelve or fourteen. Summing up a troubled year, the BSA's report for 1968 voiced alarm at youthful crime, drug use, and "the impractical flower world of the Hippie," then presented Boy Scouting as "a positive force to capture the attention and interest of youth. . . ." Though less alarmist, a successful Scoutmaster of the mid-1970s was still quite willing to classify boys moralistically as "good" or "bad."[29] Even ideas about youth development have changed less than might have been expected. The notion of adolescence as a particularly troubled time of life does not win universal acceptance today; but few social pathologies, real or imagined, have furnished more employment for professional experts. In everyday speech, the word "adolescent" is routinely used to explain any and all teenage unpleasantness. Adult hostility towards adolescent sexuality had not vanished either, although envy increasingly complicates the simple reflex of distaste. Until quite recently, adults still regarded masturbation as a malady to treat with sports and exercise programs, hoping to induce remission.[30]

Set against adult wariness of adolescence, the counterimage of boys as energetic, clean-living savages has had a durable charm. YMCA programs for younger boys long used an Indian motif; and in 1950 Clyde Brion Davis, a popular writer for and about boys, celebrated Scouting's satisfaction of the "Cro-Magnon gang instincts" of "pre-puberty boys."[31] The metaphor lost its innocence when William Golding's *Lord of the Flies* turned boyish savagery into a nightmare parable of human evil, yet the basic idea survives that for children the path of evolution leads safely upward towards civilized behavior—provided they do not climb too fast. A boy in this view must be a boy's boy before he can be a man's man; and he must stay under adult supervision, for boys' workers still regard group methods as primarily a means of indirect adult control.[32]

In another respect, continuity has been even more evident; restless teenagers in recent decades have found suburban tedium as stultifying as small-town isolation was in the 1910s. Unlike preadolescents, who professed themselves fairly satisfied, a majority of adolescents in the suburb of Levittown, Pennsylvania, studied in the 1960s, pronounced the place "endsville."[33] Yet preadolescents were the ones who flocked to adult-sponsored activities, while teenagers stayed away. If supervised busyness was the boys' workers' answer to adolescent malaise, it was working poorly in recent years.

Since 1920, character-building agencies have reached out to broader constituencies in terms of class, race, and religion as well as age. But the contours of early preferences have remained visible despite erosion.

At the start, class anxiety divided boys' work. Boys' clubs tried to pacify lower-class boys, while character-building agencies worked to strengthen middle-class lads for leadership. This did not mean total exclusion of blue-collar workers' sons, but the term "street boy" was applied loosely to bar a lot of them. By the 1910s, as class defensiveness waned, character builders reached out cautiously to broaden their base. Sons of skilled workers became Boy Scouts in large numbers, and YMCAs enrolled many working boys, although mainly young clerks rather than newsboys or factory workers.

In later decades, the trend towards wider social integration continued. Formal barriers against blacks were lowered in southern Boy Scouting during the late 1920s and 1930s, although troops were strictly segregated. Catholic Boy Scouting expanded, albeit intermittently. A few YMCAs were forced to alter their class base when changing neighborhoods marooned them amid the dwellings of the poor. More generally, urban populations changed as rural blacks and whites poured in and first and second generation immigrants gave way to third.

Since most Americans came to see themselves as middle-class regardless of their actual status (79 percent according to a 1940 survey), agencies oriented to the middle class had more room to expand than those identified with lower-class boys.[34] In addition, by using small troops, the BSA could cover the country more fully than the YMCA and boys' clubs, whose reliance on large buildings limited their range of recruitment. Already by 1939–1940, the Boy Scouts of America, with 1,062,975 boys, had far outstripped YMCA boys' work, which enrolled about 454,000 boys seventeen and under. And both these middle-class agencies were larger than the Boys' Clubs of America, which claimed 295,732 boys.[35]

Over time, the character-building agencies' sources of leadership broadened a bit as former Boy Scouts and YMCA juniors returned to serve as Scoutmasters, club leaders, or paid employees. Since early recruitment had been less selective among boys than men, the effect was to draw leaders from a somewhat wider range of social backgrounds. By 1958, only 76 percent of Scoutmasters were Protestant and only 56 percent held white-collar jobs, a decline in both categories since the 1910s. On the other hand, both figures were still much above the national averages; and among Scoutmasters who were not white-collar workers, 70 percent were craftsmen or foremen.[36] From the start, Boy Scouting had done well at recruiting the sons of skilled blue-collar workers, but not the men themselves. Now the Boy Scout movement was drawing the upper stratum of blue-collar adults into its middle-class consensus. If this process was repeated outside boys' work, it suggests a significant shift in American class relations as skilled blue-collar workers, long on a par with low-level white-collar workers as consumers, took on other middle-class roles as well. Thus a middle-class agency could slowly broaden its social base without any great shift in policy.

Ideological changes among the top leadership further encouraged broader recruitment. Although mainly symbolic, the YMCA decision in the 1930s to drop evangelical Protestantism as a prerequisite for voting membership made the Y more inviting to non-Protestants. The BSA continued to trumpet Americanism and loyalty, but the connotation of these terms was shifting. During the 1930s and World War II, democracy and equality of opportunity came to outweigh the exclusionary animus of old-fashioned 100-percent Americanism. In keeping with this new spirit, the BSA launched programs to recruit "less chance" boys (i.e., the underprivileged), although with only modest success.[37] A similar surge of concern, along racial instead of class lines, followed the civil rights movement's successes in the 1960s. In Chicago, boys' work desegregated before other YMCA programs, since adults preferred to change the young before changing themselves.[38] As government welfare programs proliferated in the 1960s, character builders, their supporters in business, and others committed to preserving voluntarism realized they had to meet the new competition with outreach of their own.[39] By the late 1960s, the BSA had succeeded to the point that nonwhite boys were about as likely to be Scouts as were whites.[40]

Rhetorically, character builders tried to please everyone with blandly positive publicity. But the readjustments of the 1960s and 1970s entailed cost and friction. For example, Chicago's metropolitan YMCA used federal money with fair success to develop inner-city programs; yet conservative board members resisted federal aid, and secretaries and laymen loyal to the ring of suburban branches had trouble accepting the new order. In many other cities political conservatives refused federal money as little better than the avails of prostitution, and schemes to help the poor and nonwhite grew only slowly at heavy cost in private charity.[41]

Coming in hard times, pressures to diversify forced painful choices. In the mid-1970s, while Boy Scouting as a whole shrank with the passing of the baby boom, the BSA held its own in large cities by diverting resources there. As we have seen, the 1972 handbook offended the BSA's established constituency by replacing woodcraft with topics more suited to the urban wilderness. Despite staff reductions in 1975, Boy Scout officials did not cut back in Harlem, and membership there rose from 1,609 to 1,737. Because volunteers were scarce in poor neighborhoods, the BSA also reversed a longstanding policy and hired paraprofessionals to lead troops. These measures succeeded, but at a cost in other areas where membership declined among the BSA's traditional middle-class constituency.[42]

There is no clear trend for the future. In a society still divided along racial and class lines, boys' workers may continue balancing the interests of different groups. On the other hand, if pressures to reach out subside, character builders could drift back into practices that tacitly favor the middle class.

If the past is any guide, such a drift is very possible. For a variety of considerations, most of which should be familiar to readers by now, persistently limited recruitment by character-building agencies even when they toyed with reaching out. One problem was that boys' clubs claimed the lower class as their preserve. Clubs sponsored few Boy Scout troops, and only in the 1960s — through federally funded programs — did they begin to work closely with YMCAs. Urban-centered programs also failed to match the success of 4-H clubs with farm boys. The BSA competed effectively in small towns; however, YMCA experiments in work with farm boys withered after 1920, and Associations declined in small towns as well.[43] The rise of organized sports did not divide boys as clearly along class or urban-rural lines, and many team players also joined the Boy Scouts; but the BSA's reluctance to sponsor sports may have hampered recruitment among lower-class boys to whom athletics seemed more manly than dress-up and badge winning. More immediate obstacles also continued to deter poor boys, notably the costs of summer camp, uniforms, and membership fees. Clyde Brion Davis complained in 1950 that although Boy Scout leaders sometimes issued free uniforms, the slow unwinding of red tape insured that "boys know just which members of a troop are 'objects of charity'. . . ."[44] And boys who got in trouble often faced exclusion under the old formula that character builders should form character, not reform it. Thus a 1970s study concluded that youngsters who come before the juvenile courts find themselves cut off from other agencies.[45]

Although major disparities in recruitment gradually declined, they refused to disappear altogether. Boy Scout membership in the South rose as the BSA welcomed black boys and the region grew more prosperous and urbanized. Yet in 1968, boys in Florida, Georgia, and the Carolinas were only 58 percent as likely to be Scouts as those in Idaho, Oregon, and Washington. Although this difference declined slightly, in 1981 southeastern boys were still only 64 percent as likely as northwestern boys to be Cub Scouts or Boy Scouts.[46] Down through the years, the BSA had trouble reaching people who were poor, fundamentalist, or farm dwellers, whereas the organization drew very well among the middle and especially the upper middle class. In "Elmtown," a small midwestern city studied in 1941–1942, A. B. Hollingshead distinguished five social strata. Boys from the top two were overrepresented in Scouting 5.5 to 1 and those from the third stratum 2 to 1, while those from the fourth level were underrepresented 0.5 to 1 and those from the bottom stratum 0.1 to 1. A national survey in the late 1950s likewise found that both Boy Scouts and YMCA juniors continued to come most frequently from white-collar families, though less disproportionately so than in Elmtown. Although their relative participation had declined, sons of skilled workers still belonged to the Boy Scouts or YMCA much more frequently than sons of semiskilled and unskilled workers. Significantly, a smaller class disparity marked participation in school clubs, suggesting that private sponsorship narrowed recruitment. Even boys' clubs drifted towards the middle, drawing well among sons of skilled workers by the late 1950s.[47] Similar patterns continued through the 1960s; for the 1968 survey which found that Scouting now recruited black boys in proportion to their share of the population nonetheless concluded that sons of "prosperous/upper middle" class parents were nearly twice as likely to be Boy Scouts as sons of "lower" class parents.[48]

Patterns of adult support and institutional alliances held Boy Scouting and the YMCA like packing in a case from their beginnings. At national headquarters and in large cities, the directors were corporate executives and other well-to-do businessmen with a smattering of professionals—conservative individuals unlikely to challenge the status quo. Similar men controlled the United Way and channeled large sums to noncontroversial agencies such as the Boy Scouts and YMCA that helped people as individuals, met middle-class needs, and did not seek basic social changes; such organizations had the broad appeal fund-raisers needed. By 1952, youth agencies of all sorts received 38 percent of the funds distributed by the average community chest—more than twice the proportion received by family service agencies, the next most generously supported category.[49] The Boy Scouts' and YMCA's public images in turn affected recruitment of volunteers, who had to accept or at least tolerate conservatism.

The BSA's institutional alliances changed only moderately. In 1981, 43 percent of all Cub Scouts, Boy Scouts, and Explorers were members of church-sponsored units. The Mormons—who found the BSA's conservative, patriotic values especially congenial—accounted for a remarkable 18 percent of the youths enrolled in these church units, even though the Latter-Day Saints made up just over 2 percent of American church members. Likewise overrepresented, although less spectacularly so, were two relatively high-status Protestant denominations that had backed Boy Scouting from the start: the Presbyterians and the United Methodist Church. Lutherans, Episcopalians, and the United Church of Christ (which had absorbed the Congregationalists) also had somewhat more than their share of youths enrolled in units under their churches' sponsorship. Roman Catholic and Baptist-sponsored units, on the other hand, were substantially underrepresented. Still fewer young people belonged to BSA groups under the sponsorship of black churches. Jewish Boy Scouts were much more likely to enlist in community-based units than in religiously affiliated groups. And almost no BSA units whatever formed under Eastern Orthodox or Pentecostal sponsorship.[50] Churches that were otherworldly in orientation or that catered to the lower class or relatively recent immigrants avoided integration into a movement representing a consensus on Americanism that retained a pronounced middle-class flavor.

Patterns of sponsorship for nonchurch units indicate only a modest broadening of the BSA's social base. The fact that nearly 26 percent of the movement's youths belonged to units sponsored by public schools, PTAs, or parents' clubs might suggest a measure of outreach into the entire community without regard to social class, although primarily among younger boys, since more than 65 percent of the youths were Cub Scouts.[51] Otherwise, predominantly middle-class backing persisted. Units sponsored by service clubs and chambers of commerce accounted for 8 percent of BSA enrollment, compared to 1 percent in units sponsored by the less prestigious fraternal orders. Sponsorship of 3 percent by veterans' clubs attested to the BSA's continuing patriotic image. As it had been since the late 1910s, backing by boys' clubs and YMCAs was negligible. Nor were farm groups significant sponsors of BSA units. Most revealing was the enrollment of nearly 4 percent of the BSA's members in units directly sponsored by business and industry, compared to less than 0.1 percent in units backed by labor unions.[52] Institutionally, the BSA in 1981 still rested upon a substantially middle-class, urban base.

Although the purposes of character-building agencies shifted somewhat as the exclusive preoccupation with adolescence faded, the organizations found secure social niches where until recently they faced only limited pressures to change. Only groups run by amateurs, such as the Boys' Brigades, fell on hard times. Boys' work gained stability by becoming a career, with the commitment that term entails; but it also took on a certain rigidity, since men were unlikely to take chances with their livelihood. Because character building did not become a full-fledged profession transcending organizational boundaries, each practitioner looked to his own agency for training, recognition, promotions, and pensions.[53] With no overarching professional standard, each agency went its own way. The BSA has remained a bureaucratic hierarchy, somewhat less centralized than in the early years but still dedicated to purveying standard programs (less so in the case of Exploring). The executive's task was and is still to find leaders and replicate units. The number of executives continued to grow — locally as well as nationally — so that even after recent cutbacks, there were 3,812 professional staff at the end of 1981. The YMCA has remained more localized, with varied programs centering mostly in YMCA buildings. An increasing share of the Associations' membership has consisted of boys rather than men; but diffusion of effort across numberless projects and the difficulty of drawing boys to a central building slowed the junior departments' growth compared to the BSA.[54]

Besides institutional momentum, what qualities have kept character-building agencies going? Most obviously, to the right ages they have offered fun, friendship, and personal achievement. Whether or not they have actually built character — a doubtful proposition, since turnover has been high and most recruits probably were fairly decent before they joined — lofty intentions have rendered the YMCA and BSA virtually proof against damaging criticism.[55] To respectable people, these organizations have answered both the yearning to believe that their sons are the hope of the future and a persistent disquietude that passive, dependent, and yet undisciplined schoolboys bode ill for their social class. Boy Scouts and YMCA juniors have seemed both reassuringly vigorous and safely under control. In addition to promising guidance for schoolboys, character builders have championed values widely regarded as essential for Americans of all ages: good citizenship, polite respect for God, and faith that character not circumstance counts in life. At least until the 1970s, when funding through the United Way declined and a shortage of adult volunteers helped shrink the Boy Scout movement, character-building agencies enjoyed a relatively secure income and supply of volunteers. Corporate gifts have supplemented private donations, and the United Way — with privileged access to employers' payrolls through the checkoff system — has channeled money to safe charities.[56] The "right" people's children have benefited. And the Boy Scouts of America in particular has offered generations of middle-class men a chance for noncontroversial service which they have accepted as a duty owed by people of their class and as a way of evincing respectability. Voluntarism, expressed in gifts of time and money, has remained ideologically important as an alternative to government action and as evidence that Americans still treasure such traditional values as individualism tempered by neighborliness.

Notes and Index

Notes

Abbreviations

AB	*Association Boys*
ABS, *RC*	Association of Boys' Secretaries of North America, *Reports of Commissions: First General Assembly, Association Workers with Boys... May 17–30, 1913* (New York, 1913)
AWB, *RP*	Second General Assembly, Association Workers with Boys, May 19–31, 1920, *Report of Proceedings,* ed. Eugene C. Foster, final rev. ed. (New York, 1921)
AY	*American Youth*
BBB	*Boys' Brigade Bulletin*
BC	*Boys' Companion* (Brooklyn, N.Y.)
Beard MSS	Daniel Carter Beard Papers, Library of Congress
BSA	Boy Scouts of America
BSA, *AR*	BSA, *Annual Report* (dated by month of issue). From 1912 through 1917 and in 1919, these were published by the BSA in New York City. In 1918, 1920, and thereafter until 1977, they appeared as either House or Senate Documents in the *Serial Set* issued by the United States Congress. Since then, they have been published by BSA National Headquarters, now in Irving Texas.
BSA, NHQ	BSA, National Headquarters. In 1969, when I did research in this collection of sources, it was stored in no clear order in boxes and filing cabinets at the Boy Scouts of America's National Headquarters, then in North Brunswick, New Jersey. Recently, the National Headquarters moved to Irving, Texas. The BSA's historical records, however, have been sorted by an archivist and are in transit. They will eventually be housed in the Rather Museum at Murray State University, Murray, Kentucky. The collection may be open in 1983. Many of the records are also being microfilmed and will eventually be available from the Rather Museum or the Boy Scouts of America.
BSA, *OR, 1922*	BSA, *Official Report of the Second Biennial Conference of Boy Scout Executives... September 12th to 19th, 1922* (New York, 1923)

BSA, *OR, 1924*	BSA, *Official Report of the Third Biennial Conference of Boy Scout Executives . . . September 6th to 15th, 1924* (New York, 1924)
BSA, *OR, 1928*	BSA, *Official Report of the Fifth National Training Conference of Scout Executives of the Boy Scouts of America . . . September 5–12, 1928* (New York, 1928)
CBC MSS	Chicago Boys' Club Papers, Chicago Historical Society
Conf., 1916	"Conference of Executive Officers, May 17–18, 1916" (stenographic report at BSA, NHQ)
Conf., 1918	"Proceedings at Conference of Scout Executives, Cranberry Lake, N.Y., Sept. 2–7, 1918" (stenographic report at BSA, NHQ)
Conf., 1919	"Extant Records of the Second National Conference of Scout Executives, Bear Mountain, 1919" (stenographic report at BSA, NHQ)
Conf., 1920	"National Conference of Scout Masters and Executives, Sept. 15–22, 1920" (stenographic report at BSA, NHQ)
EMR MSS	Edgar M. Robinson Papers, Babson Library, Springfield College, Springfield, Mass.
Exec. Conf., 1917	"Conference of Scout Executives, Feb. 2–3, Teachers College, Columbia University" (stenographic report at BSA, NHQ)
HHB	*How to Help Boys*
HS	U.S. Bureau of the Census, *Historical Statistics of the United States, Colonial Times to 1970* (Washington, 1975)
NC MSS	YMCA, National Council Papers, Public Archives of Canada, Ottawa
NEAP	National Education Association, *Addresses and Proceedings*
S	*Scouting*
Seton MSS	Ernest Thompson Seton Papers, Seton Memorial Library and Museum, Philmont Scout Ranch, Cimarron, New Mexico
SM Conf., 1912	"Conference of Scout Masters, Feb. 9, 1912" (stenographic report at BSA, NHQ)
SM Conf., 1917	"Conference of Scout Masters, Feb. 2–3, 1917, Teachers College, Columbia University" (stenographic report at BSA, NHQ)
TR MSS	Theodore Roosevelt Papers, Library of Congress
UBBA	United Boys' Brigades of America
UBBA, *OB*	First Connecticut and Rhode Island Division, UBBA, *Official Bulletin*
WWB	*Work With Boys*
YHL	YMCA Historical Library, National Council of the Young Men's Christian Associations of the U.S.A., New York City
YMCA	Young Men's Christian Association
YNAP	Young Men's Christian Associations of North America, *Proceedings*
YNA, *YB*	Young Men's Christian Associations of North America, *Year Book*. Each *Year Book* reported the previous year's statistics; thus, e.g., YNA, *YB* (1901) reported on 1900. Starting with

1903–4, however, report years ran from May 1 to April 30; thus YNA, *YB* (1921) reported on May 1920 to April 1921.

YNYP   State Association of Young Men's Christian Associations of New York, *Proceedings of the Annual Meeting*

Part I
Chapter 1: Growing Up: Boyhood, Social Class, and Social Change

1 Quotations: Hamlin Garland, *A Son of the Middle Border* (New York, 1962), pp. 73, 151.

2 Quotations: John Muir, *The Story of My Boyhood and Youth* (Boston, 1913), pp. 221, 223, 132. For other sources, see pp. 84, 251–63; Garland, *Son of the Middle Border,* pp. 6, 104, 151, 201.

3 Garland, *Son of the Middle Border,* p. 186; Muir, *My Boyhood,* p. 276.

4 Garland, *Son of the Middle Border,* pp. 160–72.

5 Harry Golden, *The Right Time: An Autobiography* (New York, 1969).

6 Leonard Covello, *The Heart Is the Teacher* (New York, 1958), p. 38 (quotation); pp. 5–72.

7 Ibid., pp. 44–45. On foraging, see p. 34; on mother, pp. 49–50. For other sources, see Golden, *The Right Time,* pp. 45–46, 64–67.

8 Lincoln Steffens, *The Autobiography* (New York, 1931), I:24–93; [Daniel Carter Beard,] *Hardly a Man Is Now Alive: The Autobiography of Dan Beard* (New York, 1939), pp. 127–63, 195–99; Ernest Thompson Seton, *Trail of an Artist-Naturalist: The Autobiography of Ernest Thompson Seton* (New York, 1948), pp. 10–106. To correct Seton's self-dramatization, cf. John Henry Wadland, *Ernest Thompson Seton: Man and Nature in the Progressive Era, 1880–1915* (New York, 1978).

9 Seton, *Trail,* pp. 103–46. In all likelihood, Seton's father merely billed him for money advanced to cover two years of rather desultory art study in London. (Wadland, *Seton,* p. 71.) On late developers, see J. M. Tanner, *Growth at Adolescence,* 2nd ed. (Oxford, 1962), pp. 220–22.

10 Carolyn Ditte Wagner, "The Boy Scouts of America: A Model and a Mirror of American Society" (Ph.D. diss., Johns Hopkins, 1979), pp. 169–70; Beard, *Hardly a Man,* pp. 191–203; Steffens, *Autobiography,* pp. 101–3.

11 Jesse Buttrick Davis, *The Saga of a Schoolmaster: An Autobiography* (Boston, 1956), pp. 14–50.

12 Bruce Catton, *Waiting for the Morning Train: An American Boyhood* (Garden City, N.Y., 1972), pp. 26–44, 151–239.

13 B. F. Skinner, *Particulars of My Life* (New York, 1976), pp. 67–185.

14 Quotations: Catton, *Waiting,* p. 133; Skinner, *Particulars,* p. 135. On Davis, see his *Saga,* p. 12.

15 Theodore Roosevelt, *An Autobiography* (New York, 1925), pp. 21–28; Carlton Putnam, *Theodore Roosevelt: The Formative Years, 1858–1886* (New York, 1958), pp. 71–128.

16 *HS,* p. 138. Specific occupational statistics are unavailable before 1900.

17 Lance Davis et al., *American Economic Growth: An Economist's History of the United States* (New York, 1972), pp. 21–55, esp. 41.

18 Douglass C. North, *The American Past: A New Economic History,* 2nd ed. (Englewood Cliffs, N.J., 1974), p. 112; *HS,* p. 242; Richard Parker, "The Myth of Middle America," *The Center Magazine* 3 (Mar.–Apr. 1970):68.

19 Davis, *American Economic Growth,* pp. 53, 404–5.

20 For the statistics, see Jürgen Kocka, *White Collar Workers in America, 1890– 1940: A Social-Political History in International Perspective,* trans. by Maura Kealey (London, 1980), pp. 156, 176; Robert K. Burn, "The Comparative Economic Position of Manual and White-Collar Employees," *Journal of Business* 27 (1954):258. On differences at other periods, see also Clyde Griffen, "Occupational Mobility in Nineteenth-Century America," *Journal of Social History* 5 (1972):322–23; Stephan Thernstrom, *The Other Bostonians: Poverty and Progress in the American Metropolis, 1880–1970* (Cambridge, Mass., 1973), pp. 298–301, 337–38.

21 On this culture, see, e.g., E. Digby Baltzell, *The Protestant Establishment: Aristocracy & Caste in America* (New York, 1964), pp. 46–225.

22 *HS,* pp. 11–12.

23 Paul Boyer, *Urban Masses and Moral Order in America, 1820–1920* (Cambridge, Mass., 1978), p. 4 (quotation); Charles N. Glaab and A. Theodore Brown, *A History of Urban America,* 2nd ed. (New York, 1976)), pp. 121–24.

24 Theodore Dreiser, quoted in Richard Sennett, *Families Against the City: Middle Class Homes of Industrial Chicago, 1872–1890* (Cambridge, Mass., 1970), p. 53.

25 Sennett, *Families;* Sam B. Warner, Jr., *Streetcar Suburbs: The Process of Growth in Boston, 1870–1900* (New York, 1970).

26 Boyer, *Urban Masses,* and below, chapters 3 and 4.

27 *HS,* pp. 8, 11–12.

28 For examples of mobility, see Robert S. Lynd and Helen Merrell Lynd, *Middletown: A Study in Modern American Culture* (New York, 1929), pp. 484–495; Glaab and Brown, *Urban America,* p. 123.

29 Timothy Jenkins, quoted in Eric Foner, *Free Soil, Free Labor, Free Men: The Ideology of the Republican Party Before the Civil War* (London, 1971), p. 17.

30 Quotations: Daniel T. Rodgers, *The Work Ethic in Industrial America, 1850– 1920* (Chicago, 1979), p. 14; Gregory H. Singleton, "Protestant Voluntary Organizations and the Shaping of Victorian America," *American Quarterly* 27 (1975):550.

31 Stow Persons, *The Decline of American Gentility* (New York, 1973), p. 14.

32 Gregory H. Singleton, "'Mere Middle-Class Institutions': Urban Protestantism in Nineteenth-Century America," *Journal of Social History* 6 (1972–73): 501–2.

33 Persons, *Gentility,* pp. 50–55, 276–97; Boyer, *Urban Masses,* p. 142.

34 Rodgers, *Work Ethic,* p. 26.

35 Kocka, *White Collar Workers,* p. 254.

36 Ibid., pp. 79, 120, 134–36, and passim.

37 Ibid., pp. 86, 92–93, 114, 132–33.

38 On these enrollments, see below, chapters 11 and 12.

39 *HS,* p. 139; Harold L. Wilensky, "The Professionalization of Everyone?" *American Journal of Sociology* 70 (1964):143.

40 E.g., Alfred D. Chandler, *The Visible Hand: The Managerial Revolution in American Business* (Cambridge, Mass., 1977), pp. 9, 338, 485; Ben Primer, *Protestants and American Business Methods* ([Ann Arbor,] 1979).

41 Robert H. Wiebe, *The Search for Order, 1877-1920* (New York, 1967), p. 112.

42 Singleton, "Protestant Voluntary Organizations," pp. 557-58.

43 C. Wright Mills, *White Collar: The American Middle Classes* (New York, 1951).

44 On salaried professionals, see Wayne K. Hobson, "Professionals, Progressives and Bureaucratization: A Reassessment," *The Historian* 39 (1977):639-58.

45 Michael B. Katz and Mark J. Stern, "Fertility, Class, and Industrial Capitalism: Erie County, New York, 1855-1915," *American Quarterly* 33 (1981):75; Frank W. Notestein, "The Decrease in Size of Families from 1890 to 1910," *Milbank Memorial Fund Quarterly* 9 (1931):183; Paula S. Fass, *The Damned and the Beautiful: American Youth in the 1920s* (Oxford, 1977), pp. 59-62, 386-91. On long-term changes in birthrates, see *HS*, p. 54.

46 Fass, *Damned,* pp. 54, 63; David M. Kennedy, *Birth Control in America: The Career of Margaret Sanger* (New Haven, 1970), pp. 39-41. Katz and Stern, "Fertility," pp. 73, 89-90, argue that parents limited fertility deliberately in order to invest in extended education for their children. But the cross-tabulations presented as evidence cannot rule out the possibility that longer education was merely an unanticipated by-product of lower fertility which resulted because smaller families could better afford prolonged schooling for their children.

47 Jeffrey P. Hantover, "Sex Role, Sexuality, and Social Status: The Early Years of the Boy Scouts of America" (Ph.D. diss., Chicago, 1976), pp. 147-61, makes this argument forcefully, although direct evidence for parental intentions is slim. My own discussion of related issues in chapter 2 focuses more closely upon the character builders' concerns, about which there is better evidence.

48 For good summaries of contemporary child-rearing advice, see Philip J. Greven, Jr., ed., *Child Rearing Concepts, 1628-1861: Historical Sources* (Itaska, Ill., 1973); Robert Sunley, "Early Nineteenth-Century American Literature on Child-Rearing," in Margaret Mead and Martha Wolfenstein, eds., *Childhood in Contemporary Cultures* (Chicago, 1955), pp. 151-62.

49 Daniel T. Rodgers, "Socializing Middle-Class Children: Institutions, Fables, and Work Values in Nineteenth-Century America," *Journal of Social History* 13 (1980):359; Daniel Calhoun, *The Intelligence of a People* (Princeton, N.J., 1973), pp. 156-65.

50 Mary Cable, *The Little Darlings: A History of Child Rearing in America* (New York, 1975), pp. 101-3; Rodgers, "Socializing," p. 361; Dorothy Ross, *G. Stanley Hall: The Psychologist as Prophet* (Chicago, 1972), pp. 124-33, 279-308.

51 Rodgers, "Socializing"; Edward Howard Griggs, *Moral Education,* 3rd ed. (New York, 1905), p. 56; R. A. Waite, "Efforts at Cooperation Which Associations Are Making," *AB* 10 (1911):98.

52 Horace Bushnell, *Christian Nurture,* intro. by Luther A. Weigle (New Haven, 1947), pp. 269-89 and passim; Griggs, *Moral Education,* pp. 203-4.

53 Fass, *Damned,* p. 89; White House Conference on Child Health and Protec-

tion, *The Adolescent in the Family* (New York, 1934), pp. 6, 133, 165–68, 342–46, 357.

54 Melvin L. Kohn, *Class and Conformity: A Study in Values,* 2nd ed. (Chicago, 1977), pp. xxvi–xlv, 17–107.

55 Conformity to authority and conformity to peer groups do not have the same class connotations. (Kohn, *Class and Conformity,* pp. 36–37.) On boys' workers' attitudes, see below, chapters 3 and 4.

56 David B. Tyack, *The One Best System: A History of Urban Education* (Cambridge, Mass., 1974), pp. 13–77.

57 Joseph M. Rice, *The Public School System of the United States* (New York, 1893), p. 98, quoted in Tyack, *One Best System,* pp. 55–56. On classroom discipline, see Barbara Berman, "Condemned by the Common Voice: The Cult of Conformity in Nineteenth Century Public Education, 1830–1890" (Paper presented to the History of Education Society, Oct. 15, 1977), p. 11.

58 Lynd, *Middletown,* p. 188. See also Raymond E. Callahan, *Education and the Cult of Efficiency* (Chicago, 1962).

59 Rodgers, *Work Ethic,* pp. 1–29. Herbert G. Gutman, "Work, Culture, and Society in Industrializing America, 1815–1919," *American Historical Review* 78 (1973):531–88, suggests that native-stock Americans went through this transformation before the Civil War, whereas other ethnic groups did so later — heightening the impression that WASPs had distinctive values.

60 *HS,* p. 168; Rodgers, *Work Ethic,* p. 106; Lynd, *Middletown,* pp. 54, 261.

61 John Duffy, "Mental Strain and 'Overpressure' in the Schools: A Nineteenth-Century Viewpoint," *Journal of the History of Medicine* 23 (Jan. 1968):63–79; Rodgers, *Work Ethic,* pp. 30–34, 94–109; Lynd, *Middletown,* p. 225.

62 Griggs, *Moral Education,* pp. 74–77.

63 "Association Boys' Work," *BC* 2 (Mar. 15, 1884), unpaged.

64 Ruth Benedict, "Continuities and Discontinuities in Cultural Conditioning," *Psychiatry* 1 (1938):161–67, esp. 167.

65 Quotations: S. N. Eisenstadt, *From Generation to Generation: Age Groups and Social Structure* (New York, 1956), pp. 168, 247. See also pp. 181–87, 232–40, 272, 293–94; and Talcott Parsons, "Youth in the Context of American Society," in Erik H. Erikson, ed., *The Challenge of Youth* (Garden City, N.Y., 1965), p. 129; Fass, *Damned,* pp. 121–22.

66 Statistics computed from U.S. Bureau of the Census, *The Vital Statistics of the United States . . . From the Original Returns of the Ninth Census* (Washington, 1872), pp. 552–71, 608–13; idem, *Fourteenth Census of the United States . . . 1920,* Vol. II, *Population* (Washington, 1922), pp. 162–81; Wilson H. Grabill et al., *The Fertility of American Women* (New York, 1958), p. 411.

67 The reduction for 1870–1900 is $1 - (.9912^{30})$, not $.0088 \times 30$. Statistics computed from the sources in note 66 plus U.S. Bureau of the Census, *Twelfth Census of the United States . . . 1900: Population,* Part II (Washington, 1902), pp. 2–5.

68 Statistics computed from the sources in notes 66 and 67.

69 N. Ray Hiner, "Adolescence in Eighteenth-Century America," *History of Childhood Quarterly* 3 (1975):253–80; Ross W. Beales, Jr., "In Search of the Historical Child: Miniature Adulthood and Youth in Colonial New England,"

American Quarterly 27 (1975): 379–98; Steven R. Smith, "The London Apprentices as Seventeenth-Century Adolescents," *Past and Present* 61 (1973): 149–61; Anne Yarbrough, "Apprentices as Adolescents in Sixteenth Century Bristol," *Journal of Social History* 13 (1979): 67–81; Richard C. Trexler, "Ritual in Florence: Adolescence and Salvation in the Renaissance," in Charles Trinkaus, ed., *The Pursuit of Holiness in Late Medieval and Renaissance Religion* (Leiden, 1974), pp. 200–64; Gerald Strauss, "The State of Pedagogical Theory c. 1530: What Protestant Reformers Knew About Education," in Lawrence Stone, ed., *Schooling and Society: Studies in the History of Education* (Baltimore, 1976), pp. 75–76; Vivian C. Fox, "Is Adolescence a Phenomenon of Modern Times?" *Journal of Psychohistory* 5 (1977):274.

70 John Gillis, *Youth and History: Tradition and Change in European Age Relations, 1770–Present* (New York, 1974), p. 2; John and Virginia Demos, "Adolescence in Historical Perspective," *Journal of Marriage and the Family* 31 (1969):632.

71 Erik H. Erikson, "Youth: Fidelity and Diversity," in Erikson, ed., *Challenge of Youth,* p. 10.

72 E.g., Yarbrough, "Apprentices," p. 68; Trexler, "Ritual in Florence," p. 201n.

73 Jonathan Edwards, *The Great Awakening,* ed. by C. C. Goen (New Haven, 1972), pp. 146–58; Hiner, "Adolescence," pp. 258–59.

74 Joseph F. Kett, "History of Age Grouping in America," in James S. Coleman et al., *Youth: Transition to Adulthood* (Chicago, 1974), p. 11n.

75 Alexis de Tocqueville, *Democracy in America,* ed. by Richard D. Heffner (New York, 1956), p. 229. On Yankee farm boys and teenage soldiers, see Joseph F. Kett, *Rites of Passage: Adolescence in America, 1790 to the Present* (New York, 1977), pp. 14–31, 39.

76 Kett, *Rites of Passage,* pp. 18–20, 38–43; Kett, "Age Grouping," pp. 10–14.

77 Allan Stanley Horlick, *Country Boys and Merchant Princes: The Social Control of Young Men in New York* (Lewisburg, Pa., 1975), pp. 11–15, 69–71, 265.

78 Quoted in ibid., p. 239.

79 Joseph F. Kett, "Adolescence and Youth in Nineteenth-Century America," *Journal of Interdisciplinary History* 2 (1971):293; Kett, *Rites of Passage,* pp. 111–13, 133; Harvey J. Graff, "Patterns of Dependency and Child Development in the Mid-Nineteenth-Century City: A Sample from Boston 1860," *History of Education Quarterly* 13 (1973):129–43; John Modell et al., "Social Change and Transitions to Adulthood in Historical Perspective," in Theodore Hershberg, ed., *Philadelphia: Work, Space, Family, and Group Experience in the Nineteenth Century: Essays Toward an Interdisciplinary History of the City* (New York, 1981), pp. 311–41.

80 Kett, *Rites of Passage,* pp. 63–65, 82–84; Hillel Schwartz, "Adolescence and Revivals in Ante-Bellum Boston," *Journal of Religious History* 9 (1974):144–58; Winthrop S. Hudson, *Religion in America* (New York, 1965), p. 129.

81 Bushnell, *Christian Nurture,* p. 4.

82 Quotations: Kett, *Rites of Passage,* p. 119; Charles W. Gilkey et al., in *Messages of the Men and Religion Movement,* vol. 5, *Boys' Work in the Local Church* (New York, 1912), p. 150; Charles C. Robinson, "Tracing Religious Stimuli," *AY* 3 (1914):16–17.

83 Anne Mary Boylan, "'The Nursery of the Church': Evangelical Protestant Sunday Schools, 1820–1880" (Ph.D. diss., Wisconsin, 1973) (quotation); Kett, *Rites of Passage,* p. 117.

84 Charles E. McKinley, "The Big Boys and the Church," *HHB* 1 (Jan. 1901):93 (quotation); Anne M. Boylan, "The Role of Conversion in Nineteenth-Century Sunday Schools," *American Studies* 20 (Spring 1979):40–46.

85 Frank Otis Erb, *The Development of the Young People's Movement* (Chicago, 1917), pp. 37–87; Myron T. Hopper, "Young People's Work in Protestant Churches in the United States" (Ph.D. diss., Chicago, 1938), p. 62.

86 Kett, *Rites of Passage,* p. 173.

87 BSA, *OR, 1922,* p. 285.

88 Frederic Palmer, "The Paganism of the Young," *New World* 6 (1897):696.

89 Kett, *Rites of Passage,* pp. 194–95; Hopper, "Young People's Work," pp. 54–55.

90 Stanley K. Schultz, *The Culture Factory: Boston Public Schools, 1789–1860* (New York, 1973), pp. 103–31; Tyack, *One Best System,* pp. 44–45. On delayed results, see John H. Ralph, "Bias in Historical School Enrollment Figures," *Historical Methods* 13 (1980):215–18.

91 Kett, *Rites of Passage,* pp. 130–31; Lee Soltow and Edward Stevens, "Economic Aspects of School Participation in Mid-Nineteenth-Century United States," *Journal of Interdisciplinary History* 8 (1977):230–41.

92 Kett, *Rites of Passage,* p. 150 (quotation); Selwyn K. Troen, *The Public and the Schools: Shaping the St. Louis System, 1838–1920* (Columbia, Mo., 1975), p. 122; *HS,* pp. 368–69.

93 Tyack, *One Best System,* pp. 200–203. For 1919, see Bureau of the Census, *Fourteenth Census . . . Population,* II:1041, 1045; III:15.

94 *HS,* p. 379. See also Callahan, *Education,* pp. 15–18, 165–69.

95 George Sylvester Counts, *The Selective Character of American Secondary Education* (Chicago, 1922), pp. 33–47. For similar statistics, see Troen, *Public and the Schools,* p. 220.

96 Bureau of the Census, *Fourteenth Census . . .Population,* II:1406.

97 John Bodnar, Roger Simon, and Michael P. Weber, *Lives of Their Own: Blacks, Italians, and Poles in Pittsburgh, 1900–1960* (Urbana, Ill., 1982), pp. 42–43, 92–96, 212–14; David Hogan, "Education and the Making of the Chicago Working Class, 1880–1930," *History of Education Quarterly* 18 (1978):228, 236–43; Modell et al., "Social Change," p. 335. On Germans, native stock, and Irish, see Claudia Goldin, "Family Strategies and the Family Economy in the Late Nineteenth Century: The Role of Secondary Workers," in Hershberg, ed., *Philadelphia,* p. 283. Goldin found that in Philadelphia in 1880, working girls under age fifteen earned 86 percent of what boys the same age did, a ratio that fell to 70 percent by maturity. She argues that economic and demographic differences fully accounted for the differences among boys from different ethnic groups; but Katz and Stern note that ethnicity markedly influenced demographic measures such as family size. (Goldin, "Family Strategies," pp. 285, 292–95; Katz and Stern, "Fertility," pp. 76–79.)

98 Goldin, "Family Strategies," pp. 283, 297; Bodnar et al., *Lives of Their Own,* pp. 35–37.

99 Goldin, "Family Strategies," pp. 297–300; Bodnar et al., *Lives of Their Own,* pp. 91–93, 147–48, and passim. On character builders' racial practices, see below, chapter 12.

100 Tyack, *One Best System,* pp. 186–91, 203–16; Jeremy P. Felt, *Hostages of Fortune: Child Labor Reform in New York State* (Syracuse, N.Y., 1965), pp. 96–127.

101 Walter I. Trattner, *Crusade for the Children: A History of the National Child Labor Committee and Child Labor Reform in America* (Chicago, 1970), pp. 115–60; Felt, *Hostages of Fortune,* pp. 128–78, 221–23.

102 Selwyn K. Troen, "The Discovery of the Adolescent by American Educational Reformers, 1900–1920: An Economic Perspective," in Stone, ed., *Schooling and Society,* pp. 239–51.

103 E.g., Mrs. John D. Townsend, "Curfew for City Children," *North American Review* 163 (1896):725–30; Lilburn Merrill, "Anti Cigarette Legislation in the United States," *AB* 4 (1905):247–48.

104 Kett, *Rites of Passage,* p. 170.

105 Modell et al., "Social Change," p. 334; Catton, *Waiting,* p. 25.

106 Kett, *Rites of Passage,* pp. 126–27, 210. See below, chapters 4 and 15, on YMCA age grading.

107 On the country boys, see Kett, *Rites of Passage,* p. 246.

Chapter 2: Character Building: Adult Ambitions and Concerns

1 BSA, *The Official Handbook for Boys* (Garden City, N.Y., 1911), pp. 14–16; C. Howard Hopkins, *History of the Y.M.C.A. in North America* (New York, 1951), p. 107.

2 BSA, *OR, 1924,* p. 481.

3 Burton J. Bledstein, *The Culture of Professionalism: The Middle Class and the Development of Higher Education in America* (New York, 1976), p. 37; James E. West, "Training Young America for Citizenship" (speech, n.d.), West File, BSA, NHQ.

4 Cf., e.g., Conf., 1920, pp. 512–15.

5 Joseph F. Kett, *Rites of Passage: Adolescence in America, 1790 to the Present* (New York, 1977), p. 105.

6 The first reference in the *Oxford English Dictionary* to "character-building" — a term which suggests deliberate, carefully planned effort, perhaps expended by one agency or individual upon *another's* character — dates from 1886, a good many decades after the new meaning of "character" gained currency. (R. W. Burchfield, ed., *A Supplement to the Oxford English Dictionary* [Oxford, 1972], I:482.)

7 Kathryn Kish Sklar, *Catherine Beecher: A Study in American Domesticity* (New York, 1973), p. 129.

8 For an example of this use of "healthy minded," see William James, *The Moral Equivalent of War and Other Essays* (New York, 1971), p. 7. On the roots of these ideas in Victorian British culture, see Bruce Haley, *The Healthy Body and Victorian Culture* (Cambridge, Mass., 1978). See Irvin G. Wyllie, *The*

Self-Made Man in America: The Myth of Rags to Riches (New York, 1966), p. 34, on character and success. On maternal nurture and the value of steady habits, see Mary P. Ryan, *Cradle of the Middle Class: The Family in Oneida County, New York, 1790–1865* (Cambridge, 1981), pp. 141–42, 160–61.

9 Stow Persons, *The Decline of American Gentility* (New York, 1973), pp. 284–85.

10 William James to Mrs. James, [c. 1878], in James McLachlan, *American Boarding Schools: A Historical Study* (New York, 1970), p. 274; Erik H. Erikson, *Identity: Youth and Crisis* (New York, 1968), p. 19.

11 Walter B. Kolesnik, *Mental Discipline in Modern Education* (Madison, Wis., 1958), p. 6. Different authors' versions of faculty psychology varied somewhat in detail. My summary follows a widely used college textbook, Joseph Haven, *Mental Philosophy: Including the Intellect, Sensibilities, and Will,* improved ed. (New York, 1882).

12 Anita Clair Fellman and Michael Fellman, "The Primacy of the Will in Late Nineteenth-Century American Ideology of the Self," *Historical Reflections* 4 (1977):28–43. See Haley, *Healthy Body,* p. 43, on stored capacity.

13 Allan Stanley Horlick, *Country Boys and Merchant Princes: The Social Control of Young Men in New York* (Lewisburg, Pa., 1975), pp. 158, 227.

14 Untitled news report, *BBB* 1 (Sept. 15, 1892):8.

15 J. Q. Adams, "The Boys' Brigade," *BBB* 1 (Apr. 1892):2.

16 E. T. Seton, "The Scouting Mind" (MS, [c. 1910–11]), copy in Seton MSS; his italics. On Baden-Powell, see below, chapter 8.

17 Paul Boyer, *Urban Masses and Moral Order in America, 1820–1920* (Cambridge, Mass., 1978), pp. viii, 65, and passim.

18 A. N. Raven, "The Country Boy: His Surroundings and Salvation," *Sunday School Times* 40 (1898):740.

19 *Physical Education in the Young Men's Christian Associations of North America,* rev. ed. (New York, 1920), p. 48.

20 J. Adams Puffer, *The Boy and His Gang* (Boston, 1912), pp. 104–5; Anthony M. Platt, *The Child Savers: The Invention of Delinquency,* 2nd ed. (Chicago, 1977), pp. 138–39; "Meeting of the Scout Commissioners of the Boy Scouts of America, Feb. 10, 1912" (steno. transcript, BSA, NHQ), p. 18.

21 Margaret F. Byington, *Homestead: The Households of a Mill Town* (Pittsburgh, 1974), pp. 120–21; "Salient Significant Facts Gleaned from the San Antonio Boy Life Survey," *Wheel of Fortune* (San Antonio, Tex.), May 6, 1921, unpaged.

22 The Boy Scouts Association, *Annual Report of the Canadian General Council . . . 1919* (Ottawa, [1920]), p. 53 (quotations); George E. Johnson, *Education Through Recreation* (Cleveland, 1916), p. 49; Paul Hanly Furfey, *The Gang Age: A Study of the Preadolescent Boy and His Recreational Needs* (New York, 1926), p. 149.

23 E.g., Lee F. Hanmer and Clarence Arthur Perry, *Recreation in Springfield, Illinois* (Springfield, Ill., 1914), pp. 5–11, 80–88. Hanmer was on the BSA executive board. On contemporary alarm outside the field of boys' work, see also Don S. Kirschner, "The Perils of Pleasure: Commercial Recreation, So-

cial Disorder and Moral Reform in the Progressive Era," *American Studies* 21 (Fall 1980):27–42.

24 "Blowing Out the Boy's Brains," *Outlook* 108 (1914):652–54 (quotation); Anthony Comstock, *Traps for the Young,* ed. by Robert Bremner (Cambridge, Mass., 1967); Jane Addams, *The Spirit of Youth and the City Streets* (New York, 1909).

25 Philip Davis, "The Boy Problem as the Press Sees It," *WWB* 16 (1916):222–26. See SM Conf., 1917, p. 45, for another expression of this view.

26 *Darkest Chicago and Her Waifs,* Jan. 1905, in CBC MSS; Walter I. Trattner, *Crusade for the Children: A History of the National Child Labor Reform in America* (Chicago, 1970), p. 111.

27 Francis Board, comment in *YNYP* 22 (1888):71; his italics.

28 Clarence McLaughlin, "A Study of the Street Boy," *HHB* 1 (July 1901):4.

29 E.g., Thomas Chew, "Character-Making on the Street," *WWB* 7 (1907):78–84; Virginia Yans McLaughlin, "Patterns of Work and Family Organization: Buffalo's Italians," *Journal of Interdisciplinary History* 2 (1971):299–314.

30 William H. McCormick, *The Boy and His Clubs* (New York, 1912), p. 53 (quotation); Jacob A. Riis, *The Children of the Poor* (New York, 1892), pp. 129–39.

31 S.A. Taggert, comment in *YNAP* 23 (1879):89.

32 News Release Notebook, BSA, NHQ, p. 20, quoted in Jeffrey P. Hantover, "Sex Role, Sexuality, and Social Status: The Early Years of the Boy Scouts of America" (Ph.D. diss., Chicago, 1976), p. 159.

33 Mrs. W. W. Ross, "Women's Auxiliary," *Watchman* 15 (1889):212.

34 On BSA efforts to segregate social classes, see below, chapter 12.

35 Clyde Griffen, "The Progressive Ethos," in Stanley Coben and Lorman Ratner, eds., *The Development of an American Culture* (Englewood Cliffs, N.J., 1970), p. 137.

36 Ryan, *Cradle of the Middle Class,* p. 13; Joseph R. Gusfield, *Symbolic Crusade: Status Politics and the American Temperance Movement* (Urbana, Ill., 1963); Boyer, *Urban Masses,* pp. 1–12, 82.

37 Herbert G. Gutman, "The Worker's Search for Power: Labor in the Gilded Age," in H. Wayne Morgan, ed., *The Gilded Age: A Reappraisal* (Syracuse, N.Y., 1963), pp. 38–68; Robert H. Wiebe, *The Search for Order, 1877–1920* (New York, 1967), pp. 1–110.

38 Josiah Strong, *Our Country,* ed. by Jurgen Herbst (Cambridge, Mass., 1963); Boyer, *Urban Masses,* pp. 125–31.

39 Quotations: editorial note, *American Brigadier* 3 (1909):80–81; H. W. Gibson, *Twenty-Five Years of Organized Boys' Work in Massachusetts and Rhode Island, 1891–1915* (Boston, 1915), p. 32.

40 E. R. Dille, "The Boy: The Raw Material," *BBB* 1 (Nov. 15, 1892):7; A. N. Cotton, report for Oct. 1912, in Boys' Work Reports, 1901–1921, YHL.

41 Henry S. Curtis, "The Boy Scouts the Salvation of the Village Boy," *Pedagogical Seminary* 20 (1913):85; A. A. Hyde, "The Story of Cheney," *AY* 1 (1912):221.

42 B. F. Skinner, *Particulars of My Life* (New York, 1976), p. 184.

43 Clyde Brion Davis, *The Age of Indiscretion* (Philadelphia, 1950), pp. 49–62.

44 Mrs. Samuel McCune Lindsay, "The Suburban Child," *Pedagogical Seminary* 16 (1909):500.

45 SM Conf., 1917, p. 16; H. E. Crowell, "The Junior," *YNYP* 23 (1889):93.

46 Boyer, *Urban Masses,* pp. 212–15, summarizes the literature on apparently antiurban reform movements.

47 Kett, *Rites of Passage,* p. 192, and below, chapters 11 and 12.

48 Luther Gulick, "Sex and Religion," *Association Outlook* 7 (1898):197–201; Sylvanus Stall, *What a Young Boy Ought to Know* (Philadelphia, 1897), pp. 84, 168; *Manual for Leaders: Pioneers: A Program of Christian Citizenship Training for Boys Twelve to Fourteen Years of Age* (New York, 1919), p. 69.

49 Wilbur F. Crafts, "Safeguarding Adolescents Against Community Moral Perils," in John L. Alexander, ed., *The Sunday School and the Teens* (New York, 1913), pp. 307–10.

50 Joseph F. Kett, "Curing the Disease of Precocity," in John Demos and Sarane Spence Boocock, eds., *Turning Points: Historical and Sociological Essays on the Family* (Chicago, 1978), pp. 183–84.

51 J. M. Tanner, *Growth at Adolescence,* 2nd ed. (Oxford, 1962), p. 152, claims a drop of three to four months per decade in the average age of menarche, although the decline was probably somewhat more gradual. For a forceful argument that Tanner has overstated the decline, see Vern L. Bullough, "Age at Menarche: A Misunderstanding," *Science* 213 (July 17, 1981):365–66. As applied to boys, the argument is necessarily inferential, since there is little direct evidence one way or the other on boys; the studies of pre-1900 changes in the age of puberty focused on girls. Thus we can only assume that the trend towards earlier puberty followed a parallel course for both sexes.

52 C. Ward Crampton, "Anatomical or Physiological Age Versus Chronological Age," *Pedagogical Seminary* 15 (1908):230–34; Bird T. Baldwin, "A Measuring Scale for Physical Growth and Physiological Age," in National Society for the Study of Education, *Yearbook* 15, part 1 (1916):11–16.

53 Howard V. Meredith, "Change in the Stature and Body Weight of North American Boys During the Last 80 Years," in Lewis Lipsitt and Charles Spiker, eds., *Advances in Child Development and Behavior* 1 (New York, 1963):70–114; Anne C. Roarke, "In Science," *Chronicle of Higher Education* 19 (Oct. 1, 1979):15.

54 Kett, "Precocity," pp. 193–204.

55 John C. Collins, "The Boys' Club," in Evangelical Alliance for the United States, *Christianity Practically Applied* (New York, 1894), p. 264; M. R. Deming, "Genesis of the Boys' Brigade," in ibid., p. 255; and below, chapters 3–7.

56 Cf. R. P. Neuman, "Masturbation, Madness, and the Modern Concepts of Childhood and Adolescence," *Journal of Social History* 8 (1975):6–7.

57 Lawrence A. Cremin, *American Education: The Colonial Experience, 1607–1783* (New York, 1970); Boyer, *Urban Masses,* p. 38. My periodization follows Daniel Scott Smith and Michael S. Hindus, "Premarital Pregnancy in America, 1640–1971: An Overview and Interpretation," *Journal of Interdisciplinary History* 5 (1975):537–60.

58 See above, chapter 1; Stanley K. Schultz, *The Culture Factory: Boston Public Schools, 1789–1860* (New York, 1973), esp. pp. 55–68, 231–37; Anne Mary

Boylan, "'The Nursery of the Church': Evangelical Protestant Sunday Schools, 1820–1880" (Ph.D. diss., Wisconsin, 1973); David J. Rothman, *The Discovery of the Asylum: Social Order and Disorder in the New Republic* (Boston, 1971), p. 209.

59 Steven L. Schlossman, *Love and the American Delinquent: The Theory and Practice of "Progressive" Juvenile Justice, 1825–1920* (Chicago, 1977), pp. 57–66, 164–68.

60 Paula S. Fass, *The Damned and the Beautiful: American Youth in the 1920s* (Oxford, 1977), pp. 71–118; Luther Halsey Gulick, "The Camp Fire Girls and the New Relation of Women to the World," *NEAP* 50 (1912):323–26.

61 M. D. Crackel, "Individual Sex Instruction," *AY* 2 (1913):70; Norman E. Richardson and Ormond E. Loomis, *The Boy Scout Movement Applied by the Church* (New York, 1915), p. 387.

62 James E. West, "Scouting as an Educational Asset," *NEAP* 54 (1916):1012. For Baden-Powell's estimate, see Boy Scouts Association, *Annual Report . . . 1919,* p. 9.

63 American Federation of Labor, *Proceedings* 32 (1912):160.

64 Bruce Catton, *Waiting for the Morning Train: An American Boyhood* (Garden City, N.Y., 1972), p. 139.

65 Galen Jones, *Extra-Curricular Activities in Relation to the Curriculum* (New York, 1935), pp. 1–21; Edmund deS. Brunner, *American Agricultural Villages* (New York, 1927), pp. 168–69. On resistance to activities, see Jesse Buttrick Davis, *The Saga of a Schoolmaster: An Autobiography* (Boston, 1956), pp. 40–46, 110–12.

66 Johnson, *Education,* pp. 29, 34; Hanmer and Perry, *Recreation,* pp. 55–59.

67 David B. Tyack, *The One Best System: A History of American Urban Education* (Cambridge, Mass., 1974), p. 47. On Harris, see p. 50. On control problems and superintendents' pessimism, see Marvin Lazerson, *Origins of the Urban School: Public Education in Massachusetts, 1870–1915* (Cambridge, Mass., 1971), pp. 127–28.

68 Joseph Kinmont Hart, *A Critical Study of Current Theories of Moral Education* (Chicago, 1910).

69 James E. Russell, "Scouting Education," *Educational Review* 54 (June 1917): 3 (quotation); Henry F. Cope, "The Character Training of the High School Boy," *AB* 7 (1908):143–45. On Baden-Powell, see Boy Scouts Association, *Annual Report . . . 1919,* p. 9.

70 Kett, *Rites of Passage,* pp. 191–92. On continued expansion of churches' clubs for their own members, see, e.g., H. Paul Douglass, *1000 City Churches: Phases of Adaptation to Urban Environment* (New York, 1926).

71 International Sunday-School Association, *The Development of the Sunday-School, 1780–1905* (Boston, 1905), p. 669; U.S. Bureau of the Census, *Religious Bodies: 1926* (Washington, 1930), I:276–87; *HS,* pp. 10, 15.

72 Adams quoted in *The Boys' Brigade in the United States of America* (San Francisco, [1891]), p. 3.

73 H. W. Gibson, *Boyology; or, Boy Analysis* (New York, 1918), p. 224; Eugene C. Foster, *The Boy and the Church* (Philadelphia, 1909), p. 9; Dille, "The Boy," p. 7; Edgar M. Robinson, "The Adolescent Boy in the Sunday School," *AB*

10 (1911):41; Howard H. Russell, "The Battle for the Boy," *American Patriot* 1 (May 1912):10; "Loss in Sunday-School Attendance, Causes of," in *The Encyclopedia of Sunday Schools and Religious Education* (New York, 1915), p. 641.

74 William Henry Roberts, "Individuality and Heredity in the Sunday-School," in International Sunday-School Association, *Development,* pp. 243–44; E. S. Lewis, "The Sunday School and the Boy," in Alexander, ed., *Sunday School,* p. 27.

75 Walter S. Athearn et al., *The Religious Education of Protestants in an American Commonwealth* (New York, 1923), pp. 290–91. Whereas there were 77 boys for every 100 girls at age twelve in urban Sunday schools, 55 at age fifteen, and just 41 by age eighteen, there were 97 rural Sunday school boys for every 100 girls at age twelve, 74 at age fifteen, and still 68 at age eighteen. (Ibid.) Athearn et al. calculated that just 39 percent of all children under age twenty-one were enrolled in Sunday school in the rural areas they investigated, compared to 49 percent in urban areas. Any community with 2,500 or more inhabitants was considered urban; all other communities were considered rural. (Ibid., pp. 52, 62.)

76 Foster, *Boy and the Church,* p. 63 (quotation); Athearn, *Religious Education,* pp. 178–79; Robinson, "Adolescent Boy," p. 44.

77 BSA, *OR, 1922,* p. 304. On women teachers, see William McCormick, "Older Boys in the Sunday School," *WWB* 9 (Nov. 1909):13; Athearn, *Religious Education,* p. 361.

78 George J. Fisher, "The Ethical Value of Physical Training," in Religious Education Association, *The Materials of Religious Education* (Chicago, 1907), p. 202.

79 McCormick, *Boy and His Clubs,* p. 27 (quotation); Ozora S. Davis, "The Endeavor Movement and the Boy," *HHB* 2 (Jan. 1902):60; Kett, *Rites of Passage,* pp. 192–95.

80 William Byron Forbush, "A Preliminary Study of the Condition and Needs of Societies of Christian Endeavor," *WWB* 4 (1904):114–25; Athearn, *Religious Education,* pp. 209–12.

81 Joe L. Dubbert, *A Man's Place: Masculinity in Transition* (Englewood Cliffs, N.J., 1979), pp. 7–39; Bledstein, *Culture of Professionalism,* pp. 20–29, 134–35.

82 Quotations: Charles E. Rosenberg, "Sexuality, Class and Role in 19th-Century America," *American Quarterly* 25 (1973):139; Dubbert, *A Man's Place,* p. 66.

83 Charles Kingsley, *Health and Education* (New York, 1874), p. 86, in Haley, *Healthy Body,* p. 119 (quotation); George M. Fredrickson, *The Inner Civil War: Northern Intellectuals and the Crisis of the Union* (New York, 1965), pp. 166–76.

84 Kett, *Rites of Passage,* pp. 173 (quotation), 189–203.

85 Theodore Roosevelt, *The Strenuous Life* (New York, 1901), pp. 1–7.

86 James, *Moral Equivalent,* pp. 7, 13, 14.

87 Roderick Nash, *Wilderness and the American Mind* (New Haven, Conn., 1967), p. 145; G. Edward White, *The Eastern Establishment and the Western Experience* (New Haven, Conn., 1968), p. 72 and passim; John Higham, "The Reorientation of American Culture in the 1890s," in his *Writing American History: Essays on Modern Scholarship* (Bloomington, Ind., 1970), pp. 80–82;

"Organization: Adopted with Little Change from Baden-Powell," in Ernest Thompson Seton, *Boy Scouts of America* (New York, 1910), p. 38.

88 Daniel T. Rodgers, *The Work Ethic in Industrial America, 1850–1920* (Chicago, 1978), pp. 30–34; Peter Gabriel Filene, *Him/Her/Self: Sex Roles in Modern America* (New York, 1974), p. 82; Wyllie, *Self-Made Man,* pp. 144–46; Hantover, "Sex Role," pp. 78–82.

89 Jürgen Kocka, *White Collar Workers in America, 1890–1940: A Social-Political History in International Perspective,* trans. by Maura Kealey (London, 1980), pp. 88, 150; and below, chapters 6, 9.

90 *HS,* p. 140; Hantover, "Sex Role," pp. 82–86; David M. Kennedy, *Birth Control in America: The Career of Margaret Sanger* (New Haven, 1970), pp. 42–47.

91 Quotations: Minutes of a Conference between Representatives of the Girl Scouts of America, Girl Guides of America, and the Camp Fire Girls of America . . . June 6 and 7, 1911, in Seton MSS; "The Resolutions," *S* 8 (Apr. 22, 1920): 21.

92 See Glenn Davis, *Childhood and History in America* (New York, 1976), p. 181.

93 Kocka, *White Collar Workers,* pp. 100–101.

94 Jeffrey P. Hantover, "The Boy Scouts and the Validation of Masculinity," *Journal of Social Issues* 34, no. 1 (1978):184–95; Hantover, "Sex Role."

95 Richardson and Loomis, *Boy Scout Movement,* p. 122; William Byron Forbush, *The Boy Problem* (Boston, 1907), p. 33.

96 Quotations: Daniel Carter Beard, letter in *Outlook* 95 (1910):697; Edward A. Krug, *The Shaping of the American High School, 1880–1920* (Madison, Wis., 1969), p. 249. For other sources, see West, "Scouting," p. 1013.

97 David R. Porter, "An Ideal Standard for American School Life," in John L. Alexander, ed., *Boy Training: An Interpretation of the Principles that Underlie Symmetrical Boy Development* (New York, 1915), p. 62 (quotation); Willard S. Elsbree, *The American Teacher* (New York, 1939), pp. 204, 554; U.S. Department of Commerce, *Statistical Abstract of the United States, 1922* (Washington, 1923), p. 105.

98 W. O. Thompson, "Character Development of Young Men When Subjected Largely to Female Instruction," *Ohio Educational Monthly* 54 (1905):432–39; F. E. Chadwick, "The Woman Peril in American Education," *Educational Review* 47 (1914):116; G. Stanley Hall, "The Question of Coeducation," *Munsey's* 35 (1906):590.

99 Gibson, *Boyology,* p. 187; Bryan Strong, "Toward a History of the Experiential Family: Sex and Incest in the Nineteenth-Century Family," *Journal of Marriage and the Family* 35 (1973):457–66.

100 Hantover, "Sex Role," pp. 99–100; Henry R. Sparapani, "The American Boy-Book: 1865–1915" (Ph.D. diss., Indiana, 1971), pp. 106–14.

101 Edgar M. Robinson, "Boys as Savages," *AB* 1 (1902):129.

102 Quotations: Thornton W. Burgess, "Making Men of Them," *Good Housekeeping* 59 (July 1914):5; James E. West, "The Real Boy Scout," *Leslie's Weekly* 114 (1912):448.

103 Barbara Welter, "The Feminization of American Religion: 1800–1860," in William L. O'Neill, ed., *Insights and Parallels* (Minneapolis, 1973), p. 307.

104 Ann Douglass, *The Feminization of American Culture* (New York, 1977), pp. 44–45; U.S. Census Bureau, *Religious Bodies, 1916* (Washington, 1919), I:40–41.

105 Henry Cabot Lodge, *Early Memories* (New York, 1913), p. 72; "A Real Boy," *Our Boys* 2 (Apr. 1884):3.

106 Howard Allen Bridgman, "Have We a Religion for Men?" *Andover Review* 13 (1890):395 (quotation); "Brotherhood Movement," in *Encyclopedia of Sunday Schools.*

107 E.g., Allan Hoben, *The Minister and the Boy* (Chicago, 1912), pp. 143–71.

108 Quotations: Luther Gulick, "Studies of Adolescent Boyhood," *AB* 1 (1902): 149–50; Ernest Thompson Seton, "The Boy Scouts in America," *Outlook* 95 (1910), p. 630. On degeneracy, see Dorothy Ross, *G. Stanley Hall: The Psychologist as Prophet* (Chicago, 1972), p. 297.

109 Quotations: Rodgers, *Work Ethic,* pp. 103–4; George M. Beard, *American Nervousness* (New York, 1881), p. 98; Richardson and Loomis, *Boy Scout Movement,* p. 304; Kett, "Precocity," p. 185.

110 Quotation: Gail Pat Parsons, "Equal Treatment for All: American Medical Remedies for Male Sexual Problems, 1850–1900," *Journal of the History of Medicine* 32 (1977):58. On these fears and contemporary remedies, see, e.g., E. H. Hare, "Masturbatory Insanity: The History of an Idea," *Journal of Mental Science* 108 (1962):1–25; John S. and Robin M. Haller, *The Physician and Sexuality in Victorian America* (Urbana, Ill., 1974), pp. 191–225; Kett, *Rites of Passage,* p. 163.

111 BSA *Handbook for Boys,* p. 260 (quotation); Winfield S. Hall, *From Youth into Manhood* (New York, 1910), pp. 37–57.

112 "The Father's Duty to a Scout," *S* 1 (Jan. 15, 1914):5.

113 Quotations: Gibson, *Boyology,* p. 18; West, "Real Boy Scout," p. 448. See Duffy, "Mental Strain," p. 72.

114 Gibson, *Boyology,* p. 25. See Richardson and Loomis, *Boy Scout Movement,* p. 123, for similar fears.

115 Luther Gulick, speech, Mar. 22, 1911, in Helen Buckler et al., *WO-HE-LO: The Story of Camp Fire Girls, 1910–1960* (New York, 1960), p. 22 (quotation); [Young Women's Christian Association], *A Handbook for Leaders of Younger Girls* (New York, 1919), pp. 7–11; [Ely List], *Juliette Low and the Girl Scouts* (New York, 1960).

116 Abby Porter Leland, "Scouting Education for Girls," *NEAP* 56 (1918):582.

117 Mrs. Theodore H. Price, "Girl Scouts," *Outlook* 118 (1918):367.

118 Girl Scouts, *Scouting for Girls,* officer's ed. (New York, [1920]), pp. 60–65; Buckler et al., *WO-HE-LO,* pp. 37–39; Hartley Davis with Mrs. Luther Halsey Gulick, "The Camp-Fire Girls," *Outlook* 101 (1912):181–89.

119 Buckler et al., *WO-HE-LO,* p. 95; Girl Scouts, *Scouting for Girls,* p. 508.

120 Buckler et al., *WO-HE-LO,* p. 55; Leland, "Scouting Education," p. 582.

121 Laura Pierce Holland, "Girl Scouts," *NEAP* 57 (1919):116; Clara Ewing Epsey, *Leaders of Girls* (New York, 1915), p. 64; Davis, "Camp-Fire Girls," p. 182.

122 Davis, "Camp-Fire Girls," p. 189.

123 See Franklin M. Reck, *The 4-H Story* (Chicago, 1951).

124 E. T. Seton, "The Boy Scouts in America," *Outlook* 95 (1910):630.

125 Ryan, *Cradle of the Middle Class,* pp. 164 (quotations), 26.

126 For a casual use of the aphorism (by Uncle Silas in reference to Tom Sawyer's mischief), see Samuel L. Clemens [Mark Twain], *The Adventures of Huckleberry Finn* (New York, 1959), p. 273. On the genre as a whole, see Anne Trensky, "The Bad Boy in Nineteenth-Century American Fiction," *Georgia Review* 27 (1973):505-9. For paintings, see *American Heritage* 24 (Dec. 1972): 68-69, 78-79.

127 W. D. Howells, *A Boy's Town* (New York, 1890), p. 68; Sparapani, "Boy-Book," pp. 4-29, 90-102; Charles Dudley Warner, *Being a Boy* (Boston, 1878), p. 213.

128 Howells, *Boy's Town,* p. 67; Warner, *Being a Boy,* pp. 188-89.

129 A. K. Boyd, *History of Ridley College* (1948), in F. Musgrove, *Youth and the Social Order* (Bloomington, Ind., 1965), p. 56. On another nineteenth-century American who admired British boyhood, see Guy Lewis, "The Muscular Christianity Movement," *Journal of Health, Physical Education, Recreation* 37 (May 1966):27.

130 J. R. de S. Honey, *Tom Brown's Universe: The Development of the Victorian Public School* (London, 1977), pp. 104-77; Haley, *Healthy Body,* pp. 141-71.

131 Theodore Roosevelt, "What We Can Expect of the American Boy," *St. Nicholas* 27 (1900):573. On the idealized schoolboy life, see, e.g., Gibson, *Boyology,* p. 92.

132 Lawrence Benedict Fuller, "Education for Leadership: The Emergence of the College Preparatory School" (Ph.D. diss., Johns Hopkins, 1974), pp. 15-16, 55, 89, 215-24, 354-410; Rodgers, *Work Ethic,* pp. 145-47.

133 Quotations: "The Hero of Manila," *Leslie's Weekly* 86 (1898):335; John Johnson, "The Savagery of Boyhood," *Popular Science Monthly* 31 (1887):798.

134 Quotations: Bruno Bettelheim, "The Problem of Generations," in Erik H. Erikson, ed., *The Challenge of Youth* (Garden City, N.Y., 1965), p. 85; Richardson and Loomis, *Boy Scout Movement,* p. 208. Bettelheim's grammar is awkward.

135 Quotations: C. H. Jackson, "The Moral Value of Physical Activities," in C. B. Horton, ed., *Reaching the Boys of an Entire Community* (New York, 1909), p. 78; BSA, *Handbook for Scout Masters* (New York, 1914), p. 105. For Roosevelt, see BSA, *Handbook for Boys,* p. 355.

136 Quoted in Richard Hofstadter, *The American Political Tradition* (New York, 1948), p. 236. On small boys' attitudes, see Ruth Hartley, "Sex Role Pressures and the Socialization of the Male Child," *Psychological Reports* 5 (1959): 458-59.

137 E.g., Sparapani, "Boy-Book," p. 1; G. Stanley Hall, "Boy Life in a Massachusetts Country Town Forty Years Ago," *Pedagogical Seminary* 13 (1906):192.

138 Winthrop D. Jordan, *White Over Black: American Attitudes Toward the Negro, 1550-1812* (Baltimore, 1969), pp. 162-63.

139 Bledstein, *Culture of Professionalism,* p. 54 and passim.

140 George E. Mowry, *The Era of Theodore Roosevelt* (New York, 1958), pp. 101-4; Richard Hofstadter, *The Age of Reform* (New York, 1955), p. 216.

141 John C. Burnham, "Essay," in John D. Buenker, John C. Burnham, and Robert M. Crunden, *Progressivism* (Cambridge, Mass., 1977), p. 12; Buenker, "Rejoinder," in ibid., p. 123.

142 For arguments and summarized evidence from voting studies against the notion that political Progressivism had a distinctively middle-class base, see David P. Thelen, "Social Tensions and the Origins of Progressivism," *Journal of American History* 56 (1969):323–41; Burnham, "Essay," p. 7; Roger E. Wyman, "Middle-Class Voters and Progressive Reform: The Conflict of Class and Culture," *American Political Science Review* 68 (1974):488–504. On ties to Roosevelt, see below, chapter 10.

143 Robert M. Crunden, "Essay," in Buenker et al., *Progressivism,* p. 72.

144 Ibid., p. 73.

145 Mowry, *Era of Theodore Roosevelt,* pp. 88–89; Dubbert, *A Man's Place,* p. 125.

146 Griffen, "Progressive Ethos," pp. 138–41; Wayne K. Hobson, "Professionals, Progressives and Bureaucratization: A Reassessment," *The Historian* 39 (1977):644.

147 Neil Sutherland, *Children in English-Canadian Society: Framing the Twentieth-Century Consensus* (Toronto, 1976), pp. 40–52.

148 Jack M. Holl, *Juvenile Reform in the Progressive Era: William R. George and the Junior Republic Movement* (Ithaca, N.Y., 1971); LeRoy Ashby, "'Recreate This Boy': Allendale Farm, the Child, and Progressivism," *Mid-America* 58 (1976):31–53.

149 John Dewey, *The School and Society* (Chicago, 1907), pp. 24–25, 30.

150 Griffen, "Progressive Ethos," p. 144 (quotation); R. Jackson Wilson, *In Quest of Community: Social Philosophy in the United States, 1860–1920* (London, 1970), pp. 87–90, 114–22, 173–74.

151 George Creel, *Rebel at Large: Recollections of Fifty Crowded Years* (New York, 1947), p. 24. See Thelen, "Social Tensions," pp. 336–37, on reaction against class strife.

152 Leo Marx, *The Machine in the Garden: Technology and the Pastoral Ideal in America* (New York, 1964), p. 226. Cf. BSA, *Handbook for Scout Masters,* p. 89.

153 P. S. Page, "Boys' Gymnasium Leaders' Corps," *AB* 1 (1902):25. Cf. Don S. Kirschner, "The Ambiguous Legacy: Social Justice and Social Control in the Progressive Era," *Historical Reflections* 2 (1975):79.

Part II
Chapter 3: Keeping Lower-Class Boys Off the Streets: The Mass Boys' Clubs

1 H. W. Gibson, *Twenty-Five Years of Organized Boys' Work in Massachusetts and Rhode Island, 1891–1915* (Boston, 1915), p. 42.

2 Frank Dawes, *A Cry from the Streets: The Boys' Club Movement in Britain* (Hove, U.K., 1975), pp. 22–34; Paul Boyer, *Urban Masses and Moral Order in America, 1820–1920* (Cambridge, Mass., 1978), pp. 135–38.

3 Evert Jansen Wendell, "Boys' Clubs," *Scribner's* 9 (1891):740; Aaron Ignatius Abell, *The Urban Impact on American Protestantism, 1865–1900* (Cambridge, Mass., 1943), pp. 95–97; Abell, *American Catholicism and Social Action: A Search for Social Justice, 1865–1950* (Notre Dame, Ind., 1963), p. 125.

4 Robert D. Cross, "Introduction," in Cross, ed., *The Church and the City,*

1865–1910 (Indianapolis, 1967), pp. xiv, xxxvi; Jacob A. Riis, *The Children of the Poor* (New York, 1892), pp. 296–97.

5 William R. Taylor, "Character Making in the Brick Church Institute," *WWB* 7 (1907):109–16; Cross, "Introduction," p. xxxvii; W. S. Rainsford, "Three Episodes in the Reconstruction of a Downtown Church," in Cross, ed., *Church,* p. 322.

6 Steven Lawrence Schlossman, "Justice through Education: Reforming the Nineteenth Century Delinquent" (M.A. thesis, Wisconsin, 1971), pp. 307–11; Winifred Buck, *Boys' Self-Governing Clubs* (New York, 1903), pp. 49–50; Charles S. Bernheimer and Jacob M. Cohen, *Boys' Clubs* (New York, 1914), p. 12.

7 P. A. Jordan, "Meeting the Boy Problem," *WWB* 12 (1912):89; Thomas Chew, "A Visit Among Some Street Boys' Clubs," *WWB* 7 (1907):34–41; George D. Chamberlain, "Boys' Clubs," *WWB* 11 (Sept. 1911):25–31; Edith Parker Thomson, "A Remarkable Boys' Club," *New England Magazine* 19 (1898):488.

8 Clyde C. Griffen, "Rich Laymen and Early Social Christianity," *Church History* 36 (1967):45–65; Abell, *Urban Impact,* pp. 36–37, 96; Thomas Chew, "What Shall We Do with Our Older Boys?" *WWB* 7 (1907):169.

9 Herbert Copeland, "A Club Run by Boys," *WWB* 8 (1908):129–30; Robert T. Handy, "Charles Stelzle," *Dictionary of American Biography: Supplement Three, 1941–1945* (New York, 1973), p. 733.

10 Steven L. Schlossman, *Love and the American Delinquent: The Theory and Practice of "Progressive" Juvenile Justice, 1825–1920* (Chicago, 1977), p. 177; Winifred Buck, "Objections to a Children's Curfew," *North American Review* 164 (1897):381–84.

11 Thomas Chew, "Character-Making on the Street," *WWB* 7 (1907):75–84.

12 Riis, *Children,* p. 217; Charles Loring Brace, *The Dangerous Classes of New York and Twenty Years' Work Among Them,* 3rd ed. (New York, 1880), pp. 80–83.

13 William McCormick, *The Boy and His Clubs* (New York, 1912), p. 44 (quotation); Charles O. Keith, "The Boys' Club and the School," *Journal of Education* 80 (1914):629–30.

14 E.g., *Our Boys* (pamphlet; New Haven, [1888], at YHL), pp. 8–15; Edward J. Gibson, "Boys' Clubs and Their Influence for Good," *WWB* 5 (1905):1.

15 Jacob Riis, "The Street Boy," *HHB* 2 (1902):26. On the role of boys in the strike, see Robert V. Bruce, *1877: Year of Violence* (Indianapolis, 1959), pp. 280–81 and passim.

16 H. J. Eckenrode and Pocahontas W. Edmunds, *E. H. Harriman* (New York, 1933), pp. 127–35; Jordan, "Boy Problem," pp. 88–89; Buck, *Clubs,* pp. 79–88; "Fourteenth Annual Boys' Work Conference," *Playground* 14 (1920):438–39.

17 "A Meeting in Behalf of Street Boys," *Juvenile Record,* Nov. 1901, CBC MSS.

18 Thomson, "Remarkable Boys' Club," p. 488; "How to Start a Boys' Club," *Review of Reviews* 7 (1893):342; Lilburn Merrill, *Winning the Boy* (New York, 1908), p. 149.

19 *Our Boys,* Annual No. 2 (New Haven, 1889), pp. 4, 12–13; Boys' Club of the City of New York, *Annual Report* (New York, 1904), p. 9. Active boys at

the Chicago Boys' Club averaged twenty-five evenings a year. (*Darkest Chicago and Her Waifs,* Jan. 1905, p. 17, in CBC MSS.)

20 Rainsford, "Three Episodes," p. 317.

21 "Police Quiet Boys at a Club Meeting," clipping, [1903], in scrapbook, 1901-03, CBC MSS (quotation); Frank Lee [pseud.], "The Slum Worker," *WWB* 10 (Dec. 1910):1-5.

22 Frank J. Mason, "Materials for Character-Making in Street Boys' Clubs," *WWB* 7 (1907):85-86 (quotation); John C. Collins, "Work for Street Boys," *Magazine of Christian Literature* 4 (1891):235; Charles Stelzle, *Boys of the Street: How to Win Them* (New York, 1904), p. 95; Thomas Chew, "How Can Street Boys' Clubs and Young Men's Christian Associations Cooperate in Work with Boys?" *AB* 4 (1905):150.

23 Taylor, "Character Making," p. 114. For similar views on discipline, see also *Our Boys,* [1888], pp. 2-3.

24 Report by A. K. Maynard for 1918-1919, Chicago Commons MSS, Chicago Historical Society; *Our Boys,* [1888], p. 2; Chew, "How Can Street Boys' Clubs," p. 149; Thomson, "Remarkable Boys' Club," p. 488.

25 Boys' Club of the City of New York, *Annual Report* (1904), pp. 22-23.

26 Quotations: Thomas Chew, "The Boys' Club View-Point," *AB* 3 (1904):71; "Boys' Clubs and the Y.M.C.A.," *WWB* 11 (Oct. 1911):64. On club policies and the CBC, see *Our Boys,* [1888], p. 3; Taylor, "Character-Making," p. 113; and "Meeting in Behalf of Street Boys," [1901]; CBC, *Annual Report* 10 (Jan. 1912):17 — both in CBC MSS.

27 Miss Abbott, "Discussion," *WWB* 8 (1908):74.

28 Quotations: Chew, "View-Point," p. 68; Chew, "What Shall We Do," p. 170.

29 Thomson, "Remarkable Boys' Club," pp. 488-89 (quotation); McCormick, *Boy and His Clubs,* pp. 38-41; "Boys' Clubs," *Outlook* 114 (1916):484.

30 George L. Denny, "The Boys' Club of Indianapolis," *WWB* 14 (1914):357.

31 Chew, "View-Point," pp. 70-71; *Darkest Chicago,* Jan. 1911, p. 20, CBC MSS.

32 William Byron Forbush, "The Beginnings of Work with Street Boys," *WWB* 6 (1906):4.

33 "Boys' Club Federation Headquarters Notes," *WWB* 15 (1915):272 (quotation); "A List of Street Boys' Clubs," *WWB* 5 (1905):48-51; William Byron Forbush, "Recent Events in the Street Boys' Club Movement," *WWB* 6 (1906):20-21; Chamberlain, "Boys' Clubs," p. 25; R. K. Atkinson, *The Boys' Club* (New York, 1939), pp. 20-21.

34 Mason, "Materials for Character-Making," pp. 85-86.

35 McCormick, *Boy and His Clubs,* p. 43 (quotation); E. M. Robinson, "The Greater Opportunity," *AY* 4 (1905):61.

36 Taylor, "Character-Making," p. 116.

37 "The Story of a Club," *Lend a Hand* 1 (1886):117 (quotation); *Our Boys* (1889), p. 2.

38 CBC, Board of Directors, Minutes, Oct. 3, 1906; CBC, *Annual Report* 14 (Jan. 1916):6-13 — both in CBC MSS.

39 Quotation: "Fourteenth . . . Conference," p. 437. See pp. 437-43 for subsequent discussion.

40 Stelzle, *Boys of the Street,* pp. 21-45; Mason, "Character-Making," pp. 89-94.

On weak clubs, see Taylor Statten, "Preventive Agencies," AB 8 (1909):224–25.

41 "Fourteenth . . . Conference," p. 438.

42 John P. Rousmanière, "Cultural Hybrid in the Slums: The College Woman and the Settlement House, 1889–94," *American Quarterly* 22 (1970):59.

43 Buck, *Self-Governing Clubs,* pp. 69–99, 138–84; Bernheimer and Cohen, *Boys' Clubs,* pp. 16–72. On results, see above, chapter 1.

44 M. E. Frampton to Lea D. Taylor, Sept. 14, 1922, Chicago Commons MSS (quotation); Winfred J. Smith, "The Volunteer Worker," *WWB* 7 (1907):165; "Editorial Comment," *WWB* 16 (1916):58–59; "Twelfth Annual Conference of Boys' Club Federation," *Playground* 12 (1918):164; "Fourteenth . . . Conference," p. 444.

45 Charles C. Keith, "Boys' Club Workers Conference," *Playground* 10 (1916):179; "Fourteenth . . . Conference," pp. 437–43.

Chapter 4: Shielding and Strengthening the Middle Class:
The Start of YMCA Junior Departments

1 C. Howard Hopkins, *History of the Y.M.C.A. in North America* (New York, 1951), pp. 4–53; Allan Stanley Horlick, *Country Boys and Merchant Princes: The Social Control of Young Men in New York* (Lewisburg, Pa., 1975), pp. 227–63.

2 Richard C. Morse, *My Life with Young Men: Fifty Years in the Young Men's Christian Association* (New York, 1918), pp. 443–44.

3 Pres. Benedict, Buffalo YMCA, *YNYP* 18 (1884):36 (quotation); Edgar M. Robinson, *The Early Years: The Beginning of Work with Boys in the Y.M.C.A.* (New York, 1950), pp. 6–7.

4 Robinson, *Early Years,* pp. 15–17; *YNAP* 20 (1875):85–92.

5 Hopkins, *History of the Y.M.C.A.,* p. 107 (quotation); Owen Earle Pence, *The Y.M.C.A. and Social Need: A Study of Institutional Adaptation* (New York, 1939), p. 15.

6 Hopkins, *History of the Y.M.C.A.,* pp. 105–18, 187–88; Robinson, *Early Years,* pp. 47, 72.

7 Quotation: Robert R. McBurney, in *YNAP* 26 (1885):87. On members, see Hopkins, *History of the Y.M.C.A.,* p. 239; *YNYP* 22 (1888):43.

8 W. W. Hoppin, "How the Young Men's Christian Association Should Meet the Wants of Young Men," *YNYP* 18 (1884):79–80; Lawrence Locke Doggett, *A Man and a School: Pioneering in Higher Education at Springfield College* (New York, 1943), p. 43.

9 Gulick, remarks in *YNAP* 28 (1889), quoted in Doggett, *A Man,* p. 52.

10 Hopkins, *History of the Y.M.C.A.,* pp. 256–57.

11 Ibid., pp. 152–68; YNA, *YB* (1901), pp. 188–209.

12 Poughkeepsie [N.Y.] YMCA, *Annual Report* (1874), p. 13; *YNYP* 18 (1884):39–40; YMCA of Buffalo, N.Y., *Annual Report* 34 (1885–86):31.

13 Emmett Dedmon, *Great Enterprises: 100 Years of the YMCA of Metropolitan Chicago* (New York, 1957), pp. 110–11 (quotation); *YNYP* 22 (1888):72.

14 Robinson, *Early Years,* pp. 73, 87; *YNAP* 26 (1885):85–86; E. G. Ackerman, "History of the Boys' Department of the Young Men's Christian Association," *Association Seminar* 12 (1903–4):139–40, 150; Morse, *My Life,* p. 412.

15 H. M. Clarke, "Work for Boys," *Watchman* 11 (1885):153; Jasper Van Vleck, *Henry Horace Webster, The Typical Young Men's Christian Association Man: The Story of a Busy Life for Busy Men* (Chicago, 1893), pp. 137–38 and passim.

16 "Boys' Work," *The Lever* 1 (Mar. 1896):11.

17 Dedmon, *Great Enterprises,* pp. 110–11 (quotation); Ackerman, "History," p. 148.

18 Quotations: H. S. Ninde et al., eds., *A Hand-Book of the History, Organization, and Methods of Work of Young Men's Christian Associations* (New York, 1892), II:358; McBurney, remarks in *YNAP* 26 (1885):87.

19 Ackerman, "History," p. 148.

20 Robinson, *Early Years,* p. 66.

21 I. E. Brown, "Association Work Among Boys," *Watchman* 11 (1885):185.

22 George H. Robinson, report in *YNYP* 24 (1890):67.

23 YNA, *YB* (1901), pp. 259–75; "Question Drawer," *YNYP* 24 (1890):63.

24 Editorial note, *AB* 3 (1904):47; Brooklyn YMCA, *Annual Report* 37 (1890): 20; and 40 (1893):14–15; *YNYP* 27 (1893):30–31; ABS, *RC*, p. 44.

25 YNA, *YB* (1891), pp. 110–39, 160–63.

26 *YNYP* 27 (1893):30–31; *YNYP* 24 (1890):68; *HS,* p. 91.

27 McBurney, remarks in *YNAP* 26 (1885):87.

28 H. E. Crowell, "The Junior," *YNYP* 23 (1889):93.

29 YNA, *YB* (1891), pp. 110–39, 160–63.

30 Gregory H. Singleton, "Protestant Voluntary Organizations and the Shaping of Victorian America," in Daniel Walker Howe, ed., *Victorian America* (Philadelphia, 1976), p. 57.

31 On the churchmen's hope, see Robert T. Handy, *A Christian America: Protestant Hopes and Historical Realities* (New York, 1971), pp. 73–150.

32 John W. Cook, in H. W. Gibson, *Twenty-Five Years of Organized Boys' Work in Massachusetts and Rhode Island, 1891–1915* (Boston, 1915), p. 34.

33 Quotation: "Boys' Work," *Watchman* 8 (1882):202. For the statistics, see Clarke, "Work for Boys," p. 153.

34 Chambers, "Boys' Work," *Watchman* 10 (1884):141 (quotation); George A. Warburton, "Boys' Work," *Watchman* 12 (1886):165; E. Clark Worman, *History of the Brooklyn and Queens Young Men's Christian Association, 1853–1949* (New York, 1952), p. 79.

35 "Boys' Department Work" (typed MS, Sept. 1900, at YHL), p. 3.

36 YMCAs and Evangelical Churches of New Hampshire, *Annual Convention* 13 (1880):11; Ninde et al., eds., *Methods of Work,* II:357.

37 Ackerman, "History," p. 148.

38 Brown, "Association Work," p. 185.

39 Quotations: "If I Should Die Before I Wake," *BC* 1 (Sept. 9, 1882), unpaged; "Association Boys' Work," *BC* 1 (Feb. 1883), unpaged; "Obituary," *BC* 2 (June 9, 1883), unpaged.

40 E.g., "Boys' Work," *Watchman* 11 (1885):82.

41 Hopkins, *History of the Y.M.C.A.,* p. 202; "Association Boys' Work," *BC* 1 (Nov. 11, 1882), unpaged.

42 For an unusually early bit of advice to separate boys by age, see "Boys' Work — A Suggestion," *Watchman* 11 (1885):77.

43 Luther Gulick, "Boys' Work Necessary," *Association Outlook* 8 (1899):166; Edgar M. Robinson, "Age Grouping of Younger Association Members," *AB* 1 (1902):4.

44 Chambers, "Boys' Work," p. 141.

45 Ninde et al., eds., *Methods of Work,* II:359; Brown, "Association Work," p. 185. On uneasiness, see Warburton, "Work for Boys," p. 165; *YNYP* 24 (1890):66.

46 Robinson, *Early Years,* pp. 44–45, 140; Ackerman, "History," pp. 95–99.

47 S. F. Dudley, "Boys' Conference — New York City," *Watchman* 11 (1885): 141; his italics. See Robinson, *Early Years,* pp. 91–94, on Dudley's earlier efforts.

48 Ackerman, "History," p. 150.

49 Ninde et al., eds., *Methods of Work,* II:358–65; Warburton, "Work for Boys," p. 165.

50 Robinson, *Early Years,* pp. 96, 119–20.

51 "Among the Boys," *The Lever* 1 (Apr. 1896):9.

52 *YNYP* 24 (1890):67; Robinson, *Early Years,* p. 63.

53 B. G. Winton and C. S. Stowitts, "What Agencies Can Be Successfully Used in Small Towns," *YNYP* 24 (1890):47.

54 Quotation: D. A. Budge, discussion in *YNAP* 26 (1885):84. For an example of the factual and moral emphases, see William A. Snyder, "Bible Study," *Empire State* 10 (1898):109.

55 Brown, "Association Work," p. 185.

56 Winton and Stowitts, "What Agencies," p. 47 (quotation); YNA, *YB* (1891), pp. 160–63.

57 "The Work Elsewhere," *Our Boys* 2 (June 1884):1. In 1900, gym course enrollments averaged 68; religious meetings averaged 39 boys. (YNA, *YB* [1901]: 259.)

58 Robinson, report in *YNYP* 24 (1890):67.

59 "Boys' Work," *Watchman* 11 (1885):33; YNA, *YB* (1901), pp. 259–75; "Association Boys' Work," *BC* 2 (Mar. 15, 1884), unpaged.

60 YNA, *YB* (1891), pp. 160–63; "Dayton, Ohio," *BC* 4 (1885):109.

61 Ninde et al., eds. *Methods of Work,* II:363; YNA, *YB* (1901), p. 259.

62 YNA, *YB* (1901), pp. 210, 259; Robinson, *Early Years,* p. 121; Jesse Buttrick Davis, *The Saga of a Schoolmaster: An Autobiography* (Boston, 1956), pp. 41–43.

63 G. M. Martin, "Recreative Games for Boys," *AB* 2 (1903):169.

64 Hopkins, *History of the Y.M.C.A.,* pp. 259–63. For extreme demands for self-control, see, e.g., Harvey Newcomb, *How to Be a Man,* 15th ed. (Boston, 1856), pp. 183–90; on difficulties with football, Luther Gulick, "Physical Department Problems," *Training School Notes* 1 (1892):78.

Chapter 5: Forerunners of Scouting:
Temperance Orders and the Boys' Brigades

1 Julia Colman, "The Work Among the Children," in *One Hundred Years of Temperance* (New York, 1886), p. 263; Mary P. Ryan, *Cradle of the Middle*

Class: The Family in Oneida County, New York, 1790–1865 (Cambridge, 1981), p. 11.

2 Charles H. Miller, "The Order of Cadets of Temperance," in *One Hundred Years,* pp. 525–26; "International Order of Good Templars," in Ernest Hurst Cherrington, ed., *Standard Encyclopedia of the Alcohol Problem* (Westerville, Ohio, 1924).

3 Colman, "Work," p. 268; "Cadets of Temperance," in *Standard Encyclopedia.*

4 Samuel Unger, "A History of the National Women's Christian Temperance Union" (Ph.D. diss., Ohio State, 1933), p. 45; *Union Signal,* Nov. 26, 1890, p. 8.

5 *Ritual of Juvenile Templars* (Boston, 1874), p. 7. Even among presumably disreputable boys committed to the Ohio Reform Farm from 1858 to 1880, 42 percent reputedly chewed tobacco, whereas fewer than 10 percent drank. (Robert M. Mennel, "'The Family System of Common Farmers': The Early Years of Ohio's Reform Farm, 1858–1884," *Ohio History* 89 [1980]:302.)

6 Joseph Haven, *Mental Philosophy,* improved ed. (New York, 1882).

7 *Ritual* (1874), p. 4 (quotation); Miller, "Cadets of Temperance," p. 528.

8 *Ritual of Juvenile Templars* (Boston, 1876), p. 25.

9 Miller, "Cadets of Temperance," p. 528; *Ritual* (1876), p. 21.

10 Quoted in Edward E. Hale, *The Ten Times One Is Ten and Lend a Hand Clubs* (Boston, 1888), p. 27.

11 Wilbur F. Crafts, "The Look-Up Legion," *Lend a Hand* 1 (1886): 114–15; untitled MS in Box 2, Howard Hyde Russell MSS, Michigan Historical Collections of the University of Michigan, Ann Arbor.

12 Quotation: William A. McKeever, "The Cigarette Boy," *Education* 28 (1908): 154. On lesser temperance and anti-cigarette societies, see David Irving Macleod, "Good Boys Made Better: The Boy Scouts of America, Boys' Brigades, and YMCA Boys' Work, 1880–1920" (Ph.D. diss., Wisconsin, 1973), pp. 1–22.

13 Quotation: "Boys' Club Is a Boon," *Chicago Post,* May 10, 1902, clipping in CBC MSS. On craps, see, e.g., pledge dated April 11, 1922, CBC MSS.

14 UBBA, Massachusetts Division, *The Boys' Brigade* (n.p., [late 1890s]), p. 1; *BC* 1–3 (1883–1885).

15 Editorial note, *Brigade Boy* 5 (1906):130.

16 E.g., Conf., 1916, p. 148. On Boy Scout and YMCA moral training, see below, chapter 14.

17 Robert Reinders, "Militia and Public Order in Nineteenth-Century America," *Journal of American Studies* 11 (1977):86–101; Richard Jensen, *The Winning of the Midwest: Social and Political Conflict, 1888–1896* (Chicago, 1971), p. 172.

18 Joseph F. Kett, *Rites of Passage: Adolescence in America, 1790 to the Present* (New York, 1977), pp. 39, 92; Charles Dudley Warner, *Being a Boy* (Boston, 1878), p. 207; W. D. Howells, *A Boy's Town* (New York, 1890), pp. 121–25.

19 Robert M. Mennell, *Thorns and Thistles: Juvenile Delinquents in the United States, 1825–1940* (Hanover, N.H., 1973), pp. 74, 103–4; YNA, *YB* (1898):114.

20 Quotations: Olive Anderson, "The Growth of Christian Militarism in Mid-Victorian Britain," *English Historical Review* 86 (1971):71, 70.

21 B. O. Flower, "Fostering the Savage in the Young," *Arena* 10 (1894):425.

22 Benjamin Harrison, "Military Instruction in Schools and Colleges," *Century* 25 (1894):468; Reinders, "Militia," p. 98. The count is from Reinders. For a revealing juxtaposition, see Barnet Phillips, "Military Instruction for Boys," *Harper's Weekly* 38 (1894):690, in an issue almost wholly given to celebrating military suppression of that summer's railroad strike.

23 Whidden Graham, "Our Schoolboy Soldiers," *Munsey's* 15 (1896):465; Henry M. MacCracken, "Military Drill in the Schools of the United States," in *Report of the Commissioner of Education, July 1898–June 1899* (Washington, 1900), pp. 479–88; Day Allen Willey, "Our Schoolboy Soldiers," *Munsey's* 27 (1902):384–92.

24 John Springhall, *Youth, Empire and Society: British Youth Movements, 1883–1940* (London, 1977), pp. 17–23.

25 Roger S. Peacock, *Pioneer of Boyhood: The Story of Sir William Smith, Founder of the Boys' Brigade* (Glasgow, 1954), p. 26 (quotation) and passim.

26 Henry Drummond, "Manliness in Boys — By a New Process," *McClure's* 2 (Dec. 1893):70 (quotation); Kett, *Rites of Passage,* pp. 201–3; *Boys' Brigade Gazette* 15 (Oct. 1906):18–23.

27 J. Q. Adams, "The Boys' Brigade," *BBB* 1 (Apr. 1892):1–4; "The United Boys' Brigades," *Knapsack* 4 (Feb. 1895), unpaged; "The New Federation," *Knapsack* 4 (Apr. 1895), unpaged; O. L. Rickard, "Annual Report," *Knapsack* 5 (Aug. 1896), unpaged.

28 Adams, "Boys' Brigade," p. 2; E. A. Girvin, "The Boys' Brigade," *BBB* 1 (Oct. 15, 1892):3; idem, "Annual Report," *Knapsack* 3 (Nov. 1894), unpaged.

29 Rickard, "Annual Report," unpaged.

30 J. S. Webster, "Battalion President's Visit to Great Britain," *BBB* 1 (Apr. 15, 1892):6; W. N. P. Dailey, letter in *Brigade Boy* 3 (1904):102.

31 *Knapsack* 3–4 (Nov. 1894–May 1895), passim; Rickard, "Report," unpaged.

32 S. F. Shattuck, report in *American Brigadier* 3 (1909):290; discussion in *Brigade Boy* 3 (1904):91.

33 Harrison, "Military Instruction," p. 469.

34 "Constitution," *Boys' Brigade Courier* 1 (Dec. 10, 1892):2; William Trotter, letter in *American Brigadier* 1 (May 1907):37; William R. Hall, "Auxiliary Teen Age Organizations," in John L. Alexander, ed., *Sunday School and the Teens* (New York, 1913), p. 355.

35 UBBA, *OB* 5 (Aug. 1901), unpaged; 5 (Nov. 1901), unpaged.

36 Gen. O. C. Grauer, quoted in UBBA, Mass. Div., *Boys' Brigade,* p. 14. Grauer quoted Harrison at length.

37 E.g., news notes in UBBA, *OB* 2 (Jan. 1898), unpaged; *American Brigadier* 1 (Dec. 1906):11–14, 48; 3 (1909):42.

38 *American Brigadier* 1 (Feb. 1907):33. See also "Camp of the First Sheboygan," *Knapsack* 3 (Nov. 1894), unpaged; "Camp Adams," *BBB* 1 (July 15, 1892):8.

39 Editorial note, *Brigade Boy* 2 (1903):185.

40 Quotation: F. L. Cleaves, "The Drill," *BBB* 2 (Feb. 1893):5.

41 On Bible study, see "What 'The Brigade' Has Done for Me," *BBB* 1 (Apr. 15, 1892):7; UBBA, *OB* 3 (Nov. 1899), unpaged. On captains' backgrounds and recruiting for the Guard, see, e.g., *American Brigadier* 1 (Dec. 1906):8; 1 (Jan.

1907):29–33; Maurice Woodhams, "Progress or Stagnation," *Knapsack* 4 (Apr. 1895), unpaged.

42 "Estimated Strength," *American Brigadier* 3 (Oct. 1909):236–37.

43 Quotations: Miller, "Cadets of Temperance," p. 525.

44 Girvin, "Boys' Brigade," p. 2.

45 Joanne Judd Brownsword, "Good Templars in Wisconsin, 1854–1880" (M.A. thesis, Wisconsin, 1960), pp. 3, 18–38, 90–92; Woodhams, "Progress," unpaged.

46 UBBA, *OB* 5 (Nov. 1901), unpaged; *American Brigadier* 3 (1909):9.

47 See pictures in *American Brigadier* 1–3 (1907–1909).

48 H. P. Bope, paper on expansion, *Brigade Boy* 3 (June 1904):86; *American Brigadier* 3 (1909):208–9, 238.

49 Kilian J. Hennrich, *Boy Guidance: A Course in Catholic Boy Leadership* (New York, 1925), p. 93.

50 Quotation: S. F. Shattuck, report in *American Brigadier* 3 (1909):290.

51 *American Brigadier* 1 (Feb. 1907):27–28; picture in UBBA, *OB* 3 (Sept. 1900), unpaged.

52 Quotation: H. P. Bope, address in *Brigade Boy* 3 (1904):41.

53 Flower, "Fostering the Savage," p. 424; *American Brigadier* 1 (July 1907):26.

54 Unger, "History," pp. 168–80; *Brigade Boy* 2 (1903):180–84. In 1912, 363 Scoutmasters claimed Brigade experience. (BSA, *AR* 3 [Feb. 1913]:19.)

55 William C. Allen, "Militarizing Our High Schools," *Journal of Education* 74 (1911):565–67; D. A. Sargent, "Should We Have Military Training in the Schools?" *NEAP* 35 (1896):920–29; "Declaration of Principles," *NEAP* 53 (1915):27.

56 Report on Camp H. P. Bope, *Brigade Boy* 2 (1903):156–57; *American Brigadier* 1 (July 1907):7.

57 Peter Karsten, "Armed Progressives," in Jerry Israel, ed., *Building the Organizational Society: Essays on Associational Activities in Modern America* (New York, 1972), pp. 217–31. For young officers' views, see various prize essays in *Journal of the Military Service Institution of the United States* 11 (1890): 337–39; 22 (1898):75–98; 46 (1910):171–226; 50 (1912):153–72; 51 (1912):94.

58 UBBA, *OB* 3 (Jan. 1900):5; 5 (Nov. 1901), unpaged; *Brigade Boy* 3 (1904):91.

59 West to Clarence H. Howard, Apr. 18, 1921, under Boys' Brigade in "Correspondence About Policies" (scrapbook, BSA, NHQ) (quotation); Springhall, *Youth,* p. 29.

Part III

Chapter 6: Adolescence and Gang-Age Boyhood:
An Ideology for Character Building

1 BSA, *Handbook For Scout Masters* (New York, 1914), p. 102.

2 See James R. Moore, *The Post-Darwinian Controversies: A Study of the Protestant Struggle to Come to Terms with Darwin in Britain and America, 1870–1900* (Cambridge, 1979), pp. 224–27, 350, and passim.

3 Dorothy Ross, *G. Stanley Hall: The Psychologist as Prophet* (Chicago, 1972),

pp. 11–12, 333; Joseph F. Kett, *Rites of Passage: Adolescence in America, 1790 to the Present* (New York, 1977), pp. 134–43.

4 Ross, *Hall,* pp. 262–308. For early work, see E. G. Lancaster, "The Psychology and Pedagogy of Adolescence," *Journal of Genetic Psychology* 5 (1897): 61–128; William H. Burnham, "The Study of Adolescence," *Pedagogical Seminary* 1 (1891):174–95.

5 C. C. Van Liew, "The Educational Theory of the Culture Epochs," *Yearbook of the Herbart Society* 1 (1895):70–86, 118–19; Robert E. Grinder and Charles E. Strickland, "G. Stanley Hall and the Social Significance of Adolescence," *Teachers College Record* 64 (1963):394. On the varied social applications of recapitulation theory, see Stephen Jay Gould, *Ontogeny and Phylogeny* (Cambridge, Mass., 1977), pp. 76–166.

6 G. Stanley Hall, *Adolescence: Its Psychology and Its Relations to Physiology, Anthropology, Sociology, Sex, Crime, Religion, and Education* (New York, 1904), I:ix–xv; idem, "The Ideal School as Based on Child Study," *Forum* 32 (1901):28–35.

7 Hall, *Adolescence,* II:71.

8 See ibid., II:145–231, 292–301; Gould, *Ontogeny,* pp. 80–86.

9 Quotations: Hall, *Adolescence,* II:72.

10 Quotations: Robinson, "Boys as Savages," *AB* 1 (1902):130; Hall, *Adolescence,* II:90.

11 Quotations: Hall, *Adolescence,* I:viii, xv; II:648.

12 Irving King, quoted in ABS, *RC,* p. 9.

13 Quotation: G. Walter Fiske, "Prolonging the Period of Adolescence for Employed Boys," *AY* 14 (1915):241, 242. On Hall's views, see Merle Curti, *The Social Ideas of American Educators,* rev. ed. (Totawa, N.J., 1966), p. 412.

14 Edwin Diller Starbuck, *The Psychology of Religion: An Empirical Study of the Growth of Religious Consciousness,* 3rd ed. (London, 1911), p. 28.

15 G. Stanley Hall, *Youth: Its Education, Regimen, and Hygiene* (New York, 1907), p. 135 (quotation); Joseph F. Kett, "Adolescence and Youth in Nineteenth-Century America," *Journal of Interdisciplinary History* 2 (1971):290; Hall, *Adolescence,* I:404.

16 Luther Gulick, "Sex and Religion," *Association Outlook* 7 (1897):37–43.

17 Hall, *Adolescence,* I:111–236; C. R. H. Jackson, "The Moral Value of Physical Activities," in C. B. Horton, ed., *Reaching the Boys of an Entire Community* (New York, 1909), p. 65. Cf. J. M. Tanner, "Growing Up," *Scientific American* 229 (Sept. 1973):36.

18 E.g., H. W. Gibson, *Boyology, or Boy Analysis* (New York, 1918), p. 103; "All Say Don't Drop the Boy," *S* 1 (Aug. 1, 1913):1.

19 Hall, *Adolescence,* I:441–45; II:292–93; Starbuck, *Psychology,* pp. 403–4.

20 E.g., "The Scout Idea," *Outlook* 95 (1910):607; Edwin Puller, "Boy Gangs," *WWB* 16 (1916):243; George Walter Fiske, *Boy Life and Self-Government* (New York, 1912), pp. 151–54. For further sources, see below, note 23.

21 BSA, *Handbook for Scout Masters,* pp. 98–102; Fiske, *Boy Life,* pp. 66, 149–57.

22 Seton to W. I. Talbot, Apr. 12, 1905, photocopy in Seton MSS.

23 Henry D. Sheldon, "The Institutional Activities of American Children,"

American Journal of Psychology 9 (1898):425–48; John Scott, "A Study of the Social Instinct and Its Development in Boy Life," *Association Seminar* 13 (1904–5):257–70, 285–308, 355–58, 365–79; T. J. Browne, "The Clan or Gang Instinct in Boys," *Association Outlook* 9 (1900):223–74; 10 (1901):8–29.

24 Quoted without page from Owen Johnson, *The Lawrenceville Stories* (New York, 1967), in Henry R. Sparapani, "The American Boy-Book, 1865–1915" (Ph.D. diss., Indiana, 1971), p. 122.

25 Luther Gulick, "A Study of Boys" (MS, n.d., at YHL), p. 49. For another example of this inconsistency, see E. M. Robinson, "A Suggested Application of the Association Idea," *AB* 7 (1908):227.

26 Henry F. Burt, "The Settlement Boys' Club and the Home," *HHB* 2 (Jan. 1902):37; Lyman Beecher Stowe, "What to Do with a Boy," *World's Work* 26 (1913):191.

27 J. Adams Puffer, *The Boy and His Gang* (Boston, 1912), pp. 10–21, 86–98, 126; James West, "Boys Who Are Boy Scouts," speech, Oct. 1922, in West File, BSA, NHQ.

28 Henry Nash Smith, *Virgin Land: The American West as Symbol and Myth* (New York, 1950), pp. 293–300.

29 William Byron Forbush, *The Boy Problem,* 6th ed. (Boston, 1907), p. 34.

30 Jean B. Quandt, *From the Small Town to the Great Community: The Social Thought of Progressive Intellectuals* (New Brunswick, N.J., 1970), pp. 54–62; Daniel T. Rodgers, "Socializing Middle-Class Children: Institutions, Fables, and Work Values in Nineteenth-Century America," *Journal of Social History* 13 (1980), p. 363.

31 Quotations: Luther Halsey Gulick, "Play and Democracy," *Charities and the Commons* 18 (1907):486; James Austin Wilder, in BSA, *OR, 1922,* p. 129.

32 Quotations: John C. Burnham, "Essay," in John D. Buenker, John C. Burnham, and Robert M. Crunden, *Progressivism* (Cambridge, Mass., 1977), p. 6.

33 Forbush, *Boy Problem*, p. 54.

34 Kett, *Rites of Passage,* pp. 233–34; Joel H. Spring, *Education and the Rise of the Corporate State* (Boston, 1972). Howard Mumford Jones, *The Age of Energy: Varieties of American Experience, 1865–1915* (New York, 1973), pp. 177–78, remarks the shift in business ideology.

35 H. P. Bope, "Address to the Annual Convention," *American Brigadier* 1 (Dec. 1906):28.

36 E.g., C. B. Gildea, "Drill and Discipline," *BBB* 1 (Apr. 15, 1892):7.

37 S. N. Eisenstadt, *From Generation to Generation: Age Groups and Social Structure* (New York, 1956), pp. 182–87, 271–94. See above, chapter 1, on theories of adolescence.

38 Elbert K. Fretwell, "The Boy, the Scout and the Citizen," in BSA, *OR, 1922,* p. 259 (quotation); Puffer, *Boy and His Gang,* pp. 86–98; L. H. Gulick, "Boys and the Gang Spirit," *Journal of Education* 74 (1911):208.

39 Quotations: BSA, *Handbook for Scout Masters,* p. 114; Forbush, *Boy Problem,* p. 23. For other source, see Ernest Thompson Seton, "Boy Scouts in America," *Outlook* 95 (1910):631.

40 Luther Halsey Gulick, "Games and Gangs," *Lippincott's* 88 (1911):84–89.

41 Theodore P. Greene, *America's Heroes: The Changing Models of Success in American Magazines* (New York, 1970), p. 261; David Riesman et al., *The Lonely Crowd: A Study of the Changing American Character,* rev. ed. (New Haven, Conn., 1961).

42 See above, chapter 4, on nineteenth-century YMCA practice.

43 BSA, *Handbook for Scout Masters,* p. 28 (quotation); Edgar M. Robinson, "Age Grouping of Younger Association Members," *AB* 1 (1902):35–36; and below, chapter 8. On adolescent as a catchword, see, e.g., BSA, *AR* 7 (Mar. 1917):22.

44 Quotations: P. F. Moriarty, "Boys' Work," *The Lever* 5 (Jan. 1901):12; "Lecture on the Boy Scout Movement Submitted by National Headquarters," n.d., in West File, BSA, NHQ; National Council of YMCAs of Canada, *The Canadian Standard Efficiency Tests,* 7th ed. (n.p., 1915), p. 12.

45 James West, remarks in BSA, *OR, 1924,* p. 195.

46 Paul Hanly Furfey, *The Gang Age: A Study of the Preadolescent Boy and His Recreational Needs* (New York, 1926), p. 9. Hall said adolescent changes *began* about age twelve, but the qualification was easy to miss. (Hall, *Youth,* pp. 1, 359.)

47 E. M. Robinson to E. T. Seton, Dec. 13, 1912, photocopy in Seton MSS.

48 Luther Gulick, "Boys' Work Necessary," *Association Outlook* 8 (1899):162. For a similar argument by an education professor, who later became one of Scouting's leading academic supporters, see James E. Russell, "What Constitutes a Secondary School," *School Review* 4 (1896):529.

49 BSA, *Handbook for Scout Masters,* p. 109 (quotation); W. H. Chapin, ed., "Boys' Department Work . . . September 1900" (typed MS at YHL).

50 Taylor Statten, "Danger Lines in Using Boys," *AY* 11 (1912):99.

51 Forbush, *Boy Problem,* p. 18 (quotation); "Important Work," *S* 1 (Aug. 1, 1913):2.

52 Review of John L. Keedy, *The Teacher's Book of the Heroic Christ* (Boston, 1907), in WWB 7 (1907):57.

53 Fiske, *Boy Life,* p. 155; R. S. S. Baden-Powell, *Scouting for Boys: A Handbook for Instruction in Good Citizenship,* rev. ed. (London, 1909), pp. 209–10, 228; BSA, *The Official Handbook for Boys* (Garden City, N.Y., 1911), pp. 7, 237–51. This use of chivalry was not unique to character builders. A similar, decidedly ahistorical and heavily moralized chivalry inspired the Victorian gentleman's code of conduct. (Mark Girouard, *The Return to Camelot: Chivalry and the English Gentleman* [New Haven, Conn., 1981].)

54 BSA, *Handbook for Scout Masters,* pp. 79–80, 102. On the oath and law, see below, chapter 9.

55 Quotations: BSA, *Handbook for Scout Masters,* p. 73; Queens Council, BSA, Report of Camp Committee, 1919, Beard MSS; BSA, *AR* 8 (Mar. 1918):5; Norman E. Richardson and Ormond E. Loomis, *The Boy Scout Movement Applied by the Church* (New York, 1915), p. 215. Strenuous athletic training does delay a girls' first menstruation. ("Menarcheal Misunderstanding," *Scientific American* 245 [Oct. 1981]:94.)

56 On boys' tastes, see below, chapter 15.

57 Quotations: Forbush, *Boy Problem,* pp. 180, 22; Starbuck, *Psychology,* p. 309.

58 Henry B. Robins, "Childhood and Youth in Relation to Church Membership," *Religious Education* 10 (1915):479 (quotation); George Albert Coe, *Education in Religion and Morals* (Chicago, 1904), p. 234.

59 Fred S. Goodman, "Bible Study by Boys," *AB* 2 (1903):26 (quotation); ABS, *RC,* pp. 63–66.

60 On the problems of professionals, see Wayne K. Hobson, "Professionals, Progressives and Bureaucratization: A Reassessment," *The Historian* 39 (1977): 656; Magali Sarfatti Larson, *The Rise of Professionalism: A Sociological Analysis* (Berkeley, Calif., 1977).

61 George E. Johnson, *Education Through Recreation* (Cleveland, 1916), p. 14 (quotation); Bernard Mergen, "The Discovery of Children's Play," *American Quarterly* 27 (1975):399–420; Luther Halsey Gulick, *A Philosophy of Play* (New York, 1920).

62 Thornton W. Burgess, "Making Men of Them," *Good Housekeeping* 59 (July 1914):3–4.

63 Quotation: Puffer, *Boy and His Gang,* p. 124. Hall lauded boys' work but seldom interposed specific advice. On his attitudes, see his *Adolescence,* II: 417–32; G. Stanley Hall to James West, Apr. 21, 1911, in "Committee on Standardization" (scrapbook, BSA, NHQ).

64 William James, *Talks to Teachers on Psychology and to Students on Some of Life's Ideals* (New York, 1962), p. 3.

65 John L. Alexander, ed., *Boy Training: An Interpretation of the Principles that Underlie Symmetrical Boy Development* (New York, 1912).

66 William Byron Forbush, *The Boy Problem: A Study in Social Pedagogy,* 2nd ed. (Boston, 1901), p. 24, appendix.

67 BSA, *Handbook for Scout Masters,* p. 97.

68 James, *Talks,* p. 90 (quotation); William James, *Psychology: Briefer Course* (New York, 1962), p. 162.

69 Edgar M. Robinson, "The Adolescent Boy in the Sunday School," *AB* 10 (1911):44 (quotation); F. A. Crosby, "Home Life," *AB* 8 (1909):257–58.

70 Forbush, *Boy Problem* (1907), p. 177.

71 Quotation: Thomas H. Briggs, *The Junior High School* (Boston, 1920), p. 245.

72 Aubrey Augustus Douglass, *The Junior High School,* Fifteenth Yearbook of the National Society for the Study of Education, Part 3 (Bloomington, Ill., 1916), p. 28.

73 On junior high goals, see Briggs, *Junior High School,* pp. 34, 250; Edward A. Krug, *The Shaping of the American High School, 1880–1920* (Madison, Wis., 1969), pp. 327–35; Spring, *Education,* pp. 104–6. On numbers, see Briggs, *Junior High School,* pp. 32, 60.

74 Ronald Tuttle Veal et al., *Classified Bibliography of Boy Life and Organized Work with Boys* (New York, 1919); BSA, *Handbook for Scout Masters,* pp. 325–26.

75 Edward Howard Griggs, *Moral Education,* 3rd ed. (New York, 1905), p. 36.

76 Joseph Lee, *Play in Education* (New York, 1915), p. 218 (quotation) and passim; *The Encyclopedia of Sunday Schools and Religious Education* (New

York, 1915). On playground leaders, see Paul Boyer, *Urban Masses and Moral Order in America, 1820–1920* (Cambridge, Mass., 1978), pp. 242–47; Dominick Cavallo, *Muscles and Morals: Organized Playgrounds and Urban Reform, 1880–1920* (Philadelphia, 1981).

77 Officers besides Gulick, Forbush, and Robinson included Thomas Chew; Ben Lindsey of the Denver Juvenile Court; Eugene Foster, who wrote for the *Sunday School Times;* and Henry F. Burt, a prominent settlement worker at Chicago Commons. ("Editorials," *WWB* 9 [July 1909]:41, 51–53.)

78 George E. Quin, *The Boy-Savers' Guide: Society Work for Lads in Their Teens* (New York, 1908), pp. 1–10, 158–85; F. Jos. Kelly, "The Clergy and the Boy Problem in the Church," *Ecclesiastical Review* 65 (1921):170–72.

79 Kilian J. Hennrich, *Youth Guidance* (New York, 1941), p. 213 (quotation); Furfey, *Gang Age.*

80 [Young Women's Christian Associations,] *A Handbook for Leaders of Younger Girls* (New York, 1919), pp. 8–10.

81 Helen Buckler et al., *WO-HE-LO: The Story of Camp Fire Girls, 1910–1960* (New York, 1961), p. 44 (quotation); ibid., pp. 43–44, 51–53, 104, 171; Anna Steese Richardson, "Growing Up Happy," *Delineator* 98 (1921):71.

82 "Wanted — 'Daddies' for Girl Scouts," *Outlook* 126 (1920):414; BSA, *OR, 1922,* p. 263.

83 *Darkest Chicago and Her Waifs,* Annual Report, Jan. 1910, in CBC MSS (quotation); Thomas Chew, "How Can Street Boys' Clubs and Young Men's Christian Associations Cooperate in Work with Boys," *AB* 4 (1905):152. On expulsions, see "Driving Them Out," *WWB* 14 (1914):79; "Editorial Comment," *WWB* 15 (1915):2–5.

84 On levels of interest, compare Robert A. Woods and Albert J. Kennedy, *The Settlement Horizon: A National Estimate* (New York, 1922), pp. 73–86, to Charles S. Bernheimer and Jacob M. Cohen, *Boys' Clubs* (New York, 1914), pp. 37, 60. For an argument stressing consensus on gang theory among settlement-type and church workers — but not mass club men — see Steven L. Schlossman, "G. Stanley Hall and the Boys' Club: Conservative Applications of Recapitulation Theory," *Journal of the History of the Behavioral Sciences* 9 (1973):140–47.

85 [E. W. Krackowizer,] "Work With Boys," *WWB* 11 (May 1911):9.

86 William McCormick, *The Boy and His Clubs* (New York, 1912), p. 70 (quotation); idem, "A Practical Magazine," *WWB* 14 (1914):43; [Krackowizer,] "Work With Boys," pp. 12–13.

87 Boys' Clubs of America, *Manual of Boys' Club Operation* (New York, 1947), p. 6. For criticism of Scouting, see BSA, *OR, 1922,* p. 366.

88 Gould, *Ontogeny,* p. 143; Ross, *Hall,* pp. 284, 364.

89 Edward L. Thorndike, *Educational Psychology* (New York, 1913), I:261.

90 J. M. Artman, "The Recognized Phenomena in the Life of the Boy," in ABS, *RC,* pp. 3–10; Conf., 1916, pp. 153–54; Conf., 1920, pp. 268–69; "Boy Gangs," *WWB* 16 (1916):243.

91 John Dewey, *The School and Society* (Chicago, 1907), p. 34; idem, "Interpretation of the Culture Epoch Theory," *Public School Journal* 15 (1896):234.

92 William H. Kilpatrick "The Project Method," *Teachers College Record* 19 (1918):319-35 (quotation); Conf., 1919, p. 130; Conf., 1920, pp. 150-61; "Projects and Adventures," *S* 6 (Dec. 23, 1920):4-6.

93 H. Parker Lansdale, "A Historical Study of YMCA Boys' Work in the United States, 1900-1925" (Ph.D. diss., Yale, 1956), pp. 65, 193-95.

94 E. K. Fretwell, "The Boy as Citizen," in BSA, *OR, 1924,* p. 77 (quotation); "The New Handbook for Scoutmasters," *S* 7 (Sept. 4, 1919):4-5; BSA, *Handbook for Scoutmasters* (New York, 1920), pp. 266-91 and passim; BSA, *OR, 1924,* pp. 87-88, 170, 278-282, 480. For Fretwell's views on adolescence and gangs, see Fretwell, "The Boy, the Scout and the Citizen," pp. 253-62.

95 Kett, *Rites of Passage,* p. 221.

96 Ross, *Hall,* pp. 376-78; Samuel M. Holton, "The Historical Development of the Formal Educational Program of the Boy Scouts of America" (Ph.D. diss., Yale, 1948), p. 274; Frederic M. Thrasher, *The Gang: A Study of 1,313 Gangs in Chicago* (Chicago, 1927). For survivals, see below, Epilogue, notes 31-32.

97 Samuel P. Hays, "Introduction," in Jerry Israel, ed., *Building the Organizational Society: Essays on Associational Activities in Modern America* (New York, 1972), p. 3.

Chapter 7: The Attempted Professionalization of YMCA Boys' Work

1 Laurence Locke Doggett, *A Man and a School: Pioneering in Higher Education at Springfield College* (New York, 1943), pp. 25-29; A. G. Knebel, *Four Decades with Men and Boys* (New York, 1936), pp. 34-56, 94-96.

2 James McConaughy, in Edgar M. Robinson, *The Early Years: The Beginning of Work with Boys in the YMCA* (New York, 1950), p. 67 (quotation); ibid., p. 113; H. S. Ninde et al., eds., *A Handbook of the History, Organization, and Methods of Work of Young Men's Christian Associations* (New York, 1892), II:356-65.

3 On professionalization, see Magali Sarfatti Larson, *The Rise of Professionalism: A Sociological Analysis* (Berkeley, Calif., 1977), pp. xi-xvi, 31-40, and passim.

4 Doggett, *A Man,* pp. 19-22, 129; Ethel Josephine Dorgan, *Luther Halsey Gulick, 1865-1918* (New York, 1934), pp. 25-28.

5 Doggett, *A Man,* p. 90 (quotation); ibid., pp. 47, 105-6, 176-88; Dorgan, *Gulick,* p. 22.

6 See, e.g., Dorgan, *Gulick,* p. 15; YMCA International Committee, Minutes, Mar., June 1899; Jan. 10, 1901 (microfilm, YHL); *Training School Notes* 6 (1897):5-6. From 1898 through 1900, *Association Outlook* published a spate of recapitulation-based articles on boys' work by Gulick and his students.

7 Dorgan, *Gulick,* pp. 98-101, 114-16; Doggett, *A Man,* pp. 141-45.

8 Quotation: Robinson, *Early Years,* p. 119.

9 Quotations: ibid., p. 125; Edgar M. Robinson, "Boys as Savages," *Association Outlook* 8 (1899):243-58. For other sources, see Robinson, *Early Years,* pp. 118-25; AWB, *RP,* p. 23; Doggett, *A Man,* p. 144.

10 Richard C. Morse, *My Life with Young Men: Fifty Years in the Young Men's*

Christian Associations (New York, 1918), pp. 268–69. For Robinson's case, see "Two Significant Letters," *Association Men* 25 (1900):199; E. M. Robinson, "The Importance of Boys' Work in the YMCA" (abstract of speech, Oct. 19, 1901), EMR MSS.

11 Robinson, *Early Years,* pp. 126–27; *Thousand Island Herald,* June 13, 1900 (YHL); First Biennial or 29th Conference of General Secretaries of the YMCAs of N. America, June 6–10, 1900 (microfilm, YHL); Morse, *My Life,* p. 413.

12 "Conversion and Adolescent Phenomenon," *Association Men* 26 (Oct. 1900): 25. The original is clumsy.

13 Quotation: Robinson to John R. Mott, May 21, 1919, in Robinson to Mott Box, YHL. Statistics: H. T. Baker to Robinson, Sept. 19, 1919, in ibid.; C. Howard Hopkins, *History of the Y.M.C.A. in North America* (New York, 1951), p. 463. On Robinson, see Knebel, *Four Decades,* p. 181; Billy Burger, *A Million Miles in New York State* (New York, 1946), p. 60; *New York Times,* Apr. 10, 1951, p. 28.

14 Oscar L. Cox, "A Viewpoint," *AB* 6 (1907):258; YNA, *YB* (1920), p. 103.

15 YNA, *YB* (1901), p. 259; (1902), p. 7; (1904), p. 9; (1921), pp. 222–23.

16 YNA, *YB* (1901–1921) gave the following memberships: 1901–39,193; 1902–37,596; 1903–50,030; 1904–54,739; 1905–61,759; 1906–67,954; 1907–70,532; 1908–82,830; 1909–91,756; 1910–103,570; 1911–112,871; 1912–120,322; 1913–131,347; 1914–123,420; 1915–160,166; 1916–161,131; 1917–152,647; 1918–181,656; 1919–199,615, plus 38,034 Hi-Y; 1920–219,376, plus 41,384 Hi-Y.

17 The regression equations used to calculate these rates take into account the figures for *every* year under consideration. Hence the results differ from those obtained by using only terminal years (1898 and 1903, for example).

18 ABS, *RC,* p. 68; Owen E. Pence, *The Professional Boys' Worker in the Young Men's Christian Association: An Occupational Study* (New York, 1932), p. 68.

19 Harold L. Wilensky, "The Professionalization of Everyone?" *American Journal of Sociology* 70 (1964):137–46.

20 Quotation: H. T. Williams, "The Intellectual Life of the Leader of Boys," in C. B. Horton, ed., *Reaching the Boys of an Entire Community* (New York, 1909), p. 233.

21 ABS, *RC,* p. 78 (quotation); ibid., pp. 77–79.

22 Ibid., p. 78; William D. Murray, "The Secretary, the Board and Self-Culture," *AB* 5 (1906):195–97; H. W. Gibson, "Personal Efficiency of the Boys' Work Secretary," *AY* 4 (1915):7.

23 ABS, *RC,* p. 79 (quotation); "The Boys' Work Secretaryship" (unsigned MS, Apr. 7, 1915, at YHL). On salaries, see Boys' Work Secretaries of Ontario and Quebec, Minutes of 5th Annual Mid-Winter Conference, Jan. 24–25, 1921, at YHL.

24 ABS, *RC,* pp. 77–78; "Boys' Work Secretaryship."

25 Quotations: W. H. Burger, "The Passing of Boy's Man," *Association Forum* 1 (Oct. 1920):13; David R. Porter, "The Boys' Work Secretaryship," *AB* 8 (1909):51.

26 John L. Alexander, "Organizations Supplementary to the Home, School and Church," in idem, ed., *Boy Training* (New York, 1912), p. 176; [E. M. Robinson], "Some Considerations for Boys' Work Secretaries," *AB* 8 (1909):84–86.

27 ABS, *RC,* pp. 69–72; Burger, *A Million Miles,* p. 58; Williams, "Intellectual Life," p. 235.

28 Quotation: ABS, *RC,* p. 77. Statistics: ibid.; "Boys' Work Secretaryship" (MS).

29 H. Parker Lansdale, "A Historical Study of YMCA Boys' Work in the United States, 1900–1925" (Ph.D. diss., Yale, 1956), p. 311; Doggett, *A Man,* pp. 141–45.

30 Harry T. Baker, "The Order of the Hourglass," *AB* 10 (1911):231–38; Gibson, "Personal Efficiency," pp. 3–9; Lansdale, "Historical Study," p. 335.

31 E. Clark Worman, *The Contribution of Silver Bay to the Professional Training of the YMCA, 1902–1952* (n.p., 1952), pp. 5–17; "History of the Lake Geneva Boys' Work School" (MS, [c. 1921]), at YHL. On attendance, see ABS, *RC,* p. 74.

32 Lansdale, "Historical Study," p. 318 (quotation); ibid., pp. 313–18.

33 Bernard Barber, "Some Problems in the Sociology of the Professions," in Kenneth S. Lynn, ed., *The Professions in America* (Boston, 1967), p. 18 (quotation); Wilensky, "Professionalization," pp. 137–46.

34 "Studies in Methods of Y.M.C.A. Boys' Work" (typed MS, [c. 1925]), in vol. 56, NC MSS. The reference is to past boys' workers. On professional commitment, see Richard H. Hall, "Professionalization and Bureaucratization," *American Sociological Review* 33 (1968):93. Not all practitioners in any profession display vast knowledge, of course, and even doctors in 1900 were notoriously ill-trained; but that was changing by 1920.

35 Canadian National Council of YMCAs, Executive Committee, Minutes, Jan. 7, 1919, in vol. 48, NC MSS.

36 "Small Clubs in the Boys' Department," *AB* 1 (1902):59–61.

37 Quotation: Roy Lubove, *The Professional Altruist: The Emergence of Social Work as a Career, 1880–1930* (New York, 1969), p. 119.

38 ABS, *RC,* p. 21.

39 Ibid., pp. 15, 24; *Physical Education in the Young Men's Christian Associations of North America,* rev. ed. (New York, 1920), pp. 163–65.

40 "Boys Are Not Tools," *AB* 1 (1902):154–55; Edgar M. Robinson, "Self-Government for Boys," *AB* 7 (1908):99–111; YNA, *YB* (1905), unpaged; (1920), p. 103.

41 Quotations: ABS, *RC,* pp. 20, 15.

42 "Do the Boy Scouts Compete with the Association?" *AY* 15 (Dec. 1916):1–2. On origins, see Lansdale, "Historical Study," pp. 170–74; *Manual for Leaders: Pioneers: A Program of Christian Citizenship Training for Boys Twelve to Fourteen Years of Age* (New York, 1919), pp. 265–66.

43 See my "A Live Vaccine: The YMCA and Male Adolescence in the United States and Canada, 1870–1920," *Histoire sociale–Social History* 11 (1978):20–22.

44 Quotation: Eugene C. Foster, "An Announcement Relative to the Forthcoming Program of Christian Citizenship Training" (flyer, 1919, at YHL). On charting, see *Manual for Leaders: Pioneers,* pp. 1–5.

45 "The American Standard Program," *AY* 15 (Dec. 1916):7; "The Standard Efficiency Tests" (MS, n.d., in Boys' Work Subcommittee Box, YHL).

46 Canadian National Council of YMCAs, Executive Committee, Minutes,

1919–1921, vol. 48, NC MSS; Canadian National Council of YMCAs, Minutes, Jan. 28, 1921, vol. 55, NC MSS; Lansdale, "Historical Study," pp. 180–93.

47 ABS, *RC,* p. 35; YNA, *YB* (1901), p. 259; (1910), p. 296; (1920), pp. 103, 188–255. On Bible courses, see editorial note, *AB* 6 (1907):244; Lansdale, "Historical Study," pp. 231–32.

48 ABS, *RC,* p. 59 (quotations); ibid., p. 63, and below, chapter 15.

49 Quotations: E. M. Robinson, "The Greater Opportunity," *AY* 4 (1915):109; idem, "Revamping Religious Work with Boys," *AY* 1 (1912):210.

50 Arthur N. Cotton, report, Jan. 1913, in ABWS, General, 1903–1928 Box, YHL.

51 Quotation: AWB, *RP,* p. 47. On Porter's views, see ibid., p. 46.

52 S. Wirt Wiley, *History of Y.M.C.A.– Church Relations in the United States* (New York, 1944), pp. 121–22; H. Paul Douglass, *How Shall Country Youth Be Served? A Study of the "Rural" Work of Certain National Character-Building Agencies* (New York, 1926), p. 28; untitled materials from 1954 Boys' Work History Consultation, YHL.

53 ABS, *RC,* pp. 40–56; "The Detroit Survey," *AB* 8 (1909):197–287.

54 E.g., M. D. Crackel and Samuel Zechar, "The Boys' Work in Cleveland," *AB* 2 (1903):116; Elwood S. Brown, "Physical Department," *AB* 6 (1907):287; editorial note, *AB* 6 (1907):229–30; AWB, *RP,* p. 32.

55 Hopkins, *History of the Y.M.C.A.,* pp. 464, 480; John R. Boardman, "The County Work with Boys," *AB* 4 (1905):156–62; C. E. Buchner, "Working with Truant, Delinquent and Neglected Boys," *AB* 10 (1911):174–82.

56 Hopkins, *History of the Y.M.C.A.,* pp. 559–61; Lansdale, "Historical Study," p. 247; and below, chapters 9, 13, 15.

57 E.g., Brown, "Physical Department," p. 287; E. Clark Worman, *History of the Brooklyn and Queens Young Men's Christian Association, 1859–1949* (New York, 1952), pp. 85, 111–18; YNA, *YB* (1920), p. 103; BSA, *AR* 10 (Apr. 1, 1920):56.

58 Quotations: ABS, *RC,* pp. 16, 12.

59 Unidentified source in Hopkins, *History of the Y.M.C.A.,* p. 576 (quotation); ibid., pp. 456–57.

60 "From Our Mailbag," *AY* 15 (Mar. 1916):14.

61 Quotation: editorial note, *AB* 5 (1906):321.

62 "Open Forum on 'Service Membership'," *AY* 15 (Dec. 1916):3. See below, chapter 14, note 21, on pledges.

63 See Hall, "Professionalization," p. 103; Association of Employed Officers, *Report of Commission on the Boys' Work of the Young Men's Christian Association* (n.p., 1921), pp. 2–3; Policy Adopted by Canadian National Boys' Work Committee, June 1918, in National Boys' Work Committee Minutes, YHL.

64 Pence, *Professional Boys' Worker,* pp. 27–35.

Chapter 8: The Invention of Boy Scouting

1 John Henry Wadland, *Ernest Thompson Seton: Man and Nature in the Progressive Era, 1880–1915* (New York, 1978), p. 313 and passim. See "Ernest

Thompson Seton's Boys," *Ladies' Home Journal* 19 (May 1902):15, 41, through ibid. (Nov.):15; Ernest Thompson Seton, *Two Little Savages: Being the Adventures of Two Boys Who Lived as Indians and What They Learned* (New York, 1903).

2 Wadland, *Seton,* pp. 176–208, 282–337; *Trail of an Artist-Naturalist: The Autobiography of Ernest Thompson Seton* (New York, 1948), pp. 111, 170, 220.

3 E. T. Seton, *Manual of the Woodcraft Indians: The Fourteenth Birch-Bark Roll* (Garden City, N.Y., 1915), p. 21 (quotation); idem, "The Woodcraft Movement" (MS, [1927], at BSA, NHQ).

4 Ernest Thompson Seton, *The Birch-Bark Roll of the Woodcraft Indians,* 5th ed. (New York, 1906), pp. 2–5, 12–13, 21, 28–45; Edgar M. Robinson, "Ernest Thompson Seton: An Unforgettable Personality" (typed MS, [1941]), in EMR MSS; interview by Joseph Wyckoff with Len Clark, George White, Al Fienel, and Tom Hillegas [former Seton Indians], Sept. 9, 1966 (typescript at BSA, NHQ).

5 E. T. Seton to W. I. Talbot, Apr. 12, 1905, in Seton MSS; Seton to Editorial Board, Apr. 21, 1911, in Seton File, BSA, NHQ.

6 E.g., Wadland, *Seton,* pp. 43–44; Brooks Atkinson, "A Puritan Boyhood," *Massachusetts Review* 15 (1974):353. Boys even copied the book by hand. (Clyde Brion Davis, ed., *Eyes of Boyhood* [Philadelphia, 1953], p. 320.)

7 E.g., Robinson, "Seton"; C. R. Warthew, "The Wild Indians of Roanoke," *AB* 5 (1906):84–87; *Manual for Leaders: Pioneers: A Program of Christian Citizenship Training for Boys Twelve to Fourteen Years of Age* (New York, 1919), pp. 210–30; C. Howard Hopkins, *History of the Y.M.C.A. in North America* (New York, 1951), p. 554.

8 New York *Herald,* Oct. 11, 1903, magazine section, p. 3; M'Cready Sykes, "Making a New American Boy Through Woodcraft," *Everybody's Magazine* 23 (1910):481. Seton's journals (photocopies in Seton MSS of originals at the American Museum of Natural History, New York) show that boys' work took only a fraction of his time. Up to 1915, just eighteen boys had become sagamores. (Seton, *Manual,* p. 26.)

9 Howard Bradstreet to Seton, Jan. 11, 1910, photocopy in Seton MSS; Seton to William T. Hornaday, Dec. 19, 1911, in Hornaday MSS, Library of Congress.

10 Robinson, "Seton"; John L. Alexander to Seton, Oct. 27, 1914; J. P. Freeman to James West, Oct. 31, 1931, both in Seton File, BSA, NHQ.

11 Daniel Carter Beard, *Hardly a Man Is Now Alive: The Autobiography of Dan Beard* (New York, 1939). See next note for further sources.

12 E.g., Allan Richard Whitmore, "Beard, Boys, and Buckskins: Daniel Carter Beard and the Preservation of the American Pioneer Tradition" (Ph.D. diss., Northwestern, 1970), pp. 88–92; Daniel C. Beard, "Flat-Boating for Boys," *St. Nicholas* 8 (1881):696–703; "Dan Beard and the Boys," *Recreation* 24 (1906):171.

13 Quotations: "Dan Beard's Own Page for Boys," *Woman's Home Companion* 34 (Aug. 1907):33; Daniel C. Beard, *The Buckskin Book of the Boy Pioneers of America* (n.p., 1912), p. 3.

14 Beard to Mr. Annis, Feb. 16, 1906; Beard to Frank Morse, Jan. 2, 1909; John

C. Derr to Joseph R. Swan, Feb. 1, 1909; *Pictorial Review* to Beard, Aug. 25, 1914; Colin H. Livingstone to Beard, Jan. 18, 1919, all in Beard MSS.

15 "Dan Beard and the Boys," *Recreation* 21 (1905):523–24. On boys' restlessness, see "Special Announcement to the S.D.B.," *Woman's Home Companion* 36 (Feb. 1909):34; Patrick Griffin to Beard, Dec. 27, 1909, in Beard MSS.

16 E. E. Reynolds, *The Scout Movement* (London, 1950), p. 3 (quotation); idem, *Baden-Powell: A Biography of Lord Baden-Powell of Gilwell* (London, 1943), p. 20; William Hillcourt, with Olave, Lady Baden-Powell, *Baden-Powell: Two Lives of a Hero* (New York, 1964), pp. 8–150; R. S. S. Baden-Powell, *Aids to Scouting for N.C.O.'s and Men,* rev. ed. (London, 1906). The revisions were minor.

17 Ralph D. Blumenfeld, "The Boy Scouts," *Outlook* 95 (1910):617; Brian Gardner, *Mafeking: A Victorian Legend* (London, 1966), p. 213 and passim; Hillcourt, *Baden-Powell,* p. 222.

18 [R. S. S.] Baden-Powell, *Lessons of a Lifetime* (New York, 1933), p. 258; "General Baden-Powell on the Boys' Brigade," *Boys' Brigade Gazette* 12 (1904):157.

19 R. S. S. Baden-Powell, "Scouting for Boys," *Boys' Brigade Gazette* 14 (1906):150, is a full outline, including tests. For other sources, see Baden-Powell to Seton, Aug. 1, 1906, in Seton MSS; the same, Oct. 31, 1906, in Seton File, BSA, NHQ; Reynolds, *Scout Movement,* pp. 7–13. Baden-Powell was going ahead with plans for Scouting before he met Seton.

20 E. K. Wade, *Twenty-One Years of Scouting: The Official History of the Boy Scout Movement from Its Inception* (London, 1929), pp. 41–44.

21 Percy Everett, "The Start of It All . . . Brownsea Island," *Victorian Scout,* Oct. 1957, pp. 5–9, in Baden-Powell File, BSA, NHQ.

22 Reynolds, *Scout Movement,* pp. 24–25; R.S.S. Baden-Powell, *Scouting for Boys: A Handbook for Instruction in Good Citizenship,* rev. ed. (London, 1909).

23 Baden-Powell, *Scouting for Boys,* pp. 19, 48–50; James E. West to Theodore Roosevelt, Jr., Dec. 23, 1940, in Seton File, BSA, NHQ; R. S. S. Baden-Powell, "The Scoutmaster's Training Course," *S* 2 (Oct. 1, 1914):6; (Nov. 1, 1914):6.

24 Baden-Powell, *Scouting for Boys,* pp. 31–37.

25 [Boys' Brigade Executive,] *The Boys' Brigade Manual* (Glasgow, 1914), pp. 44–46.

26 R. S. S. Baden-Powell, *Boy Scouts: A Suggestion* (London, 1907); John Springhall, *Youth, Empire and Society: British Youth Movements, 1883–1940* (London, 1977), p. 58; W. McG. Eager, *Making Men: The History of Boys' Clubs and Related Movements in Great Britain* (London, 1953), pp. 380–82; Paul Wilkinson, "A Study of English Uniformed Youth Movements, 1883–1935: Their Origins, Development, and Social and Political Influence" (M.A. thesis, Univ. of Wales, [1968]), p. 78.

27 Baden-Powell, *Scouting for Boys,* p. 178 (quotation; his capitals); ibid., pp. 184, 270–91.

28 Quotations: ibid., pp. 284, 49.

29 See ibid., pp. 233, 289; Baden-Powell, "Scoutmaster's Training Course," *S* 2 (Oct. 1, 1914):7; ibid., *S* 2 (Dec. 1, 1914):6–7. The inclusion of reading and

writing in the original Scout tests attested to Baden-Powell's low expectations. (R. S. S. Baden-Powell, *Scouting for Boys* . . . [London, (1908)], p. 37.)

30 Quotations: Earl of Meath, "What the Boy Scout Movement May Do for Britain," *Windsor Magazine* 31 (Dec. 1909):55; Lieutenant-General Baden-Powell, *Boy Scouts Scheme* (n.p., [1907]), p. 13. On the church attendance policy, see Wade, *Twenty-One Years,* p. 93.

31 Quotations: Baden-Powell quoted in Reynolds, *Scout Movement,* p. 1; Baden-Powell, *Boy Scouts Scheme,* p. 5. For some memberships, see John Onslow Springhall, "Youth and Empire: A Study of the Propagation of Imperialism to the Young in Edwardian Britain" (D.Phil. thesis, Sussex, 1968), p. 348.

32 Bruce Haley, *The Healthy Body and Victorian Culture* (Cambridge, Mass., 1978), pp. 160, 258–60; Baden-Powell, *Scouting for Boys,* pp. 276–77; Mark Girouard, *The Return to Camelot: Chivalry and the English Gentleman* (New Haven, Conn., 1981), esp. 253–58.

33 Springhall, *Youth,* pp. 15–16, 53–54.

34 Baden-Powell, *Scouting for Boys,* p. 127 (quotation); ibid., pp. 122–23.

35 Baden-Powell said the working class were unhappy because they were too intellectual. (Baden-Powell, "Scoutmaster's Training Course," *S* 2 [Dec. 1, 1914]:7.)

36 Baden-Powell, *Scouting for Boys,* p. 118 (quotation); ibid., pp. 182–85.

37 Paul Wilkinson, "English Youth Movements, 1908–1930," *Journal of Contemporary History* 4 (Apr. 1969): 9–11; Bernard Semmel, *Imperialism and Social Reform: English Social-Imperial Thought, 1895–1914* (Cambridge, Mass., 1960), pp. 112, 216–20; G. R. Searle, *The Quest for Efficiency: A Study in British Politics and Political Thought, 1899–1914* (Berkeley, Calif., 1971), pp. 2–3, 66, 92–95.

38 Richard Price, *An Imperial War and the British Working Class: Working-Class Attitudes and Reactions to the Boer War* (London, 1972), pp. 73–80, 95, 130, 238–40, and passim.

39 Quotation: Baden-Powell, *Scouting for Boys,* p. 11. On the militarism controversy, see ibid., p. 301; Reynolds, *Scout Movement,* pp. 49, 68; *The Times* (London), Sept. 4–28, 1909; Springhall, "Youth and Empire," pp. 258, 294–320. On the clubs, see Price, *Imperial War,* p. 223. Nonconformist and working-class suspicion of the Boys' Brigade inspired the creation in 1899 of a moderately successful Boys' Life Brigade for ambulance work, though it merged with the regular Brigade in 1926. (Eager, *Making Men,* p. 324; Roger S. Peacock, *Pioneer of Boyhood: Story of Sir William A. Smith, Founder of the Boys' Brigade* [Glasgow, 1954], pp. 122–23.)

40 R. S. S. Baden-Powell to Major, The Earl of Lanesborough, Jan. 9, 1910, on exhibit at the Canadian Scouting Museum, Ottawa (quotation); Baden-Powell, *Scouting for Boys,* p. 275.

41 Samuel Moffat, "Observations of the Boy Scout Movement in England," *AY* 3 (1914):157–58 (quotation); Springhall, *Youth,* p. 8; idem, "Youth and Empire," pp. 204, 246; Wilkinson, "English Youth Movements," p. 14; Boy Scouts Association, Canadian General Council, *Canadian Boy Scouts: Report of Officer Commanding the Canadian Boy Scouts' Contingent to England, 1911* ([Montreal, 1912]), pp. 4–6.

42 Baden-Powell considered *Aids to Scouting* central to his plans. The Seton Memorial Library has the copy he gave Seton on December 10, 1906.

43 Baden-Powell's badges each rewarded a cluster of skills; Seton's coups were for isolated feats. Seton intermittently pressed his claim to have originated Scouting but weakened his case by charging that Baden-Powell had radically altered it. Letters that he submitted to the BSA in 1927 showed that Baden-Powell openly borrowed only some games and tracking irons. Baden-Powell took more, but the issue is too complex to argue here in detail. For Seton's case, see the letters in the Seton MSS; Brian Morris, "Ernest Thompson Seton and the Origins of the Woodcraft Movement," *Journal of Contemporary History* 5, no. 2 (1970):189–90.

44 *Woman's Home Companion,* Nov. 1909 to Sept. 1910.

45 John R. Gillis, *Youth and History: Tradition and Change in European Age Relations, 1770–Present* (New York, 1974), p. 139. The closest Baden-Powell came to listing his sources was a 1918 deposition, reprinted in BSA, *Handbook for Scoutmasters: A Manual of Leadership,* 2nd ed. (New York, 1926), pp. 477–79.

46 Baden-Powell, *Scouting for Boys,* pp. 296, 303; J. Clifford Banham, "The Psychology of Scouting," *Headquarters Gazette,* reprinted in *S* 3 (June 15, 1915):3; (July 1, 1915):3.

47 Quotation: Moffat, "Observations," p. 159.

48 T. Manners Howe, "The World's New Order of Chivalry," *Graphic* (London), Sept. 17, 1910, clipping at BSA, NHQ (quotation); Baden-Powell, *Scouting for Boys,* pp. 30, 292; Percy Everett, *The First Ten Years* (Ipswich, U.K., [1948]), p. 67.

49 P. Jacques Sevin, *Le Scoutisme* (Paris, 1933), pp. 158–59.

50 Erik H. Erikson, *Childhood and Society,* 2nd ed. (New York, 1963), pp. 258–60.

51 Seton, *Trail,* pp. 54–72, 107–15. On Peter Pan and his creator, James Barrie, cf. Alison Lurie, "The Boy Who Couldn't Grow Up," *New York Review* 22 (Feb. 6, 1975):11–15.

52 Henrietta Grace Baden-Powell, letter, Mar. 24, 1884, in Hillcourt, *Baden-Powell,* p. 101 (quotation); ibid., pp. 47–62, 333–36; Carolyn Ditte Wagner, "The Boy Scouts of America: A Model and a Mirror of American Society" (Ph.D. diss., Johns Hopkins, 1979), pp. 21–24.

53 Billy [William Harold] Burger, *A Million Miles in New York State* (New York, 1946), p. 11 (quotation); Jasper Van Vleck, *Henry Horace Webster* (Chicago, 1893); *New York Times,* Apr. 10, 1951, p. 28. Bryan Strong, "Toward a History of the Experiential Family: Sex and Incest in the Nineteenth-Century Family,"*Journal of Marriage and the Family* 35 (1973):460–64, suggests that mother-dominated Victorian families often engendered problems like Burger's. If, as Peter Blos suggests, preadolescent boys normally have unconflicted relations with their fathers, Seton and Baden-Powell, who missed this, may have tried to construct a surrogate experience. ("The Initial Stage of Male Adolescence," *The Psychoanalytic Study of the Child* 20 [New York, 1965]:148–49.)

54 E. M. Robinson to Seton, Dec. 13, 1912, photocopy in Seton MSS; Beard to W. P. McGuire, Sept. 11, 1918, Beard MSS; Baden-Powell, *Boy Scouts Scheme,* p. 13.

55 Baden-Powell, quoted in Everett, *First Ten Years,* p. 80.

56 Sir R. Baden-Powell, *Rovering to Success* (London, 1922).

57 Leslie Paul, *Angry Young Man* (London, 1951), p. 53 (quotation); BSA, *OR, 1924,* p. 185; Wilkinson, "Uniformed Youth Movements," pp. 88, 99. For a caustic view of Scouting as a letdown, see Evelyn Waugh, *A Little Learning* (Boston, 1964), p. 89.

58 Springhall, *Youth,* p. 90; Sevin, *Le Scoutisme,* p. 179.

59 Springhall, "Youth and Empire," pp. 221–49.

60 Reynolds, *Scout Movement,* pp. 47–77; Wade, *Twenty-One Years,* p. 83.

61 Springhall, "Youth and Empire," p. 217; Wade, *Twenty-One Years,* pp. 81–82.

62 Springhall, *Youth,* pp. 61–62; Sevin, *Le Scoutisme,* pp. 59, 63.

63 Wilkinson, "Uniformed Youth Movements," pp. 127–61; Heinz Reichling, *Ernest Thompson Seton und die Woodcraft Bewegung in England* (Bonn, 1937), pp. 67–69, 89.

64 Letter from "A Worker," *The Times,* Sept. 13, 1909; Springhall, *Youth,* pp. 90–96. On general working-class views, see Price, *Imperial War,* p. 4.

65 Springhall, *Youth,* pp. 121–22; Price, *Imperial War,* pp. 73, 240.

66 Long accounts of Baden-Powell's Canadian tour may be found at the Canadian Scouting Museum and in the Dr. John A. Stiles Collection housed there.

67 Beard, *Buckskin Book,* p. 6 (quotation); ibid., pp. 3, 12.

Chapter 9: The Organization and Expansion of the Boy Scouts of America

1 Raymond Callahan, *Education and the Cult of Efficiency* (Chicago, 1962).

2 Edwin R. Lampshire and Ralph W. Ellis, Jr., "Early History of the Boy Scouts of America in Springfield, Massachusetts" (MS, 1923, Marsh Library, Springfield College); J. A. Van Dis to William D. Murray, Oct. 22, 1934, at BSA, NHQ.

3 Edgar M. Robinson, "Recollections of the Early Days of the Boy Scouts of America" (typed, 1940s, YHL); R. Woodland Gates to John L. Alexander, July 23, 1910, in Alexander File, BSA, NHQ.

4 E. M. Robinson to A. N. Cotton, Feb. 1, 1930, in Boy Scouts–YMCA Box, YHL; Robinson, "Recollections."

5 "Reports and Minutes, 1910" (scrapbook, BSA, NHQ), esp. Minutes of Meeting for Organization of the Boy Scouts of America, June 21, 1910.

6 Sidney Brooks, "England's Boy Army," *Harper's Weekly* 54 (Mar. 26, 1910): 9–10; John L. Alexander to Colin Livingstone, June 14, 1910, Alexander File, BSA, NHQ; National Scouts of America, *Circular No. 1* (Manlius, N.Y., n.d.); Peter Bomus to Lee Hanmer, Oct. 24, 1910, in "Early History, 1910" (scrapbook, BSA, NHQ).

7 John L. Alexander to E. M. Robinson, Aug. 2, 1910, in "Early History"; San Francisco *Examiner,* May 18, 1910, in historical files, BSA, NHQ; "Confidential Copy of Memoranda with Regard to American Boy Scouts" (MS, late 1911), Beard MSS. An example of the confusion can be seen in Joseph F. Kett, *Rites of Passage: Adolescence in America, 1790 to the Present* (New York, 1977), following p. 211. Photographs show Scouts with rifles, but they

are members of the United States Boy Scouts, a successor of the Hearst group, and not the BSA.

8 John L. Alexander's reports to Committee on Organization, in "Reports and Minutes, 1910"; idem, *Boy Scouts* (n.p., 1910); Ernest Thompson Seton, *Boy Scouts of America: A Handbook of Woodcraft, Scouting, and Life-Craft* (New York, 1910); *New York Times,* Sept. 24, 1910, p. 8; R. S. S. Baden-Powell et al., "The Boy Scout Movement," *The Churchman* 28 (1910):711–13.

9 Quotation: "Address by Baden-Powell at the Waldorf-Astoria, Sept. 23, 1910" (MS in Baden-Powell File, BSA, NHQ). Cf. Robert H. Wiebe, *The Search for Order, 1877–1920* (New York, 1967), p. 24.

10 E. M. Robinson, "Ernest Thompson Seton" (typed MS, in EMR MSS), p. 19; Edward Knapp to BSA, Feb. 11, 1911, in Alphabetical File, BSA, NHQ; Reports of Div. of Recreation, Child Hygiene Dept., Russell Sage Foundation, at BSA, NHQ.

11 Ernest P. Bicknell to Luther Gulick, Nov. 2, 1910, in "Early History, 1910"; Roy Lubove, "James Edward West," *Dictionary of American Biography,* Supplement Four (New York, 1974), pp. 871–72.

12 Theodore Roosevelt to James West, Dec. 27, 1912; Oct. 3, 1913, in TR MSS.

13 Editorial Board to Executive Board, Jan. 17, 1911, at BSA, NHQ.

14 James West, "Historical Statement to the National Training School" (typed, 1932, at BSA, NHQ).

15 Executive Board, Minutes, Mar. 3, 1911, at BSA, NHQ; James West to Jeremiah Jenks, Apr. 8, 1911, in "Committee on Standardization" (scrapbook, BSA, NHQ).

16 James West, report to Executive Board, Feb. 14, 1911, at BSA, NHQ.

17 R. S. S. Baden-Powell to James West, Apr. 14, 1911, in Beard MSS; Oscar Handlin, *Race and Nationality in American Life* (Garden City, N.Y., 1957), p. 80.

18 BSA, *The Official Handbook for Boys* (Garden City, N.Y., 1911), pp. 14–16; R. S. S. Baden-Powell, *Scouting for Boys: A Handbook for Instruction in Good Citizenship,* rev. ed. (London, 1909), pp. 39, 48–50. On whistling, see undated suggestions by Joseph Lee, W. D. Murray, and E. T. Seton in "Committee on Standardization."

19 BSA, *Handbook for Boys,* p. 18 (quotation); Baden-Powell, *Scouting for Boys,* pp. 32–33; Ernest Thompson Seton, revisions on April 11 version, in "Committee on Standardization."

20 BSA, *Official Handbook for Boys,* p. 43 (quotation); ibid., pp. 24–43.

21 Ibid., p. v.

22 SM Conf., 1912, p. 9.

23 William D. Murray, *The History of the Boy Scouts of America* (New York, 1937), p. 400; Samuel D. Bogan, *No Larger Fields: The History of a Boy Scout Council, 1910–1963* (Hamden, Conn., 1966), p. 13.

24 On Weber's ideas, see Amitai Etzioni, *A Comparative Analysis of Complex Organizations: On Power, Involvement, and Their Correlates* (New York, 1961), pp. 106, 204.

25 Committee on Organization, Minutes, June 23, 1910, in "Reports and Minutes, 1910"; Executive Board, Minutes, Nov. 22, 1910, in Beard MSS.

26 Committee on Organization, Oct. 31, 1912 (list at BSA, NHQ); West, "His-

torical Statement"; Richard C. Morse, *My Life with Young Men: Fifty Years in the Young Men's Christian Association* (New York, 1918), pp. 443–53.

27 BSA, *AR* 3 (Feb. 1913):28. Maryland Scouters wanted a state organization and St. Paul men resented loss of a projected regional headquarters. (H. Laurance Eddy to James West, Sept. 13, 1911; John L. Alexander to West, Oct. 24, 1911; transcripts of BSA, 6th Annual Meeting, 1916, pt. 3, all at BSA, NHQ.)

28 Executive Board, Minutes, May 29, 1912, Beard MSS.

29 Ibid., Feb. 19, 1915, Beard MSS; John R. Boardman, "New Organization Plan for Greater New York," *S* 3 (June 1, 1915):1–3. See also Conf., 1916, p. 262; W. E. Severance to James West, Dec. 21, 1918, Beard MSS.

30 BSA, *AR* 4 (Apr. 1914):15; 7 (Mar. 1917):14, 106; Mark M. Jones, *Report on a Survey of the Boy Scouts of America* (privately printed, 1927), pp. 5–6.

31 BSA, *Handbook for Boys,* p. vii; Executive Board, Minutes, June 18, 1912, and Mar. 29, 1915, Beard MSS; *Who Was Who in America* (Chicago, 1942–73); *Dictionary of American Biography* (New York, 1937–74); *National Cyclopaedia of American Biography* (New York and Clifton, N.J., 1898–1974); biographical lists at BSA, NHQ; obituaries in the *New York Times.* Murray, *History of the Boy Scouts of America,* pp. 547–48, is unreliable.

32 BSA, *AR* 11 (Aug. 1921):67–74. The twelve were Alfred W. Dater, president of Stamford Gas and Electric; Lewis B. Gawtry, an executive with Consolidated Gas in New York; Walter W. Head, an Omaha banker and insurance executive; Myron T. Herrick, a banker and diplomat; John S. Hoyt; Arthur Letts, a department store owner from Los Angeles; Harold McCormick, president of International Harvester; John M. Phillips, a wealthy oilman; George D. Porter, an investment banker; G. Barrett Rich, a Buffalo insurance and real estate man; Bolton Smith, an investment banker in Memphis; and James J. Storrow, a wealthy banker who had worked to consolidate the administration of Boston schools. See William T. Doherty, "The Impact of Business on Protestantism, 1900–1929," *Business History Review* 28 (1954):143–48. Similar self-perpetuating elite boards ran church agencies. See Paul M. Harrison, *Authority and Power in the Free Church Tradition* (Princeton, 1959), p. 50.

33 BSA, *AR* 4 (Apr. 1914):88.

34 On lax standards see, e.g., letter from G. Barrett Rich, *S* 1 (Oct. 15, 1913):8; Lorillard Spencer to James West, Dec. 30, 1912, Beard MSS; SM Conf., 1917, p. 15. On Scoutmasters' dropout rates, see BSA, *AR* 4 (Apr. 1914):19.

35 BSA, *AR* 4 (Apr. 1914):14. See also Conf., 1919, p. 55.

36 Conf., 1916, p. 157.

37 E.g., Minutes of a Meeting [c. Nov. 1910] of E. Stamford White, John D. Shoop, and F. A. Crosby, Historical Files, BSA, NHQ; lists in "Reports and Minutes, 1910"; Boy Scout Council, Peru, Ind., Minutes, Mar. 11, 1912, Contributions File, BSA, NHQ; "Field," *S* 5 (Dec. 15, 1917):15.

38 Quotations: BSA, *AR* 4 (Apr. 1914):14; "Scout Movement Begun by Best Men of Dayton," *S* 1 (Mar. 1, 1914):1. Cf. David B. Tyack, *The One Best System: A History of American Urban Education* (Cambridge, Mass., 1974), pp. 139–41.

39 SM Conf., 1912, p. 96.

40 Executive Board, Minutes, Mar. 27, 1913, and John Hendrig to James West,

Dec. 26, 1913, both in Beard MSS; Executive Board, Minutes, Sept. 22, 1913, at BSA, NHQ; "Membership Plan Adopted," *S* 1 (Sept. 1, 1913):1–2.

41 James West, "Opening Address and First Assignment, 18th National Training School" (typed MS, n.d., at YHL) (quotation); BSA, *AR* 7 (Mar. 1917):88–89.

42 Conf., 1916, pp. 74–90.

43 Frank Otis Erb, *The Development of the Young People's Movement* (Chicago, 1917), p. 66 (quotation); James E. West, "Play Leaders and Boy Scout Activities," *Playground* 5 (1911–12):279; idem, "Historical Statement."

44 Executive Board, Minutes, May 7, 1914, and Mar. 29, 1915, Beard MSS; BSA, *AR* 6 (Feb. 1916):47; 7 (Mar. 1917):127–30; 10 (Apr. 1920):30.

45 H. Paul Douglass, *How Shall Country Youth Be Served? A Study of the "Rural" Work of Certain National Character-Building Agencies* (New York, 1926), p. 100; BSA, *AR* 10 (Apr. 1920):50, 116; 12 (Mar. 1922):140.

46 Canadian General Council of the Boy Scouts Association, *Policy, Organization and Rules for Canada, March, 1916* (Ottawa, 1916), p. 8; BSA, *OR, 1924,* p. 449.

47 BSA, *AR* 7 (Mar. 1917):60–62, 90, 117; 10 (Apr. 1920):96–98.

48 "Another Echo of the Convention," *S* 7 (Mar. 20, 1919):2.

49 BSA, *AR* 6 (Feb. 1916):33; 7 (Mar. 1917):17–18, 91; 8 (Mar. 1918):28.

50 BSA, *AR* 3 (Feb. 1913):42; 5 (Feb. 1915):62; Murray, *History of the Boy Scouts of America,* p. 406; Peter A. Soderbergh, "The Great Book War: Edward Stratemeyer and the Boy Scouts of America," *New Jersey History* 91 (1973): 235–48.

51 E.g., William D. Murray, *As He Journeyed: The Autobiography of William D. Murray* (New York, 1929), p. 349.

52 James West to New York Knife Co., May 2, 1913, Beard MSS; Committee on Badges, Awards, and Equipment, Minutes, July 30, Sept. 12, 1912, at BSA, NHQ.

53 BSA, *AR* 8 (Mar. 1918):76, 80; 9 (Mar. 1919):133; 10 (Apr. 1920):24.

54 BSA, *AR* 10 (Apr. 1920):23; W. Lloyd Warner et al., *The Emergent American Society,* vol. I, *Large-Scale Organizations* (New Haven, 1967), pp. 305–7.

55 Alfred D. Chandler, Jr., *Strategy and Structure: Chapters in the History of the Industrial Enterprise* (Cambridge, Mass., 1962), p. 37.

56 Executive Board, Minutes, June 26, 1914, Beard MSS. See also Harold F. Pote, *Fifty Years of Scouting in America and the Pioneers* (n.p., [c. 1966]), p. 19.

57 Franklin D. Elmer to James West, Mar. 30, 1916, Beard MSS (quotation); West to G. Barrett Rich, Jr., Dec. 28, 1917, Beard MSS.

58 E.g., Pote, *Fifty Years,* pp. 17–18; West to Daniel C. Beard, May 4, 1914, and Mortimer Schiff to Beard, May 24, 1918, both in Beard MSS.

59 Pote, *Fifty Years,* p. 16; S. A. Moffat, "Memorandum to Mr. West Regarding Boy Scout Movement in England" (typed, [c. 1914]), Beard MSS.

60 "A Memorial Addressed to the National Headquarters of the Boy Scouts of America . . . February, 1914," at BSA, NHQ.

61 Robinson, "Seton," pp. 19–21; extract from Minutes, 3rd Annual Meeting, National Council, Feb. 11, 1913, at BSA, NHQ; Seton to Executive Board, Dec. (n.d.), in Seton File, BSA, NHQ,; Executive Board, Minutes, Jan. 29, 1915, Beard MSS.

62 Seton File, BSA, NHQ, esp. E. T. Seton to Executive Board, Nov. 21, 1912; Resolutions for National Council with memorandum by James West, Feb. 27, 1913; Seton to Colin Livingstone, Dec. 28, 1914.

63 *New York Times,* Dec. 6, 1915, p. 6.

64 Conf., 1916, p. 91 (quotation); Conf., 1920, p. 19.

65 U.S., *Statutes at Large* (1916), 64th Cong., 1st sess., ch. 148, secs. 7, 5. See U.S. Congress, House, *Congressional Record,* 64th Cong., 1st sess., 1916, 53, pt. 3:2895.

66 U.S., *Statutes at Large* (1916), 64th Cong., 1st sess., ch. 134, sec. 125.

67 James West to Daniel Carter Beard, May 18, 1917, and Jan. 4, 1918, both in Beard MSS. The USBS's story can be followed in *Uncle Sam's Boy* 1 (1918–19).

68 Executive Board, Minutes, Oct. 5, 1914, and Apr. 9, 1917, both in Beard MSS.

69 James West to E. M. Robinson, Dec. 2, 1918, Beard MSS; E. C. Foster to A. N. Cotton, Oct. 20, 1920, in Boy Scouts–YMCA Box, YHL.

70 Conf., 1916, p. 87; E. E. Reynolds, *The Scout Movement* (London, 1950), p. 45.

71 BSA, *AR* 4 (Apr. 1914):46–49; Committee on Merit Badges, Awards, and Scout Requirements, Minutes, Feb. 23, 1916, and 1911–20, at BSA, NHQ.

72 Frederick K. Vreeland to Dan Beard, Feb. 15, 1917, Beard MSS.

73 Conf., 1916, p. 204 (quotation); BSA, *OR, 1924,* pp. 206, 490.

74 Conf., 1916, p. 196; West's report in "Extract of Discussion at the Annual Meeting, March 1920," Beard MSS.

75 BSA, *OR, 1922,* pp. 327–34. The BSA introduced Achievement Badges for handicapped boys in 1923. (Samuel M. Holton, "The Historical Development of the Formal Program of the Boy Scouts of America" [Ph.D. diss., Yale, 1948], pp. 107–9.)

76 BSA, *AR* 7 (Mar. 1917):16.

77 BSA, *AR* 10 (Apr. 1920):117.

78 BSA, *AR* 12 (May 1922):60.

79 Ibid., p. 61 (quotation); ibid., pp. 37–39, 59–62; BSA, *AR* 11 (Aug. 1921):45–48.

80 Jones, *Report,* p. viii (quotation); Pote, *Fifty Years,* pp. 8–11, 17–19.

81 BSA, *AR* 7 (Mar. 1917):13; 10 (Apr. 1920):84–87; 12 (May 1922):58–59, 109; Murray, *History of the Boy Scouts of America,* p. 259.

82 E. M. Robinson to James West, Mar. 24, 1911, Robinson File, BSA, NHQ.

83 Biographical lists in *S* 2 (Jan. 15, 1915):3; E. M. Robinson to John R. Mott, Sept. 19, 1919, in Robinson to Mott Box, YHL; biographical sketches in *S* 6 (Oct. 31, 1918):7; Conf., 1920, p. 437.

84 Conf., 1920, pp. 824–62; William H. Burger to Arthur N. Cotton, Feb. 25, 1921, and "Relationships Between the YMCA and the Boy Scouts" (typed, May 4, 1923), both in Boy Scouts–YMCA Box, YHL.

85 "Orienting the Council Office," *S* 8 (Mar. 11, 1920):3 (quotation); Douglass, *How Shall Country Youth Be Served?* p. 108.

86 *S* 3–5 (May 1915–Dec. 1917); BSA, *OR, 1924,* pp. 41–43.

87 BSA, *OR, 1922,* p. 78; Robert H. Shaffer, "Career Opportunities with the Boy Scouts," *Occupations* 19 (1941):568.

88 Conf., 1916, p. 102; Conf., 1918, p. 48; BSA, "Annual Meeting" 6 (1916), parts 3, 4 (typed transcript, BSA, NHQ); BSA, *OR, 1922,* p. 304.

89 BSA, *OR, 1922,* p. 179 (quotation); ibid., p. 136; BSA, *OR, 1928,* pp. 341–50.

90 E.g., BSA, *OR, 1922,* p. 116; BSA, *OR, 1924,* pp. 243–50, 284–98.

91 Conf., 1916, p. 150.

92 Murray, *History of the Boy Scouts of America,* pp. 348–50. On using psychology, see Conf., 1920, pp. 514–15.

93 Quotations: Lynn L. Marshall, "The Strange Stillbirth of the Whig Party," *American Historical Review* 72 (1967):455n., 455, 468; Peter M. Blau and W. Richard Scott, "Dilemmas of Formal Organization," in Amitai Etzioni, ed., *Readings on Modern Organizations* (Englewood Cliffs, N.J., 1969), pp. 140–41.

94 Douglass, *How Shall Country Youth Be Served?* pp. 114–15. See also BSA, *OR, 1922,* p. 186.

95 David B. Tyack, "Bureaucracy and the Common School: The Example of Portland, Oregon, 1851–1913," *American Quarterly* 19 (1967):476.

96 Idem, "City Schools: Centralization at the Turn of the Century," in Jerry Israel, ed., *Building the Organizational Society* (New York, 1972), p. 60.

97 BSA, *OR, 1928,* pp. 399–402. Cf. Warner, *Emergent American Society,* I:305–7.

98 Conf., 1916, pp. 14–15.

99 Porter R. Lee et al., *Report of a Study of the Interrelation of the Work of National Social Agencies in Fourteen American Cities* (New York, [1923]), p. 55.

100 Incidents in order: Conf., 1916, pp. 219, 137.

101 James West to E. M. Robinson, Sept. 26, 1911, and West to E. T. Seton, Aug. 13, 1912, both in Seton File, BSA, NHQ.

102 BSA, *AR* 7 (Mar. 1917):132–33; Exec. Conf., 1917, p. 26.

103 James West, report to Executive Board, May 6, 1911, Beard MSS.

104 Conf., 1920, p. 233; Conf., 1919, p. 55.

105 Douglass, *How Shall Country Youth Be Served?* pp. 42–50, 104, 128–32, 156.

106 James West to Langan J. Foard, Mar. 20, 1923, under Religious Policy, in "Correspondence About Policies" (scrapbook, BSA, NHQ).

107 Incidents in order: Conf., 1916, pp. 174–80; Conf., 1920, p. 220.

108 SM Conf., 1917, p. 15; Exec. Conf., 1917, pp. 111–29, 156–57.

109 BSA, *OR, 1924,* p. 465.

110 S. A. Moffat to John L. Alexander, Nov. 16, 1911, at BSA, NHQ (quotation); BSA, *Bulletin No. 1: Scouting for Boys* (New York, 1911), p. vii; John L. Alexander to William D. Murray, May 31, 1911, Alexander File, BSA, NHQ; SM Conf., 1917, pp. 202–10.

111 "Self-Training for New Scoutmasters," *S* 6 (Feb. 15, 1918):4; SM Conf., 1917, p. 299; Exec. Conf., 1917, pp. 106–7.

112 "First Aid," *S* 7 (Dec. 11, 1919):2 (quotation); Conf., 1919, pp. 53–54.

113 Conf., 1916, pp. 153–54.

114 "Training the Scoutmaster for His Job," *S* 8 (Feb. 12, 1920):7; BSA, *AR* 10 (Apr. 1920):60–68; Jones, *Report,* p. iii.

115 Jones, *Report,* pp. 28–35.

116 Ibid., pp. ii–viii, 38–40.

117 Samuel P. Hays, "Introduction," in Israel, ed., *Organizational Society,* p. 1 (quotation); Robert D. Cuff, "American Historians and the 'Organizational Factor,'" *Canadian Review of American Studies* 4 (Spring 1973):19–31.

118 Quotations: Hays, "Introduction," pp. 2–4, 7.
119 Samuel P. Hays, "The Politics of Reform in Municipal Government in the Progressive Era," *Pacific Northwest Quarterly* 55 (1964):157–69; Tyack, *One Best System,* pp. 126–98.
120 Quotations: Wiebe, *Search for Order,* pp. 111, 112, 166.
121 Wayne K. Hobson, "Professionals, Progressives and Bureaucratization: A Reassessment," *The Historian* 39 (1977):644.
122 BSA, *OR, 1924,* p. 140.
123 Hobson, "Professionals," p. 650.
124 Ibid., pp. 653–54.
125 Cf. Wiebe, *Search for Order,* pp. 128, 147–61.
126 Roy Lubove, *The Professional Altruist: The Emergence of Social Work as a Career, 1880–1930* (New York, 1969), p. 51.
127 I am extrapolating from Steven L. Schlossman, *Love and the American Delinquent: The Theory and Practice of "Progressive" Juvenile Justice, 1825–1920* (Chicago, 1977), pp. 137, 154–55, 250.

Part IV
*Chapter 10: Boyhood, God, and Country:
Creation and Defense of a Public Image*

1 H. Paul Douglass, *How Shall Country Youth Be Served? A Study of the "Rural" Work of Certain National Character-Building Agencies* (New York, 1926), pp. 157–59.
2 Billy Burger, *A Million Miles in New York State* (New York, 1946), p. 30.
3 BSA Exec. Board, Minutes, Jan. 17, 1911, Beard MSS; BSA, *AR* 2 (Feb. 1912): 12; 3 (Feb. 1913):38; 4 (Apr. 1914):31–33; 10 (Apr. 1920):40–43.
4 Conf., 1920, pp. 323–37. For a good clipping file, see the Charles Deere Velie MSS, Minnesota Historical Society, St. Paul.
5 Quotations: "How Men and Money Are Building the Future for American Boys," *S* 4 (Apr. 15, 1917):15; "The Buck," *S* 8 (Feb. 26, 1920):3.
6 Peter A. Soderbergh, "The Great Book War: Edward Stratemeyer and the Boy Scouts of America," *New Jersey History* 91 (1973):244. As an example of such novels, see Archibald Lee Fletcher, *Boy Scouts in Alaska, or, The Camp on the Glacier* (Chicago, 1913).
7 Joseph B. Ames, "Under Boy Scout Colors," *St. Nicholas* 44 (1917):810–16. F. H. Cheley published a tale of YMCA camping, but the YMCA dime novel never caught on. *Buffalo Roost* (Cincinnati, 1913).
8 S. A. Moffat, "How Scout Masters Can Make Their Camps Most Successful," *S* 2 (June 15, 1914):1. On Boy Scout heroism, see also Will Oursler, *The Boy Scout Story* (Garden City, 1955), p. 211; Conf., 1918, pp. 1–2.
9 Harold Horne, "Why the Nation Supports the Boy Scouts," *Review of Reviews* 59 (1919):625 (quotation); Charles W. Eliot, *The Training of Boy Scouts* (n.p., n.d.).
10 Gary Dean Best, *The Politics of American Individualism: Herbert Hoover in Transition, 1918–1921* (Westport, Conn., 1975), pp. 93–94.

11 BSA, *OR, 1924*, pp. 395–96.

12 A. A. Hyde, "The Story of Cheney," *AY* 11 (1912):224.

13 Chicago Scouts did teach signaling at an Officers' Training Camp. Stuart P. Walsh, *Thirteen Years of Scout Adventure* (Seattle, 1923), p. 126.

14 "The Ranger," *S* 5 (Aug. 15, 1917):6; Lewis Atherton, *Main Street on the Middle Border* (Chicago, 1966), p. 327.

15 Harold P. Levy, *Building a Popular Movement: A Case Study of the Public Relations of the Boy Scouts of America* (New York, 1944), p. 26.

16 Quotation: BSA, *OR, 1928*, p. 275. For examples of such activities, see BSA, *AR* 7 (Mar. 1917):36–43; Ashley Piper, "A New Moral Force," *Outlook* 121 (1919):265. For views for and against marching, see Minneapolis *Journal*, Oct. 6, 1917; BSA, *Scout Masters' Bulletin No. 5* (New York, 1912).

17 BSA, *OR, 1928*, p. 274; BSA, *OR, 1922*, p. 193; SM Conf., 1917, p. 42.

18 "To Every Scout," *S* 6 (May 1, 1918):1–2.

19 News note in *S* 2 (Dec. 1, 1914):1; *Minneapolis Tribune*, Oct. 23, 1920. Robert M. Crunden has observed that Progressive reformers, coming out of a secularized Protestant tradition, "were seeking moral and psychological satisfactions, and the act of moral indignation, followed by public criticism and legislative activity was satisfying *in itself*, quite apart from whether it ever did any good." (Crunden, "Essay," in John D. Buenker, John C. Burnham, and Robert M. Crunden, *Progressivism* [Cambridge, Mass., 1977], p. 75.)

20 Photograph in BSA, *AR* 4 (Apr. 1914):29. On middle-class clubs' charities, see Robert S. Lynd and Helen Merrell Lynd, *Middletown* (New York, 1929), pp. 460–61.

21 James E. West, "Trained for Citizenship: The Boy Scout," *Review of Reviews* 54 (1916):647.

22 Levy, *Popular Movement*, p. 34. As an example of West's letters to university presidents, see James West to J. G. Shurman, Apr. 20, 1911, in "Committee on Standardization" (scrapbook, BSA, NHQ).

23 Illinois State Federation of Labor, *Report of the Committee on Schools: The Boy Scout Movement . . . Oct. 15–20, 1917* (New York: BSA, n.d.), p. 12.

24 Forbush to James West, Apr. 20, 1911, in "Committee on Standardization."

25 BSA, *AR* 7 (Mar. 1917):103, 104 (quotations); William D. Murray, Suggestions, May 2, 1911, in "Committee on Standardization"; James West, "Historical Statement to the National Training School" (typed MS, 1932, at BSA, NHQ).

26 Livingstone to James West, Feb. 8, 1917, Beard MSS.

27 West to Livingstone, Feb. 15, 1917, Beard MSS; Edward Roberts Moore, "What Is a Boy Scout?" *Commonweal* 21 (1935):278; BSA, *AR* 7 (Mar. 1917):103.

28 BSA, *AR* 7 (Mar. 1917):103.

29 Russell E. Richey and Donald G. Jones, eds., *American Civil Religion* (New York, 1974), pp. 15, 60; Henri Van Effenterre, *Histoire du Scoutisme* (Paris, 1961), p. 52.

30 Quotation: B. Burgoyne Chapman, "Impressions of Some Dangers and Problems in Y.M.C.A. Boys' Work," *AY* 2 (1913):12. For ministers' views,

see John L. Alexander, ed., *Sunday School and the Teens* (New York, 1913), p. 320.

31 C. Howard Hopkins, *History of the Y.M.C.A. in North America* (New York, 1951), pp. 515–19, 590–92.

32 W. Stephen Bush, "'The Making of a Scout,'" *S* 1 (Oct. 1, 1913):7.

33 "Scouting Endorsed by Boards of Education," *S* 7 (Feb. 20, 1919):8; U.S. Congress, House, Committee on the Judiciary, *Boy Scouts of America,* 64th Cong., 1st sess., 1916, H. Report, p. 1.

34 Secretary to James West, Feb. 17, 1917, under Reformation and Balance in "Correspondence About Policies" (scrapbook, BSA, NHQ) (quotation); Norman E. Richardson and Ormond E. Loomis, *The Boy Scout Movement Applied by the Church* (New York, 1915), pp. 147–48.

35 BSA, *AR* 7 (Mar. 1917):72–73. For examples of a film and a cartoon, see "Knights of the Square Table," *S* 5 (July 15, 1917):11; cartoon in *S* 7 (June 19, 1919):15.

36 On immigrants, see news note in *S* 2 (Aug. 1, 1914):1. On the uniform, see BSA, *The Official Hand Book for Boys,* rev. ed. (New York, 1914), p. 69.

37 West, "Historical Statement."

38 BSA, *Hand Book for Boys* (1914), pp. 70–71; "The Boy Scout Rally," *Outlook* 103 (1913):698; Conf., 1916, p. 70.

39 Conf., 1916, pp. 58–59; Conf., 1918, pp. 39–41; BSA, *AR* 10 (Apr. 1920):25.

40 *New York Times,* Sept. 24, 1910, p. 8 (quotation); Howard J. Hickok, "Honorable Mention Essay," *Journal of the Military Service Institution of the United States* 51 (1912):192–94.

41 Alexander, ed., *Sunday School,* p. 319; Winthrop Lane, "The Camp Fire Girls," *Survey* 28 (1912):320; Jeffrey P. Hantover, "Sex Role, Sexuality, and Social Status: The Early Years of the Boy Scouts of America" (Ph.D. diss., Chicago, 1976), p. 251.

42 BSA, *The Official Handbook for Boys* (Garden City, N.Y., 1911), proof copy, p. 180; final copy, p. 209; David Starr Jordan to Lee F. Hanmer, Oct. 13, 1910, in "Early History, 1910" (scrapbook, BSA, NHQ).

43 BSA, *Handbook for Scout Masters* (New York, 1914), p. 73.

44 Quotations: BSA, *AR* 3 (Feb. 1913):5; Rich quoted in *S* 2 (July 1, 1914):8.

45 "What War Is—Just One Battle," *Boys' Life* 4 (Nov. 1914):7.

46 "President Livingstone's Statement," *S* 2 (Nov. 1, 1914):1.

47 Theodore Roosevelt to James West, Nov. 31, 1915, vol. 94, ser. 2, TR MSS (quotation); Leonard Wood to James West, Nov. 9, 1914, box 276, ser. 1, TR MSS.

48 *Statistical Abstract of the United States, 1921* (Washington, 1922), pp. 124–25.

49 BSA, *AR* 6 (Feb. 1916):20.

50 C. Ward Crampton, "A Physical Training Not Confined to Hard Muscles," *S* 4 (May 15, 1916):3; *New York Times,* May 5, 1916, p. 10.

51 "National Education Association Endorses Policy of the Movement," *S* 3 (Nov. 1, 1915):1; "New York State Boys to Register December 3rd," *S* 6 (Nov. 28, 1918):3.

52 BSA, *AR* 6 (Feb. 1916):19.

53 James West to Briton Hadden, Aug. 3, 1927, Seton File, BSA, NHQ (quota-

tion); "Headquarters Correspondence on Questions of Policy," *S* 4 (June 15, 1916):6.

54 Richardson and Loomis, *Boy Scout Movement,* p. 23.

55 BSA, *Handbook for Boys* (1911), pp. 239–40, 338–39.

56 Quotations: BSA, *AR* 7 (Mar. 1917):104; Conf., 1918, p. 41.

57 E.g., BSA, *AR* 10 (Apr. 1920):102; Samuel D. Bogan, *No Larger Fields: The History of a Boy Scout Council, 1910–1963* (Hamden, Conn., 1966), p. 7; B. F. Skinner, *Particulars of My Life* (New York, 1976), p. 86.

58 BSA, *AR* 7 (Mar. 1917):24 (quotation); ibid., p. 12.

59 Quotation: E. T. Seton to Editorial Board, Apr. 21, 1911, Seton File, BSA, NHQ.

60 *New York Times,* Mar. 26, 1914, p. 1; Mar. 27, 1914, p. 10. There is a long correspondence dealing with Seton's situation in the Seton File, BSA, NHQ.

61 *New York Times,* Dec. 7, 1915, p. 4 (quotation); ibid., Dec. 6, 1915, p. 6.

62 Ibid., Dec. 11, 1915, p. 22; Dec. 13, 1915, p. 6; Theodore Roosevelt to James West, Dec. 14, 1915, in Seton File, BSA, NHQ.

63 E. M. Robinson to James West, Feb. 2, Dec. 14, 1915, both in Seton File, BSA, NHQ. Robinson's paraphrased remarks are from the first letter.

64 Exec. Board, Minutes, Feb. 18, Mar. 11, 1918, Beard MSS; "Shall We Have Hun Leadership?" *S* 6 (Aug. 1, 1918):8; clipping, Sault Ste. Marie newspaper [1918], at BSA, NHQ; Daniel Beard to H. O. Hunter, Apr. 4, 1917, Beard MSS.

65 "Get Ready for Victory Loan," *S* 7 (Mar. 20, 1919):1.

66 "Are We 100% Loyal?" *S* 6 (July 1, 1918):8; BSA, *AR* 9 (May 1919):34. In the second drive, 9.3 percent of all Boy Scouts sold ten or more bonds. (Statistical table in *S* 6 [Mar. 15, 1918]:15.)

67 William D. Murray, *The History of the Boy Scouts of America* (New York, 1937), pp. 101–36. On fears of neglect, see BSA, *AR* 8 (Apr. 1918):66.

68 "By the President of the United States: A Proclamation," *S* 7 (June 5, 1919): 6; Armstrong Perry, "Half a Million Scouts," *Independent* 97 (1919):269–70.

69 James West to E. T. Seton, Nov. 10, 1914, Seton File, BSA, NHQ.

70 YNA, *YB* (1919), p. 21. On the CCTP, see above, chapter 7.

71 Quotations: "Questions Inspired by 4,000 Strikes," *S* 8 (Jan. 29, 1920):3; BSA, *AR* 10 (Apr. 1920):29; "Neglected Boyhood Breeds Bolshevism," *S* 7 (Apr. 10, 1919):7. On Cincinnati, see "A Factor in Nation," *S* 6 (Dec. 12, 1918):3.

72 "The Chairman's Message," *S* 7 (June 12, 1919):4. For the Hartford paper's comments, see "Try a Little Scouting," *S* 7 (Dec. 18, 1919):3.

73 BSA, *AR* 11 (Aug. 1921):31; B. W. Folger to Daniel Beard, Mar. 30, 1920, Beard to M. L. Schiff, Apr. 22, 1920, James West to Frank Presbrey, May 21, 1920, and West's report to Exec. Board, Dec. 27, 1920, all in Beard MSS.

74 BSA, *AR* 10 (Apr. 1920):37–41; Murray, *History of the Boy Scouts,* p. 442.

75 BSA, *Handbook for Scoutmasters: A Manual of Leadership,* 2nd ed. (New York, 1920), p. 355 (quotation); BSA, *AR* 13 (Dec. 1923):15.

76 BSA, *Handbook for Scoutmasters* (New York, 1937), I:491, quoted in Edwin Nicholson, *Education and the Boy Scout Movement in America* (New York, 1940), p. 68. Note that the boys' interpretation constituted sufficient evidence.

77 Paul Wilkinson, "A Study of English Uniformed Youth Movements, 1883–

1935" (M.A. thesis, Univ. of Wales, [1968]), pp. 116–22; James West to Hubert S. Martin, June 7, 1921, in "Committee on Standardization."

78 BSA, *AR* 12 (May 1922):27 (quotation); Mortimer Schiff to Daniel Beard, Apr. 23, 1920; BSA, *OR, 1924,* pp. 347–51; BSA, *OR, 1928,* pp. 320–23.

79 S. N. Eisenstadt, "Archetypal Patterns of Youth," *Daedalus* 91 (1962):43.

80 Uncertain source for quotation in Charles E. Strickland, "Juliette Low, the Girl Scouts and the Role of American Women" (paper at Conference on the History of Women, St. Paul, Minn., Oct. 1977), p. 12. I am much indebted to Strickland's paper. On the planning for Camp Fire Girls, see Helen F. Buckler et al., *WO-HE-LO: The Story of Camp Fire Girls, 1910–1960* (New York, 1961), pp. 11, 27–33.

81 "Thousands Applaud Girl Scouts as They March through Back Bay," unidentified clipping in historical scrapbook, vol. 5, at Boy Scouts of Canada, National Council Library, Ottawa. See also Mary Rothschild, "Is a Girl to Guide? Some Comments on the Origins of Girl Scouting and the Boy Scout-Girl Scout Controversy" (paper at the Berkshire Conference, 1978), p. 8.

82 Strickland, "Juliette Low," pp. 9–11. The shift in publicity can be traced in the 1910–14 and 1919–21 volumes of the *Reader's Guide to Periodical Literature.*

83 Gladys Denny Shultz and Daisy Gordon Lawrence, *Lady from Savannah: The Life of Juliette Low* (Philadelphia, 1958), p. 299; Rothschild, "Is a Girl," pp. 9–13.

84 "The Resolutions," *S* 8 (Apr. 22, 1920): 21; BSA, *OR, 1924,* pp. 343–44.

85 BSA, *OR, 1922,* pp. 356–63; Rothschild, "Is a Girl," pp. 8–15.

86 Nicholson, *Boy Scout Movement,* pp. 73–75; Murray, *History of the Boy Scouts,* pp. 481–82.

87 "'Wet' and 'Dry,'" *S* 5 (July 1, 1917):9; "Concise Council Report," *S* 6 (Dec. 19, 1918):8; BSA, *AR* 7 (Mar. 1917):42–43, 104.

88 *New York Times,* Jan. 30, 1911, p. 3.

89 Daniel Beard to Colin H. Livingstone, Sept. 10, 1919, Beard MSS. For biographical sources, see above, chapter 9, notes 31 and 32. Besides West, eight of the twenty-six board members in 1920 have more than ten letters in the TR MSS. West, Jenks, Neill, and Goethals held offices or served as consultants under Roosevelt. In addition, TR's son Theodore and George W. Perkins, Jr., the son of his financial backer in 1912, were on the board.

90 R. W. DuBose, Jr., "A Discussion of the Boy Scout Movement in America During the 20's and 30's" (paper, Univ. of California, 1962, at BSA, NHQ), pp. 8, 14.

91 Cf. Peter G. Filene, "An Obituary for 'The Progressive Movement,'" *American Quarterly* 22 (1970):20–34.

92 Hopkins, *History of the Y.M.C.A.,* pp. 497–504; Exec. Committee, Minutes, 1919–1921, in NC MSS.

93 Emory S. Bogardus, *The City Boy and His Problems: A Survey of Boy Life in Los Angeles* (Los Angeles, 1926), p. 114 (quotations); George J. Fisher to John F. Moore, Apr. 24, 1923, in Boy Scouts-YMCA Box, YHL; BSA, *OR, 1922,* pp. 163–64; AWB, *RP,* pp. 39–40.

94 Douglass, *How Shall Country Youth Be Served?* p. 159 (quotations); ibid., pp. 129, 156, 160.

95 Conf., 1920, pp. 851–56.

96 Quotations: Carmine Tolatta, in "Scoutmaster's Round Table," *S* 10 (Jan. 1922):8; Levy, *Popular Movement,* pp. 78–79.

Chapter 11: Winning Institutional Support and Volunteer Leaders

1 E.g., "This Number," *WWB* 8 (1908):243; George J. Fisher, "The Physical Life of the Adolescent," in John L. Alexander, ed., *The Sunday School and the Teens* (New York, 1913), pp. 225–26.

2 Wilbur F. Crafts, "Safeguarding Adolescents Against Moral Perils," in Alexander, ed., *Sunday School,* p. 319 (quotation); Ann Douglas, *The Feminization of American Culture* (New York, 1977), p. 78 and passim.

3 Quotations: Letters from B. M. Lewis, J. Spencer Voorhees, and H. A. Jump, *WWB* 6 (1906):208, 210, 207.

4 A. B. Mackintire, "The Captains of Ten," *WWB* 8 (1908):2–29; Perry Edwards Powell, *The Knights of the Holy Grail and Boy Scouts: A Solution of the Boy Problem* (Cincinnati, 1911); review in *AY* 11 (1912):39.

5 William R. Hall, "Auxiliary Teen Age Organizations," in Alexander, ed., *Sunday School,* pp. 339–54; James Standishstreet, *Ritual, Rites and Ceremonies of the Junior Order of Messenger Boys* (Toledo, 1913); C. C. Robinson, "A Program of Boys' Work for a Local Church," *AY* 11 (1912):102–4.

6 William Byron Forbush and Frank Lincoln Masseck, *The Boys' Round Table: A Manual of the International Order of the Knights of King Arthur,* 6th ed. (Potsdam, N.Y., 1908), pp. 15–24, 75–95, 118–45; William Byron Forbush and Dascomb Forbush, *The Knights of King Arthur: The Merlin's Book of Advanced Work* (Oberlin, 1916), pp. 25, 51.

7 Quotations: William O. Brosard, "Some Experiences with Boys in a Lumber Town," *WWB* 7 (1907):128, 129, 132. See Forbush, *Merlin's Book,* p. 36, for Forbush's attitude.

8 William B. Forbush, *The New Round Table* (Boston, 1925), p. 12.

9 H. Paul Douglass, *1000 City Churches* (New York, 1926), pp. viii, 323; Edmund deS. Brunner et al., *American Agricultural Villages* (New York, 1927), pp. 200–1.

10 West to Exec. Board, Apr. 10, 1916, Beard MSS (quotation); BSA, *AR* 12 (Mar. 1922):140.

11 See Table 6; Jeffrey P. Hantover, "Sex Role, Sexuality, and Social Status: The Early Years of the Boy Scouts of America" (Ph.D. diss., Chicago, 1976), p. 221.

12 S. A. Moffat to John L. Alexander, Nov. 16, 1911, at BSA, NHQ (quotation); Conf., 1916, pp. 173–74; BSA, Annual Meeting 6 (1916), part 3 (transcript at BSA, NHQ).

13 H. Paul Douglass, *How Shall Country Youth Be Served? A Study of the "Rural" Work of Certain National Character-Building Agencies* (New York, 1926), p. 203n (quotation); ibid., p. 130; BSA, *AR* 9 (Mar. 1919), Table D; 12 (May 1922):142; 16 (Aug. 1926):157; R. W. Dubose, Jr., "A Discussion of the Boy Scout Movement in America During the 20's and 30's" (paper, Univ. of Calif., 1962, at BSA, NHQ).

14 Conf., 1920, pp. 556–61; BSA, *OR, 1924*, pp. 543–44; Norman E. Richardson and Ormond E. Loomis, *The Boy Scout Movement Applied by the Church* (New York, 1915), p. 16.

15 James West to Albert J. Watson, Oct. 9, 1916, under Religious Merit Badge in "Correspondence About Policies" (scrapbook at BSA, NHQ); Committee on Merit Badges, Awards, and Scout Requirements, Minutes, Feb. 23, 1916, at BSA, NHQ.

16 Conf., 1918, pp. 68–70; Douglass, *How Shall Country Youth Be Served?* p. 93. See above, chapter 9.

17 Norman E. Richardson to James West, Dec. 6, 1918, Beard MSS; Douglass, *How Shall Country Youth Be Served?* p. 209; BSA, *AR* 12 (May 1922):139; Walter S. Athearn et al., *The Religious Education of Protestants in an American Commonwealth* (New York, 1923), p. 236.

18 BSA, *AR* 10 (Apr. 1920):41–43; BSA, *OR, 1922*, pp. 163–64; Forrest B. Fordham, *Our Church Plans for Youth* (Philadelphia, 1953), p. 57.

19 Above, chapter 6; Edgar M. Robinson, "Some Bible Class Difficulties," *AB* 3 (1904):4–7; S. Wirt Wiley, *History of Y.M.C.A.-Church Relations in the United States* (New York, 1944), pp. 35, 111.

20 H. W. Gibson, "Church-Association Cooperation in Work with Boys," *AY* 17 (Mar. 1918):2; (Apr. 1918):15–16; Wiley, *Y.M.C.A.-Church Relations,* pp. 89–111.

21 ABS, *RC*, p. 19. See, e.g., Allan Hoben, *The Minister and the Boy: A Handbook for Churchmen Engaged in Boys' Work* (Chicago, 1912), pp. 168–69, on clergymen's views.

22 H. Parker Lansdale, "A Historical Study of YMCA Boys' Work in the United States, 1900–1925" (Ph.D. diss., Yale, 1956), pp. 174–92.

23 Douglass, *How Shall Country Youth Be Served?* pp. 90–91, 129–31, 162.

24 Richard J. Jensen, *The Winning of the Midwest: Social and Political Conflict, 1888–1896* (Chicago, 1971), p. 77n. For denominational finances, see U.S. Bureau of the Census, *Religious Bodies, 1916* (Washington, 1919), I:58, 72.

25 Catholics were overenumerated relative to Protestants. I have adjusted using estimates from H. K. Carroll, *The Religious Forces of the United States . . .* (New York, 1893), p. xxxv, and Jensen, *Winning of the Midwest,* p. 86.

26 C. J. Carver, "Here and There in Christian Vocations," *AY* 19 (June 1920):22. See also National Advisory Committee for Co-operation in Boys' Work, Minutes, May 10, 1917, and Jan. 7, 1918, in Canada, National Boys' Work Committee Box, YHL.

27 Jensen, *Winning of the Midwest,* pp. 58–88; Paul Kleppner, *The Cross of Culture: A Social Analysis of Midwestern Politics, 1850–1900* (New York, 1970), pp. 69–91.

28 *Statistical Abstract of the United States, 1910* (Washington, 1911), p. 110.

29 Sunday school enrollments for 1906, 1916, and 1926 in thousands: Northern Baptist—851; 1,029; 1,053; Southern Baptist—1,015; 1,666; 2,346; Congregational—638; 655; 597 (cf. 1895—678); white Methodist—3,968; 5,851; 5,897; Presbyterian—1,511; 1,947; 2,002; Episcopal—464; 489; 479. U.S. Bureau of the Census, *Religious Bodies: 1926* (Washington, 1930), I:276–87; *1916*, II:240. See Samuel W. Dike, "The Retarded Growth of the Sunday School," *Sunday School Times* 40 (1898):443–44, on 1890s patterns.

30 *Appleton's Annual Cyclopedia* (New York, 1895); Myron T. Hopper, "Young People's Work in Protestant Churches in the United States" (Ph.D. diss., Chicago, 1938), p. 62.

31 Douglass, *1000 City Churches,* pp. 123–25, 173–79; Lewis Atherton, *Main Street on the Middle Border* (Chicago, 1966), p. 260.

32 Quotations: Richardson and Loomis, *Boy Scout Movement,* p. 384; Franklin D. Elmer, "Community Co-ordination Through the Boy Scouts," *Religious Education* 8 (1913–14):490–91.

33 BSA, *OR, 1924,* p. 545 (quotation); BSA, Division of Relationships, "Fifty Year Highlights" (mimeographed, Dec. 1959), pp. 37–38.

34 *The Boy-Savers' Guide: Society Work for Lads in Their Teens* (New York, 1908), p. 40 (quotation); "Holding the Youth to the Church," *Ecclesiastical Review* 56 (1917):527–28.

35 Oscar Bélanger, *Le Scoutisme: Sa valeur éducative* (Montreal, 1935), pp. 1–7.

36 Quotations: D. J. Connor, "The Priest and Summer Camps for Boys," *Ecclesiastical Review* 48 (1913):541; "Catholic Boy Scouts," *Literary Digest* 45 (1912): 724. For an example of early Catholic concern, see Henry C. Thompson to James West, Oct. 5, 1911, Beard MSS.

37 E.g., Cardinal O'Connell to H. B. Converse, Jan. 17, 1917, Beard MSS.

38 "Catholics Heartily Endorse Scout Program," *S* 7 (Aug. 28, 1919):2. On the National Catholic War Council, see Aaron I. Abell, *American Catholicism and Social Action: A Search for Social Justice, 1865–1950* (Garden City, N.Y., 1960), pp. 192–225.

39 Hugh L. McMenamin, quoted in "Boy Scout Program a Common Platform for All Creeds," *S* 7 (Feb. 13, 1919):1; Kilian J. Hennrich, *Boy Guidance: A Course in Catholic Boy Leadership* (New York, 1925), p. xiv.

40 BSA, *OR, 1924,* p. 544.

41 "Two Archbishops Laud Principles of Boy Scout Organization," *Catholic Action* 19 (Aug. 1937):3–4; BSA, *AR* 27 (June 1937):140–41; 29 (July 1939): 161.

42 George Q. Morris, "Thirty-Five Years of Scouting in the Church," *Improvement Era* 51 (1948):313; BSA, Div. of Relationships, "Highlights," pp. 16, 22.

43 Wiley, *Y.M.C.A.-Church Relations,* pp. 65–67; Robinson, "Bible Class," pp. 9–10; C. C. Robinson, "A Plan for Work Among Factory Boys," *AB* 7 (1908): 239.

44 Edward A. Krug, *The Shaping of the American High School, 1880–1920* (Madison, Wis., 1969), p. 249 (quotation); Committee on the Reorganization of Secondary Schooling, *Cardinal Principles of Secondary Education,* Bureau of Education Bulletin, 1918, No. 25 (Washington, 1918), pp. 10–11.

45 Spencer R. Smith, "Report of the Committee on the Influence of Fraternities in Secondary Schools," *School Review* 13 (1905):3–10.

46 A. N. Cotton, "Schools," *AB* 8 (1909):263 (quotation); Douglass, *How Shall Country Youth Be Served?* p. 158.

47 Richard L. Flynn, "The Campaign of Friendship at Kansas City," *AY* 4 (1915): 73. Cf. Robert S. Lynd and Helen Merrell Lynd, *Middletown: A Study in Modern American Culture* (New York, 1929), p. 396.

48 David R. Porter, "Association Work in City High Schools," *AB* 7 (1908):160

(quotation); A. N. Cotton to E. M. Robinson [1915], in Boys' Work Reports, YHL.

49 Report of the Boys' Work Committee, Mar. 11, 1920, in Boys' Work Reports, YHL; Lansdale, "Historical Study," pp. 80–88.

50 C. O. Davis, "Training for Citizenship in North Central Association Second-ary Schools," *School Review* 28 (1920):275; BSA, *AR* 3 (Feb. 1913):14.

51 Ray O. Wyland, *Scouting in the Schools: A Study of the Relationships be-tween the Schools and the Boy Scouts of America* (New York, 1934), pp. 34–39; BSA, *AR* 12 (May 1922):139–40; Phillip R. Kunz, "Sponsorship and Or-ganizational Stability: Boy Scout Troops," *American Journal of Sociology* 74 (1968–69):673.

52 Exec. Conf., 1917, pp. 76–80; Emory S. Bogardus, *The City Boy and His Prob-lems: A Survey of Boy Life in Los Angeles* (Los Angeles, 1926), p. 114.

53 James West to Milton Fairchild, Apr. 18, 1916, Beard MSS; West to H. D. Shedd, Feb. 26, 1917, under School Troops in "Correspondence About Policies."

54 Leonard V. Koos, "Analysis of the General Literature on Extra-Curricular Activities," in National Society for the Study of Education, *Yearbook* 25 (1926), II:22; Joseph G. Masters, "General Survey of Practices," ibid., II:41.

55 Walter Kaulfers, "Practical Aspects of the School-Scout Program," *Educa-tion* 49 (1928):272–76.

56 "Teacher-Scoutmasters," *S* 8 (June 3, 1920):1. See American Federation of Labor, *Proceedings* 32 (1912):158, on the Chicago Teachers' Federation, and below, Table 6, on teachers as Scoutmasters.

57 Arthur B. Leach, "A Personal Letter to Superintendents," *WWB* 10 (Dec. 1910): 14–15; Exec. Conf., 1917, p. 75. On troubles with the YMCA, see above, chap-ter 9.

58 "Editorial Comment," *WWB* 17 (1917):253.

59 George J. Fisher to B. W. Folger, Aug. 19, 1920, Beard MSS.

60 Conf., 1920, p. 149; BSA, *AR* 12 (Mar. 1922):139.

61 BSA, *OR, 1924,* p. 113; BSA, *OR, 1928,* p. 186.

62 Quotations: SM Conf., 1917, p. 199; Fisher to Folger, Aug. 19, 1920; SM Conf., 1917, p. 201.

63 Terms adapted from Milton M. Gordon, "Assimilation in America: Theory and Reality," *Daedalus* 90 (Spring 1961):263–85.

64 Douglass, *How Shall Country Youth Be Served?* p. 29.

65 "Troops in Industries," *S* 9 (Sept. 1921):3; BSA, *AR* 12 (May 1922):139.

66 Owen Earle Pence, *The Y.M.C.A. and Social Need: A Study of Institutional Adaptation* (New York, 1939), p. 256; YNA, *YB* (1920), pp. 103, 196.

67 "Employment," *AB* 9 (1910):270 (quotation); Lansdale, "Historical Study," pp. 110–25.

68 Thomas C. Cochran, *Railroad Leaders, 1845–1890: The Business Mind in Ac-tion* (Cambridge, Mass., 1953), pp. 210–12; Pierce Williams and Frederick E. Croxton, *Corporation Contributions to Organized Community Welfare Ser-vices* (New York, 1930), pp. 48–70.

69 Roy Lubove, *The Professional Altruist: The Emergence of Social Work as a Career, 1880–1930* (New York, 1969), pp. 212–14; Williams and Croxton, *Corporation Contributions,* pp. 214–19.

70 Clyde Griffen, "The Progressive Ethos," in Stanley Coben and Lorman Ratner, eds., *The Development of an American Culture* (Englewood Cliffs, N.J., 1970), p. 148.

71 David Kennedy, *Over Here: The First World War and American Society* (New York, 1980), pp. 132-33 and passim.

72 BSA, *OR, 1922*, p. 85; BSA, *OR, 1928*, pp. 257-69.

73 Williams and Croxton, *Corporation Contributions*, p. 49 (quotation); ibid., p. 48; Pence, *Y.M.C.A.*, p. 182.

74 BSA, *OR, 1922*, p. 179; BSA, *OR, 1924*, pp. 390-91; BSA, *OR, 1928*, pp. 43, 341-47; Porter R. Lee et al., *Report of a Study of the Interrelation of the Work of National Social Agencies in Fourteen American Communities* (New York, n.d.), p. 55.

75 E.g., Lee, *Report*, p. 56; Lansdale, "Historical Study," pp. 342-44.

76 Conf., 1920, pp. 853-55; Douglass, *How Shall Country Youth Be Served?* p. 138.

77 Table 4, note (g); Kunz, "Sponsorship," pp. 668, 673; Raymond Moley, Jr., *The American Legion Story* (New York, 1966), p. 141.

78 Atherton, *Main Street*, p. 267 (quotation); Fred M. Hansen, "The Practical Program of a Village Commercial Club," *American City* 8 (1913):398.

79 Allen Eaton, *A Bibliography of Social Surveys* (New York, 1930), pp. 22-23, 255; "Rotary Backs Scouting Program," *S* 7 (Feb. 27, 1919):1-3; BSA, "Highlights," pp. 49-50.

80 C. Howard Hopkins, *History of the Y.M.C.A. in North America* (New York, 1951), pp. 601-4; Lynd, *Middletown*, p. 465; BSA, *OR, 1924*, pp. 389-99; interleaved sheet in Mark M. Jones, *Report on a Survey of the Boy Scouts of America* (New York, 1927).

81 Quotations: AWB, *RP*, pp. 31, 34. See also Pence, *Y.M.C.A.*, p. 257.

82 "Lawlessness and the Training of the Young," *Century* 81 (1911):472-73; Allan Richard Whitmore, "Beard, Boys and Buckskins: Daniel Carter Beard and the Preservation of the American Pioneer Tradition" (Ph.D. diss., Northwestern, 1970), pp. 226, 258.

83 Ernest Thompson Seton, *Boy Scouts of America: A Handbook of Woodcraft, Scouting, and Life-Craft* (New York, 1910), pp. 32-36; *New York Times*, Dec. 8, 1912, p. 20. On the IWW, see the *Times*, Mar. 10, 1912, p. 1.

84 American Federation of Labor, *Proceedings* 32 (1912):159; John Price Jones to James West, Oct. 10, 1911, Beard MSS.

85 American Federation of Labor, *Proceedings* 32 (1912):160-61.

86 Executive Board, Minutes, Oct. 8, 1917, Beard MSS; "In Time of Strike—*Do Not Rush In!*" *S* 7 (June 19, 1919):5.

87 N. W. Webster in BSA, *OR, 1922*, p. 211.

88 Ibid., pp. 84, 210-14; "Labor and Scouting" (typed MS, c. 1965), at BSA, NHQ.

89 Quotations: E. M. Robinson, "Methods of Grouping Boys," *AB* 1 (1902): 199; ABS, *RC*, p. 24.

90 "Do the Boy Scouts Compete with the Association?" *AY* 15 (Dec. 1916):1-2.

91 Eugene C. Foster, "Announcement Relative to the Forthcoming Program of Christian Citizenship Training" (1919), at YHL (quotation); F. A. Crosby, "The

Relation of Summer Activities to the Year Round Work With Boys," *AB* 10 (1911):250.

92 "Report of Minnesota Research Commission, 1924" (typed MS in A.B.W.S. General, 1903–1929 Box, at YHL); Douglass, *How Shall Country Youth Be Served?* pp. 93–103.

93 BSA, *AR* 3 (Feb. 1913):19; 12 (May 1922):141–42; U.S. Bureau of the Census, *Census of Population: 1950,* vol. II, *Characteristics of the Population,* pt. 1, pp. 1–96. The census lacked such statistics before 1940.

94 The BSA did not report statistics for 1920. *HS,* p. 139. Service workers made up 4 percent of the male labor force; 1 percent is the rounding error.

95 In Chicago, clerks made up almost three quarters of this category. (Hantover, "Sex Role," p. 223.)

96 George S. Counts, "The Social Status of Occupations: A Problem in Vocational Guidance," *School Review* 33 (1925):16–27. On small-town ministers, see Atherton, *Main Street,* p. 170.

97 Conf., 1916, pp. 123–138, 247; Exec. Conf., 1917, pp. 104–6; BSA, *OR, 1922,* p. 146.

98 Quotations: BSA, *AR* 6 (Feb. 1916):47; Richardson and Loomis, *Boy Scout Movement,* pp. 155–56.

99 Hantover, "Sex Role," p. 246 (quotation); BSA, *OR, 1924,* p. 93.

100 Other motives mentioned at least twenty times were service (34), helping the church (29), building character (28), helping boys through adolescence (23), preoccupation (23), and moral (24), physical (21), and mental (20) development of boys. Recomputed from Hantover, "Sex Role," pp. 244–45.

101 A. B. Cohn, "Why Some Scoutmasters Lose Out," *S* 7 (Feb. 13, 1919):7.

102 "Guns That 'Kick,'" *S* 4 (Sept. 1, 1916):4; "Embarrassed by Volunteers," *S* 6 (Dec. 19, 1918):2; BSA, *AR* 11 (Aug. 1921):8.

103 Quotations: Cohn, "Scoutmasters," p. 7; BSA, *OR, 1922,* pp. 142–43.

104 BSA, *AR* 12 (May 1922):141. See also BSA, *AR* 3 (Feb. 1913):20.

105 Quotations: E. J. B. Gorman, in "College Students as Scout Leaders," *S* 3 (Sept. 1, 1915):2; extract from Scoutmasters' applications in *S* 7 (June 19, 1919): 9. For other sources, see Conf., 1916, pp. 121–22; Hantover, "Sex Role," pp. 236–41.

106 Athearn, *Religious Education,* pp. 359–65.

107 Quotations: Robert G. McPhail, in "College Students as Scout Leaders," p. 2; extract from Scoutmasters' applications, *S* 7 (June 19, 1919):8. See also "First Aid for Recruiters," *S* 5 (July 15, 1917):10.

108 See above, chapter 10, notes 10, 11; Paul Boyer, *Urban Masses and Moral Order in America, 1820–1920* (Cambridge, Mass., 1978), pp. 60–61.

109 Conf., 1916, p. 127 (quotation); ibid., pp. 123–26; William D. Murray, *History of the Boy Scouts of America* (New York, 1937), pp. 212–14.

110 "What There's In It For the Scoutmaster," *Scout Leader* 1 (Nov. 1923):2.

Chapter 12: Recruiting a "Fine Lot of Lads"

1 E.g., Robert S. Lynd and Helen Merrell Lynd, *Middletown: A Study in Modern American Culture* (New York, 1929), p. 308; Murray Hausknecht, "The

Blue-Collar Joiner," in Arthur B. Shostak and William Gomberg, eds., *Blue-Collar World: Studies of the American Worker* (Englewood Cliffs, N.J., 1964), pp. 208–11.

2 William D. Murray, *As He Journeyed: The Autobiography of William D. Murray* (New York, 1929), pp. 336–37; Ernest Thompson Seton, *Boy Scouts of America: A Handbook of Woodcraft, Scouting, and Life-Craft* (New York, 1910), p. 57.

3 Exec. Board, Minutes, Nov. 22, 1910; Dec. 21, 1914; May 21, 1918; BSA, *OR, 1922,* p. 145; Rosa Lowe to James West, May 18, 1918, Beard MSS.

4 Bolton Smith to Rosa Lowe, May 8, 1918, Beard MSS.

5 James West to George Fisher, Apr. 25, 1923, under Colored Question in "Correspondence About Policies" (scrapbook, BSA, NHQ).

6 Interview with Stanley Harris, Mar. 12, 1967 (transcript at BSA, HNQ).

7 *Our Boys* (New Haven), Annual No. 2 (1889), p. 7; *Darkest Chicago and Her Waifs,* Jan. 1910, p. 20, CBC MSS; "Suggestions to Scout Masters," *S* 1 (Oct. 15, 1913):6; BSA, "Annual Meeting" 6 (1916), pt. 4 (transcript, BSA, NHQ).

8 BSA, "Annual Meeting" 6 (1916), pt. 5.

9 BSA, Division of Relationships, "Fifty Year Highlights" (mimeographed, Dec. 1959), p. 69; Henry P. Fairchild, *Conduct Habits of Boy Scouts* (New York, 1931), p. 35.

10 R. M. Wheat, "The Scout Movement and the Colored Boy," on A. W. Anthony to Daniel Beard, Mar. 26, 1924, Beard MSS; BSA, *OR, 1928,* pp. 324–28.

11 Harris interview; Stanley A. Harris, "Negro Youth and Scouting: A Character Education Program," *Journal of Negro Education* 9 (1940):372.

12 Jesse E. Moorland, "The Y.M.C.A. Among Negroes," *Journal of Negro History* 9 (1924):135; George R. Arthur, *Life on the Negro Frontier* (New York, 1934), pp. 23–46.

13 J. E. Moorland, "For the Colored Boys of the Nation," *AY* 15 (May 1916):6; idem, "Work for Negro Boys," Apr. 8, 1920, in Boys' Work Reports, YHL; YNA, *YB* (1920), p. 103.

14 E. M. Robinson to John R. Mott, Oct. 22, 1917, in Robinson to Mott Box, YHL.

15 Robinson to Fletcher S. Brockman, May 6, 1918, in Robinson to Mott Box.

16 AWB, *RP,* p. 28 (quotation); "Living Conditions," *AB* 9 (1910):279.

17 Exec. Board, Minutes, Oct. 5, 1914, Beard MSS.

18 BSA, *OR, 1924,* pp. 542–43; "Extracting the Hyphen," *S* 10 (July 1922):4. In Jerome Weidman, *Fourth Street East: A Novel of How It Was* (New York, 1971), p. 182, the hero's mother thought the BSA would turn boys into "pogromniks."

19 M. P. Willett to Lorillard Spencer, Jr., Feb. 22, 1911, in Alphabetical File, BSA, NHQ; above, chapter 1; Leonard Covello, "The Influence of Southern Italian Family Mores upon the School Situation in America," in Francesco Cordasco and Eugene Bucchioni, eds., *The Italians* (Clifton, N.J., 1974), pp. 543–63.

20 Report of Scout Troop 24, July 15, 1924, Box 6, Chicago Commons MSS, Chicago Historical Society. On Worcester, see BSA, "Annual Meeting" 5 (1915, transcript at BSA, NHQ), p. 24.

21 Quotations: BSA, *OR, 1924,* p. 191; BSA, "Annual Meeting" 5 (1915), p. 57; BSA, *OR, 1928,* p. 464. On preindustrial habits, see Herbert G. Gutman, "Work, Culture, and Society in Industrializing America, 1815-1919," *American Historical Review* 78 (1973):531-87. Boys' workers often played ethnic favorites, admiring Jewish boys, for instance. E.g., Winifred Buck, *Boys' Self-Governing Clubs* (New York, 1903), pp. 182-83.

22 Henry Pratt Fairchild, *The Melting Pot Mistake* (New York, 1926). See above, chapter 9, note 17.

23 Fred H. Rindge, Jr., "Can the Young Men's Christian Association Help the Church to Reach the Unreached Boy?" *AB* 10 (1911):104-5.

24 Quotations: "A Valuable Statement on Boys' Work," *Association Men* 25 (1900):391; "Studies in Methods of Boys' Work" (typed MS, c. 1925), in NC MSS.

25 E.g., editorial notes, *AB* 5 (1906):109; 8 (1909):28; ABS, *RC,* pp. 30-31.

26 Frederic Milton Thrasher, "The Boy Scout Movement as a Socializing Agency" (M.A. thesis, Chicago, 1918), pp. 40-41.

27 Quotations: Norman E. Richardson and Ormond E. Loomis, *The Boy Scout Movement Applied by the Church* (New York, 1915), pp. 147, 42. See also SM Conf., 1917, p. 49.

28 Quotations: Exec. Conf., 1917, p. 79; Frederic M. Thrasher, "The Boys' Club and Juvenile Delinquency," *American Journal of Sociology* 42 (July 1936):74.

29 "A Good Suggestion," *S* 1 (Feb. 1, 1914):4 (quotation); Lewis W. Dunn, "What the State Boys' Conference Means to the Churches," *AB* 10 (1911):113-17.

30 A. J. Taylor, "Man with Man in Scouting," *Southern Workman* 64 (1935):109.

31 Buck, *Self-Governing Clubs,* p. 175; SM Conf., 1917, pp. 74-79, 193-94.

32 ABS, *RC,* p. 53 (quotation); "Classes of Working Boys," *AB* 9 (1910):254-55.

33 "Executive Board Playing Santa Claus," *S* 8 (Jan. 1, 1920):4 (quotation); BSA, *Official Hand Book for Boys,* rev. ed. (New York, 1914), end papers; Mark M. Jones, *Report of a Survey of the Boy Scouts of America* (New York, 1927), pp. 49-51.

34 "The Problem of Troop Finances," *S* 2 (Jan. 1, 1915):7; SM Conf., 1917, pp. 187-91; Exec. Board, Minutes, Jan. 24, 1916, Beard MSS; BSA, *AR* 7 (Mar. 1917):127.

35 "Applying the Tests," *S* 6 (Oct. 3, 1918):8 (quotation); Conf., 1919, p. 39.

36 See James West, speech to International Boys' Work Conference, Dec. 2, 1924, in West File, BSA, NHQ; and BSA, *Hand Book for Boys* (1914), p. 69, on the uniform as democratic. On McDonald, see Conf., 1916, p. 247.

37 Daniel Beard to George D. Pratt, Apr. 24, 1912, Beard MSS.

38 "New Light on the Scouts," *WWB* 17 (1917):258-59.

39 "Editorial Comment," *WWB* 17 (1917):252-53 (quotation); SM Conf., 1917, p. 174.

40 Jeffrey P. Hantover, "Sex Role, Sexuality, and Social Status: The Early Years of the Boy Scouts of America" (Ph.D. diss., Chicago, 1976), pp. 170, 182. In Minneapolis, upper white-collar men were overrepresented as fathers of Boy Scouts a bit more than 3:2 compared to the city's male labor force; lower white-collar and skilled blue-collar workers were each overrepresented about 6:5; semiskilled workers were underrepresented 3:5; and unskilled workers were underrepresented 1:2 or a bit more. ("Survey Shows Value of Boy Scout

Work," clipping from unidentified newspaper, c. Aug. 1918, in vol. 2, Charles Deere Velie MSS, Minnesota Historical Society, St. Paul; U.S. Bureau of the Census, *Fourteenth Census of the United States . . . 1920. Population* [Washington, 1921], I:67, 112, ibid. [Washington, 1923], IV:168-85.) The local BSA executive, Ludvig S. Dale, reported fathers' occupations for Boy Scouts in Hennepin County, whereas the census reported occupations for males in Minneapolis, but the city accounted for 92 percent of the county's population. More troublesome were Dale's vague occupational labels. His desire to show maximum social diversity, plus my guesswork, probably produced lower differences between the top and bottom classes than really existed. My occupational classification followed Stephan Thernstrom, *The Other Bostonians: Poverty and Progress in the American Metropolis, 1880-1970* (Cambridge, Mass., 1973), pp. 290-92. On wartime income trends, see above, chapter 1, note 20.

41　Walter S. Athearn et al., *The Religious Education of Protestants in an American Commonwealth* (New York, 1923), pp. 224-32; Ray O. Wyland, *Scouting in the Schools: A Study of the Relationships between the Schools and the Boy Scouts of America* (New York, 1934), pp. 106-25.

42　Fairchild, *Conduct Habits,* p. 36. The samples were not strictly random.

43　Wyland, *Scouting,* pp. 113, 132-33; Jerome Davis, "Effects of Occupations and Racial Background on the Boy Scouts of Connecticut," *Sociology and Social Research* 18 (1933):43-51.

44　Wyland, *Scouting,* p. 72n.; William D. Murray, *History of the Boy Scouts of America* (New York, 1937), p. 390.

45　*Fourteenth Census . . . Population, 1920* (Washington, 1922), II:162; *Statistical Abstract of the United States, 1910* (Washington, 1911), p. 102; ibid., *1922* (Washington, 1923), p. 105; George Sylvester Counts, *The Selective Character of American Secondary Education* (Chicago, 1922).

46　H. Paul Douglass, *The Springfield Church Survey* (New York, 1926), p. 337. In New Haven, Y boys were 22 percent Catholic, 9 percent Jewish, and 23 percent foreign—low figures for an eastern city. ("Correspondence," *AY* 4 [1915]:86.)

47　E.g., C. C. Robinson, "Among Employed Boys," *AY* 16 (Feb. 1917):10; Report of Boys' Work Committee, June 12, 1919, in Boys' Work Reports, YHL.

48　"A Comparison of Membership Groups," *AY* 16 (Oct. 1917):13.

49　*Fourteenth Census . . . Population,* IV:376. On census undercounting, see Walter I. Trattner, *Crusade for the Children: A History of the National Child Labor Committee and Child Labor Reform in America* (Chicago, 1970), p. 241; David Stern et al., "How Children Used to Work," *Law and Contemporary Problems* 39 (Summer 1975):99-100.

50　E.g., Emmett Dedmon, *Great Enterprises: 100 Years of the YMCA of Metropolitan Chicago* (New York, 1957), pp. 170-73.

51　"Employment," *AB* 9 (1910):266-68; AWB, *RP,* p. 31.

52　"Editorial Comment," *WWB* 15 (1915):363.

53　"Classes of Working Boys," *AB* 9 (1910):254-56.

54　BSA, *AR* 12 (May 1922):139; U.S. Bureau of Education, *Biennial Survey of Education, 1918-1920* (Washington, 1923), pp. 505, 538; Wyland, *Scouting,* pp. 112-14; SM Conf., 1917, pp. 17, 294.

55 Chicago Boys' Club, *Annual Report* 10 (Jan. 1912):17, in CBC MSS.

56 H. Paul Douglass, *1000 City Churches: Phases of Adaptation to Urban Environment* (New York, 1926), pp. 132–38, 276; Thernstrom, *Other Bostonians,* p. 40; Alan Booth and Nicholas Babchuk, "Personal Influence Networks and Voluntary Association Affiliation," *Sociological Inquiry* 39 (1969):179–88.

57 Quotations: Roger S. Peacock, *Pioneer of Boyhood: The Story of Sir William A. Smith, Founder of the Boys' Brigade* (Glasgow, 1954), p. 57; Leslie Paul, *Angry Young Man* (London [1951]), p. 51. See also John R. Gillis, "The Evolution of Juvenile Delinquency in England, 1890–1914," *Past and Present* no. 67 (May 1975):116–25.

58 Stuart P. Walsh, *Thirteen Years of Scout Adventure* (Seattle, 1923), p. 14 (quotation); BSA, Research Service, *Scouting in Less-Chance Areas* (New York, 1939), p. 7.

59 "The Ranger," *S* 6 (Sept. 1, 1918):6.

60 "The Ranger," *S* 7 (Jan. 2, 1919):4.

61 Quotations: Emory S. Bogardus, *The City Boy and His Problems: A Survey of Boy Life in Los Angeles* (Los Angeles, 1926), p. 118; Joseph F. Kett, *Rites of Passage: Adolescence in America, 1790 to the Present* (New York, 1977), p. 227.

62 Philip D. Fagans, "The Greatest Need of the Employed Boy," *AB* 9 (1910):237; C. C. Robinson, "The Democratic Spirit in Boys' Work," *AB* 8 (1909):60.

63 "Existing Agencies," *AB* 9 (1910):296.

64 Quotation: H. T. Confer, "The Adolescent Boy and the YMCA" (Master's thesis, Springfield College, n.d.), quoted in H. Parker Lansdale, "A Historical Study of YMCA Boys' Work in the United States, 1900–1925" (Ph.D. diss., Yale, 1956), p. 57. For other sources, see C. C. Robinson, "The Approach to the Problem of the Wage-Earning Boy," *AB* 8 (1909):279; idem, "A Plan for Work Among Factory Boys," *AB* 7 (1908):237.

65 M. P. Willett to Lorillard Spencer, Jr., Feb. 22, 1911, in Alphabetical File, BSA, NHQ.

66 Scoutmaster Leonard, in SM Conf., 1917, p. 300 (quotation); James West in *Report of Conference: Boy Scouts of America and the Public Schools at the 49th Annual Meeting of the Department of Superintendence of the National Education Association* (n.p., n.d.), p. 15; SM Conf., 1917, pp. 171, 247, 299–301. William A. Westley and Frederick Elkin, in "The Protective Environment and Adolescent Socialization," *Social Forces* 35 (1957):246n., suggest that working-class boys are less likely than middle-class boys to discuss their doings with parents. To such boys, the character builders' supervision may have seemed intrusive compared to boys' club methods.

67 Boys' Club of the City of New York, *Annual Report* (1904), p. 20.

68 E.g., Margaret F. Byington, *Homestead: The Households of a Mill Town* (Pittsburgh, 1974), pp. 116–17.

69 Robert Coles, "The Politics of Middle-Class Children," *New York Review* 22 (Mar. 6, 1975):13–16. On fears about immigrant youth, see Burdett G. Lewis, "Boys' and Girls' Organizations," in Bureau of Education, *Proceedings: Americanization Conference . . . May 12–15, 1919* (Washington, 1919), p. 385.

70 See above, chapter 1, note 54; Lynd, *Middletown,* pp. 142–44.

71 Wyland, *Scouting,* pp. 116–41.

72 Statistics computed from BSA, *AR* 12 (May 1922):8, 110–37; *HS,* p. 14. Data for 1920 were unavailable.

73 BSA, *AR* 5 (Feb. 1915):68; BSA, "Annual Meeting" 6 (1916), pt. 4; Samuel P. Hays, "The Politics of Reform in Municipal Government in the Progressive Era," *Pacific Northwest Quarterly* 55 (1964):157–69.

74 Kett, *Rites of Passage,* p. 252, makes similar points. A computerized analysis of all U.S. cities with 25,000 or more inhabitants in 1920 shows a moderate inverse correlation between city size and the ratios of Boy Scouts or YMCA juniors to boys aged 10–14 (r = −.43 to −.48), but much lower positive associations with the percentage of boys native-born or Protestant. Size itself mattered. Since the Y and Boy Scouts recruited only a minority of the boys in any town, these results do *not* mean that they enlisted a lot of Catholics and foreign-born boys.

75 SM Conf., 1917, pp. 15–16. See above, chapter 2, note 45; chapter 4, note 28. On continuing class divisions, see below, Epilogue.

76 The percentage of troops in towns from 1,000 to 5,000 rose from 15.6 in 1916 to 19.2 in 1921. (BSA, *AR* 7 [Mar. 1917]:45; 12 [May 1922]:8.)

77 See above, chapter 2; Edmund de S. Brunner et al., *American Agricultural Villages* (New York, 1927), pp. 158–59, 183–85, 300–302.

78 H. Paul Douglass, *How Shall Country Youth Be Served? A Study of the "Rural" Work of Some National Character-Building Agencies* (New York, 1926), pp. 51–56, 189; H. Paul Douglass, *The Suburban Trend* (New York, 1925), pp. 177–78.

79 Computed from YNA, *YB* (1920), pp. 188–253; U.S. Bureau of the Census, *Sixteenth Census . . . 1940: Population* (Washington, 1942), I:32–49.

80 I. B. Rhodes et al., *The Problem of the Small City Young Men's Christian Association* (n.p., 1921), p. 9; "A Significant Quotation," *AY* 4 (1915):279.

81 Owen Earle Pence, *The Y.M.C.A. and Social Need: A Study of Institutional Adaptation* (New York, 1939), p. 296.

82 ABS, *RC,* p. 38; Douglass, *How Shall Country Youth Be Served?* p. 240.

83 Quotation: "The Association and the Country Boy," *AB* 6 (1907):188. On views of country boys, see above, chapter 2.

84 "Boys' and Girls' Club Work in the United States," *Bulletin of the Pan American Union* 50 (1920):303; Franklin M. Reck, *The 4-H Story: A History of 4-H Club Work* (Chicago, 1951), pp. 96–125; Brunner, *Villages,* p. 150. The fourfold approach echoed the YMCA. Cf. W. H. Kendrick, *The Four-H Trail* (Boston [1926]).

85 Garland A. Bricker et al., *Solving the Country Church Problem* (Cincinnati, 1913), pp. 263–77; YNA, *YB* (1921), pp. 278–93.

86 Willett M. Hays to James West, Apr. 12, 1911, and Jeremiah Jenks to West, Apr. 20, 1911, both in "Committee on Standardization" (scrapbook, BSA, NHQ); BSA, *The Official Handbook for Boys* (Garden City, N.Y., 1911), pp. 24–40.

87 BSA, *OR, 1922,* pp. 401–2; BSA, *OR, 1924,* p. 418.

88 William M. Hall, "Nostalgic Journey," *Scout Memorabilia* 4:1 (1969):3–5; BSA, *OR, 1924,* pp. 409–16.

89 O. H. Benson, "A Good Use for Free Time," *Journal of Education* 110 (1929): 159 (quotation); Murray, *History of the Boy Scouts of America*, p. 368; BSA, *OR, 1928*, pp. 402–23.

90 BSA, *AR* 16 (Aug. 1926):164. Cf. BSA, *OR, 1928*, p. 409.

91 Quotations: BSA, *OR, 1924*, 212, 412. For further discussion, see ibid., pp. 209–212.

92 Brunner, *Villages*, p. 203 (quotation); ibid., pp. 185, 302.

93 BSA, *OR, 1924*, p. 210; William L. Bowers, *The Country Life Movement in America, 1900–1920* (Port Washington, N.Y., 1974), pp. 102–27; Brunner, *Villages*, pp. 97–100.

94 "Helpful Hints," *S* 3 (Dec. 1, 1915):11; Brunner, *Villages*, p. 215.

95 Douglass, *How Shall Country Youth Be Served?* p. 78.

96 Kett, *Rites of Passage*, p. 245.

Part V
Chapter 13: Camping: An Organized Setting for the New Boyhood

1 William H. H. Murray, *Adventures in the Wilderness* (Boston, 1869), p. 24, quoted in Roderick Nash, *Wilderness and the American Mind* (New Haven, 1967), p. 116.

2 Quotations: Charles K. Taylor, "When Boys Go Camping," *Independent* 90 (Apr. 7, 1917):68; Jacob A. Riis, *The Children of the Poor* (New York, 1892), pp. 160–61. For Muir's prescription, see John Muir, "The Wild Parks and Forest Reservations of the West," *Atlantic* 81 (Jan. 1898):15. On boys' vigor and appetites, see "Boys' Branch, Newburgh, N.Y., in Camp," *Watchman* 11 (1885):177; "Camp Conference," *WWB* 3 (1903):158.

3 News note in *BC* 1 (June 3, 1882), unpaged; "Work for Boys," *Watchman* 11 (1885):152; report by George H. Robinson, *YNYP* 24 (1890):67.

4 E.g., "Junior Department," *Watchman* 12 (1886):167.

5 H. S. Ninde et al., eds., *A Hand-Book of the History, Organization, and Methods of Work of Young Men's Christian Associations* (New York, 1892), II:364 (quotation); Edgar M. Robinson, *The Early Years: The Beginning of Work with Boys in the Y.M.C.A.* (New York, 1950), pp. 76–86.

6 Riis, *Children*, pp. 153–73; James Beaumont Whipple, "Cleveland in Conflict: A Study in Urban Adolescence, 1876–1900" (Ph.D. diss., Western Reserve, 1951), p. 302; Stanley M. Ulanoff, "The Origin and Development of Organized Camping in the United States, 1861–1961" (Ph.D. diss., New York Univ., 1968), p. 31.

7 Carlos Edgar Ward, *Organized Camping and Progressive Education* [Nashville, 1935], p. 30; Boys' Club of the City of New York, *Annual Report* (1904), pp. 16–20.

8 E. T. Seton, "The Birch-Bark Roll Camp," *St. Nicholas* 39 (1912):269.

9 H. W. Gibson, *The History of Organized Camping* (n.p., n.d., reprinted from *Camping Magazine* 8 [1936]), chapters 1, 2, 4; Porter Sargent, *A Handbook of Summer Camps*, 10th ed. (Boston, 1933), pp. 100–115; Elizabeth Balch, "The Boys' Paradise: A Summer Visitor's Account of Camp Chocorua," *St.*

Nicholas 13 (1886):604–7; C. Hanford Henderson, "The Day's Program," *WWB* 3 (1903):164–83.

10 "Third Annual International Encampment, Knights of the Holy Grail . . . Aug. 18–28, 1908" (flyer at YHL); "Camp Nutt," *American Brigadier* 3 (1909): 304.

11 E.g., "Camp Adams," *BBB* 1 (July 15, 1892):1–9; "Camp of the First Sheboygan," *Knapsack* 3 (Nov. 1894), unpaged; Gibson, *Camping,* chapters 1, 4.

12 E.g., "Camp Adams," p. 8; Elias G. Brown, "The Sanitary Care of a Boys' Camp, *AB* 1 (1902):48–51, 110–21.

13 Minott A. Osborn, ed., *Camp Dudley: The Story of the First Fifty Years* (New York, 1934), p. 20; Gibson, *Camping,* chapter 6.

14 Quotations: "Camp Adams," p. 1; Edgar M. Robinson, "Character Making in Boys' Camps," in *The Materials of Religious Education* (Chicago, 1907), p. 214.

15 George Robley Howe, "How to Interest Boys in Nature Study," *AB* 5 (1906): 70–76. See also Peter J. Schmitt, *Back to Nature: The Arcadian Myth in Urban America* (New York, 1969), pp. xvii, 86–95.

16 Quotations: "Boys' Branch, Newburgh," p. 177; Peter Blos, *On Adolescence: A Psychoanalytic Interpretation* (New York, 1962), p. 61.

17 Quotations: Jay Mechling, "The Magic of the Boy Scout Campfire," *Journal of American Folklore* 93 (Jan.–Mar. 1980):40; Edgar M. Robinson, "Association Boys' Camps," *AB* 1 (1902):87. My own Boy Scout experience in the 1950s was closer to the 1970s pattern reported by Mechling than to the standards Robinson favored.

18 George E. Johnson, *Education through Recreation* (Cleveland, 1916), pp. 63–71.

19 Untitled note in *BC* 1 (June, 24, 1882), unpaged.

20 BSA, *Handbook for Scoutmasters,* 2nd ed. (New York, 1920), pp. 385–86.

21 Gibson, *Camping,* chapters 4, 5.

22 Matthew Crackel, in Billy Burger, *A Million Miles in New York State* (New York, 1946), p. 40 (quotation); YNA, *YB* (1901), p. 259; (1916), pp. 254–95. On fees, see editorial note, *AB* 3 (1904):133–34; Camp Dudley, Prospectus, 1911, at YHL.

23 "Boys' Branch, Newburgh," p. 177 (quotation); news notes in *Men* 22 (1896): 363–64.

24 Robinson, "Association Boys' Camps," p. 101 (quotation); Osborn, *Camp Dudley,* pp. 31–33; Edgar M. Robinson, "What Some Prominent Men Think About the Boys' Camp," *AB* 2 (1903):66–75.

25 Harvey Smith and Irving Cobleigh, "Some Interesting Things About Camp Tuxis," *AB* (1904):121.

26 Osborn, *Camp Dudley,* pp. 58, 128–29; E. M. Robinson to John R. Mott, July 3, 1915, in Robinson to Mott Box, YHL; H. Parker Lansdale, "A Historical Study of YMCA Boys' Work in the United States, 1900–1925" (Ph.D. diss., Yale, 1956), pp. 212–13.

27 H. W. Gibson, "Camping as a Character Maker," *AY* 4 (1915):115 (quotation); Osborn, *Camp Dudley,* pp. 121–27; "When Cleveland Boys Go Camping," *AY* 19 (June 1920):37.

28 Osborn, *Camp Dudley,* p. 148; Robinson, "Association Boys' Camps," pp. 71, 82; M. D. Crackel, "Self-Operative Discipline in Camp," *AB* 8 (1909): 119–21.

29 H. W. Gibson, "Camps Durrell and Becket," *AB* 5 (1906):118–21; Osborn, *Camp Dudley,* pp. 28–32, 72–76, 102; entire issue on camping, *AY* 19 (Apr. 1920).

30 Quotations: Edgar M. Robinson, "The Experimental Woodcraft Camp," *AB* 9 (1910):116; "Camping on Champlain" (prospectus for Camp Dudley, 1912), at YHL. See also E. Clark Worman, *History of the Brooklyn and Queens Young Men's Christian Association, 1853–1949* (New York, 1952), pp. 101–7.

31 Colin Livingstone to James West, Oct. 13, 1924, in Seton File, BSA, NHQ (quotation); Resolutions for the National Council Meeting [early 1913], ibid.; Committee on Badges, Awards, and Scout Requirements, Minutes, Jan. 26, 1914, at BSA, NHQ.

32 Ernest Thompson Seton, *Manual of the Woodcraft Indians: The Fourteenth Birch-Bark Roll* (Garden City, 1915), pp. xv, 10–42; *The Totem Board* 4 (Jan. 1921):5, 7; *Woodcraft Totem Board* 5 (Dec. 1922):2–3.

33 D. C. Beard, "Boy Scouts of America," *American Review of Reviews* 44 (1911):437; William D. Murray, *As He Journeyed: The Autobiography of William D. Murray* (New York, 1929), pp. 349–50; Daniel Beard to James West, Nov. 26, 1912, and Gifford Pinchot to Daniel Beard, Jan. 25, 1916, both in Beard MSS.

34 E.g., Daniel Beard to Colin H. Livingstone, Nov. 12, 1924, Beard MSS.

35 Allan Richard Whitmore, "Beard, Boys, and Buckskins: Daniel Carter Beard and the Preservation of the American Pioneer Tradition" (Ph.D. diss., Northwestern, 1970), p. iv; Lyman Berry, interview by Sherron Cummings, Jan. 26, 1968, transcript at BSA, NHQ; Colin H. Livingstone to Beard, Mar. 13, 1924, Beard MSS.

36 E.g., Exec. Conf., 1917, p. 250; BSA, *OR, 1924,* pp. 361, 439–44.

37 BSA, *The Official Handbook for Boys* (Garden City, N.Y., 1911), pp. 16–43; BSA, *OR, 1922,* p. 329.

38 SM Conf., 1912, pp. 49–65; SM Conf., 1917, pp. 55–68; BSA, *OR, 1922: Report of Commission on Scout Mortality and Turnover* (New York, 1922), p. 18; BSA, *OR, 1928,* p. 58.

39 Stuart P. Walsh, *Thirteen Years of Scout Adventure* (Seattle, 1923), pp. 15–16, 115–19, 148–73; BSA, *Handbook for Scoutmasters* (1920), p. 61.

40 "On the Hike," *S* 8 (Apr. 22, 1920):7 (quotation); Walsh, *Adventure,* p. 72.

41 John Lovett Morse, "Athletics in the School," *S* 3 (Mar. 1, 1916):5.

42 *Boys' Life* 2 (July 1912):49–64; S. A. Moffat, "How Scout Masters Can Make Their Camps Most Successful," *S* 1 (June 15, 1914):2; SM Conf., 1917, pp. 63–65.

43 Quotations: BSA, *Official Handbook for Boys* (1911), p. 145; BSA, *Handbook for Scoutmasters* (1920), p. 59.

44 BSA, "Annual Meeting" 6 (1916), pt. 5 (transcript at BSA, NHQ).

45 "'Outsiders' Help Scout Camps," *S* 1 (July 15, 1913):5; miscellaneous camp reports in *S* 2 (July 1, 1914):3; Conf., 1916, pp. 47–49. Even so, cost deterred some poor boys. See, e.g., C. H. West to James West, Feb. 14, 1916, Beard MSS.

46 BSA, *AR* 11 (Aug. 1921):56. On sites, see, e.g., Lyman Berry interview; Jacob A. Swisher, "The Boy Scouts in Iowa," *Palimpsest* 34 (1953):51-97.

47 Letter from unnamed Scoutmaster, *S* 2 (Aug. 1, 1914):4.

48 B. F. Skinner to Mother, July 9, 1918, in B. F. Skinner, *Particulars of My Life* (New York, 1976), p. 89 (quotation); ibid., p. 87; Conf., 1918, pp. 59-63.

49 James West to Exec. Board, Oct. 9, 1916, Boy Scouts-YMCA Box, YHL; Exec. Board, Minutes, Dec. 10, 1917, Beard MSS; "Standard Requirements for Boy Scout Camp," *S* 6 (May 15, 1918):8-12; "Scout Executive and Two Scouts Lose Their Lives," *S* 2 (Sept. 1, 1914):1.

50 Samuel A. Moffatt, comp., *Boy Scouts' Diary* (New York, 1913), p. 3 (quotation); Daniel Carter Beard to M. B. Sackett, Mar. 3, 1917, Beard MSS.

51 See Lyman Berry interview on Beard fires. On facilities, see camp reports in *S* 2 (Aug 1, 1914):7; pictures in *S* 2 (June 15, 1914):1; 8 (June 3, 1920):8-9; E. S. Martin to Beard, Jan. 8, 1914, Beard MSS; Conf., 1916, pp. 27-29; "Boy Scouts in Camp at Lake Minnetonka," Minneapolis *Tribune,* July 14, 1918.

52 Quotation: "Teach Camping in Camp," *S* 6 (May 15, 1918):4. On trips and facilities, see "Hundreds of Scouts Enjoy Life under Canvas," *S* 3 (Aug. 15, 1915):1-3; Queens Council, Report of Camp Committee, 1919, Beard MSS. Frank F. Gray, a New Jersey executive, interpreted back to nature literally and let the boys go nude, but mothers protested and the council required trunks except for inspection and swimming. (Luther Edmonds Price, *Eagle Rock Scouting* [Montclair, N.J., 1937], p. 29.)

53 BSA, *Official Handbook for Boys* (1911), p. 148; Conf., 1916, p. 30; Charles Morris, "Ain't We Got Fun," Minneapolis *Journal,* Aug. 7, 1921; "Camp Reports," *S* 3 (Sept. 1, 1915):3.

54 BSA, *AR* 11 (Aug. 1921):57. On wives, see Conf., 1918, pp. 70-72.

55 "Summer Program," *S* 6 (July 15, 1918):13; BSA, *AR* 11 (Aug. 1921):57.

56 E.g., camp reports in *Boys' Life* 3 (Nov. 1913):22; Norman E. Richardson and Ormond E. Loomis, *The Boy Scout Movement Applied by the Church* (New York, 1915), p. 334.

57 BSA, *Official Handbook for Boys* (1911), p. 153; E. S. Martin to Daniel Beard, Jan. 8, 1914, Beard MSS.

58 Skinner to Mother and Papa, n.d., in Skinner, *Particulars,* pp. 87-88.

59 BSA, *Official Handbook for Boys* (1911), pp. 160-61 (quotation); Conf., 1916, pp. 99-100; Richardson and Loomis, *Boy Scout Movement,* pp. 331-32.

60 Quotations: "Camp Delmont's Initiation," *S* 7 (Aug. 28, 1919):4; "Boynton Three's Initiation," *S* 7 (Sept. 18, 1919):4. On the fast, see "Delmont," pp. 4-5.

61 Ralph Graham, "Making Good in a Boys' Camp," *St. Nicholas* 44 (1917):839.

62 Executive Weston, in "The Eighth Law," *S* 7 (Aug. 28, 1919):8 (quotation); Joseph B. Ames, "Under Boy Scout Colors," *St. Nicholas* 44 (1917):812; Walsh, *Adventure,* pp. 56-57, 109-14. The BSA often checked stories such as Ames's. For an elaborate interpretation of a rough game as a manifestation of male anxiety regarding female sexuality and of campfires as a form of male bonding, see Jay Mechling, "Sacred and Profane Play in the Boy Scouts of America," in Helen B. Schwartzman, ed., *Play and Culture* (West Point, N.Y., 1980), pp. 206-13; Mechling, "Boy Scout Campfire," pp. 35-56.

63 BSA, *OR, 1922,* pp. 156-67. On Baden-Powell, see Carolyn Ditte Wagner,

"The Boy Scouts of America: A Model and a Mirror for American Society" (Ph.D. diss., Johns Hopkins, 1979), p. 243.

64 Quotations: Conf., 1918, pp. 58, 61. On instruction at council camps, see Exec. Conf., 1917, p. 227.

65 BSA, *AR* 11 (Aug. 1921):56. On assistants, see Conf., 1916, pp. 35, 93–97.

66 "First Class Council Camps," *S* 6 (June 15, 1918):14.

67 Conf., 1916, pp. 74–104; Conf., 1919, pp. 38–40; BSA, *OR, 1922,* pp. 166–67.

68 Conf., 1916, pp. 41–43; Exec. Conf., 1917, p. 235.

69 BSA, *OR, 1928,* pp. 65, 273; Wagner, "Boy Scouts," p. 352.

70 Samuel D. Bogan, *No Larger Fields: The History of a Boy Scout Council, 1910–1963* (Hamden, Conn., 1966), p. 6; Seton Journal, Sept. 1, 1910, Seton MSS; Ernest Thompson Seton, *Boy Scouts of America: A Handbook of Woodcraft, Scouting, and Life-Craft* (New York, 1910), p. 63.

71 Conf., 1916, p. 60; SM Conf., 1917, pp. 268, 283–84; "Applying the Tests," *S* 6 (July 1, 1918):6.

72 Samuel P. Hays, *Conservation and the Gospel of Efficiency: The Progressive Conservation Movement, 1890–1920* (Cambridge, Mass., 1959).

73 W. D. Howells, *A Boy's Town* (New York, 1890), p. 208 (quotation); picture in *American Brigadier* 1 (June 1907):30; Harlan H. Ballard, *Handbook of the St. Nicholas Agassiz Association* (Pittsfield, Mass., 1882); "The Agassiz Association," *American Boy* 2 (Jan. 1901):90.

74 BSA, *AR* 3 (Feb. 1913):40; BSA, *Hand Book for Boys* (New York, 1914), pp. 163–81; W. T. Hornaday to James West, Feb. 17, 1915, and Hornaday to E. S. Martin, Nov. 20, 1922, both in Beard MSS.

Chapter 14: Adult Instruction and Boys' Responses

1 E.g., SM Conf., 1917, p. 165.

2 Quotations: Letter from George R. Sikes, *S* 2 (May 1, 1914):4; BSA, *AR* 6 (Feb. 1916):19. By 1927, the BSA offered a palm for each five badges beyond Eagle. (Samuel M. Holton, "The Historical Development of the Formal Educational Program of the Boy Scouts of America" [Ph.D. diss., Yale, 1948], p. 176.)

3 "The Ranking Eagle," *S* 7 (Nov. 13, 1919):35–36 (quotation); BSA, *AR* 4 (Apr. 1914).

4 BSA, *AR* 11 (Aug. 1921):44; Conf., 1920, pp. 517–29. See, e.g., "Brothers Break Records for Speed in Scout Advancement," *Minneapolis Journal,* Mar. 12, 1922, clipping in Charles Deere Velie MSS, Minnesota Historical Society, St. Paul.

5 Quotations: Scoutmaster Newcomb in SM Conf., 1917, p. 322; "What Are the Answers?" *S* 4 (Aug. 1, 1916):5. See also Norman E. Richardson and Ormond E. Loomis, *The Boy Scout Movement Applied by the Church* (New York, 1915), p. 96.

6 BSA, *OR, 1922,* p. 103; "Scouts and Athletics," *Scout Leader* 2 (Dec. 1924):32.

7 BSA, *AR* 10 (Apr. 1, 1920):68; BSA, *AR* 16 (Aug. 1926):178.

8 Quotations: Erik H. Erikson, *Identity: Youth and Crisis* (New York, 1968),

p. 123; Sandra Bem, "The Measurement of Psychological Androgyny," *Journal of Consulting and Clinical Psychology* 42 (1974):156, in Jay Mechling, "Male Gender Display at a Boy Scout Camp," in R. Timothy Sieber and Andrew J. Gordon, eds., *Children and Their Organizations: Investigations in American Culture* (Boston, 1981), p. 152.

9 Unnamed Scoutmaster in SM Conf., 1917, p. 179 (quotation); Holton, "Educational Program," pp. 19-27, 57-58; and above, chapter 2, note 11.

10 On boys' long hours of play, see Paul Hanly Furfey, *The Gang Age: A Study of the Preadolescent Boy and His Recreational Needs* (New York, 1926), p. 33.

11 "A First Aid Criticism," *S* 6 (June 15, 1918):11. Cf. "Be Fair to the Boy," ibid., p. 8.

12 See above, chapter 9, note 112; "The Fruit of Experience," *S* 5 (Sept. 1, 1917):3; and a series of articles all entitled "Applying the Tests," in *S* 6 (Feb. 15, 1918): 13; (Apr. 1, 1918):15-16; (June 1, 1918):14; (Sept. 11, 1918):7.

13 "The New Handbook for Scoutmasters," *S* 7 (Sept. 4, 1919):4-5 (quotation); "Applying the Tests," *S* 6 (Dec. 12, 1918):7.

14 "A Statement of Policy About Merit Badges," *S* 2 (Nov. 1, 1914):1; Comm. on Merit Badges, Awards, and Scout Requirements, Minutes, Feb. 23, 1916, at BSA, NHQ; SM Conf., 1917, p. 168.

15 "Map of 14-Mile Hike," *Minneapolis Tribune,* Jan. 20, 1918, vol. 2, Velie MSS (quotation); other clippings in this volume and Conf., 1920, p. 535.

16 Conf., 1916, pp. 297-301; "What Is a Fair Examination," *S* 8 (Mar. 11, 1920): 4.

17 Quotation: Joseph Adelson, "The Political Imagination of the Young Adolescent," *Daedalus* 100 (1971):1030. On the Personal Health badge, see BSA, *The Official Hand Book for Boys,* rev. ed. (New York, 1914), p. 51.

18 Barry J. Wadsworth, *Piaget's Theory of Cognitive Development,* 2nd ed. (New York, 1979), pp. 96-116; Michael D. Berzonsky, "Formal Reasoning in Adolescence: An Alternative View," *Adolescence* 13 (1978):278-88.

19 Cf. David Elkind, *Children and Adolescents: Interpretive Essays on Jean Piaget,* 2nd ed. (New York, 1974), p. 101.

20 On the rules, see BSA, *Handbook for Scoutmasters,* 2nd ed. (New York, 1920), p. 177; on badges won, BSA, *AR* 11 (Aug. 1921):44.

21 Quotations: "Making Membership Real," *AY* 15 (Nov. 1916):1-2; A. R. Freeman, "I Want to Join the 'Y,'" *AY* 19 (Mar. 1920):22. See also editorial note, *AB* 5 (1906):321-22; and above, chapter 7, note 62.

22 "The Standard Efficiency Tests" (MS, n.d.), Boys' Work Sub-Committee Box, YHL; "The American Standard Program," *AY* 15 (Dec. 1916):7.

23 YNA, *YB* (1910), p. 296; (1920), p. 103; G. M. Martin, "Recreational Games for Boys," *AB* 2 (1903):169; *Physical Education in the Young Men's Christian Associations of North America,* rev. ed. (New York, 1920), pp. 114-15.

24 Conf., 1920, p. 530 (quotation); BSA, *AR* 7 (Mar. 1917):8.

25 Holton, "Educational Program" p. 112 (quotation); BSA, *Hand Book for Boys* (1914), pp. 40, 359-91. On the flag, see James West, "Training Young Americans for Citizenship" (speech, n.d.), West File, BSA, NHQ.

26 Robert D. Hess, "Political Socialization in the Schools," in William R. Looft, ed., *Developmental Psychology: A Book of Readings* (Hinsdale, Ill., 1972),

pp. 418-19; Fred I. Greenstein, *Children and Politics,* rev. ed. (New Haven, 1969), pp. 31-42.

27 Greenstein, *Children and Politics,* pp. 130, 138.

28 *The Live Wire,* Oct. 9, 1918, in vol. 2, Velie MSS (quotation); Florence Woolston, "Billy and the World War," *New Republic* 17 (1919):369-71.

29 Adelson, "Political Imagination," pp. 1022-27.

30 Harold P. Levy, *Building a Popular Movement: A Case Study of the Public Relations of the Boy Scouts of America* (New York, 1944), pp. 83-92; Edwin Nicholson, *Education and the Boy Scout Movement in America* (New York, 1940), pp. 64-106.

31 BSA, *AR* 12 (May 1922):24-25; and above, chapter 10. On troop activities, see H. Paul Douglass, *How Shall Country Youth Be Served? A Study of the "Rural" Work of Some National Character-Building Agencies* (New York, 1926), pp. 147, 152.

32 Ray O. Wyland, *Scouting in the Schools: A Study of the Relationships between the Schools and the Boy Scouts of America* (New York, 1934), p. 115.

33 Edgar M. Robinson, "Self-Government for Boys," *AB* 7 (1908):111 (quotation); ibid., pp. 99-111; idem, report, Dec. 16, 1915, in Boys' Work Reports, YHL.

34 "What Are Your Boys Thinking About?" *AY* 15 (May 1916):6-7.

35 *The Elevator* (Toronto), n.v. (Apr. 1910), unpaged. On the very low levels of service by YMCA and Boy Scout groups alike, see Douglass, *How Shall Country Youth Be Served?* pp. 152-53.

36 David Elkind, "Understanding the Young Adolescent," *Adolescence* 13 (1978):133. On Boy Scout service, see above, chapter 10, notes 14-20; Woolston, "Billy," p. 369.

37 BSA, *The Official Handbook for Boys* (Garden City, N.Y., 1911), pp. 15, 16. Even Jenks had to fall back upon a utilitarian principle from outside the law to resolve conflicts. BSA, *OR, 1924,* pp. 49-50.

38 BSA, *AR* 7 (Mar. 1917):79. See SM Conf., 1917, pp. 73-92, on troop practices. Cf. David M. Kennedy, *Birth Control in America: The Career of Margaret Sanger* (New Haven, 1970), pp. 66-68, on contemporary morality.

39 Lawrence Kohlberg and Carol Gilligan, "The Adolescent as a Philosopher: The Discovery of the Self in a Postconventional World," *Daedalus* 100 (1971): 1067.

40 Ibid., p. 1070.

41 "Typical Troop Problem — Tobacco," *S* 6 (June 1, 1918):12. See above, chapter 5, notes 14-15, on the Brigades. The Scoutmaster's misdeed is described in C. F. Sesinger to Theodore Roosevelt, Aug. 8, 1911, Box 171, Ser. 1, TR MSS.

42 Quotation: unidentified Scoutmaster in Emory S. Bogardus, *The City Boy and His Problems: A Survey of Boy Life in Los Angeles* (Los Angeles, 1926), p. 116.

43 Scoutmasters' Reports File, BSA, NHQ.

44 "Two Telephone Calls," *S* 8 (Jan. 1, 1920):16.

45 Quoted in "The Boy Scout Movement at Its Best," *AY* 3 (1914):29.

46 BSA, *Official Handbook for Boys* (1911), p. 18 (quotation); Conf., 1920, pp.

520–37; William D. Murray, *History of the Boy Scouts of America* (New York, 1937), p. 232.

47 Quotation: Committee on Merit Badges, Awards, and Scout Requirements, Minutes, Feb. 23, 1916, at BSA, NHQ. For an account of a modern troop whose leaders have taken a much less formalistic approach, insisting upon responsible behavior as a prerequisite for promotion to Eagle Scout, see Mechling, "Male Gender Display," p. 142. Similar expectations could have prevailed in early Boy Scout troops, but this seems unlikely in view of the high degree of formalism which marked early twentieth-century moral instruction.

48 Quotations: "What 'The Brigade' Has Done for Me," from the *Church Gleaner,* in *BBB* 1 (Apr. 15, 1892):7; W. J. Hart, "The Saving of 'Billy,'" *S* 3 (July 15, 1915):7.

49 Mark A. May and Hugh Hartshorne, *Studies in the Nature of Character,* vol. I, *Studies in Deceit* (New York, 1928), pp. 362–67, 400.

50 Henry P. Fairchild, *Conduct Habits of Boy Scouts* (New York, 1931). Fairchild classified ex-Scouts as non-Scouts, thus failing to allow for the fact that older boys, who were mostly non-Scouts by this definition, had more court trouble. Nor did he consider whether differences in social class or ethnicity biased either law enforcement or his raters' assessments. Albert R. Monson and Harl R. Douglass, "A Comparison of School Records and Ratings of Boy Scouts and Non-Scouts," *School Review* 45 (1937):764–68, found that teachers did not rate Boy Scouts above non-Scouts on character, but fewer Boy Scouts came before the juvenile court.

51 Quotations: Jeremiah Jenks, *Life Questions of School Boys* (New York, 1912), p. 10; W. H. Thomson, "The Decline in Biblical Instruction," *Association Monthly* 2 (1871):143.

52 Francis P. Miller, Report on Visits to Boys' Secretaries, c. 1915, in Boys' Work Reports, at YHL.

53 Morton White, *Social Thought in America: The Revolt against Formalism,* new ed. (Boston, 1957).

54 Furfey, *Gang Age,* p. 35. On high school students, see Sidney S. Tedesche, "Salient Significant Facts Gleaned from the San Antonio Boy Life Survey," *Wheel of Fortune* (San Antonio), May 6, 1921, unpaged. See also Conf., 1920, p. 525.

55 YNA, *YB* (1921), p. 217; Philo R. Brooke, "Manual Training for Association Boys," *AB* 6 (1907):60–65; Clarence C. Robinson, "Problems of the Working Boys' School," ibid., pp. 66–70; BSA, *AR* 5 (Feb. 1915):64–65; BSA, *OR, 1922,* p. 334.

56 BSA, *AR* 11 (Aug. 1921):44; SM Conf., 1917, pp. 161–77.

57 Quotation: "Leaving School," *S* 7 (May 15, 1919):25. On taking any job, however badly paid, cf. the favorable advice of Charles H. Parkhurst, *Talks to Young Men* (New York, 1897), pp. 6–7.

58 E.g., *Uncle Sam's Boy* 1 (July 1918):23; Douglass, *How Shall Country Youth Be Served?* p. 158; "The Scout and His School," *S* 7 (Nov. 13, 1919):15–16.

59 "A Vocational Quiz Blank," *AB* 7 (1908):216 (quotation); ibid., pp. 210–18.

60 C. J. Carver, "Here and There in Christian Callings," *AY* 19 (June 1920):22.

On limited counseling, see Douglass, *How Shall Country Youth Be Served?* p. 152.

61 Frank Lee, "Moloch and the Boy," *WWB* 9 (Jan. 1909):31 (quotation); Bryan Strong, "Ideas of the Early Sex Education Movement in America, 1890–1920," *History of Education Quarterly* 12 (1972):153; "A Symposium on Sex-Knowledge," in C. B. Horton, ed., *Reaching the Boys of an Entire Community* (New York, 1909), p. 48.

62 Joseph Flint, "Sex Instruction for Boys," *HHB* 1 (July 1901):32.

63 M. D. Crackel, "Individual Sex Instruction," *AY* 2 (1913):71–72 (quotation); William Byron Forbush and Frank Lincoln Masseck, *The Boys' Round Table: A Manual of the International Order of the Knights of King Arthur,* 6th ed. (Potsdam, 1908), pp. 120–21; Mel B. Rideout, "Physical Examinations for Boys," *AB* 2 (1903):166–68.

64 Douglass, *How Shall Country Youth Be Served?* pp. 152–53. For a note on Boy Scout activity, see "Sex Hygiene Lectures," *S* 1 (Aug. 15, 1913):8. Such notices were rare.

65 R. S. S. Baden-Powell, *Scouting for Boys: A Handbook for Instruction in Good Citizenship,* rev. ed. (London, 1909), pp. 196–97; "Sex Education Literature for Boys and Men," *AY* 12 (Apr. 1913):74–84; and above, chapter 2, notes 110–12.

66 Clarence C. Robinson, "Physical Fitness Message to Employed Boys," *AY* 19 (July 1920):11; Bryan Strong, "Toward a History of the Experiential Family: Sex and Incest in the Nineteenth-Century Family," *Journal of Marriage and the Family* 35 (1973):457–66.

67 Quotations: H. W. Gibson, *Boyology or Boy Analysis* (New York, 1918), p. 190; Crackel, "Sex Instruction," p. 72; Gibson, *Boyology,* p. 199. See also Winfield S. Hall, "Instruction Regarding Sex," in John L. Alexander, ed., *Boy Training* (New York, 1912), pp. 91–93.

68 Max J. Exner, "The Sex Factor in Christian Character Training," in *The Place of Boyhood in the Nations of the World: Being the Report of the Second World Conference of Y.M.C.A. Workers among Boys . . . 1923* (Geneva, n.d.), p. 190.

69 "Boys' Questions," *AB* 5 (1906):267 (quotation); Baden-Powell, *Scouting for Boys,* p. 196. On boys' admissions, see editorial note, *AB* 3 (1904):246.

70 Crackel, "Sex Instruction," p. 72.

71 Edgar M. Robinson, "Association Boys' Camps," *AB* 1 (1902):76.

72 See above, chapter 13. Cf. Alfred C. Kinsey et al., *Sexual Behavior in the Human Male* (Philadelphia, 1948), pp. 168–71. As Jay Mechling notes, Boy Scouts of the 1970s called each other "homo" as a routine bit of teasing—a practice equally common when I was of Boy Scout age in the 1950s. Although boys at neither time took the epithet seriously, it suggests a tradition of wariness that may have limited experimentation. (Mechling, "Male Gender Display," p. 155.) On other insults as a way for boys to distance themselves from homosexuality, see also Jay Mechling, "The Magic of the Boy Scout Campfire," *Journal of American Folklore* 93 (Jan.–Mar. 1980):45.

73 "Giving the Invitation," *AB* 3 (1904):53.

74 Montreal YMCA, *Annual Report* 56 (1907):27; YNA, *YB* (1921), p. 217.

75 Quotations: Forbush and Masseck, *Boys' Round Table,* p. 26; National Boys' Work Board of the Religious Education Council of Canada, *The Mentors' Manual: A Handbook for Leaders of Trail Ranger Camps and Tuxis Squares,* 3rd ed. (n.p., 1923), p. 186.

76 C. C. Robinson, report, Dec. 1915, in Boys' Work Reports, YHL (quotation); Arthur N. Cotton, "A Continuous Campaign of Friendship," [early 1910s], in Hi-Y to 1937 Box, YHL.

77 Canadian Standard Efficiency Tests Committee, *The Canadian Standard Efficiency Tests* (n.p., 1915), p. 20.

78 Quotations: "Interviews with Strangers," *AY* 15 (Oct. 1916):12; Arthur N. Cotton, "Significant Experiences in My Work This Year," [c. Dec. 1913], in Boys' Work Reports, YHL.

79 "A New Form of Decision Card," *AB* 8 (1909):96.

80 Edgar M. Robinson, "The Forward Step Meeting for Older Boys" (typed MS, n.d.), E. M. Robinson Letters and Statements Box, YHL.

81 C. N., in A. N. Cotton, "Talks to High School Boys and Girls," (typed, n.d.), Hi-Y to 1937 Box, YHL (quotation); Albert M. Chesley, "Emotionally Explosive," *AY* 15 (June 1916):6; Cotton, Report for Oct. 1912, in Boys' Work Reports, YHL.

82 R. E. C., N. Y.; R. D. W., Col.; R. M. S., Col., all in Cotton, "Talks."

83 B. Burgoyne Chapman, "Impressions of Some Dangers and Problems in Y.M.C.A. Boys' Work," *AY* 2 (1913):12.

84 Edgar M. Robinson, "Was This an Accident?" *AY* 4 (1915):11-14.

85 "After Many Days," *AY* 18 (Apr. 1919):4.

86 "A College Boy's Letter," *AY* 3 (1914):321.

87 Quotations: Cotton, "Significant Experiences"; Francis P. Miller, report for Dec. 1915, in Boys' Work Reports, YHL.

88 Quoted in Eugene C. Foster, "By Way of Conclusion," *AB* 8 (1909):284.

89 Richard L. Flynn, "The Campaign of Friendship at Kansas City," *AY* 4 (1915): 76-77; "Fifteen Older Boys' Conferences," *AY* 15 (Dec. 1916):8-9.

90 YNA, *YB* (1910), p. 296; (1920), p. 103; (1921), p. 217.

91 BSA, *AR* 11 (Aug. 1921):44; Conf., 1920, pp. 849-50. Boys found the two badges hard to earn. (Committee on Merit Badges . . . , Minutes, Feb. 23, 1916, BSA, NHQ.)

92 "Boy Scout Lore Sticks in Minds, Essays Reveal," *Minneapolis Journal,* May 22, 1921, p. 3.

93 Scout authorities worried that the physical benefits of summer camp would not carry over into the year. ("Make Them Prove It," *S* 5 [Sept. 1, 1917]:6.)

94 National Boys' Work Board, *Mentors' Manual,* pp. 191-92.

95 Joe L. Dubbert, *A Man's Place: Masculinity in Transition* (Englewood Cliffs, N.J., 1979), p. 115.

96 There is still disagreement. Compare Peter Blos, *On Adolescence: A Psychoanalytic Interpretation* (New York, 1962), and Erikson, *Identity,* with Daniel Offer, *The Psychological World of the Teenager: A Study of Normal Adolescent Boys* (New York, 1969), esp. pp. 183-92, and Frederick Elkin and William A. Westley, "The Myth of Adolescent Culture," *American Sociological Review* 20 (1955):680-84. For a substantial recent bibliography and an argu-

ment that turmoil generally is not normative in adolescence, see Jeffrey R. Mitchell, "Normality in Adolescence," in Sherman C. Feinstein et al., eds., *Adolescent Psychiatry,* vol. 8: *Developmental and Clinical Studies* (Chicago, 1980), pp. 200-213.

Chapter 15: Group Experience, Membership Turnover, and Age Stratification

1 BSA, *Special Bulletin* (New York, Oct. 1911), p. 40.
2 E.g., "How to Do It," *S* 1 (Oct. 1, 1913):2; Norman E. Richardson and Ormond E. Loomis, *The Boy Scout Movement Applied by the Church* (New York, 1915), p. 269; Conf., 1919, p. 38.
3 Edgar M. Robinson, "Boys as Savages," *AB* 1 (1902):128 (quotation); I. E. Vining, "Influencing Character through Hiking," *S* 1 (Aug. 15, 1913):2.
4 Conf., 1916, pp. 25-26; Conf., 1920, pp. 460-61.
5 John L. Alexander to James West, Jan. 23, 1912, at BSA, NHQ; "Problems of General Interest Discussed in Correspondence," *S* 3 (Jan. 1, 1916):14.
6 Conf., 1920, p. 269 (quotation); BSA, *Report of the Commission on Scout Mortality and Turnover* (New York, 1922), pp. 11, 18-19.
7 R. H. Nodine, "Troop Meeting Programs," *S* 6 (Sept. 26, 1918):10.
8 "Plans Meetings Months Ahead," *S* 4 (Dec. 1, 1916):2; "Arrangement of Meetings," *S* 4 (June 15, 1916):5.
9 "Troop Meeting Programs," *S* 7 (Aug. 21, 1919):4-5.
10 *Lowry Hill Scout Record,* Dec. 17, 23, 1919, Box 1, Charles Deere Velie MSS, Minnesota Historical Society, St. Paul. Against formal self-government, cf. SM Conf., 1917, pp. 182-86; "From the Scout Field," *S* 3 (Oct. 1, 1915):5.
11 SM Conf., 1917, pp. 87, 92, 211-12; Richardson and Loomis, *Boy Scout Movement,* p. 107; "The Boy's Point of View," *S* 4 (Nov. 1, 1916):6.
12 "Maintain Scout Service," *S* 6 (July 15, 1918):1-2. The thirty week estimate is from H. Paul Douglass, *How Shall Country Youth Be Served? A Study of the "Rural" Work of Certain National Character-Building Agencies* (New York, 1926), p. 145. Walter S. Athearn et al., *The Religious Education of Protestants in an American Commonwealth* (New York, 1923), p. 124, comments on meeting places.
13 BSA, *OR, 1922,* p. 166 (quotation); BSA, *OR, 1924,* pp. 466-67; BSA, *OR, 1928,* pp. 274-76.
14 Walter Kaulfers, "Practical Aspects of the School-Scout Program," *Education* 49 (1928):270; BSA, *OR, 1922,* pp. 239-41.
15 YNA, *YB* (1906), p. 280; (1921), p. 217. On the organization of a boys' branch, see, e.g., Cecil M. Daggett, "The St. Louis Boys' Work," *AB* 5 (1906):61-69.
16 Anonymous boy in George W. Hinckley, "The Unique Value of Conferences of Older Boys," *AY* 1 (1912):66 (quotation); editorial note, *AB* 8 (1909):93.
17 Anonymous respondent in ABS, *RC,* p. 17 (quotation); Harvey L. Smith, "The Tuxis System of Character Building," in C. B. Horton, ed., *Reaching the Boys of an Entire Community* (New York, 1909), pp. 128-31.
18 Anonymous respondent in ABS, *RC,* p. 17.

19 ABS, *RC,* pp. 17-18; Owen Earle Pence, *The Y.M.C.A. and Social Need: A Study of Institutional Adaptation* (New York, 1939), p. 157.
20 BSA, *The Official Hand Book for Boys,* rev. ed. (New York, 1914), p. 20; William D. Murray, *History of the Boy Scouts of America* (New York, 1937), p. 238.
21 E.g., Conf., 1918, pp. 33-36; BSA, *OR, 1924,* p. 186; Richardson and Loomis, *Boy Scout Movement,* p. 188.
22 E.g., "The Patrol and the Patrol Leader," *S* 4 (Feb. 1, 1917):6.
23 Richardson and Loomis, *Boy Scout Movement,* p. 193; Conf., 1918, p. 2.
24 Conf., 1919, pp. 39-40.
25 Conf., 1918, p. 2 (quotation); SM Conf., 1912, pp. 60-61; BSA, *OR, 1924,* pp. 190-92.
26 SM Conf., 1912, pp. 51-52; BSA, *OR, 1922,* p. 414; Conf., 1916, p. 52.
27 Conf., 1918, pp. 3, 33; SM Conf., 1912, pp. 65-70.
28 Ft. Deerfoot to Frank I. Morse, n.d., Beard MSS. See above, chapter 14, on boys' politics.
29 "From the Scout Field," *S* 3 (Oct. 1, 1915):5; Minutes of the Lightning Athletic Club, 1920-21, Box 6, Chicago Commons MSS, Chicago Historical Society; Daniel Carter Beard to Ft. Washington No. 1102, May 8, 1908, Beard MSS.
30 BSA, *Handbook for Scout Masters* (New York, 1914), p. 114.
31 Richardson and Loomis, *Boy Scout Movement,* pp. 183-84; SM Conf., 1917, pp. 2-3; "The Patrol and the Patrol Leader," *S* 4 (Jan. 15, 1917):6; "Topics and Opinions at the Vancouver P. L. Convention," *Scout Leader* 1 (Jan. 1924): 8; "How Scoutmasters Choose Patrol Leaders," *S* 8 (Jan. 1, 1920):14.
32 SM Conf., 1917, p. 10 (quotation); ibid., pp. 182, 239-240, 296.
33 Boy Scout officials increasingly recognized this. Richardson and Loomis, *Boy Scout Movement,* p. 181; "Better Troops Through Patrol Organization," *S* 10 (Nov. 1922):12; E. DeAlton Partridge, *Leadership Among Adolescent Boys* (New York, 1934), pp. 37-38.
34 BSA, *Scout Mortality,* pp. 13-14; BSA, *OR, 1924,* p. 192; Conf., 1918, pp. 32-33.
35 "Hints for Patrol Leaders," *S* 6 (July 15, 1918):6; "Better Troops," p. 11; Lorne W. Barclay, "Landmarks in the Patrol System," *S* 11 (Mar. 1923):8.
36 Richardson and Loomis, *Boy Scout Movement,* pp. 200-2; SM Conf., 1917, pp. 5-8; BSA, *OR, 1924,* p. 182.
37 Charles W. Eliot, "Discussion," *School Review* 7 (1899):631-32, in James McLachlan, *American Boarding Schools: A Historical Study* (New York, 1970), p. 281. American Boys' Brigade publications were full of reports of boy officers chosen solely for drill proficiency. On caning, see Noel Annan, "Victorian Swish," *New York Review,* July 19, 1979, p. 21.
38 Quotations: R. S. S. Baden-Powell, "The American Boy Scouts" (MS, n.d.), and idem, Memorandum before leaving America, [c. Mar. 11, 1912], both in Beard MSS. On Smith, see news note in *American Brigadier* 1 (July 1907):20.
39 "Scouting Invaluable to American Youth," *S* 7 (Mar. 6, 1919):2; Samuel A. Moffat, "Observations of the Boy Scout Movement in England," *AY* 3 (June 1914):155-56; E. E. Reynolds, *The Scout Movement* (London, 1950), pp. 35-36, 91-93.

40 R. S. S. Baden-Powell, *Scouting for Boys: A Handbook for Instruction in Good Citizenship,* rev. ed. (London, 1909), p. 209. British Brigade offices were graded by age. (*The Boys' Brigade Manual for the Use of Officers* [Glasgow, 1914], p. 28.)

41 Quotations: Baden-Powell, Memorandum, c. Mar. 11, 1912; idem, Report after Spending Two Months in Canada, Oct. 4, 1910, in Dr. John A. Stiles Collection, Boy Scouts of Canada, National Council Library, Ottawa; Stuart C. Godfrey, in SM Conf., 1917, p. 234.

42 Moffat, in Conf., 1916, p. 106; Executive Shayne in BSA, *OR, 1924,* p. 191.

43 Anonymous boy in Emory S. Bogardus, *The City Boy and His Problems: A Survey of Boy Life in Los Angeles* (Los Angeles, 1926), p. 117.

44 Anonymous Scout in "Ye Troop Almanack," *S* 8 (June 3, 1920):2.

45 Frederic M. Thrasher, *The Gang: A Study of 1,313 Gangs in Chicago,* abridged (Chicago, 1963), p. 197 (quotation); Richardson and Loomis, *Boy Scout Movement,* p. 184; SM Conf., 1917, p. 193.

46 Jay Mechling, "Male Gender Display at a Boy Scout Camp," in R. Timothy Sieber and Andrew J. Gordon, eds., *Children and Their Organizations: Investigations in American Culture* (Boston, 1981), pp. 138-60.

47 Unnamed secretary in "The Boys' Work Clinic," *AY* 18 (Mar. 1919):16.

48 P. S. Page, "Boys' Gymnasium Leaders' Corps," *AB* 1 (1902):24; Frank M. Smith, "Why a Boy Should Be a Bible Class Teacher," *The Lever* 14 (Mar. 1909):17.

49 "Do You Entrust Leadership to Your Older Boys?" *AY* 20 (Jan. 1921):34-37; YNA, *YB* (1906), p. 280; (1921), p. 217.

50 Abel J. Gregg, *Boys' Work Advances* (New York, 1934), pp. 12-13; untitled materials, 1954 Boys' Work History Consultation, at YHL.

51 For a summary, see Philip R. Newman, "Social Settings and Their Significance for Adolescent Development," *Adolescence* 11 (1976):409-10.

52 Murray Brooks, "The Appeal of Work with Boys to the College Undergraduate," *AB* 9 (1910):209 (quotation); Frederick H. Zbinden, "Keep At It," *S* 2 (Dec. 1, 1914):5.

53 "Reproduction of One of the First Membership Blanks Received At Headquarters," *S* 1 (Oct. 15, 1913):2; BSA, *AR* 3 (Feb. 1913):20; 6 (Feb. 1916):38; Douglass, *How Shall Country Youth Be Served?* p. 102. The 1½ hour estimate is in Athearn, *Religious Education,* p. 76.

54 Quotation: SM Conf., 1917, p. 68. On troubles getting men to hike, see BSA, "Annual Meeting" 6 (1916), pt. 4, transcript at BSA, NHQ.

55 BSA, *OR, 1924,* pp. 92-93, 468.

56 BSA, *AR* 12 (Mar. 1922):141; Bogardus, *City Boy,* p. 115.

57 Quotations: anonymous Scoutmaster and Curtis Culin, Jr., in "From the Scout Field," *S* 3 (Nov. 1, 1915):9.

58 YNA, *YB* (1919), p. 127; Association of Employed Officers of the YMCA's of North America, *Report of Commission on the Boys' Work of the Young Men's Christian Association* (looseleaf, 1921, at YHL), pp. 2-3.

59 ABS, *RC,* p. 24 (quotation); ibid., pp. 13-15.

60 H. E. Montague, "High School Honor Boys," *AB* 7 (1908):85.

61 Nathaniel Alexander Owings, *The Spaces In Between: An Architect's Journey* (Boston, 1973), pp. 17, 18 (quotations); ibid., p. 19.

62 YNA, *YB* (1910), p. 296.

63 Above, Tables 3 and 4, and below, note 65; Mark M. Jones, *Report on a Survey of the Boy Scouts of America* (privately printed, 1927), pp. 27-28.

64 William McCormick, *The Boy and His Clubs* (New York, 1912), p. 88; "One Year's Work at Denver," *AY* 16 (Feb. 1917):6; editorial note, *AY* 19 (Mar. 1920): 22.

65 Potential members included boys twelve to fifteen in 1910 and all who turned twelve through 1920. I assumed that 60 percent of each year's YMCA juniors were new. U.S. Bureau of the Census, *Thirteenth Census of the United States . . . 1910: Population* (Washington, 1913), I:310; idem, *Fourteenth Census of the United States . . . 1920: Population* (Washington, 1923), II:162.

66 Jones, *Survey,* pp. 27-28; BSA, *OR, 1928,* pp. 362, 366. If all Boy Scouts had joined at twelve and left at eighteen, there would have been 17 percent annual turnover, but the rate should have been lower as long as the BSA recruited increasing numbers of young members each year.

67 BSA, *Scout Mortality,* p. 20; BSA, *OR, 1922,* p. 101. The conflicting facts that only 14 percent blamed a collapsed troop for their departure and that nearly a third of former Boy Scouts had been registered with defunct troops suggest that boys often quit first and *then* the troop fell apart.

68 Jones, *Survey,* p. 27.

69 P. Jacques Sevin, *Le Scoutisme,* 3ᵉ éd. (Paris, 1933), p. 158.

70 "Rochester's Find Yourself Campaign," *AY* 18 (Apr. 1919):15; William Boyce, undated MS [c. 1912], Boyce File, BSA, NHQ.

71 AWB, *RP,* p. 48.

72 Quotations: Amitai Etzioni, *A Comparative Analysis of Complex Organizations: On Power, Involvement, and Their Correlates,* rev. ed. (New York, 1975), p. 10.

73 Conf., 1920, p. 289.

74 Athearn, *Religious Education,* p. 229. New Scouts in 1925: age twelve — 43%; thirteen — 24%; fourteen — 16%; fifteen — 9%; sixteen — 5%; seventeen and above — 3%. Jones, *Survey,* p. 10. The average Boy Scout's "life" in 1927 was still nineteen months. BSA, *OR, 1928,* p. 360.

75 According to a 1926 survey, Boy Scouts who joined at twelve and reached first class averaged 3.3 years membership; those who remained tenderfeet averaged 1.4. Those who joined at sixteen and reached first class averaged only 1.4 years; those who remained tenderfeet averaged .9. Jones, *Survey,* p. 25.

76 Editorials, UBBA, *OB* 5 (Aug., Sept. 1910), n.p.; SM Conf., 1917, pp. 292-309.

77 For source, see above, chapter 2, Table 1.

78 Above, chapter 2, note 52. The criteria for pubescence approximated Stage 3 in J. M. Tanner, *Growth at Adolescence,* 2nd ed. (Oxford, 1962), p. 33.

79 Paul Hanly Furfey, *The Gang Age: A Study of the Preadolescent Boy and His Recreational Needs* (New York, 1926), pp. 11-12; Rolf E. Muuss, *Theories of Adolescence* (New York, 1966), pp. 4-9.

80 BSA, Exec. Board, resolution, Apr. 1, 1911, on James West to Daniel Beard,

Nov. 4, 1911, Beard MSS; Baden-Powell, *Scouting for Boys,* p. 30; Conf., 1916, pp. 303–11.

81 H. E. Montague to James West, Apr. 22, 1911, in "Committee on Standardization" (scrapbook, BSA, NHQ); West to M. L. Schiff, Apr. 20, 1925, in Beard MSS; H. R. Randall, "Advocates Lower Age Limit," *S* 2 (Dec. 1, 1914):5; BSA, *OR, 1924,* p. 277.

82 B. F. Skinner, *Particulars of My Life* (New York, 1976), pp. 86–89; William R. Hall, "Auxiliary Teen Age Organizations," in John L. Alexander, ed., *The Sunday School and the Teens* (New York, 1913), p. 355.

83 Percy Everett, *The First Ten Years* (Ipswich, U.K., 1948), p. 67; Sevin, *Scoutisme,* pp. 148, 158–62.

84 Anonymous boy in Bogardus, *City Boy,* p. 116 (quotation); Edgar M. Robinson, "Age Grouping of Younger Association Members," *AB* 1 (1902):34–35; "Retaining the Interest of the Older Scout," *S* 6 (Jan. 15, 1918):13.

85 Sevin, *Scoutisme,* pp. 162–65; Conf., 1916, pp. 141–44, 202–5.

86 H. W. Gibson, *Boyology, or Boy Analysis* (New York, 1918), p. 225.

87 Quotations: Hulse to D. C. Beard, Feb. 7, 1920, Beard MSS; William C. McCormick, "The Big Boys and the Church," *HHB* 1 (Jan. 1901):92; Taylor Statten, "Boy Scouts of Toronto," *AB* 9 (1910):92. The BSA has changed its promotional name to "Scouting/USA" in order to remove the word *boy.* (*New York Times,* Feb. 23, 1977, p. B2.)

88 SM Conf., 1917, p. 311 (quotation); "Why I Joined the Boy Scouts of America," *S* 5 (July 15, 1917):4; "The Ranger," *S* 6 (Nov. 7, 1918):4.

89 "The Influence on Boys of Books They Enjoy," *S* 2 (July 1, 1914):3.

90 Boys advertised in *Scouting* 3–7 (May 1915–Dec. 1919) as missing from home. Notices before and after those dates were rare. On Sunday school dropouts, cf. Table 1, above in chapter 2.

91 On West's view, see above, chapter 6, note 45. On boys quitting, see above, chapter 12, note 66; SM Conf., 1917, p. 301; BSA, *Scout Mortality,* p. 13.

92 BSA, *OR, 1922,* p. 189 (quotations); BSA, *OR, 1924,* p. 96.

93 Quotations: BSA, *Handbook for Scout Masters* (1914), p. 106; Bogardus, *City Boy,* p. 114; "Retaining the Interest of the Older Scout," *S* 6 (Feb. 1, 1918):14. See Furfey, *Gang Age,* pp. 1–11, on boys' attitudes, and above, chapter 8, notes 52–54, on the founding fathers.

94 "Retaining the Interest of the Older Scout," *S* 6 (Mar. 1, 1918):13; SM Conf., 1917, pp. 122–24; Conf., 1920, p. 310; James West's secretary to W. B. Holcombe, Mar. 27, 1917, under Joint Hikes in "Correspondence About Policies" (scrapbook, BSA, NHQ).

95 H. Parker Lansdale, "A Historical Study of YMCA Boys' Work in the United States, 1900–1925" (Ph.D. diss., Yale, 1956), p. 49. A boys' club in Philadelphia found that girls preferred the glamor of the dance halls. (George D. Chamberlain, "The Mass Boys' Club," *Advancement* 2 [Sept. 1913]:2–3, in CBC MSS.)

96 A. D. Jamieson and Kirkham in BSA, *OR, 1922,* p. 75.

97 Above, chapter 8, note 15; Alvin Marsh to Dan Beard, Dec. 6, 1912, Beard MSS; BSA, *AR* 11 (Aug. 1921):44. Such badges accounted for only 15 percent of those awarded in 1920.

98 T. R. Croswell, "Amusements of Worcester School Children," *Pedagogical Semi-*

nary 6 (1899):229–230. Boys much preferred standard sports to the simplified games assigned by teachers and playground supervisors. (George E. Johnson, *Education Through Recreation* [Cleveland, 1916], pp. 39, 48–49.) A survey over Easter found that 71 percent of grammar school boys played baseball, while only 11 percent engaged in Scout-style activities, though it was early to hike. (Lee F. Hanmer and Clarence Arthur Perry, *Recreation in Springfield, Illinois* [Springfield, 1914], p. 24. See also Henry D. Sheldon, "The Institutional Activities of American Children," *American Journal of Psychology* 9 [1898]:425–48.)

99 Edmund deS. Brunner et al., *American Agricultural Villages* (New York, 1927), p. 215. Teenage boys increasingly specialized in a few forms of play, notably baseball and football. (Zach McGee, "A Study in the Play Life of Some South Carolina Children," *Pedagogical Seminary* 7 [1900]:468. See also Joel H. Spring, "Mass Culture and School Sports," *History of Education Quarterly* 14 [1974]: 493–94.)

100 E.g., unidentified clipping, Sault Ste. Marie newspaper, 1917, in historical files, BSA, NHQ; *Lowry Hill Scout Record,* Dec. 17, 1919, Velie MSS; "The Ranger," *S* 6 (Dec. 26, 1918):4; SM Conf., 1917, p. 299.

101 Cf. James S. Coleman, *The Adolescent Society: The Social Life of the Teen-ager and Its Impact on Education* (New York, 1961), esp. p. 309.

102 SM Conf., 1917, pp. 298–99.

103 Quotation: "Here's the Way to Keep Him Always a Scout," *S* 4 (Sept. 1, 1916): 1. See also BSA, *OR, 1922,* p. 75.

104 Conf., 1916, pp. 189–99; SM Conf., 1917, pp. 125–27, 316; BSA, *OR, 1928,* p. 114.

105 Table 10; and above, chapter 9, note 115.

106 I. B. Rhodes et al., *The Problems of the Small City Young Men's Christian Association* (looseleaf sheets, 1921, at YHL), p. 12. In Cleveland, 20 percent of elementary school boys played basketball, compared to 64 percent of high school boys. (Johnson, *Education,* p. 57.)

107 "A Comparison of Membership Groups," *AY* 16 (Oct. 1917):13.

108 C. H. Barnes to E. M. Robinson, Dec. 5, 1914, Boys' Work Reports, YHL.

109 Boys' Work Committees of the Rotary Club and the YMCA, *Some Salient Facts Gathered from Trenton's Boy-Life Survey* (Trenton, N.J., 1922), pp. 9, 27.

110 Robert S. Lynd and Helen Merrell Lynd, *Middletown: A Study in American Culture* (New York, 1929), pp. 216–17. See also Bogardus, *City Boy,* pp. 117–19.

111 H. W. Gibson et al., *Ungrasped and Undeveloped Opportunities among Young Men from 18 to 21 Years of Age* (looseleaf sheets, 1921, at YHL).

112 Philip R. Newman and Barbara M. Newman, "Early Adolescence and Its Conflict: Group Identity Versus Alienation," *Adolescence* 11 (1976):265.

Conclusion and Epilogue

1 Barbara Gillis, "Scout's Honor," Boston *Globe,* July 12, 1979 (quotation); Daniel Yankelovitch, Inc., *Is Scouting in Tune with the Times?* (mimeographed, July 1968), pp. 82, 110, and passim.

2 Cf. Joseph F. Kett, *Rites of Passage: Adolescence in America, 1790 to the Present* (New York, 1977), p. 266.

3 Computed from population figures by single year of age in the decennial U.S. censuses of population, plus the sources for Tables 10 and 13 and BSA, *AR* 64 (May 1974):31. The enrollment of girls as Explorers since 1968 and the BSA's failure to report membership by single year of age preclude equivalent calculations for later years, but the decline since the mid-1970s is incontestable.

4 For observational data, see Raymond Montemayor and Roger Van Komen, "Age Segregation of Adolescents In and Out of School," *Journal of Youth and Adolescence* 9 (1980):371–81.

5 Boys and adults were at war over smoking well before 1900.

6 Cf. James S. Coleman, "Youth Culture," in idem et al., *Youth: Transition to Adulthood* (Chicago, 1974), pp. 112–25.

7 E.g., Frederic M. Thrasher, "The Boys' Club and Juvenile Delinquency," *American Journal of Sociology* 42 (July 1936):66–80. Recidivism among juvenile offenders and high dropout rates from high schools point in the same direction.

8 Quotation: John R. Gillis, *Youth and History: Tradition and Change in European Age Relations, 1770–Present* (New York, 1974), p. ix.

9 See above, chapter 6, note 94.

10 BSA, *OR, 1924,* p. 196 (quotation); H. W. Hurt, *Younger Boy Character Education Research* (New York, n.d.), p. 108 and passim; H. Parker Lansdale, "A Historical Study of YMCA Boys' Work in the United States, 1900–1925" (Ph.D. diss., Yale, 1956), pp. 55–57.

11 Robert D. Cuff, "American Historians and the 'Organizational Factor,'" *Canadian Review of American Studies* 4 (Spring 1973):22, summarizing Alfred D. Chandler, *Strategy and Structure: Chapters in the History of Industrial Enterprise* (Cambridge, Mass., 1962).

12 BSA, *OR, 1922,* p. 20; BSA, *OR, 1924,* pp. 195–207, 419.

13 Robert Baden-Powell, *The Wolf Cub's Handbook* (London, 1916); "Headquarters Correspondence on Questions of Policy," *S* 4 (Aug. 1, 1916):6; Junior Boy Scouts, in "Correspondence About Policies" (scrapbook, BSA, NHQ); BSA, *OR, 1924,* pp. 200–2.

14 William D. Murray, *History of the Boy Scouts of America* (New York, 1937), pp. 378–81; Samuel M. Holton, "The Historical Development of the Formal Educational Program of the Boy Scouts of America" (Ph.D. diss., Yale, 1948), pp. 197–202; BSA, *Pack Organization Training Course: How to Organize a Cub Pack* (New York, 1939); Ann W. Nally and James D. Nally, "50 Years of Cub Scouting: A Long Look Back," *S* 68 (Jan.–Feb. 1980):26–29, 66–67; (Mar.–Apr. 1980):32, 48–52.

15 BSA, *AR* 62 (Nov. 1972):131; 65 (Apr. 1976):46–47; Jack W. Berryman, "From the Cradle to the Playing Field: America's Emphasis on Highly Organized Competitive Sports for Preadolescent Boys," *Journal of Sport History* 2 (1975): 112–31.

16 Erik H. Erikson, in *Childhood and Society,* 2nd ed. (New York, 1963), pp. 258–61, describes this age group as striving towards pride in accomplishing tasks.

17 BSA, *OR, 1924,* pp. 103, 447, 487–89; BSA, *AR* 15 (Mar. 1926):142.

18 Murray, *History of the Boy Scouts of America,* p. 377.

19 Holton, "Educational Program," pp. 244–54; Will Oursler, *The Boy Scout Story* (Garden City, 1955), pp. 176–77; BSA, *Exploring* (New York, 1958); BSA, *AR* 59 (July 1969):22.

20 BSA, *AR* 35 (June 1945):8; 64 (May 1974):11, 29; 65 (Apr. 1976):4.

21 These rates may be a bit high, as the BSA may not have taken full account of boys who came and went within a single year. Persistence = (membership at year's end − new members during year) / (membership at start of year). Calculated from BSA, *AR* 65 (Apr. 1976):46–47.

22 Survey Research Center, Institute for Social Research, University of Michigan, *A Study of Boy Scouts and Their Scoutmasters: A Report of Four National Surveys* (Ann Arbor, 1960), pp. 53–54; Nally, "50 Years" (Mar.–Apr.), p. 51. See also BSA, *AR* 36 (June 1946):91.

23 BSA, *AR* 12 (May 1922):27, 102; BSA, *AR* 64 (May 1974):9, 20. But for an account of a three-week troop camp much more intensive than early council camps, see Jay Mechling, "Male Gender Display at a Boy Scout Camp," in R. Timothy Sieber and Andrew J. Gordon, eds., *Children and Their Organizations: Investigations in American Culture* (Boston, 1981), pp. 138–60.

24 "Scouting for the 70's," *S* 60 (Mar.–Apr. 1972):2–5, 61; Yankelovich, *Is Scouting in Tune,* p. 88 and passim.

25 "Coming Soon: Our New Boy Scout Handbook," *S* 67 (Jan.–Feb. 1979):28–30, 58; "Boy Scouts—Trying to Make a Comeback," *U.S. News and World Report* 86 (May 7, 1979):87–88; BSA, *AR* 72 (1982):146, 176–86.

26 BSA, *AR* 72 (1982):87, 94, 97.

27 BSA, *AR* 62 (Nov. 1972):27; 72 (1982):2, 187; U.S. Bureau of the Census, *1970 Census of Population,* vol. 1, *Characteristics of the Population,* part 1, *United States Summary,* section 1 (Washington, 1973), p. 1–265.

28 "The YMCA and the Boy Scouts" (typed MS, c. 1927), at YHL; Mayer N. Zald, *Organizational Change: The Political Economy of the YMCA* (Chicago, 1970), p. 41.

29 Quotations: BSA, *AR* 59 (July 1969):5; Mechling, "Male Gender Display," p. 152.

30 Ann Sieg, "Why Adolescence Occurs," *Adolescence* 6 (1971):377–47. As late as 1961, a survey of graduating medical interns found half believed that masturbation often causes insanity. (Steven M. Dranoff, "Masturbation and the Male Adolescent," *Adolescence* 9 [1974]:170.)

31 Quotations: *The Age of Indiscretion* (Philadelphia, 1950), pp. 71, 62. Davis urged that Boy Scouting begin at age nine, not twelve. See also Oursler, *Boy Scout Story,* pp. 106–9.

32 William Golding, *Lord of the Flies* (New York, 1955). Edgar Z. Friedenberg turns a romantic version of the metaphor to critical ends, presenting adult supervision of teenagers as colonialism in which the youth worker seeks "to wean the young from savagery." What savagery? Noble, one presumes. (*Coming of Age in America: Growth and Acquiescence* [New York, 1965], p. 4.)

33 Herbert J. Gans, *The Levittowners: Ways of Life and Politics in a New Suburban Community* (New York, 1967), p. 206.

34 Burton J. Bledstein, *The Culture of Professionalism: The Middle Class and the Development of Higher Education in America* (New York, 1976), p. 3.

35 M. M. Chambers, *Youth-Serving Organizations* (Washington, 1941), pp. 21–27.

36 Survey Research Center, *Study of Boy Scouts,* pp. 65, 69. In 1958, only 56 percent of American church members were Protestants, although Jewish and Catholic memberships tend to be exaggerated. In 1960, only 34 percent of the country's male labor force held white-collar jobs. (*HS,* pp. 391, 139.)

37 Quotation: above, chapter 12, note 44. See also C. Howard Hopkins, *History of the Y.M.C.A. in North America* (New York, 1951), pp. 519–21.

38 Zald, *Organizational Change,* pp. 146–52. The fact that Boy Scout groups were smaller and often tied to neighborhood institutions made it easier to divide up the community and buffered the strains of integration.

39 Ron Chernow, "Cornering the Goodness Market: Uncharitable Doings at the United Way," *Saturday Review,* Oct. 28, 1978, p. 17.

40 Yankelovich, *Is Scouting in Tune,* p. 29.

41 Zald, *Organizational Change,* pp. 159–228.

42 Chip McGrath, "The Gang in Red Berets," *New York Times Magazine,* Dec. 21, 1975, pp. 6–7, 48–52.

43 Zald, *Organizational Change,* p. 193; Hopkins, *History of the Y.M.C.A.,* pp. 583–85.

44 Davis, *Age of Indiscretion,* p. 70. In 1973, the BSA subsidized camping for 39,515 needy Scouts and non-Scouts. (BSA, *AR* 64 [May 1974]:3.)

45 Anthony M. Platt, *The Child Savers: The Invention of Delinquency,* 2nd ed. (Chicago, 1977), p. 191.

46 Earlier, the South Central region was the most underrepresented. In 1921, the proportion of boys enrolled there was only 28 percent that of the Northwest. In 1960, it was 43 percent. (BSA, *AR* 12 [May 1922]:104; 51 [June 1961]: 166–67; 59 [July 1969]:67; 72 [1982]:146, 176–86.)

47 August B. Hollingshead, *Elmtown's Youth: The Impact of Social Classes on Adolescents* (New York, 1961), p. 292. In the 1950s survey, 33 percent of the sons of business and professional men were Boy Scouts, 33 percent of the clerical workers' sons, 24 percent of the sons of skilled workers, 14 percent of the sons of semiskilled and unskilled workers, and 8 percent of the sons of farm operators. For the YMCA, the respective percentages were 7, 7, 4, 2, and 1; for 4-H and other farm groups, 4, 6, 9, 7, and 36; and for boys' clubs, 2, 1, 4, 2, and 0. The sample comprised only 1,242 boys. The respective figures for school activities were 19, 15, 15, 12, and 9. (Survey Research Center, Institute for Social Research, University of Michigan, *A Study of Boys Becoming Adolescents: A Report of a National Survey of Boys in the 11 to 13 Age Range* [Ann Arbor, 1960], p. 18.)

48 Yankelovich, *Is Scouting in Tune,* p. 29.

49 Chernow, "Cornering the Goodness Market," pp. 15–18; Zald, *Organizational Change,* pp. 204–7; F. Emerson Andrews, *Corporation Giving* (New York, 1952), p. 154.

50 Forty-eight percent of all BSA units were church-sponsored — only a little below the proportion in the 1910s. Because church-sponsored troops were a bit

below average size, though, the number of youths enrolled (all boys except some of the Explorers) may be a better measure of effective support for the BSA. One can construct an index of representation by dividing each denomination's percentage of the enrollment in church-sponsored units by that denomination's percentage of total U.S. church membership and then multiplying the result by 100. Although the results are at best a rough measure, a figure above 100 suggests overrepresentation, while one below 100 indicates underrepresentation. In the following results, because their share of U.S. church membership is generally overstated relative to other religious bodies, the index numbers for Roman Catholics and especially Jews are somewhat too low: Latter-Day Saints, 817; Presbyterian, 346; United Methodist, 289; United Church of Christ (now including the Congregational churches), 140; Lutheran, 134; Episcopal, 116; Roman Catholic, 52; Baptist, 42; African Methodist Episcopal and African Methodist Episcopal Zion (combined), 26; Jewish, 10; Orthodox Christian, 4; Assemblies of God, 3. Black and Southern Baptists presumably lower the Baptist figure. (BSA, *AR* 72 [1982]:90; U.S. Bureau of the Census, *Statistical Abstract of the United States, 1981* [Washington, 1981], pp. 52–53.)

51 A somewhat smaller percentage of BSA units were school-sponsored — 20 percent — but they were above average size. (BSA, *AR* 72 [1982]:92.)

52 Unit sponsors by percentage of BSA boys (and girls) enrolled in 1981: churches, 43.1; parents' clubs, PTAs, and public schools, 25.8; service clubs, 8.2; industry and business, 3.6; veterans' groups, 3.0; groups of citizens, 2.1; fire departments, 1.6; military units, 1.4; law enforcement agencies, 1.2; hospitals, 1.1; fraternal orders, 1.0; private schools, .8; settlement houses, .8; professional and scientific societies, .7; playgrounds and recreation centers, .4; schools for the handicapped, .4; governmental bodies, correctional institutions, district committees of Scout councils, men's clubs, housing projects, .2 each; Office of Economic Opportunity, .1; Grange and Farm Bureau (combined), .1; boys' clubs, .09; YMCAs, .07; labor organizations, .06; unclassified and other sponsors under .1 percent, 3.3. (BSA, *AR* 72 [1982]:90–92.) Industry supported Exploring as a form of vocational guidance, but business-sponsored Cub and Boy Scout units also enrolled twenty-six times as many boys as those backed by labor unions.

53 Owen E. Pence, *The Professional Boys' Worker in the Young Men's Christian Association: An Occupational Study* (New York, 1932); Robert H. Shaffer, "Career Opportunities with the Boy Scouts," *Occupations* 19 (1941):567–69.

54 BSA, *AR* 72 (1982):75; Zald, *Organizational Change,* p. 73.

55 H. Paul Douglass, *How Shall Country Youth Be Served? A Study of the "Rural" Work of Certain National Character-Building Agencies* (New York, 1926), pp. 155–60.

56 Chernow, "Cornering the Goodness Market," p. 16. More than mere access has been involved, as employers have pressured employees to give. ("Donors' Backlash," *Wall Street Journal,* Jan. 12, 1982, p. 1.) On the 1970s decline, see "Boy Scouts — Trying," pp. 87–88.

Index

Abbott, Jacob, 16

Adams, Rev. John Quincy, 42, 88

Addams, Jane, 33, 92, 152

Administrative models: military, 90–91, 161; amateur, 143, 156; school, 152; business, 153, 155, 158, 165, 295, 350n32. *See also* Bureaucracy

Adolescence: and boys' clubs, xiv, 114; in historical writing, xiv–xv; theories of, 19–20; social class and, 19–28, 100; forerunners and origins of, 20–22; adult concerns about, 23, 28, 50, 107, 115, 241, 258, 266, 299; character builders concentrate on, 97, 105–6, 114, 115–16, 158, 295; early use of term, 98; G. Stanley Hall on, 98–101; age limits of, 101, 102, 106, 112, 292, 337n46; romanticism manipulated, 107, 286; BSA response to, 107–8, 253, 258, 266, 280–81, 288–89, 297; distraction from, 107–8, 264, 277; YMCA response to, 108, 238, 258, 259–65, 266, 287–89; and junior high schools, 112; knowledge of gives character builders authority, 112, 118, 119, 122, 124; and Catholic boys' work, 113; and girls' work agencies, 113–14; and British Scouting, 141–42; public approves concern for, 187, 204; crises of, 244, 262–64; turmoil exaggerated, 266, 379–80n96; peer groups in, 275; developmental tasks of, 288; recent changes in, 291, 293. *See also* Preadolescent boys; Puberty; Religious conversions

Adventure, 173, 236, 244

Agassiz Association, 246

Age: and boys' response to character building, xvi, 291; boys seek status with, 27–28, 283; of puberty, 37, 38, 280–81, 320n51; of physical growth, 38; early teens critical, 38, 43, 106, 284; of Sunday school pupils, 42–43, 137; *vs.* masculinity as boys' concern, 46, 283; for relaxing home restraints, 47, 48, 296; of idealized boyhood, 55; in boys' clubs, 68–69; of YMCA boys, 77–79, 287–89, 299; in temperance societies, 85; of religious conversion, 100, 108; in British Scouting, 141, 142, 282; in woodcraft groups, 142; and political thinking, 253; and moral development, 255–56; of Boy Scouts, 278, 280–82, 286, 287, 289, 291–92, 296, 298, 383n74, 383n75; in Boys' Brigades, 280, 283; of runaway Boy Scouts, 284; of boys' interest in girls, 284; of recreational tastes, 285, 385n99; of Cub Scouts, 292, 298; of Explorers, 291–92, 299. *See also* Adolescence; Older boys; Preadolescent boys

Age limits: in boys' clubs, 38, 114; in YMCA, 72, 74, 105–6; in Boys' Brigades, 89, 281; of gang age, 97, 101–2; of culture epochs, 101; in BSA, 106–7, 149, 296, 297, 387n31; in girls' work, 113–14, 184; in Catholic boys' work, 113

Age mixing: decline of, 21–22, 28; in farm groups, 228

Age stratification: and character building, 4, 28; in schools, 24, 27; among boys, 27–28, 282, 292–93, 297; by social class, 28, 293; in boys' clubs, 70; in YMCA, 72, 74, 77–79, 287, 299; in BSA, 272, 297; in British boys' work, 273, 382n40; in boys' recreation, 286–87

Alcott, Louisa May, 53

Aldrich, Thomas Bailey, 52

Alexander, John L., 54, 113, 122, 146, 183, 239

Altruism, 103, 104, 105. *See also* Good
turns
Alverson, O. C., 245
Amateurism, 91, 143, 156, 161–62
American Boy Scouts, 147. *See also*
United States Boy Scouts
American Cadets, 157, 259
American Federation of Labor, 40, 204
Americanism, BSA's: and revision of pro-
gram, 148; in 1910s and 1920s, 156, 180,
181, 182–83, 186, 209; and church rela-
tions, 192, 196–97, 198, 201, 304; alarms
immigrants, 215; in 1930s, 301
American Legion, 182, 191, 203
Anti-intellectualism, 41, 50, 244, 346*n35*
Assistant Scoutmasters, 282
Association of Boys' Secretaries of North
America, 123
Athletics. *See* Sports
Atkinson, John F., 66, 68
Authoritarianism, and Boy Scouts, 253–54
Authority, in Scout troops, 274

Babcock, W. H., 227
"Bad" boy, 53, 54, 256
Baden-Powell, Robert S. S.: character-
building methods, 31, 157, 249, 250;
criticizes British society, 32, 46, 136–37;
on control of boys, 40, 41, 137; sources
for Boy Scouting, 54, 137, 140–41, 240,
347*n42*; boyhood, 133, 347*n53*; career,
133–34, 136; and Seton, 134, 140,
345*n19*, 347*n43*; begins Boy Scouting,
134–35; public persona, 135, 139; and
working class, 137, 144, 177, 204, 245–
46*n29*, 346*n35*; on military training,
139; and other boys' workers, 140–41,
200; boyishness, 141–42; relations with
mother, 142; controls British Scouting,
143; in Canada, 144; and formation of
BSA, 144, 145, 147; ideas differ from
BSA, 148, 149, 150, 273, 281; further
innovations, 158, 164, 282, 295; backs
internationalism, 183; forms Girl
Guides, 184; racist joke, 212; criticizes
Boy Scouts in U.S., 244, 273; on sexuality, 260, 261
Ballantine, William G., 118
Baptist churches and members, 192, 193,
196, 197, 304, 360*n29*, 389*n50*
Baptist Young People's Union, 23

Barclay, Lorne, 163, 182, 272
Baseball, 52, 110, 224, 285, 385*n98*,
385*n99*
Basketball, 82, 286, 287, 385*n106*
Beard, Daniel Carter: boyhood, 6, 7; criti-
cizes schools, 47; career, 132; *vs.* Seton,
133, 239; and Baden-Powell, 140, 145;
boyishness, 141–42; role in BSA, 147,
151, 154, 239; criticizes BSA, 156, 157,
239; political attitudes, 181, 182, 185;
on Boy Scouts' social class, 218; popu-
larity with boys, 239; and outdoors,
242, 246. *See also* Sons of Daniel
Boone
Beard, George M., 49
Beecher, Henry Ward, 18
Benedict, Ruth, 19
Benson, O. H., 228
Beresford, Admiral Charles, 134
Bethune, George, 22
Bettelheim, Bruno, 54–55
Bible study, 80, 81, 90, 126, 192, 252, 258,
262, 275
Big cities, character builders' problems in,
76, 150, 224–26
Birthrates, 15, 46
Black boys: problems, 25–26; in BSA,
212–14, 217, 301, 302; in YMCA, 214,
301
Black churches, 194–95, 389*n50*
Blacks, as Scoutmasters, 193, 213
Blos, Peter, 236, 347*n53*
Blue-collar workers: status of, 11–13; and
BSA, 13, 206, 222, 301, 333, 388*n47*
Board, Francis, 34
Boer War, 134, 136, 139
Bogan, Samuel, 149
Bogradus, Emory, 223
Bolshevism, fear of, 182, 183
Bomus, Peter, 147, 151
Booth, Charles, 136
Bope, Henry P., 91, 104
Borden, Matthew C. D., 65
Boredom, boys', 175, 269, 279, 297, 300
Boyce, William D., 146, 227, 279
Boyhood: idealized American, 52–53, 54,
58–59; British, 53–54, 138; prolonging,
55, 107–8; BSA style of, 55, 115, 285;
in early YMCAs, 77–79; *vs.* childhood,
78–79; age span of, 97, 99; Scoutmas-
ters nostalgic for, 208–9. *See also* Gang

Boyhood (*continued*)
  age; Preadolescent boys; Savages, boys
  as; Small-town boyhood
Boy Pioneers, 133
Boy problem, the, 33, 148
Boys. *See* Black boys; Boyhood; Farm
  boys; Immigrant boys; Lower-class boys;
  Middle-class boys; Older boys; Younger
  boys
Boys, American and British compared,
  273, 274, 279
Boys' activities: foreshadow character
  building, 86–87, 236
Boys as leaders: in Sons of Daniel Boone,
  133, 272; in Britain, 138, 273, 382*n40*;
  authoritarianism and, 271–72; in Boys'
  Brigades, 273, 381*n37*. *See also* Boy
  Scout patrols; YMCA boys: as leaders
Boys' Brigade, British: origins, 87–88; uniform, 88; membership, 88; boys' social
  class, 88, 346*n39*; and Boy Scouting,
  92, 134, 136, 140–41
Boys' Brigades, American: early history,
  85, 88; pledge, 85, 256; boys' social
  class, 88; compared to British, 88, 90,
  273; membership, 88, 90, 278; organization, 88, 90–91; uniforms, 88, 91, 92;
  and churches, 88, 91–92, 280; ages in,
  89, 280, 281, 283; military training, 89–
  92, 235, 276; religious activities, 90; and
  National Guard, 90, 92; decline, 90, 92,
  93; officers, 91, 276; and BSA, 91, 92,
  93, 104, 209, 210; individualism in, 104;
  camps, 235, 236; discipline, 235, 273;
  boy officers, 273, 381*n37*
Boys' brotherhoods, 196
Boys' Club Federation, 69, 70, 71
Boys' club members: social backgrounds,
  68, 69, 217, 303, 388*n47*; ages, 68–69,
  114, 293; racial integration, 213; attendance, 328*n19*
Boys' Club of the City of New York, 64,
  66, 68
Boys' clubs: and adolescence, xv, 114;
  goals of, 3, 67–69, 70–71; small, 6;
  compared to character-building agencies, 63, 66, 67–71, 114; types of, 63–64;
  church-sponsored, 63–64, 189; religious
  activities of, 64, 68; sponsors and supporters, 64–65; workers in, 65, 69, 70,
  71; arguments for need, 65–66; member-

ships, 66, 69; discipline in, 66–67; programs, 66–68, 70; moral training in, 67;
  character-building expectations in, 67–
  68, 69–70, 71; and YMCA, 68, 77, 80,
  81, 302; numbers of, 69; job training in,
  70; mass methods, 70–71; and BSA,
  70–71, 114, 119, 200, 209, 210, 300, 304,
  389*n52*; pledges in, 85; British, 137,
  140; camps, 224, 235
Boys' Clubs of America, 69, 114, 300
Boy Scout executives: powers and duties,
  158–64 *passim,* 193, 245; numbers, 159,
  305; background and training, 159–62;
  and Scoutmasters, 162–64, 190–91, 211,
  244–45
Boy Scouting: purposes, 47, 107, 110, 115,
  163, 175, 280–82; in fiction, 155, 173;
  international, 183
— British: political affinities, 136, 137,
  138; military elements, 139; administration, 143; membership, 143; rivals to,
  143, 144; boys' response to, 143, 282;
  social class in, 144
— British and American compared: program, 148–50, 244, 295; administration,
  153, 156, 157, 158, 164; goals, 273; boys'
  response, 279, 282
Boy Scout patrols, 104, 138, 140, 215, 242,
  271–73, 381*n33*
Boy Scout program and activities: sources,
  130, 134–37, 140–41; Americanization,
  148–49; games, 243, 285; rituals, 244,
  286; 1970s revisions, 298
— badges: British, 135; American, 149;
  BSA control of, 154, 155, 156; and first
  class rank, 158, 298; and school grades,
  224; types available, 227, 352*n75*,
  374*n2*; types earned, 240, 251–52, 259,
  384*n97*; numbers won, 248, 249, 252;
  examinations for, 250.
— camps: attendance, 152, 219, 241–42,
  245, 297–98; cost, 217, 241, 388*n44*; activities and schedule, 236, 241–45, 247;
  troop camps, 241, 242, 244, 245,
  387*n23*; living conditions, 241–43;
  campfires, 243, 274; mass camps,
  244–45, 270
— character building: techniques, 31, 175,
  248; as goal of BSA, 187, 216; results
  of, 257–58, 276, 377*n50*
— instruction: in citizenship and patrio-

tism, 176, 180, 181, 207, 253–55; military, 178–80; techniques, 250–51, 269

— moral training: Boy Scout motto, 18, 135, 137, 145; Boy Scout oath, 29, 86, 135, 148–49, 175, 256–57, 273; Boy Scout law, 135, 137, 149, 175–77, 255–57; boys' response, 149, 256–57, 276, 377*n47*; formalism, 255, 299, 376*n37*; in troop setting, 256

— outdoor activities: foreshadowed by boys, 53, 385*n98*; admired by public, 172, 186, 204; boys' interest in, 224, 279, 285; conservation in, 240, 246; de-emphasized, 240, 298. *See also* Boy Scout program and activities—camps; Hikes

— promotion requirements: outlined, 135, 149, 298; enforcement and testing, 157–58, 162, 163; most difficult, 163, 164, 217, 249–50

— service projects: described, 173–75, 246; limits on scope of, 174–75, 185, 254, 297; in wartime, 181; admired by public, 187

Boy Scouts: individual enthusiasts, 8, 277–78; Sunday school attendance, 192; relations with girls, 260, 284–85; relations with Scoutmasters, 274, 276, 277

— advancement in rank: pressures on boys, 245, 248, 251, 276, 374*n2*; rates of, 248, 249, 297, 298; and duration of membership, 383*n75*

— age: limits, 106, 149, 281, 297; older boy problems, 272, 283, 284, 381*n33*; of recruitment, 280, 281, 296, 383*n74*, 383*n75*; of runaways, 284; of current members, 286, 287, 289, 291, 292; and grade in school, 287

— backgrounds of: social class, 13, 47, 218–21, 257–58, 300, 303, 366–67*n40*, 388*n47*; in BSA publicity, 177; race, 213, 301; BSA social outreach, 216, 219, 274, 301, 302; religious affiliations, 219; family size, 219

— character of: tests of, 257–58, 377*n50*

— departure from Scouting: reasons for, 224, 240, 278–79, 282, 284–85, 383*n67*; frequency by years of membership, 278; frequency by age, 280, 281; Scoutmaster's reaction to, 286. *See also* Boy Scouts—membership

— membership: by size of municipality, 36, 190, 224–26, 302, 369*n74*, 369*n76*; aggregate, 153, 154, 297, 298, 300; turnover, 153, 154, 164, 278–80, 290, 297, 383*n66*, 387*n21*; regional, 158, 302–3, 388*n47*; duration of, 278, 280, 383*n74*, 383*n75*; as share of all American boys, 278, 291

— responses to program: reasons for joining, 171, 173, 281; surveyed by age, 291; summarized, 293–94

Boy Scouts of America: badge Americanized, 148; publications, 149, 154, 155, 163, 180, 298; finances, 151, 152, 155, 181–82, 202, 203, 303, 305; legal monopoly, 156–57; Congressional charter, 156–57, 181; religious policies, 160, 176, 186, 187, 191–92, 197, 198; World War I projects, 175, 181, 243, 253, 254, 357*n66*; U.S. president's role in, 178; citizenship rules, 180, 181, 182

— expansion and success: cumulative membership, xi; reasons for, xi–xii, xiv, xvii, xviii, 290, 293–94, 300; administrative strategies for, 153, 154, 158, 164, 165–66

— organization: early development of, 146–48, 150–56; National Council, 150; local councils, 150, 152, 153, 159, 161–62, 202, 203; executive board, 150–51, 156, 181, 185, 213, 350*n32*, 358*n89*; centralization, 150–59, 161–62, 164, 193, 213, 270, 350*n27*; registration system, 152; national headquarters, 153–56; National Court of Honor, 154, 173; Supply Department, 155, 246; bureaucratic features, 156, 158–59, 160–61, 295, 305; administrative models, 156, 161, 295; power of paid staff, 158–59, 161–62, 166; district committees, 158–59, 225; volunteers in, 166–67, 193; summarized, 210–11

— political positions: antiradicalism, 181, 182, 198; demands on Scoutmasters, 183, 357*n76*; contemporary affinities, 184–86; nonpartisanship, 186; contrasted to foreign youth groups, 294; shifts in 1930s, 301

— publicity and public image: social class in, 34, 177–78, 223; public attitudes towards BSA, 162, 186–87, 290, 305; serious tone, 171, 175, 187; techniques, 172;

BSA publicity and public image (*continued*) use of boys' achievements, 172–73, 248–49; service projects and, 173–75; policy statements and, 175–80; nationalism in, 178, 181–83; military issues in, 178–80, 348–49*n7*; outdoor activities and, 182, 186; problems with word "Boy," 283, 384*n87*
— relationships and comparisons with: Girl Scouting, 50, 183; Boys' Brigades, 91, 92, 104, 152, 334*n54*; other boys' work agencies, 136, 151, 200; public schools, 152, 157, 161, 162, 163, 191, 199–200, 253, 269, 270, 271; immigrants, 157, 175, 177, 197, 201, 215–17; 365*n18*; churches, 176, 178, 190–98; Camp Fire Girls, 183–84; parents, 186, 187, 216, 237; boys' clubs, 191, 200, 300, 304, 389*n52*; Sunday schools, 191–92, 280; farmers, 227–28; Progressive reform, 253, 255, 355*n19*. *See also* YMCA and BSA
— standards and standardization: role in BSA growth, 150, 164; enforcement problems, 162–64, 250, 281; criticized, 164; in policy statements, 175–80; of uniforms, 178; in camping, 239, 242, 245; rigidity of, 286, 295
— statements of purpose: gravity of, 171, 175, 187; formulas used, 175, 182, 216; by Scoutmasters, 208, 364*n100*; in 1960s, 299
— uniform: BSA monopoly of, 157; described, 178, 183; blacks not to wear, 213, 214; cost of, 217, 302; mocked by other youths, 222–23, 283, 284, 291
Boy Scout troops: troop committees, 153, 162; collapse of, 153, 269, 278, 279, 383*n67*; institutional sponsors of, 162, 188, 191–200, 203, 204, 205, 221, 303–4, 388–89*n50*, 389*n51*, 389*n52*; cohesion and group loyalty, 174, 243, 245, 269–72; meetings and activities, 199, 242, 269, 271, 276–79, 285; size and structure, 268–69, 270, 271, 282
Boys' Life, 149, 155, 179, 255
Boys' Life Brigade, 346*n39*
Boys' work: organizational unification of, 69, 113, 114; consensus within, 113; rivalries within, 114, 200
Brady, Cyrus Townsend, 179

Brainerd, Cephas, 74
British Boy Scouts, 143
British influences: on American boys' work, 40, 54, 64; on concepts of boyhood, 54
Britton, S. C., 204
Brooks, Murray, 276
Brosard, Rev. William, 190
Brown, I. E., 77–78, 81
BSA. *See* Boy Scouts of America
Buck, Winifred, 217
Bureaucracy, 13–14, 155, 161, 165, 166. *See also* Boy Scouts of America—organization
Bureau of Municipal Research, 155
Burger, William H., 122, 142, 347*n53*
Burgess, Thornton W., 110
Burnett, Frances Hodgson, 48
Burroughs, John, 239
Burt, Henry F., 102, 339*n77*
Bushnell, Horace, 17, 23
Business ethos, in BSA, 151, 152, 160, 190–91
Business firms: support YMCA, 201, 202; support BSA, 201, 202, 304, 389*n52*
Businessmen, role in BSA, 151, 152, 160, 201–4, 206, 350*n32*
Busyness: in YMCA, 81, 238; as remedy for adolescence, 107–8, 300; in Boy Scouting, 138, 172, 243, 246; boys as paragons of, 277, 278

Cadet corps, 52, 85, 86, 87, 92, 189. *See also* Boys' Brigades, American
Cadets of Temperance, 83–84, 85, 87
Camp Dudley, 237, 238
Camp Fire Girls, 50–51, 113, 132, 183–84
Campfires, 131, 134–35, 237–38, 243–44, 245
Camping: effect on boys, xviii; and stereotypes of boyhood, 54, 102; role in character building, 233–34; origins of organized, 234–36; and older boys, 285
Camps: private, 235, 237; organizational, 237. *See also* Boys' clubs: camps; Boy Scout program—camps; YMCA camps
Canada: YMCA in, 125, 186, 196; Boy Scouting in, 139, 144, 153, 197
Canadians: in U.S. boys' work, 40, 54, 182
Captains of Ten, 189
Career lines, boys', 5, 22, 25–26

Carey, Arthur, 156, 256

Carnegie, Andrew, 92, 151, 178

Catholic Boys' Brigade, 91, 198

Catholics. *See* Roman Catholic churches and members

Catton, Bruce, 7, 8

Chamberlain, Joseph, 138, 139

Chandler, Alfred D., 295

Character: definitions of, xvi, 29–30, 44, 89, 248, 257; and middle-class identity, 17, 29, 207; Baden-Powell's views of, 138; age of development, 294–95. *See also* Boy Scouts—character of

Character builders: social class of, xvii, xviii; expertise of, 165–66; successes summarized, 289–90, 293–94, 305; values summarized, 305

Character building: definitions of, xi–xii, 3–4, 30–31, 73–74, 80, 93, 100, 249; and middle class, 3–4, 18, 56–57, 203; and child rearing, 17; goals of, 18, 29, 32, 38–44, 51, 112, 289–90; and boys' clubs, 67–72; early ideas of, 82, 83, 85, 93; recapitulation theory reorients, 109, 110, 111; Seton's methods of, 131–32; Baden-Powell's methods of, 135, 138, 295; in schools, 198; at camp, 233–34; results summarized, 265–66; in 1920s, 295; first use of term, 317n6. *See also* Boy Scout program and activities—character building

Cheating, tests of, 257

Chew, Thomas, 65, 67, 68, 114, 339n77

Chicago, Illinois: YMCA of, 74, 127, 301; BSA in, 152, 202, 208, 218

Chicago Boys' Club, 67, 68, 69, 70, 85, 221–22, 328n19

Chicago Teachers' Federation, 200

Childishness, boys' fear of, 184, 283, 284

Child labor, 25–26

Child-rearing techniques, 4, 9, 15–17, 22, 224

Children's literature, 16, 19, 103

Child study movement, 16, 98

Child welfare movement, 26, 57, 177

Chivalry, 70, 97, 101, 107, 137–38, 189–90, 337n53

Christian Citizenship Training Program, 125, 193, 252, 263

Christian Endeavor Society, 23, 196

Christian nurture, 23, 80, 109, 126

Churches: boys' work of, 88, 91–92, 189–90, 192, 226; and British Boy Scouting, 137, 143, 144; as BSA unit sponsors, 190–98, 303–4, 388–89n50, 389n52; memberships of, 193, 194–95, 360n25, 388n36; farmers', 228

Cigarettes, 85, 254. *See also* Smoking

Citizenship: YMCA version, 173–74; BSA training in, 174–85, 253, 254

City boys, 5–6, 32–33, 43, 298, 302

City life, 10, 32, 36–37, 49, 55

City missions, 64, 65

Civil religion, in BSA, 176

Class conflict, fears of, 58, 66, 87, 136, 137, 138, 149, 177–78

Clergymen, Protestant: roles in BSA, 160, 190–91, 202, 206, 207, 225; need boys' work, 189–90; roles in YMCA, 192, 193, 205

Clerical workers: income, 12; masculinity concerns, 46; in YMCA, 73; as Scoutmasters, 206, 364n95

Cognitive stages, 251, 255

Cohn, Judge A. B., 208

Cold Water Army, 83

College attendance, Boy Scouts', 219

Collins, Rev. John C., 64

Commercial entertainment, 33, 136

Committee for Christian Workers, 64

Community chest, 173, 202, 203, 303. *See also* United Way

Community integration, 200–201, 203

Comrades (YMCA group), 299

Comstock, Anthony, 33

Conformity, xvii–xviii, 140, 201

Congregationalist churches and church members, 192, 193–95, 196, 360n29

Conservation, 185, 246

Control of boys: character builders seek, xv, xvi, 29, 32, 273, 300; adults want, 16–17, 54–55; methods for, 39, 89, 99–100, 233, 238, 244, 270; churches need, 42–44; *vs.* masculinity, 47, 55, 283, 286; problems maintaining, 79–80, 264–65, 274, 293, 294; boys' work supporters want, 188, 204; teachers want, 198–99; in Cub Scouting, 296. *See also* Independence; Social order and control

Cooley, Charles, 103

Cooperation, teaching, 101, 103, 104–5

Cotton, Arthur N., 262, 263, 264

Countryside: BSA in, 225, 226, 228; YMCA in, 227
Covello, Leonard, 5, 6, 58
Crackel, Matthew, 260, 261
Craft, Henry K., 214
Crafts, Rev. Wilbur F., 85
Crane, Zenas, 65
Creel, George, 58
Crockett, David, 145
Crosby, F. A., 111
Crowell, H. E., 76
Cub Scouting, 292, 295–98, 303–4, 387n21
Curfew ordinances, 26, 65
Curtis, Henry S., 36, 113

Dale, Ludwig S., 152
Dater, Alfred W., 350n32
Davis, Clyde Brion, 36, 299, 302
Davis, Jesse, 7, 8
Debs, Eugene V., 176
deGroot, E. B., 284
Demographic trends: ratio of boys to men, 20; in 1970s, 298
Demos, John, 21
Demos, Virginia, 21
Dependency, extension of boys', 22–23, 24, 26, 27, 38, 45, 100–101, 109
Dewey, Admiral George, 54
Dewey, John, 58, 115, 295, 296
Discipline, 17, 66–67, 89–90, 273, 274. *See also* Control of boys
Doggett, Laurence L., 118
Drill, military: praised for boys, 31, 88–89; as recreation, 86, 87, 89; decried for boys, 92; in BSA, 183, 269; Girl Scouts', 184. *See also* Military activities and training
Drill, physical, 82, 252
Drinking, boys', 34, 36, 84, 85, 332n5
Drummond, Henry, 88, 98
Dudley, Sumner, 72, 74, 80, 142, 234, 236, 237
Dulaney, Benjamin L., 151
Durieux, A. H., 223

Eagle Scouts: badge requirements, 149, 157, 251, 377n47; numbers of, 248, 297, 298
Education: and social background, 4–5, 7, 8, 16; extension of, 24–26
Edwards, Jonathan, 21

Efficiency, zeal for, 147–48, 160, 165, 190–91, 245, 248
Eisenstadt, S. N., 19, 27, 104, 183
Eliot, Charles William, 273
Elks, 191, 203
Elles, Sir Edmund, 139
Elmer, Franklin D., 196–97
Emotions, fear of, 51, 107–8
Employed Boys' Brotherhood, 220
Energy, boys', admired, 52, 53, 55, 56, 59, 102, 186
Episcopal churches and members, 192, 193–95, 196, 304, 360n29, 389n50
Epworth Guards, 88
Epworth League, 23, 196
Erikson, Erik H., 21, 30, 141, 249, 386n16
Ethnocentrism, 35–36
Evolution, 97, 98–99
Expertise, technical: in character building, xvii, 57, 116, 164, 165–66; in Progressive reform, 165, 166
Explorer program, 291, 292, 296–97, 298–99, 303–4, 305, 387n21
Extracurricular activities, schools', 17, 40–41, 200, 303, 388n47

Faculty psychology, 30–31, 83, 84, 110–11, 138, 140, 266
Fagans, Philip, 239
Fairchild, Henry Pratt, 216, 257–58
Fallows, Rev. Samuel, 91
Family life: middle-class, 10, 17, 40; criticized, 34
Family size, 15–16, 313n46
Farm boys: lives of, 4–5, 21, 28, 51, 227; idealized by character builders, 32, 52, 227; in BSA, 228; in YMCA, 302
Farm clubs, 51, 227, 388n47
Farmers: numbers, 8–9; income, 9; separate from middle class, 11; resist urban character building, 205, 206, 227–28, 304; 388n47, 389n52
Farm labor, in boys' work, 235, 243, 252
Fathers: relations with sons, 4, 5–6, 6–7, 8, 16; criticized by character builders, 40, 47–48; involvement in character building, 171, 268
Federal Council of Churches, 192
Federated Boys' Clubs, 69, 114
Feminization, fears of, 46–48
Fighting, boys', 53, 55

Finley, John H., 151
First aid, 135, 163, 172, 249–50
Fisher, George J., 44, 158–59, 162, 200, 205, 241
Fiske, George Walter, 100, 101
Flint, Rev. Joseph, 260
Forbush, William Byron, 47, 103, 107, 108, 111, 112, 113, 123, 141, 176, 189–90, 262
Formalism: in character building, 251, 253, 254, 255, 258; revolt against, 258
Forward Step, in Y boys' work, 126, 263, 264, 265
Foster, Eugene C., 44, 339*n77*
France, Boy Scouting in, 176, 197
Freeman, A. R., 252
Fretwell, Elbert K., 104, 115, 295
Friendly Indians (Y group), 299
Frontier, closing of, 45–46, 102–3
Fun, boys' demand for, 171, 175, 276–77
Furfey, Paul H., 281

Galpin, Charles, 228
Gang age: in character-bulding theory, 97–98, 112, 113, 115, 227; limits of, 101, 102, 292
Gangs: studies of, 102; praised, 102, 103, 110; condemned, 102, 116, 274; use to control boys, 104
Garland, Hamlin, 4, 5, 239
Gawtry, Lewis B., 350*n32*
General Alliance of Workers with Boys, 69, 113, 114, 339*n77*
Gentry class, 11, 14, 15, 30
George Junior Republic, 58
Gibson, H. W., 50, 241, 261
Gillis, John, 21
Girl Guides, 184
Girls: draw boys from BSA, 284–85; at YMCA parties, 284–85; in Explorer units, 297, 299; wages, 316*n97*; age of puberty, 320*n51*
Girls and boys compared: Sunday school membership, 42–43; youth work, 50–52; socialization, 51–52; adult expectations of, 53
Girl Scouting: BSA opposes, 46, 114, 183–84; origins and program, 50–51, 113, 183
Girvin, E. A., 90
Goethals, George W., 151

Golden, Harry, 5, 6
Golding, William, 299
Goodman, Fred S., 108
Good turns, 136, 137–38, 256
Grauer, O. C., 89
Gray, Frank F., 283, 373*n52*
Gregg, Abel J., 115
Griggs, Edward H., 16, 17
Group loyalties, boys', 268–69, 270, 277–80, 294
Group orientation: in Progressive Era, 103, 105; in character building, 104–5
Gulick, Charlotte Vetter, 50, 183
Gulick, Luther, 49, 50, 73, 82, 101, 102, 103, 106, 112, 113, 118–19, 147, 183
Gymnastics, 70, 73, 81–82, 223

Habits, 31, 67, 111, 115, 138, 263, 264, 295
Haeckel, Ernst, 99
Hall, G. Stanley: child-rearing advice, 16; boyhood and career, 98; views on adolescence, 98–101, 106, 266, 295, 337*n46*; influence on boys' workers, 109–15, 118, 123, 131, 141, 143, 338*n63*
Handicapped boys, 157, 158, 352*n75*
Hanmer, Lee F., 46, 147, 151
Hantover, Jeffrey P., 47, 208, 218
Hargrave, John, 143
Harriman, Edward H., 64, 66
Harris, Stanley, 214
Harris, William Torrey, 41
Harrison, Benjamin, 88–89
Hartshorne, Hugh, 257
Hays, Samuel P., 116, 165, 166
Hays, Willett M., 227
Hazing, 238, 244
Head, Walter W., 350*n32*
Hearst newspapers, 146, 147, 157
Hennrich, Kilian J., 113, 198
Herrick, Myron T., 350*n32*
High school boys: in YMCA, 220, 221, 287–88; and Boy Scouting, 284, 285–86; recreational tastes of, 285
High schools: enrollments, 24–25; sexuality in, 37, 263–64; YMCA clubs in, 120, 199, 220, 221, 288; Boy Scout troops in, 199
Hikes, 178, 236, 240–41
Hillcourt, William, 298
Hinckley, George W., 151
Hoard, Rev. Guy V., 260

Hollingshead, A. B., 303
Homosexuality, 208, 261, 378*n72*
Hopson, S. W., 29
Hornaday, William T., 246
Housman, W. J. B., 161
Howells, William Dean, 53, 246
Hoyt, John Sherman, 151
Hughes, Thomas, 53
Hulse, E. P., 283
Hurt, Harold W., 115, 165, 295, 296

Immigrant boys: work, 25; in YMCA,
    214–15, 216, 367*n46*; political attitudes,
    224. *See also* Boy Scouts of America—
    relationships: immigrants
Income, differences in, 9, 12
Independence, boys seek, 28, 79–80, 224,
    283–84, 286–87
Indian motif in boys' work, 131, 132, 140,
    147, 156, 239, 240, 244
Individualism, 104, 105, 228, 273, 289–90
Industrial Workers of the World, 182, 204
Instincts, 97, 99, 102, 110, 111, 115, 295
Intellectual training: schools' stress on de-
    cried, 41, 49; in character building, 251,
    253, 265
International Order of Good Templars, 84

James, William, 30, 45, 110, 111, 179
Jemison, David, 189
Jenks, Jeremiah, 148, 151, 216, 258,
    358*n89*, 376*n37*
Jensen, Richard, 196
Jewish boys, 198, 219, 264, 366*n21*, 367*n46*
Jews, BSA support by, 194–95, 304,
    389*n50*
Johnson, George, 110
Johnson, John, 54
Johnson, Owen, 102
Jones, John Price, 172
Jones, Mark M., 164
Jump, Rev. H. A., 189
Junior high schools, 112, 287
Juvenile delinquency: and courts, 33, 39,
    127, 167, 302; remedies for, 39, 58, 66;
    BSA response to, 177, 216, 257; Boy
    Scouts' rates, 257, 377*n50*
Juvenile Templars, 84–85

Kappa Sigma Pi, 189
Keith, Charles, 65

Kett, Joseph F., xiv–xv, 45, 86, 229
Kibbo Kift Kindred, 143
Kilpatrick, William H., 115
Kingsley, Charles, 45
Kipling, Rudyard, 295
Kirkham, Oscar A., 285
Kiwanis clubs, 191, 203
Kleppner, Paul, 196
Knapp, Seaman, 227
Knebel, A. G., 117
Knights of Columbus, 191, 203
Knights of King Arthur, 111, 189–90, 209
Knights of the Holy Grail, 189, 235
Kocka, Jürgen, 11–12
Kohlberg, Lawrence, 255–56
Krackowizer, E. W., 114

Labor unions, 162, 177, 182, 204–5, 304,
    389*n52*
Laura Spellman Rockefeller Foundation,
    214
Lee, Joseph, 113
Leisure time: boys', 4, 5, 6–8, 40, 227,
    278; middle-class, 18
Letts, Arthur, 350*n32*
Lindsey, Benjamin B., 339*n77*
Lipscomb, Dr. W. N., 250
Livingstone, Colin H., 147, 151, 156, 176,
    179, 186
Lodge, Henry Cabot, 48
Lone Scouting, 227–28
Look-Up Legion, 85
Loomis, Ormond, 207
Low, Juliette Gordon, 50, 184
Lower-class boys: lives of, 5–6, 28; charac-
    ter decried, 34, 136–37; and YMCA, 77,
    79, 214, 216, 217, 223–24, 301, 303,
    388*n47*; and British Scouting, 137, 138,
    144, 222, 345–46*n29*, 346*n35*; and BSA,
    215–16, 218, 219, 301, 302, 303, 388*n44*,
    388*n47*; and boys' clubs, 221–22,
    368*n66*. *See also* Boys' clubs; Street
    boys
Loyal Temperance Legion, 84
Lubove, Roy, 166
Lutheran churches and church members,
    193–95, 196, 197, 304, 389*n50*

McAdoo, William Gibbs, 182, 185
McBurney, Robert R., 74, 76
McCormick, Harold, 350*n32*

McCormick, William, 64, 65, 114, 200, 218, 283

McDonald, L. L., 215, 218, 242

McRae, Milton L., 151

Manliness: character builders' concern for, xv, xvi, 122, 132, 133, 208; maturity or masculinity, xvi, 45, 46, 283, 286–87; clergymen worry about, 189, 190–91. *See also* Masculinity

Manual training, 47, 67–68, 70

Marshall, Lynn, 161

Martin, E. S., 295

Marx, Leo, 58–59

Masculinity: fears of loss by men and boys, 32, 44–49; *vs.* religious commitment, 44, 48; notions of, 45, 145, 266; as goal of BSA, 46, 47, 110, 183–84, 249, 289; boys' concerns about, 46, 184, 283, 286–87; small boyhood as haven of, 53, 55, 103, 142; *vs.* control in character building, 55, 184; as YMCA goal, 73, 78–79, 223, 289; through camping, 234, 238, 244. *See also* Muscular Christianity; Strength

Mason, Frank, 67, 69

Masturbation, 37, 49–50, 53, 101, 260, 261, 263, 264, 299, 387n30

Mathiews, Franklin K., 33, 155, 283

May, Mark, 257

Mead, George, 295

Mechling, Jay, 274

Methodist churches and church members, 192, 193–95, 196, 304, 360n29, 389n50

Middle class: superiority assumed, xvi, 34, 207; boundaries of, xvii, 11, 218–19, 300, 301; values of, xvii–xviii, 56–59, 105; class identity, 10–15, 27, 30, 35, 36–37, 173, 175; use of term, 13; child rearing by, 15–16; supports BSA, 47, 193, 196, 201–4, 206–7, 209–10, 304; supports YMCA, 201–5. *See also* White-collar occupations

Middle class, new: and character building, xvi, xvii, xviii, 14–15, 103; nature of, 14, 165, 202

Middle-class boys: sample lives, 6–8; fragmented socialization, 17–18, 32, 51–52, 58–59, 277; adult demands upon, 27–28; age grading among, 28, 292–93; anxieties regarding, 32, 36, 39, 44–50; to be protected and strengthened, 34, 35, 76, 216; barred from boys' clubs, 68; favored by YMCA, 73, 74–77, 82, 210, 216, 302; favored by Boys' Brigades, 88; ideal adolescents, 100; in Scouting, 144, 218–19, 303, 366–67n40, 388n47; favored by BSA, 210, 216, 302; in YMCA, 388n47

Military activities and training: equivalents for, 45; in Boys' Brigades, 87–88, 89, 91, 92; in British Scouting, 139, 140, 144; by BSA rivals, 146, 147; in BSA, 152, 156, 178–80, 204–5, 208, 215, 250, 253; in high schools, 179; at camp, 235, 243; boys' interest wanes, 281, 283. *See also* Cadet corps; Drill, military

Miller, Francis, 264

Mills, C. Wright, 14

Moffat, Samuel A., 139, 141, 154, 163, 173, 190–91, 274

Moody, Dwight, 73, 87

Moore, George W., 214

Moorland, Jesse, 214

Moral education: techniques, 16, 41, 253; in YMCA, 81, 93, 199, 263; and activity programs, 93, 253; Seton on, 131–32; in Scouting, 135, 136, 149; and cognitive stages, 255–56

Moralism: *vs.* spirituality, 57, 177, 196–97, 263; in character building, 165; in YMCA, 174, 177, 263

Morgan, Lewis Henry, 101

Mormon churches and church members, 194–95, 198, 303–4, 398n50

Morrell, Rev. Charles, 31

Morse, John Lovett, 241

Morse, Richard C., 150

Mothers and sons, 6, 16, 48, 142, 268, 347n53

Muir, John, 4–5, 234

Murray, William D., 151, 176

Murray, William H. H., 234

Muscular Christianity, 45, 48, 53–54, 59, 81, 87, 172

Naismith, James, 82

National Catholic War Council, 197–98

National Education Association, 92, 172, 180, 198, 199

National Guard, 86, 87, 90, 92, 152, 178, 208

National Scouts of America, 147

Nativism, 9, 35, 157, 181, 182, 198, 215–16, 217, 301

Nature, attitudes towards, 5, 59, 140, 235–38, 240, 245–46

Nature study, 140, 240, 246

Neill, Charles P., 151, 358*n89*

Newsboys, 223, 279

Nurture, steady, 16–17, 23, 24, 27, 30–31

Oates, J. F., 119

Older boys: in YMCA, 80, 262, 275, 287–88; in British Scouting, 142, 282; British and American treatment compared, 272, 273; in BSA, 280, 282–86, 291–92, 296–97

Oosterhuis, Klaas, 215

Order of Woodcraft Chivalry, 143

Organizations, growth of large, xii, 14, 17, 46, 103, 104

Owings, Nathaniel Alexander, 277–78

Parents: relations with children, 17, 25–26, 27, 368*n66*; criticized, 34, 111–12, 137; fears for sons outdoors, 236–37, 271; weaning boys from, 268, 296. *See also* Fathers; Mothers and sons

Pastoral ideal, 59, 245

Patriotism, 224, 253. *See also* Americanism

Patrol leaders. *See* Boy Scout patrols

Paul, Leslie, 143

Pearson, C. Arthur, 134, 135, 139

Pedophilia, 208

Peer groups, 19, 27–28, 275. *See also* Gangs

Perkins, George W., Jr., 151, 358*n89*

Perrigo, Oscar, 89

Phillips, John M., 350*n32*

Physical growth, trends in, 38

Physical training, 265

Piaget, Jean, 251

Pioneers (YMCA group), 299

Play, 18–19, 33, 82, 109–10

Playgrounds, 33, 113, 127

Pledges, 16, 84, 85–86, 135, 190, 252, 256, 263

Polish National Council, 215

Political views, boys', 253–54, 272

Porter, David R., 47, 122, 123, 126, 199, 262, 264

Porter, George D., 350*n32*

Powell, Perry Edwards, 189

Pranks, boys', 36, 52, 240, 244

Pratt, George D., 151, 246

Preadolescent boys: character builders like, 55, 78, 141–42; boys' clubs favor, 69; and Scouting, 141, 142, 253, 281–82, 284, 297, 299, 387*n31*; behavior, 236; eager joiners, 296, 300

Precocity, 37–38, 50–54, 100–101, 108, 283–84, 297, 299

Presbrey, Frank, 151

Presbyterian churches and members, 192, 193, 196, 304, 360*n29*, 389*n50*

Primitivism, 59, 140, 144

Professionalization: in American life, 11, 13, 14, 121, 165–67, 342*n34*; in boys' work movement, 71, 109, 111, 114, 116–29, 160, 161, 166, 205; criteria of, 121; *vs.* bureaucratization, 166

Progressive Era: values of, xvi–xviii, 76–79, 103, 105, 145, 294; institutional changes in, 164–67

Progressive reform: and character builders, xvi–xvii, 56–59, 127, 173–74, 175, 184–86, 210–11, 355*n19*; characteristics of, 35, 56, 57

Psychology, 111, 114–15, 126, 160, 163, 164, 294–95. *See also* Faculty psychology; Recapitulation theory

Puberty, 21, 22, 100, 114. *See also* Age: of puberty

Puffer, J. Adams, 33, 104, 110

Quin, Rev. George E., 113, 197

Racial policies, 213–14, 301, 388*n38*

Racism, 212–14

Rauschenbusch, Walter, 123

Raven, A. N., 32

Recapitulation theory, 99–101, 109–14, 116, 143

Recreation, 36, 52, 285, 286–87, 293, 385*n98*. *See also* Play

Religious conversions: nineteenth-century, 23; in YMCA, 80, 108, 118, 119, 126, 193, 254, 261–64; and adolescence, 100, 101; age for, 100, 108; at camp, 234, 237–38; in Sunday school, 261

Religious proselytizing, 64, 68, 191–92, 198, 199, 214–15

Republican party, 56, 185

Rice, Joseph, 17
Rich, G. Barrett, 179, 350*n32*
Richardson, Norman, 24
Riesman, David, 105
Riis, Jacob A., 34, 66, 147, 234
Rindge, Fred H., 216
Robins, Henry B., 108
Robinson, Clarence C., 223, 254, 262
Robinson, Edgar M.: opinions, 48, 75, 99,
    106, 112, 113, 131, 262, 268, 282; life
    and activities in YMCA, 105-6, 118-19,
    122, 123, 124, 126, 142, 214, 254, 263,
    264; involvement with BSA, 146, 147,
    151, 157, 159, 181, 182, 239; and
    YMCA camps, 234, 236, 238, 261,
    371*n17*
Robinson, George H., 81
Rockefeller, John D., Jr., 151
Rodgers, Daniel T., 16
Roman Catholic boys' work, 64, 113, 197,
    198
Roman Catholic churches and members:
    and BSA, 193-95, 197-98, 201, 215, 219,
    304, 389*n50*; and YMCA, 197, 198, 215,
    220, 367*n46*
Roosevelt, Franklin D., 175
Roosevelt, Theodore: boyhood, 8; as
    model of character, 30, 45-46; on boys,
    54, 55; role in BSA, 57, 148, 178, 179,
    180, 181, 182, 185, 186, 358*n89*
Roosevelt, Theodore, Jr., 151, 182
Rosenwald, Julius, 214
Rotary clubs, 191, 203
Rote learning, 250, 251, 255
Rover Scouting, 142-43, 282
Rowntree, Seebohm, 136
Russell, Charles E. B., 140
Russell, Howard H., 85
Russell, James E., 41
Russell Sage Foundation, 147
Ryan, Mary P., 52

Sage, Mrs. Russell, 151
Sargent, D. A., 92
Savages, boys as: conceptions of, 52, 53,
    101-2, 116, 299, 387*n32*; virtues of, 55,
    102; and character building, 99, 113,
    131, 132, 140, 141, 241; resistance to,
    190; at camp, 236, 244, 373*n52*
Schiff, Mortimer L., 46, 151, 183
Schools, preparatory, 54, 221, 235, 273

Schools, public: criticized, 17, 18, 29, 40-
    41, 47, 49, 50, 65, 137, 199, 200; Eng-
    lish, 53-54, 137-38; and BSA, 199-200,
    250, 251, 304, 389*n51*, 389*n52*. *See also*
    Extracurricular activities; High schools;
    Teachers
Scott, John, 102
Scout, frontier, 132, 133, 239
Scout Commissioners, 152, 161-62, 202
Scoutmasters: control of, 143, 152, 153,
    156, 162-63, 176, 181, 183; quit BSA,
    152, 153, 154, 276; do not follow pro-
    gram, 152, 178, 281; numbers of, 154;
    training for, 154, 163-64; religious pref-
    erences, 192, 193-95, 301; ages, 206;
    education, 206, 207; occupations, 206,
    207, 225, 301, 364*n95*; recruitment, 207;
    motives, 207-10, 364*n100*; family status,
    208; experience in youth work, 209,
    210; relations with boys, 240, 244, 256,
    274, 275-77, 286; role in troop, 250,
    269, 271; BSA experience, 276; time
    commitment, 276; shortage in 1970s,
    302, 305
Sea Scouting, 296
Sennett, Richard, 10
Service: and middle class, 13, 14, 173,
    175, 202, 209-10; by YMCA boys, 173,
    254. *See also* Boy Scout program—
    service projects
Service clubs, 203, 304
Seton, Ernest Thompson: boyhood, 6-7,
    311*n9*; views on boyhood, 32, 49, 52,
    101, 104-5, 106; founds Woodcraft In-
    dians, 130-32, 344*n8*; values and opin-
    ions, 131, 145, 235, 239; personality,
    131, 141-42; influence on Boy Scouting,
    134, 140, 141, 240, 347*n43*; influence on
    other youth work, 143, 183, 227, 238,
    239; role in BSA, 147-51 *passim*; ouster
    from BSA, 156, 181, 239; politics, 180-
    81, 185; *vs.* Beard, 239, 246
Sex segregation, 47, 51, 103, 184, 284, 297
Sexual impurity: alarms boys, 7, 261, 263,
    264; alarms youth workers, 37, 50; dis-
    traction from, 108. *See also* Masturba-
    tion
Sexual purity: instruction, 48, 49, 260-61,
    263-65; 378*n64*; value of, 49, 264; of
    preadolescent boyhood, 53, 55, 142
Shattuck, S. F., 91

Shaver, Waldo, 214–15
Sheldon, Henry, 102
Signaling, 135, 174, 175, 250
Singleton, Gregory H., 14, 15
Skinner, B. F., 7–8, 36, 242, 243, 281
Small cities and towns: defensiveness, 10, 36–37; character builders' success in, 76, 189, 190, 193, 211, 224–27, 229, 369n76
Small-town boyhood: activities, 5, 36, 52, 293–94; nostalgia for, 52–53, 58–59
Smith, Bolton, 213, 350n32
Smith, Charles F., 250
Smith, Harvey, 270
Smith, Sir William, 87, 273
Smoking, 26, 49, 84, 85, 174, 256, 263
Snedden, David, 218
Social class: demarcation of, 11–13; in character building, 74–75, 144, 205–7, 212, 215–21, 300–301, 303, 304. See also Lower-class boys; Middle class; Social segregation in boys' work
Social Gospel, 35, 42, 196
Social order and control, xvi, 35, 66, 76, 137, 145, 290, 291. See also Control of boys
Social segregation in boys' work, 34, 36, 76, 216–17, 222, 225, 302
Sons of Daniel Boone, 132–33, 272, 285
Southworth, I. S., 215
Spencer, Lorillard, Jr., 185, 186
Sports: in schools, 40–41, 53; spectator, 46, 49, 136; in boys' work, 68, 189, 242, 249. See also Baseball; Basketball
Springfield College, 118, 123
Spring-Rice, Cecil, 55
Starbuck, Edwin D., 100, 101, 108
Statten, Taylor, 107
Steffens, Lincoln, 6, 7
Stelzle, Charles, 65, 70, 141
Stern, Walter T., 68
Stokes, Wyndham H., 83–84
Storrow, James J., 350n32
Street boys, 33–34, 65, 67, 69, 73, 74, 77, 216
Strength: hopes of building, 44, 45, 47, 88–89, 234; fears of loss, 49, 241; vs. control, 51
Strong, Josiah, 35
Styles, John A., 240
Suburbs, 36, 150, 226, 300
Sunday schools: early history, 10, 23;

membership growth, 42; enrollment by sex and age, 42–43, 284, 322n75; problems holding boys, 42–44, 87, 137, 280, 284; urban vs. rural, 43, 322n75; teachers, 44, 163, 209, 276; criticized, 44, 48, 112; sports in, 189, 192; membership by denomination, 196, 360n29; boys' complaints about, 283
Surveys of boy life, 127, 165
Swimming, 157, 241, 242, 251, 252

Taft, William Howard, 178
Taggert, S. A., 34
Taylor, William, 67, 69–70
Teachers: and extracurricular activities, 40–41; men as, 46, 47; women as, 47, 200; and BSA, 199–200, 202, 206, 207; and YMCA, 205
Temperance societies, 83–85, 189
Tennyson, Alfred Lord, 190
Terry, Seth Sprague, 151
Thorndike, E. L., 114, 296
Thrasher, Frederic M., 116
Tocqueville, Alexis de, 22
Traffic, Boy Scouts direct, 174, 175, 182
Turner, Frederick Jackson, 102–3

Uniforms: drill corps', 86; Boys' Brigades', 88, 91, 92; Girl Scouts' and Camp Fire Girls', 184. See also Boy Scouts of America—uniform
United Boys' Brigades of America. See Boys' Brigades, American
United States Boy Scouts, 157, 348–49n7
United States government, 156–57, 227, 301, 302
United Way, 303, 305, 389n56. See also Community chest
Upper class, 11, 87, 193, 196, 221. See also Gentry class
Urbanization. See City life

Vane, Sir Francis, 143
Verbeck, William, 147, 151
Veterans' clubs, 304, 389n52
Vocational guidance, 47, 127, 137, 140, 196, 258–59, 262, 297
Vocational training, 70, 81, 227, 252, 259
Voluntarism, 10, 13, 14, 15, 167, 202, 302, 305. See also Service

Voluntary associations: and social class, 11, 13, 212; and churches, 42, 196; and reform, 56, 90; administration of, 150, 152–53, 161

Volunteers, 161, 166–67, 188, 211. *See also* Scoutmasters

Vreeland, Frederick K., 157

Walker, George G., 269

Walsh, Stuart, 240

Wandervögel, xv*n*

Warner, Charles Dudley, 52, 53

Watson, John B., 295

Webelos Scouting, 297

Weber, Max, 150, 161

Webster, Henry Horace, 74

Welter, Barbara, 48

West, the American, 45–46

West, James: views on boys' work issues, 40, 47, 92–93, 106, 108; views on Boy Scouts, 48, 50, 177, 213, 218, 224, 227, 271; boyhood and career, 147–48, 296; role and activities as Chief Scout Executive, 148–51, 155–59, 164, 172, 176, 178, 181, 184, 204, 213, 286, 295; views on BSA administration, 152, 160, 162, 190, 199; views on BSA program and policies, 175, 176, 192, 253, 286, 295, 296; political views, 179, 180, 182, 183, 185, 358*n89*

Westlake, Ernest, 143

White, Morton, 258

White-collar occupations, 9–13, 46, 206, 301, 388*n36. See also* Middle class

Wiebe, Robert H., 14, 165, 166

Wilderness, 45–46, 235–36, 245, 246

Will, power of, 31, 47, 84, 249

Williams, George, 72

Wister, Owen, 45–46

Wolf Cub program, 295–96

Women: masculine fears of, 44, 46, 47, 283; as Sunday school teachers, 44, 283; in work force, 46, 47; as teachers, 47; kept out of boys' work, 79, 200; boys' workers' relations with, 142

Women's Christian Temperance Union, 84, 92

Wood, Gen. Leonard, 179

Woodcraft, 140, 143–44, 235–36, 239, 240, 242–43, 285, 384*n97*

Woodcraft Indians, 130–32, 344*n8*

Woodcraft League, 239

Work: farm boys', 4, 228; other boys', 5–8 *passim,* 25–26; boys' part-time, 7, 8, 25, 26, 217, 219; surrogates for, 18, 247, 290; changing nature of, 18, 314*n59*

Working boys: prospects and numbers, 25, 100, 220, 259, 316*n97*; in YMCA, 204, 216, 220, 221, 223; in BSA, 217, 218, 219, 224

Working-class boys. *See* Lower-class boys

Work With Boys, 113, 114

World War I, xviii, 139, 173, 179–82, 183, 184

Wyland, Ray O., 215, 219, 224

YMCA, parent body and men's programs: purposes, 10, 22, 29, 45, 46; age limits, 72; federal structure, 72, 73; general secretaries, 72, 73, 74, 117, 118; early history, 72–74; buildings, 74, 127–28, 201, 202; fund raising, 186, 201, 202–3, 301, 303, 305; for blacks, 214; Protestantism and, 301

YMCA and BSA—compared regarding: response to adolescence, 108–9, 258, 260, 266; organization, 150, 152, 159, 164, 165, 166, 268–69; training of workers, 161; expansion, 166–67, 300; public image, 172, 182, 186–87; political attitudes, 185, 254; supporters, 188, 196; volunteers' backgrounds, 205, 206; recruitment of boys, 220, 225, 226–27, 287, 289; camping, 241–44 *passim*; character building, 265–66

—competition between: in program, 125; for staff, 128, 159, 160; BSA advantages, 182, 187, 193; trading criticisms, 186, 187, 205; local, 203, 226–27

—other relationships: influence on program, 125, 149; organizational help, 127, 140, 146–47, 150, 152; troop sponsorship, 157, 191, 200, 304, 389*n52*; transfer of staff, 158, 159, 160

YMCA boys: socioeconomic background, 68, 73–77, 79, 82, 127, 214, 216, 217, 220, 221, 223, 287, 300, 303, 367*n46*, 388*n47*; eagerness, 74; religious response, 76, 192–93, 259, 262, 265; group cohesion, 77, 80, 275, 277; age, 77–80, 287–89, 299; total membership, 78, 120–21, 278, 299, 300, 305, 341*n16*;

YMCA boys (*continued*)
  as leaders, 79–80, 124, 254, 270, 275;
  relations with boys' secretaries, 124, 270,
  274–75, 277; market power, 128, 279;
  quitting, 153, 274–75, 278, 279, 293–94;
  by size of town, 193, 226, 228, 369*n74*;
  religious backgrounds, 196, 198, 215,
  367*n46*; activity preferences, 252, 259,
  331*n57*; sexual concerns, 260–65; ideal
  boys, 264, 277; attendance, 278
YMCA boys' secretaries: professionalization, 13, 109, 121–29, 205; religious experiences, 23; pre-1900 forerunners, 74,
  79, 117; turnover, 117, 121, 129, 277;
  training, 118–19, 122, 123, 129, 161;
  numbers, 119; rewards, 121–22; job
  problems, 121–28 *passim,* 211, 260, 261,
  274–75, 277; motives, 122; previous
  jobs, 122, 123; later jobs, 122, 123, 159,
  160; age, 122, 129
YMCA boys' work: political position, 127,
  173–74, 254, 301; publicity and public
  image, 171–72, 173, 174, 176–77, 182,
  186, 187, 290, 305
— activities and program: early, 72–73;
  moral and religious training, 80–81, 85,
  126, 176–77, 192, 193, 237–38, 252, 258,
  259, 262–65, 275; physical, 81–82, 252;
  varied clubs, 81, 124; character-building,
  100, 248, 289–90; standardized, 125,
  277; building-centered or not, 127–28;
  localized, 171; wartime, 182; citizenship

  training, 182, 254; surveys, 203; older
  boys' conferences, 217, 259; parties, 252,
  284–85. *See also* Christian Citizenship
  Training Program
— organization and administration: supervision, 40, 74, 119; start of separate, 74;
  costs and incentives, 75, 119, 295; fees,
  75, 217; city size, 76; group size, 80,
  277; number of branches, 93, 94, 121;
  use of volunteers, 124, 167, 188, 205,
  211, 237, 276; fund raising, 172, 203
— relationships and comparisons with:
  boys' clubs, 68, 74–75, 77, 80, 81, 119,
  223–24, 302; parent YMCA, 74, 128,
  150; Boys' Brigades, 104; churches and
  clergy, 127, 176–77, 188, 192–93, 196,
  262, 265; schools, 193, 199, 221, 262–
  65
YMCA camps, 234–38, 247, 261
Young Converts' Association, 79
Younger boys, 281, 285, 291, 295–96, 299
Young Men's Christian Association. *See*
  YMCA
Young people's societies, 23, 44, 153
Young Women's Christian Association, 50,
  113
Youth: breadth of term, xv, 19; premodern, 21; in late 1800s, 22; groups, American and foreign compared, 183, 294;
  culture, 293

Zald, Mayer N., xii

JACKET DESIGNED BY BRUCE GORE
COMPOSED BY METRICOMP, GRUNDY CENTER, IOWA
MANUFACTURED BY CUSHING-MALLOY, INC., ANN ARBOR, MICHIGAN
TEXT AND DISPLAY LINES ARE SET IN TIMES ROMAN

Library of Congress Cataloging in Publication Data
Macleod, David I.
Building character in the American boy
Includes bibliographical references and index.
1. Boy Scouts of America. 2. YMCA. I. Title.
HS3313.M25 1983   369.43'0973   83-47763
ISBN 0-299-09400-6

DATE DUE

OCT 1 6 2009			

DEMCO 38-296